Sardar Vallabhbhai Patel

Sardar Vallabhbhai Patel
INDIA'S IRON MAN

Balraj Krishna

RUPA

Published by
Rupa Publications India Pvt. Ltd 2013
7/16, Ansari Road, Daryaganj
New Delhi 110002

Sales centres:
Allahabad Bengaluru Chennai
Hyderabad Jaipur Kathmandu
Kolkata Mumbai

ISBN: 978-81-291-2450-0

10 9 8 7 6 5 4 3 2 1

Typeset in Palatino LT Std by Mindways Design, New Delhi

Printed at Yash Printographics, Noida

To my father, Gauri Shankar

1885-1975

A nationalist to the core, at 19 in 1904 he joined Lala Lajpat Rai's volunteer corps and served in Kangra earthquake relief; in 1905, he boycotted foreign cloth for good, in answer to the call of the Bengal Partition leaders; and in 1921, he responded to Gandhi's call to give up imported sugar, and stuck to his decision till indigenous production started a decade and a half later. He was my inspirer and financial support when I devoted myself to Sardar Patel's biography. He had in him the spirit of the times, having been born in the year the Indian National Congress was established (1885). He was considerably influenced by the militant nationalism of Tilak, Lajpat Rai and Bipin Chandra Pal. He was a close friend of revolutionary Bhagat Singh's father, Sardar Kishen Singh. A neo-Hindu of Swami Dayanand's Arya Samaj, he adhered to resurgent Hinduism, and discarded caste to contribute to Hindu unity. Later, he developed great affinity for Sardar Patel. He desired I should write this biography, which is in fulfillment of his wish.

Contents

Appendices

Acknowledgements

I was privileged to receive, either through interviews or through correspondence, personal memoirs from many, which helped me build up Sardar Patel's image as the Iron Man of India: bold, blunt and shrewd; principled and uncompromising on national matters; to a degree ruthless in the face of a crisis, otherwise benign, even persuasive when that served purpose. Some of my contributors were British; the rest were Indians. Among the former were Lord Mountbatten, General Sir Roy Bucher, Air Marshal Sir Thomas Elmhirst, Sir Hugh Garrett (an old ICS), Andrew Mellor, the *Daily Herald* correspondent, and C.W.E. U'ren, the British Indian Police officer who served an arrest warrant on Patel in the pre-dawn swoop on August 9th, 1942. "Quit India" was his guilt.

There were nearly a dozen members of the ICS, the implementers of the transfer of power, who generously offered me their help. They included such distinguished members of the Service: C.S. Venkatachar, H.V.R. Iengar, K.B. Lall, Vishnu Sahay, C.D. Deshmukh, C.M. Trivedi, H.M. Patel, K.P.S. Menon, Shavax Lal, N. Senapati, B.R. Patel and the redoubtable V.P. Menon, Patel's right-hand man in the elimination of the Princely Order.

I was a recipient of similar generosity from elderly veteran Indulal Yagnik, Bardoli warhorse Kalyanji Mehta, Ashabhai Patel of Ras, K.M. Munshi, M.R. Masani, Lalji Mehrotra, Mahavir Tyagi, Thakur Jaswant Singh (of Bikaner), Mehr Chand Khanna, Bhim Sen Sachar, S. Ramakrishnan (Bharatiya Vidya Bhavan), Begum Aizaz Rasul (UP Muslim Leaguer), G.M. Sadiq, Humayun Kabir, Nityanand Kanungo and Khushwant Singh.

To each one of them I offer my deepest gratitude for helping me make this biography of Sardar Patel what it has turned out to be.

Balraj Krishna
181, Mehr Naz, Cuffe Parade,
Mumbai 400 005

Preface

Common talk among the members of the Indian Civil Service post-Independence used to be: "If the dead body of the Sardar were stuffed and placed on a chair, he could still rule."[1] Vallabhbhai Patel's face commanded such obedience. Princes, politicians and administrators called upon him with certain trepidation, fearing the scorn of his eyes; much worse, the rap of his caustic tongue. Air Marshal Sir Thomas Elmhirst, India's Air Chief, saw in his eyes the same "fierce, piercing look" as of Kamal Ataturk or Winston Churchill.[2] General Sir Roy Bucher, India's Army Chief, was once witness to his fear, and wrote: "I personally never saw him other than absolutely composed and determined to uphold law and order throughout India. Later I was to see him in a rage, and realised how his colleagues were dominated."[3] Patel's hold over the party was absolute. He had been the builder of the party machine; he was, hence, the master of party affairs. None could challenge his authority, or did so at his cost. Eight months before his death, Lord Mountbatten pleaded with him for Nehru: "With your support, Jawaharlal cannot fail..."

Patel judged people instantly. He had the courage to reprimand the erring. He did so judiciously, though treating everyone with the same yardstick. There were two exceptions: Gandhi and Nehru. He spared them with a difference. To Gandhi, he was respectful as his guru; to Nehru, considerate as his Prime Minister. In national matters he was "harder than steel", but "softer than a flower in personal and private relations."[4]

Patel never walked over a "fallen" enemy. Post-Independence, when he wielded power, this was particularly so in the case of the Princes who had surrendered to him on losing their "battles". They included such powerful ones as the Nawab of Bhopal who had intrigued on behalf of Jinnah to dismember India; the Nizam of Hyderabad who waged a war of "independence" at Jinnah's behest; and C.P. Ramaswami Aiyar, Diwan of Travancore, who was the first to raise the banner of revolt by declaring that Travancore would be independent simultaneously with the lapse of Paramountcy. The Jamsaheb of Nawanagar had earlier played into the hands of Sir Conard Corfield, the powerful Secretary of the Political Department, in the latter's proposed formation of an independent confederation of the Kathiawar States outside the proposed Indian Union. Many considered it a miracle when a single meeting with Patel turned him into an ardent supporter of the Sardar's plan to unify these States as a unit of the Indian Republic.

There was a glaring contrast between the attitudes of Nehru and Patel towards the Princes. One instance in particular may be mentioned. Nehru felt annoyed over the Jamsaheb's membership of the Indian delegation to the UN General Assembly in 1949, and blurted, "I am damned if I send him on our delegation. He and his diamond buttons!" Foreign Secretary K.P.S. Menon reported Nehru's reaction to Patel who kept quiet for a few seconds and said, "I have given my nomination and I stick to it. Panditji accepted the nomination without further ado."[5]

Patel's helping hand reached high and low alike. The Nawab of Bhopal's son-in-law, the Nawab of Pataudi, along with his family, was trapped in communal rioting in his state capital. Patel responded to Bhopal's appeal by sending an emissary in his car to get the news and render whatever help was needed. I too was a recipient of Patel's large-heartedness. Lahore was in the grip of communal holocaust. My younger brother, Yuvraj Krishan, was to sit for the first competitive examination of the newly-formed IAS replacing the ICS, being held in July 1947. In May I had forewarned the British Chairman of the Federal Public Service Commission (later UPSC), of the grave communal situation prevailing in Lahore. I got a shock in early June when communication reaching us stated that the centre for the candidates would be the Islamia College, which was located in an area under 72-hour curfew. What could be done at that late stage? I wondered. All the leaders were neck-deep in the transfer of power. My instinct forced me to write to Patel, even when I was uncertain if he could spare a few minutes. I had a most pleasant surprise on the third or fourth day, when a telegram from Patel's office informed me of the change of the centre to a safer locality. Further, each candidate was asked telegraphically whether he would take the examination at Lahore or Simla.

I was instantly won over. I said to myself: Here's a man of action, caring as much for the common folk as for the better placed. Pre-Independence, we, the young in Lahore and elsewhere, did not pay much attention to Patel. The charisma of Gandhi, Nehru and Subhas cast a spell on us. We revered Gandhi as a Mahatma; we admired Subhas Chandra Bose as a radical; but we loved Nehru as our "uncrowned king". We even sought identification with Nehru by donning the Jawahar jacket in a spirit of national pride. Patel's one act considerably enhanced my esteem for him. He gained such esteem from the people in the Punjab and the NWFP during the months which followed Partition. He was one man who saved the lives of millions stranded in West Pakistan by arranging their expeditious pull-out.

Post-Independence, Patel's two historic achievements won him universal praise: the country's administrative unity through the IAS replacing the ICS; and the integration of the Princely States. Both at lightning speed, which made hard-core Communist M.N. Roy say that had Kashmir remained with Patel, the solution would have been reached soon after Partition. Similarly, India might have been spared humiliation at the hands of the Chinese in 1962 had Nehru pursued Patel's advice given prior to his death.

Some of the British administrators ruling over India thought very highly of Patel. A special mention needs to be made of Sir Hugh Garrett (ICS). He was 88 in 1968 when he wrote me a short but sweet letter from the UK, on reading my letter to the Editor of the *Daily Telegraph*. It reads: "I, who knew him very well, always called him Vallabhbhai… He was a pillar of the Congress party, but that in no way caused ill-feeling on my side, nor, I hope, did he feel any against me… (once) he came to see me and related how a fakir had built a tomb in the middle of a road in the city's outskirts. He said the fakir had threatened him with a sword. He asked if I would deal with the situation. He did not want a police or magisterial case. I accordingly got my car and went to the place and found it as stated. I spoke to the fakir and ordered removal of everything within two hours. I went back and found it all done. Later, of course, I had much to do with him, but I had faith in him. He was honest and frank… Of all the Indians I ever met, I place him as the greatest."[6]

A no less worthy tribute is paid by another member of the "Steel Frame", Philip Mason, in the *Dictionary of National Biography* (Oxford): "Patel has been compared to Bismarck, but the parallel cannot be carried far. Patel was courageous, honest and realistic, but far from cynical." And on his demise, the *Manchester Guardian* (now the *Guardian*) wrote: "… He was the organiser, the disciplinarian, the party boss. In the Congress, he was what the Americans call the 'hatchet man' of the party. This is not a gracious role, but a revolutionary party cannot be effective without a determined and rather prosaic chief of staff. Without Patel, Gandhi's ideas would have had less practical influence and Nehru's idealism less scope. Patel was not only the organiser of the fight for freedom, but also the architect of the new State when the fight was over. The same man is seldom successful both as rebel and statesman. Patel was the exception."[7]

Patel was a tower of strength and hope to Gandhi and the Congress. He was his Deputy Commander in the Kheda satyagraha (1917), Hero of Bardoli, whom the British called Lenin (1928), "John the Baptist" to Gandhi in the Salt satyagraha (1930); the Party Boss who directed and supervised the functioning of the Congress Governments post-1937 provincial elections. And he even defeated Subhas Bose in the challenge he posed to Gandhi.

Prior to the transfer of power on August 15th, Patel shepherded into his pen almost all the Princes, with the notable exception of Kashmir and Hyderabad – the latter's integration was a brilliant achievement. Accession prior to August 15th prevented the States from becoming independent with the lapse of Paramountcy. Such independence would have led to a far greater and a far more serious confrontation with the States than with Pakistan.

Vinoba Bhave called Patel "the accurate bowman of Gandhi's struggle, his disciple and his GOC. He knew no retreat..." For over three decades he was to the Indians what Churchill was to war-time British. Such a man was called the "master-builder" by M.N. Roy, who even speculated: "What will happen to India when the master-builder will go, sooner or later, by way of all mortals?"[8]

During the Cabinet Mission parleys in 1946 in New Delhi, a Jain *muni* visited Patel. After lavish praise, he ventured to suggest: "Sardar Saheb, you must write India's history." Patel had a hearty laugh, and said, "We do not write history. We make history." And Patel did make history, comparable to those of Asoka and Akbar, for which Nehru appropriately called him "builder and consolidator of New India".

Part I

1

The Child, the Land, the People

Eighteen years after India's first war of independence, which the British called the Indian Mutiny, a boy was born on October 31, 1875, at Nadiad, in the Kheda district of Gujarat, nearly 40 miles south-east of Ahmedabad. The year was significant. It witnessed the maturing of nationalistic stirrings since 1857. In 1875, Bankim Chandra wrote his immortal song *Bande Mataram*; while in 1876, Surendranath Banerjea established his political party, the Indian Association. In 1883, the Association held the All-India National Conference, which its President, Ananda Mohan Bose, called "the first stage towards a National Parliament,"[1] and which proved to be a precursor of the Indian National Congress in 1885. In promoting such a development, Allan Octavian Hume, called the Father of the Congress, seemed to have acted on a certain foreboding; and because of that the National Congress was to provide, according to what he told the Viceroy, Lord Dufferin, "a safety valve for the escape of great and growing forces generated by our own action."[2]

The boy's father had participated in the 1857 war; and he himself was to grow into a great, fiery, relentless freedom fighter, while his birth-place was to be the storm-centre of another freedom struggle—a unique agrarian non-violent revolt in 1917 launched by Mahatma Gandhi for the first time in India after his return from South Africa in 1915. The boy was named Vallabhbhai

Zaverbhai Patel, later known to millions of his countrymen as Sardar Patel—a title he earned not by virtue of his birth, but for his unique leadership in Bardoli satyagraha in 1928. He was the fourth son of Zaverbhai Galabhai Patel, a petty land-owner from Karamsad, a small village about five miles from Anand. In keeping with Hindu tradition, Patel's birth took place in his maternal uncle's home at Nadiad.

Patel's origins were humble. His parents were of average means. Like others in the village, they had no formal education; nor did they possess even the limited sophistication of the city middle classes, let alone of the rich like the Nehrus. His environment, therefore, lacked the city glitter; they were rather rustic. Yet, he grew into a great Indian—the unifier and consolidator of a vast country—of the size of a sub-continent—that faced disintegration on the eve of Britain's decision to relinquish her Indian Empire, and which in the process got nearly submerged in administrative and political chaos. Out of the depths of such a cataclysm, Patel pulled a floundering nation to stability.

A people are shaped physically, mentally or otherwise by the land they live in. And the land makes them hardy, honest, and self-respecting. Like some other notable areas in India, this has been true of Punjab as the sword arm of India, which bore the brunt of many foreign invasions from the north-west; and it was from that land that Patel's ancestors, the Patidars, are reported to have migrated to Gujarat some centuries past. In a way, Kheda too was uniquely situated, "crossed by so many of the chief lines of traffic between upper and central India and the coast," the Gulf of Cambay separating it from the Arabian Sea.

Like Punjab, Kheda had had "settlements of very great antiquity." Between AD 746-1290, it was ruled by different Rajput dynasties. Towards the end of the 14th century, it passed under the rule of the Muslim kings of Ahmedabad, and in 1573 transferred to the Mughals. Todarmal, Akbar's legendary Revenue Minister, had Kheda surveyed in 1590. Between 1720 and 1750, the district was "the scene of almost unceasing conflicts between the Marathas and the Musalman viceroys and nobles."[3] Except for a period of ten years when it was in the hands of the Babi family of Ahmedabad, Kheda was ruled either by the Peshwa or the Gaikwar. In 1803, under the Treaty of Bassein, the Gaikwar ceded to the British Nadiad, Matar and Mahudha, and "granted in perpetual gift the fort and town of Kheda as a proof of his friendship and as testimony of his sense of the benefit he received from the alliance with the Honourable Company's Government."[4] In 1805, the British turned Kheda into a large military station.

Towards the end of the first decade of British occupation, there grew in Kheda stiff opposition to the new administrative set-up which had drastically curtailed "the chief's independence in his own village, so carefully respected during the early years of British rule... and he suffered at once from a loss of position and of revenue."[5] According to the *Bombay Gazetteer*: "The results of the British rule were not unmixed good. The chiefs and large landholders felt weakened and depressed, the district officers, and among them the heads of villages, were stripped of power and influence, and the men of capital suffered both as traders and money-lenders."[6] In Nadiad, "the opposition was the keenest." Under the influence of the Desai community, some village headmen "refused to collect the revenues." The British succeeded in breaking down the opposition. Assistant Collector Capt. Barnewall was sent to arrange a settlement directly with the cultivators. He came down upon the leaders with a heavy hand. Four Desais from Nadiad were, in 1814, convicted of "conspiracy and sentenced to five years' imprisonment and a fine of "1,000."[7] Non-cultivating classes too seethed with discontent. The Rajput Girasias, the Kolis and the Bhats, having lost their former position, were turning into outlaws. On the night of March 17, 1826, a Koli by the name of Govindas Ramdas and his 500 strong armed followers "attacked the town of Thasra with the object of driving out the British officer and establishing himself as a ruler."[8]

The British, however, continued to govern Kheda with a firm hand. John Malcolm, Governor of Bombay Presidency, who visiting Kheda in 1830, admitted that the revenue "rates were high and ought in some cases to be lowered." He said, "The cultivators' condition should never be lost sight of. For a time they may go on paying a high rent, but the strain must gradually impoverish them, and in the end will cause a sudden, large and inevitable defalcation in the public revenue."[9] Malcolm's visit was in connection with the distressing condition of the cultivators. Collector Williamson had earlier "ascribed the various tumults and risings of the Gujaratis to their families, which frequently reduced whole families and villages to the state of broken men." In 1826 a fall in prices of agricultural produce had set in and "rapidly increased till the collapse of 1831... To meet these difficulties, rates were considerably lowered, and by postponing the dates of revenue instalments, further relief was given. In the next year, after a further reduction of rates, all complaints ceased."[10] Such were the early years of British rule of Kheda.

The name Kheda comes from *Ketaka*, the Sanskrit form of *Kevda*—the sweet-scented *Pandanus*. Central Kheda, comprising Nadiad, Anand and Karamsad, is called the charotar or "godly land—a tract of most fertile and well-tilled soil; the people, skilful cultivators and rich, live in large, well-built villages. Their fields, yielding the choicest crops, are sheltered by high hedges, and the whole country is clothed with rows and clusters of large shapely trees."[11] Kheda's population of 782,733 lived in an area of 1,600 square miles, or 489.20 to the square mile, which was quite high for the year 1877. The district, with a breadth varying from 25 to 40 miles, stretched towards the north-east for over 60 miles along the right bank of the river Mahi, which separated it from the Panch Mahals, Baroda and Broach on the east, south-east and south. To the south-west lay Cambay, and to the west, the river Sabarmati, with Ahmedabad beyond. The region's prosperity can be gauged from the total realisable land revenue of Rs.19.30 lakhs in 1877.

Kheda's economy was of the middle class; "though there were no men of great wealth, there was no class of landless labourers."[12] A happy, fairly prosperous middle-class contributed to the Patidars' thrifty habits, hard-working disposition and enterprising spirit. A few, ignoring social prejudices, crossed the seas to East

Africa in search of better fortunes. Kheda's social and political awakening was evident from its having in 1874 four local Gujarati newspapers; the *Kheda Niti Prakash* which first made its appearance in 1856, the *Kheda Vartman* which was started in 1860, the *Nadiad Duniadad* and *Mahudha Adal Insaf.** During 1877-78, Kheda had 190 Government schools, or on an average, one school for every three inhabited villages, with 14,930 pupils on the rolls.

It was during such awakened times of the century that Patel was born amongst a people who were bold, courageous and virile, but honest and self-respecting. Their moderate middle-class affluence gave them a certain cohesion and independence of spirit, largely contributed by the compact, well-knit community of Patidars they belonged to. Patel's father, Zaverbhai, was a Leva Patidar—a class of cultivators known for their sober, simple character, quiet nature, industrious habits, honest disposition and straightforward dealings. Not only were they among the best farmers in Gujarat, but, perhaps, the whole of India. They were "probably descendants of the leading men among the original settlers in Gujarat... known as men of family or *kulia*; the rest as men of no family or *akulia*."[13]

Since the Patidars hailed from Punjab, this speaks volumes on their being skilled cultivators and their love for cattle—the main occupations of the Aryans. In about the 12th century, A.D. Siddharaj Jaisingh, ruler of Gujarat, arranged for the migration of about 1800 families from the Ganga-Jamuna Doab, with the ostensible object of having the jungles abounding the Kheda region converted into cultivable land. To give these hardy, ingenious people sufficient inducement, the Raja introduced a system called *narva*, under which the land went to the head of the family and, thus, ensured undivided inheritance. The migrants were settled in 12 Kheda villages, of which the most important were six: Nadiad, Vaso, Karamsad, Bhadran, Dharmaj and Sojitra. The Patidars from these were considered to be superior to the rest.

**Niti Prakash* (moral luminary), *Vartman* (news), *Duniadad* (world redresser) and *Adal Insaf* (pure justice).

Alla-ud-din Khilji's conquest of Gujarat ushered in unsettled conditions. Many well-to-do towns or villages were looted by unruly peasants. During A.D. 1460-1511, Mahmud Begara, as ruler of Gujarat, not only "added glory and luster to the kingdom of Gujarat, but brought about normalcy in Kheda by making one Patidar the owner of village lands. These were given in perpetuity, though on payment of *nazrana* to the state. Such Patidars were allowed to have their own police, and were invested with powers to try civil and criminal cases. Karamsad seems to have been given to Patel's ancestors, of whom Galabhai was his grandfather and Nathabhai and Sakhidas his great-grandfathers. They owned about 40 acres of land.

Galabhai, Zaverbhai's father, was the only son of Sakhidas, who, in turn, happened to be the only son of Nathabhai. On Sakhidas's death, Zaverbhai and his brothers inherited 10 acres of land each. Zaverbhai was thus, a petty landlord of moderate means. According to the Administration Report for 1875-76, there were 107,918 landowners in the Kheda district, of which 62,501 owned upto 5 acres, 25,866 between 5 to 10 acres, 14,227 between 10 and 20 acres and 4,557 between 20 and 50 acres. While Zaverbhai belonged to the second category, his father, Galabhai, was from the last. Having come from a family which had founded Karamsad, Zaverbhai enjoyed considerable status and esteem. Most of the Patidars sought his advice in matters of dispute.

Possessing a well-built physique, Zaverbhai was of commanding personality, resolute mind and domineering disposition. Whenever he reproached anyone, "he was listened to quietly and none dared talk back to him"[14]—a trait he passed on to Patel. In 1905, when the 30-year old Patel was practising at Borsad, 76-year old Zaverbhai, clad in white and walking erect, arrived there one day, unexpected. With humility and respect for his father, Patel immediately put aside his *hukha*, got up and asked, "Motakaka, what has brought you here? If you had sent me word, I would have myself come to Karamsad. That would have also given me a chance to meet Ladbai" (his mother). Zaverbhai said, "Since my work is in Borsad, what was the point in asking you to come to Karamsad? And what is the good of your enjoying such high reputation and great influence in the district, if, in spite of it, a warrant can be issued against our Maharaj (priest) and the police threaten to arrest him?" Patel could not hold back his sarcastic tongue, "A warrant against the Maharaj! He is the incarnation of God Purushottam. How could anyone dare think of arresting him who has the power of setting us free from the bonds of this world!" Patel's attempt to advise his father that he ought to give up the company of *sadhus* angered Zaverbhai and he retorted, "That is not what I came to discuss. All I want you to do is to have the warrant cancelled, if one has been issued."[15]

Having issued such a firman, he left Patel's office with the same abruptness with which he had entered. Patel himself was in this regard his father's image: firm, determined and demanding; and like his father too, he was least tolerant of injustice, and ever ready to fight it out. Both father and son were of independent temperament and hated flattery. A deeply religious man, Zaverbhai was a believer in the Swaminarayan cult. Most of his time was spent in the Swaminarayan temple at Karamsad. Even at 85, in 1914, he often walked to Vadtal, about 20 miles from Karamsad, to offer prayers on full moon day at the main Swaminarayan temple there. Many a time Patel, as a boy, accompanied his father, and often fasted with him twice a month. But he never grew orthodox, and gave up fasting and formal prayers as soon as he moved out of Karamsad, though he never became agnostic or irreligious.

Patel, along with his elder brother, Vithalbhai, had also inherited from his father the great quality of becoming a firebrand freedom fighter. It is well known that Zaverbhai, moved by nationalist fervour, had joined the Rani of Jhansi in the 1857 war of Independence. When it petered out, Zaverbhai was taken prisoner by Malharrao Holkar. One day Holkar was playing chess within sight of his prisoner, and whenever he made a wrong move, Zaverbhai made bold not only to point out the mistake, but suggested, instead, the right one. Astonished and pleased, the Holkar not only returned to Zaverbhai his freedom, but the two struck up a friendship. His son exhibited similar genius in making the right moves on the country's chessboard in his settlement with the Princes.

Zaverbhai, who lived to the age of 94, had five sons, whom he gave names bearing religious significance. In order of seniority, they were: Somabhai (meaning the sun), Narsibhai (Narsingh god), Vithalbhai (Vithalnathji), Vallabhbhai (Vallabhacharya) and Kashibhai (Kashi or Varanasi). The first two engaged themselves in agriculture; the middle two, turning out to be more enterprising, became barristers and India's foremost fiery political leaders, and the youngest a practising lawyer. In his strong, stout build, in his power of endurance and capacity to bear hardship, in his fearless, bold temperament, in his determination, firmness and resoluteness, Patel was like his father.

Patel's mother, Ladbai, also moulded his character. She came from Nadiad and was 18 years younger than Zaverbhai. She was gentle, an expert housekeeper who looked after her guests well, and friendly by nature, "tended to look upon her neighbours' work and troubles as her own". It is said of her that "until she died in 1932 at the age of 85, she ran the house and cooked every meal". From her, Patel inherited motherly instincts—the spirit of service that was so dominant in her, also a taste for cleanliness, and the orderliness he observed throughout his life. Like all Hindu mothers of her times, she narrated to her sons the epics, the *Ramayana* and the *Mahabharata*, which seemed to have had a great impact on her two sons—both Patel and Vithalbhai. These great epics instilled in Patel's mind warrior-like qualities, and awakened in him a restless spirit, and an irresistible desire to fight against injustice—first at school and later, on the political stage of India.

2

Genius of a Schoolboy

Patel possessed an ingenious mind as a schoolboy—far from the ordinary. Even when he had no particular academic distinction to his credit, some of his eventful school-life happenings did cast shadows of the man he was ultimately going to be. He was a rebel whose exceptional organisational abilities were recognised by his schoolmates and teachers.

Patel's early schooling took place in the typically rural setting of Karamsad, where he grew, in his own words, "in the open spaces of a village" free from the "restrictions and limitations" of town-life, on terms of "complete equality with his fellow children", having "his share of black eye like any others", rolling on dusty streets, or being "pushed into the village pond with the same vigorous and unexpected rap on the knuckles as any other child." Reminiscing about his early life once, Patel said, "It was in this atmosphere of equal give-and-take that I grew up with all the zest for life that only a village child can have and all that sturdiness and determination which grow out of a healthy atmosphere and daredevilry and juvenile buoyancy and of impish pranks, mirth and laughter."[1]

Patel completed seven standards of Gujarati from the Government school at Karamsad. He was by then seventeen or so. A lower standard teacher, a real shirker, was in the habit of dismissing questions asked by the boys with the petulant remark, "Why do you ask me? Learn for yourself." For Patel this was a lesson in self-reliance then, and during later life. He was practically self-taught. But he learnt a great deal from his father, who used to take him to the fields every morning and teach him tables and simple sums. This apart, such company gave Patel deep knowledge of the people, the fields and the villages in the neighbourhood, and the experience thus gained stood by him some twenty-eight years later in the Kheda satyagraha launched by Gandhi.

Patel had no inclination to stay in his village. Though less vocal by temperament, his ambitions were as high as Vithalbhai's who was already studying English at Nadiad and was staying with his maternal uncle. Zaverbhai could not send Patel there, as he did not want to burden his brother-in-law with the responsibility of his second son as well. A private English school up to the third standard opened at Karamsad, which Patel joined, though for a year only. Thereafter, he was sent to Petlad, where the local school had English up to the fifth standard.

By imbibing the environment of Karamsad in the company of his father, Patel became a true son of the soil—more rural than urban in outlook. At Petlad, away from his sheltered family life at Karamsad, he had a different experience: the rich experience of community living, necessitated by the family's frugal circumstances. He collected half a dozen students who jointly rented a house. Each boy, when he went home on a Sunday, brought back with him enough foodgrains to last a week; and during the week each member of the small community cooked meals by turns. Patel was the organiser, and the leader.

Patel was keen to pursue his study of English. The desire seemed to be in keeping with the prevailing spirit of the times. Socially, the language had already become a status symbol; but, more importantly, it had opened the gates to higher employment in service for Indians, or a more respectable and lucrative position in one of the newly thrown open professions—particularly the legal. Zaverbhai had no recourse this time but to send Patel to Nadiad and allow him to stay with his maternal uncle. Here the world grew still bigger for Patel; and he had better opportunities for sharpening his talents as a rebel student leader. He once admitted, "I yielded to none in the captaincy of mischief or of sly attempts to hoodwink one's elders."[2]

In the very first year at Nadiad, in his sixth standard, he organised a strike in his school which lasted three days. It was over a fellow student whom a haughty, high-handed teacher, taking pride in caning boys, had turned out of class for failing to bring from his parents the fine-money imposed on him the previous day. Even though he himself was a boy, Patel could not stomach such injustice. At his call, the class staged a walkout. To make matters worse, he persuaded the entire school to go on strike. He even organised picketing! He conducted his operations from the headquarters he had set up in the travellers' rest-house at Nadiad, which he had taken possession of and where the strikers rested by turns. On the third day of the agitation, the headmaster thought it prudent to reach an "honourable" settlement with Patel on the assurance that no excessive and unjust punishment would be meted out in future. Patel was then hardly eighteen. Immediately thereafter, he taught a lesson to another teacher who was running the private business of selling paper, pencils and exercise books and openly forced the boys to buy from him. This time Patel organised an effective boycott of him. The teacher was so shaken with fear that he gave up his sidelines.

Patel had "no patience with an indifferent teacher". Nor did he "spare a lazy one". He and his classmates used to make fun of a teacher who had the habit of coming late to the class. He punished Patel with the task of writing one to ten. Not complying with this, the teacher went on increasing this "doublefold for each day that went by" until it became Patel's task "to write out the sums 200 times". Patel explained later, "I wrote on the slate just the figure 200 and took it to my teacher with an innocent air. The teacher asked me where the *padas* were (meaning in Gujarati both sums and buffaloes). I told him I could write only 200 when the *padas* (buffaloes) ran away! The teacher was all sound and fury. I was presented before the headmaster, who, instead of punishing me, took the teacher to task for not knowing the correct method of prescribing tasks."[3]

Such successful adventures established Patel's leadership in school. No less was his reputation built as an agitator. And he grew bolder to accept a bigger challenge in the civic life of Nadiad. One of his teachers was standing for municipal elections. His opponent, a wealthy, influential person, was too confident of his success. Unwisely, he declared in a moment of uncalled for pride that, if he were defeated, he would have his moustache shaved! A moustache was in those days a symbol of masculine pride, class consciousness and status ego, but shaving it off meant disgrace. The fighting instinct in Patel stirred him into action. He accepted the challenge on behalf of his poor, humble teacher. He worked with "such resolute will and steadfastness that his teacher scored a resounding victory over his opponent."[4] His impishness did not let him rest at that. He led a procession of some 50 boys to the house of the defeated candidate, taking with him a barber to round off the affair!

Patel, thus, became the unquestionable leader of the small student community of Nadiad. He enjoyed the confidence and backing of almost all the boys in his school, including the seniors. To keep them as a well-knit body, he started a "club" where at night the students assembled not merely to pursue their studies, but to sort out their common problems and seek remedies. Patel's influence, at that young age, was acknowledged even by some teachers, some of whom sought his help to seek redress of their grievances against the headmaster!

From Nadiad, Patel moved to Baroda to join a school there. But his stay did not last longer than a month. During this short period he gave ample evidence of his irrepressible, rebellious nature. Since he preferred to opt for Gujarati in place of Sanskrit, much against the wishes of his class teacher, the later tauntingly called him *mahapurush* (a great man). Once when Patel could not bear it, he sarcastically asked him, "If all of us studied Sanskrit, whom would you teach Gujarati?" But he had a more serious clash with his teacher of mathematics in the Government High

School at Baroda. One day the teacher found himself confused trying to do an algebraic problem. Patel had the audacity to stand up and say, "Sir, you don't know how to work it out!" In sheer irritation, the teacher threw a challenge, "Well, if I do not know how to do it, come here and be a teacher yourself." Undaunted, Patel went to the board and not only solved the problem, but impudently occupied the teacher's chair! The headmaster sent for Patel and warned him to behave himself, to which he retorted, "I do not wish to study in a school where there are teachers of such type."[5]

Patel passed the Matriculation examination from the Nadiad High School in 1897. He was 22. Reminiscing later in the Yeravada jail in 1932, Patel humorously narrated to Gandhi and Mahadev Desai what his maternal uncle thought of his future, "My uncle was an overseer in the municipality. He thought I wouldn't pursue my studies, and, therefore, he would find a job for me. He told me: "Come to the municipality. I will get you a *mukudam's* (mate's) job and you will start earning immediately."[6] Many Indians of his class and status were entering life like that in those days. Patel might have followed their example. Once a mate, he might have remained a mate, having had no engineering qualifications. But fate seemed to have destined him to be different—one who was to shape India's destiny as much as his own.

In spite of his failure in Matriculation the previous year, Patel was a bright boy—gifted with an ingenious mind bent more towards agitational activities than studies. Towards teachers who were just and honest, he always had kindly thoughts and showed them the highest regard. He almost revered them. Years later, in 1938 when he was the Congress party boss and Chairman of the Congress Parliamentary Board, Patel happened to be on a visit to Baroda. Someone told him that his English teacher in the Baroda High School, Manchershaw Wadia, wished to come and pay his respects to him. Jokingly, he asked, "Is Mr. Wadia still alive?" He hurriedly got up and left for Wadia's house. Meanwhile, Wadia too had left his place to meet Patel. Both met somewhere halfway. According to a witness: "The Sardar bent down to touch his old teacher's feet. Mr. Wadia, filled with great emotion, lifted him up and embraced him, tears of boundless joy rolling down his cheeks."

3

Pleader Whom the Police Feared

Zaverbhai, as Patel admitted in 1921, had "no means to enable me to fulfil my ambitions."[1] He came from a middle-class family, lived a humble and pious life and died in the temple he loved.[2] Patel had, therefore, to devise his own means to achieve his ambitions: first, to become a pleader, and after that, a barrister. During those days a Matriculate could become a lawyer by taking the Pleaders examination. Since he had neither the money nor the time to spend on higher studies, he took the short-cut and became a pleader in 1900.

Where was he to start his practice? His resources were limited. But his independent nature did not permit him to accept the offer of his brother, Vithalbhai, and some others to join them as their junior. He did not want to start life like that; it didn't matter if that meant coming up the hard way. His choice fell on Godhra. Vithalbhai, who had practised there since 1895, had shifted to Borsad. Patel could hopefully take over some of his practice to begin with. Moreover, Godhra, being a small town of 4,000 inhabitants, suited his means.

In July 1900, Patel and his wife, Javerbai, arrived at Godhra, bringing with them hardly anything, barring a handful of household articles and a few legal books. With borrowed money he rented a small house and opened a modest office. While Javerbai arranged her kitchen and their living-room, Patel devoted himself to the setting up of his office—arranging his books, table and chairs; even fixing his nameplate on the front door, which read: Vallabhbhai J. Patel, District Pleader, Godhra.

It was a humble beginning. The realist in Patel suffered from no illusions of immediate success. Luck, however, smiled upon him not before long. The first year ended with his earning Rs.600—on an average of Rs.50 a month. That was a considerable amount in 1900 in any Indian city, let alone a small town like Godhra. The success earned him a name. But his independent nature and aversion to flattery made him not too popular a figure among his professional colleagues. This was particularly felt in the local club, where others showed a certain coldness towards him. Ignoring them, Patel continued riding the wave of success. But he always looked for a change for the better. An opportunity arrived two years later.

Bubonic plague broke out at Godhra. A friend named Ramjibhai was stricken with it. Being a bachelor, he had none to look after him. He sent for Patel, who nursed him as best he could, but Ramjibhai did not survive. Returning from his cremation, Patel discovered that he too had caught the disease. Overruling the protests of his wife, he sent Javerbai to his parents at Karamsad, while he himself, saying goodbye to Godhra, proceeded to Nadiad where he stayed alone till he recovered fully.

In 1920, Patel shifted to Borsad. It was a taluka headquarters and had the highest number of criminal cases not only in Kheda district of which it formed a part, but in the whole of Bombay Presidency. The people were simple, honest, but virile. They did not hesitate committing acts of violence for which, in the eyes of the British officials, they appeared to be criminals. To deal with them with a stern hand, the Government made special arrangements: appointment of a First Class Resident Magistrate, and for the Government Pleader for Ahmedabad to appear for the prosecution. No opportunity could have been better than this for Patel to become a criminal lawyer of repute.

Patel's move from Godhra to Borsad was also for another reason: to be nearer to Vithalbhai who had got into hot water with the local magistracy. He had annoyed the Resident First Class Magistrate, the Mamlatdar and the First Class Sub-Judge by getting a commission appointed to inquire into complaints of bribery and corruption against a former Sub-Judge. They all looked for an occasion to wreak vengeance on Vithalbhai. Patel's "operation rescue" was a camouflaged move. The brothers lived apart though they secretly helped each other financially in times of need. Patel would not talk to his brother in public. This gave the impression that the brothers were not on good terms. But like a shrewd lawyer, Patel waited patiently for an opportunity when he could retrieve the situation for Vithalbhai and restore his status and prestige. The opportunity came soon. Patel happened to be engaged in a case in which the Mamlatdar was involved. No one except he could save the Mamlatdar's approaches, but finally agreed to help him only on Vithalbhai's recommendation! The judiciary was left with no choice but to patch up with Vithalbhai.

There was a highly dramatic incident in Borsad. One day when Patel appeared in the court of a British Sub-Judge, he found him sitting in his chair without wearing his gown. If it was hot and humid for the judge, it was no less for the gowned lawyers. Patel decided to squarely deal with such blatant disrespect for a tradition the British had themselves handed down for strict adherence in the courts. As soon as the judge asked Patel to begin his arguments, he quietly got up, betrayed no emotion, and then slung a stinging surprise on the judge by declaring, "As the Hon'ble Judge is not properly dressed, this seems to be no court!" Those present in the court-room were stunned. And without losing a minute, Patel turned his face to leave when the judge retrieved the situation by putting on the gown and offering his apologies. None before Patel had shown such fearlessness. The incident proved his audacity and established his reputation as a dauntless lawyer in the whole of Borsad taluka. It also boosted his practice. What equally contributed to his success was his extraordinary thoroughness in the preparation of his cases. He would accept only a few, but charged high fees.

As a criminal lawyer, Patel mostly took up the defence of those involved in police cases for murder, dacoity and similar cases. He chose this line because of his being a fighter; also, because the early termination of these cases brought him quick money. He was in a hurry to earn as much as he could in the shortest possible time, so as to be able to proceed to England to become a barrister. Since he always appeared against the police, it was natural that he should have earned their displeasure. That worried him the least. He remained unconcerned and undaunted. His deep understanding of human nature, his thorough analysis of the circumstances of the case and his penetrating cross-examination helped him win more than 90 per cent of the cases. This meant loss of face for the police.

The authorities in Bombay got perturbed. It was obvious that as long as Patel was at Borsad, there could be no hope for the police prosecution to win. So it was decided to shift the criminal court from Borsad to Anand, a distance of 15 miles. That meant a great distance during those days. The authorities thought Patel would stay on at Borsad. But he belied their hopes. While other lawyers jointly engaged a *tonga* for going to Anand, Patel had one of his own. Besides the driver, a servant would accompany him to carry his books. He wanted to impress upon others his superior status, especially when he intended to deal with the bureaucracy not as their inferior but as their equal.

Anand made no difference to Patel. Nor did it benefit the police. Patel's success remained unchecked. Police prestige continued to suffer, with Patel winning almost all the cases against them. Acquittal seemed to be the rule rather than an exception. Since the authorities failed in their objective, the criminal court was shifted back to Borsad after a year's unsuccessful experiment. This put an additional feather in Patel's cap. He established his reputation as the pleader whom the police feared.

Patel's fame soared higher still; and he grew bolder. His brushes with the magistrates became more frequent. There is, for instance, the typical story of the looking-glass. During the court proceedings, a magistrate adopted a devious method to nonplus the accused by asking him to see his face in a looking-glass while being cross-examined. Patel put an end to this by objecting to the procedure, and demanded that the court should make note of it. Fearing that the incident, if recorded, would assume seriousness in Patel's deft hands, the magistrate, getting somewhat nervous, dismissed the court, called Patel to his chambers and almost begged of him not to insist upon the incident being recorded.

Vithalbhai was jovial and carefree, never willing to shoulder responsibility—even of his family. The younger brother was serious-looking, reserved, never letting anyone have a peep into his heart and mind. Yet, Patel was kind-hearted, full of sympathy for the underdog, endowed with a sense of subtle, sarcastic humour. His professional career as a pleader had many instances of the latter. He had appeared before the Collector in an appeal case in which a goldsmith had been sentenced to six months imprisonment by the lower court on charge of trespass with the intention of committing adultery with a woman. The Collector, a Britisher, happened to be drunk while conducting the court proceedings. He left it to his Sarishtedar to take up cross-examination. Patel took it to be an insult. Without hesitation, he declared, "I haven't come to conduct the case before the Sarishtedar. I was under the impression that I had to conduct it before the Collector." This unexpected boldness gave a jolt to the Collector, and brought him to his senses. Without argument or delay, he himself assumed charge of cross-examination. During the course of the proceedings the Collector asked Patel, "Is adultery a crime?" Patel's sarcastic reply caused considerable amusement to those present in the courtroom, but embarrassment to the Collector, "No, Sir. In all advanced countries, adultery is not an offence. But in this backward country, the *sadhus* and magistrates of the lower court, religious, narrow-minded Brahmins (meaning the Sarishtedar) look upon such an offence as serious."[3]

Patel practiced at Borsad for nearly eight years, till the year 1910, during which period he had built a name for himself as a most successful criminal lawyer. He had set up a happy home too, with a daughter, Maniben, and a son, Dahyabhai, born in 1904 and 1905. Towards the closing years of his Borsad stay, a great personal tragedy befell him: the death of his wife. He bore it with rare fortitude and courage. About mid-1908, Javerbai suffered from acute intestinal trouble and later in the year had to be shifted to Bombay for treatment. She was to undergo an operation as soon as she regained her strength. Meanwhile, Patel was to appear in a murder case. To utilise the intervening period, he returned to Borsad, leaving Javerbai in the charge of his brother, Vithalbhai, who had been practising at Bombay since his return from England as a barrister. The operation became necessary during Patel's absence, and was performed successfully. He was informed of this. But soon after, Javerbai's condition suddenly deteriorated, and she died on January 11, 1909.

When Javerbai died, Patel was thirty-three. The tragedy shattered his home life. He children were only four and five years old respectively. And he had yet many important things to achieve in life. Brushing aside pressures from his parents and relations, he decided not to marry for the second time. Such a decision was also in keeping with the family tradition. His two elder brothers, Somabhai and Vithalbhai, had lost their wives at 35, and so did his younger brother, Kashibhai, at 32.

Even at that young age, there was an iron-like quality in Patel's character. He never wavered in the decisions he once took and pursued them with an astonishingly strong determination.

4

A Great Ambition Fulfilled

Patel wanted to be a great man, and in those days to become a great man meant to become a lawyer or a barrister. His obsession for the latter had been aroused by his occasional brushes with barristers from Ahmedabad visiting Borsad. They were pompous, status conscious, commanding not only higher prestige but also higher fees. Patel could not suffer them. The only way he satisfied his ruptured ego was by jesting at them. He seldom missed an opportunity when he could display his superiority. But the real solution, he knew, lay in his becoming a barrister himself.

Patel had to overcome two hurdles: first, how to finance his visit to London; second, how to set aside any objection from his family. "I was told", he once admitted, "that only if I could get seven to ten thousand rupees, I would be able to proceed to England. No one was likely to give me so much money. I realised finally that if I wanted to go to England, I had to earn the money myself. I, therefore, studied very earnestly for my law examination and resolved firmly to save sufficient money for a visit to England." Patel was "anxious to go overseas to see the people of England, who, living 7000 miles away, were able to rule us for so long", as also "to imitate the British and their ways closely."[1] Without that, he felt, he couldn't be a successful barrister. Such a metamorphosis, physical as well as mental, most educated Indians of his times had slavishly undergone. Patel was no exception. And neither was Gandhi.

In an effort to cross the second hurdle, Patel contrived an ingenious device as a test case to break any possible social barrier. Along with three other friends, he hatched a plan, instigating one of them, Lakshmishankar Karunashankar, to secretly leave for England to become a barrister. Lakshmishankar was chosen because he had the financial means to put the plan into action. Unlike others, he belonged to rich parents, his father being a money-lender from Borsad. At the instigation of Patel and others, he stole money from his father's safe, returned to Nadiad where the others waited for him, and from there he was packed off to Bombay *en route* to England. Lakshmishankar's father kept on enquiring about his son. But all were tight-lipped. The secret was out only when Lakshmishankar sent his father a cable from Aden asking for more money. On his return, whenever Lakshmishankar reminded Patel that, as originally planned, it was now his turn to go, he would give the evasive reply, "I am preparing for it."

That was literally true. Patel had to have enough money to implement his plan. Leading a simple, austere life, and practising as much as he could, he saved enough from his earnings as a pleader. By 1905 he was ready to fulfil the second ambition of his life. A passage was arranged through Thomas Cook & Sons. But Fate played a joke on him to upset his plans. Addressed as V.J. Patel, his passport and other travel documents, which carried no photographs those days, were delivered by mistake by the postman to Vithalbhai who too had been nursing the hope of going to England to become a barrister. But he had saved no money. Exercising an elder's prerogative in a Hindu family, Vithalbhai took it to be his opportunity first—not the younger brother's, no matter if the latter had sweated to save money for this visit. As a true Hindu, Patel bowed to his brother's wishes without a grumble. Not only did he surrender his travel documents to Vithalbhai, but also willingly agreed to bear his entire expenses.

Even with this sacrifice on Patel's part, the elder brother still faced another problem. With whom was he to leave his wife? Again, the younger brother came to his help by willingly putting up his sister-in-law at his Borsad house. Hardly a few days had passed when the two women quarreled seriously. Since his sister-in-law had no place to go to and Patel had taken upon himself the responsibility of looking after her during Vithalbhai's absence, he underwent another sacrifice. He sent his wife to his in-laws, and let her remain there till he could honourably "return" his sister-in-law to his brother on Vithalbhai's return from England.

Vithalbhai returned to India in 1908. Meanwhile, Patel had continued to collect the required money once again by working still harder at the Bar. He would have proceeded to England without further delay but for his wife's death in January 1909. A year later in August, he managed to leave for England.

Being reserved by nature, Patel had kept his plan a closely guarded secret. The earlier one, though a secret, had been betrayed by the postman. This time too, none knew about it except Vithalbhai with whom he had to correspond in order to gain some knowledge of the country he was to visit and the studies he was to pursue. Another person who could merely smell the plan was his younger brother, Kashibhai, who, in the true style of a detective, had spied on him. He had collected bits of torn letters Vithalbhai had written to Patel, which he pieced together to know the secret. But as a dutiful brother, he kept it to himself, not letting even their parents know. A day prior to his departure from Borsad, Patel disclosed his plan to two of his friends, Dr. Jivanlal Bavabhai Dave and Tulsidas Garibdas Patel, as he wanted them to look after Kashibhai, who had come to Borsad after qualifying as a pleader and who was to take over his brother's house and practice.

Patel had kept the whole of Borsad guessing: What was he up to? Nobody knew. On the departure day when a *ghorra garry* was being loaded with his luggage, the postmaster ventured to ask Patel if he was leaving for England. To such a simple query, the answer was evasive, "It is not yet certain." Its coldness dampened the courage of the postmaster. He felt dissuaded to pursue the matter further, but ruefully commented after Patel had left, "Look at this fellow! He has left. But he talked to me so evasively." Patel continued to be an enigma even on his return from England. Instead of going to Karamsad to see his parents, he went to Borsad. When asked for the reason, his simple reply was, "I had gone from Borsad. So I have come back to Borsad."

Patel was thirty-five when he sailed for England. He was seen off at Bombay by none excepting Vithalbhai. Even when he was mature, experienced, worldly-wise, not given to fun, frolic or frivolity like other young men of his times, he did believe that "it was the best policy to imitate the foreigner". He had accepted what he had been taught to think: "that the people of our country were of poor character and unworthy, and that it was only the foreigner ruling over us who was good and had the ability to improve our condition. We could only be slaves."[2] He admired the British and had faith in their invincibility. Yet, he was devoid of sentimentalism. He had a clear-cut objective before him: a definite, determined purpose for which he was going to England—to return home as a barrister within the shortest possible time.

On board the ship, Patel put on the European dress for the first time. Till then he had worn a *dhoti*, turban, a long coat often unbuttoned, and open slippers that required no socks to wear. Another change he underwent was the use of a fork and knife at the dining table. Almost all the passengers were Europeans. Seeing western life so closely, there could have been many temptations for Patel. But he was not the person to allow distractions to take him away from the only purpose of his journey to England. In the fulfillment of it, he had begun serious studies on board the vessel itself, and completed Roman Law before reaching Marseilles.

His lone Indian companion on board was a Thakur from Kathiawar, whose company he kept in London too on landing, by staying at Hotel Cecil. But it was far beyond his means. He was to live in England within his savings. Therefore, he moved out the next day, and put up with a friend for a couple of days before finally shifting to a moderately-priced boarding house at 23, Aldrige Villa, Bayswater.

Patel joined the Middle Temple. Straightaway he plunged into serious studies, devoting not less than eleven hours each day. His limited means imposed many hardships on him. Unable to possess many of the books he badly needed, he depended on the Middle Temple library, which was about ten to twelve miles away from the place of his residence. Daily he walked up that much distance both ways. He reached the library at nine in the morning and stayed on till six in the evening, in between taking his frugal lunch and tea.

Soon after joining the Middle Temple, Patel took an examination in Roman Law in which he stood first. The full course of studies meant twelve terms, four in a year. One who passed with honours could take the final examination on the completion of the sixth term, which meant cutting down the total period of three years to half. Patel qualified for such a concession. He stood bracketed "first" in the preliminary examination in the paper on Equity, sharing the prize of Rs 5 with one G. Davis, who later entered the Indian Civil Service and retired as the Chief Justice of the Sind High Court. Patel took the final examination in June 1912, and was called to the Bar on January 27, 1913. He obtained a first class first, winning the prize of Rs 50.

Patel did not desire to stay in England a day longer than was necessary. Having passed the final examination in June 1912, he considered it a waste of time to stay on till January 1913 for the Call Night—not even bothering about the solemn grandeur of the occasion which filled many a would-be great man with a sense of pride. He was very keen on returning home immediately. His savings were just enough for that and he had come to London straight from Borsad without visiting his parents at Karamsad. Above all, Ahmedabad—the city of his dreams—was beckoning him to come and fulfil the second ambition of his life: to start practising as a barrister on par with the barristers with whom he had crossed swords earlier at Borsad as a district court pleader. He had also no desire to see the famed beauty of cities like Naples and Venice or make a trip to Switzerland to see the splendour of the Alps. No attraction, however alluring, could change his mind or purpose.

Patel, therefore, applied for an exemption on the basis of his excellent record at the Inn. His request was given due consideration by the Constitution Committee, which, however, feared that a precedent once set up would attract others to take advantage of it, thus lowering the solemnity and dignity of the Call Night. Patel's request was, therefore, turned down, and he had to live in England for the next six months or so. He utilised the time to extensively tour the British Isles.

The Call Night on January 27, 1913 was no ordinary night for Patel. It symbolised the culmination of his unremitting toil over a year and a half. It was the fulfillment of his most cherished ambition, for which he had laboured for well over a decade. On the Call Night, in the Middle Temple Hall assembled the students whose Call had been approved by the British Parliament. The atmosphere was somber and exuded the dignity of the Honourable and Learned Society of Barristers. The ceremony was tradition-bound. The students, pre-eminent among whom was Patel for having stood first, took their places in the order in which they were to be called. Like the others, he too wore a wig and gown over a dark suit. The Master Treasurer, the Master Reader and the other Masters sat on the dais. Each student was individually presented to the Master Treasurer by the Master Reader. The former called him "in the name of the Bench... to the Degree of the Utter Bar". Thereafter, in keeping with the ancient tradition, Patel entered his name at the Cupboard in the Book containing the Roll of the Barristers of the Inn. The ceremony concluded with a dinner with night.

Prior to the Call, Patel was required to find out a Bencher who could propose his name and another who could second it. But Patel knew none. He chose one from the list of Benchers, and approached him. Not only did he willingly agree to oblige Patel, but even found a supporter for him. He turned out to be a cousin of the Chief Justice of the Bombay High Court, Basil Scott. The night after the Call, he invited Patel to dinner. But the latter had to regretfully decline it, as he was sailing home the very next day. But the Bencher, pleased with Patel's performance in the Bar examination, volunteered to give him a letter of introduction to Basil Scott.

Patel reached Bombay on February 13th. He called upon Basil Scott, who was extremely courteous in his welcome, solicitous in advising him to set up practice in Bombay, and even offered him a job in the Government Law School. But Patel's heart was in Ahmedabad, where he was to build up a lucrative practice. So, he politely refused the kind offer of the Chief Justice.

The new barrister caused a flutter in the Ahmedabad Bar. Patel was "a smart young man, dressed in well-cut clothes, with a felt hat worn slightly at an angle, stern and reserved, his eyes piercing and bright, not given to many words, receiving visitors with just a simple greeting but not entering into any conversation, and of a firm and pensive expression, almost as if one looked down upon the world with a sort of superiority complex, talking with an air of confidence and superiority whenever he opened his lips... His personality and demeanour, attracted them (the junior Bar), but they had mixed feelings of respect, awe and, perhaps, of subdued resentment at the way he seemed to look at others."[3]

It did not take Patel long to conquer the barrister-dominated Bar. For he stood head and shoulders above others at cross-examination: penetrating enough to unnerve even well-prepared, hardened witnesses. He possessed that rare quality: "a quick judgment of men" by a mere piercing glance at the witness; he knew the type of person he was, which determined his attack in cross-examination. "In conducting cases, he always exhibited a thorough mastery of facts, a proper and correct estimate of the opponent's points and line of attack, and a carefully planned defence and attack."[4]

What mattered above all was the fearlessness with which he dealt with the court—something unheard of in 1913-14, when Gandhi had not yet arrived in India. G.V. Mavalankar gives the instance of a murder case. During the sessions trial, Patel had "a straight thrust at the judge" for his refusal to grant bail on the police plea that, being a Kheda case, the accused should be taken to be "a dangerous person". Patel could not stomach this. He himself was from Kheda. He declared with rare boldness: "I regret very much to note that no accused from Kheda gets a fair trial in this court. If there is insufficient evidence, it is suggested that the accused, being a Kheda man, must have tampered with it. Since the district is considered to be criminal, whether there is evidence or not, it is thought that the accused must be convicted. That appears to be the reasoning of this court. If this were not the case, I do not see why bail should not have been granted in a case like this where there is not even *prima facie* evidence of the guilt of the accused."

According to Mavalankar, "the judge was stunned at this frontal attack". He, therefore, spoke in a condescending tone: "Mr. Patel, you were obviously in an excited mood when you made such a serious allegation against the court. We will adjourn and meet after half an hour."[5] He went into his chamber and, without waiting for the half-hour to be over, passed orders granting bail to the accused. But Patel's ultimate success lay in his acquittal.

Thus did Barrister Patel storm the Ahmedabad courts and the Bar with his domineering personality: bold, fearless, competent and totally dedicated to his profession.

5

A Rebel Enters Municipal Politics

In 1905, when the Bengal Partition agitation was sweeping the land, Patel was quietly building up his legal practice at Borsad. Being the son of a rebel, his mind must have been disturbed by the happenings in the country. But he saw no reason to allow himself to be carried away from his immediate goal of life: to earn enough for a passage to England and return as a barrister. He could become one not before 1913, by which time Vithalbhai had already given up his legal practice and entered public life by joining the Bombay Legislative Council. Once again it fell to Patel's lot to support his brother. There was an understanding between the two, as Patel admitted, that "one of us should serve the country; and the other, the family." He added with his characteristic well-meaning humour, "My brother gave up his flourishing practice and started on a career of public service, while I bore the burden of maintaining the household. I had, thus, to commit all the sins, and he performed all the good deeds; but I reconciled myself with the thought that I could claim at least a share in his good work!"[1]

Barrister Patel merrily practised at Ahmedabad from 1913 onwards. His hitherto hurt ego as a pleader of Borsad found satisfaction from his great success in the law courts—against the very barristers and lawyers who had wounded his pride earlier. Now, as a barrister amongst them, he too enjoyed the same status, and his confidence in his ability as a criminal lawyer got a further fillip. Courts apart, he took pleasure in establishing his supremacy even in the Gujarat Club, where his professional colleagues gathered to pass their leisure hours gossiping over cups of tea. Since the club was located opposite the courts and his house nearby, he spent his evenings there playing bridge against the same barristers and lawyers.

The fame of Patel's skill as a bridge player spread in no time among the club members. To one member in particular, this was like a thorn in his flesh. He was senior Barrister Wadia, who took pride in his having introduced the game in the club. Wadia also had a high opinion about himself. He refused to accept Patel's superiority, and had vowed to defeat his rival. His ego made him raise the stakes so high as to have lost on the first day Rs.200 to Rs. 300 and on the second day Rs.400 to Rs.500. Fearing that worse might happen on the third, Mrs. Wadia besought Patel to cancel the game. He readily obliged the lady, as he himself was adverse to playing such high stakes, but had been forced by the challenge thrown by Mrs. Wadia's husband. Nevertheless, it was a common joke in the club that a quarter of Barrister Wadia's earnings went into Barrister Patel's pocket!

While Patel was leading a quiet, prosperous, comfortable life between the courts and the Gujarat Club, a crisis was brewing in the Ahmedabad Municipality. An amendment of the District Municipal Act in 1914 permitted the appointment of an ICS officer as the head of a self-governing institution. The purpose was to curb the powers of Municipal Councillors to be elected in 1915. The Government camouflaged its real intentions through a devious device; by first making *ad hoc* appointments of non-ICS Indian officers for short spells. Most of them served only for six to seven months. M.A. Dixit was there for 17 days, while Bhaishankar Nanubhai Bhatt just for one day! Finally came the appointment of J.A. Shillidy, ICS, in November 1915. With this the Government's real intentions became known.

The move to appoint an ICS officer as Municipal Commissioner was strongly criticised by the Councillors. They apprehended loss of whatever limited authority they enjoyed. Shillidy was a blue-blooded bureaucrat, who meant to rule with the firm hand of an autocrat, ignoring the proclaimed principles of self-government granted to the people. There was friction between him and the Councillors over his unconstitutional interference in the working of the municipal administration. He spent money as he wished, without reference to the appropriate municipal body. He chose to usurp the President's right to correspond with the Government. Further, considering himself above municipal rules and regulations, he absented himself from work without intimation to the President. On many occasions his actions were adversely commented upon by the President and the Secretary, both of whom were mild-tempered, public-spirited gentlemen pitted against an arrogant, assertive, self-opinionated British Municipal Commissioner.

The administration of the Municipality was in a chaotic state. The Administration Report for 1916-17 stated: "It was found everywhere that there was little organization, duties were carelessly defined and procedure was negligible..." Its author, the President of the Municipality, R.B. Ramanbhai, further stated:" the efficiency of the municipal staff is at a low ebb. Complaints on the part of the public against delays and corruption by municipal servants have been rife... it cannot be denied that they are founded on a substratum of truth. Good roads, good conservancy and good water supply are the three elements of municipal administration... in none of these is the Municipality in a position to show satisfactory work..."[2] The seriousness of the affairs invited adverse comment even from among some of the public-spirited citizens of Ahmedabad. It was also discussed at length by the Bombay Provincial Conference at its 16th session held at Ahmedabad in October 1916 under the Presidentship of Mohammad Ali Jinnah, the creator of Pakistan in 1947, who in those days was the epitome of secular politics in India. The conference recommended abolition of the office of the Municipal Commissioner. Patel had attended the conference as a visitor in the company of Vithalbhai, but had taken no part in its deliberations.

Mere protests and resolutions could not have resolved the situation. Some leaders of public opinion realised that "only someone with Vallabhbhai's skill, shrewdness and fearlessness could organise the agitation for the abolition of the post of the Municipal Commissioner".[3] It involved a battle of wits with the dictator-like British Municipal Commissioner, who could have been outwitted and defeated only by one who possessed dauntless courage and an ingenious legal brain: indeed, "a person with tough temperament, rough manners and indomitable spirit", which alone could "match the arrogance, obstinacy and irritability of Shillidy." And so, "a search for such a person was going on till the eyes of some of the members of the Gujarat Club fell upon Vallabhbhai who was well-known among his colleagues for qualities of sustained labour, blunt repartee and a tendency of delivering telling blows on his adversaries."[4] A born fighter, Patel yielded to the persuasion of friends. He got elected in an election held on January 5, 1917, which was nevertheless declared invalid and set aside. In a fresh poll that took place on May14, Patel was elected unopposed.

A rebel, thus, entered municipal politics. Patel's presence stirred the drooping spirits of the Councillors, injecting into them a new life, much to the dislike and discomfort of Shillidy. Patel sought to curb the self-acquired power of the Municipal Commissioner through forthright, determined, constitutional moves. As an essential prerequisite, he had first to forge unity among the docile and spineless Councillors. They were afraid of incurring Shillidy's displeasure. Patel counselled them that unless they shed their fears, they would not achieve anything. Their servile attitude gave direct encouragement to the Municipal Commissioner to ride roughshod over them and humiliate them. It was sheer coincidence that about this time Gandhi too had started delivering his first lessons in self-respect from the same city—Ahmedabad.

Patel took two steps to defeat Shillidy. Both were constitutional. The first put monetary limits on the purchase transactions. Those already authorised by the General Board were to be entertained by the Municipal Commissioner. The second required of the latter to accept any one of the tenders recommended to him by the Board. Patel got a resolution passed by the Board which called upon the Municipal Commissioner to furnish a statement of purchases made by him since 1914-15, and added insult to injury by suggesting that the Managing Committee should scrutinise it before its submission to the Board. It was an attempt to establish the Board's authority over the Municipal Commissioner.

In a battle of wits between Patel and Shillidy, the latter had to eat humble pie on quite a few occasions. Nearly 75,000 gallons of municipal water were supplied to the British officers and others in the Cantonment area at a "very nominal rate" of 2 annas and 6 pies per 1,000 gallons, whereas for the same water the city rate-payers paid 8 annas per 1,000 gallons. Not satisfied with this concession, the Cantonment authorities took law into their own hands and "tampered with the meter to receive more water surreptitiously."[5] Not only that, during the hot summer months when there was no water available in some localities of the city, army officers in the Cantonment callously wasted scarce water. The citizens of Ahmedabad also suffered in another way. The water supplied in the taps was often muddy and impure, accounting for the high incidence of typhoid cases. This was largely due to "the incompetence of the Municipal Engineer, V.M. Macassey, in whose appointment Shillidy and Pratt… had taken a prominent but 'back-door' part".[6] Nobody had up to then dared question the Municipal Commissioner. Only Patel did—and could. He had the issue set right to the satisfaction of the citizens of Ahmedabad by getting the subject transferred to the Sanitary Committee of which he was the Chairman.

There was also Shillidy's clever move to change the constitution of the Schools Committee whereby it could be transformed into an independent body to be directly under him. Because of the formidable opposition built up by Patel, Shillidy had to drop his proposal. It was submission to the Board's verdict on both the issues. He could, however, not forget the insult heaped on him. For Patel, it was no victory to celebrate. He looked for the opportunity when he would "net" Shillidy and force his removal from the post. Not before long, Patel had his prize catch. A small lake in Ahmedabad had been transferred to the Municipality by the Government in 1914 with the object of filling it up because of its abominable smell and also because it bred mosquitoes. Near this lake was a match factory owned by a Municipal Councillor, Fateh Mohammed Munshi, who used it for seasoning his timber. He was a favourite of Shillidy. In return for his war contribution, he claimed ownership of the lake. This was rejected both by the lower courts and the Bombay High Court. Shillidy, however, did not implement the Government decision to fill it up, thereby helping Munshi to continue making use of the lake. Not satisfied with the manner in which the lake issue was being treated, F.G. Pratt, Commissioner of Northern Division, intervened to establish the Municipality's claim over the lake. In spite of that, Shillidy acted contrary to that, circumventing it by recommending to the Government to give away the lake to Munshi on a permanent lease.

This was the opportunity Patel was angling for. On June 7, 1917, he charged the Municipal Commissioner with "deliberate insubordination" and demanded his removal. For Shillidy, it became an issue of prestige. Without consulting the Board, he wrote to the Government that the Municipality did not require the lake, whereby he wanted to let Munshi make use of it as hitherto. This would have at least vindicated his honour. It mattered little to him that the area involved was about 53,000 square yards of municipal land worth Rs.10 lakhs (at 1917 price) which, because of its proximity to the railway station, was bound to appreciate in value soon. Patel saw in this Shillidy's failure in not protecting the Municipality's ownership rights. A further indiscretion on Shillidy's part was that in the letter to the Government, approved by the Board, Shillidy had arbitrarily deleted thirteen significant words. Patel considered this an administrative "crime", and, therefore, unpardonable. Through a Board's resolution, he demanded Shillidy's removal from the post of Municipal Commissioner. The facts of the case being overwhelmingly against Shillidy, the Government was left with no alternative but to bow to the wishes of the Councillors. And for the first time in India, perhaps, such an action was taken against a British ICS official. It was a victory for Patel—the first shining feather in his cap.

Patel's next encounter was with Pratt, who wanted to exercise greater influence over municipal affairs through the appointment of two more Britishers, besides the Municipal Health Officer. In his bureaucratic pride and high-handed way, he ignored the claims of two fully qualified Indians. The British Municipal Engineer was from the railways. He possessed no knowledge of municipal work. He displayed no competence in the conduct of his new job. Because of such incompetence, he got into trouble. There was an acute shortage of water in certain parts of the city—so much so that the Gujarat Sabha held a protest meeting under Gandhi's presidentship. A copy of the resolution passed was sent to the President of the Municipality, the Collector and the Commissioner. This was about the second half of 1917, when Patel had already become a prominent member of the Sabha. A protest from the Sabha, but more particularly from Gandhi, could not be ignored. As Chairman of the Sanitary Committee, Patel had to devise a strategy to tackle the situation which involved the Commissioner indirectly and the Municipal Engineer directly.

On receipt of a copy of the resolution, Pratt invited the two Secretaries of the Sabha to see him. One of them was G.V. Mavalankar.

Impertinently, Pratt asked them, "Why has this resolution been sent to me? What have I to do with the Municipality?" He took this stand under the District Municipal Act. When one of the Secretaries ventured to suggest that he could use his good offices with the Municipality, Pratt took it to be an oblique reference to his hand in the appointment of the Municipal Engineer. In a fit of anger, he could not restrain himself from saying, "If you have any grievance, go to the Municipal Hall. Do not let the Municipal Committee have peace till you get what you want. If you still do not get water, go to their houses and burn them."[7] This served as fuel to the firebrand Patel. Fearing at the same time that Patel might use such indiscretion on his part to his advantage, Patel tried to amend matters before they got out of hand, by arranging a visit to Ahmedabad by the Consulting Engineer to the Bombay Government.

Accompanied by Pratt, the Municipal Engineer, Patel as Chairman of the Sanitary Committee and the Consulting Engineer went round the city on an inspection tour. During the course of discussion, when Patel wished to offer a suggestion and had hardly uttered the words, "The best way to meet the situation to my mind is", Pratt cut him short with the insulting remark, "The best way, Mr. Patel, is for your committee to cooperate with the Municipal Engineer and not to non-cooperate." Patel was not the man to pocket such insolence. He at once retorted, "The best way is to dispense with the services of this incompetent officer whom you have foisted on the Municipality... when the Secretaries of the Gujarat Sabha waited on you in deputation, you had the impertinence to advise them to burn our houses! Why burn our houses? Why not burn the bungalow of the fellow who is at the root of the trouble?"

Pratt was stunned. He was speechless. He never expected such a drubbing from an Indian. Pratt was a proud Englishman, much senior to the rest, and he was the all powerful Commissioner of Northern Division. Yet, he realised he had gone too far. In an attempt to soothe Patel, he calmly observed, "Mr. Patel, you do not appear to be in a mood to discuss..."

To this Patel retorted, "How do you expect me to be?"[8] The acrimonious atmosphere not only put an end to a discussion of the issue under investigation by the Consulting Engineer from Bombay, but the inspection had to be given up. Patel's victory lay in the resignation of the Municipal Engineer on Pratt's advice.

But a long drawn out battle between Patel and Pratt was fought over education. Patel attempted to rescue education from British control and influence, "to remove their strangulating hold from the municipal schools."[9] Under Patel's leadership, the majority of the Councillors decided to end Government control of municipal schools by refusing to accept Government grant. The Deputy Education Inspector was debarred from inspection of schools; also from conducting the final examinations. A protest lodged by the Education Inspector was rejected by the General Board of the Municipality. This sparked off a bitter controversy. Ignoring the Board's decision, the Deputy Education Inspector wrote to the Chairman of the Schools Committee, Patel, of his intention to visit the schools and conduct examinations. The master tactician in Patel coolly informed the Collector that the examinations had already been held! Not willing to bear this insult, the Deputy Education Inspector warned the Chairman that if the 4th Standard examination were not held under his auspices, the boys would not be admitted to Government-run English middle schools.

The Collector now entered the fray by declaring in a letter that the Schools Committee's resolution was *ultra vires* and directed its non-compliance. Further weight—rather fuel—was added to the controversy with the Commissioner joining the issue. But Patel was not a man to be cowed by such a strong combination. He called a meeting of the Board. He showed rare courage in suggesting that the Collector's letter be filed, and he be simply informed of the examinations having already been conducted. Further, he was to be told that not only had great care been taken in formulating the new education policy, but the Municipality was merely respecting the wishes of the tax-payers, which it was bound to under the Municipal Act. Patel's suggestion was endorsed by the majority of the Councillors.

The Deputy Education Inspector ingeniously thought of using Government grant as a weapon to the municipal schools, and announced his decision to examine their accounts. Patel was quick to act in conveying to him the counter-decision of the Municipality not to accept Government grant, thereby making the examination of accounts unnecessary. Yet, the Deputy Education Inspector insisted on inspection of the schools. This forced Patel to announce bluntly that municipal schools were not to be inspected by Government Inspectors. He instructed the teachers not to permit any Inspector to visit their schools. The situation took a dramatic turn when an Assistant Deputy Inspector attempted to conduct an inspection of one of the schools. Patel boldly severed all links with the Government by asking the latter to withdraw all the 300 odd teachers. He confronted the Government with an embarrassing situation. He simultaneously assured the teachers of their pay and pension in terms of the Civil Service Regulations. He even offered release to those who desired to go. Only three did so. The remaining 297 decided to stand by Patel. He also defeated the Government in its decision to open new schools; and when it ordered the Superintendent of the municipal schools to revert to his parent department, he, in obedience to Patel's advice, resigned from Government service.

The local Government at Ahmedabad having met with failure in its "battles" with Patel, the Presidency Government at Bombay asked Pratt to handle the situation. Pratt and Patel were old foes, and it was expected of the former to fight "tooth and nail" and reduce the recalcitrant Councillors into submission. He was confronted with the challenge the Government faced in the refusal of the municipalities of Ahmedabad, Surat and Nadiad to accept Government grant. Pratt took two steps: one, to call for a report on the working of the three municipalities; and, second, to invite people to sue a municipality for misuse of its funds. Thereby Pratt wanted to sow seeds of dissension among the Councillors, and to break the solid front Patel had forged. But the latter out-manoeuvred the Government by getting the Board to record that Pratt was inciting the tax-paying citizens against the Municipality, and this made it difficult for the latter to do its duty. This put the Government in the dock. The Board further recorded that the Municipality understood better than the Government the educational requirements of the people, and that all municipal actions ought to be in accordance with the citizens' wishes.

Since the dispute was not resolving itself—nor could Patel be outwitted—the Minister of Education, Raghunath Paranjpe, stepped into the scene. He visited Ahmedabad and held discussions with the local leaders. At their very first meeting, Patel bluntly asked him as to what would happen if any compromise reached between them was rejected by the Governor. It was a double-edged attack on the ICS officers whose advice the Governor could not ignore, and the so-called popular Ministers who mattered little in comparison with the former. This was much to the discomfiture of Paranjpe. Being a Minister in those good old days, he least expected it. When Patel had left the meeting, he remarked, "Look at the impertinence of this man. He talked to me in such a manner."

The Government decided to get tougher directly. It held the Municipality responsible for obstructing Government Inspectors from inspecting municipal schools, as also not allowing them to hold examinations. On the Government's instructions, Pratt issued a directive to the President of the Municipality to comply with his order by calling a meeting of the Board on December 17. Patel outwitted Pratt by holding a meeting of the Board five days earlier, and, instead of carrying out his instructions, the Board proposed to the Government to revise the rules to enable municipalities to run their primary schools themselves with their own resources. On this, Pratt ordered the President to divest the Schools Committee, of which Patel was Chairman, of administrative powers over schools, and transfer such powers to the Deputy Education Inspector. Since the latter required money to run them, Pratt further ordered the President to place at his disposal Rs.72,000 within seven days. Patel proved his cleverness in defeating Pratt's plans by ordering the closure of schools on a month's holiday.

That did not end the controversy. Nor did Patel stop at that. He managed with 17 Councillors to issue a signed leaflet which placed the whole matter of primary education before the public of Ahmedabad. The issue caused considerable concern. Ignoring public sentiments, the Government took over schools in Surat and Nadiad. No simultaneous action was taken in Ahmedabad. Before the Government could take action, Patel had the Schools Committee declare Pratt's order illegal, and advised the President of the Municipality that it would consider it improper if he handed over the administration of schools to the Deputy Education Inspector without first consulting the Committee or its Chairman, Patel. Nor should Rs.72,000 be transferred as directed by Pratt but the latter had already withdrawn this amount from the Imperial Bank with the Agent's connivance. The Deputy Education Inspector attempted to have the schools reopened, but failed. The boys boycotted by absenting themselves, while the municipal teachers refused to accept their salary from him.

The Board condemned Pratt's withdrawing municipal money from the bank, and advised him to put it back without delay. Pratt's action also annoyed the moderate Councillors. Patel then called a meeting of the Schools Committee, which resolved that the teachers be paid from the Municipal Treasury. Acting upon such authority, he asked the Personal Assistant to the Chief Officer to arrange for payment by noon that day. Realising his failure to outwit and outmanoeuvre Patel, Pratt had the Municipality suspended on February 9, 1922. In such action lay Pratt's defeat, as it amounted to his withdrawal from the "battlefield".

Patel, however, continued his fight. He called the Government action illegal. He organised a People's Education Board, which had instant success. Soon there were 43 schools run by it, including 13 for girls. These schools had 270 teachers, 65 per cent of whom were professionally qualified, and a total of nearly 8,400 pupils, of whom over 900 were Muslims and over 2,000 girls. These schools incurred a monthly expenditure of Rs.10,000. Patel raised Rs.1.25 lakhs through public subscription. In comparison, in 57 Government-run schools there were less than 2,000 pupils and 250 teachers. The situation drifted along for two years. In the end the Government lost patience and reinstated the Ahmedabad Municipality in February 1924. It was a double victory for Patel. The People's Education Society was allowed by the Municipality to run its schools—and that too with a municipal grant of Rs.1.50 lakhs. The Director of Education was not happy over this, though legally he could not object to it. The Government sought a compromise, which Patel generously accepted. While the People's Primary Education Board agreed to close down its schools, the Municipality decided to absorb all its teachers. The fight, thus, came to a happy end. But it "engendered in the citizens genuine interest in the work of the Municipality and confidence in their own ability to run the administration."[10]

Patel was temperamentally fair and judicious. He dealt with Englishmen and Indians with the same yardstick. If he could not bear the haughty, patronizing attitude of the former, he refused to suffer the incompetence of the latter. Caste, colour or social status did not influence him. What concerned him was how best he could safeguard the interests of the Municipality, and thereby serve the public whose elected representative he was. A number of rich, influential citizens had not been paying taxes for quit some time. One such defaulter was a Government pensioner, a Khan Bahadur and an honorary first-class magistrate. Patel got every pie out of him by employing "a judicious mixture of threats and persuasion"[11]—a weapon he successfully employed later with the Princes.

Within the Municipality, the Water Works Engineer, R.C. Wadia, was not only incompetent but apathetic towards his duties, sure in his mind that nothing could happen to a person of his seniority and influence. On not a few occasions he ignored the advice of the Municipal Engineer and the President. When two big fires broke out in Ahmedabad within a period of four months, on neither occasion was there sufficient water to put them out. Further, out of the four engines in the water works, only one worked. With one engine working continuously for twenty-four hours, the tanks overflowed at night causing much waste of scarce water. Repeated warnings form the Municipal Engineer had had no effect on Wadia and city suffered from an acute shortage. Patel had to step in to get Wadia removed from municipal service—not till the case against him was complete and fully substantiated by documents.

More significant was the case of a wily intriguer, I.R. Bhagat, in whose appointment as Municipal Secretary, Patel had a hand.

Bhagat had no consideration for that. He proved too clever for everyone, including Patel whose final exit from municipal politics was largely due to him. Bhagat was yet to complete his probation in his first job when he managed his promotion to a newly created higher post of Personal Assistant to the Municipal Commissioner. Patel was opposed to this, and he wrote to the President and the Municipal Commissioner pointing out "the illegality of the decision". While this was going on, serious differences developed between the Acting Municipal Commissioner, D.K. Bhave, and his Personal Assistant. Bhagat was stopped from issuing any communication under his signature. Patel condemned this as "a lamentable lack of discipline" on Bhagat's part, and sought the Board's approval. But the wily Bhagat outmanoeuvred Patel. He managed the matter to be dragged on; and in July 1919 the Municipal Commissioner's post was abolished by the Government on the recommendation of the Board. In the process, Bhagat got himself appointed as Chief Officer.

Bhagat was the Acting Chief Officer when Patel became President of the Municipality. He continued to work in a high-handed manner. Patel and Bhagat clashed on the question of the issuance of cheques by the latter without the prior permission of the former. Bhagat, however, could not be stopped. When the question of his confirmation came up before the Board, Patel was shocked to see the majority voting in favour of Bhagat, including some of his party. Patel considered this as a personal defeat. With this resignation, he bade good-bye to municipal politics.

Years later, when Patel was India's Deputy Prime Minister, he learnt of Bhagat's financial plight. Bhagat had lost all he had earned at the race-course, including his spacious bungalow at Ahmedabad. Patel invited Bhagat to New Delhi, promising him a good job. By then Bhagat was in poor health, and was not fit to travel. He declined the good, sincere offer with profound thanks, and confessed to a friend of Patel's greatness in possessing a large, generous heart. Behind a forbidding exterior, Patel's heart beat with warmth and affection. And yet, he was a hard taskmaster. He could not tolerate deliberate negligence. To him, insubordination to a superior was anathema. His reaction towards the guilty was "swift and violent".

Early in 1922, the municipalities of Ahmedabad, Nadiad and Surat were suspended for the disobedience shown to the Government on many occasions. Over the previous years, Patel had "fought valiantly both against the forces of chaos and confusion within the Municipality, as well as against the Government outside it. On both these fronts he scored brilliant victories."[12] Within a few months of his election to the Municipality, not only did he establish his authority, but proved his mettle: an iron will to fight his way to victory, also his ability as a leader of indomitable courage, devoted to public causes, and one who could outwit his opponent through a well-planned strategy.

Patel always remembered those years with nostalgia. Years later, in 1940, while addressing the Municipal Employees Association he recalled, "It is a matter of pride with me that I have devoted the best part of my life here. I recall those years with great satisfaction. I even occupied a place in the hearts of sweepers. I did nothing special for them. Still they remember me. Indeed, all big and small here remember me with kind thoughts. The reason is that I listened to everyone's woes—not from the high chair I was given, but by sitting amidst them."[13] This was despite the fact that he was "a hard taskmaster" who possessed the "innate tendency of exacting hard work from the employees"; but, as the Board recorded, "he was always keen to see that sincere and industrious persons were suitably rewarded for their devotion and hard work."[14] Of him, Alfred Master, a former Municipal Commissioner in Ahmedabad, has recorded, "I remember Mr. Vallabhbhai J. Patel as a most efficient Chairman of the Sanitary Committee, who stood aloof from the domestic and political intrigues in which some of his fellow Councillors indulged."[15] And of his days with the Municipal Corporation, Patel stated in 1948: "... I served Ahmedabad Municipality to the best of my ability. I had unalloyed happiness in the tasks which I performed then. After all, to all of us, to serve our own city must give unmitigated pleasure and satisfaction which I cannot get in any other sphere. Further, to cleanse the city of the dirt is quite different from cleansing the dirt of politics."

Such a stern and severe, impartial and public-spirited young man of 42 came in direct contact with 48-year-old Gandhi for the first time in November 1917 at the Gujarat Political Conference held at Godhra. It was at this conference that Gandhi made a statement of great significance when he said, "If we are unable to run our village administration skillfully, honestly and justly, how can we justify our demand for the independence of our country?"[16] Steeped in rural culture, Patel fully agreed with this. He had proved it by his actions in running the civic administration of Ahmedabad. People saw in him a new leader in-the-making; a relentless fighter, great administrator and skillful negotiator.

6

Gandhi's Disciple

Gandhi returned home from South Africa in 1915. On landing at Bombay on January 9th, he was given a hero's welcome. He had been triumphant in his first-ever non-violent satyagraha, and, as a result, a luminous glow of a halo hung around him. Indians looked to him with great expectations for their political emancipation. At an all-Bombay reception on January 12th, Pherozeshah Mehta spoke of the people's hopes when he called Gandhi "a hero in the cause of Indian independence", and went on to say, "So long as we have Indians like Mr. Gandhi and Indian women like Mrs. Gandhi, we need not despair of our country… they are possessed of the highest qualities of courage, heroism and capacity of endurance and suffering."[1] Jinnah was no less eloquent at a reception given by the Gujaratis of Bombay on January 14th, when he said that here in India, Gandhi would not only be "a worthy ornament, but also a real worker whose equals there were very few". Complimenting Gandhi and Mrs. Gandhi for their "trials and sufferings and sacrifices", Jinnah was profuse in his praise, "Such a son of India and such a daughter of India had not only raised the reputation of India, but had vindicated the honour of the great and ancient land."[2]

Soon thereafter Gandhi set up an ashram at Ahmedabad on the banks of the Sabarmati river, which attracted the elite of the city. Some went to him out of curiousity; others seemed to be impelled by veneration for the new saint. Patel did not belong to either category. For more than a year he remained unconcerned by Gandhi's presence in Ahmedabad. Rather, he was an unabashed scoffer; "a smart young man dressed in tip-top English style"; "the bridge-player, chain-smoking barrister, sardonically scanning the Indian political scene from the seclusion of his "fritters club" at Ahmedabad"; who at first "kept himself cynically and sarcastically aloof". Being a barrister himself, Gandhi felt attracted towards the people of his own clan in the Gujarat Club—in the hope that they would understand him better than the less sophisticated commonfolk. This was about the beginning of 1916. One day while Gandhi was addressing a group of elders in the club, Patel was delightfully enjoying his game of bridge. Mavalankar, who was watching the game by his side, recalls, "When I got up to go... Vallabhbhai passed very sarcastic remarks, discouraging me from going... was very skeptical and critical about Gandhi's ideas and plans... brutally blunt in expressing his view."[3]

Patel moved towards his future guru only in 1917, in the year of Gandhi's three victories in quick succession: one, the Viceroy's compliance with his request to abolish indentured labour by a fixed date; two, the removal by a Viceregal decree of the much-hated Customs barrier at Viramgam in Kathiawar to which Gandhi belonged; and three, Gandhi's victory at Champaran in Bihar against the British indigo planters in May 1917. The last one was unique. It rocketed the future Mahatma to all-India fame. Tilak had given people the political *mantra*—"Swaraj is my birthright, and I will have it"—which had electrified the atmosphere in the country. It was, however, left to Gandhi to translate that *mantra* into action: to turn it into a reality by carrying it to India's teeming millions in her villages. In Champaran, it was a new spectacle of a great surge of thousands of indigo cultivators rising to Gandhi's call. Such an eventuality was hitherto unthinkable. Gandhi emerged as a great leader of the oppressed peasantry.

Champaran had a sweeping effect on Patel's mind: an effect that was deep, far-reaching and life-long. It moved a mind that was resolute and analytical; a mind not influenced by sentiment, but governed by reason. One summer afternoon at the Gujarat Club, Patel, Harilal Desai, both Secretaries of the Gujarat Sabha, and G.V. Mavalankar, joint Secretary, were, as usual, gossiping when the news of Champaran was received. Gandhi's preference for imprisonment to abandonment of his inquiry into the indigo planters' high-handedness "electrified all of us", writes Mavalankar, "Desai jumped up and waving his hand exclaimed, Mavalankar, here's a brave man. We must have him as our President of the Gujarat Sabha."[4] True to his nature, Patel quietly listened without betraying emotions. In reality, as the coming months unveiled, he was more "electrified" than the other two. In Gandhi's Champaran victory, Patel saw the beginnings of a new agrarian revolution, which was most welcome to him as a son of the soil. Gandhi appeared to him to be the man who had arrived in Kheda in 1917 to carry out such a revolution. This realization irresistibly drew Patel towards Gandhi.

In June 1917, Gandhi again hit the headlines. He showed unusual boldness on Mrs. Annie Besant's internment by drafting a mass petition to be passed at public meetings throughout India. It was a radical departure from earlier politics. Besides pleading for Mrs. Besant's freedom, the petition appealed to Secretary of State Montagu, and Viceroy Chelmsford to grant the reforms formulated by the Congress-League scheme under the Lucknow Pact of December 1916, to which Tilak and Jinnah were signatories. Whom did Gandhi represent? Not the Congress nor the Home Rule League. He had yet no place in either. He represented the Gujarat Sabha, which was established in 1884 to petition people's grievances to the Government.

One such public meeting was held at Borsad. Patel brought with him copies of the petition from Ahmedabad on behalf of the Gujarat Sabha, while Indulal Yagnik proceeded to Borsad from Bombay with the same copies printed by the Home Rule League. They met at Nadiad. Yagnik found in Patel a man of stern disposition. He "felt rather nervous", and was "put out by seeing the proud barrister in person... dressed tip-top in western style, complete with a high starched collar, a coloured necktie, a velvet hat", and a pair of black shining shoes. He had his collars laundered not in Ahmedabad, but by Bombay's best laundry. Barrister Patel traveled Second Class—a luxury for Indians in those days. Despite his forbidding appearance, Patel greeted Yagnik with "a friendly twinkle in his eye", and thus "placed me completely at ease", and laid "the basis of a human bond" that endured during their lifetime.[5]

Patel's participation in the meeting at Borsad was the beginning of a great change in him. His interest in politics had been kindled. This became all the more clear towards the end of 1917 at the Provincial Political Conference organised by the Gujarat Sabha at Godhra, where Patel had started his legal practice 17 years earlier. Gandhi presided. Both Tilak and Jinnah were present. Patel attended as an ordinary delegate and did not speak at all, but a significant change was noticeable in his person. The European dress had gone; instead, he wore a *dhoti*, a long loose shirt, an *alpaca* and a waistcoat. An Indian black cap had replaced the English felt hat; and his shining black shoes had given place to ordinary *chappals*.

The conference appointed a permanent committee with Gandhi as the President, and Patel and Yagnik as Secretaries. The conference proved a turning-point in Patel's life. At a meeting of the Sabha's working committee, Gandhi stated, "The time has come when we need wholetime workers—not those who shall be like seasonal birds." He began asking one by one those present if they would accept his proposition. The first was a barrister from Ahmedabad, who declined by saying, "I am not a *sanyasi*. I have a family, and children." Then came Patel's turn—also a barrister with two motherless children and other family responsibilities. Patel did not take a second to give his consent.[6] He placed his life at the disposal of his future guru. From then onwards the scoffer turned into Gandhi's *chella* (follower) and developed an unquestioned loyalty and devotion to Gandhi. Many nicknamed him Gandhi's "blind follower".

7

Gandhi's Deputy Commander

No prophet has ever succeeded without a deputy: without the unstinted loyalty of a devoted, self-sacrificing disciple, endowed with extraordinary organisational ability. Asoka, Lenin, Vivekananda—all belonged to the same class. Without Asoka, Buddha would not have been a universal figure, worshipped by a multitude of humanity. Marx, in spite of his intellectual brilliance, needed a Lenin to give practical shape to his political and economic thoughts. But for Vivekananda, Ramkrishna Paramhansa's fame would not have reached America and Europe.

So was Patel to Gandhi. His choice as number two during the Kheda satyagraha made Gandhi say with pride, "A leader's skill is judged by his competence in selecting his assistants for the execution of his plans."[1] Patel's assistance was the most significant contribution to Gandhi's satyagraha movement in India. He helped Gandhi build a strong, disciplined, non-violent army of satyagrahis and also a party machine capable of conducting a fight against the British for nearly three decades. With a view to keeping such a machine in trim and high gear, Patel maintained party discipline by even being ruthless to some of the stalwarts turned rebels. Patel was the *only* disciple whom the guru permitted to launch and lead satyagrahas independent of him. Not so was the case with Nehru or Rajagopalachari: the former in later years became his "heir-apparent", while the latter his "conscience-keeper". But it was Patel who served him as his "Deputy Commander".

Gandhi discovered Patel only on the "battlefield" of Kheda during the latter half of 1917—not earlier when he was Secretary of the Gujarat Sabha with Gandhi as its President. In Kheda, for the successful conduct of the satyagraha, Gandhi looked for a number two. "Who should be my Deputy Commander?" he asked himself. He considered some of the colleagues around him. Patel appeared to him "a stiff-looking person". Gandhi wondered whether he would be able to do what he wanted. Closer scrutiny convinced him that he must secure his help.[2] Gandhi never had to regret his decision.

Even though Champaran had given Gandhi his all-India fame, it stood no comparison with Kheda. At the former, Gandhi had only posed a threat to the British indigo planters. His victory was a mere walk-over. In Kheda, Gandhi's challenge was to the authority of the British over land revenue—a sensitive issue as it was the very foundation of their Indian Empire. Commissioner Pratt voiced the grave apprehension that worried the British, "In India, to defy the law of land revenue is to take a step which would destroy all administration. To break this law, therefore, is different from breaking all other laws."[3] Gandhi was preaching rebellion in asking the peasants to withhold payment of land tax. Pratt was equally prophetic when he told the Kheda peasants, "If you fight about land revenue today, the whole country will fight about it tomorrow."[4] The Government could not afford to face Gandhi's challenge lightly in Kheda which was not the case in Champaran.

The issue involved at Kheda was most simple, though blown out of all proportion by the officials. Excessive monsoon rains in the district during 1917 had completely ruined the *kharif* crop, while an epidemic of rats and other pests had heavily damaged the *rabi* crop. Revenue rules permitted a postponement of the entire assessment if the yield was estimated to be less than 25 per cent, and a complete remission in the event of a failure of the crop in the following year. On behalf of the peasants, Gandhi only demanded a postponement of land revenue recovery not its total remission. Under the signatures of over 18,000 peasants, an application was submitted to the Government on November 15, 1917. Another was signed by several thousand members of the Nadiad and Kathalal Home Rule Leagues. The Bombay Government refused to interfere with the Commissioner's authority, which encouraged the local officials to believe that the Government, being "paternal", knew best the peasant's requirements and sought nothing but their welfare. This misconceived thinking led the officials to conclude that "the peasants were complaining only because they had been instigated and their emotions worked up by agitators. So, if the Government accepted the demands of the peasants, it would be the agitators who would gain in reputation, while the reputation of the officers would decline. Thus, to Government officers, the fight on this occasion was one chiefly of prestige."[5]

That was not so with Gandhi and his Deputy Commander, Patel. The guru and the *chella* were fighting for a just cause. Their reasonableness lay in their plea to postpone recovery of land revenue till a full inquiry had been conducted by the Government. Gandhi had even shown his willingness to accept a non-Indian as chairman of a committee of inquiry. Patel and he had taken up a brief on behalf of the peasants only when they had been fully satisfied with the justness of their losses, and their sufferings. The Bombay Government showed callous disregard for the peasants' plight by letting the Commissioner ride roughshod over people's hopes and aspirations to secure justice.

The local English bureaucrats dubbed Gandhi, Patel and their associates agitators, while for themselves they adopted a self-styled paternal role that, they assumed, enjoined upon them the right to decide the fate of their "children". Pratt told the Secretaries of the Gujarat Sabha, which was negotiating for a just compromise with the Government and later led the satyagraha movement, that "the responsibility for proper administration in Kheda district is that of the Collector."[6] He even held out the threat, "If I do not hear from you by tomorrow, I shall write to the Government recommending that your Sabha should be declared illegal."[7] In Gandhi's assessment, the Commissioner had "finally shown his true colours".[8]

Without caring to clasp the hand of friendship Gandhi had extended, the Commissioner, under pressure from the taluka revenue officers, came down on the people with a heavy hand. Some peasants were forced to sell their land in order to pay up the revenue, while others had to borrow money at 75 per cent interest. In one instance, "six Harijan cultivators were made to hold their toes for two hours and were released only when they promised to pay up their land revenue dues. These men were obliged to borrow money at 37½ per cent interest. Many others were kept imprisoned illegally until they promised to pay up... One Muslim cultivator was compelled to marry off his 10 year old daughter so as to borrow Rs.15 from his son-in-law in order to pay up his revenue dues."[9] Such high-handedness on the part of local officials came to light in a letter to the Editor in The *Times of India* of Bombay, the facts being the outcome of a thorough inquiry conducted by Amritlal V. Thakkar.

Gandhi happened to be in Champaran. He was much perturbed over the happenings in Kheda. He advised the Sabha to start immediately a strong movement for "ensuring the postponement of land revenue and the suspension of the recovery work" which, he thought, would be "the only correct reply to the arrogance of the Commissioner and the threat he issued." Since Gandhi was launching in India his first agrarian satyagraha movement, he had not only to prepare the masses to join it on certain well-defined principles, but also educate his immediate lieutenants. He wanted the latter "to stand by the side of the public fearlessly", as also to understand the spirit of the struggle he was launching. He advised them, "You may be arrested for doing so, but you must regard that as the fulfillment of your work. That is satyagraha."[10] To the workers down in the line his advice was, "If we do our duty fearlessly, the public too will draw from it a wonderful object lesson. It is understandable that the officials are very annoyed. How can they like to see a public alive to its rights? I hope that none of you will lose heart. If on this occasion we do our duty to the utmost, we shall be well on the way to independence."[11]

Simultaneously, Vithalbhai Patel and Gokuldas Parekh, members of the Provincial legislature from Gujarat, were searching for a compromise formula with the Government in Bombay. They had talks with Revenue Member G. Carmichael, who not only refused to intervene, but displayed a hardened attitude. This encouraged the Collector of Kheda to hold out a threat on January 14, 1918, "If anyone, influenced by the wrong advice which is being given to them, refused to pay up his land revenue dues, I shall be compelled to take stringent legal measures against him." To this, Gandhi gave an equally bold reply, "The Government may do what it likes. If the hardship is genuine and the workers skilful, they cannot but achieve success."[12] The Sabha too defended its position by observing that "it represents the whole of Gujarat, and many residents of Kheda district are its members. It... claims to speak on its behalf. It is not desirous of inciting the peasants of Kheda district, but only to assist them in their time of difficulty."[13]

Gandhi was not spoiling for a fight. He was anxious to prove his duty as a satyagrahi: to explore all avenues of reaching an amicable settlement. He explained his stand on February 4th, the day he arrived in Bombay from Champaran, "If the Commissioner had given the Government the right advice, all would have been well. The appointment of an independent inquiry committee was the obvious answer... the people have only two weapons: either they may rise in rebellion, or they may practice satyagraha—non-violent non-cooperation."[14] Gandhi was opposed to the former, but was anxious to secure success under the latter. He, therefore, met the Governor on the 5th itself, accompanied by Dinshaw Wacha, Parekh and Vithalbhai. The Governor was assisted by Revenue Member Carmichael, and Commissioner Pratt.

Gandhi's compromise effort was spurned. The Governor's Secretary informed him that His Excellency "is not satisfied that any advantage would be gained by appointing an independent commission." This did not dampen Gandhi's spirits. As a true satyagrahi, he still continued correspondence with the Commissioner in an attempt to prevent the Government from taking "steps which can leave only bitterness behind." The Government's attitude made a simple matter taste bitter. In many cases the officials' language was, Gandhi thought, "unbecoming and unnecessarily painful."[15] The Commissioner preferred to dismiss summarily Gandhi's complaints.

Gandhi knew that satyagraha was the only answer to the Government's high-handed behaviour and open threats of dire consequences, which hurt the dignity and pride of the self-respecting, virile peasantry of Kheda. He was yet averse to precipitating action, unless he personally satisfied himself, no matter if his trusted workers had earlier collected unfailing evidence of the prevailing situation. He instructed the Gujarat Sabha executive to carry out, in addition to what had already been done, a detailed on-the-spot inquiry into crop estimates. A decision to that effect was taken by the executive at Patel's Ahmedabad residence on February 16th, the day the Commissioner had replied to Gandhi's letters of the 10th and 11th.

With this the scene of activity shifted from Ahmedabad to Nadiad, in Kheda, where Gandhi, along with Patel and some twenty others, moved on the 16th itself. He opened his camp office in the local orphanage, and carried out his personal on-the-spot inquiry into the conditions of the peasants. Prior to his departure from Ahmedabad, he had made the last attempt at compromise by writing to the Commissioner: "I would like to reassure you that it is not my intention just to start an agitation, or to encourage a futile agitation. I am going to Kheda district in search of Truth... Although I have the full assurance of reputable leaders of the district, I feel it my duty to verify the facts for myself. If you are able to postpone the land revenue recovery work until my inquiry is completed, it will help a great deal in reducing the discontent that has now spread among the people."[16] Gandhi's request was rejected, as the Commissioner saw "no reason whatever for postponing the recovery of land revenue."

As supreme commander, it was necessary for Gandhi to know

intimately the people who were to form his army, as also the area of his operations. He divided his lieutenants into groups, each one was to conduct inquiries in a number of villages. Before the week was out, 425 villages, out of a total of 600, had been surveyed. Gandhi and Patel together carried out inquiries in about 60 villages. Their joint operations were at Gandhi's bidding. He had laid the condition that one of the Sabha workers should accompany him and devote all his time to the campaign until it was completed. Narhari Parikh records that "as no one else was prepared to give up his other activities wholly, Vallabhbhai offered his services, much to Gandhi's delight."[17] This was the first time Patel was working so close to Gandhi—and that too on a battlefield. More than Gandhi's other colleagues, he enjoyed two distinct advantages: first, he belonged to Kheda, born and brought up on its soil and amidst its environment, and had practised as a lawyer at Borsad earlier in the century. Second, being the son of a peasant, he knew and understood the people better than others. He acted as his master's interpreter to the villagers. Both worked together night and day, moving about in the countryside on foot, covering long distances, quite often over hot sands, "exhorting, encouraging, bullying good-humouredly when necessary". Kheda brought about a complete transformation in Patel's life. He gave up his legal practice in order to devote his entire time in his master's service.

Gandhi launched the satyagraha on March 22, 1918 at a public meeting of peasants at Nadiad. His inspiring words to them were, "It is intolerable that the Government should forcibly recover assessment. But that has become the practice in our country. However truthful the people, and however just their case, the Government refuses to believe them and insists on having its own way. There must be justice, and injustice must be ended... That people would tell lies for the sake of saving at the most a year's interest—for they are asking only for a postponement of assessment—is inconceivable. It is an insult to all of us that the Government dares to make this accusation. I would, therefore, tell you that, if the Government does not accept our request, we should declare plainly that we shall not pay land revenue, and will be prepared to face the consequences... the Government may recover the assessment by selling our cattle and our movable property, confiscate *jagirs* and even put people in jail on the ground that they are not law-abiding. I do not like this charge of lawlessness."[18] This amounted to defying British authority by refusing to pay land revenue; also to conduct the fight on an economic issue that affected all classes alike, whether Hindus or Muslims. "The people", as Gandhi explained, "are fighting for a principle, while the officials are fighting for their prestige. The peasants of Kheda have ventured to take up cudgels in the interests of justice and truth."[19] It was a non-sectarian, non-communal, non-political fight.

The satyagraha had run for a few days when Gandhi had to leave for Indore to preside over the Hindi Sahitya Sammelan. He handed over charge to his deputy commander on March 30th. In his new position, Patel displayed unmistakable evidence of the great qualities of leadership he possessed, so complementary to his master's. If Gandhi had a *bania's* suave, courteous veneer hiding his firmness and determination, Patel had the bluntness of a soldier and the astuteness of an organiser. In a fighting speech at Nadiad the same day, Patel gave a grim but prophetic warning, "This fight will act as a spark which will set the whole country afire", which it did, being the precursor of the satyagrahas Gandhi and Patel launched thereafter. Another truth Patel uttered was, "The brave man (Gandhi) who has inspired this fight is capable of converting the cowardly into the bravest of persons, and in India, Kheda district is the land of brave men." He also told the peasants, "A state ought to be proud of a people who are strong and determined. There is nothing to be gained from the loyalty of a cowardly and cringing public. The loyalty which you get from a fearless and self-respecting people is the loyalty which a Government should welcome... it is only if you are prepared to face hardships now and get the Government to change its policy, that you can remove the source of hardship for all time."[20]

In public speeches during Gandhi's absence, Patel always

struck the same inspiring strain, attempting to build up his master's image of one who had taught them the new *mantra* of Truth and *ahimsa*, who had injected into their hearts and minds courage and fearlessness, and who had infused into them a feeling of unity to fight against the Government for justice. Addressing peasants at Ras on April 18th, Patel advised them, "Stick to the path the Mahatma has shown you. You should give up violence, any thought of loot or use of underhand means. Instead, you should take to the path of *dharma*—the path of Truth and Justice. Don't misuse your valour. Remain united. March forward in all humility, but fully awake to the situation you face, demanding your rights with firmness. Have no fear of the tehsildar."

Satirically, Patel narrated the story of an ass, "You know, the owner first puts a maund of load on the back of the ass. If the ass bears this without reluctance, the owner increases the load by another half a maund, and, finally, raises it to two maunds! Likewise, as you submit to the Government in carrying loads on your backs, you too are made to carry heavier loads. Up till now you have borne them patiently. Throw them off now. Give up fear too. Follow Truth. Then only the Government will say that the people of Kheda are not devoid of manliness."

Then, switching over from a satirical tone to an appeal, Patel said, "Even if the heavens fall, you should not forsake your pledge. And if you carry it through to success, Kheda's will be the first name in the history of India's freedom struggle. All of India's eyes are focused on you... The Government will have to do justice to the peasants' demand. It cannot oppose a united public... In the fulfilment of your pledge lies your prosperity, and also of the coming generations."[21]

In the beginning the Government thought that by merely taking away their dearly loved cattle, the peasants would be cowed and pay up the land revenue. This did not work. So, a more drastic step was taken in the confiscation and auctioning of their lands. Lest people's morale should crack under mounting pressures, Gandhi, Patel and their colleagues moved from village to village, injecting into the people a fresh dose of elixir to strengthen their hearts and steel their determination, imploring them to honour the pledge they had taken. In Patel's own village, Karamsad, things were not shaping well. Some non-landholders seemed to be willing to avail themselves of the auctions. Patel was deeply hurt. He implored them, "When I see the condition of this village today, I am reminded of my childhood days, when the elders of the village carried themselves with such dignity that the revenue officers accepted their advice and sat most humbly in front of them. Today, the position is quite the reverse. I see you frightened of the officials. This is clearly due to lack of unity amongst yourselves. If even on an occasion like this you are not able to get rid of disunity, when will you be able to do so?"[22]

Gandhi's loyalty to the British could not yet be doubted. He possessed deep faith in their law-abiding character. He was unusually polite in manners, courteous in speech and ever willing for a compromise. Pratt thought of making capital out of Gandhi's innate goodness. Since it was difficult for him to reach the boycotting peasants through his officials, he hit upon the ingenious device by asking Gandhi to help him address them. A meeting of over 2,000 was arranged on April 22nd. Desiring not to embarrass Pratt with his presence, Gandhi sent Patel to the meeting as an observer.

Pratt took advantage of the opportunity and exploited it. Since he had been in the Gujarat administration for 28 years, he thought he could act as the people's *mai-bap* (mother-father) and deliver them a paternal sermon, full of threats as well as cajolery. Cleverly, he attempted to establish a direct rapport with them by calling Gandhi, Mahatma, and drew thereby loud cheers; and thereafter he appealed to them, "Today is our turn. Pray listen to my speech and hear my advice... The power to fix assessment is in the hands of the Government and the officers of the Government... We are the final arbiters of a legal right you may fight in a court of law. The sole authority to issue orders in the matter rests in the hands of the officials. It is not in the hands of Mr. Gandhi, nor of Mr. Vallabhbhai. You may bear fully in mind that any amount of your effort in this matter is bound to be futile. My words are final orders. They are not my personal orders, but are the orders of His Excellency Lord Willingdon. I have a letter from His Excellency in which he has been pleased to say that he would confirm whatever orders I may pass in the matter and every word that I may say. This is Lord Willingdon's letter. You may, therefore, understand that it is not I who say this. It is His Excellency Lord Willingdon."

Thereafter, Pratt attempted to deflate Gandhi's influence by paying him a left-handed compliment, "Mahatma Gandhi is an exceedingly good and saintly soul. And whatever advice he gives you, he does with the purest of intentions and in the full consciousness that it is in your interest. His advice is that you should not pay the assessment, because thereby you would safeguard the interests of the poor... Do you mean to say that the Government does not protect them? Is not the Government solicitous of their welfare?" The moment Pratt said that the Home Rulers would not go to jail, someone from the audience shouted, "Sir, if you send us, we will go." This was an oblique reference to the rumour that Gandhi would be sent to jail. Pratt scotched the rumour at once by categorically stating, "During the passive resistance campaign in South Africa, Mahatma Gandhi had to go to jail. But under this Government such a thing will not happen... The jail is not a fit place for him. I repeat that Mahatma Gandhi is a most saintly character."

Simultaneously with such a flattering statement, Pratt attempted to build up his own position with the clever observation, "The fight of the Government is not with the peasants; if children kick their parents, the latter are pained but not angered... I have 28 years of experience of administration of land revenue assessment and of land revenue legislation. Mahatma Gandhi is my friend. He has passed the greater part of his life in South Africa and has been here for only two or three years. In the domain of knowledge, letters and religion, he is a great authority. His advice on these subjects must be right. But in matters of administration and land revenue assessment, his knowledge is limited. I claim better knowledge." He capped his ingenuity with the stern warning,

"I have come here only to give you a final word of advice... if you do not pay the assessment, your lands will be confiscated. Many people say, "This won't happen." But I say that it will... Those who are contumacious will get no lands in future."[23]

Pratt seemed satisfied with his performance. In Gandhi's absence, he thought he had carried the day. His bureaucratic arrogance, however, blinded him to the fact that he was landing himself in hot water. By expressing his willingness to hear people speak out their minds, he stirred up a hornet's nest, in the mistaken hope that they would support him. Over a dozen peasants rose, one after another, to express their views with stunningly brutal frankness. Besides, by telling a lie about the Ahmedabad millhands calling off their strike, Pratt had provided Patel with a hammer to nail the lie onto him. Mistakenly, he had stated that the vow they had taken had no sanctity, when a similar vow by the millhands had already been broken.

Patel was at the meeting only as an observer; he was not to speak. This had given Pratt satisfaction and relief. But, unwittingly, he gave him an opportunity to come out from his self-imposed silence when he sought his opinion in regard to what Narsinhbhai from Karamsad had said that their fight was not intended to embarrass the Government. Patel jumped at the opportunity to say, "The speaker does not deny that ours is a fight. He admits it is. What he means to say is that it is not intended to embarrass the authorities."

Before Patel could proceed further, Pratt, out of nervousness, asked him whether he was going to make a speech. Patel replied that he was going to refer to the question of the millhands' strike only. Whereupon Pratt remarked rather ruefully, "Well, you may go on. But today is our turn."

Patel, however, observed, "I was one of the workers during the trouble, and I say that there was no breaking of the millhands' vow... Mr. Pratt himself graced the last meeting of the millhands when the terms of the compromise were declared." And then he did not spare Pratt by answering his left-handed compliment to Gandhi with the shrewd observation, "He says he has a great regard for Mr. Gandhi (the Commissioner interjecting: "Yes, of course"). Mr. Gandhi has a great regard for Mr. Pratt, and so have I. But it was Mr. Pratt who had said on that occasion that the millhands should always follow Mr. Gandhi's advice and they would not fail to get justice. I also say likewise that if you follow Mr. Gandhi's advice in this matter, you are sure to get justice at Mr. Pratt's hands. Here also the Commissioner may, if he so wishes, get a committee appointed and we would willingly accept its decision as not inconsistent with our vow."[24] Patel netted Pratt nicely. But Pratt's discomfiture was complete with some of the irritating questions asked by the peasants, which gave proof of their boldness and unity.

An uneducated Narsinhbhai (Karamsad) had cogently argued, "If the rich among us paid their share, the poor would have to follow suit, and suffer the consequences." Another peasant sarcastically observed, "The Government is our *mai-bap*. We are gratified to have the rare privilege of seeing you, Sir, today. I implore you as the representative of the *mai-bap* to visit our villages to ascertain the condition of our crops. We have no grains in our houses. The scourge of plague is upon us..."

Pratt replied arrogantly, "I do not want to answer any question regarding other things. Speak up whether or not you are going to pay." The third peasant exhibited still greater ingenuity when he told Pratt, "What is intolerable is that the word of an ordinary Talati should be accepted as true, while what a respectable peasant says should be rejected as false. We know from the Hindu Shastras that Harishchandra renounced his whole kingdom for the sake of truth. To give up a small piece of land for the sake of truth is of no account therefore. We took the vow with the fullest deliberation and knowledge, and we are not going to swerve therefrom even though the sun should change its course. And if, in spite of this, the *sarkar mai-bap* decides to deal death to us, we will not fail."

The fourth one poured ridicule by making a humiliating offer, "I have seen the Commissioner only today (for the first time). He is a very good man. We ought to pay the money. But as the Commissioner himself has said that 80 per cent of the assessment has already been paid, the question is only of 9 months' interest on the small balance. If things stand thus and if unity between the rulers and the ruled can be brought about, I am ready to contribute Rs.1,000 towards the loss of interest sustained by the Government."

An exasperated Pratt said, "The Government is not hard pressed for money. You need not pay a single rupee more than what it due." Such exasperation reached its limits when, answering the fifth peasant whether it was fair to confiscate land worth Rs.4,000 for recovering of Rs.4 revenue, Pratt stated, "Yes, that is a matter for the Government's discretion. It is not a question of Rs.4, but it affects 36 crores of people. If you are allowed to do as you are doing, the whole nation would also do the same." To Gandhi, for a revenue of Rs.4 lakhs to confiscate over 150,000 acres of land worth over Rs. 3 crores was "unreasonable and unjust". Pratt abruptly ended the dialogue with the peasants with the remark, "I have finished. The final decision rests with you. To a *sanyasi* the loss of property may not matter at all. But you are not *sanyasis*!"[25]

This was Pratt's parting dig at Gandhi. It was unbecoming, not only in the latter's absence but also because Gandhi had arranged the meeting for him. More than that, it reflected his frustration over his having been cornered and subjected to a fusillade. Patel testified Pratt's plight in a Press statement, "... the Commissioner, who thought that the people would certainly be frightened, hearing the bold answers of the peasants and witnessing a sight never seen or heard of in his twenty-eight years of political experience, went away completed amazed."[26]

The situation looked grave. Pratt's threat was a clear indication that the Government was poised for action. To allay any doubts and fears on the part of peasants, Gandhi issued a pamphlet, in which he stated: "The Commissioner has issued many threats. He has even said that he will see to it that these do not remain empty threats... He seems to regard the relationship between the Government and the people as similar to that between parents and children. If so, has anyone seen in the whole history of the world an instance of parents having turned their children out of their homes for having resisted them in a non-violent manner?"[27]

The fight went on unabated. Gandhi, as the supreme commander, took every opportunity to explain his stand and the genesis of the dispute. His was a fight for justice—indeed, for Truth. It evoked such wide response as to have drawn into it for the first time large numbers of women from villages, who fought shoulder to shoulder with their menfolk. Their presence at public meetings proved of "extraordinary importance"—adding a certain colour and light-heartedness, but above all dignity; and, more importantly, it gave confidence and courage to their menfolk. Such normally shy and reticent women displayed unusual bravery when some among them publicly declared, "Let the Government take away our cattle and our ornaments, and confiscate our fields. But our men will not depart from their pledge." Their boldness was a great revelation to Gandhi himself. He was heartened to say, "My experience in Kheda and Champaran convinces me that, if only the leaders move amongst the people and mix freely with them, within two years very significant things can be achieved."

Kheda had by then attracted all-India attention and support. A public meeting held in Bombay on April 23rd, was presided over by Vithalbhai Patel. Gandhi, as the main speaker, referred to Pratt's unfounded allegations and said, "It is not barristers or pleaders who are behind this fight, but the peasants themselves. After the conference at Godhra, some peasants thought that they must, through their efforts, protect their own interests. They wrote to me that they wished to ask for justice from the Government and inquired if I would help them. Thus, this fight was not started by agitators from outside, though of course it has acquired importance as a result of outside assistance."[28]

Tilak had moved the main resolution at this meeting. Stating that the Kheda peasants' agitation was not new, he disclosed, "In 1896, a similar situation had arisen in Kolaba district and we had a difference of opinion with the same Mr. Pratt. On that occasion, the land of many peasants was confiscated." Tilak asserted, "The land belongs to the peasant, but the Government reduces him to beggary in order to recover a single year's land revenue assessment... An independent commission ought to be appointed to settle the very complicated question."[29] Jinnah was not far behind others in lending his support to Gandhi's Kheda satyagraha. His telegram stated: "Am firmly convinced Kheda distress question should be inquired into immediately by an independent committee. I sympathise with the object of the meeting and with the ryots in their struggle."[30]

From Bombay, Gandhi proceeded to New Delhi on an urgent call from the Viceroy and from there to Bihar. In his absence from Gujarat, Patel assumed command of the fight for the second time. He had already proved great qualities of leadership. His speeches and the pamphlets he issued kept up the spark Gandhi had lit with inspiring words. Patel told the peasants, "A fierce *dharma-yudh* (righteous war) has been going on between the people and blind authority... notices of confiscation have been enforced in the case of some leading men's houses; fines imposed; standing crops taken possession of. Even threats of arrests held out. But people have remained undaunted, while officers have betrayed their helplessness over their failure. It was then that the Commissioner stepped in, and addressed the peasants at Nadiad. He gave them serious threats; even read out the Governor's letter to impress upon them his authority to act. But the peasants showed rare courage in answering his threats. He was surprised to see such fearlessness for the first time in his twenty-eight years of administrative career. And, no wonder, he left the meeting in sheer desperation."[31]

Patel further stated, "The peasants took all this cheerfully. In the net result, the Government was recovering no money at all... So the Government gave up confiscations and restarted auctions of movable properties. In order to give the peasants as much trouble as possible—even when there was other property which could be auctioned—they took charge of milk-giving buffaloes and kept them in the sun. They separated them from their calves. This reduced the price of buffalo by half. Even so, the peasants adhered to their pledge patiently and bore whatever hardships they were called upon to bear."

Patel's advice to them was truly Gandhian, "The longer the fight lasts, the stiffer is the test which the public will have to pass. But without such hardships, they cannot have this unique experience... If the Government oversteps the limits, is itself angered and harasses us, we, on our part, should not act unreasonably, never be impolite or lose our temper... always be peaceful. Even the hardest of hearts can be conquered by love. The more the opponent is stiff, the more should our affection go out to him. Only then shall we be able to win. That is the significance of satyagraha."[32]

Yet, Patel could not surrender his peasant's sturdy independence on some marginal issues. He accepted Gandhi's operational strategy and the principles governing the satyagraha. But he could not subscribe to Gandhi's advice to the peasants to willingly accept suffering by voluntarily surrendering their cattle. He preferred that they should save their cattle from attachment by deliberately not letting them remain near their houses. And that is what the peasants did.

The struggle, which was launched on March 22nd, continued through the months of April, May and part of June. Its uniqueness lay in the peasants, both men and women, standing firmly behind Gandhi and Patel, willingly accepting any punishment inflicted on them. Not only were their cattle and standing crops seized, but also the ornaments and household utensils of the women. All the 600 villages showed a rare determination and a remarkable solidarity, which surprised many a visitor from outside. The Bombay newspapers, which published eyewitness accounts, paid glowing tributes to the peasants for their courage and spirit of sacrifice. One instance drew particular commendation. A trusted lieutenant of Gandhi and Patel, Mohanlal Pandya, was arrested, along with four leaders of village Nawagam, where a batch of 200 satyagrahis undertook to remove onions from the fields. Five of them were charged with theft and sentenced to 10 to 20 days of jail. A crowd had collected in the courtroom to witness the trial, which was not defended. Gandhi, addressing the crowd outside, said, "This is a case in which, I have no doubt, we can appeal without any difficulty. It was not because our case was weak that neither Vallabhbhai nor I asked a single question. We did not cross-examine witnesses although any independent magistrate, having any knowledge of law, would have at once seen that this was not a case of theft at all. Nevertheless, we shall not appeal. A satyagrahi should not appeal. The right course for him is to undergo imprisonment."[33] On the day Mohanlal Pandya was released, Gandhi and Patel walked seven miles on foot to offer him and others a hero's welcome at the gates of the jail.

Gandhi's fight was transparently clean and unquestionably upright, free from malice, hatred, or cunning. Such a fight, as the *Bombay Chronicle* reported, "promises to be memorable in the history of this country... In the course of a fortnight (during April), he and his lieutenants had covered over 400 villages... A brave little band of workers had gone round amongst the villagers, tramping the country in the scorching sun, and induced over 2,500 peasants to take a vow. The peasants, who had been emasculated by centuries of petty tyranny by petty officials, have, under the elevating influence of Gandhi's teachings, imbibed an entirely new spirit of self-respect and have assumed the noble role of passive resisters."

Gandhi made the bold declaration that, if the Government confiscated their lands, it would be "an act of spoliation and theft that would shake the foundations of the British authority in India."[34] Gandhi's sincerity and the righteousness of his satyagraha had pricked the conscience of many village revenue officials, some of whom openly offered their sympathies. One Talati, after hearing Gandhi at a meeting held at Vadthal on April 18, publicly said, "with engaging and pathetic candour", that "he had his sympathy for all present, but that he had to obey at the Government's behest simply because the unfortunate problem of bread faced him cruelly."[35]

This was indicative of the winds of change. The Government seemed to have lost control over the situation. Consequently, a dramatic development took place on June 3rd, when Gandhi, in the company of Patel, reached Uttersanda, a village three miles from Nadiad. On alighting from the train he was informed of the Mamlatdar's desire to see him. He and Patel were informed of the Government's decision to suspend assessment till the next year. The Talati was called to the meeting to give the good news to the peasants assembled, whom Gandhi addressed thereafter, "A few days back when I had an interview with the Collector, I had made suggestions to that effect. I told him that if he would act up to my suggestions, the struggle would soon terminate. Such an order has now been issued by the Mamlatdar. It was the first condition of our struggle that the day the assessment dues of the poor were suspended, those who could afford to pay should at once pay up the revenue... We must thank the Mamlatdar for this kind order... How bitterly did we feel when we were told the Government was right and that we were wrong? Now the Government says that it leaves it to us whether to pay the revenue or not."[36]

That was vindication of the cause for which the struggle had been launched. Gandhi and Patel, therefore, announced termination of the satyagraha on June 6th. In a joint statement they stated: "Until today it was a matter of honour not to pay up the land revenue; now it will be a matter of honour to pay it up. Whoever has the means to pay should do so, and thereby show that where there is no conflict between man-made law and spiritual law, the satyagraha has no hesitation in honouring the man-made law."

Paying rich tributes to the people of Kheda, Gandhi and Patel said, "By their courage the peasants of Kheda have drawn towards them the attention of the whole of India. For the past six months they have shown great loyalty to truth, fearlessness, unity, firmness and self-sacrifice... The public of Kheda have rendered great service to themselves, to the struggle for independence and to the State (Empire)."[37]

The success of the Kheda satyagraha sent a wave of jubilation throughout Kheda. Village after village, small and big, had victory celebrations full of gusto but tempered by sobriety. An eyewitness confirmed that the "rejoicings, characterised everywhere by a spirit of moderation and always free from anything like frantic mirth, have unmistakably proved the wonderful hold the Mahatma has secured over the people of Kheda, their deep sense of gratefulness for what has been achieved, as also their appreciation of the moral significance of the campaign. For, everywhere people flocked in their thousands, small villages rocked with their tumultuous rejoicings, and every village that followed, tried to vie with the one that preceded in the measure of its reception and in the volume of its gratefulness." People were "fully, and some even painfully, conscious that the material result has been almost nil. But they are more conscious—and it is that consciousness that has been vivid more than anything else throughout these celebrations—that they have reaped fruits that will forever abide, that they have for ever freed themselves from the mortal fear of the *sarkar*... They are conscious that never was such rich political education given them."[38]

The meeting at Nadiad was called to do honour to Gandhi. The faces of the large mass of people glowed with unbounded joy over a victory won through weapons of *dharma*; but no less over their newly aroused hopes and aspirations. Such faces also radiated a new sense of dignity and a pride unmarred by any traces of hatred. Gandhi was felicitated by the people of Kheda for the exemplary conduct of the first passive resistance movement in India; as also to express their gratitude for kindling amongst them a new spirit of fearlessness.

In his reply to the address presented to him, Gandhi paid glowing tributes to Patel for the role he played as his deputy commander, "The choice of my lieutenant was particularly happy... without the help of Vallabhbhai we could not have won the campaign. He had a splendid (legal) practice, he had his municipal work to do, but he renounced all and threw himself into the campaign."[39]

Patel's speech reflected the humility of a disciple, "In India, it is customary with gods and *mahatmas* not to keep to themselves the offerings given to them, but distribute them amongst their worshippers. Mahatmaji has, likewise, given me all that was given to him, even when I did not do much... On my behalf and on behalf of my co-workers I wish to say that unless the people of Kheda had not shown courage and forbearance, we could not have achieved anything in this fight. Therefore, whatever honour has been bestowed upon me, I would like to pass it on to the people of Kheda, who really deserve it."

Patel further observed, "For hundreds of years India has suffered from a chronic disease (slavery). No doctor had so far been able to cure it. Those who made efforts up to now merely administered sweet medicines, which failed to be effective. Some people felt, how could one who advised them to fight against the Government treat the disease? But never forget, this doctor's (Gandhi's) mind and heart are filled with the burning desire to serve the people... I congratulate Mahatmaji for having led Kheda to the forefront of India's struggle for independence."[40]

Of historic significance was the fact that, in Gandhi's admission, "the flag of satyagraha was unfurled" in Kheda district.[41] But an equally significant fact was that Gandhi was still loyal to the Empire. Before winding up the Nadiad meeting, he converted it into a recruiting centre and asked for *guru dakshina* in the form of recruits for the war Britain was fighting against Germany. His reasoning sounded the very opposite of his total *ahimsa* of later years, which he was to preach so uncompromisingly. He reminded his audience of their "utter want of strength and capacity to defend themselves." He asked them "to decide for themselves if the present was not the opportunity wherewith they could shake themselves free of that weakness and effeminacy, adding, "Joining the army was the only remedy to clear that reproach and it behoved all of them to furiously think of the significance of the juncture and to strike the nail when it has hot. Only by preparing for the war could the martial instinct be revived in them, and if the present opportunity was allowed to go, another would never be coming."

From the all-India angle and future of India's struggle for

freedom, the Kheda satyagraha had double significance. With it, Gandhi had ushered in a new era in India's freedom struggle, and no less significant was the fact that, to quote the Congress historian, Pattabhi Sitarammayya, "It brought two great men together. It was the beginning of Vallabhbhai's public life. He burnt his boats and gave Gandhi cooperation and allegiance which grew with the years."[42]

8

Birth of a New Congress

The 36th Congress, held at Ahmedabad in December 1921, was momentous, even unprecedented, in its historic significance. It surpassed in many ways the earlier sessions since 1885. It was Gandhi's child, born out of the non-cooperation resolution passed the previous year at the Calcutta Congress which gave a new direction to Gandhi's Rowlatt Act agitation, the Khilafat protest and the Non-Cooperation Movement. But the Ahmedabad Congress marked a turning point in the history of the Congress as a party. Unmistakably, it bore the stamp of two personalities—Gandhi and Patel: one, the inspirer; the other, the organiser.

At Ahmedabad, Patel's role was in his capacity as Chairman of the Reception Committee; also, as deputy commander to Gandhi in Gujarat. By 1921, Gandhi had the entire Congress under his sway. The Ahmedabad Congress appointed him "the Dictator for the whole country, following the precedent of the Bengal Congress Committee which had appointed the Deshbandu (C.R. Das) as the Dictator for the province."[1] In that capacity, Gandhi gave the Congress a new character, rather a new direction—a well-knit, highly organised party organisation of elected representatives, which was revolutionary in concept and outlook. Never was it so earlier.

Earlier to Ahmedabad, the British-inspired Congress of Hume, of the Moderates under Gokhale and even of the radicals under Tilak was "a constitutional party and mainly a talking body."[2] Now under Gandhi, it shed that character and became a mass organisation. From a body of a few highly intellectual and patriotic individuals who enjoyed the status of acknowledged patriarchs in the provinces they belonged to, the new party now became a party of the masses, poised for an organised fight against the British. Gandhi achieved that by giving the party a new radical constitution, a nationwide base, a new uniform policy that created organizational unity and strength, and a new ideology that inspired party members with greater aspirations that soon grew from self-rule within the Empire to complete independence. At the Ahmedabad Congress, Gandhi created greater party homogeneity by giving the Congress the tricolour as India's national flag; Hindi as the country's *lingua franca* and *khadi* as the official wear for all Congressmen—more as a matter of national pride than convenience.

Thus, while Gandhi, as the leader, invested the Congress with the character of a national political party, Patel proved the party's backbone throughout thereafter. As deputy commander to Gandhi in the Kheda satyagraha, Patel had helped Gandhi infuse a revolutionary spirit into the people. His role in helping Gandhi build his all-India strength, not his stature, was not inconsequential. He got Gandhi the strong backing of a monolith Congress party in Gandhi's home province. Strength at home meant strength outside, or abroad, was Patel's concept of power then and later as a strategist.

As Chairman of the Reception Committee at Ahmedabad, Patel made the Congress session memorable by making it leave the beaten track. For the first time in a Congress session, he implemented some of the basic Gandhian principles and made a model of it to be emulated thereafter at the subsequent sessions. Cleanliness, sanitation and simplicity, pursued under his personal supervision, were the hallmark of the Ahmedabad Congress, which was completely devoid of "the usual outer glamour and show."[3] In this he used with advantage the experience and knowledge of sanitary affairs he had acquired while in the Municipality. There was hardly any ungainly sight. Nor were there any foul-smelling pools of stagnant water. He had specially got constructed water works to provide adequate supply of water for an assembly of over 15,000.

Patel introduced many striking innovations. The main *pandal* was tastefully decorated for the first time in *khadi*; it was a sight to see *khadi* all around—"on the walls, on the roof and as matting." An eye-witness recorded, "The Congress *pandal* is a huge affair. It at once strikes the imagination and arrests the attention of the spectator. It is huge and imposing." The gates impressed people by their massiveness. Not only did they "complete the illusion of a huge fort", but with its emblem of the universal *charkha* in the centre, "lent both dignity and beauty to the pavilion."[4] The *pandal* and the tents, whose beauty lay in their white simplicity and streamlined effects, were erected at a cost of just rupees three and a half lakhs.

For the first time, too, not a single chair was to be seen in the whole pavilion. Chairs and benches would have alone cost Rs.70,000. Whereas in the truly egalitarian Indian tradition, everyone was made to sit on the ground, even the leaders, though they sat on a slightly raised platform to enable the audience to have a view of them. This was totally unlike the western practice of sitting in chairs followed at the previous Congress sessions. The squatted assembly also contrasted with the earlier such meetings in their domination by a few suited-booted arm-chair gentlemen politicians. The Congress under Gandhi seemed to have shed its earlier bourgeois image, and assumed instead a mass character. Patel's innovations at the session projected the temper of the changed times within the party. All this added to Gandhi's all-India prestige and acceptance by the masses as a leader who was ushering in a revolution.

An innovation that was considered ingenious was the manner in which the problem of shoes and chappals was solved so easily and so simply. None was permitted to enter the *pandal* with these on. Patel offered each person—and there were over 15,000 of them—a small *khadi* bag at a nominal cost, in which they were to carry them inside. In this he had a double motive: not only did the sale of *khadi* fetch the organisers good money, but it avoided the employment of volunteers to take care of them and the usual scramble that follows at the close of such sessions. This also helped the Congress Volunteer Corps maintain discipline and cleanliness "in a praiseworthy manner." It was a sight to see Gujarati girls as volunteers for the first time, and young people taking up the broom to sweep the *pandal* and its environs.

As Chairman of the Reception Committee, Patel made "the briefest speech in Congress history"; and the number of resolutions moved were also the smallest—altogether nine. Appropriately, Patel observed, "We had hoped that we would meet to celebrate the establishment of Swaraj, and therefore, endeavoured to arrange a reception befitting such an occasion. But, though we do not meet to celebrate that happy event, God in His abundant mercy has sent us suffering to try us and make us worthy of so precious a gift." That was in true Gandhian fashion—an abiding, fatalistic faith in God. He considered recent imprisonments, assaults, forcible searches and breaking open of Congress offices and national schools as "a certain sign of the approaching Swaraj, as a balm for the wounds inflicted upon our Muslim brothers and the Punjabis."[5] He also observed, "I truthfully claim that we have endeavoured to be non-violent in thought, word and deed… The best proof of this is Hindu-Muslim unity… I say with a sense of pride that our friendship is from the heart, and that we are working closely together in promoting national causes. In a similar way, we have established amicable friendship with the Parsis, the Christians and other communities."[6]

Patel also stated, "The use of *khadi* in the construction of the various *pandals* and Khadi Nagar is, in my opinion, a striking demonstration of our work in the direction of *swadeshi*"—a concept which had been passionately advocated earlier by Tilak, but now religiously adopted by Gandhi as part of the freedom struggle and as a cardinal principle of the Congress constructive programme especially in the villages. Another point Patel made with pride was in regard to the untouchables, "We have, perhaps, made the greatest advance in the matter of untouchability. Our suppressed countrymen freely attend our meetings." Under the constructive programme, Patel said, 31,000 boys and girls were studying in national schools in Gujarat. These had been started under Gandhi's inspiration, but ran under Patel's supervision. Gujarat had 110,000 spinning wheels producing no less than two lakh pounds of *khadi* every year. In all these and other constructive Gandhian activities, Patel's was the organising genius; and he had the pride to claim , "We have spent about Rs. 5 lakhs in organizing *swadeshi*."[7]

C.R. Das was to preside over the Ahmedabad Congress but couldn't. He had been arrested in connection with the protest organised in Calcutta against the visit of the Prince of Wales to India. Gandhi, therefore, commented in *Young India*, "The arrest of our President-elect need not disturb us. His spirit will preside over our deliberations. We know what message he has for the country. He has become the living embodiment of it. Certainly no Congress has ever met under happier auspices than this... That many of the best of us are in gaol is Swaraj."[8] In place of Das, Hakim Ajmal Khan presided over the session. In his welcome address Patel said, "Though Deshbandhu is not in our midst in body, his pure, patriotic and self-sacrificing spirit is with us. In Hakim Ajmal Khan, who is an embodiment of Hindu-Muslim unity, we have one of the greatest and noblest of our countrymen."

The Ahmedabad Congress was an inspiring spectacle of men and women pouring in thousands into the city and the Khadi Nagar in such high spirits as to be brimming with "ardent patriotism and disciplined enthusiasm for the national cause"[9]—that of freedom for the country. And so economically superb was the handling of the finances of the Congress session that Patel saved enough money to build with it the present Congress House in Ahmedabad city.

The Ahmedabad Congress was revolutionary insofar as it brought about a total change in the people's outlook. According to an eyewitness: "Fear had been cast off by the people. A sense of self-respect developed in the nation. Congressmen realised that service and self-sacrifice were the only means of winning public confidence. The prestige of the Government was materially shaken, and people had received good lessons regarding the ideology of Swaraj."[10] The Ahmedabad Congress was, in M.R. Jayakar's opinion, "a signal mark of the complete triumph at this date of Gandhi's views, surmounting all opposition."[11]

And, thus, Ahmedabad saw the birth of a new Congress under Gandhi's leadership. As the right-hand man of Gandhi, Patel's contribution to Gandhi's success was significant and far-reaching—second only to the master's.

9

Nagpur Satyagraha

The Nagpur Flag satyagraha had its origin in Jabalpur, not in Nagpur. In August 1922, Hakim Ajmal Khan visited Jabalpur as a member of a committee inquiring into the possibilities of starting civil disobedience in the country. He was given an address of welcome by the Congress members of the Municipality in the Town Hall, over which they hoisted the national flag. What caused a flutter among the British rulers in India and among the British MPs in London was the rebellious spirit displayed in this connection by the Municipality in rejecting a resolution suggesting that the national flag and the Union Jack be flown together. The incident was looked upon not only as an insult to the Union Jack, but an affront to the British Crown. The minds of British MPs were filled with grim apprehension and indignation. The Secretary of State for India had to assure the MPs that this would not be permitted to happen again.

In March 1923, when the Congress Working Committee was to meet at Jabalpur, the Municipality passed a resolution similar to the earlier one—to hoist the national flag over the Town Hall. It was disallowed by the District Magistrate. Not only did he prohibit the flying of the national flag, but also the holding of a public meeting in front of the Town Hall. This provoked the launching of an agitation on March 18th. The national flag was hoisted by the Congress members of the Jabalpur Municipality.

The District Magistrate ordered the flag to be pulled down. The police exhibited their overzealousness by trampling the national flag under their feet. The insult to the flag sparked off an agitation. All the Congress members of the Municipality resigned, and a satyagraha was immediately launched by the Jabalpur District Congress Committee. Defying the prohibitory order, Congress volunteers took out a procession, carrying the national flag in front and aloft. Among the participants were the well-known revolutionary, Pandit Sundarlal, and the Hindi poetess, Subhadra Kumari Chauhan. The latter had written a most inspiring poem in Hindi on the heroine of the 1857 war of independence, Rani Laxmibai of Jhansi. Both were arrested. Sunderlal was sentenced to six months' imprisonment.

At this moment the Nagpur District Congress entered the fray to vindicate the honour of the national flag. In true Gandhian style and spirit, the decision was announced publicly, as also the route of the procession to reach Sadar Bazar, where a public meeting was to be held after marching through the Civil Lines, where most of the ruling European class lived. The procession was taken out on April 13th, the anniversary of the Jallianwala Bagh tragedy. It was stopped at the entry of the Civil Lines. Ten volunteers stepped forward holding the national flag to offer satyagraha. They were mercilessly beaten. Some of them were even "dragged along the road and flung into the open drains."[1] The satyagrahis, nevertheless, remained peaceful. The Congress decided to fight by shifting the centre of the satyagraha from Jabalpur to the provincial capital at Nagpur, and placing it under a unified command.

The satyagraha at Nagpur started on May 1st and continued upto August 18th. Thereafter, for a period of two weeks it turned into a battle of wits between Patel and the unrelenting local bureaucracy. The latter looked upon a settlement between the Congress and the Government as loss of face, to avoid which, they put every hurdle in the way of its implementation, resulting in the release of nearly 2,000 imprisoned volunteers not earlier than September 3rd. The first commander of the satyagraha was

Jamnalal Bajaj. On his arrest, the Congress Working Committee asked Patel to take charge of it.

On arrival in Nagpur on July 22nd to take charge of the satyagraha, Patel found himself in the midst of a situation far from satisfactory—one that was not according to his way of thinking and working. The volunteers' camp was in police possession. He himself was without organised assistance. And, above all, volunteers had to be arranged from other parts of India. Patel, however, wrote to a friend, "This is, indeed, a stimulating struggle. If only the people are united, it would be possible to make the Government yield within a week. But here we have an orchestra in which every player plays whatever tune he likes. All the English newspapers are either opposed to the struggle, or are indifferent. The public men seem interested only in getting their own point of view accepted. The Government of the day is very determined. In spite of these difficulties, we have to see that everyone's attention in the country is focused on Nagpur". The struggle was after Patel's heart. As a soldier, he always itched for a fight.

Patel's first act was to organise his "forces", which he did by asking the provinces to specify "the number of volunteers they must send and the dates on which they must arrive. Volunteers should continue coming every day so that at least fifty would be available for arrest at the railway station."[2] Volunteers thus started pouring into Nagpur from all parts of the country, and they comprised all communities and classes—educated and uneducated, practising High Court lawyers, school teachers, college students, as also zamindars and businessmen. He proceeded on the assumption that the Government would prolong the struggle in order to see that it tapered off for want of adequate supply of volunteers. He even planned to enlist women into the movement in the belief that "that cannot fail to arouse the country"; and he sent word to Kasturba, Gandhi's wife, "to be ready to go to jail."[3] The movement continued unabated. Volunteers daily offered satyagraha and filled the Nagpur jail. The railway authorities tried to restrict, though without success, the issue of tickets for Nagpur.

Vithalbhai arrived in Nagpur to render whatever assistance

he could to his brother. Even when the two were in the opposite Congress camps, locked in a bitter controversy, political differences never overshadowed their love for each other. Vithalbhai thought that he would be able to help Patel secure the Swarajists' support in their stronghold in Nagpur, as also the officials' sympathetic attitude. The Governor of the Central Provinces, Frank Sly, and Vithalbhai had been co-students at the Inns of Court in London, and he was also on friendly terms with the Home Member of the Governor's Council, Moropant Joshi. His visit was, therefore, as much welcome to Patel as to the authorities. Not only were the latter apprehensive of intensification of the movement under Patel, whose ability and capacity to carry satyagraha to a successful end was acknowledged by friend and foe alike, but the Government realised that the movement under Patel was gathering momentum.

The Home Member gave an inkling of the Government's desire for a settlement by stating in the Provincial Legislative Assembly that no one had any objection to the national flag being taken out in a procession; and that, if permission for doing so was sought in accordance with the rules laid down, it would be given. The small European community was opposed to it. The anomaly in the situation lay in the fact that in Britain the Government had taken no action against the British Bolshevik party members for taking out the Red flag in a procession through the streets of London and shouting slogans in front in the Houses of Parliament. How could it be otherwise in India? The Europeans were provoked by the Commissioner of Nagpur Division. The latter, who was Secretary of the ICS Association, had threatened to fire on the procession when it passed it front of his bungalow. The provincial Government was thus in a dilemma: how to avoid bloodshed; and how to resolve the issue. Its desire for a settlement was genuine. The Home Member, therefore, arranged a meeting between the Governor and Patel, at which Vithalbhai was also present.

The prohibitory order was to expire on August 17th. Before it could be renewed, Patel took the Government by surprise by issuing a statement on the 16th, which clarified some of the misconceptions concerning the satyagraha Government propaganda had attempted to spread. Lest his objective was further misconceived either by the Government or by his political opponents and the public, Patel announced that on the 17th, "instead of a batch of three volunteers as usual, a procession of five volunteers will start from Sadar Bazar through the Civil Lines... If they are prevented by the authorities, the struggle will assume a new phase." This squarely fixed the Government on the horns of a dilemma, it being both a warning and an olive branch.

Patel said, "We (non-cooperators) have been accused by no less a person than His Excellency the Governor of the Central Provinces that we claim an absolutely unrestricted right, unheard of in any civilised country, to use public thoroughfares for processions... that is not the case... I desire to make it clear that the Nagpur satyagraha struggle has been started in order to vindicate our elementary right against arbitrary and unjustifiable interference and abuse of law... the organisers of the processions never intend to cause annoyance to any section of the public... The Working Committee has also instructed me to repudiate most emphatically the suggestion contained in the speech of the Home Member of the Central Provinces Government that the national flag processions were being organised to offer an insult to the Union Jack."[4]

It was a shrewd, masterly move, which put the Government in a quandary. What was it to do with the order that was expiring on the 18th? If renewed, the Government ran the risk of facing Patel's threat of the struggle assuming a new phase of intensified activity; if it wasn't, it would amount to accepting a defeat without a settlement that would make the Government lose face. The Home Member met Patel on the 16th evening itself and sought a settlement, offering to allow the procession to pass through the Civil Lines on the 18th, provided the Congress thereafter called off the satyagraha. That was acceptable to Patel, who asked for unconditional release of prisoners. The Home Member agreed to this, and, on securing the Governor's consent, confirmed the settlement in writing.

No fresh order was issued on the 17th. But the British Superintendent of Police prohibited the taking out of a procession through the Civil Lines under the Police Act, unless his permission was obtained. Patel felt intrigued. Did it mean a *volte face* on the part of the Government? He, however, went ahead with his plans. Instead of seeking permission, he merely wrote to the Superintendent of Police of his intention to take a procession on the 18th through the Civil Lines, indicating both the hour and the route. At midday one hundred volunteers set out with the national flag. The Superintendent of Police accompanied the mounted police. The processionists halted near the railway bridge which had earned the appellation of Flag Bridge, and also at the National Flag square. Loud slogans rent the air along the entire route, which was lined up with policemen. Complete silence was, however, observed in front of the church in the Civil Lines. This was an indication of Patel's conciliatory attitude towards the European community. The procession reached its destination without being stopped by the police. Patel declared, "The honour of the national flag stands vindicated. Our right to take out processions on public roads in a peaceful and orderly manner has been restored. I regard this as a triumph of truth, non-violence and suffering. By the grace of God, I am now in a position to announce that the Nagpur satyagraha campaign successfully closes on this auspicious Gandhi Day in a manner entirely in consonance with the spirit of the teachings of Mahatma Gandhi."[5]

In announcing the termination of the satyagraha, Patel had kept his word. Now it was the Home Member's turn to fulfil his promise: the release of prisoners. Over this a storm of protest was raised by the local European ICS officers, especially the Commissioner of Nagpur Division and the Deputy Commissioners of the districts, who, as members of the Indian Civil Service, could directly approach the Secretary of State, even over the head of the Viceroy. The Government of India was approached to resolve the dispute between them and the Provincial Government. In such a situation, the Governor and the Home Member, signatories to a written agreement with Patel, looked for an opportunity to repudiate it. Vithalbhai, mistakenly, provided it by hailing it as a victory for the Congress. The police contradicted the claim that the procession was allowed to go through with their permission; therefore, there could be no question of victory. The Governor considered this a violation of the agreement. Patel saved the situation by disowning his brother, by saying that Vithalbhai had no connection with the satyagraha, and that his visit to Nagpur was in his capacity as a Swarajist leader. He, therefore, demanded of the Provincial Government to honour the agreement reached with him.

Patel's resoluteness surprised both the Governor and the Home Member. Since they had already committed themselves in writing, they seemed to be badly caught. Therefore, they pressed the Government of India for authority to release the prisoners. The Civil Servants, ignoring the Governor's involvement, carried their war against the Provincial Government to London by representing their side of the case to the Secretary of State. With every day that passed, Patel's position became more difficult in the eyes of the public. Some anti-Congress newspapers carried a virulent campaign of character assassination. Patel was accused of lowering the Congress' prestige by compromising with the Provincial Government, especially in his seeking an interview with the Governor, as also approaching the Superintendent of Police for permission to take out the procession. In actual fact, Patel hadn't sought permission; he had merely informed him.

Patel was full of anguish. But he maintained his silence, which was necessary in the sort of situation both he and the Provincial Government were in. He wrote to Mahadev Desai: "I am in a fix... I have sealed my lips. The Government is opposed to any pronouncement being made... I feel Vithalbhai had been indiscreet. What he said had caused a terrible commotion in the Civil Service... Had Vithalbhai not been indiscreet in Bombay, I might well have left here on the 22nd along with the released prisoners." Patel had to change his strategy. He disclosed to Desai, "I have got the Commissioner in a tight corner. Many Civil Service officers are of his way of thinking. They feel that the settlement means complete defeat of the Government, and so they appear to have opposed the release of the prisoners... If they do not release the prisoners, the local Government's prestige and honour will be damaged; and if they are released, the civilians will be enraged... the Correspondent of *The Times of India* has suggested that I applied to the Superintendent of Police for permission. He has been caught out. I have been able to bring to light his secret conspiracy. It was he who had instigated *The Pioneer* to write against the Government, and caused the delay in the release of prisoners. The Government for the moment is completely baffled. It must, however, come to some decision in the next few days."[6]

Patel got hold of "a curious piece of evidence", of highly damaging nature. The Commissioner of Nagpur himself had been writing highly malicious stories in *The Statesman* and *The Times of India*. The former on August 21st carried his message under the headlines: "Satyagraha to cease: Leaders to Submit to Authority", while the latter on August 20th published a verbatim copy of the same "from its Nagpur correspondent". Sarcastically Patel observed, "Reading the two together, it is difficult to make out whether the correspondent of *The Times of India* is the Commissioner of Nagpur, or the Commissioner of Nagpur is the correspondent of *The Times of India*. It is possible that the inadvertence of *The Statesman*, unlike its Bombay contemporary, in publishing it as a message from the Commissioner of Nagpur, instead of "from its own correspondent", has exposed him."

Patel also disclosed, "The Commissioner of Nagpur was not authorised to issue the statement that has been wired by him to *The Statesman*." Further, "the Government of the Central Provinces are unable to control the journalistic activities of the Commissioner. On a former occasion also he had brought the Government into trouble by his activities in this direction in connection with this very movement, in spite of orders not to meddle with the affairs of the Government." Patel shrewdly avoided alienating the Governor and the Home Member by openly acknowledging "the genuine desire of the Government for an honourable end of the struggle"; but the "Government cannot escape responsibility for his (Commissioner's) action in the end."[7]

Patel had the trump card in his hand. He decided to break his silence. He delivered the last blow by warning the provincial Government that, if the prisoners were not released within the next 24 hours, he would have no choice left but to publish his correspondence with the Governor. He also threatened to restart the satyagraha. This would have been damaging to the prestige of the Governor and the Home Member. Finding no alternative, they conveyed to the Secretary of State their intention to resign if he did not agree to the release of the prisoners prior to the expiry of the stipulated period. A cable came back immediately from London accepting the release of prisoners. While this took place within the period stipulated by Patel, it also coincided with the Commissioner being packed off on leave preparatory to retirement.

The volunteers were set free on September 3rd. As a finale to the satyagraha, they took out a victory mark through the Civil Lines with the national flag flying high right in front. Patel, however, shared the fruits of victory with the Government as a true Gandhian, when he stated at a public meeting the same evening, "I must place on record my conviction that the Government has been most desirous of bringing this struggle to an honourable conclusion... I can truthfully say that I am not in the least elated over our victory. All honour goes to those who went to jail and suffered all manner of hardships... All honour goes to the Congress Committee of Nagpur which showed an amazing organising capacity and was tireless in its efforts. They all will always look back with pride upon this struggle which was fought with weapons of purity and fearlessness. It will fill the people with faith in the superiority of the weapons of truth, non-violence and self-sacrifice."[8]

In a post-satyagraha speech in Ahmedabad, Patel explained, "As long as the Government order remained, the fight continued. When the District Magistrate withdrew it, and the Superintendent of Police began acting under his normal powers, I informed him of the manner in which I proposed to fight him... In advising the volunteers to maintain silence while passing in front of the Christian church, as also the houses of Europeans, I was asking them only to act in a manner which was courteous and in keeping with our dignity. I wanted the British to appreciate that it was not our intention to hurt their feelings in any way. We were opposing only what we considered to be an improper step of the Government."[9]

The Nagpur Flag satyagraha was a victory which Patel did not claim as his, but Gandhi's. He admitted that he had put into action at Nagpur his earlier apprenticeship under Gandhi in the Kheda satyagraha. In the hands of Patel, Gandhi's satyagraha triumphed against the might of the British over a sensitive, prestigious issue—the flag. It was another shinning feather in Patel's cap. With the vindication of the national flag's honour, his prestige soared high. He was well-placed in the higher hierarchy of national leaders.

10

A Satyagraha to Fight Dacoits

Hardly had Patel wound up the Nagpur Flag satyagraha when he was called upon to lead another satyagraha in the Borsad taluka in Gujarat. It was a satyagraha to fight dacoits, who were terrorising the villages around Borsad. The people suffered from dual tyranny: that of the local officials and of the dacoits. The dacoits committed robberies and murders unchecked, while the high-handed officials connived with the dacoits. To cover up their failure, the police blamed the people for providing shelter to the dacoits. The people maintained that the police were in collusion with the dacoits. Without caring to look into the people's allegations, the Government accepted the advice of the local officials that more police were required to cope with the problem and that the people must bear the expenses to be incurred on the additional police. A punitive tax of over Rs.2.40 lakhs was imposed on the taluka, payable by all above the age of sixteen. The Government's action was unjustified and arbitrary.

Prior to agreeing to lead the fight, Patel, like Gandhi in Kheda, decided to institute first a personal inquiry. He deputed two of his trustworthy colleagues, Mohanlal Pandya and Ravishankar Maharaj, to go from village to village and prepare for his study a factual account of the situation. This account revealed the sordid story of the two most dangerous and most feared dacoits—Babar Deva of village Golel and Ali from Borsad town itself. The faulty, misconceived operation of the Criminal Tribes Act had turned many good people into hardened criminals. Babar Deva was one of them. He was required to make his appearance every morning and evening at the local police station. For failure to do so one morning, he was sentenced to six months' imprisonment. As he was scrupulously honest in his behaviour, Babar Deva's pride was deeply hurt, and, on escaping from prison, he turned into a confirmed outlaw. Anyone reporting to the police of his whereabouts was dealt with brutally. Some had their noses cut off, while some were nailed to trees. Suspecting that his wife was conspiring to have him arrested, he murdered her; and so was the fate of some of his relations. He must have committed some 22 murders. The police, far from taking action, often gave names of informants to Babar Deva. In one particular instance, a Rajput, serving as an informant, took a police party to a place where Babar Deva and his men had gathered under a tree. Instead of approaching the spot quietly and arresting him, the police beat a boy who happened to be there, and thereby helped the dacoits run away on hearing the boy's screams. Under such unchecked conditions Babar Deva and his gang roamed the countryside on horseback and used firearms.

Ali, the other notorious dacoit, took to dacoity in a bid to escape the arm of the law after he had murdered a lawyer in broad daylight in Borsad. He lodged his loot with a friend in Uttarsanda. Under pressure from the police, this man got Ali arrested. Fear of Ali's revenge began to haunt him. To get over it, he suggested to the police that if Ali was set free, he would help them arrest Babar Deva through Ali. The police welcomed the plan, and Ali was released. As planned, he invited Babar to meet him. But Babar smelt a rat and did not turn up. The fertile brain of Ali's friend now worked in a more ingenious direction. He suggested that the police allow Ali to indulge in dacoities, with a view to making Babar get over his suspicions. For implementation of their plan, the police supplied Ali with firearms; in return, they had a share in Ali's booty.

The report submitted by Mohanlal Pandya and Ravishankar

Maharaj satisfied Patel that the people were absolutely innocent. According to the report, the outlaws committed robberies at night, while the police committed them during the day! But the latter wrongly held the people as collaborators of the dacoits. The police were charged with dishonesty, as they gave "the outlaws guns and ammunition and filled their pockets by sharing the looted property."[1] Patel spoke at the Borsad taluka conference, 'In Golel, the outlaw (Babar) assaulted the punitive police. The people saw the District Magistrate and said that they could not pay the fine. The Mamlatdar also reported that it was impossible to realise a fine from people who, not being contumacious, were too poor to pay it. This he had stated in his letter P.O.L. 245 dated Borsad, February 16th. He protested against the imposition of any further burden, and went on to record, "No villager seems willing for the continuance of the additional police in the villages." The District Superintendent of Police disagreed with the Mamlatdar, who was the man on the spot, and insisted that the impost should be continued. His reasons were that Babar and his gang were still at large; that though Babar killed Shibhai in broad daylight, no evidence was forthcoming."

An enraged Patel asked, "What are the policemen in the village doing? How are the people to furnish evidence if the police are impotent to do so?... the funniest part of the affair is that the Collector disagreed with the Superintendent of Police, and he reported entirely differently to the Commissioner. A copy of his letter is in my possession. He was against the continuation of the additional police in either of the villages because the additional police are useless to prevent Babar's being sheltered in the villages... The Commissioner disagreed with the Collector and the Mamlatdar; he felt that the Superintendent of Police had given solid reasons for the continuance of the police in the two villages for another year and issued orders accordingly. That was in June. How all of a sudden in October the Government resolved to impose the police on the whole taluka, passes comprehension." Patel ridiculed the whole affair with the caustic remark, "When Babar could not be got hold of, the police made friends with his new genius (Ali), and sought to get rid of an outlaw with the help of another outlaw, and provided him with arms and ammunition. Oh, the pity and the shame of it! The Government ceased to rule, making room for the outlaw. Who is going to punish the Government for having leagued with this outlaw? God alone! The Government surely knows what number of murders and dacoities Ali has committed, having been armed by the Government itself... I hold the Government responsible for all the misdeeds of that miscreant Ali."

Critically but logically Patel argued, "The only reason assigned by the Government for punishing a whole people is that they do not provide information or evidence. Let us see how far this is true. Babar has to his credit 22 murders. Not one of the victims was a rich man. He did not murder them for the mere fun of it. He murdered them as they were informants. If after 22 such informants had been murdered, the Government seriously argues that the people do not give information, shall we ask how many policemen were murdered? An informant was crucified to a tree by Babar... A first class magistrate was waylaid by an outlaw on his way from Wasad to Borsad. The outlaw gave a smack on his face, and wrestled the rifle from his hands. The poor fellow had to plead that he was an ordinary clerk and not a magistrate to escape with his life! A Government with such a magistracy has no title to exist; and has surely no title to punish a people." Patel further argued, "All these things go to show that the Government knows that the people are innocent. But the Government has no money. It still wants to hold its head high before the Princely States in the vicinity. Those States have imposed on their villages additional police to protect them from those very outlaws, but they have not taxed their people. Our Government apes those States in imposing the police, but it tries to find out money from the people's pockets. Well, if it wants money, let it beg of us. But why should it cast a slur on our name? Why should it asperse our behaviour? Treat us as criminals and extort the cost of the police fine!"

Patel complained, "Those who can be charged with the utmost complicity in the crimes are exempted, viz. the Government servants. My information is that every petty village officer knows the whereabouts of these outlaws, but is afraid of them." Patel, therefore, asked his audience, "What, then, should you do?" And promptly gave the answer, "Do not for a moment think that you are fighting for the paltry amount of two rupees and seven annas... You have been fined because of your complicity in the crime; because you are suspected of sheltering the outlaws and befriending them. I ask you to fight only if you are convinced that no power on earth has the right to impugn your character. Let us plainly tell the Government that we are honourable men of character. We shall not sign certificates of our bad behaviour with our own hands. We refuse to pay the fine."

Patel's advice was: "to fight like Gandhi's men. His men do not need a stick or a sickle. They need brave backs to receive blows. Do not be tempted into anger. Do not be tempted into violence... we shall not recognise the police. Let us have our own volunteer corps. I ask you to raise a corps from among yourselves."[2]

That was a revolutionary step unheard of so far. Patel could speak with confidence; and he spoke from a position of strength—strength he had gained with the possession of a secret circular issued by the District Superintendent of Police. The latter had advised all Sub-Inspectors and head constables "to turn a blind eye to dacoities and offences committed by Ali, as he had undertaken to assist in the arrest of Babar Deva."[3] Patel's fight against the Establishment was not an easy one. In true military fashion, Patel drew up the battleline. He divided his volunteer corps into platoons. Each was to defend non-violently a group of villages. He made Borsad his headquarters, from where he conducted his satyagraha. He infused a new spirit and discipline into his volunteers and the general public, through the regular issue of leaflets, which carried his instructions in regard to what they were supposed to do from time to time, what sort of vigilance they were required to maintain, and, above all, how to have unity among the ranks.

The first of such leaflets read:

> "Only by carrying out your pledges can you retain your self-respect. The Government will confiscate your property, take away your cattle and will have no hesitation in attaching for the recovering of Rs.2.50, property worth Rs.25,000. All that you should bear patiently. Under no circumstance should you pay a pie or react violently. The Government has adopted for itself the untruthful and dishonest path. Truth is on your side. If you adhere to the principle of non-violence, you are bound to succeed. Anyone who is honest and who practices non-violence can never lose."[4]

Such an honest, straightforward appeal touched the heart of the simple-minded people, and steeled their determination to fight against injustice on Gandhian principles under Patel's leadership. Patel secured the strategic, all-important support of Borsad town by making a similar appeal to its residents amongst whom he had lived as a fiery lawyer at the beginning of the century:

> "Borsad has assumed large responsibilities. If you are determined, others will follow you. But if you weaken, others will suffer. It is not a question of two or three rupees. We are not beggars that we cannot afford to throw away two or three rupees, but the Government wants to take that much money after calling us the associates of dacoits. If the Government admits that its finances are poor and that its authority has vanished, we shall be quite prepared to take over the administration."[5]

Borsad's response to Patel's appeal was instantaneous and most heartening. He secured a firm assurance that none from the town would come forward to bid for the attached property. The response carried the resolve of all communities—Hindus, Muslims and others. It made it obligatory that anyone buying attached property should be made to pay a token fine of Rs.50. The Government started the attachment work in all seriousness, wielding the baton of authority as menacingly as possible. The

Mamlatdar and his entire staff suspended normal duties to devote themselves wholetime to the task assigned to them. Non-violent defence organised by Patel's "platoons" proved most astonishing, reducing official operations to a comic drama. A volunteer was stationed atop a tall tree at the entrance to a village. On sighting an attachment party, he would beat a drum, and thereby signal the menfolk to make haste to lock up their houses with their womenfolk inside, so as to avoid attachment, and take their cattle outside the village for grazing. Only present to welcome the party were the village urchins, who would follow it singing and shouting, creating all sorts of exasperatingly ludicrous scenes. Such a novel way of boycott lasted throughout the period of satyagraha. Village after village presented a picture of desolation during the day with houses locked, while at night life returned to normal—houses opened and lighted, market place bustling with activity, and women going to fetch water after dark. Under the law attachments could not be carried out after sunset.

The satyagraha was still in progress when Patel had to leave Borsad for Kakinada to attend the Congress session there. In Bombay, in a public speech he caused a flutter among Government circles with his embarrassing disclosure, "I have been able to secure copies of certain official correspondence, and with the help of these papers have exposed the Government's disgraceful policy. If that is regarded as an offence in law, let the Government prosecute me... In order to arrest one outlaw, Government officers thought it wise to seek the assistance of another outlaw, to furnish him with arms and ammunition, and to allow him to commit dacoities and murders at will. What reply does the Government have to this public charge which I make? None, so far as I can see. The Government, in fact, has betrayed the people. Who can prosecute the Government for it? It is the Government which is the confederate of the outlaws, and yet it is the same Government that has now come forward to collect punitive fines from the innocent public. Could there be a better illustration of a thief punishing a magistrate?"[6]

The Governor, Leslie Wilson, who had just assumed charge,

felt shocked by such serious allegations being publicly made against the Government. He asked his Home Member, Maurice Hayward, to proceed to Borsad and conduct an on-the-spot investigation. Hayward arrived in the town on January 4, 1924. First, he acquainted himself with the background of the satyagraha from the Commissioner, the Collector and other officials, and thereafter held, as if, an open court to which were invited some 150 selected men. These men chose one Ramabhai as their spokesman. To let Hayward judge the issue impartially, Patel, his lieutenants and volunteers absented themselves from the meeting.

Ramabhai conducted his evidence with remarkable courage, independence and fearlessness and in a manner that was truthful and convincing. He told the Home Member that the people had given up the thought of representation to the Government for loss of confidence in the officials. Complaining of harassment, he pointed to the Deputy Superintendent of Police and said, "That gentleman went, only two days ago, to village Nisraya and threatened the people that if they did not pay the tax, he would send to their village the outlaws who had visited Jhalund." When the Deputy Superintendent of Police defended himself with a denial, a villager from Nisraya got up to say that he was not telling the truth. On the Home Member's calling for suggestions as to how the outlaws could soon be arrested, Ramabhai bluntly told him, "If the police department continues to be as it is today, not only will the existing outlaws not be arrested, but new ones will be created... Inspector Maganlal, who is also sitting here, is a personal friend of outlaw Ali... If your officers encourage the outlaws in this manner, instead of arresting them, how can you ask us to pay a tax? Only if you get rid of such corrupt police, would it possible to bring the outlaws to book. Since the commencement of this movement, several outlaws have written to the satyagraha camp that they are anxious to reform themselves if only they are given an opportunity."[7]

The Home Member felt convinced of the righteousness of Patel's fight. He ordered immediate stoppage of further attachment of property; and, on his return to Bombay on January 8th, the

Government made an announcement which fully vindicated Patel. It stated, "The Governor-in-Council has resolved that the cost of the extra police, who have already been enlisted in, shall be met during the current year from general revenues and that the Legislative Council shall be asked to vote funds for the continuance of operations during the next financial year... The Governor-in-Council believes that the people of Borsad... will respond to this policy of liberality by cordial assistance and cooperation in the further operations necessary for suppressing the violent crimes from which their taluka has so long suffered."[8]

It was a victory for Patel. He had been fully vindicated. He ordered immediate withdrawal of the satyagraha; and in a statement reflecting grace, charm and humility he said, "Once again there has been a triumph of truth, non-violence and penance. This victory has been as quick as our struggle was just. It is unique in that both the parties have won. It has admitted its mistake openly and with courage. The Government has, thus, gained a victory by admitting the truth and declining to follow the normal practice of refusing to admit a mistake for fear of loss of prestige. We would be failing in our duty if we did not congratulate most sincerely His Excellency the Governor of Bombay, Leslie Wilson, for showing so much moral courage... Our victory lies in the Government's withdrawal of the charge made against us."[9]

Victory celebrations on a grand scale were held in Borsad on January 12th. Nearly 30,000 people joined them. Participants came from as far as Ahmedabad and Bombay. The presence of women in large numbers electrified the whole atmosphere, then, as also earlier, during the satyagraha. Men added colour of their own: "Patidars, confident of their achievement and of their importance; fine, well-built Baraiyas and Patanwadias with their long sticks and their hubble-bubbles, and Garasias with large turbans." It was not a motley crowd; but a gathering of proud, disciplined soldiers of Patel who had carried the satyagraha to a glorious finish.

Addressing the huge gathering, Patel said, "Your relatively small quarrel with the Government is over but our main, bigger quarrel (for independence) is still unresolved... During this short struggle, consider what great sacrifices you have made, what courage you have exhibited, what unity you have maintained, and what enthusiasm you have shown. It is only because you have proved yourselves capable of these that you have been able to gain what you wanted. You have not succeeded because of my skill or cleverness. Today, we have gained this victory because we walked along the road shown by the great saint who is now in jail."

Patel then pleaded with the people, "Let sweetness and friendship reign hereafter... Make friends with the Talati, the Mukhi, the Ravania... and the police. Forget all about the attachments carried out by them... And to the outlaws, let me say, a real outlaw does not keep running about with a little gun, robbing and murdering the innocent. A real outlaw does not require a weapon. Whoever harasses a defenceless person, or robs or murders innocent informers, is a disgrace to his community."[10]

The day Borsad celebrated its victory, Gandhi was operated upon for appendicitis in the Sassoon Hospital at Pune. From his sick-bed, he greeted Patel with the words, "Welcome, the King of Borsad."

That was a befitting tribute from the master. On his recovery, Gandhi wrote in the *Young India* of April 6th, "These achievements (both in the Kheda and Borsad satyagrahas) are a great tribute to Vallabhbhai's magnificent organizing and administrative ability. And he has collected around him in the process, a band of devoted workers of like mind and ability. The Borsad satyagraha is a magnificent example of the public activity, governed wholly by public consideration." It was Gandhi's view that "the satyagraha struggle at Borsad was in many ways superior to that in Kheda", because "the latter was merely a vindication of the honour of the people... In Borsad, however, there was a complete victory for satyagraha: honour was vindicated and the object was achieved after a straight struggle."[11]

11

Fighting Gujarat Floods

It was Saturday, July 23, 1927. Public and privates offices had already closed for the week-end. About late evening, a gloom started gathering ominously. And soon a heavy downpour began in Ahmedabad. It was to continue with unabated fury for a week or so. Since the rain on Saturday was unusually heavy for hours at a stretch, many hopefully expected it to spend its fury by Sunday evening. But it didn't. That caused worry to many. But most of it to Patel. He was President of the Ahmedabad Municipality. Sitting in his Ahmedabad house, he felt restless, worried by a premonition that the rain was going to bring upon Gujarat no ordinary calamity. His restlessness would not let him sleep, even when it was past midnight. Undeterred, he decided to have a round of the city.

The night was dark and windy. The desolate look of the streets and houses made everything menacingly gloomy. Alone he walked along Gandhi Road in pouring rain. On the way he knocked at the door of a friend, Harilal Kapadia, who was shocked to see him at that late hour—and that too, completely drenched. Patel warmed himself with a hot cup of tea, and also changed into his friend's clothes at the latter's persuasion. Soon after, accompanied by Kapadia, he set out on his tour of the city. Till late hours he moved from street to street. Armed with first-hand knowledge of the situation, he reached the Municipal Engineer's house, woke him up and took him to the Municipal office. The staff concerned with the situation were summoned. Before day-break, arrangements were complete for the drainage of the rain-water accumulated in the low-lying areas of the city. Yet 6,000 houses collapsed in Ahmedabad, rendering thousands homeless. In one week, it had rained 52 inches as against the annual average of 30 inches—a record for over half a century or more.

The countryside presented a grimmer picture of misery and devastation. Over 4,000 villages were marooned in five to six feet deep water which stretched for miles around. Some villages had been swept away by the swift-flowing current of swollen rivers. Not a few were submerged by flood water. More than 50 per cent of the houses had collapsed. Mile upon mile of fertile agricultural land was covered with water, totally ruining the crop. At many places receding waters had left a few feet of sand. Kheda district suffered worst, with 100 inches of rainfall. Over 72,000 houses had collapsed. Kheda town looked like an oasis in a vast expanse of water. As the waters kept rising, many families had to seek shelter on tree-tops for five to six days at a stretch, going without food and even sleep. In one particular instance, 61 Bhils of a small village, on the bank of the Dhadhar river, took shelter on two small trees adjacent to each other. On the fifth day of their stay, "children and old people started falling down through sheer exhaustion, and were dragged away by the current. In this way 31 out of the 61 lives were lost".[1]

Patel faced a great challenge, seemingly insurmountable. He had to reach people hovering between life and death, trapped in almost inaccessible places. It had taken him three days to reach the Sabarmati ashram in Ahmedabad itself. The problems in the countryside were stupendous. He asked for a list of volunteers to be prepared immediately. Lakshmidas Purushottam Asher, who was on a visit to Ahmedabad from the Bardoli ashram where he worked on a hand-operated cotton-ginning machine, took the list to Patel at the latter's residence. Asher was carrying a roller with him. After he had scrutinised the list, Patel asked him, "Why is not your name in the list?" Asher explained the particular errand on which he had come from Bardoli and was likely to go back soon. Patel retorted, "If Gujarat goes under, who will ply your *charkha*? Leave your roller in my house and go for relief work."[2]

That sounded like the command of a leader. Asher became Patel's right-hand man in the relief work. Others to join soon were Amritlal Thakkar, Narhari Parikh, Maganlal Gandhi, Dr. Chandulal and Kishorilal Mashruwala. Each one of them was appointed a Corps Commander at the relief centres at Nadiad, Anand, Mehmadabad, Broach and Baroda. In order to reach their headquarters, both Asher and Thakkar had to cross a broken bridge by catching hold of supports. Under the direction of Corps Commanders, relief reached each and every hamlet, no matter how far it was located and what circumstances it was in. Patel's volunteers, numbering over 2,000, travelled under the most trying conditions. On occasions they risked their lives by swimming across deep waters to reach starving people stranded in their marooned village houses.

In spite of its vast administrative set-up, the Government could not collect correct and full information. But Patel had with him vital information within eight days of the stoppage of rain—even when post and telegraph and railway communications had completely broken down. The Collector of Ahmedabad called upon Patel with a wire from the Presidency Government at Bombay, and Patel complied with the request to provide details of the flood havoc in the district. Patel even responded to the call from the Collector of Kheda for prompt supply of essential commodities, such as rice and kerosene. Patel, on his part, was equally keen to secure Government assistance, as the magnitude of the problem was so big. He was for mutual cooperation. "It is not a political issue", he explained. "It is one of compassion for human life and of humanism."[3]

Patel's forceful and forthright speeches and articles were reasoned, matter-of-fact, incontestable. His information of the calamity was most authentic and up-to-date. His organization of relief reached the remotest hamlet. Compared to the "speed and zeal with which Vallabhbhai acted on this occasion, the

Government appeared to have moved at a snail's pace."[4] He, thus, won the confidence of the Government. As a result, not only did the Finance Member of the Presidency Government at Bombay, Chunilal Mehta, visit Nadiad for personal discussions with the local officials, but even the Governor, Leslie Wilson, undertook a weeklong tour of the affected areas. Patel was shrewdly quick to give him the praise he deserved, "The Hon'ble Governor Saheb undertook a week-long tour of the affected areas. He visited many villages and inspected a number of relief centres. He was much moved by the plight of the people in the countryside. In keeping with the circumstances, his tour was devoid of the usual pomp and show—and no receptions either; instead, he freely mixed with the people in order to have a correct assessment of the situation... he promised to render all possible help. Everywhere not only did he express satisfaction over relief work, but had a word of praise for the volunteers too."[5]

Earlier, the Commissioner of the Northern Division had announced, by way of relief, a free gift of Rs.2,000 and Rs.15,000 as *taquavi* loans to every taluka. Patel wasn't in favour of free gifts, because "the peasant of Gujarat is self-respecting. He doesn't want to live on charity. Even at the cost of his life, he would refuse to accept donations... the relief centres have, therefore, opened cheap grain shops. More than his stomach, he looks to his lands and fresh sowing. What he needs are seeds. If within eight days he doesn't get seeds, for a year his land will remain without a crop. This is the Government's duty to provide."[6]

Patel disclosed that he had asked the Commissioner for a crore of rupees. He had pleaded with him not to treat the calamity as a minor one, arguing, "You may not worry yourself about giving relief in regard to foodstuffs and other immediate necessities. It is clear, however, that the people will need a great deal of money in order to bring their land once again under cultivation and to rebuild their houses."[7] Patel laid emphasis on the implementation of the plan outlined by Purushottamdas Thakurdas at the Nadiad conference of the relief workers. The plan wanted the Government to make a provision of Rs. 1 crore and 30 lakhs. Patel's' assessment began to be appreciated by the authorities, particularly after the Governor's tour. Patel was invited to Pune for a conference, where he got what he wanted—the Government's sanction of Rs. 1 crore and 30 lakhs towards loans.

The fame of Patel's humanitarian work travelled across the seas to reach England, making tremendous impact. So much so that before the Government made an announcement, the King Emperor and Secretary of State Birkenhead announced their personal donations of Rs.2,000 and £10. These were, indeed, token contributions, intended essentially to bring about an atmosphere of goodwill. The Government relief plan was what Patel had already initiated. His relief measures were not only amazingly quick in their implementation, but were most judiciously planned and executed. Being himself a farmer's son, he had correctly analysed the needs of the people. His first step was to make available adequate supplies of foodgrains and clothing through cheap—not free—shops. External aid was to be limited, so as not to make of them "helpless dependents" The second step was to arrange for distribution of seeds, which the Government, he knew, would take time to do through *taquavi* loans. Delay would have prolonged—and even aggravated the calamity. Sowing operations were also to provide the peasant with employment, and spare him from suffering the humiliation of a beggar. The third step was to rebuild 72,000 village houses.

Hugh Garrett, an ICS who had served in Gujarat from 1919 to 1938, worked in close association with Patel for a number of months as the Government's special officer for flood relief. Garrett appreciated Patel's organizing qualities, his devotion to duty without any communal bias, and his being "a pillar of the Congress party". Garrett had developed "faith in him" and considered Patel absolutely "honest and frank". One day when the two were together, he asked Patel if he would have any objection to his recommending to the Government to confer some honours or titles on him and his colleagues in appreciation of their commendable relief work. The suggestion was well-meaning, but it amused Patel. He told Garrett, "Our delight is in doing service to the people. We are not anxious for publicity or fame."[8]

Glowing reports of the great human drama Patel had enacted in Gujarat reached the far corners of India. His brother Vithalbhai, then President of the Central Legislature, could not resist reaching Nadiad from Simla towards the end of September "to work under Vallabhbhai". In December, the Viceroy and Lady Irwin visited Gujarat to see for themselves the much-acclaimed achievement of Patel and his volunteers. A garden party was given in their honour at Nadiad on December 12th by Vithalbhai, with all the principal workers participating in it. In a speech on the occasion, the Viceroy acknowledged, "From what I have seen and heard, I am satisfied that, if the volunteers of the Gujarat Provincial Congress Committee had not reached the flood-affected areas in time, the loss of life, instead of being negligible, would have been very heavy. The credit for preventing such a calamity goes to the volunteers of the Provincial Congress Committee."[9]

Patel's victory over the unprecedented calamity was one which no other agency could have accomplished—not even the Government, with its vast resources in money and materials, if not men. The Finance Member, Chunilal Mehta, unreservedly praised Patel's "alertness and organizing ability", and said that "in Gandhi's absence, Vallabhbhai had taken his place and discharged his duties creditably... the discipline and the ability which the volunteer workers had shown was the result of years of training given to them by Gandhi and Vallabhbhai."[10] Gandhi on his part wrote in the *Navajivan*: "Vallabhbhai is a seasoned soldier, and he has no other occupation than that of service. He has got an efficient agency of workers under him."[11] Patel had trained these workers like a loving patriarch, and inspired them with the ideals of service which Gandhi had been preaching.

12

The Lenin of Bardoli

The dazzling success of the Bardoli satyagraha helped Patel climb to new heights of political eminence. In a most apt description, Gandhi said, "Vallabhbhai found his Vallabh (God) in Bardoli."[1] It was the fulfillment of the fond hope with which his parents had named him after Vallabhacharya. Mrs. Annie-Besant declared: "Let us Bardolise the country".[2] Motilal Nehru, the Congress President in 1928, in a letter to Gandhi described Patel as "the hero of the hour", and counseled that "the least we can do to appreciate his public services is to offer him the Crown"[3] he himself was wearing. The British, out of fear, called him Lenin. Judging from the total obedience Patel commanded and the iron discipline he had imposed on the 87,000 non-cooperating peasants, they came to the conclusion, to quote *The Times of India*, that Patel had "instituted there a Bolshevik regime in which he plays the role of Lenin."[4]

The Lenin of Bardoli was, however, every inch a Gandhian—in thought, in speech, in action. His heavy moustache no doubt gave him the stern looks of Bismarck or Stalin; yet he was unlike them. With the farmer's staff in hand, he led his armless army just wearing the peasant's crude countrymade *chappals*, his *jubba*, waistcoat and *dhoti* made from coarse homespun *khadi*. And his disciplined army of men and women non-violently faced a fully armed opponent. Such non-violence lay in their willingly surrendering to his command to make sacrifices and undergo suffering, which made Gandhi remark, "Only the Sardar can evoke such discipline."[5] Patel's comment, however showed his humility when he stated: "I have been with him (Gandhi) almost since he returned to India... Even so, I keep him away from my work. We are not likely to regain our capacity for leadership and wait for his guidance... I told him to go to Bardoli only after I was arrested."[6]

The immediate cause of the satyagraha was the arbitrary enhancement of land revenue by the Government in 1927. But the seeds of the satyagraha had been sown by Gandhi himself earlier during the Non-Cooperation Movement when he had selected the taluka as the "staring point of one of the biggest experiments in history."[7] Gandhi's choice of Bardoli had a historic background. Its people knew Gandhi from his South African satyagraha days, when the United Patidar Society of Johannesburg had given him valuable support. Both the President and the Secretary of the Society were from Bardoli. The people of Bardoli were industrious, skilful and thrifty: "their frank and open faces bear a natural stamp of purity"; and they had "a sense of sacredness about their pledges and their vows."[8]

The invitation to Gandhi in 1921 had come from two brothers, Kalyanji Mehta and Kuverji Mehta. Since 1911 they had been running the Patidar Vidyarthi Ashram in Surat, which imparted preliminary education to boys proceeding to South Africa. From 1920 onwards, answering Gandhi's call for non-cooperation, they turned out from their school students imbibed with national spirit. Kalyanji Mehta claimed that the British, when they first came to India, had landed at the Surat port and had established their first factory there. Since "from Surat they had extended their domain over the rest of the country, it was only appropriate that Surat should set afoot a movement to say farewell to them".[9] He and some other public spirited men from Surat saw in the Bardoli satyagraha such a movement—an opportunity to throw the British out of India.

Gandhi had visited Bardoli in 1921 to satisfy himself through personal on-the-spot inquiries. He had a number of meetings with village representatives. He had also consulted a former Diwan of Cambay, Mahadev Rao, who belonged to Bardoli and had settled there on retirement. He had told Gandhi that the people of Bardoli were simple minded and straight forward; though not conversant with politics, they were capable of giving a fight, and were ready for the proposed satyagraha—at least fifty per cent of them. Thus satisfied, Gandhi had sent an ultimatum to the Viceroy, a decision regarding which the Congress Working Committee had taken at Surat on January 31, 1921. But the satyagraha never took off. It was given up about the time it was to start because of the Chauri Chaura riots in Uttar Pradesh in which 21 policemen were burnt alive. The Bardoli workers, who had put in months of preparations, were opposed to such a decision. As Gandhi's deputy, Patel took the decision in his stride and said, "He is our Commander. We are fighting the battle on his principles. We should, therefore, follow him." Bardoli, nevertheless, suffered frustration. In such a situation of gloom and despair, it fell on Patel to keep the people's spirits buoyed up. This he accomplished through Gandhian constructive work from the four principal centres at Bardoli, Sarbhon, Varad and Vankaner—places which distinguished themselves later in the Bardoli satyagraha of 1928; and the work so carried out had "bound the villagers to the workers with a tie of indissoluble union."[10]

The announcement of the new land revenue settlement towards the end of 1925 made Bardoli seethe with discontent. Such revenue settlements, as a rule, were carried out every 30 years, primarily to assess the economic condition of agriculturists. The previous one had taken place in 1896. A fresh one was due in 1926. An Indian member of the Provincial Civil Service, M.S. Jayakar, who was Deputy Collector of Surat, was entrusted with the job. He had no earlier experience of such work. Arbitrarily, therefore, he recommended an unjustifiable increase in the total assessment for the taluka of over 30 per cent. The report was not published. A copy could be seen for reference only at the taluka court. A former revenue officer and an ICS, H.B. Shivdasani, while speaking in the Presidency Council in March 1927, described this as "not fair", and argued, "We all know how very backward the villagers are, and how very lazy they are, and we cannot expect them to walk 20 miles to the taluka town to see the report which is in English."[11]

Earlier in January, Bardoli peasants had met in a conference. In March, a deputation of peasants, headed by Council members Bhimbhai Naik and Shivdasani, had waited on the Revenue Member, J.L. Rieu. Instead of being given a patient hearing, they were shown scant courtesy. In May, Naik submitted a representation to the Revenue Member which was critical of the Settlement Officer's report. The Settlement Commissioner in 1896 had admitted that "the general conclusion from all the recorded statistics is that the taluka in 1896 was either over-assessed or assessed right up to the full limit of half the rental value."[12] In 1900-1, G.V. Joshi had proved that the incidence of land revenue on population in the Bombay Presidency was far heavier than in any other Indian province (as much as Rs.2 per head of population); the incidence on cultivated acreage was the highest in the Gujarat districts (as much as Rs.4 per acre); and that in Surat district, of which Bardoli was a part, it was the highest in Gujarat (as much as Rs. 5.90 per acre).

Not only was the system of assessment arbitrary, the peasants were given no right of appeal, as the Bombay Revenue Jurisdiction Act excluded the jurisdiction of civil courts in matters concerning assessments. Such an Act was brought into force following a Bombay High Court judgement against the Settlement Officer in an assessment suit in 1873. A member of the Bombay Legislative Council had, therefore, complained, "so far as the administration of the land revenue system is concerned, the reforms have proved to be a curse. The doors of the law courts are barred against the peasant by statute; and the Government of India's power of interference are considerably limited. On account of the division of functions and the devolution of larger powers, the Government of India will not exercise their superior authority of official control. Land revenue is a provincial subject and also a reserved subject... in provincial reserved subject, local Government possess acknowledged authority of their own."[13]

In 1919, the Joint Parliamentary Committee had recommended that "the process of revising land revenue assessments ought to be brought under closer regulation by statute as soon as possible", it had pointed out that "the people who are most affected have no voice in the shaping of the system, and the rules are often obscure and imperfectly understood by those who pay the revenue." In 1924 the Bombay Legislative Council made an identical recommendation regarding statutory regulation by stating that "no revision be proceeded with and no new rates under any revised settlement be introduced till the said legislation is brought into effect."[14] The resolution was opposed by the Government. Because of the majority voting in its favour, the Government appointed a Land Revenue Assessment Committee to go into the issue. This proved to be a stalling move, as the committee did nothing over the next three years.

In 1927, the Legislative Council passed another resolution by a majority of 52 against 29 votes, "reaffirming the principle of the resolution as amended and carried by it by a majority on the 15th March 1924."[15] For the second time the Council recommended to the Governor-in-Council that "he would be pleased to give immediate effect to it by introducing the necessary legislation... and pending such legislation, to issue orders to the revenue authorities concerned, not to collect the assessment enhanced in revision after the 15th March, 1924." A year passed without action on the suggested legislation. Meanwhile, the Government issued a resolution on the Revenue Assessment Committee's report, which turned out to be most unsatisfactory. Of the twenty-two members of the committee, thirteen appended a joint or separate minutes of dissent. The Government resolution, accepting the view of the official members, resolved that "rental value must be adopted as the sole basis for fixing the assessment." The committee had recommended that the assessment should not exceed 25 per cent of the net profits, whereas the Government decided to "adhere to the present practice of regarding 50 per cent of the rental value as the maximum limit."[16] This authorised the action taken by the Settlement Commissioner. The Government even rejected the committee's recommendation that the Settlement Officer "shall have the assistance of two representatives of the peasants elected by the Taluka Local Board in preparing his settlement."[17]

The Government of India's Resolution of January 16, 1927 supported the provincial Government's stand by stating; "Assessments cannot be dictated by the theorist in his study... they can only be safely worked out by the Settlement Officer in the village and on the fields."[18] This in itself proved a theorist's view. M.S. Jayakar had no previous experience of assessment work, and yet he wrote his report "after visiting the principal villages of the taluka in a superficial way, without meeting or discussing the question with the local people, or giving the local people any opportunity to put forward their point of view."[19] He himself admitted that his report had been "revised in accordance with the Settlement Commissioner's instructions."[20] According to some, Settlement Commissioner Anderson "practically rewrote the report."[21] Whereas Jayakar had grossly misjudged the prosperity of the taluka on the basis of which he had recommended higher assessment, the Settlement Commissioner, though accepting his data on sales and rentals, practically discarded Jayakar's report. The Government, thus, had two conflicting reports:—the Settlement Commissioner's recommending a 29 per cent increase, and the Settlement Officer's 30 per cent. The Government decided on 22 per cent.

Petition-making had, thus, failed. In September 1927, a few thousand peasants met at a conference at Bardoli. Dadubhai Desai, MLC, presided. It was unanimously resolved to withhold payment of the enhanced amount. Unmoved by public opinion, voiced through the Legislature and the people outside it, the Government ordered collection of revised assessment from February 5, 1928. Frustration overtook the people. In their hour of distress, their minds turned to Patel—the hero of many a battle in the past. Kalyanji and Kuverji, along with some others, called on Patel at Ahmedabad and requested him to give a lead to the Bardoli peasants. Patel laid down some conditions, and asked them to come back after giving due consideration to his warning against the dire consequences of a satyagraha campaign which might be indefinitely prolonged. This was around January 20th, whereas the collections were to begin from February 5th. The taluka leaders, as desired by Patel, visited villages to ascertain people's resolve. They reported "a unanimity and keenness about offering satyagraha."[22] They added force to their request by bringing with them, on their second visit, such seasoned "soldiers" as Darbarsaheb Gopaldas, Mohanlal Pandya and Ravishankar Maharaj, who were ready to join the satyagraha. All of them had been Patel's trusted lieutenants in earlier battles. Nothing could have been more assuring to Patel than their help and the peasants' resolve. Since Gandhi's consent was still required, Patel told them, "You go and see Bapu. I will follow you."

A long conversation took place between Gandhi and Kalyanji, at the end of which, on Patel's testimony that Bardoli's cause was just, Gandhi said, "Well, then, there is nothing more to be considered. Victory to Gujarat."[23]

Patel went a step further. He had an assurance from each village that full tax would not be paid, and that in the meetings addressed by him half of those present would be women. Asked to explain this, he merely said, "You will understand it later."

Patel arrived in Bardoli on February 4th—a day prior to the start of the collection of the enhanced land revenue—to preside over a conference of peasants, who not only accepted his contention not to precipitate matters, but left it to him to chalk out a course of action he considered best. Patel really felt for the oppressed peasants, but outwardly he looked harsh and firm, though quiet. He did not appear to be a man in a hurry. He still wanted to examine and cross-examine the people before leading them into the battle. Besides conferring with his workers, he met representatives from some 80 villages. When satisfied, he addressed a public meeting of about 10,000 peasants whom he told with his characteristic bluntness, "I shall stand by the side of anyone who is prepared to take risks. In 1921, we were on the point of being put to test, but unforeseen circumstances intervened and we had no opportunity of giving a demonstration of our strength. Now the hour has struck. But are you really ready?"[24] He warned them against reaching a hasty decision. He gave them seven days to think it over.

Patel had a double purpose in the postponement of the satyagraha by a week; first, to administer shock therapy to the people with a view to steeling their resolve; secondly, to explore possibilities of a compromise through the Gandhian principle of negotiation. Three members of the Legislative Council present at the conference stated that they had "exhausted every constitutional means at their disposal." Therefore, they entrusted "their case to one who could take them along the path on non-violent resistance and suffering."[25] Patel's generalship of the satyagraha was now accepted by one and all. His immediate task at Bardoli was over. He returned to Ahmedabad on February 5th. On the 6th, he wrote to the Governor, drawing his attention to "the flagrant injustice" being done under the revised settlement. He suggested to the Governor "to afford a fair opportunity to the people to place their case before an impartial tribunal clothed with adequate authority", and warned him that unless that was done, "with all my anxiety to avoid a serious conflict with the Government, I would have no alternative but to advise the people to refuse to pay the assessment, and peacefully and quietly suffer the consequences of the refusal. Should Your Excellency think it necessary that we should meet in the matter, I would gladly wait on you."[26]

Patel was not unknown to the Governor, Leslie Wilson. He had met him during the Gujarat floods, and had won his high praise for relief work. Yet, instead of gracefully accepting the suggestion for a meeting, Wilson sent a reply through his Private Secretary, with the curt remark that Patel's letter "has been sent to the Revenue Department for official consideration and disposal."[27] The Government did not communicate till February 11th, whereas the final date for the payment of the first instalment was the 15th. Patel returned to Bardoli on the 12th. Once again he talked to the peasants with his usual bluntness, "I still ask you to think twice before you take the plunge. Do not derive comfort from the feeling that you have as your leader a fighter like myself. Forget me and forget my companions. Fight, if you feel that you must resist oppression and injustice. Do not take the plunge lightly. If you fail miserably, you will not rise again for several years. But if you succeed, you will have done much to lay the foundations of Swaraj."[28]

Patel was hurt by the Governor's curt reply, and that too through his Private Secretary. His speeches became more firm, determined and even challenging. "We have", he told a conference of the peasants, "done everything we could. Now there remains only one way—to oppose force with force. The Government has all the paraphernalia of authority and has the physical strength of the armed forces. You have the strength of truth and your capacity to endure pain. These are the two rival forces. The Government's stand is unjust. It is your duty to oppose it... If you make up your mind that you will not give even a single pie—no matter what the Government may do, no matter how many confiscations it may carry out, no matter how many fields it may take away—the Government will not be able to collect the revised land revenue which you are unwilling to accept."

Patel then strengthened the hearts of the peasants with the argument that, "the Government does not have in its possession any weapons with which it can compel you to modify your decision. But do not make up your mind because you have confidence in me. You must rely on your own strength, on your own courage, on your ability to be ruined in the course of this fight, if necessary. When you take this decision, remember that you are taking it as a pledge. But if you have at the back of your mind the fear that against this powerful Government you will not be able to stand firm, for heaven's sake do not enter the fight. If, on the other hand, you are satisfied that this Government is not prepared to listen to any fair proposal and that by failing to stand up to it, you will only ruin yourselves and your children, and, in addition, lose your self-respect, then alone you should undertake this fight. This is not merely a question of an increase of a lakh of rupees or so, or of 37 lakhs in 30 years, but a question of truth and falsehood—a question of self-respect."[29]

The conference passed a resolution, which was supported by representatives of the villages and communities in the taluka. The representatives comprised all—Patidars, Vanias, Christians, Parsis, Muslims and backward classes. The resolution stated: "This conference of the people of Bardoli taluka resolves that the revision settlement... is arbitrary, unjust and oppressive, and advises all the occupants to refuse payment of the revised assessment until the Government is prepared to accept the amount of the old assessment in full satisfaction of its dues, or until the Government appoints an impartial tribunal to settle the whole question of revision by investigation and inquiry on the spot."[30]

As soon as the fight began, Patel discerned some chinks in the satyagrahis' armour. There were a few who "cherished the old mentality of tendering the old assessment", whereas Patel had counseled non-payment of the total. A more serious weakness was that "amongst the different communities there was nothing like cohesion": the Raniparaj, the "meekest of the meek" were likely "to bend under the first blow"; the Vanias, with heavy stakes in land, "might not hold out until the last", the Anavlas, "proud and defiant, were still sitting on the fence and their calculating nature made them hesitate to join the fray until the campaign was in full swing"; the attitude of the Muslims of Surat was "hardly encouraging and might easily contaminate Bardoli", and "the mild Parsis—who could be sure about them?" The Patidars, Patel's own community, were the only ones with "a closely knit organization" on whom he could implicitly reply; and his sermon to the weak and the vacillating was: "Having now entered into the water, you must learn to swim".[31]

Patel's trusted lieutenant Mohanlal Pandya wrote to Patel after touring the taluka: "The atmosphere fills me with doubt and dismay. Can these be the men and women who intend to engage themselves in a fierce struggle against the Government in a few days? No one seems to me to be in fighting trim... They are going about their business as though nothing has happened. Are these the people you want to go to war against a mighty Government? I do not despair, but let us not overrate our strength. May God keep your honour!"[32] Patel was not dispirited by the prevailing uncertain climate. He knew how to weld these people into a unified fighting force, and make them exude courage, hope and buoyancy. He told a group of peasants' representatives, "If you can give me only a hundred true men who will fight unto death, I assure you that success is certain." But he wanted all the 17,000 landholders to join the fight, and "not to reap the unmerited benefit of the suffering of a hundred."[33]

The Government was alarmed by the new spirit of rebellion that swept Bardoli. The Commissioner of Northern Division, W.W. Smart, who was holidaying at a seaside resort, was ordered to return and camp at Surat, so as to be 15 to 20 miles from Bardoli town, the headquarters of the struggle. The District Collector, not knowing what was happening in his taluka as he had paid no visit for some time, was asked to visit Bardoli immediately. On arrival, to his shock and dismay, he found a chilling welcome. With all the shops shut and doors of all the houses closed, Bardoli town was under a total boycott. He got no conveyance to go to a nearby village, Sarbhon, where he reached with great difficulty. Far from a welcome awaiting him, as on earlier occasions, his arrival was signaled by young, enthusiastic volunteers by the beat of a drum, following which the streets at once bore a deserted look and the door of every house was shut. He sent for the village Patel, who had the courage to tell him, "The people will not listen to us. They are indifferent to forfeitures and confiscations."[34] Annoyed over his humiliation and helplessness, he ordered the Talatis to prepare plans for auction of land and seizure of buffaloes. To effect these speedily and subject the people to terror, "a number of Pathans of questionable character were brought in from Bombay."

Undeterred, the peasants reacted "in a firmer manner than ever before to fight against the Government, and they imposed a most severe form of boycott of the officers." The officers, in Patel's view, were not their enemies. He, therefore, ordered that the peasants should remain unflinching in their resolve not to pay land revenue and even deny the officers the use of a bullock-cart or labour, but the officers were not to be harassed by stoppage of supply of essential commodities like milk, vegetables, foodstuffs or medicines, as also the services of a barber or a washerman. Denial of the latter he considered as "not satyagraha but cruelty."[35] He kept control over the situation by not letting people form into a crowd to watch the attachments and thereby allow officials to create disturbances; and, secondly by prohibiting anyone, including his Sector Commanders, from speaking in public. When the struggle was on, there should be, he declared, one leader, one voice. He kept the right of speaking in public to himself. This avoided expression of divergent views, and ensured that the Sector Commanders and his *sainiks* would busy themselves with the actual battle. Such a step denied the Government an opportunity to incite violence and drive a wedge between the leader and others.

Patel organised the satyagraha on the military pattern. He himself was the Supreme Commander or *Senapati.* Directly under him were Sector Commanders or *Vibhapatis*. Under each Commander were volunteers called *sainiks* or soldiers. The battlefield covered about 92 villages. He had horse-riders to bring him messages from the remotest ones. The battle itself involved some 87,000 peasants from the Bardoli taluka and Valod Mahal. Operationwise, there were 18 sectors, 12 being in the former and six in the latter. Bardoli served as the HQ of the Supreme Commander, who had, like a General, his personal staff to help him carry out his various duties. Patel's Personal Secretary, Swami Anand, conducted the Supreme Commander's correspondence, as also looked after dissemination of war information. The Master of Ceremonies was Kalyanji Mehta, who programmed Patel's movements. The Editor of publications, *Patrikapati,* was Jugatram Dave. He was also in charge of the publication division, called *Satyagraha Prakashan Vibhag*. The most significant publication was *Larat-ki-Patrika,* the war bulletin. Kalyanji Mehta's brother, Kuverji, was the Conciliator, who moved from village to village to know of possible breaches of the pledge the peasants had taken and to mend them. Lastly, an Ambassador in Manilal Kothari toured India to brief important opinion-builders like Tej Bahadur Sapru, M.R. Jayakar and Srinivasa Sastri.

The war bulletin, carrying Patel's stirring speeches and satyagraha news, was published daily and distributed amongst the Bardoli peasants as well as others. Handwritten copies used to reach Surat before midnight; and the following morning the Tapti Valley Railway would bring bundles of printed issues which volunteers would collect at different stations *en route*, and would go at galloping speed to "the villagers waiting anxiously for the *Patrika* every morning and devouring the contents with avidity."[36] From 5,000 copies at start, the number soon rose to over 15,000. More than 10,000 copies were distributed in Bardoli alone. Outside Bardoli, every important Gujarat town and village received the war bulletin. The *Patrika* also served English newspapers in Gujarat and outside as valuable source material for publication. To sustain the peasants' enthusiasm further, Patel organised a *bhajan mandli*—a troupe of musicians which went from village to village at night, like India's traditional bards, singing national and religious songs. The troupe included a story-teller who regaled the peasants with inspiring anecdotes and sarcastic gibes. Besides, a women workers' unit moved among the village womenfolk to keep their spirits high, and also of their menfolk.

Sector Commanders were some of Patel's tried and trusted lieutenants from his past battles. They included reputed men like Ravishankar Maharaj at Sarbhon, Darbarsaheb Gopaldas at Bamni, Mohanlal Pandya at Varad, Dr. Chunilal Mehta and his wife at Vedchhi, Makanji Desai at Madhi, Dr. Chandulal at Valod, Ambalal Patel at Balda, Naranbhai at Buhari, besides Sharda Mehta and her husband, Dr. Sumant Mehta, Patel's daughter Maniben Patel and Mithuben Petit of the multi-millionaire Parsi family of the Petits from Bombay. Abbas Saheb Tayabji and Imam Saheb Abdul Kadar Bavazir (of the Satyagraha Ashram of South Africa fame) placed their services at Patel's disposal to take care of the Muslims in the taluka.

The fierceness of the battle lay in the people's sufferings. Over

87,000 peasant satyagrahis, along with their womenfolk, children and their "beloved cattle", voluntarily locked themselves up in their "small and insanitary houses for over three months" to avoid attachments by officials. Giving an account of such a horrifying and yet brave situation, K.M. Munshi wrote to the Governor: "As I passed through villages—silent, empty and deserted with sentinels posted at different ends—I saw women peeping through barred windows, and on being reassured, they opened the doors. I went inside and I saw the darkness, the stench, the filth, and men, women and children herded together for months in the same room with their beloved cattle—miserable, lacerated and grown pale with disease. As I heard their determination to remain in that condition for months rather than abandon their cattle to the tender mercies of the *japti* (attachment) officer, I could not help but think that the imagination which conceived the dire *japti* methods, the severity with which they were enforced and the inhuman policy they represented were difficult to find outside the pages of a history of medieval times."

Munshi tried to impress upon the Governor the grimness of the situation by bluntly telling him, "The cheap sneers of lofty bureaucrats, the disproportionately severe sentences for technical offences, the thunders of arrogant proclamations, the official sabre-rattlings have ceased to excite anything but ridicule." Munshi asked the Governor to appreciate the reverence people had for Patel. "Your *japti* officer", he told him, "has to travel miles before he can get a shave. Your officer's car which got stuck would have remained in the mud but for Vallabhbhai, officially styled 'agitator living in Bardoli'... The Collector gets no conveyance at the railway station without Vallabhbhai's sanction. In the few villages which I visited, not a man, woman, was either sorry for the step taken or is shaken in his or her faith, and as Vallabhbhai passed through village after village, I saw men, women and children coming out to greet him in spontaneous homage. I saw illiterate women, old and young, in their tatters, placing on his forehead the auspicious mark of victory *(kum-kum)*, laying at his feet, for their sacred cause, their hard-earned rupee or two and singing in their rustic accents, songs of "the misdeeds of the hapless Government"."[37] Invariably, the women would be half of the audience—seldom numbering less than 500 to 1,000 and sometimes even 2,000. Such meetings would continue till past midnight.

The *modus operandi* of Patel's *sainiks* was very simple. The pattern was the same as in the Borsad satyagraha. Perched on treetops, the *sainiks* would beat the drum at the sight of attachment officers approaching a village. Hearing which, the peasants hurried to their houses to lock themselves up inside with their family and cattle. In their absence, or non-presence, as the law provided, no attachment work could be carried out. Nor did the law permit execution of work after the day was over. When the sun went down, life returned to the villages. With that would begin Patel's operations too. As Supreme Commander, he moved from one village to another, addressing public meetings, or conferring with his Sector Commanders, or even talking to volunteers, giving them on-the-spot instructions on the strategy to follow. He had made it a practice to visit each village every alternate night. And each night he covered a distance of 15 miles or more. A friend had placed at his disposal an old Ford. The roads being unmetalled and dusty, a light rain turned them slushy. Often the car would get stuck in the mud. Patel, not minding his age (53), would get down and, along with Swami Anand, Kalyanji and others, push it to make it run again. If it didn't work he would walk up to a nearby village to fulfil his engagement. He would return to his HQ not before daybreak. And before going to bed, he would attend to dispatches received from his Sector Commanders, and reports brought from Government officers by his informants.

Patel's speeches always cast a spell—irresistible, overpowering—and the villagers sang a song of an old saint whose refrain was: "all our sorrows have ended, now that the Master has come."

Most touching was the conversation between Patel and an old woman, whom he happened to have asked, "I hope, old mother, you are not afraid."

She promptly replied, "Why should I be afraid, when you are here to protect us?" To another question whether she liked the Pathans and policemen at her doors, she answered, "But for them, the Sardar (Patel) would not have graced my house."[38] To the peasants Patel sounded like an oracle, who spoke their idiom with "a peculiar flavour of the soil", and those words haunted their minds long afterwards.

Sharda Mehta, who with her husband, Dr. Sumant Mehta, were Patel's Sector Commanders, said "He speaks like one inspired. Every word of his comes from the depths of his heart. The situation before him gives him the language, and his earnestness carries his hearers at once to a lofty plane."[39] They were captivated by "the burning fire in the speaker's eyes and the masculine vigour of his tone."[40] And Patel had told them, "I want to inoculate you with fearlessness. I want to galvanise you with new life. I miss in your eyes the flash of indignation against wrong."[41] Mahadev Desai and others felt that they had never before "heard such brilliance in his language, or seen such indignation in his eyes... The villagers were moved by the extraordinary eloquence of his speeches and by his astonishingly simple yet effective popular similes and analogies."[42]

Frank, forthright, blunt, Patel's speeches were torrents of biting sarcasm against the Government. He would also chasten the peasants for their weaknesses, with well-meaning ridicule, "The Government has, like a wild elephant, run amuck. It thinks it can trample anything and everything under its feet... priding itself on having trampled in the past even lions and tigers to death, and scorning the little gnat defying him. I am teaching the little gnat today to let the elephant go on in his mad career, and then get into his trunk at the opportune moment. The gnat need not fear the elephant. The elephant can never trample it to death, but the gnat can certainly prove formidable to the elephant."[43] Patel asked the peasants if they wished to live the life of a bullock, "Should you die and seek re-birth as a bullock! But I want to see the people of Gujarat full of fire and courage. They may be weak physically, but that does not mean that they cannot have the heart of a lion."[44]

Rustic words alone could move rustic people. But such people, in Patel's view, occupied an unrivalled position. He told them, "On the peasants depend millions; the peasant depends on none... In this world the only genuine producers are the peasants and the labourers. All others merely live as parasites on them."[45] Then he dispelled their fears over confiscation of their lands. Would they take the lands away to England? he sarcastically asked. The worst that could happen was that the lands would be transferred to the Government in its books. Forfeiture was an empty threat. No one could unjustly deprive the peasants of their land and get away with it. If that happened, it would be clear that there was no Government in the country. "It will then be robbers with whom we shall be dealing. I say, let the robbers come in."

Patel's was the language of a revolutionary, who openly preached rebellion, though of the Gandhian type. His *sainiks* bore no arms, not even wooden staves! Patel no doubt carried one himself as a leader—a symbol of his status as Supreme Commander. The Government felt perturbed. According to official assessment, Patel was speaking the language of Lenin. *The Times of India* flashed on its front-page such headlines: *"Bolshevik Regime in Bardoli"*; *"Mr. Vallabhbhai Patel in the Role of Lenin"*. The newspaper's correspondent, an Englishman, wrote, "Iron discipline prevails in Bardoli. Mr. Patel has instituted there a Bolshevik regime in which he plays the role of Lenin. His hold on the population is absolute. The women of Bardoli have been taught amazingly seditious songs with which they incite their men to hate the Government, to obey only the wishes of their Commander-in-Chief, Mr. Patel, and to be ready to die, if need be, in defence of their rights."[46]

Reuter's follow-up despatch to London had the desired effect in awakening the British lion from his slumber; and in the House of Commons Lord Winterton admitted that in the Bardoli no-tax campaign Patel had achieved "a measure of success." Diehard Conservative hawks like Michael O'Dwyer, former Governor of Punjab, who was responsible for the Jallianwala Bagh massacre in 1919 at Amritsar, fretted and fumed and cried for "prompt enforcement of the law of conspirary."[47] Such fears and anger on the part of the British could not be entirely unfounded and misconceived. A member of the Bombay Legislative Council, Shivdasani, had stated earlier: "If Bardoli stands firm until the last, this fight will be the first nail in the British coffin."[48]

The Commissioner of the Northern Division, Smart, in a letter addressed to a Surat medical practitioner, Dr. D.J. Edul Behram, described Patel and his companions as "a swarm of agitators who are living on them (the people of Bardoli) and misguiding them", but expressed his willingness "to investigate the case of any village which can show reasonable grounds for supposing that it has been wrongly grouped." He alleged that "the agitators now in Bardoli are the same men who had conducted the no-tax campaign in Kheda district in 1918."[49] The Congress Working Committee considered the letter as "highly offensive and unworthy of a high official."[50] But a calm, confident Patel, whom Smart had called "a personal friend", offered Smart the facility he had arranged earlier for Pratt in the Kheda satyagraha: a meeting of 17,000 Bardoli peasants whom Smart could address. Patel's composure was also due to his having defined his position earlier: "I regard myself as a watchman responsible for the peace of the taluka. I hold myself responsible to the man (Gandhi) who is now watching the movement from his peaceful abode in Sabarmati. I prize more than anything else his name and his work which I cannot allow to be besmirched by a single mistake or error."[51] Patel had also stated: "The peasants today are like the road-metal crushed flat under a steamroller, which let us call the Anderson Patent Steamroller!"[52] Anderson was the Settlement Commissioner.

Hereafter Patel's tongue became sharper and more biting, and he looked for opportunities when he could ridicule the officials and thereby keep up the morale of his people. While addressing women at a public meeting, he tickled them with the comment, "Oh! It seems to me that, by remaining in the house all day and night, your buffaloes are fast becoming white like white women."[53] Why was women's participation in public meetings and in the satyagraha so necessary? Patel thought, without their participation they could not bear up against the confiscation of household goods. They must fight shoulder to shoulder with their menfolk. The heroism of the simple, unsophisticated but steel-hearted women of Bardoli not only inspired their men, but contributed to Patel's success. Women would often stand in front of their locked doors, laughing derisively at the attachment officials much to the latter's embarrassment and humiliation. Women went a step further when they threatened to boycott their husbands if they faltered. Once when some attached buffaloes started bellowing from inside the nearby police station Patel shouted, "Listen to the bellows of these buffaloes. Reporters! Write it down and report that in the police station at Valod, the buffaloes make speeches!... listen to these buffaloes, which tell you that justice has disappeared from this kingdom."[54] A Mamlatdar was leading a party of Pathans in search of buffaloes. Patel ridiculed him by calling him "Buffalo Tiger".

The Government's reign of terror was described by Patel in a telling manner: "Armed policemen marching, and men with rifles on horseback parading through streets!"[55] He exhorted the peasants with the advice: "Render all police perfectly useless by your peaceful behaviour."[56] He even told them: "Even if a handful from amongst you fall victim to their wiles, don't be alarmed. Don't flinch from your resolve. Even a victorious army has its casualty list, and has its deserters. If blacklegs are discovered, understand that it is so much dirt and stain washed away. Challenge the Government to take up your land and carry it, if they can, to England. Challenge them to surround the taluka with machine-guns and aeroplanes. We have no armed force, but we have a better and a purer force to pit against it—the force of truth, the force of our allegiance to our pledge." On another occasion he told them, "Let them capture your buffaloes and other property. They cannot capture your souls."[57]

By the end of May, Bardoli had earned all-India fame, as "it has stood the fire beyond all expectations; it had belied all the gloomy forebodings of doubters and cynics."[58] Mahadev Desai wrote in the *Young India* a graphic account of his travel in the region in the third week of May: "As the up-train takes you to Valsad, it is a discussion about Bardoli going on amongst the passengers that wakes you up in the early hours of the morning. One who has been on the scene of operations describes in vivid detail the *Pathan-raj* in the taluka... I had occasion to travel by a day train too. The Bardoli publicity leaflets were in the hands of many passengers. Some of them were reading Vallabhbhai's speeches aloud, and discussing the situation. As I passed through the streets of Navsari with my haversack on my back, a Parsi came running after me to ask if I had the Bardoli leaflets in my haversack!"[59] Patel's war bulletins enjoyed such popularity.

Not only Gujarat but the whole of India had woken up to realise the grimness of the situation in Bardoli through Patel's war bulletins. As Mahadev Desai had discovered, Bardoli had become by now "the cynosure of all eyes." And there was an irresistible urge among many to pay a visit and personally witness the breathtaking spectacle Patel had created. Senior Congress leaders—Muslims, Hindus, Sikhs and Parsis—came there from many places in India. Maulana Shaukat Ali and Maulvi Mahomed Baloch were "delighted at the wonderful atmosphere of solidarity and unity in Bardoli."[60] Two non-Congress Councillors from Bombay, Joshi and Pataskar, visited Bardoli with a critical mind but were compelled to say, "We had come to scorn, but have stayed on to praise."[61] Nine members of the Legislative Council sent in their resignations to the Governor, and demanded an independent inquiry. They said: "When a Government, forgetful of its own obligations, commits grave breaches of law and ruthlessly attempts to trample underfoot such noble and law-abiding people, it is but fair and proper for us, as a protest against the high-handed policy of the Government in that taluka, to resign our seats on the Bombay Legislative Council."[62] Patel was in Bombay for a day to meet the members of the Congress Working Committee. He was warmly greeted by Motilal Nehru, who humorously asked someone, who happened to be an insurance agent, for how much he would be prepared to insure Patel's freedom!

As days passed, the satyagraha picked up more and more

strength, and there were bursts of brilliant flashes of Patel's fighting mood, which also revealed his genius for detail. The ease with which he exposed the absurdity of the Government figures reminded some of Lloyd George. Patel told the peasants in a reassuring manner, "Let there be no mistake. Your land will come back to you knocking at your door... The world knows that among the purchasers are *chaprasis* and policemen and a few butchers who were specially persuaded to come from Surat."[63] Speaking on Bardoli Day celebrations throughout India on June 12th, Patel said, "So long as a square foot of land, belonging to a peasant or to a participant in this fight, remains forfeited, this fight will continue. For the sake of such land, thousands of peasants are ready to die. This is not a charity performance for the Government to hand over land to some kerosene merchant from Broach! He who buys such land drinks the life-blood of the peasants."[64]

In another speech, he ridiculed the local officials by observing, "If you regard this Government as a bullock-cart, it may be said to have two wheels: one, the village Patel and the other, the Talati. Or, you may say that they are the two bullocks of the government bullock-cart. Day and night these bullocks are whipped and abused. But now and again the Government lets them suck... molasses. It tastes sweet, and so they forget the beating and the abuses, and start pulling the cart once again."[65]

By mid-June the satyagraha reached its climax: 63 Patels and 11 Talatis of the Bardoli taluka resigned. Gandhi congratulated them with such soothing words, "In the final result, it is sacrifices such as these which will bring independence to us."[66] The resignations were a blow to the Government machinery. They dampened the spirits of officials, but injected new courage into the satyagrahis. In one instance, a satyagrahi's wife bade him a befitting farewell; Take care that no weak word escapes your lips... Don't think of me or the children. Be courageous. Answer all questions boldly and in a manly way. What a pity, they didn't prosecute me! I would have shown them what the women of Bardoli can do."[67] That was the revolution Patel had brought about in Bardoli.

Firm, determined and relentless in resolve to keep the fight on,

Patel was yet, like Gandhi, ever willing to enter into negotiations for an honourable compromise. At the all-India level, Vithalbhai Patel, President of the Central Legislative Assembly, presented the Bardoli case to the Viceroy. At the provincial level, Munshi wrote to the Governor about the unconstitutional position of the Government. He also warned the Government that their determination to refuse the reasonable request of the people "will result either in the elimination of the existing peasants in Bardoli or in bloodshed; and, in either case, will result in deep and lasting embitterment."[68] Other leaders who lent support to the movement included Purushottamdas Thakurdas, Pundit Hridaynath Kunzru, Motilal Nehru and Tej Bahadur Sapru. Purushottamdas carried a useful dialogue with the Government and the Commissioner. Motilal said, "I gather that the Bombay Government is prepared to agree to a fresh inquiry, but it insists on the payment of all revenue dues under the present assessment before holding the inquiry. This is an extraordinary position to take up. If the assessment is *prima facie* wrong and unjust and merits reconsideration, it is manifestly absurd and illogical to demand payment of any dues under it."[69] Sapru suggested that an independent inquiry should be made not only into the grievances of the people of Bardoli with regard to the enhanced assessment, but also into the allegations made regarding the methods employed in enforcing payment and dealing with the situation generally.

The satyagraha reached a critical stage with thousands of peasants pledging their support to it at the district conference held at Surat, Broach, Nadiad and Ahmedabad. In a grim warning to the Government at Broach, Patel said, "If the Government means to devour the land, I warn it that the conflagration will spread over the whole of Gujarat, and it will realise not a farthing in Gujarat next year... The Government may think it has far greater strength than Ravana had, but let the mighty Government remember that it has to deal not with one Sita but 87,000 satyagrahis."[70] At Nadiad he advised the peasants, "Keep quiet and watch with sympathetic interest. I shall give you the signal when your turn comes. Today, the immolation of Bardoli is enough. Out of its ashes will rise numerous Bardolis."[71] And to the peasants of Bardoli, his message was, "Do not be anxious for a premature settlement. You know what happens if you pluck and taste an unripe mango. It will simply set your teeth on edge. On the other hand, if you allow it to ripen, it will drop itself in due season and your patience will be rewarded with its delicious flavour and sweet juice... When the time is ripe for a settlement, we shall know it without being told by anyone."[72]

On July 13th the Viceroy conferred with the Governor at Simla. There was an evident climb-down, though not yet complete, on the Governor's part in a statement on his behalf; "It is His Excellency's obvious duty to uphold the supremacy of the law. But it is also his duty, as the representative of the King Emperor, to see that hardship and suffering are not inflicted on so large a number of persons."[73] Following this, the Commissioner sent a message to Patel that the Governor was arriving at Surat and would like to meet him on the 18th. Along with his six lieutenants, Patel met the Governor for a total of six hours. No settlement could be reached. The Governor insisted on payment of the enhanced assessment, or, alternatively payment by a third party on behalf of the Bardoli peasants of a deposit equivalent to the enhanced assessment. Patel could not accept such a suggestion, while the Governor rejected his terms. The British-owned *The Pioneer* and *The Statesman* thought that the Government's conditions were unreasonable. The former wrote: "The main point that must be made, and made without delay, is that no impartial observer of the Bardoli dispute, possessed of the plain facts of the case, can resist the conclusion that the peasants have got the right on their side, and that their claim for an examination of the enhanced assessment by an impartial tribunal is just, reasonable and fair."[74] *The Pioneer* described the Government's terms as a case of "putting the cart before the horse." *The Leader* felt that the terms were tantamount to a demand for complete surrender on the part of the Bardoli peasants. Mrs. Besant's paper, the *New India*, wrote: "If Birkenhead remains obstinate, then an agitation should be set up in Parliament to make him change his mind." In *The Hindu's* view, "the Governor has given up an excellent opportunity of securing a satisfactory settlement."

Ignoring such criticism, the Governor held out a threat in his opening address to the Legislative Council on 23rd, "The main point at issue is not the justice or injustice of the revised revenue assessment in Bardoli, whether the writ of His Majesty the King Emperor is to run in a portion of His Majesty's domains. The Government is, therefore, prepared to meet the situation with all the power it possesses."[75] Patel was quick to reply, "I must confess that I was unprepared for the threatening address of His Excellency the Governor. But threats apart, I want to remove the confusion that the speech is consciously or unconsciously intended to create." He explained that, "the people of Bardoli are not fighting in order to have the right of civil disobedience vindicated. They are fighting through civil disobedience—or whatever name the method adopted may be given—to induce the Government either to waive the enhancement, or, if it is not convinced that the enhancement is improperly made, to appoint an impartial, independent body to inquire into the matter. The only question, therefore, is that of justice or injustice of the re-assessment. And if the Government is prepared to have the question examined by a "full, open and independent inquiry", it must surely accept the logical consequence of the proposition it itself lays down, namely, not to insist upon the payment of the enhancement which is in dispute, and to restore the people to the condition they occupied before the struggle commenced."[76]

Meanwhile, the Council Members from Surat were carrying on negotiations with the Government at Pune. Patel's presence there was considered necessary, as they felt that the Government was anxious to reach a settlement, but it was concerned with the preservation of its prestige. In this respect, Chunilal Mehta, a senior Member of the Governor's Council, who was equally anxious for a settlement, played a notable role. In their draft letter, the MLCs from Surat had told the Revenue Member, "We are glad to be able to say that we are in a position to inform the Government that the conditions laid down by His Excellency the Governor in his opening speech to the Council, dated July 23rd, will be fulfilled." Patel was totally opposed to this. Mehta, however, assured him, "That is not your concern. If the members are agreeable to addressing the letter, you need not worry as to how, when and by whom the conditions will be fulfilled. You will pay the old assessment after the inquiry is announced."[77] That was a way to save the Government's prestige, and yet achieve the objective. Patel was not to be a party to the offer. Nor was he compromising in any manner. Yet, he agreed to let Mehta play his game on the presumption that, to quote Mahadev Desai, "he knew the mind of the Government better than anyone of us and his patriotism had, at this great moment, got the better of his officialdom." According to Mahadev Desai, who was one of the negotiators, "If the Government was content with clutching at the shadow of prestige, Vallabhbhai could not be content without the substance. All he wanted was a full, independent, judicial inquiry and a restoration of the status quo. The Government was perfectly agreeable, provided here too it could have its prestige intact."[78]

Since Mehta's "diplomacy was beyond our wits", a compromise was reached; and the institution of an inquiry was announced by the Government exactly on the terms Patel had suggested. The inquiry committee vindicated Patel's stand. Comprising Reginald Maxwell (later Home Member of the Viceroy's Executive Council) and Robert Broomfield (later a High Court Judge), the committee recommended an increase in the settlement rates of 5.7 per cent as against 22 per cent sanctioned by the Government. Consequently, the Government announced restoration of lands confiscated and sold, release of all prisoners and reinstatement of Patels and Talatis who had submitted their resignations. To make matters move swiftly and smoothly, the Government replaced Collector J.E.B. Hartshorne, who had often declared that sold lands would never be restored, by Hugh Garrett, who persuaded the purchasers to return the lands. Satisfied with the Government's decisions and the action it took so promptly, Patel thanked all concerned, including the Government. At the same time he instructed the peasants, "Now we have to pay up the old assessment, not the enhanced one. I hope you will keep yourselves in readiness to pay the old assessment."[79]

And thus ended the Bardoli satyagraha, "pursued by a peaceful peasantry with truth and patient suffering... against an enemy who could any day have crushed them to atoms. But the Bardoli peasants demonstrated to the world that truth and non-violence cannot be crushed." Mahadev Desai described the Bardoli settlement as "the third of the Sardar's successful campaigns—the third milestone that he had the honour of laying on the road to Swaraj." He further wrote: "The Nagpur victory was the vindication of a technical right. The Borsad victory, won after a very short and swift campaign, only redressed a local grievance, and though no victory could have been more signal and decisive, the campaign, because of its swiftness, failed to draw the nation's attention to the extent that the Bardoli campaign had drawn."

In Mahadev Desai's assessment: "The Bardoli triumph was unique in that it compelled not only the nation's but the whole Empire's attention, and the justice and moderation of the people's demand won practically the entire nation's sympathy. It was unique in that it was fought by perhaps one of the meekest of the talukas in India, in that it affected the Revenue Department, whose dispositions, it was up to now believed, not even the gods may question; and in that it compelled a mighty Government, pledged to crush the movement, to yield within a fortnight of the pledge. It was unique in that the leader of the campaign shed all ideas of personal prestige, and also in that the Governor of the province... did all that he personally could to bring about peace... That is why Gandhi and Vallabhbhai emphasised in their speeches, throughout the week after the settlement, the duty of congratulating the Governor as much as that of congratulating those who had won the campaign."[80]

Bardoli rocketed Patel to great fame. He shone in the luminous glow of his great victory, though his elation seemed to be like that of a shy bride. Congratulations poured in from all parts of India and abroad. Gandhi was the first to pay a most deserving tribute to Patel, "without whose firmness as well as gentleness, the settlement would have been impossible." As President of the Calcutta Congress, Motilal Nehru called it "a splendid triumph", and described Patel as "that matchless general" and the peasants as "the Balaklava battalion of Bardoli." Srinivasa Sastri wrote to Gandhi from Johannesburg: "Vallabhbhai Patel has risen to the highest rank. I bow to him in reverence." Lala Lajpat Rai wrote in his newspaper, *The People*: "The settlement of the Bardoli dispute... is a notable triumph of the popular cause... it is a moral victory for truth and justice, and conclusively shows that the government is susceptible to the pressure of public opinion if properly organised." In Rajagopalachari's view: "Vallabhbhai's part in Indian history has been great." Madan Mohan Malaviya wrote to Patel: "The first signal triumph of satyagraha was in Champaran. The second and equally great has been in Bardoli." Subhas Chandra Bose wired: "All India rejoices with you on glorious victory. All honour to satyagrahis and their leader."

Among the Muslim leaders, Maulana Shaukat Ali and Shuhib Qureshi wired congratulations to "our brave brothers, their Sardar and co-workers." Sarojini Naidu, in a message to Gandhi, said: "Your dream was to make Bardoli the perfect example of satyagraha. Bardoli has fulfilled itself in its own fashion, interpreting and perfecting your dream." Richard Gregg wrote to Gandhi: "Heartiest congratulations to the Bardoli peasants, to you and Vallabhbhai Patel. It has been a superb struggle and will be a telling example to the whole country in methods and tactics."[81]

At the Calcutta session of the Congress in 1928, President Motilal Nehru moved a resolution congratulating those who had contributed to the success of the Bardoli satyagraha. The audience clamoured to see the hero, who reluctantly stood up in his place from amidst the delegates from Gujarat. Not satisfied, the people insisted upon his appearing on the stage. Patel in his shyness declined to oblige them. He was forcibly pushed to the dais. There were repeated cheers for quite some time. Overwhelmed by such a spontaneous show of affection, Patel spoke a few words, "I thank you for having congratulated the peasants of Bardoli. If you are genuinely appreciative of what they have done, I hope you will follow in their footsteps."[82]

In a speech in Bombay on May 4, 1929, Patel referred to the comparison made earlier between the Bolshevik revolution in Russia and the Bardoli satyagraha and said, "The Bardoli satyagraha was considered to be an imitation of Bolshevism, and I was given the title of an Indian Lenin. But my entire knowledge of Lenin is limited to what I have learnt from Pandit Jawaharlal Nehru's small book, *Soviet Russia*. I admit I am completely ignorant of the Soviet system."[83] However, by calling Patel the "Indian Lenin", the British did him a great honour; and Bardoli placed Patel on a new pinnacle of glory and greatness, equalled by none in the Congress except Gandhi. Bose rightly forejudged the Bardoli satyagraha as "the precursor of the larger fight that (Gandhi) was to wage in 1930"[84]—the Salt satyagraha. Bardoli, indeed, put a new life into Gandhi. According to British historian Judith Brown, for Gandhi Bardoli meant, "reevaluation of his public role": dissolving "many of his doubts, born of the debacle and violence of the early 1920s, about the viability of satyagraha in India... It revived his faith in the power of non-violence and in the potential for a mass struggle."[85] As a consequence, in the Salt satyagraha, Gandhi became "a Messianic figure, striding out staff in hand, to lead the confrontation with the British, compelling respect for his fearlessness."[86]

Bardoli was a great personal triumph for Patel. He was the recipient of a most endearing, life-long title—far nobler, much more satisfying and even glorifying than any high-sounding and well-acclaimed titles. Like Gandhi becoming Mahatma a decade earlier, the title of Sardar was conferred upon Patel as a token of the Bardoli people's appreciation, reverence and faith in his powers of command and judgment as a leader in times of crisis. The conferment came not in a glittering durbar hall, but at a village public meeting amidst the rustic environment of Nanifalod, in Bardoli taluka, when a tall, sturdy farmer, Kuverji Durlabh Patel, got up from amidst the crowd and shouted in a clear, loud voice, "You are our Sardar. I welcome you."[87]

An ordinary word, meaning only a leader. But it possessed extraordinary power because of an inherent truth; and so powerful as to leave an imprint on the sands of Indian history. It brought to surface the qualities of a Sardar that Patel had within him. Bardoli proved him to be a true and great leader. The word also mirrored, from India's traditional viewpoint, a Sardar's qualities of sincerity, simplicity and truthfulness that Patel had exhibited. The speaker, Kuverji Durlabh Patel, little realised that what he had spontaneously uttered had the potential of making history. From that moment onwards Patel came to be known as Sardar Vallabhbhai Patel—not the Sardar of Gujarat alone, but of the whole of India, and accepted as such by the high and low within the party and outside. For Patel it was a historic transformation. It set him on the road to all-India leadership.

13

"John the Baptist" in Dandi March

Patel earned the appellation of "John the Baptist" during Gandhi's Dandi March, or Salt satyagraha, of 1930. He was to Gandhi what St. John was to Christ. St. John was the forerunner and Baptist of Jesus. Patel played precisely the same role in the Dandi March. Gandhi was Christ-like: a frail body dominated by hallowed looks, and an oracular voice that inspired an apostle's reverence, as well as the hope of resurrection for his people. Patel was John-like: strong-bodied, and a forerunner of Gandhi in the Salt satyagraha, who "baptised" people on the route the master was to follow to Dandi, a small, little-known seaside village on Gujarat's west coast near Surat, where Gandhi broke the law prohibiting the manufacture of salt from sea water—a simple act that turned into a symbol of national defiance and aroused worldwide attention for its revolutionary implications.

Dandi was Patel's choice. So were the leaders of the March. They were his most trusted lieutenants since his earlier satyagrahas. The march was historic in its fulfillment of Gandhi's promise to launch a campaign in protest against the British refusal to comply with the Complete Independence Resolution passed at the Lahore Congress in December 1929. Its most significant aspect was that

Patel went ahead of it as "John the Baptist". Gandhi admitted in his speech at Napa on March 18th that "Vallabhbhai had come ahead of him to smoothen his own path."[1] The Congress historian, Pattabhi Sitaramayya, described Patel's role in its true historic perspective: "While yet Gandhi was making preparations... Vallabhbhai went before his master to prime up the villagers for the coming ordeals... When Vallabhbhai was moving in advance as Gandhi's forerunner, the government saw in him John the Baptist, who was the forerunner of Jesus nineteen hundred years ago."[2] Patel was arrested at Ras, sentenced to three months' imprisonment and lodged at Sabarmati jail at Ahmedabad.

In his speech at Navagaon, Gandhi admitted that the Government had arrested Patel because "it feared that if he were free, he and not the Government would rule over the district."[3] As Sitaramayya records, "with his arrest and conviction, the whole of Gujarat rose to a man against the Government: 75,000 people gathered on the sands of the Sabarmati" and resolved: "We the citizens of Ahmedabad determine hereby that we shall go the same path where Vallabhbhai has gone."[4] The Millowners Association also passed a resolution, condemning Patel's arrest, and closed down all the mills in Ahmedabad. The Municipality lodged its protest by keeping the administrative offices closed. And so were the schools in the city. Businessmen recorded their protest by closing their shops in Ahmedabad and in many other towns of Gujarat. Ras, where Patel was arrested, surpassed all. Village officers submitted their resignations. Landlords surrendered their special rights. A country liquor licensee was so moved that he pledged never to sell alcohol. Over 500 men and women from Ras got themselves registered as satyagrahis. Many villages in Borsad and Bardoli talukas followed on the heels of Ras with equal fervour.

Far in Delhi, the capital of India, Madan Mohan Malaviya moved a resolution in the Central Legislative Assembly, condemning government action in arresting Patel without a trial. The resolution was lost by 30 votes against 55, but during the course of the debate many members were critical of the government. Speaking on the occasion, Jinnah said, "According to the Home Member, Sardar Vallabhbhai Patel had delivered many speeches before he was arrested... Were those speeches against law? The point at issue is whether the Sardar committed any breach of law. On that point no information has been given to us. If he had made speeches earlier in which he had committed breaches of law, and was about to deliver one further speech of the same kind, then the right course for the district authorities was to have taken action against Sardar Vallabhbhai Patel for those earlier offences. It was improper for them to serve upon him an order which cuts at the root of the principle of freedom of speech." Jinnah asserted, "The Government of India is setting a precedent with very serious implications."[5]

The 241-mile march from Ahmedabad to Dandi, with seventy-one satyagrahis, began on March 12th, whereas Patel had been arrested earlier on the 7th. How far Patel could smoothen Gandhi's path was evident from the manner with which people obeyed his instructions to remain non-violent, the extent to which the atmosphere had been electrified, and the spectacular way the people had been buoyed up by his arrest. The District Superintendent of Police confirmed, "Mr. Gandhi appeared calm and collected. He is gathering more strength as he proceeds. His lieutenants, like Darbar Gopaldas and Ravishankar Vyas (Maharaj), are also getting bolder and arouse the feelings of the people of this taluka by using Vallabhbhai's arrest as their trump card."[6]

Patel's arrest became the main burden of Gandhi's speeches. At Wasna, Gandhi paid a most handsome tribute to Patel, "I may die at any moment, but the future generations will see that my prophecy was correct. Vallabhbhai was not a fit person for arrest. He should have been rewarded by the Government. What wrong did Vallabhbhai do in Bardoli? He befriended the people which was the duty of the government. He managed the administration of Ahmedabad; and the Collector and the Commissioner were astounded by his work. I could succeed in Kheda district on account of Vallabhbhai, and it is on account of him that I am here today."[7] At Nadiad, Gandhi told his audience, "You must understand that the imprisonment of Vallabhbhai is equivalent to the imprisonment of the whole of Kheda district."[8]

And thus Gandhi continued with his march from village to village, along the path laid by Patel, amidst excited, thrilled, surging crowds. William Shirer, an American correspondent representing the *Chicago Tribute* and other major newspapers, who was a witness to the march, wrote: "The procession soon became a triumphal march. The villages through which the marchers passed were festooned in their honour. Between the villages, peasants sprinkled water on the roads to keep the dust down and threw leaves and flower petals on them to make the going on foot easier. In nearly every settlement hundreds abandoned their work and joined the procession until the original band of less than one hundred swelled to several thousand by the time the sea was reached... Some of Gandhi's followers began to compare the march to the journey of Jesus to Jerusalem, and there was much reading of the New Testament along the way. To add to the comparison, someone in the party picked up a donkey to follow in the wake of Gandhi."[9]

Jawaharlal Nehru wrote: "Today the pilgrim marches onward on his long trek—the fire of a great resolve is in him and surpassing love of his miserable countrymen... And none that passes him can escape the spell, and men of common clay feel the spark of life." Patel's contribution to the spark was great. His arrest proved as historic as Gandhi's march to Dandi.

Earlier, prior to visiting Ras on March 7th, Patel delivered a stirring speech at Broach on February 11th, in which he told his listeners, "Within the next eight or ten or fifteen days, civil disobedience will have begun. There will take place non-violent breaches of law. Such offences will be committed by individuals who are devotees of non-violence—who have no anger, nor any jealousy, and about whose purity and goodness there can be no two opinions." Referring to a recent remark by a British politician that when Gandhi was arrested in 1922, not a dog had barked in India, Patel remarked, "This is true; also not. We had at that time planned to start a struggle in Bardoli, but Gandhi decided to put it off. When two Rajputs (warriors) decide to battle, and one of them refuses to strike, the other should refrain from attacking. But here, our opponent was not a Rajput and he attacked by arresting Gandhi, who had directed his followers to refrain from continuing the struggle and to do nothing which would result in their being arrested." Patel asserted, "This self-restraint was misinterpreted. Even the Viceroy himself was compelled to admit that he did not know what he would have done, had the Congress forced the issue. The Governor of Bombay had gone so far as to remark "Swaraj was there for the taking... Let there be innumerable arrests so that the world may find out for itself whether the dog is capable of barking or not, when it wants to."[10]

Patel turned to the two bogeys the British had deliberately spread in order to defeat Gandhi's satyagraha: one was Hindu-Muslim internecine war; the other was about the Afghans invading the country if they left India. Patel, therefore, asked, "Have you come across a single Muslim who says the salt tax is good and should be maintained? ...They also consider the land tax as unjust. No Muslim has asked the people to take to drinking. It is the title-holders who make the Hindus and Muslims fight. Muslims in villages, in fact, never think of a fight... The rulers also threaten that if they go away, the Afghans will come in. Or, the Pathans! And that not a single unmarried girl's honour will be safe. Haven't they reduced us to such a helpless state after 150 years of their rule? If thirty-three crores of us cannot protect ourselves, then what is left of us to do is to commit suicide! But to tolerate such talk is a great insult."[11]

Patel then ridiculed some other myths spread by the British: especially the British claim of being "trustees in India". Patel sarcastically asked: "But whose trustees? Who went to England to crown them and invite them here? Such talk can no longer be acceptable. No one will accept their threats... The Government says that it has given us peace. But of what use is this peace to us? People are suffering from hunger. There is no blood in our veins, nor luster in the eyes." Calling Gandhi the Saint of Sabarmati, Patel said, "That man at Sabarmati, with a handful of bones, has shaken the Empire with his spinning wheel. That is real wonder. He has built hopes in you... Aren't you going to fulfil them? Wisdom will dawn on the people just as light follows sunrise... Freedom's first page is being written in Gujarat's history."[12]

From Broach, Patel went to Ras. Awaiting his arrival were thousands of villagers—tall, burly people, wearing colourful dresses, and, above all, brimming with enthusiasm. They had gathered under a large banyan tree outside Ras to welcome their Sardar. He was not scheduled to speak, but was to address a public meeting at the nearby village, Kankapura. It was hurriedly decided by the local leaders that he should address those gathered. A Sub-Inspector of Police came to know of this from a village sweeper. The Collector, Shillidy, was immediately informed. He was the same person whom Patel had earlier thrown out of the Ahmedabad Municipality. He naturally looked upon it as an opportunity to avenge himself by arresting Patel. The police party which had gone to Kankapura was hurriedly called to Ras. Patel opened his speech by saying, "Sisters and brothers. Are you ready for the satyagraha?" A loud, resounding "yes" rent the air. This did not amount to a speech. But a Magistrate promulgated prohibitory orders under Section 144 of the Indian Penal Code, and arrested Patel.

A police party escorted Patel to Borsad for a trial. The Collector was brought from the travellers' bungalow to the Magistrate's Court. Some pleaders and other gentlemen were cleared out of the courtroom. Patel was asked to sit in the adjoining room all by himself with the door closed, whereas in the courtroom the Collector, the Magistrate and the Deputy Superintendent of Police sat down to start a farcical trial. Called upon to say why he should not be convicted for "disobeying directions given", Patel replied, "I do not want to defend myself. I plead guilty." According to Patel, "the Magistrate was too dense to understand the law. He did not know under what section he was to convict me. He took about an hour and half to write out a judgment of eight lines."[13] The judgment was read out—only the portion which referred to the sentence saying that "as the maximum sentence permissible was only three months and 500 rupees fine, he could not impose a greater punishment."[14] Patel had made no speech. He had uttered a few words only, which did not amount to his intention to disobey the order. Yet he was arrested prior to the promulgation of Section 144.

From Borsad, Patel was taken to Ahmedabad and lodged in the Sabarmati jail in a cell meant for prisoners awarded capital punishment. He was treated "just like an ordinary criminal". The cell was locked up for the night at 5.30 p.m. on weekdays and at 3.30 p.m. on Sundays. He told Mahadev Desai and Acharya Kripalani who visited him, "I was afraid I might not get sleep on the first day, but fortunately there has been no difficulty about that. I have been sleeping like a log." He had feared that it would be "hard to sleep on the floor', with no bed and no mattress. A blanket had been provided, and he had to sleep inside the cell in hot weather. He was refused a lantern at night for the first few days. Regarding food, Patel told Mahadev Desai, "As good, or as bad, as one can expect to get in jail."[15] Jowar gruel was doled out at breakfast. Patel did not take it, for fear of getting dysentery. Next on the menu were jowar *roti* and *dal*, or *roti* and a vegetable served for lunch every alternate day. Since he suffered from toothache, Patel would "soak it up in water and get along splendidly."

Patel asked Mahadev Desai to send him a cake of soap, which, the Jailor said, should be unscented, and also his shaving kit. The Jail Superintendent said, "No razor is allowed. But we shall allow you facilities for a shave." Patel retorted, "I know what kind of a shave you will give me!" The Jailor interrupted the Superintendent with evidently better knowledge of jail rules, "In this case, Sir, a razor might be allowed, provided he does not keep it with him. We shall give it to him when he wants it."

Patel quipped, "Quite all right. But why not give me a razor and allow me to shave the others as well?—required in prisons for good behaviour. This remark of Patel caused laughter amongst those present. When Desai and Kripalani were to take leave of him, Patel said, "Don't worry about me. I am as happy as a bird. There is only one thing over which I am rather unhappy." He paused to give the answer a dramatic touch of suspense. The Superintendent and the Jailor looked curiously at each other. Pressed to come out with what was in his mind, Patel mischievously said, "It can't be said." On insistence, he slowly stated, "Well then, one thing, and one only, worries me, and that is that all the people in charge of the jail are Indians! It is through us Indians that they work this inhuman system."

Patel's arrest had no valid ground. According to the Home Member of the Government of India, he had delivered many speeches before he was arrested; whereas Patel had told G.V. Mavalankar, "The only 'speech' I made was in reply to the Magistrate's question. I said to him that I would make a speech, and on that expression of my intention I was arrested... The District Superintendent of Police gave me no warning... I made to attempt to speak, but I simply mentioned my intention, although I would certainly have spoken if I had not been arrested... No evidence was recorded in my presence; nor was I examined during the five minutes that I was in the courtroom."[16] Further, neither was a complaint read out to Patel, nor was any witness examined. The lawyers of Ahmedabad, who held him in the highest esteem, felt very agitated. The Bar Association passed a resolution. G. Davis, the District Judge, who happened to be Patel's co-student in Britain in the Bar, had it dispatched to the High Court.

Ras staged an epic struggle over Patel's arrest. Its people were proud of the arrest having been made in their village. After Patel had been driven away to Borsad, the assembled audience of young, old and women decided to launch a non-violent, non-cooperative campaign. This involved non-payment of land revenue, closing down of milk dairies and liquor shops in the villages, besides boycott of Government officials. Gandhi's arrival at Ras on March 19th on his way to Dandi, was befittingly celebrated with the resignations of village officials—the Police Patel (mukhi), Revenue Patel, Mamlatdar, guards and sweepers. One late evening, news reached Ras that Government officials were coming at night to surround the village and confiscate property of non-cooperators. The villagers made an unusual decision: to abandon the village. By this time it had become dark and the time for the arrival of officials was nearing. In less than half an hour's time, four hundred families packed whatever they could carry on their shoulders, locked their houses, and moved across to the Baroda State territory about a quarter of a mile away. Working as a team, they put up temporary grass-huts for shelter near the villages of Zarola and Vasana. Happily, they called their 'march' *hijarat*. The Ras émigrés lived a life of untold hardships for five to six months. Unseasonal heavy rains added much to their suffering. But they bore the hardships with courage, cheer and determination. According to one of their leaders, Ashabhai Patel, "They were living for Gandhi and their Sardar."[17]

H.N. Brailsford, a British author-journalist who toured the area, confirmed how Gandhi and Patel had "mesmerised the crowds". Gandhi "is devotedly loved, and so too is his lieutenant, Vallabhbhai Patel. I asked a group of forty or fifty villagers why they faced the risks and hardships. The women, as usual, answered first, and voiced their feeling of personal loyalty. "We'll pay no taxes," they said, "till Mahatmaji and Vallabhbhai tell us to pay." Then the men, slowly collecting their thoughts, voiced their economic grievances, "We won't pay because the tax is unjust"... Finally, they added, "We're doing it to win Swaraj"... Many villages were totally abandoned. I could see through the windows that every stick of property had been removed. In the silent street, nothing moved till a monkey skipped from a roof across the lane... the people had moved across the frontier of British India into the territory of independent Baroda. There, close to the boundary, they camped in shelters of matting and palm leaves, the ground cumbered with their chests and their beds, their churns and the great clay-coated baskets that hold their grain. In the hot autumn days, life was just tolerable for hardy villagers in these conditions... Even in Baroda, these refugees were not always safe. Their camps had more than once been invaded and the Gaekwar's territory was violated by the armed British Indian police under an Indian official, who beat with their lathis not only their own people but the Gaekwar's subjects also."[18]

During their absence from Ras, their houses were broken open and whatever the people had left behind was looted. At the time of their leaving, crops were getting ready. The police encamped on the outskirts of the village, and the Government officials got the crops harvested for sale. Lands were also confiscated, and sold. Nothing could make the people resile from their resolve. It was only on the conclusion of the Gandhi-Irwin Pact that the *hijarat* was over, and the people returned to their houses in Ras. They "entered the village in a procession, happy and gay, led by a band. The village bore a festive look, decorated with colourful flags and buntings."[19] Their faces bore no bitterness or remorse. Hardships had been willingly undergone for a cause. Much to Patel's regret, the Gandhi-Irwin Pact did not provide for the return of lands to the owners. Patel felt sore over his failure in his efforts to have it incorporated in the pact. He, however, comforted the villagers with the soothing words, "Don't worry about your land. It will come back to you knocking at your door."

In 1932 Gandhi and Patel visited Ras. They asked the people if they could launch a no-tax campaign—this time by staying in the village. The answer was in the affirmative. Far from being disheartened by earlier hardships and sufferings, their hearts had been steeled and their confidence in Gandhi and Patel redoubled. They underwent a second round of suffering and sacrifice after Gandhi's arrest on his return from the Round Table Conference. Again the crops were ready. And again they were harvested and sold. Lands were confiscated. This time the police pitched their tents in the midst of fields. One hundred and fifty policemen conducted the operations. One hundred and nine peasants courted arrest, including some women and old men. Between 1932 and 1939, the people of Ras had no means to maintain themselves. From jail, Patel came to their rescue by ordering Ahmedabad industrialists that each family be given one buffalo (in all 400 buffaloes), Rs.3 per day per adult, and Rs.1.50 per day per child for two years from 1933. The most constructive aid was the provision of 450 maunds of cotton and 300 spinning wheels. Some were given jobs in the textile mills at Ahmedabad, whereas the children of the village were provided with free education. In 1934, when some houses got burnt in a fire in Ras, Patel got them repaired without delay. Such was the rapport between the leader and his followers. His promise to Ras was fulfilled in 1939 when the Congress Government returned confiscated lands to their owners. The event was celebrated through a festival. Patel presided over it. With that, a decade long Gandhian struggle came to a victorious end, and Patel's promise was fulfilled. Ras had gloriously lived, sacrificed and suffered to make the Dandi March one of the most successful satyagrahas of Gandhi.

Gandhi's Dandi March was an event in history even greater than his Non-Cooperation movement or the Bardoli satyagraha. For the first time the satyagrahis faced merciless blows of armed policemen with unparalleled acts of heroism, suffering and dauntless courage. They bore all this with absolute calm. The ferocity of attack attracted world-wide sympathy, especially from the American journalists who had flown out to India to witness Gandhi's miracle. The classic dispatch of Webb Miller of the *United Press* read:

> "...Suddenly, at a word of command, scores of native policemen rushed upon the advancing marchers and rained blows on their heads with their steel-shod lathis. Not one of the marchers even raised an arm to fend off the blows. They went down like tenpins. From where I stood, I heard the sickening whack of the clubs on unprotected skulls. The waiting crowd of marchers groaned and sucked in their breath in sympathetic pain at every blow. Those struck down fell sprawling, unconscious or writhing with fractured skulls or broken shoulders... The survivors, without breaking ranks, silently and doggedly marched on until struck down... They marched steadily, with heads up, without the encouragement of music or cheering or any possibility that they might escape serious

> injury or death. The police rushed out and methodically and mechanically beat down the second column. There was no fight, no struggle; the marchers simply walked forward till struck down... The police commenced to savagely kick the seated men in the abdomen and testicles and then dragged them by their arms and feet and threw them into the ditches."[20]

In another dispatch, Webb Miller wrote in *New Freeman*: "In eighteen years of reporting in twenty-two countries, I have never witnessed such harrowing scenes as at Dharasana. Sometimes the scenes were so painful that I had to turn away momentarily. One surprising feature was the discipline of volunteers. It seemed they were thoroughly imbued with Gandhi's non-violent creed."[21]

Vincent Sheean called Dandi "a symbol of imperishable power over the imaginations of men". Other American journalists discovered in the Dandi March a meaningful comparison with the Boston Tea Party which was the harbinger of the country's independence. Like the latter, the former was undertaken in fulfillment of the Independence Resolution passed at the Lahore Congress in December 1929. According to William Shirer, "The day after the Boston Tea Party, John Adams had predicted that it would arouse the country and have "important consequences"." He considered it "an Epocha in history"; and so was the Dandi March. The Americans wanted to see for themselves Gandhi's miracle. In Shirer's words: "The struggle in America had been bloody. His would be bloodless, but just as relentless."[22] Such a bloodless struggle, much to their wonder, shook Viceroy Irwin exactly in the same way as Gandhi's Non-Cooperative Movement had shaken Viceroy Reading a decade earlier. As a witness, Shirer has recorded: "The British authorities at first were flabbergasted. They could not understand it."[23] Irwin was forced to reach a settlement with the Mahatma in the Gandhi-Irwin Pact.

Dandi once again placed Gandhi on top of the political ladder. He acquired undisputed command of the Congress party and people's veneration for him touched new heights. In Gandhi's most spectacular bloodless revolution, Patel's contribution was second only to that of the master. He had played John the Baptist to Jesus Christ.

14

President of Karachi Congress

Patel, who was to be crowned Congress President at the Lahore Congress on the recommendation of Motilal Nehru, got the crown at the Karachi Congress held in March 1931. The two sessions stood poles apart. They reflected the contrasting personalities of the two Presidents. Lahore was an effervescent affair, high-sounding and effusive—a euphoria of pious hopes built on the ultimatum to the British to declare within a year their clear intention regarding India's independence. Karachi was a grim, business-like session, lacking in luster, flutter and the high-flown excitement of Lahore, where, to use Gandhi's expression, "an uncrowned king" majestically rode a white horse followed by a surging crowd of excited men and women, with balconies of buildings *en route* bulging with them; and the President-elect Jawaharlal Nehru, "an embodiment of youthful ardour and indomitable enthusiasm for independence, lent a special glamour to the vast concourse assembled in the Congress pandal."[1] Karachi's grimness lay in the hostile climate Gandhi and Patel faced on the Mahatma's failure to save Bhagat Singh and his two revolutionary associates from the gallows, as also the barrage of criticism on Gandhi's compromise decision to participate in the Round Table Conference as the sole Congress nominee following the Gandhi-Irwin Pact, even against the advice of Nehru and Patel.

Nehru, however, admitted that the Karachi Congress was "an even greater personal triumph for Gandhi than any previous Congress had been." He had also stated that "the President, Sardar Vallabhbhai Patel, was one of the most popular and forceful men in India with the prestige of victorious leadership in Gujarat."[2] The Karachi Congress was in a way comparable to the Ahmedabad Congress held a decade earlier in 1921. The Ahmedabad Congress had given birth to a new Congress under Gandhi, with Patel as his deputy. At Karachi, Patel was again by Gandhi's side—even arriving there together to face a hostile demonstration. This time he was the Congress President-elect.

Patel's choice as Congress President had a history behind it. In 1928, Motilal Nehru had proposed his name in consideration of his spectacular success in the Bardoli satyagraha. Yet, Motilal had in the same breath, talked of his son Jawaharlal. Besides writing to Gandhi, he had conveyed his innermost feelings to Subhas Chandra Bose. "...Vallabhbhai Patel was the hero of the hour, and the first choice should go to him. Failing him, however, the next best choice was Jawaharlal."[3] Motilal's was the legitimate wish of a father to see his son as the Congress President during his life-time. He seemed to have had the premonition of time running out for him. He was 70, and ailing; and he died in 1931 before the Karachi Congress. But he had his wish fulfilled in seeing his son wear the crown earlier. Gandhi's preference for Jawaharlal to Patel in 1929 was for different reasons. By putting the crown on his head, he wanted to wean Nehru away from the radicalism he had taken to since his return from the Soviet Union in 1927.

At the Karachi railway station, a large crowd of agitated young men "greeted" Gandhi and Patel with black flags and staged an unruly demonstration. This was an emotional upsurge following the execution of Bhagat Singh, whose "name was as widely known all over India and was as popular as Gandhi's."[4] Patel stood behind Gandhi when the latter faced an explosive situation. Gandhi's response to the demonstrators was tactful. It was "friendly and quiet". It mollified the agitated minds.

Gandhi took the sting out of their anger by thanking them for offering him and Patel "black" flowers rather than throwing these at them! Gandhi still commanded their respect, and the demonstration could not be termed a revolt, but only a protest. For Gandhi had made sincere efforts with Irwin, the Viceroy, to save the lives of Bhagat Singh and others. He had told him, "In not allowing yourself to be persuaded by me, you are losing a very fine opportunity of winning the hearts of the youth of this country. If, therefore, you are determined to hang these men, by all means do so before the Congress session is held, so that Sardar Patel and I can face whatever our young men may have to say in their anger at the session. We should not like to run away from their anger."[5]

In his desire not to aggravate the people's frenzied temper, Patel delivered an unusually short, business-like Presidential address, free from the customary frills and catchy rhetoric. His boldness lay in his support to Gandhi on the extreme excitement caused by the executions. Patel soothed the angered mind of the youth by stating, "Young Bhagat Singh, Sukhdev and Rajguru were executed a few days ago. It roused countrywide deep resentment. It is true that I do not identify myself with their cult; and I do not believe that political murder is less reprehensible than any other. Yet, my head bows down to Bhagat Singh and his comrades for their patriotism, their daring and their sacrifice. The executions have been carried out in the teeth of opposition. This proves how heartless is the Government." Patel counselled that "provocation and frenzied anger should not make us falter in our principles." He called the Government soulless as it believed in a policy of repression. But in the fight against it, weapons had no place. By staying firm on the path of non-violence, the people would immensely justify their ability for freedom. "God", he added, "may grant peace to the soul of these brave patriots. Their families should draw consolation from the fact that the entire nation shares their bereavement."

In an oblique reference to the Bardoli and Salt satyagrahas, Patel stated, "India has shown to the world that the use of non-violence on a mass scale is no longer a dream of the visionaries. Nor is it a false concept, but a proven reality. Up to now, mankind had looked upon violence as a goddess. Even though harassed by it, it had no faith in the success of non-violence. Our successful use of it has raised new hopes for the future. Many had doubted the capacity of the peasants to participate in a non-violent battle. Many had even feared that there would be outbreaks of large-scale violence. But we have falsified such doubts and fears by the people's bravery and unheard of spirit of sacrifice. By calling upon women and children to participate, Gandhi gave evidence of the uniqueness of his battle." He stated, "From the viewpoint of non-violence, ours has been a great struggle in the world. That many nations, especially the Americans, have expressed their sympathy and given encouragement has been for us a matter of no small satisfaction."

Despite disagreement with Gandhi over the Gandhi-Irwin Pact—its failure to return confiscated lands to Bardoli peasants and to those who had participated in the Salt-satyagraha, Patel appealed to the delegates to accept the pact. His reasoning was that of a loyalist, "The members of the Working Committee are your trusted representatives. You cannot reject the agreement to which they have given their consent. But you can express your no-confidence against the committee, and have a more trustworthy committee. If we do not accept the agreement, we shall be held responsible for its failure, and last year's labours will go waste. As satyagrahis, we should not only be always ready for a compromise, but also be eager to work for it. Therefore, when we felt the door was opened for peace, we preferred to Irwin's assurance on behalf of the British Government and the hopes generated by the RTC and said, "Our countrymen (non-Congressmen) attending the RTC (1) have demanded a completely responsible government. The British delegates having given recognition to such a demand, the Prime Minister, the Viceroy and some of our representatives at the RTC asked for Congress support. This made the Working Committee feel that, if an honourable settlement could be reached and we can attain complete independence, the Congress should in that case accept the invitation to attend the RTC and lend its support to other groups in framing a constitution." By way of a sop to the critics, he added, "If we meet with failure, nothing can stop us from returning to our present path of struggle and sacrifice."

Contrary to the pronouncements of radicals like Nehru and Bose, Patel lent his powerful support to Gandhi who did not believe in India's complete severance of the British connection on achieving independence. Patel struck a realistic note, "Since India has been drained for nearly 200 years, we will need outside help in many matters. Such help we will certainly take from the British, provided their intentions are clear and just. As an example, we will need the services of men possessing military knowledge... This should assure retention of British officers, or a small British force, for the benefit of the country. But the control of the army, whether those serving it are Indians or the whites, has to be in our hands... We will gratefully accept their advice. But we shall not accept their hegemony. The reality is that the British army is in occupation of our country. It is wrong to say it is for our protection. It is only for safeguarding British interests...."

In regard to the complete independence resolution passed at the Lahore Congress, Patel satisfied the restive youth with the statement, "We are not retracing our steps from the resolve. But complete independence does not mean that we shall have no relations with Britain, or any other power. In our mutual interest, we must look to cooperation with other countries. And if we have to attain independence through discussion and agreement, it would be right to admit that we shall have to maintain a relationship with Britain. I am aware of a powerful section of people in the country which advocates that prior to considering such cooperation, we must first snap our connections. I am not in favour of this, as such thinking is influenced by weakness and distrust."

Patel also referred to two other issues. One was the proposed Federation; the other, communal unity. "The Federation", he said, "is a welcome thought. But it has many complexities. The Princes joining it will not agree to severance of their relations with Britain. But if they join in all sincerity, the proposed Federation will be a real gain. Their joining should in no way be a hindrance to our march towards democracy. I hope the Princes will not adopt such preconditions as would prove contrary to our concept of independence. We need not press them for a declaration to march in step with the present times. Nevertheless, they will have to grant such fundamental rights to their people as are given to people in the rest of India. Residents of every part of the Federation must enjoy such rights, protected by a common court of law. It will not be too much to hope that in the Federal legislature, the State subjects will have the right of representation."

Patel said that "communal unity is the most important issue, to which the Congress made its attitude abundantly clear at the Lahore Congress... As a Hindu, I accept the principle laid down by our past President, namely, to hand over to the minorities pen, paper and ink and ask them to write down their demands. I am ready to put down my signature. But there seems great haste in doing things in this manner. It may be a short cut. For this the Hindus shall have to be brave and large-hearted. But we should not have such a fragile unity as would break under the slightest strain. What we need is the unity of hearts."[6]

The address reflected the realism of a seasoned soldier-politician, who, more than others in the party, appreciated Gandhi's position vis-à-vis the Gandhi-Irwin Pact, as also the execution of Bhagat Singh and others. From that point of view, the Karachi Congress gave strong support to Gandhi at a time when he was in the midst of raging criticism. The atmosphere at Karachi, tense at the very start, was at last relaxed. This enabled Patel to assert the position Gandhi and he occupied in India's politics by speaking in the final summing-up as Congress President, "Gandhi is now almost 63 years old. I am 56. Should we, the old, be not more anxious for independence than you" the young? Because we are interested in seeing India independent before we die, it is we who are far more anxious, and in a hurry, than you. You talk of workers and peasants. But I can claim that I have become old in the service of the peasants. Hardly any one of you could have made the peasants sacrifice their person and their property so much as I have. Why are you agitating yourselves unnecessarily? You are not going to be old soon... Don't let your energies get wasted. Keep your weapons bright and shining. You have before you plenty of work—abstinence from alcoholic drinks, use of khadi and cultivation of self-purification. All these activities give the people incredible strength."[7]

Diplomatically, Patel also soothed Nehru by offering him a glowing tribute, "Many feel shocked when Pandit Jawaharlal puts forward a programme of activities. Why are they afraid of him? He has nothing but love for the poor, and has hostility towards none." Patel then referred to the zamindars and said, "Why should we frighten the people by saying that the zamindars will make them lose their land? The zamindars are miserable creatures. Even a sepoy of the Government can frighten them. But God lives in their hearts too. Let us act in such a way that they too realise that, and throw in their lot for the good of the people."[8]

The Karachi Congress was notable for two other things. One was the presence of Abdul Ghaffar Khan's Khudai Khidmatgars (God's servants) from the NWFP, popularly known as the Redshirts for their colourful uniform. Their leader was to be known thereafter as the "Frontier Gandhi." They drew special attention and applause of the delegates and visitors alike. Later that year, the Redshirts became an integral part of the Congress party. The other no less significant feature was Patel's insistence on the entire proceedings of the session being conducted in Hindi—the country's national language after independence—which was in line with the policy of Indianisation of the Congress which Gandhi and Patel had initiated at the Ahmedabad Congress in 1921.

If at Lahore the youth had dominated, at Karachi the Old Guard re-established its leadership under Patel. This was to continue thereafter. In handing over the reins of the party to Nehru at Lahore, Gandhi was not merely bowing down to Motilal's wishes, but allowing the radical, restless youth of the party to give vent to their feelings. He could not have allowed this to continue for ever; and a necessary balance between them and the Old Guard was essential. Such a balance was restored at Karachi.

At Karachi, Patel acquired a new status, next only to Gandhi's. Of this, William Shirer, an American journalist who covered the proceedings of the Congress session, writes, "There was one figure in Karachi, little known in the West but a power in India, who deserves mention. Next to Gandhi, it was Vallabhbhai Patel, India's nearest thing to an old Tammany Hall boss, who ran the convention. Under Gandhi's guidance, it had been Patel, a bald-headed, walrus-moustached, tough-minded, pragmatic peasant lawyer, who built up the Congress to a formidable national political party, the only one there was in India. He was the boss of the machine."[9]

The Karachi Congress thus sowed the seeds of Patel's becoming by 1934 the *de facto* party boss—an undefined post as powerful as the General Secretary of the Communist Party in Soviet Russia.

15

A "Mother to Gandhi"

Patel, the "iron man" of India, had a stern, granite-like face and penetrating hawkish eyes, which showed his soldierly qualities: daring, disciplined and even ruthless. He revealed his true character, rather humorously, when he told Gandhi in the Yeravada jail in 1932, "Who has attained immortality by reading and writing? They live for ever who are either victorious, or go down fighting bravely."[1] He said so because basically he was a fighter. Behind the hard exterior and stern mind of such a man, pulsated a warm heart: a heart as soft as rose petals; a heart that "overflowed with devotion and fidelity towards Gandhi."[2] Hidden in its deep recesses were Patel's motherly qualities of service and sacrifice. Such motherly qualities of Patel were discovered by Gandhi after nearly a decade and a half of their association—in the Yeravada jail where the two, along with Mahadev Desai, had been lodged. Gandhi's discovery was the outcome of their living together in an atmosphere free from the din and dust of the battlefield on which the two had waged many a battle. The discovery was also the outcome of the new guru-disciple relationship Patel had built with Gandhi in the Yeravada jail.

Gandhi and Patel were together in the Yeravada jail from January 4, 1932 to May 8, 1933. On his release, Gandhi issued a statement in which he said, "One of the greatest joys of my life was that I had an opportunity of staying in prison with the Sardar. I knew of his invincible courage and of his burning love for our country, but never before had I the good fortune of spending as much time with him as I was able to do during these sixteen months. His affection and love overwhelmed me and reminded me of my dear mother. I would never have imagined that he possessed such qualities of maternal affection." Gandhi's judgment of Patel was based on personal experience he had had during their prison life. Whenever he was "in the slightest degree indisposed," Gandhi admitted, "he would be immediately by my side, and would pay personal attention to the smallest of my needs."[3]

Patel nursed Gandhi with the devotion and care of a mother. At the same time, he did not spare the master—chaffing at some of his personal fads and even illogical political views, which, because of his loyalty, he would never make public. Patel's indulgence was without malice. He enjoyed a privilege which no other colleague of Gandhi did. And Gandhi, on his part, reciprocated with a corresponding open-heartedness. He felt much regaled by Patel's good-intentioned sardonic humour. It was an amusing sight to see the two indulge in bantering. In this, Patel always had the upper hand, may be because, as Gandhi sarcastically put it, he had "a longer tongue than mine." However, in a letter to Srinivasa Sastri, who had inquired about his health, Gandhi wrote: "Sardar Vallabhbhai is with me. His jokes make me laugh until I can laugh no more—not once, but several times every day."[4]

Living together for sixteen months was a wonderful experience as much for Patel as for the master himself. Since the former looked upon the latter as a demi-god, he found soulful satisfaction in the service he rendered so devotedly, unrestrained by consideration of age or status. Patel was 57, while Gandhi was his senior by six years only. Of such relationship, Mahadev Desai records: "It is inspiring to others to see with what immense devotion the Sardar prepares his drink of soda, washes dates for Bapu, or runs to fetch a *datan* (twig for brushing teeth) if he happens to have forgotten to fetch one." In whatever manner he served the master, Patel had the genius for animating ordinary, dull routine jobs with a tinge of humour—a dig at Gandhi for his fads, and his being too exact and inflexible in his thinking, habits and actions, personal or political.

Soon after he had taken over certain daily duties towards Gandhi, Patel jokingly complained to Mahadev Desai, "How could I imagine that I would be staying with Bapu! Had I known it, I would have inquired from Kaka (Kalelkar) of his needs. Bapu never says a word about his wants. He hasn't left for others the washing of his clothes. Whatever he has on him (a loincloth only) he washes it before he comes out of the bathroom."[5] It was a daily routine with Patel to peel and crush almonds for Gandhi, prepare his *datan*, morning drink of an ounce of honey, five grams of baking soda and fresh lime in eight ounces of warm water, wash dates in fresh water and read for him newspapers. When lemons became somewhat dearer, Gandhi suggested tamarind instead, especially when there were many tamarind trees in jail. Patel turned the whole matter into a joke by telling Gandhi, "Surely, you know, tamarind water causes rheumatism and weakens the bones."

Gandhi asked in sheer innocence, "Is Jamnalal Bajaj not drinking it?" Alluding to Bajaj's fat body, Patel impishly said, "Tamarind water cannot reach his bones!"

Gandhi said, "But, at one time I too had taken a lot of tamarind."

Patel replied, "At that time you could digest even stones. Not now!"

One day out of sheer mischief, Patel asked Gandhi, "How many dates should I wash?"

"Fifteen," was the reply.

But Patel argued, "What difference would there be between fifteen and twenty?"

Gandhi said, "In that case ten, as there would be no difference between ten and fifteen!"

On another occasion, while preparing Gandhi's *datan* as usual, Patel humorously grumbled, "Bapu has only a few teeth left; yet, he keeps on rubbing them!" He even made fun of Gandhi's preference for using baking soda in almost every drink. He would offer a solution to a difficult problem with the sarcastic remark, "*Soda dalo na*" (add soda). When a 70-year-old pensioner, troubled by asthma, asked Gandhi to suggest if he should undergo Nature cure, Patel volunteered to suggest, "Write to him to undergo (like Gandhi) a fast, take boiled vegetables and *kashifal* and drink soda!"

A man wrote that he did not like his wife as she was ugly. What should he do? Patel asked Gandhi to tell him to solve this problem by taking his eyes out, and thereafter he would not have to suffer her ugliness! Another person wanted to oblige a friend by marrying for the second time one of his three daughters, as in their community there was a dearth of bridegrooms. Patel's advice was that he should oblige his friend fully—by marrying all three!

Patel's day would begin with Gandhi at a quarter to four in the morning with prayers. Thereafter, Gandhi would make the poor man recite Sanskrit *slokas* (religious incantations)! It was a Herculean task, as Patel's knowledge of the language was nil, and his pronunciation was atrocious. But he had on his side a great asset—determination. At 57 he started learning Sanskrit, of which Gandhi wrote to Pyarelal, "Vallabhbhai is running with the speed of an Arab horse! The Sanskrit book seldom leaves his hands. Never could I have had such a hope from him."[6] Patel made "incredibly rapid progress" in Sanskrit. He surprised Gandhi one day by telling him in Sanskrit what he should write to someone. Gandhi inquired of Mahadev Desai whether Patel had learnt the Sanskrit phrase recently. He was told, "From tomorrow he is going to read the *Gita*. Once that happens, he will put before you original interpretations! All I can say is: Heavens help us all!"

While going to bed one night, Mahadev Desai asked Patel if he was ready to begin the study of the *Gita* the following day. Patel replied with a Sanskrit quotation, meaning, "Do it now, not afterwards. It is you who has to do it."

Mahadev Desai reported to Gandhi, "The fact of the matter is that he likes studying Sanskrit. So far, it seems, he has never had the time to be a student. Now he is like a child with a new toy in his hands! He feels as if the gates of paradise have been thrown open to him."[7]

Patel's skill in odd manual jobs drew no less praise from Gandhi. He wrote to Pyarelal, "In envelope-making, none can equal him in speed. He makes them without any kind of measurement. With naked eye he makes his estimates, and his envelopes come out absolutely equal in size. And yet he does not appear to spend much time over it." Speaking of Patel's skill, Gandhi further wrote: "What astonishes me is the method with which he works. Whatever has to be done, he does it immediately. Now that he has taken to spinning, he adheres to schedule strictly, and his daily output is increasing. Hardly ever does he forget anything with which he is entrusted; and where there is so much method, there can hardly be anything like rush or confusion."[8] Accuracy, precision, promptness and unwavering determination were the hallmarks of his character then, and later when, in the post-Independence India, they shaped him into the Great Administrator—whose decisions were instant, and invariably correct. Such qualities of Patel helped him successfully counter confusion and work effectively in the headlong rush of cataclysmic events leading to the transfer of power in 1947.

Patel used to make envelopes from discarded wrappers and other paper from Gandhi's Sunday mail from the Wardha ashram. Patel called this jocularly "Homeward Mail Day" (after the mail from Britain for Englishmen in India). One day, Gandhi entrusted Patel with the task of binding a book whose cover had come off. Gandhi was surprised to see the job done to his entire satisfaction. He asked Patel during one of their morning walks, "Vallabhbhai, do you have the inclination for doing odd jobs (so well) since childhood, or have you acquired it in prison? Were you a craftsman already or have become one now?"

Patel replied, "There is nothing like that. I have had no previous experience. When I see anyone doing something, I try to pick it up."

There upon Gandhi told him, "It means that it is an in-born

gift. Das could not even thread a needle, while Motilal could do a number of things."[9]

How independent and assertive Patel was is revealed by the heart-to-heart talks the two had on the many problems the country faced. They showed what a practical, down-to-earth outlook Patel had on the problems that were to plague India later and lead to her Partition. He did not share Gandhi's faith in the British politicians. No matter whether they were Conservatives, Liberals or Labourites, Patel's view was: "They are all tarred with the same brush. If that were not so, how could Samuel Hoare speak in this manner in Parliament."[10] On another occasion, he bluntly told Gandhi, "They all have no sense of shame. You will come round to my view in time..."[11] For Patel, Hoare, MacDonald, Willingdon and even Irwin were birds of a feather, not only uncompromising and unconcerned with India's aspirations, but bent upon dividing Indian opinion and thereby strengthening their rule. On receipt of a letter from Hoare when Gandhi spoke of his courtesy, Patel pulled his leg by telling Mahadev Desai in his presence, "If Bapu were to give up the fight, they will all write nice letters, just as Sikhs would like him much more if he were to keep long hair."[12] One day Patel said, "Never before were the people of England so united against India as they are today."

Gandhi thereupon explained, "The people of England have always been united on the question of India. If they give up India, they will turn into beggars. It is in their self-interest to cling to India."[13]

Alluding to Gandhi's spirit of compromise with all, especially with Irwin in the Gandhi-Irwin Pact, Patel told him one day, "You can compromise with anyone. How does this matter to you? After all a *bania* has no pride in his moustache (like a Rajput warrior) and lets it hang down!"

Gandhi was quick to retort, "See, that's why I had it shaved off!"[14] Patel even made fun of Gandhi for sending the Government, now and again, some complaint, caustically remarking, "Every few days Bapu must send some complaint to the Government, lest they think he is a spent force!"[15]

On another day, the doctor who came to examine Gandhi remarked that according to Lord Reading, Indians spent as much as Rs.16 lakhs a day on feeding beggars. Patel could not restrain himself from observing, "Yes. But a larger sum is spent on dacoits." The doctor could not catch the meaning. Patel exclaimed, "These so many dacoits who have come from Britain! They are no better than looters."[16]

One day when Gandhi was scanning through the pages of some books by an English writer, he asked Patel, "What could be the Bible of the British?"

Pat came a caustic reply, "Pound, shilling and pence." Since one of the books had said the same, Patel instantly quipped, "See how much I know about the British!"[17]

Patel was equally critical of Gandhi in regard to some of his pet ideas and habits: non-violence, fasting and Indian Muslims, to mention the major ones. When Gandhi started covering the steaming hot tumbler of his morning drink with a piece of cloth in order to save tiny insects from falling into it, Patel could not help poking fun at him, "We cannot practice your non-violence to such limits!"[18] And when someone asked Gandhi foolishly as to how one should avoid violence in the trampling of ants "when we walk on this earth with our three-maund body", Patel offered an equally foolish suggestion, "Tell him, he should walk with his feet on his head!" Patel did not spare Gandhi even in the matter of spinning with his left-hand, which was a newly acquired fad Gandhi was experimenting with. He told him with his usual bluntness, "I see no advantage in this. Why can't you stick to that to which you are accustomed? You cannot acquire a new skill after a certain age." On Gandhi's insistence that he was making progress, Patel ridiculed the affair by using a Gujarati proverb that "advice does not influence an incorrigible mind". Gandhi's persistence invited the comment, "For heaven's sake don't broadcast this, lest the whole ashram starts spinning with the left hand!"

When Gandhi attempted one day to ply a newly-designed *charkha* after a two-hour struggle to make it work, Patel, who impishly "bubbled with laughter" all the time over Gandhi's latest fad, told him, "You will waste more cotton than you will spin."[19] Next time when Gandhi sat down to ply the new *charkha*, he looked at Patel with a twinkle in his eye and mischievously said, "Of course it will work, unless it suffers from your curse!" Gandhi succeeded for a while, and then something went wrong. When Patel got up from his mid-day nap, Gandhi was still struggling with the *charkha*. Patel could not restrain from pointing an accusing finger at "the waste lying on the floor" and remarked cynically, "You have spun a lot! Now stop it."[20]

Patel did not go the whole hog with Gandhi in his fasting. When he suddenly announced his decision to go on a fast in protest against Ramsay MacDonald's Communal Award, Patel felt very angry and told him, "You should have given notice about your fast. Four days' notice is not enough. You are doing injustice both to the people and to the Government. We cannot explain your position. People will say, you write a letter which only the writer can understand. One fast has just ended; and another is about to begin! How can the Government understand your non-cooperation? You behave as if others are your subordinates."[21] When his second fast coincided with the start of the first RTC, Gandhi asked Patel rather mockingly, "Well, Vallabhbhai, what have you to say?"

An irritated Patel said, "You should now allow the people to have some peace. Those who have gathered there (in London) will do what they want (unconcerned with the fast). Then, why should you hold a threat and make the people feel worried? Others will conclude that this man has nothing else to do, and talks of a fast in season and out of season. Some may take it to be an excuse for release."

Gandhi teased Patel with the question, "Is the Congress President (Patel) giving his refusal?"

In the same mood, Patel said, "Yes". And then added, "You seem to be testing us. You are such a person that if we say, "yes", you will say "no"; and if we say "no", you will say "yes".

Seeing the tables turned on him, Gandhi said, "Then I must undertake the fast."

Patel laughed away Gandhi's obduracy, but suggested, "If you have to fast, then it should be against those who are going for the RTC."

Gandhi thereupon said, "Such a fast you should undertake. I give you my permission." Patel replied, "Why should I fast? If I undertake it, these people will let me die. They are your friends and might listen to you."[22]

On a later occasion, Patel told Gandhi, "Your undertaking a fast so frequently has no meaning. You will simply make your fast appear cheap. They will cease to carry weight with the people as well as with the Government."[23] On another day, prior to retiring for the night, Patel poured out his anger, "Many times you announce your decisions without consulting your colleagues, and thereby embarrass them. You got published your temple-entry settlement without consulting Rajagopalachari, which gave rise to new situations. The Harijans turned against him. And so were the members of the Justice Party and the orthodox caste Hindus. Why do you, thus, complicate matters and make the position of those working on a solution difficult? You must correct your habit."[24]

On the issue of the Communal Award and the intended fast, Patel told Gandhi, "Not before long, everything will become clear and be understood. Today, what shall we gain by arguing with you? Whatever was to happen, has happened. If you had taken my advice, there would have been no announcement of the Communal Award. The announcement was a direct consequence of your letter."[25]

As a practical man, Patel believed that Gandhi would be unable to please either of the two Hindu groups on the issue of temple-entry. Answering Mahadev Desai's fear that "we might get crushed between the millstones of the orthodox and the Ambedkarites", Patel said, "Only if we get in between the two. I say, we shouldn't. We should keep aloof, letting the two fight each other. Instead, Bapu tells the orthodox that he was one of them, and to the other that he is a 'touchable' turned untouchable. In such a situation, one is bound to get crushed between the two."[26]

Far from that, Patel wanted the Congress to build its fighting power for the political struggle against the British.

Another major issue of disagreement was Gandhi's pro-Muslim policy of appeasement; and his claim to represent the Muslims. Patel felt that by fasting, Gandhi pricked the conscience of the Hindus only, and not of the Muslims. He asked him one day, "Are there any Muslims who will listen to you?"[27] On another occasion, he ruefully remarked, "The Muslims are keeping mum and are offering no opinion. But they are co-operating with the Government and shall continue doing so."[28] He had his usual dig at Gandhi when the latter was one day practising Urdu in a note-book, "You may have to ask God to let you be reborn as an Urdu *munshi*!" Then added sarcastically, "If you can have your way, you may even write with your feet."[29]

In that quiet, uncontaminated climate of the jail, free from the harsh glare of public controversy and in the company of his most trusted colleagues, Gandhi for the first time, perhaps, revealed how much sorrow and pain were caused to him by the Muslims' attitude towards him in the case of the Kohat communal rioting and at the RTC. Gandhi said in a depressed tone, "Whom should I tell the insults I have borne on behalf of the Muslims? For their sake I have drunk bitter cups of sorrow."[30] One day while reading an Urdu school text-book, Gandhi admitted, "The book pours out maximum poison. It was prescribed by the Government as text-book before the Hindu-Muslim conflict began; and today's Muslim youth has been brought up on such books."[31] On another occasion Gandhi referred to a fourth standard Urdu primer of Lahore's *Anjuman-i-Himayat*, and regretfully observed, "The reading of this book makes one sad. It appears the Muslim children are taught violence and bloodshed from their childhood."[32]

Gandhi told Patel and Mahadev Desai one day, "Iqbal's opposition to (single) nationhood is shared by many Muslims. Some speak out; others don't. Iqbal now repudiates his *Hindustan Hamara* song."[33] On another day, Gandhi asked Mahadev Desai to draw Patel's attention to the distorted version of the same song in a Government school text-book in Urdu. The song propagated

Pan-Islamism, and its first two lines read: *Chino-Arab hamara, Hindustan hamara; Muslim hain hum, watan hai sara jahan hamara* (from China to Arabia the whole territory is ours; India is ours; we are Muslims, and the whole world is ours). Gandhi sadly commented, "The Muslim boys are brought up on such education. The book hasn't a single lesson which should teach the Muslim boys that this country is theirs and they should take pride in her. Not only that, as a result, the Muslims have developed enmity with others."[34]

Gandhi's regret was that all this was happening despite what he had done or undergone for the sake of Hindu-Muslim unity. He led the Khilafat agitation, boldly bearing attacks from senior Congress leaders, Hindu leaders and even the saintly Britisher, C.F. Andrews. And it was at the RTC, which could have provided India with an opportunity to gain independence in 1931, that Gandhi had met his Waterloo at the hands of the Muslims. Maulana Shaukat Ali had told the American journalist William Shirer, "If the Hindus don't meet our demands this time, we're going to make war on them. We ruled the Hindus once. We at least don't intend to be ruled by them now."[35] Gandhi had to admit to "an inglorious end" to his years of labours. According to Shirer, "This failure, as Gandhi often said, was the greatest cross he ever bore."[36]

During Gandhi's fast, as Mahadev Desai confirms, Patel's sense of humour had dried up, but "blossomed again" as soon as the fast ended. One day when Gandhi was being given a sponge bath, Patel took out from the cupboard a few towels. Gandhi said, "I would like to have an account of these."

Patel answered, "Why should an account be given to you? We had taken you to be lost. We didn't know that you will come back to ask for an account!" He good humouredly complained to Gandhi's wife, "Look at his tyranny. He made Malaviya wear *khadi*, "touch" the untouchables, drove him to jail, took him to England and won't be satisfied until he makes him agree to eat with the Harijans—and even make him agree to their matrimonial alliances with others."[37]

During their sixteen-months companionship in the Yeravada jail, Patel played the role of a perfect "mother"—not only personally looking after Gandhi's daily needs, but also administering Gandhi a mother's admonition in an effort to chasten morals with ridicule. He was, nevertheless, first and last, the Mahatma's disciple.

One day while conversing, Gandhi asked Patel, "Under Swaraj, which portfolio should be allotted to you?" Patel answered, "A wandering minstrel." Thereupon Gandhi disclosed rather distressingly, "Das and Motilal used to talk in terms of allotment of their portfolios. Mohammad Ali and Shaukat Ali wanted to become Education Minister and the Army Commander-in-Chief." And further added as if with a feeling of relief, "Saved from an embarrassment that we didn't get Swaraj, and none could become anything!"[38]

During his fast and prior to his release on May 8, 1933, Gandhi told Mahadev Desai, "... how great has been God's kindness to me that I have had the companionship of a brave man like Vallabhbhai?"[39] On his being brought back to the Yeravada jail on June 2nd, the first inquiry he made was about Patel. But the latter had been shifted to the Nashik jail. Growing sad, Gandhi remarked, "The nest is there, but the bird has flown." He pined for the companionship he had enjoyed for sixteen months, and he often repeated a line from the Sanskrit play *Bhartrihari*, "Oh! God, this is a wound which will not heal even by practising *yoga*."[40] What Gandhi sadly missed and pined for was Patel's "maternal affection".

16

The Party Boss

The mid-thirties saw Patel assuming a new role—that of the party boss, in his capacity as Chairman of the all-powerful Congress Parliamentary Board. The Board had been constituted to fight the provincial elections in 1937 under the Act of 1935, which purported to grant autonomy to the provinces. The Congress, under the Old Guard or the Gandhiites, had since the Karachi session moved away from the early policy of boycott and confrontation to that of parliamentary politics. Patel, supported by Rajendra Prasad and Rajagopalachari, spearheaded the change. He had confessed to Gandhi earlier in the Yeravada jail, "Government officials are harassing the peasants so much that we can give them protection only by entering into the government."[1] Gandhi shared his view, provided his cooperation with the government took the country towards independence. As Chairman of the Board, Patel became the virtual boss of the party.

The radical change brought about a conflict within the party. The lone opponent was Nehru, whom Gandhi mollified adroitly as he did not wish to alienate him. In fact, in view of the forthcoming elections, Gandhi could ill-afford an inter-party conflict marring the Lucknow Congress, being held in April 1936. He resolved the situation by proposing Nehru as President. But Gandhi did so without Nehru's prior consent. The latter was in Germany. Gandhi wrote him on October 3, 1935: "Your letter about the wearing of the next year's crown was delightful. I was glad to have your consent. I am sure that it would solve many difficulties, and it is the rightest thing that could have happened for the country." Gandhi thought it fit to explain further: "Your Presidentship at Lahore was totally different from what it would be at Lucknow. In my opinion, it was comparatively plain sailing at Lahore in every respect. It won't be so in any respect at Lucknow. But these circumstances I cannot imagine anybody better able to cope with than you."[2] Persuasion also came from the Congress Socialist Party. Formed in 1934 and controlling one-third of the delegates to the AICC at the Bombay session in 1935, the Socialists, along with the Communists, dreamed of capturing the party machine through Nehru's election.

When Nehru accepted the Congress Presidentship, he claimed to be unaware of "the new alignments, a hardening of party lines within the Congress", to which, some thought, he had contributed no less by lending his support to the Socialists. Differences had surfaced between him and Gandhi, and between him and the Old Guard. To assuage Nehru's hurt feelings, Gandhi wrote to him: "I understand your deep sorrow... there is not enough reason for all the grief and disappointment you have left. Let me assure you that you have not lost a comrade in me. I am the same as you knew me in 1917 and after. I have the same passion that you knew me to possess for the common goal (of complete independence)... But I fancy that I have the knack for knowing the need of the time. And the resolutions are a response thereto. Of course, here comes in the difference of our emphasis on the method or the means... Greatest consideration has been paid to the Socialists... I have found them as a body to be in a hurry... I have looked up the dictionary meaning of socialism. It takes me no further than where I was before I read the definition."

This was an attempt to pacify Nehru over what he himself called the "spiritual defeat", to mollify his high-flown sentiments, to curb his radicalism and to keep him tied to the party moorings—a party, which under Patel's command, had begun to be more and more in the hands of the Old Guard. Gandhi's restraining efforts lent support to the Old Guard's frank dialogue with Nehru. On their behalf, Rajendra Prasad wrote to Nehru on December 19, 1935: "I know that there is a certain difference between your outlook and that of men like Vallabhbhai, Jamnalal (Bajaj) and myself, and it is even of a fundamental character. But, I suppose, that has been there all these years, and yet we have worked together. Now that Bapu has in a sense withdrawn himself (primary membership resignation)... these differences may become more marked. But I believe, unless a radical change comes to be made in the programme and methods of our work, it will still be possible for all of us to continue to work together."

Prasad argued: "It is not right to put it as if it were a question of acceptance or non-acceptance of offices... no one wants to accept offices for their own sake. No one wants to work the Constitution as the government would like it to be worked. The questions for us are altogether different. What are we to do with this Constitution? Are we to ignore it altogether and go our way? Is it possible to do so? Are we to capture it and use it as we would like to use it, and to the extent it lends itself to be used in that way? Are we to fight it from within, or from without, and in what way? It is really a question of laying down a positive programme for dealing with the situation created by the introduction of this Constitution in the light of the circumstances as they exist."[4]

Nehru's election as Congress President was, thus, under conflicting circumstances. Though realising that "the President did not mean the party's conversion to socialism", Nehru attempted to wrest power from the Old Guard not so much through direct confrontation as through radical resolutions. In such a situation, the right-wing leaders under Patel's direction "played their cards most skillfully", allowing the Working Committee, which was of the new President's choosing, to pass the proposals mooted, but getting them rejected by the AICC, whereby the responsibility for such rejection was of the Congress as a whole and not of a group of individuals. Neither to Gandhi, nor to the Old Guard, the radical resolutions were accepted. The proposal to allow collective affiliation of trade unions and peasant leagues with the Congress would have shifted the balance of power into the hands of the Leftists outside the party.

Nehru's election had also raised the radicals' hope of active participation by the Congress in agitations in the Princely States. Such a hope suffered a damp squib by Gandhi's policy of non-intervention, with which Patel was in full agreement. Patel was against involvement in the struggle of the States people against their rulers, unless circumstances forced the Congress to do so. His reasoning was sound: the States people were yet incapable of undertaking such a struggle. Such an ability, he believed, should be first brought about through an awakening among them—and thus "gradually make them capable of putting up a fight". This was a defeat for Nehru's Left-wing supporters. Nehru suffered a further defeat in respect of his two other proposals: the Congress participation in the "Imperial war" in Ethiopia; and rejection of the proposal not to contest the provincial elections. The last was a major victory for Patel and other Rightists.

Nehru was bitterly disappointed. He wanted to resign. "After much mental conflict" he changed his mind, because "our whole organization might have been shaken up by it." His defeat in wresting power from the Old Guard was obvious. And yet, he gave expression to his radical views in his address as Congress President at Lucknow on April 14, 1936. He delivered "a direct snub to the Old Guard", when he charged the Congress with "the spirit of disunity", which he ascribed to the "gradual divorce of its middle-class leadership from the masses"; and even observed: "The Congress must be not only *for* the masses; as it claims to be, but *of* the masses." According to him, the party had become "a prey to authoritarianism and a battleground for rival cliques fighting for control, and, in doing so, stooping to the lowest and most objectionable tactics." He also deplored the Old Guard's refusal to broaden the party base by permitting trade unions and peasant leagues to have collective affiliation to the Congress, and thereby denying the formation of a "joint anti-imperialist front". Such radicalism was dismissed as empty rhetoric; and it looked ludicrous in comparison with Patel's most successful peasant and worker movements in Gujarat—the like of which no other Congress leader, other than Gandhi, had led so far.

Gandhi felt distressed over two things: Nehru's insinuations against his colleagues of the Old Guard, and that what he had said was a contradiction of the basic principles Gandhi had attempted to implement since 1920. At Lahore, Nehru had declared himself to be a Socialist and Republican; at Lucknow, "he reached the logical fulfillment of Socialism—namely, Communism"[6]; in consequence, "the address pleaded for pure Communism in a country which had had its own traditions built up through at least a hundred and thirty centuries of progress."[7] In a letter of April 30, 1936, to Agatha Harrison, Gandhi wrote: "Jawaharlal's way is not my way. I accept his ideal about land, etc. But I do not accept practically any of his methods. I would strain every nerve to prevent a class war."[8]

"The Old Guard's views were none other than Gandhi's, and their "fight" against Nehru was Gandhi's fight—to save the party from disruption by the Communists. Theirs was a fight for the survival of Gandhism. Gandhi wrote to Nehru on May 29th: "Your statement… has given much pain to Rajen Babu, C.R. and Vallabhbhai. They feel, and I agree with them, they have tried to act honourably and with perfect loyalty towards you as a colleague. Your statement makes you out to be the injured party."[9] Gandhi wrote again on July 15th: "They have chafed under your rebukes and magisterial manner, and, above all, your arrogance of, what has appeared to them, your infallibility and superior knowledge. They feel that you have treated them with scant courtesy and never defended them from the Socialists' ridicule and even misrepresentation." Gandhi, therefore, bluntly asked Nehru, "Why do you resent their majority being reflected in all sub-committees, etc? Is it not the most natural thing? You are in office by their unanimous choice, but you are not in power yet. To put you in office was an attempt to find you in power quicker than you would otherwise have been. Anyway, that was at the back of my mind when I suggested your name for the crown of thorns." And then in the same breath Gandhi urged Nehru,

"Keep it on, though the head be bruised. Resume your humour at the committee meetings. That is your most usual role, not that of a care-worn, irritable man ready to burst on the slightest occasion."[10]

Gandhi's rebuke sobered Nehru. His intervention also made Patel and other Old Guard members withdraw their letter of resignation from Nehru's Working Committee. They told Gandhi, "We feel that the preaching and emphasizing of Socialism, particularly at this stage, by the President and other Socialist members of the Working Committee, while the Congress has not yet adopted it, is prejudicial to the best interests of the country and to the success of the national struggle for freedom... We feel the Congress should still follow the ideals, and the line of action and policy, which it has been following since 1920." They also told Nehru, "The effect of your propaganda on the political work immediately before the nation, particularly the programme of election, has been very harmful, and we feel that, in the situation created, we cannot shoulder the responsibility of organizing and fighting the coming elections."[11] The Old Guard's apprehensions were not baseless. Nehru had drafted into the Working Committee Socialists like Jayaprakash Narayan, Narendra Deva and Achyut Patwardhan, who were soon to become, though unwittingly, a shadow of the Communist Party, which not before long "overwhelmed" the former. "The CSP and the CP became familiar terms. Conspiracy cases conducted by the Government unfolded these truths to an ignorant public."[12]

Patel saw what was going on; and his shrewd sense of judgment aptly described the Congress Socialists, in 1936 itself, as mere "sappers and miners" of the Communist Party. He feared, what Minno Masani and other Socialists came to realise later, that "many of the gains of the Socialists would ultimately accrue to the Communists." Patel correctly sensed that the Communists sought entry into the Congress through the Congress Socialist Party, as their own party was banned by the Government. He, therefore, felt worried about "the respectability that the united front (formed by the Communists and the Socialists) gave the

Communists and the way it assured them a foothold in Indian politics, which otherwise would have been difficult." Besides doubting the wisdom of the Socialists' political strategy, Patel queried a definition of Socialism. Knowing there would be none, sarcastically he observed, "The Socialists are not agreed regarding the definition of Socialism. Different people put forward different meanings. There are 84 castes among the Brahmins, whereas it would seem there are 85 different types of Socialists!"

Masani made a confession which Jayaprakash Narayan repeated later, "Though I used to be annoyed at that time with Sardar Patel's attacks at the Congress Socialist Party, looking back I feel that he was justified when he made the charge of the Socialists being 'sappers and miners' of the Communist Party. I myself found it necessary in 1939 to resign from the Congress Socialist Party over the issue of alliance with the Communists. In 1941 Jayaprakash Narayan himself arrived at the same conclusion."[13] Another top Socialist, Yusuf Meherally, appreciating Patel's position in the party, dramatically put it that Rajagopalachari was "the brain trust of the Gandhi group, just as Sardar Patel is its directing hand."[14]

In selecting his colleagues on the Working Committee, Nehru dropped some second-line Old Guard leaders like Sarojini Naidu and Purushottam Das Tandon, but accommodated some young, fire-brand Socialists. Rafi Ahmed Kidwai and some other close friends of Nehru looked upon this with "dismay and incredulity". Kidwai wrote to Nehru on April 20th: "I have passed the last few days in agony. Apparently you were our only hope; but are you going to prove an illusory one?... You were given an opportunity of reshuffling the Working Committee. You have excluded Tandon, Nariman, Pattabhi, Sardul Singh... They have manoeuvred to isolate you from the middle men. We have been weakened both in the AICC and the delegates. And the Working Committee you have formed is bound to prove more reactionary than the one it has replaced. It may be that my vision is narrow. I rely more on the number of heads than on ideological discourses."[15]

Patel accepted membership of the Working Committee "with

great hesitation". As a strategist, he counterbalanced Nehru's move by getting Bhulabhai Desai on the Working Committee. With provincial assemblies in mind, Patel wanted his inclusion for his proven ability as a parliamentarian in the Central Legislative Assembly, where the Congress party had "marshaled its forces under his able leadership"; and he had "brought to the assembly the same prestige and glamour as Motilal himself had." Desai was not acceptable to Nehru: but, as Gandhi has recorded, he swallowed "the Bhulabhai pill in the interest of the cause."

Gandhi, thus, helped preserve the party unity with a view to promoting parliamentary politics. It was a return to what the Swarajists had advocated a decade earlier. The Congress had nearly got tired of boycotts and non-cooperation. The freedom struggle was entering upon a new phase of parliamentary democracy. The Old Guard was not without misgivings. But it seemed pragmatic in its approach: to try its hand at it through office acceptance in the provinces; and it was averse to missing an opportunity which other political parties were bound to cash in on. Boycott would have thrown the Congress into isolation. The Old Guard was guided by the thought that the elections, to borrow Nehru's words, "brought us into intimate touch not only with millions of voters but also others."[16] Nehru fell in line with others and strained himself to the utmost in the electioneering work. His great consolation was that his performance was superb. He was intoxicated by the adulation he received from India's teeming millions: to use his own words, from the "surging crowds, with an enthusiasm bordering on frenzy and shining eyes with unspoken pledges looking through them." But he had confided to a friend earlier that in the Working Committee he had been "completely isolated, and there was not a single member to support me."[17]

While Nehru managed the platform, Patel built up and controlled the party machine. As Chairman of the Congress Parliamentary Board, he supervised the all-important task of selecting Congress candidates, and later guiding the Congress Ministries in the provinces. This post turned out to be the most significant and powerful, as the Board was to be "in close and constant touch with the work of the Congress parties in all legislatures in the provinces, to advise them in all their activities and to take the necessary action in the case of an emergency." It was, thus, a combination of Nehru's electioneering performance and Patel's sound, firm party strategy that got the Congress a thumping victory. Gandhi's success in achieving the Nehru-Patel combination was more of an arrangement than real unity of hearts.

At the Faizpur Congress, the Right-Left controversy again reared its head. The names of Patel and Nehru were suggested for the Presidentship by either side. Nehru fired a shot by issuing a statement that before his name was considered, Congressmen must bear in mind that he believed in socialist principles and programmes. Patel did not react to such an emotional outburst. He played it cool. His role at Faizpur was more skilful than earlier in Lucknow. He withdrew in Nehru's favour, but issued, what Sitaramayya describes as, "a timely rejoinder which helped the President-designate discover his bearings."[18] Patel was, however, diplomatic in describing Nehru as "the best person to represent the nation"; but was bold to say at the same time, "My withdrawal should not be taken to mean that I endorse all the views Jawaharlal stands for. Indeed, Congressmen know that on some vital matters my views are in conflict with those held by Jawaharlal. For instance, I do not believe in the inevitability of class war. Whilst I detest imperialism and admit the destructive inequality between the capitalist class and the famishing poor, I do believe that it is possible to purge capitalism of its hideousness." He further explained, "I believe that when the masses awake to the sense of their terrible condition, they will know how to deal with it. There is no difficulty in my subscribing to the doctrine that all land and all wealth belong to all. Being a farmer, and having identified myself with the peasantry for years, I know where the shoe pinches." Nehru's approach was ideological; Patel's was practical, born out of what he had been himself—the son of a peasant and a leader of peasants.

On the issue of parliamentary programme, Patel's approach

was no less pragmatic. He told Nehru, "There is, again, no difference of opinion about the objective. All of us want to destroy the imposed Constitution. How to destroy it from within the legislatures is the question... The question of 'holding office' is not a live issue today. But I can visualise the occasion when the acceptance of office may be desirable to achieve the common purpose... I am no more wedded to the parliamentary programme than to the acceptance of office... We might in the course of events be driven to such an acceptance, but it shall never be at the cost of self-respect or through a compromise of our objective."

Patel bluntly stated, "The Congress President has no dictatorial powers. He is the chairman of a well-knit organisation. He regulates the proceedings and carries out decisions of the Congress as they may be arrived at from time to time. The Congress does not part with its ample powers by electing any individual, no matter who he is."[19]

Patel's definition of the powers of the President was identical to the views expressed by Motilal Nehru in 1921, "... every president owes his position to, and derives his authority from, the persons who elect him... he can, in no case, have powers larger than those of the whole body of his electors, and it is open to the latter, or their representatives, to restrict his powers within as narrow limits as they choose."[20]

Patel's statement had the desired effect. A mollified Nehru stated, "It would be absurd for me to treat this Presidential election as a vote for Socialism or against office acceptance... I do believe political independence is the paramount issue before the country, and the necessity for a joint and united action for its achievement is incumbent on all of us."[21] In his Presidential address, Nehru merely stated that the Congress stood for complete democracy and the establishment of a democratic State, avoiding to call it a Socialist State, though he hoped that events would automatically lead to Socialism. Patel too believed in Socialism, but of the Gandhian type and not Marxian. The Faizpur Congress ended on a subdued note. To Patel it mattered little if Nehru felt

Sardar Vallabhbhai Patel, India's Iron Man

A rebel student leader

Vallabhbhai as a lawyer at Godhra

Leaving for the Bar-at-Law, 1910

The two brothers: Vithalbhai and Vallabhbhai,
on latter's return from UK

Gandhi's 'Deputy Commander' in the Kaira satyagraha

Gandhi's GOC

Jawaharlal Nehru and Sardar Patel

Gandhi's great support

(top) Sardar with Anthony Eden, Deputy Prime Minister, UK, during his visit to India

(below) L to R: Pandit Nehru, Lady Mountbatten, Manibehn Patel, Lord Mountbatten, Sardar Patel, Amrit Kaur, Sardar Baldev Singh and Dr. Rajendra Prasad.

With Arthur Henderson, Under Secretary of State for India, U.K., on successful conclusion of negotiations on Covenanted Services

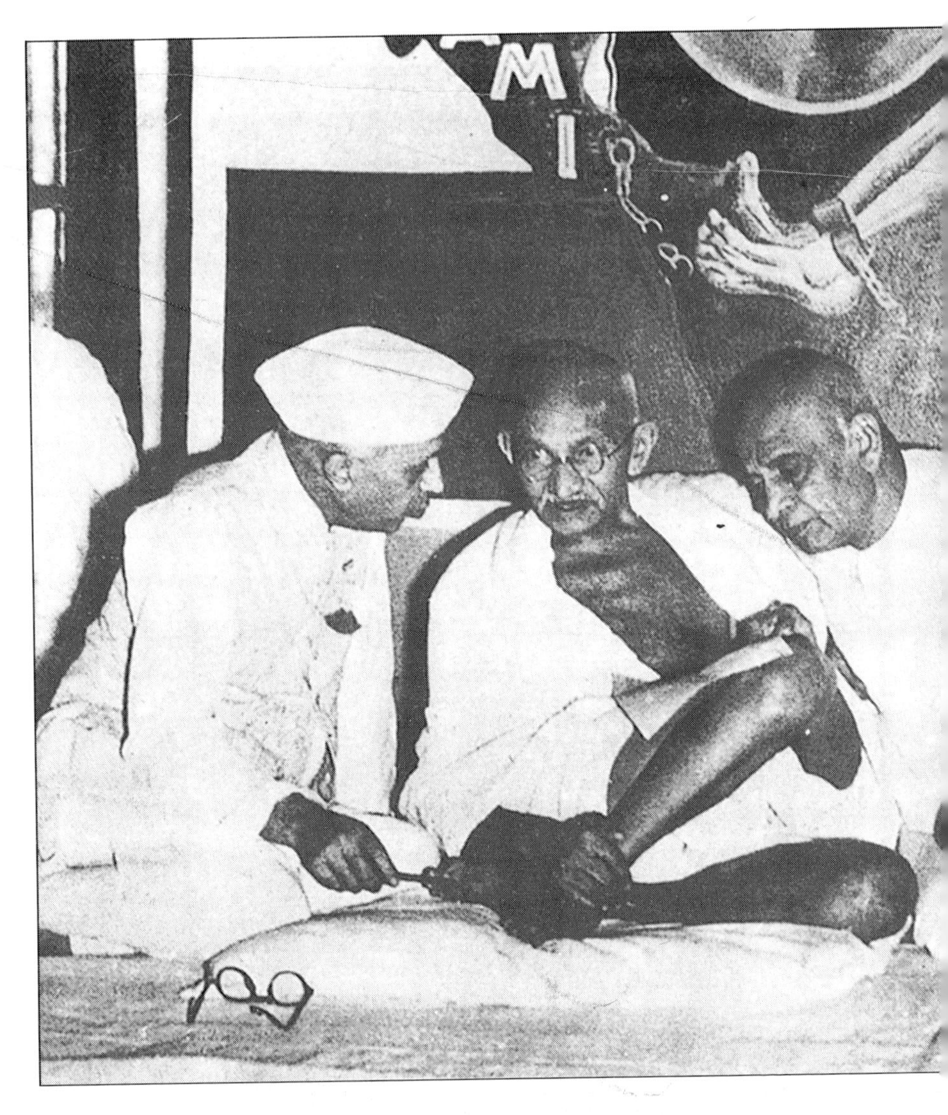

The Troika: Nehru, Gandhi, Patel

(facing page) Patel and Nehru: a study in contrasts –
a unique combination of rugged strength and alluring softness,
as if of Siva and Vishnu
(Photo : Mrs. Homai Vyarawalla)

Sardar with his brother Vithalbhai Patel

Sardar with the Maharaja of Gwalior, who, while presenting a portrait of him to Parliament in 1954, said:
"Here is the man whom I once hated. Here is the man of whom I was later afraid. Here is the man whom I admire and love"

(top) The Simla Conference (1945); The Sardar on his way to the meeting

(below) In Simla, along with Dr. Rajendra Prasad, Pattabhi Sitaramayya, Dr. Khan Sahib and other Congress leaders

pleased by describing the Congress "a powerful joint front of all the anti-imperialist forces in the country."[22]

With the Congress winning the elections in eight out of eleven provinces, Patel moved further in his position as Chairman of the Congress Parliamentary Board, and thus outpaced the President in the race for supremacy. He had fully realised that he was "entrusted by the Congress with the work of organising the elections and seeing that it achieved success at the polls."[23] Yet, in a message to Congressmen elected to the legislatures, Patel paid glowing tributes to Nehru for his "wonderful cooperation" and "inspiring lead"; and to Rajendra Prasad, Govind Ballabh Pant and Bhulabhai Desai for their "untiring efforts and willing cooperation."

As Chairman of the Parliamentary Board, Patel took into his hands the responsibility of explaining the task before the Congress to provincial Ministers and legislators. He told them, "The first stage of our work is over, and we are now on the threshold of the next stage, which will require all our energy and time, at least in the immediate future. If we show the same determination and unity as we exhibited in a remarkable degree in winning the elections in our legislative programme, whatever that be, I have no doubt that we will once again confound our enemies and hasten the day of Swaraj." He further said, "I dare say that Congressmen who will be present at Delhi will strain every nerve to keep up a solid, united front, however much we may disagree on the methods of our approach to our common goal, and loyally abide by the decision of the Congress Executive, whatever that decision might be." Patel made himself clear when he said, "The Congress objective of ending the Government of India Act would not be achieved unless the hands of the Congress legislators are strengthened by those outside in the country by carrying on extra-parliamentary activities..."[24]

Patel's statement, which preceded the meeting of the AICC and the Congressmen elected to the legislatures on March 19th and 20th, established two facts: first, whereas the Congress President ceased to be effective with the expiry of his one-year term, Patel's functions as Chairman of the Congress Parliamentary Board did not end with the winning of the elections, but extended, and even widened, in the conduct of parliamentary affairs in the provinces, through the imposition of a new discipline the Congress Ministers and legislators were not known to. Such discipline was not only essential for the maintenance of party unity and strength, but also for proper conduct on their part. As Chairman of the Board, Patel was to ensure this. He was, thus, operationally more effective than the President, with tight control over the Congress ministries.

Second, Patel's was an attempt at establishing the authority of the Congress Executive as a body above the Congress President and even himself. His main concern seemed to be to usher in a healthy democratic practice of majority rule, rather than allow the new democratic process in evolution to become subservient to an individual's dictatorial or "magisterial" behaviour. Since the Congress had never enjoyed power in the past and its decisions did not require such legislative sanctions as now, Patel himself, as Chairman of the Board, was anxious to draw his strength from the Congress Executive. He realised that the new burdens and responsibilities he carried were far bigger and more arduous and complex than those of the Congress President. The new challenges required enforcement of strict discipline and suppression of fissiparous tendencies, or anti-party activity, with an iron hand. Such responsibilities sat squarely on his broad shoulders as the party boss; and his was the only iron hand which could effectively handle the complexities of the new situation.

Not before long Patel faced three major confrontations: two concerned him as Chairman of the Parliamentary Board, while the third was a challenge to Gandhi. The first two were with K.F. Nariman and N.B. Khare; the third was with Subhas Chandra Bose. Nariman, being Chairman of the Bombay Provincial Congress Parliamentary Board expected to be the leader of the Legislative party and by virtue to that the Premier of Bombay Presidency. The party, instead, elected B.G. Kher. The Parsi-owned Gujarati newspapers and the Parsi-owned English newspaper, the *Bombay Sentinel*, carried a campaign of vilification against Patel, the allegation being that he had brought to bear pressure on the members in the election of Kher. Nariman clarified his position by publicly stating, "Whatever claims or grievances an individual might have, he must cheerfully and ungrudgingly accept the freely and properly obtained verdict of the majority. I would be less than honest if I were to say that an event like last Friday's election does not hurt. I have enough sense of discipline and public duty, however, not to allow my personal feelings to affect the national work. As long as Kher remains the elected leader of our party, we must pledge him our wholehearted and devoted cooperation in the difficult task which lies ahead of him."[25]

This ought to have closed the unhappy episode. But the vilification campaign continued. In spite of his earlier statement, Nariman himself jumped into the fray by reopening the matter in a letter to Nehru, the Congress President. Along with Patel, the three others whom he accused were Shankarrao Deo, Gangadharrao Deshpande and Achyut Patwardhan, the Socialist leader. All the three publicly stated that "it was certainly not the Sardar's intention to ask us to work against Nariman."[26] Nehru acted impartially in writing to Nariman: "You refer to secret meetings and the like. The impression created in my mind is that you are allowing your imagination to carry you away from facts... It surprises me that you should wish to pursue this matter in the way you have done and make serious charges without any real basis."[27]

The correspondence with Nehru continued for nearly a month. Nariman was given an opportunity to explain his point of view before the Congress Working Committee. He was found to be not specific; nor was he desirous of reconsidering the decision reached by the committee earlier.

Upon this, Nehru wrote to Nariman: "Your letters... are lacking in clarity and, therefore, it is difficult to see what you want and what your precise allegations are. You keep reiterating that you are being persecuted and that you want protection from this persecution. At the same time you say that you do not want the matter to be reopened. You then go on to say that, if it is to be reopened, you want to have a full inquiry. All this is very confusing."[28]

Patel, who had so far remained "studiously silent", now publicly stated, "... I have never, directly or indirectly, influenced this election."[29] The irrepressible Nariman came out with a series of counter-statements. This irritated Nehru, who had to tell Nariman, "I find that you have again launched a fierce campaign and those who champion you in the Press are out again for everybody's blood... So far as I am concerned, since the Working Committee unfortunately does not enjoy your confidence, you can go to the Privy Council or the League of Nations, or any other tribunal in which you have confidence."[30] With Nehru slamming the door on him, Nariman now conducted his campaign through correspondence with Gandhi. He didn't spare him either. In his anxiety to settle the matter judiciously, Gandhi had an inquiry conducted by him and Justice Bahadurji. Nariman argued his own case, whereas Patel refrained from participation.

Arbitration was sought in regard to two issues: (a) Nariman's conduct in the elections to the Central Legislature in November 1934, betraying the interests of the Congress; and (b) whether Patel was guilty of using his influence in preventing Nariman's election as leader of the Congress party in the Bombay Legislature in 1937. Bahadurji's verdict in regard to the first was that "the facts stated indicate entire absence of a desire on the part of Nariman to win the election for himself,[31] resulting from his indifference to the filing of his nomination papers which carried an address other than his own. This had disqualified him from being on the Assembly electoral rolls; and this had incurred the displeasure of Patel, who had the frankness to admit that to be the reason for his not extending support to Nariman in 1937. About the latter, the report revealed: "The question of electing the leader was first considered by and among Messrs. Deshpande, Deo and Patwardhan in, or about, the last week of February 1937. They appear then to have made up their mind that neither Nariman nor Munshi would be the right person. Their idea was that Sardar Vallabhbhai Patel should be the leader, and failing him, Kher should be elected... As Sardar Vallabhbhai persisted in his refusal, they suggested the name of Kher, and asked Sardar Vallabhbhai's opinion on the question."[32]

Bahadurji's verdict was: "Sardar Vallabhbhai made no attempt to influence the vote of anyone... the charge against Nariman in respect of the election of 1934 is proved and the charge made by Nariman against Sardar Vallabhbhai Patel is not proved."[33] In his concurring note, Gandhi said, "My analysis of the situation is that Nariman overestimated his hold on the legislators and felt the keenest disappointment over his defeat. His judgment became warped... His advisers and the newspaper propaganda kept up the illusion."[34] Like the earlier occasion, when he had accepted the decision of the Working Committee, this time too, Nariman, on being given by Gandhi the choice between the publication of the award and a frank statement by him accepting the findings, stated: "I have studied them (findings) carefully and must accept them as findings arrived at by judges who were judges of my choice, and whom I have the privilege of regarding as my friends... I am convinced that in the matter of the election of 1934, I neglected my duty as a responsible office-bearer of the Congress, and gave some of my friends cause to feel that my neglect amounted to a grave breach of trust. In the matter of the election of the leader of the Bombay Parliamentary Party in 1937, I am sorry to confess that I misjudged the general position, and on the strength of statements made by some of the legislators, I felt a grievance which I allowed my friends and a part of the Press to share with me. As a result, considerable bitterness was aroused, and Sardar Vallabhbhai Patel was even charged by a section of the Press with having acted through communal prejudice. I have publicly stated before, and I do so now, that this charge was entirely unfounded and whatever the Sardar did, or did not do, was from a sense of public duty. I am sorry that the agitation should have taken a personal aspect and even a communal aspect."[35]

With this admission, the curtain ought to have finally been pulled down on the controversy. But it wasn't. Nariman staged another somersault. He got a favourable verdict on the arbitrators' findings from Barrister Velinker. This was the last straw that broke the camel's back. The Congress Working Committee, at its meeting in Calcutta, concluded that Nariman's "conduct has been such as to prove him unworthy of holding any position of trust and responsibility in the Congress organisation."[36] In a fit of anger Nariman charged Gandhi, Nehru and Bahadurji with favouritism. Gandhi asked Patel to seek the opinion of Bhulabhai Desai or Motilal Setalvad, Bombay's foremost lawyers. Convinced of the justness of his case and knowing his strength within the party, Patel decided otherwise, allowing the controversy to die in silence. Ten years later, Nariman apologised to Patel; and the latter took him back into the Congress.

The Khare episode had graver implications. Nariman's was a party affair; in Khare's case, the British Governor of the Central Provinces, of which Khare was the Premier, exploited the opportunity to damage Congress prestige and power. Khare merely played into his hands. The episode originated in "a very serious error of judgment" on the part of Minister of Law and Justice Shareef in a case of rape of a thirteen-year-old Harijan girl by some people, including a Class I officer of the Education Department. Without consulting his Cabinet colleagues, Shareef directly recommended to the Governor their release on grounds of mercy. Patel called for Shareef's explanation, and asked the Congress Parliamentary Party to investigate the matter. Shareef regretted his action and offered to resign, but Khare offered him protection. Communal colour was lent to the matter with the Muslim League jumping into the fray by stating that the Congress Parliamentary Board had no right to interfere. An agitated public took the matter to the High Court, which confirmed the sentences of the accused. The issue did not end with this. A further inquiry was conducted by a retired judge of the Calcutta High Court, Manmatha Nath Mukherji, whose judgment went against Shareef.

This led to a crisis of confidence, which resulted in the surfacing of serious differences between Khare and some of his Cabinet colleagues from the Hindi part of the province. There were charges of bribery and corruption against some belonging to Khare's group. Three of the Ministers submitted their resignations. At this stage, Patel stepped into the dispute in order to heal the rupture. At a meeting at Panchmarhi on May 24, 1938, they withdrew their resignations. But Khare had something up his sleeve. This time, as planned, two Ministers siding with Khare, submitted their resignations to him. Khare had submitted a report to Patel on what he had done to implement the Panchmarhi settlement and had left the matter in Patel's hands. But he kept back information about the two resignations he had deliberately secured, obviously with the purpose of submitting them to the Governor along with his own, and, thereby, pave the way for the formation of a new Ministry, independently of the Congress.

Khare did not wait for the Working Committee meeting called for July 23rd. Nor did he keep the Parliamentary Board informed about his plans. On the 19th, Khare declared his intention to resign as Premier and asked his colleagues to hand over to him their resignations as well. The three Mahakoshal Ministers refused to do so unless instructed by the Parliamentary Board. Ignoring the latter, Khare submitted to the Governor his resignation and the two resignations he had already secured. The Governor lost no time in holding a meeting with the three Mahakoshal Ministers after midnight but failed in coaxing them to follow the others. On the morning of July 21st, the Governor accepted the resignations of Khare and his two colleagues, terminated the office of the other three recalcitrant Ministers and invited Khare to form a new Ministry, which he did at once and took the oath of office the same day. It was a plot engineered by Khare in league with the Governor.

The Parliamentary Board met on July 22nd and the Congress Working Committee the following day. Khare, along with his new and old colleagues, attended these meetings. After the matter had been gone through carefully, Khare was told that his conduct did not befit the high position that he held. Consultations among Khare and his colleagues took place in a closed room. On coming out, they informed the Parliamentary Board that they had committed an error, which they would set right by submitting their resignations. On the 23rd at Nagpur, they did so. The Congress Working Committee now took the matter in its hand. It advised Khare to call a meeting of the Congress Legislative Party to consider the resignations and elect a new one in Khare's place. Against the advice of the Congress President, Khare announced his intention to offer himself for re-election. He remained adamant. After he had met Gandhi, he gave the impression of having given up the idea. But he was dilly-dallying to gain time.

The Working Committee passed a resolution to the effect that "Dr. Khare was guilty of grave errors of judgment which have exposed the Congress in the Central Provinces to ridicule and lowered its prestige." Further, his action helped the Governor use his special powers for the first time since the assumption of office by the Congress. Khare was also declared guilty of indiscipline in accepting the Governor's invitation to form a new Ministry without reference to the Parliamentary Board; and, as a result, Khare had proved himself unworthy of holding any position of responsibility in the Congress organisation. The resolution, behind which was the iron hand of Patel, did not spare even the Governor. He was held guilty of forcing a crisis, as "he was anxious to weaken and discredit the Congress insofar as it lay in his power to do so."[37] He was accused of "unseemly haste" in not only accepting the resignations of the Ministers, but going so far as to have demanded the resignations of the recalcitrant Ministers as well; and, on their refusal to oblige him, dismissed them, and, thereby, helped Khare to form a new Ministry.

The Working Committee resolution sparked a bitter anti-Patel campaign by Khare and a section of the Marathi Press. In a public statement on August 5th, Patel corrected the "several gross mis-statements and serious allegations" made by Khare, "Dr. Khare's assertion that the Premiership of the Central Provinces was thrust on him is entirely untrue. From the very beginning, he was anxious to be elected leader of the Congress party in the C.P. and Berar Assembly and he first asked me and then Pandit Jawaharlal Nehru to help him in this respect by presiding over the party meeting convened to elect the leader of the party. Neither of us agreed to preside, as the President of the Mahakoshal Provincial Congress Committee had warned us of the situation. At that time he had enlisted D.P. Mishra's support for himself, exploiting the differences which then existed between Ravi Shankar Shukla and Mishra." Patel also disclosed that in the Shareef episode, Khare presented the Working Committee "with a *fait accompli*", and that he "went to the extent of threatening the Working Committee that he would resign if it went against his party's decision."[38]

A Nariman-type controversy raised its head. An anti-Congress campaign was whipped up, particularly in Maharashtra, against Patel by such critics of the Congress as Ambedkar, Munje and even Nariman, laying the accusation of naked fascism. Gandhi had to intervene by commenting that Khare "should have rushed not to the Governor but to the Working Committee and tendered his resignation." Khare "erred grievously in ignoring or, what is worse, not knowing this simple remedy." Gandhi declared Khare "not only guilty of gross indiscipline in flouting the warnings of the Parliamentary Board, but he betrayed incompetence as a leader by allowing himself to be fooled by the Governor, or not knowing that, by his precipitate action, he was compromising the Congress."[39] Gandhi was also highly critical of the Governor's role. He thought "the Governor betrayed a haste which I can only call indecent", and that his action "killed the spirit of the tacit compact between the British Government and the Congress."[40]

Supporting Patel's role, Gandhi expressed the view that "... the Congress must be in the nature of an army ...the Congress, conceived as a fighting machine, has to centralise control and guide every department and every Congressman, however highly placed, and expected unquestioned obedience. The fight cannot be fought on any other terms."[41] Such centralised control Gandhi had placed in Patel's hand, and it was Patel's responsibility to shepherd Congress Ministers and legislators. Such responsibility Patel could discharge only as an effective party boss, no matter who wore the annual President's crown. In his confrontation with Patel, Khare failed to elicit the support of even Subhas Bose, the then Congress President. Bose concurred with Gandhi and Patel that Khare had committed grave disciplinary offence, and thought the action taken against him was lenient. The Governor, despite the part he had played, was impressed by Patel's quiet, firm, judicious role. At the end of the political drama, he remarked that Patel had "added a few inches to his political stature."[42]

The third confrontation Patel had as party boss was with the fiery and radical Subhas Bose, whose popularity among the youth was next only to Nehru's. Nehru had nearly compromised his position with Gandhi and the Old Guard after the Lucknow and Faizpur Congress. But Bose had laid low. His re-election after Faizpur at Tripuri, in the wake of a great controversy, was conceded by Gandhi as a personal defeat. This emboldened Bose, who had thrown two challenges to the Old Guard so as to wrest party control. The first was a bogey raised to overwhelm Congressmen, especially those in the AICC, that the Old Guard was "contemplating to come to some kind of a settlement with the British Government in regard to the Federal scheme." The second was a serious attempt at reversal of the Congress policy of parliamentary programme, which had been initiated by Gandhi under Patel as Chairman of the Congress Parliamentary Board, by advocating resumption of civil disobedience on a mass scale. Prior to his election, at a meeting of the Bengal delegates to the Tripuri Congress held at Jalpaiguri, Bose had suggested a six-month notice to Britain, ignoring the assessment arrived at earlier by Nehru: "Civil disobedience was finally killed for all practical purposes by the suspension of it in May 1933... even without that suspension, it would have gradually petered out. India was numbed by the violence and harshness of repression. The nervous energy of the nation as a whole was for the moment exhausted, and it was not being re-charged."[43] Gandhi wanted to re-charge it through a parliamentary programme. Nehru being an opponent of such a programme and neutral insofar as Bose was concerned, Patel was Gandhi's choice for shouldering the onerous and most unpopular responsibility of implementing it.

It also meant a confrontation with the redoubtable Bose. Patel acquitted himself with rare boldness, tact and diplomacy.

Patel's first act was to dispel the confusion Bose was deliberately causing by stating, "We have not accepted office in order to carry out a few reforms. We accepted office with a view to moving towards a far greater objective—complete independence, which is the only remedy for all our ills. If by accepting office our ability to move towards that goal is increased, well and good. But if by accepting office we find that our final goal is jeopardised, we must immediately give up office."[44] The Congress hadn't hesitated in taking an uncompromising stand in Uttar Pradesh and Bihar, where the Governors refused to accept their Ministers' recommendation to release political prisoners. The conflict was resolved only when the Governors had relented. But Patel's boldness lay in catching the bull by the horns by objecting to Bose's re-election. In a joint statement with six of his Working Committee colleagues, Patel argued, "It is a sound policy to adhere to the rule of not re-electing the same President except under very exceptional circumstances... The Congress policy and programmes are not determined by its successive Presidents. If it were so, the constitution would not limit the office to one year... The position of the President is, therefore, that of a chairman. More than this, the President represents and symbolises, as under a constitutional monarchy, the unity and solidarity of the nation."[45] This circumscribed the status and powers of Bose as President.

Bose, however, stuck to his guns. With a view to maligning the Old Guard, he repeated his trump card, "It is widely believed that there may be a compromise on the Federal scheme between the Right Wing of the Congress and the British Government during the coming year. It is imperative in the circumstances to have as President one who will be an anti-Federationist to the core of his heart."[46] Patel was quick to nail the lie, "I can only say that I know of no member who wants the Federation of the Government of India Act. And after all, no single member, not even the President for the time being of the Congress, can decide on such big issues. It is the Congress alone that can decide... even the Working Committee has no power to depart from the letter and the spirit of the declared policy of the Congress. I wholly dissent from the view that the President of the Congress has any powers of initiating policies, save by consent of the Working Committee. More than once the Working Committee has asserted itself in the teeth of opposition of Presidents, who, be it said to their credit, have always bowed to the will of the Working Committee... the matter is not one of persons but of principles, not of Leftists and Rightists, but of what is in the best interest of the country."[47]

As a result of the bitter controversy whipped up by Bose, Nehru veered round to Patel's way of thinking, as he too felt that Subhas Babu should not stand for Presidentship. Yet Bose defeated Pattabhi Sitaramayya by 95 votes. In the *Harijan* of February 2, 1939, Gandhi confessed that "from the very beginning I was decidedly against his re-election... I do not subscribe to his facts or the arguments in his manifestoes. I think that his references to his colleagues were unjustified and unworthy. Nevertheless, I am glad of his victory. And since I was instrumental in inducing Dr. Pattabhi not to withdraw his name as a candidate when Maulana Saheb withdrew, the defeat is more mine than his." Gandhi went on to say that Bose, "instead of being President on the sufferance of those whom he calls Rightists, is now President elected in a contested election. This enables him to choose a homogeneous Cabinet and enforce his programme without let or hindrance." Gandhi, however, felt pained to observe that the Congress is fast becoming a corrupt organisation in the sense that its registers contain a very large number of bogus members", and feared that "the only thing that may possibly be affected by the changes is the parliamentary programme."[48]

Gandhi's statement had a magical effect on the minds of the Congress delegates to the Tripuri Congress. Most of them felt that, had Gandhi expressed himself earlier, Bose might not have been elected. To Patel, the situation appeared quite serious. Bose's was a challenge to Gandhi; more than that to Gandhism. He wanted to face it constitutionally as a party man. He was confident of success, as he carried the majority of the Working

Committee with him. As a first step, he felt that Bose should prepare resolutions for the coming Congress session at Tripuri in consultation with those who were in accord with him—primarily to bear responsibility for the decisions taken. It was also thought that Bose should be allowed a free hand in whatever he wanted to do. The Working Committee met at Wardha on February 9th. Bose could not attend owing to high fever. In his absence, thirteen members submitted their resignations, which the President-elect accepted on the 26th.

It was amidst such an acrimonious atmosphere that the Tripuri Congress was held. On arrival, Bose again took ill, and could not leave his bed. The Presidential procession was taken out with his portrait placed in a chariot drawn by 52 elephants symbolising the 52nd session of the party. Owing to the resignation of its thirteen members, the Working Committee could not meet. The session had two resolutions to consider: one by President Bose for the consideration of the AICC; the other by the resigned members of the Working Committee, which the Subjects Committee accepted by a big majority. Bose's resolution proposed an ultimatum to be given to the Government of civil disobedience to be started at the end of six months. The other resolution, proposed by Govind Ballabh Pant and supported by about 160 members of the AICC, was an effort to save Gandhi's face. It proposed that, in view of the controversies in connection with the Presidential election, "it is desirable that the AICC should clarify the position and declare its general policy. The committee declares its firm adherence to the fundamental policies of the Congress, which have governed its programme in the past years under the guidance of Mahatma Gandhi." The resolution further stated: "In view of the critical situation that may develop during the coming year, and in view of the fact that Mahatma Gandhi alone can lead the Congress and the country to victory during such a crisis, the committee regards it as imperative that the Congress Executive should command his implicit confidence and requests the President to nominate a Working Committee in accordance with the wishes of Gandhi."[49]

Gandhi's statement had already upset Bose's applecart by causing a rethinking among the members of the AICC. Now, Pant's resolution, on behalf of the Rightists, caused another dent in Bose's side. The wide support gained by the resolution became still wider, following news from Rajkot that Gandhi had ended his fast on a settlement reached with the Ruler. This set Gandhi's spirit hovering over Tripuri. Amidst such an atmosphere,an ailing Bose was brought to the meetings of the AICC and the Subjects Committee on a stretcher. A suggestion to refer Pant's resolution to the AICC, so as to save all the unpleasantness in the open session, was resisted with force by Bose's supporters, leading to complete pandemonium, "paralyzing all proceedings for well nigh an hour"; it was "one that had not been witnessed since Surat (1907) or even at Surat."[50] An appeal from his brother, Sarat Bose, restored order. Pant's resolution was withdrawn, and the session was postponed. With a view to avoiding repetition of such unseemly scenes, the following day's proceedings were held by keeping visitors out. There was still an abortive attempt to cause disturbance. Finally, however, Patel's resolution was passed.

Subhas Bose felt particularly "angry and bitter against Sardar". The new situation had created many challenges for him. First, was he to submit to Gandhi in the selection of his new Working Committee? Second, how was he to face the prospect of the power of the President being cut and that of Patel as Chairman of the Parliamentary Board strengthened, with the principle laid down in an AICC resolution in June 1938? The resolution stated that "in administrative matters, the Provincial Congress Committee should not interfere with the discretion of the Ministry, but it is always open to the Executive of the PCC to draw the attention of the Government privately to any particular abuse or difficulty. In matters of policy, if there is a difference between the Ministry and the PCC, reference should be made to the Parliamentary Board."[51] Third, Gandhi's Congress had categorically rejected Bose's policy of hastening the fight with the Government and coming "to grips with the British straightaway."

From Tripuri, Bose went to a place near Jharia to recoup his shattered health. For nearly a month he did not appoint a new Working Committee. And when he convened a meeting of the AICC in Calcutta for the purpose, rowdy scenes dominated it. Many a time physical conflicts marred the proceedings. In order to avoid any wrong impression being created, Patel had not gone to Calcutta. Since the deadlock could not be resolved in his favour, Bose thought it fit to submit his resignation from the Presidentship of the Congress. His place was taken over by Rajendra Prasad, a protégé of Patel. At the Tripuri session, in M.N. Roy's apt description, the Sardar sat on the dais, a figure of granite, confident of strangling the ambitious upstart. The picture was reminiscent of that of Stalin when the latter walked up and down in the background of the platform, smoking his pipe with a grim but cynical smile."[52] The occasion was the wresting of power by Stalin. But Patel had none of Stalin's cunning, nor did he have his diabolical game of capturing absolute power.

M.N. Roy also thought that "in 1938, Subhas Bose could have made history, for good or evil. His weakness plus the Sardar's iron will frustrated his ambition and saved the Gandhian Congress."[53] In Sarat Bose's view, Patel was "the shining light" of the ruling coterie.[54] And even a defeated Subhas Bose acknowledged that "the Gandhian Wing had this tactical advantage that it was the only organised party within the Congress, acting under a centralised leadership."[55] Such leadership was centralised in Patel as Chairman of the Congress Parliamentary Board—a position more or less analogous to the General Secretary of the Communist Party in the Soviet Union. He enjoyed the power to watch and guide the Congress Ministers, to pull up defaulting partymen, to smother revolts even by stalwarts, and thereby discipline the vast array of Congressmen in a country of the size of a sub-continent. Patel's muscle power was complementary to Gandhi's soul force. Had Patel not used, judiciously, democratically and promptly, his "muscle power" to protect Gandhi and the Gandhiites, the Congress, ripped by internal discord and disunity, could have gone the way of the All-India Trade Union Congress, which had slipped out of Congress hands into those of the Communists, and who were manoeuvring under the directions of the Communist International.

17

The God that Failed

The Second World War, which broke out on September 3, 1939, caused serious differences within the Congress party. Congress leaders clashed over whether or not to cooperate in the war effort. Anti-Fascist Nehru, with sympathies for the Allied cause, preferred "a contingent fight" for freedom against the British in India—contingent upon failure to secure a negotiated settlement. Anti-Imperialist Subhas Bose favoured "an immediate fight". Opposed to Nehru and Bose was Gandhi, who ingeniously offered the British moral support under the policy of non-embarrassment, in the belief that by allowing the Congress Ministries to remain in office, he would be able "to manoeuvre a declaration of *Pooran Swaraj* or Dominion Status". Patel wavered between his loyalty to Gandhi and the realities of the newly emerging situation.

There were, as a consequence, two serious developments within the Congress: first, a gradual decline from then onwards in Gandhi's hold over the party; and, second, the drifting away of Patel from Gandhi, and Gandhi's losing his strongest support both within the party and in his satyagrahas. The first indication of such a drift was when Patel expressed himself in a public speech in Bombay on October 26, 1939, "Gandhi says when the enemy is stuck deep in difficulties, we should cooperate with him. But we ask, what about the enemy who will later strangle our throats? In the 1914 war, Rs. 100 crores were voted by India through a resolution of the Legislative Assembly. On termination of the war, we got Jallianwala Bagh... We, therefore, ask them: 'What are your war aims?' They say, why do you ask that when we are in difficulties. We thought, in their difficulties they will speak the truth. But they say, 'We do not know why we are fighting.' ... They frighten us by saying: 'If we go away, do you know who will follow us?' We say, 'Yes. Perhaps, the Germans and Hitler. If you (the British) say their shackles will be of iron while yours are of silver, even then we feel yours are heavier! You may be better than them; but if you are going to throttle us later, let both of you get destroyed, and we shall take care of what happens to us thereafter." Patel characterised the Secretary of State's declaration through the Viceroy as "full of arrogance" and likened it, for the appreciation of his Indian listeners, to that of Ravana, and went on to observe, "They think if India doesn't offer cooperation, they can force her. Let me forewarn them that the days of 1914-17 are gone. In Europe, they shall be engaged in the war, in India they shall have to impose army rule. If you need help, seek Gandhi's blessings."[1]

Soon after on November 5th, at Ahmedabad, Patel told the Gujarat Provincial Congress Committee, "The war is between two powers—the one led by Germany is Nazism, the other by the Imperialism of France and Britain. India has been dragged into it without her consent. Had she been independent, she would have taken a decision like America." (aloofness). In his view, "India has nothing to choose between British Imperialism and German Nazism. If these powers are fighting to strengthen the foundations of their empires and thereby give some permanence to India's slavery, there is then no basis for us to side with either." He ridiculed the Secretary of State's plea that "at a time when life is sticking in my throat, don't raise such difficult issues" with the terse remark, "He has uttered the truth. But when they are not in difficulties and we raise the issue, they simply frown upon us." Declaring that "this war is going to be long drawn-out", Patel observed, "all the curtains of this drama haven't yet been raised.

We do not know what is behind the Russo-German pact. Until the facts come to light, we need not rush to launch a fight against the Government. The Congress should take each step after full consideration... Don't be in a hurry for a fight. In any decision, we should be guided by our experience of the past satyagraha... In India, no one can launch a struggle by keeping Gandhi aloof."[2] The drift on Patel's part, unlike that of Nehru, was not ideological. Patel could not yet accept completely dissociating himself from Gandhi politically.

The following day, Patel struck a more realistic note in a public speech, "Our sympathies are with Britain. But she would desire to maintain her empire, whereas we wish destruction of Imperialism in the same way as of Nazism." He recalled, "Four days after India had been dragged into the war, the Viceroy addressed the Legislative Assembly in the absence of Congress members. He did not even mention their absence. Nor did he refer to Gandhi's offer of unconditional cooperation. I call this political craftiness of the British! Later, the Viceroy called senior Congress leaders for talks; and the Muslim Leaguers too. Up to that it seemed all right. But thereafter he invited anyone who put up a demand, no matter if he were an oil dealer, a betel-seller or a cobbler! He created a Round Table Conference atmosphere. His published speech revealed that, no matter what happened to the world, British Imperialism cannot change its colours. It was then that the Congress proposed that the war shouldn't be used as an excuse for not spelling out the war aims." Ridiculing the British claim that "India was their sacred Trust", Patel bluntly asked, "Who gave this Trust to you? ... Robert Clive and men like him? In reply, the Congress says that it has the Trust of the Indian people." The Viceroy, Patel added, says "the Hindus and the Muslims are not one. But why should you meddle between them? The Viceroy says he would continue with his efforts towards unity. But such efforts on his part would be absurdly impossible. The Congress, therefore, wishes to prepare an atmosphere similar to the one at the time of the Dandi March, which had instantly set the whole of India aflame."[3]

On November 8th, Patel further clarified himself at the

Working Committee meeting held at Ahmedabad, "India's situation is different from that of other countries. If just two bombs were dropped on Bombay Harbour, we haven't got even crackers to fire in reply! In India we have only paper tigers. If we were invaded like Poland, all will be over in an hour and a half."[4] Patel believed that if the British were to give India her freedom, the Congress would offer full support in the war. He, therefore, advocated not only the training of young men in warfare, but also Indianisation of the Army, which the Congress Parliamentary Party had repeatedly asked for. Such an approach was anti-Gandhian, but pro-Nehru. Further, even when he was, on Gandhi's admission, his strongest pillar, Patel's basic character wasn't the same as Nehru's: it was diametrically opposite, though it had been moulded in line with Gandhi's. He had said of himself in 1938 during the Rajkot satyagraha, "I am a fighter by instinct and vocation; and I love fighting."[5] Yet, he seemed to be in agreement with Gandhi insofar as the continuance of the Congress Ministries was concerned. This was typical of him as the party boss and as an administrator, who saw obvious political gains in holding on to power. Linlithgow's thinking tallied with Patel's. He had written to the King that "Jinnah had become alarmed by the defection of a growing number of Muslims from the Muslim League to the Congress", because the Ministers could "help their friends" and "inconvenience their opponents."[6] Such defections, however probable, could not have taken place because of the Congress giving up power in the provinces. The Editor of *The Hindu*, K. Srinivasan, at his meeting with Linlithgow early in February (1940), "blamed Nehru for 'the dreadful blunder' of withdrawing the provincial Ministers from office."[7]

The withdrawal was a triumph for the Congress Left—a triumph which had serious political repercussions. It threw the Congress into the wilderness and gave Jinnah absolute freedom to play a game that strengthened his position with the British and helped him, in the end, get Pakistan. The inappropriateness of the resignations lay in their being most inopportune and untimely, especially when Linlithgow had formed a favourable opinion of the Congress leaders and the Congress as a party. He considered the latter to be "the only one worthy of the name, and certainly the only one possessing an active and widespread organisation in the constituencies."[8] It was an achievement due to Patel's effective Chairmanship of the Congress Parliamentary Board. In Patel, Linlithgow had found "a sense of humour, a shrewd and active brain and a strong personality... Patel clearly saw the point about avoiding speculative hypothesis as a basis of argument."[9]

Congress failure to evolve the right political strategy in the non-Congress Muslim majority provinces was equally ominous, even when prospects for the Congress seemed favourable. The Muslim League had failed to form a League Ministry in any one of them; and, more importantly, the Muslim Premiers had refused to accept Jinnah's ideology and his leadership. Jinnah had no representative character then, and even later, in the provinces which were to form his Pakistan in 1947. The political scene being so dismal for Jinnah, the Congress could have clinched a political deal with the Premiers of Punjab, Bengal and Sind, and thereby buried Jinnah's future Pakistan in 1937 itself, rather than allowing him to trot ominously on the political horizon and pose a threat a decade later. Punjab had a Hindu-Muslim-Sikh coalition in the Unionist Party under Sikander Hyat Khan; in Bengal, it was the Krishak Proja Party under Fazlul Huq, then a nationalist Muslim; and in Sind, an uncommitted Ghulam Hussain Hidayatullah, had formed a Hindu-Muslim coalition independent of the Muslim League. None owed allegiance to Jinnah. Fazlul Huq had, in fact, made "earnest efforts to form a Ministry in cooperation with the Congress",[10] and in December 1941, in a Cabinet reshuffle, he got rid of some of the League Ministers. More than the Congress leaders, Sikander Hayat Khan realised the dangerous communal implications of Pakistan. As early as 1938, he had prophetically told Penderel Moon, "Pakistan would be an invitation to the Muslims to cut the throat of every Hindu bania... Pakistan would mean a massacre."[11]

Congress failure in strategy, in the Congress and non-Congress provinces, was the outcome of its high-minded, airy-fairy, ivory-tower outlook, its lack of party homogeneity and its ideological cobwebs as represented by the Congress Left under Nehru. The party had adopted four attitudes with devastating consequences: First, its non-concern towards the provincial Governments in Punjab, Bengal and Sind. Second, its overconcern with the Centre, which suited Jinnah most as a centralist who had no base even in the Muslim-dominated provinces; and it was at the Centre that the British could help Jinnah build himself as a counterpoise to the Congress on an all-India basis. Third, the Congress aloofness from the Viceroy and the British Civil Servants, without appreciating that it were they who would hand over power to India ultimately. And, fourth, its undue, out of proportion concern with the overthrow of the 1935 Constitution and severance of the British connection. On the transference of power in 1947, not only did the Congress adopt the same Constitution, but even agreed to the continuance of its membership of the Commonwealth. In 1937, however, Nehru, as Congress President, was hostile towards provincial autonomy, the creation of a Federation and the Viceroy himself. This earned the Congress distrust of the British as much as of the Princes. Nehru's favouring agitation in the States, contrary to a Gandhi-Patel policy, antagonised the Princes and drove them away from the Federal idea. It seemed not to have been appreciated that only a Federation, no matter on what basis, could have preserved India's unity.

More than the external factors, the Congress suffered from an internal malaise. Nehru had compromised with Gandhi at the time of becoming Congress President. But he reasserted his ideological beliefs not before long in two respects: first, in forcing the resignation of the Congress Ministries; secondly, in confronting Gandhi over the issue of Congress support to Britain in the war. Besides Azad and Rajagopalachari, he had won over Patel to his side, which really mattered because of the latter's hold over the party. Patel said in a speech on July 18, 1940, "Gandhi says that if the Congress, which has followed the path of non-violence for the past twenty years, were to give it up, it would land itself in difficulties. We are, however, placed differently... India's internal condition is such that we do not have the strength to face external danger through non-violence." He argued further, "Since assuming power in the provinces, we had to resort to violence to some extent... We do not have the far-sightedness of Gandhi; but we cannot go as far as Gandhi can. And we do not wish to be a burden to him, nor a hindrance." Patel conceded that, in consideration of Gandhi's universal love, his offer of unconditional help to Britain was the right thing in principle, but expressed the blunt truth, "If I were to follow such a principle, then I ought to be become a *sadhu*. I cannot persuade my family members to adopt it. Except for Gandhi, none in the Congress has been able to do that. That's why it is universally impracticable."[12]

Addressing the Gujarat Provincial Congress Committee at Ahmedabad on July 19th, Patel referred to Gandhi's article in which he had expressed the hope that "the Sardar would definitely return to him", and replied, "I have told Gandhi that if you order me to follow you, I, who am so much devoted to you, will do so blindfolded. But he says that it is not for him to say that, and I should follow the path I consider right." Patel said, "How can I be untrue to him, and play him false?" Patel didn't mince words in saying, "In the prevailing situation, it is not possible for the Congress to adopt total non-violence. This is beyond our capacity. In assessing the capacity of the country, Gandhi and we differ. Such a matter cannot be left to an individual. We have to carry the party and the country with us. It is beyond my comprehension as to how we can meet the challenge of those committing atrocities on society without the use of violence."[13] As regards the future, Patel pointed out, "We have also to decide whether, on gaining freedom and authority, we can run the country without the army. If we say that as soon as we get power, we shall disperse the army, we shall be never given authority." He, however, assured Gandhi that "if temporarily non-violence has to be given up in the larger context, it does not mean that the Congress workers will have to give up their pledge of non-violence in their conduct of the freedom struggle."[14]

The resignation of the Congress Ministries was "as unexpected as it appeared to many, uncalled for." Whether or not Patel subscribed to Nehru's way of thinking is not known; nor was he in any way responsible for the Congress policy towards the Allied war, even when he had moved away from Gandhi. As a disciplined Congressman, he adhered to the majority view in the Congress Working Committee, which was at that time dominated by Nehru, especially in regard to the decision to resign from the Ministries; and "once the step was taken, the whole future hung thereon, and the situation created by this momentous step opened out, before even Gandhi's vision, a yawning gulf."[15] Gandhi found himself "out of tune with the Working Committee."[16]

By mid-1940 Germany had overrun Denmark, Norway, the Netherlands and Belgium, and Paris fell to the Nazis without struggle. Nehru thought the Congress could no longer remain passive. The Working Committee met at Delhi on July 3rd and passed a resolution demanding complete independence and establishment of a provisional National Government as "a prerequisite to the Congress throwing full weight in the efforts for the effective organisation of the defence of the country."[17] The resolution was ratified by the AICC at Pune on July 7th, whereupon Gandhi issued a statement in self-defence. The framer of the Delhi resolution was Rajagopalachari; and Gandhi betrayed a sense of defeat and dismay when he said, "His persistency, courage and utter humility brought him converts. Sardar Patel was his greatest prize."[18] In his hour of defeat, Gandhi could not overlook the fact that in all his satyagrahas, Patel's contribution had been most vital; and that they were parting company for the first time. He wrote in the *Harijan* how people found it to be a difficult choice whether to follow him or Patel; and advised them, as he did to Nityanand Kanungo, "to follow the Sardar so that they can come back to him when the Sardar returned."[19]

Gandhi was fighting against his lieutenants. In order to disclaim his responsibility, he asserted that if Nehru were to have his way; he "should bear the responsibility for the negotiations and to that end, he should be made the President", so that he could "take the reins in his hands."[20] Since this was beyond the competence of the Working Committee, the constitutional hurdle was circumvented by constituting a War Sub-Committee with Nehru as its President, and Patel and Azad as its two members. At a time when the Congress had offered support between "a free India and a free Britain", the Viceroy's August 8th statement not only proved disappointing but it created a new hurdle. It came in "all too suddenly"; for, in his January speech at the Orient Club in Calcutta, the Viceroy had built hopes by talking of Dominion Status within the Westminster Statute. Now in his August offer he spoke of "a free and equal partnership" in the proposed expansion of the Governor-General's Executive Council and the establishment of a War Advisory Council; but he attempted to satisfy the British Government's "inability to transfer government to any system whose authority was directly denied by large and powerful elements."[21]

The August offer hardened the attitude of the minority groups, especially the Muslim League. This blocked the way to the formation of a National Government. Some still hoped that a way might be found to reach a settlement, and tentatively arranged a meeting between Linlithgow and Patel in Bombay, where the former had gone on a visit. According to Kanji Dwarkadas, an invitation to Patel was about to be issued on behalf of the Viceroy, but was withheld by his Private Secretary, Gilbert Laithwaite, in view of Azad's refusal to the Viceroy's invitation to him as Congress President. Azad had stated that "he saw no basis for a settlement in the August 8th proposals." He regretted that "he did not think it necessary to come all the way to Bombay to have any further talks with the Viceroy." Laithwaite felt that "as the Congress President had refused to meet the Viceroy, it would not be fair to ask the Sardar to meet the Viceroy as that would lower the Viceroy's prestige." In Kanji Dwarkadas's assessment, "Vallabhbhai was disappointed. What a great opportunity was thus lost for a settlement, which foundered on the rocks of pride, prestige and suspicion!"[22] Gandhi and Patel were "not happy over the Maulana's reply to the invitation of the Viceroy and thought he should have explored further by seeing him... Gandhi further felt that the door must be kept open and room should be left for the standpoint of his colleagues."[23] A meeting between Linlithgow and Patel could have borne some fruit in view of the Viceroy's opinion of Patel, and Patel's assurance to the Viceroy on the fall of Paris that the Congress would support Britain in the war if she gave India Dominion Status.

A bewildered Congress, losing all its enthusiasm, returned to its old position. A disheartened Patel publicly stated on September 8th, "Now, at Bombay, we shall return to Gandhi's leadership of the Congress, and we shall do whatever he says. We shall patiently watch, no matter if they form a provisional Government... Let them have Jinnah and Savarkar together in it. We shall see from outside what the cat and the mouse do inside."[24] In a hard-hitting speech, Patel said, "Our patience has exhausted. The British Government has begun to show itself in its true colours. It has begun to create divisions amongst us. Let the British Government do what it wants, but the nationalism that has developed in the country cannot be smothered in this manner." Ridiculing the British assertion as to "what will happen to us if they leave the country", Patel bluntly observed, "Surely, this is a strange question. It is as if a watchman were to say to his employer, 'what will happen to you if I were to leave you?' The answer will be, 'You go your way. Either we shall engage another watchman, or we will learn to keep watch ourselves.' But this watchman of ours not only doesn't go away, but keeps on threatening his employer!"[25]

Gandhi was once again the generalissimo of the Congress. He launched the individual satyagraha on October 17th. The first to offer satyagraha was Vinoba Bhave. The second was Nehru, who was arrested prior to the day on which he was to offer himself for satyagraha. The next to be arrested was Patel on November 17th. By the end of the month, most of the erstwhile Ministers and Parliamentary Secretaries, as also members of the AICC, were in jail. The individual satyagraha produced no results; and Gandhi reached no end. He was faced with a dilemma. Should he replace the current individual satyagraha with the mass civil disobedience the radicals were demanding? His mind was torn with conflict. He was apprehensive of violence breaking out. Once mass civil disobedience was declared, Gandhi confessed, they could not stop it; if stopped, the people would be crushed. Gandhi also sensed that there was no atmosphere for it. He was in a fix. As an alternative, he thought of a fast. This too was found not practicable. Finally, he had to call off the individual satyagraha, as many second-rankers in his "army" brought shame to him and the party by defaulting. The year 1941 rolled on without a perceptible change in the situation.

Gandhi called off the second phase of the individual satyagraha in June 1941. Gandhi faced a mini revolt in the party. Rajagopalachari was already openly critical of Gandhi. He was joined by Nehru and Azad on their release. Patel remained with the master. At the Working Committee meeting held at Bardoli on December 23, 1941, Gandhi was relieved of "the responsibility laid upon him by the Bombay resolution." Instructions issued by the committee to Congressmen read: "Recent developments in the world situation have brought the war near to India's frontiers. This may lead to internal dislocation in certain parts of the country. There is a possibility of some cities being subjected to aerial attack."[26] Patel, along with Rajendra Prasad, Kripalani and P.C. Ghosh, declared their intention of exercising independent judgment at the next AICC meeting.

Gandhi made his position clear in his advice to the Gujarat members of the AICC at Ahmedabad, "Rajaji thinks that all of us should go to war fully armed, but it may not be the opinion of all... I do not want to send workers to jail nowadays, when their services can be better availed of in allaying panic." Gandhi's greatest support now was Patel, who presided over the meeting and said in favour of Gandhi, "More critical times await us. Our responsibilities will increase, and at that time we cannot look to the Government; for they are engrossed in their own responsibilities. We shall have to decide for ourselves."[27] At the AICC meeting, Nehru was bitterly critical of Gandhi. When the

AICC met at Allahabad in April-May 1942, not only was the party suffering from internal dissensions on ideological grounds, but the war had cast its ominous shadows over eastern and southern India. There was "symbolic" bombardment of Kakinada and Visakhapatnam, leading to some evacuation in Madras and some other places on the East Coast of India. There was also the sighting of Japanese ships in the Bay of Bengal. On that, at Allahabad, Rajagopalachari moved a resolution which was defeated by a majority of 120 to 15.

The defeat was due to the stand Patel took. About this, Gandhi had made sure earlier. Lest he lost Patel for the second time, Gandhi wrote to him on April 14th, prior to the latter's proceeding to Allahabad, in a tone which was more of a command than anything else: "If the Congress adopts the policy of violence, in my opinion, you must leave it. This is not the time to suppress one's views… It matters little if people spurns you, or praise you to the skies. I would like you to read carefully whatever I am writing in the *Harijan* on the subject." To make himself doubly sure, Gandhi wrote to Patel again prior to the meeting on April 22nd: "…stand firmly by your views. It is your duty to leave the Congress if it does not accept clearly the policy of non-violent non-cooperation. There must be the strongest opposition to any proposal to bring troops from outside or to destroy everything in territories likely to be invaded."[28]

At Allahabad, Nehru could not have his way. He suffered defeat at the hands of Patel. Gandhi's modified draft, moved by Rajendra Prasad, was accepted by the Working Committee. This helped Gandhi regain the command of the party, largely due to Patel's vigorous lead to the Old Guard. His speech was most hard-hitting, not sparing either Nehru or Rajagopalachari: the former in regard to Cripps, the latter in regard to Jinnah. Patel told the members, "There are two distinct opinions in the committee. Ever since the outbreak of the war, we have tried to pull together. But it may not be possible on this occasion. Gandhi has taken a definite stand. If his background is unsuitable to some members of the committee, there is the other background which is unsuitable to us." In a rebuttal to Nehru, Patel called Cripps "a clever fellow" who had "gone about saying that his Mission has not been a failure. The draft is a perfect reply to his propaganda." Patel told Rajagopalachari, "I am not in favour of making any approach to Jinnah. We have made repeated attempts and courted many insults. The Congress today is reeling under two blows: one, Cripps's; and the other, Rajaji's resolutions, which have done enormous harm. I have placed myself in the hands of Gandhi. I feel that he is instinctively right in the lead he gives in all critical situations... It is time the door (to negotiations) is finally closed after the repeated insults heaped upon us."[29]

At Allahabad, for the first time since the outbreak of the war, Patel strongly asserted his loyalty to Gandhi. This had a sobering effect on the voting. Nehru could not reconcile himself to Gandhi's draft, even when it was modified to accommodate him. Both the drafts—Gandhi's and Nehru's—were put to the vote. Nehru's was defeated by 6 to 11 votes. Even Socialist members Narendra Dave and Achyut Patwardhan could not see eye to eye with Nehru and voted against his draft. The Allahabad meeting, thus, served as a prelude to the Working Committee meeting at Wardha, when Gandhi was reinstalled as the Supreme Commander. In this achievement of Gandhi, Patel's support was most crucial. In regard to withdrawal of British rule from India, the committee made it clear that "the Congress has no desire whatsoever to embarrass Great Britain or the Allied Powers in their prosecution of the war... Nor does the Congress intend to jeopardise the defensive capacity of the Allied Powers. The Congress is, therefore, agreeable to the stationing of the armed forces of the Allies in India, should they so desire, in order to ward off and resist Japanese or other aggression."[30]

Patel once again became an outspoken mouthpiece of Gandhi, as also his main backbone in the party. As a disciplinarian he could not shut his eyes on Rajagopalachari, who had turned anti-Congress and who had anti-party plans up his sleeve after Allahabad. Soon he came out in the open with defiance of the Congress High Command, when he got the Madras Legislature to pass two resolutions: the first supported the creation of Pakistan; the other aimed at "reforming" the Congress Ministry in Madras even when it was out of office. The first meant open rebellion; the second would have undermined the authority of the Congress Parliamentary Board—and the Congress as a party—by creating an autonomous legislature in Madras. Patel saw the Khare episode repeating itself. He had to curb such gross indiscipline on the part of Rajagopalachari, even through he was Gandhi's close relation and a senior Congress leader. He acted with speed to nip the evil while it was still budding. As Chairman of the Parliamentary Board, Patel secured Rajagopalachari's resignation by July 15th, both from membership of the Madras Legislative Assembly and the primary membership of the Congress. Patel was prompted by two considerations: to discharge his duty as Chairman of the Board; and to safeguard Gandhi's position by killing opposition to the Mahatma. His action had the hallmark of an administrator's capacity to act with speed before events could overtake him, and, no less, his integrity in placing the party above personal relationship. Patel handled Rajagopalachari with the same yardstick as he had others earlier on three occasions: Bose, Khare and Nariman.

Simultaneously with the tightening of party discipline, Patel raised his strong voice in support of Gandhi at public meetings. Towards the end of July, he spoke at Ahmedabad, "The Cripps Mission was a bad coin. Its makers had evil designs. It smelt of untruthfulness and betrayal. At the time of leaving India, Cripps went back on his promises and blamed the Congress for his failure. It was then that the Congress decided to act. The Mission's scheme was intended to convert American opinion in Britain's favour."[31] Earlier Patel had condemned the Cripps offer for its other design—the conceding of Pakistan. He regretfully observed, "We parted company with Gandhi (at Pune) to ask people to join the armed forces, provided a National Government were set up in India. We could secure people's support only if we could make them feel that the country belonged to them. There was no response to our offer. The Congress then realised that the Government, by showing such disregard, did not value our offer; and (that) if the Congress remained silent, its very existence might be jeopardised."[32]

Patel bluntly stated, "Everyone realises that India is likely to be invaded. But the country is filled with so much hatred towards the British that ninety-nine and three quarters of the population say that it is better if this demon leaves us, no matter if another one follows him. People feel elated when they hear of German or Japanese victories... We have praise for the bravery with which Russia is fighting. It is so because the people there are fighting for the preservation of their freedom. But what have the Indians to fight for? Where is our freedom? That is why Gandhi says: 'Leave India'." Patel ridiculed Britain's assertion that she "shall get back Burma" with the remarks, "Why didn't the Burmese side with them? Indians wish to know, why did they flee from Burma when there were no (communal) hurdles? Can they give us a guarantee that the Indians will not meet with the same fate as did the Burmese? However, from there they came away in a cowardly manner, allowing the people to be crushed... They say: 'It is our responsibility—rather duty—to defend India'. We have no faith in such an assertion. What responsibility did they show towards defending Burma? They only claim that in the end victory will be theirs! But when will that happen? We have our doubts about it." Patel further said: "Some people tell us, 'it is the people's war'. Which people? Russia and China can say so. But how can India when it wasn't her people's war?" He mentioned that until recently the Communist party was illegal. But now the Communists had been released so that they could fight the Congress.

Explaining further the Congress position, Patel said, "In Wardha, the Working Committee had decided that we can face an attack only after we have gained independence. Radio Japan daily cries hoarse: 'We do not wish to capture even an inch of Indian territory. We are fighting to drive the British out.' Some of our people have joined hands with the Japanese. They claim this to be a matter of pride. Subhas Babu is also there (in Japan).

But we have not to believe Radio Japan. Nor should we rely upon Moscow to free us. The Congress has, therefore, decided not to look to anyone for help. The British must understand this, and leave the country for good. But they will not... We must free ourselves before the Japanese invasion."[33] Referring to Gandhi's coming fight, Patel said, "It will be a sum total of all the movements conducted since the Rowlatt Act of 1919. It will aim at pulling down the Government machinery through stoppage of the railways, closing down of posts and telegraph, giving up of Government jobs and closure of schools and colleges. Such, indeed, will be the struggle."[34]

As "Quit India" drew nearer, Patel's speeches grew stronger and sharper in tone. On August 2nd, he asked a huge gathering on Bombay's Chowpatty sands, "to break the chains of slavery" under Gandhi's 'Do or die' call. "Cripps", he said, "is telling the Americans that the Congress resolution is an invitation to Japan and Germany; and, therefore, the Americans should help British in crushing India. If Britain is seeking America's help, India seeks God's. How strange, a fully armed people should be asking for America's help in suppressing forty crore unarmed Indians!" Calling the British rule as "the blackest period of Indian history", Patel stated, "India is being made a war zone. If we do not fight now, then someone else might replace the British who have been here for the past 200 years... We must fight to ensure that we do not suffer the fate of Burma and Malaya."[35]

And thus India moved towards her fateful day in history—the 9th of August. On the midnight of the 7th, Patel, seconding the "Quit India" resolution—"Go away British"—moved by Nehru at the Working Committee meeting, made a forceful speech in which he said, "We have waited for three years. Gandhi said, let us not embarrass Britain in the midst of her difficulties... Now his patience has exhausted; and the war is knocking at India's door." He explained, "Our struggle is to save India from falling into the hands of the Japanese. Who would believe the British? How many times have they talked of India's safety and defence! When they were getting a beating in Malaya, they said, 'Let them come to

Singapore! We shall settle scores with them there'. Singapore was claimed to be an impregnable fort. Armery had said time and again that under any circumstances Singapore will be defended. But such a fort fell like a house of cards!... Now even Burma has gone in the twinkling of an eye, and the enemy forces are on India's frontier." Patel, therefore, asked, "If the British were to suffer similar defeats, what will happen to us (in India)? Are we to continue as slaves? To avoid such a fate, we have to free ourselves and stand on our own."

Continuing in a sarcastic tone, he said, "They hold out the promise of giving us freedom at the end of the war. But how are we to believe them? Who knows whether they would be there to do that! Or, whether they would have by then the power to give us freedom. If at the end of the war we are in the hands of another power, how would Britain give us freedom? At that time where shall we be looking for Churchill?... Cripps had raised hopes, but proved a great disappointment. His proposals meant that even if we become independent, India will have many partitions and foreign troops will remain in the country... A Socialist Cripps has today turned into an Imperialist." Patel referred to the Atlantic Charter and said, "Someone asked Churchill: 'Where is India's place in that?' He replied: 'There can be no place for India in it, as the Charter is for Europe only. The Indian issue is one of domestic concern.' Whom should the British hand over power? In the British Parliament a question was raised in regard to a statement by me. Someone said: 'Patel says, the Congress does not want power. Give it to anyone—but to Indians.' I say, you hand over power even to dacoits, but go away. We shall thereafter settle amongst ourselves. But hand it over to the Indians. Leave this country. Otherwise, we shall have to fight you. You claim you have given India peace. But the truth is that you have turned India into a graveyard."

Regarding the Congress plan of action, Patel said, "We shall obey Gandhi and do as soldiers do... If the Government arrests Gandhi... then it becomes the duty of every Indian to secure the country's freedom through whatever means... The fight has to be short and swift... Before the arrival of the Japanese, we must become independent and be prepared to fight them... As long as Gandhi is there, he is our Commander-in-Chief. On his arrest, everyone will be free to act on his own, and the responsibility for this will be of the British. Even for lawlessness, they shall be responsible. The nation cannot withhold itself for fear of lawlessness. No other way is open to us. We must be independent, Slavery cannot be tolerated any more."[36]

The 9th of August dawned with a gloom cast over Bombay. It spread in no time over the rest of the country. In many a city, town and village people seethed with anger over the manner in which Gandhi and other leaders had been arrested in a single swoop, early that morning before the city rose to life. Violence broke out in many parts of India. Not willing to wait till Gandhi had had his proposed meeting with the Viceroy, the Government had struck a pre-dawn blow, so as to make the Congress reel under its impact. When the British Indian Police officer, C.W.E. U'ren, arrived at Patel's residence, he got ready in no time to accompany him. Where was he being taken? He was not told. Nor did he bother to know. Maniben, his daughter, asked him whether the detention documents were in order. "Mainly, I think, to pacify her," writes U'ren, "the Sardar... having scanned them rapidly, nodded his head. He was most dignified throughout, and his example to the other two (Maniben and Kripalani) made my task a comparatively simple one."[37] Before it was broad daylight, Patel, Nehru, Azad and other members of the Working Committee had been brought to Victoria Terminus, where a special train awaited to take them to Ahmednagar Fort near Pune to spend the next three years of their captivity there.

Life in Ahmednagar Fort was peaceful. It was free from the day-to-day anxieties of a hectic public life. It was, on the other hand, a happy community life. They were a group of twelve top Congressmen, brilliant in so many diverse ways, who "spent nearly a thousand days counting the hours of the day, the days of the week, the weeks of the month and the months of the year... together in a building, eating at a common table, chatting, playing, joking and very rarely quarrelling... Here were men from 42 to 68, bachelors and married men, men with no children and men with several, a few also who lost their wives and remained widowers." Sitaramayya, a member of the group, further records: "Maulana (Azad) by position (as Congress President) is the foremost citizen of the abode, Vallabhbhai the most wise, Jawaharlal the most active, Dr. Syed Mahmood the most sedate, Asaf Ali the most contemplative, Pandit Pant the most astute, Dr. Ghosh the most scientific, Shankarrao Deo the most serviceable, Kripalani the most professorial, Narendra Deva the most scholarly and Mehtab the most artistic." The twelfth was the writer, Dr. Pattabhi Sitaramayya, who became the Congress historian.

"Vallabhbhai", writes Sitaramayya, "if he can be described in one word, is a man of common sense as all Patidars must be. He is a man of few words; but they are words of wisdom. He exercised the privilege of the old and is mischievous to a degree. He has the taciturnity of a statesman. His is the superior levity of age, and he has none of the inferior gravity of the snob. His malady, which occasioned his medical release from Yeravada in 1941, has been his companion and his curse, but his good cheer enables him to face death with a joke on his lips." Patel "is the oldest of the group, approaching 70 in age. He is called Sardar in spite of the Congress disavowing all titles, but that does not include those titles of popular origin signifying the people's appreciation of a leader. Gandhi himself always called him 'the Sardar'." According to Sitaramayya, "the Sardar has definite views. He makes up his mind instantly and adheres to the decision generally, though he is open to conviction and change. He is extremely alert and equally extremely anxious to inform himself. He has a genius for detail. No detail is too insignificant for him, whether it be in understanding the war situation or interpreting the latest speech of Amery or the Viceroy. He is most affable and has no aristocratic bearing or reserve. He has a wit all his own. In conversation he chokes you with laughter by a play of his sharp and incisive wit, by the display of his wisdom and by the apt citation of hundreds of proverbs in Gujarati. His loyalty to Gandhi is proverbial. Of him it can be truly said:

> 'His is not to reason why,
> His is but to do and die'."[38]

In prison, Patel's was the first room from the north. Next to him were those of Azad, Asaf Ali, Nehru and Dr. Syed Mahmood. Patel did his three to four miles daily morning walk without fail, while Nehru, as "president of the planting committee, and also the digger and delver", had taken upon himself "the whole onus of preparing the flowerbeds... Vallabhbhai gives his expert's attention to the plants that have sprung up."[39] But one field in which Patel towered above the group was card-playing. "Two parties are hard at work—the afternoon party post-lunch and the evening party pre-supper. Vallabhbhai is the leader and he has a reluctant following that has to be ordered into it, except perhaps Kripalani who pairs with Vallabhbhai and gets comments and criticism in abundance."[40] Towards the end of August, the Surgeon-General of Bombay, Major-General Candy, an elderly Irishman, visited Ahmednagar Fort "to make out the Government's promised report about the health of the members of the Working Committee." He happened to have known Patel as Health Officer in the Ahmedabad Municipality when Patel was its Chairman. In a light-hearted vein he told Patel, "I am getting old and a little peevish."

Patel retorted, "If you are old and peevish at 56, what should I be?"

Candy put down Patel's age at 58 and his at 54, but was astonished to hear Patel say, "It is 67, and I am looking forward to another 33 years!"[41]

Three years thus passed with the Congress leaders hibernating in the Ahmednagar Fort. They simply lived a life of idleness and remained oblivious about the developments in India and abroad. Judging "Quit India" in its historical perspective, Gandhi's wisdom in launching the movement is questioned by some. Was Gandhi compelled to take such a sudden, precipitate step following "the crushed hope" due to the failure of the Cripps Mission? And he had characterised the Cripps proposals as "a post-dated cheque on a crashing bank". Or, was it due to the Japanese victories which appeared to have convinced him that Britain was going to lose the war soon? Or, was it due to the anxiety that, with Britain losing the war, India's freedom would pass into the hands of new masters? Lack of evidence makes assessment merely speculative, especially when Gandhi "had not formulated any detailed programme of action to be followed by the people in the event of a British refusal to accept the Congress demand"; and "stranger still was the fact that none of his colleagues had chosen to demand from him any clear plan of action. Men like Vallabhbhai Patel, Rajendra Prasad and J.B. Kripalani were ready to put their implicit trust in any course of action that the Mahatma might recommend. Maulana Azad did not share Gandhi's optimism that a settlement might yet emerge. Jawaharlal Nehru was torn by conflicting emotions."[42]

The war ended on May 8, 1945. A month later Patel and other members of the Working Committee were released from Ahmednagar Fort. During the three years they were there, Patel admitted, "India had seen many changes. And so had the world. But inside the jail we were completely in the dark. On coming out only we could learn about these."[43] The changes in India distressed him very much. On reaching Pune, he went straight to Gadgil's residence, and told him how upset he was about the propaganda done by Gandhi and other Congress leaders about Rajagopalachari's formula which conceded Pakistan; and also about Bhulabhai Desai's negotiations with Liaquat Ali Khan, with Gandhi's blessings, on the possibility of forming a joint National Government at the Centre. His opposition to such negotiations were on three grounds: first, these had no approval of the Working Committee; second, the reported move of Desai was apparently for assuming power himself at the Centre, and third, his fear of the Congress losing face with Jinnah's repudiation of support. That is what Jinnah did, not much later.

Patel, in fact, was against any talks with Jinnah since he always proved not merely uncompromising and insulting, but a malicious wrecker. He wanted to throw him into isolation and let him stew in his own juice. Patel, therefore, strongly disapproved Gandhi's talks with Jinnah in 1944, which Rajagopalachari had arranged during Patel's absence in prison. On his coming out, he wrote to Gandhi a politely-worded letter of dissent which was indicative of his having moved further away from the master: "In matters of love, the party that loves less has the upper hand."[44] Patel seemed to have considered the Gandhi-Jinnah Bombay talks as the "Munich of India" insofar as Gandhi's spirit of conciliation was interpreted as a gross weakness of the Congress as a party.

Patel appeared to have regretted that their three years in jail had made the Congress surrender the political field to Jinnah, who had cleverly capitalised on a situation of vacuum created by the absence of the Congress. He had considerably strengthened his position in the provinces. Earlier in February 1942, Fazlul Huq, who in 1940 had moved the Lahore resolution of the Muslim League on Partition, declared that the resolution could not be applied to Bengal. It was with the help of the European group that Jinnah had him replaced by a more loyal follower, Nizam-ul-Din, early in 1943. And because of the official patronage given to Jinnah, the Muslims by and large had come to look upon him as their spokesman; more so in the Muslim minority provinces than in the Muslim majority provinces of Punjab, Sind, Bengal and the NWFP, none of which was too keen on getting Pakistan in spite of their being the ultimate beneficiaries. It was, however, on the failure of Gandhi that Jinnah built his dream of Pakistan.

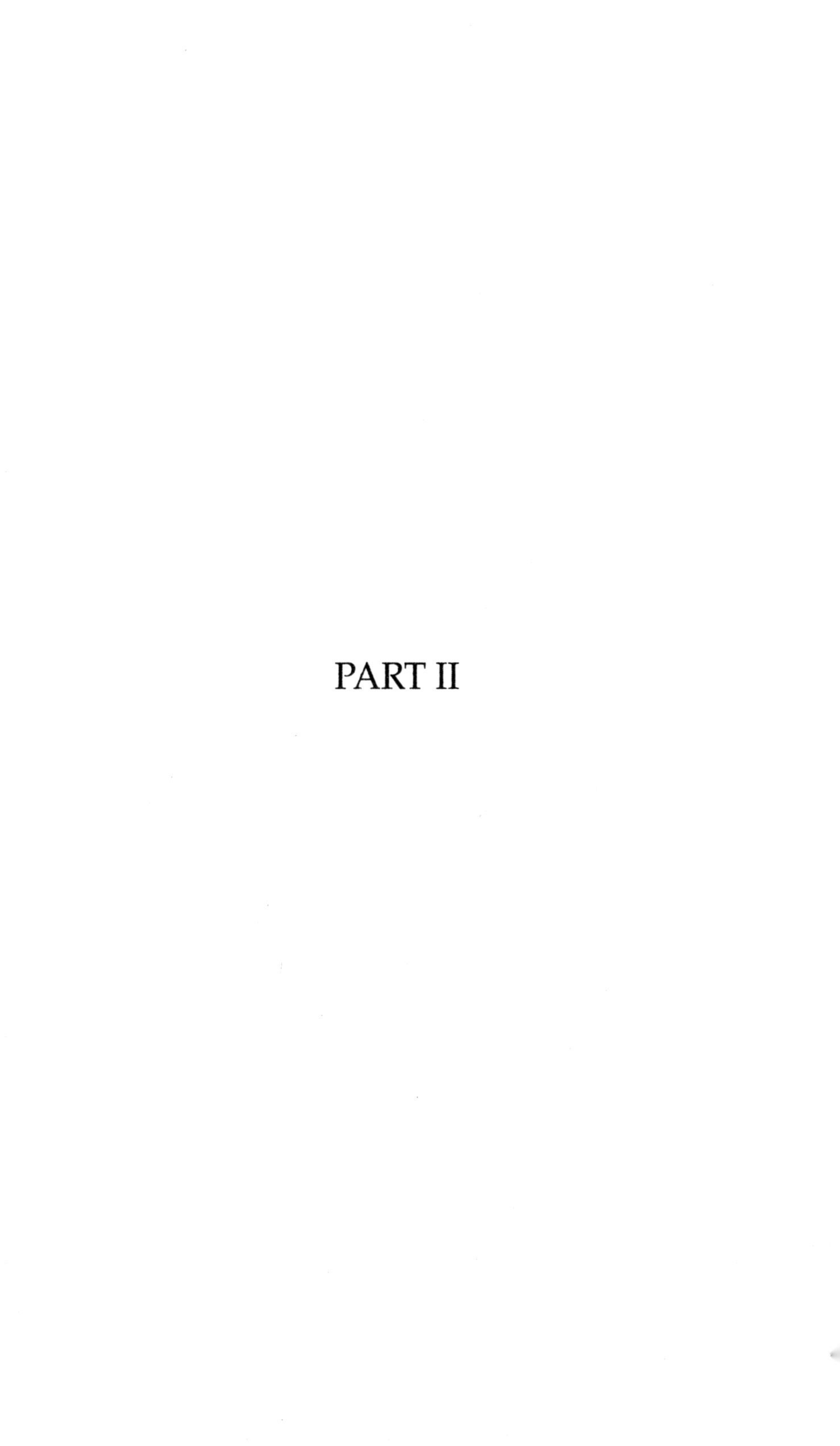

PART II

18

Churchill's "Imperial Strategy"

Winston Churchill had won the war in 1945. But as a down-to-earth realist, he was not blind to the reality he faced: the inevitable prospect of losing the 150-year old Indian Empire, which, to him, was the "most precious jewel in the British Crown". It was the beginning of the end, which he wanted to face resolutely. Glowing with the pride of a victor, the dogged fighter in Churchill was not prepared to let the eclipse be at least total, or too soon. He wanted Britain to hold on to the sub-continent in some effective way under the "Imperial strategy" he got prepared soon after the war was over.

Earlier in March 1945, Churchill had defined his "Imperial strategy" to mean India's "partition into Pakistan, Hindustan and Princestan".[1] In a complete withdrawal from the sub-continent Churchill saw "serious implications for Britain's communications and bases between the Middle East and South-East Asia". This included the preservation of the Indian Ocean between Aden and Chittagong as a zone of peace.

Churchill had agreed with Viceroy Lord Wavell that the Congress, under the influence of pro-Soviet Nehru, was "unlikely to cooperate with Britain on military matters and foreign policy", whereas the Muslim League would be "willing to do so".[2] This way Britain expected continuation of her control over the sub-continent's borders with Afghanistan and Russia. The latter through Gilgit which in north-west Kashmir was already under the control of British-dominated Gilgit Scouts. It was, therefore, in Britain's interest to create a Pakistan that would have "political stability" and "economic viability" through two Pakistans—one in the West and the other in the East. Creation of Pakistan was, thus, imperative for the success of Churchill's "Imperial strategy".

Churchill had ordered the framing of his "Imperial strategy" soon after the war was over in May 1945. The "strategy" had, in fact, started taking shape earlier in 1942. The British Labour was as much a part of it as were the Conservatives. On 2nd March, Secretary of State Amery wrote to A. Harding: "Here is the Document as drafted by the India Committee under Attlee's chairmanship... what Linlithgow and I were agreed upon in July 1940... This is the first public admission of the possibility of Pakistan, i.e. an India divided between the Muslim and Hindu parties."[3]

Such a commitment on Britain's part was within four months of the Muslim League's Pakistan resolution passed under Jinnah's presidentship at the Lahore session earlier in March 1940. On 24th March, Amery wrote to Viceroy Lord Linlithgow: "Jinnah, I should have thought, will be content to realise that he has got Pakistan in essence, whether as substantial or as a beginning point."[4]

Yet, little could Churchill, or anyone else in Britain, could foresee that in the end the shots would be called by none other than Sardar Patel, whom Lord Wavell had later called: "Vallabhbhai Patel, India's Bismarck, the man of iron from Gujarat."[5] As a result, the transfer of power took place on Patel's two major conditions. One: division of Punjab and Bengal, which rendered Jinnah's Pakistan "moth-eaten and truncated". Second: despite Britain's solemn promise to the Princes to grant their independence simultaneously with India and Pakistan with allegiance to Britain, Patel forced Britain to deny them membership of the Commonwealth. This resulted in the dissolution of the Chamber of Princes, which placed power in the hands of Patel to deal with each prince individually, thereby denying them their collective bargaining power.

In this manner Patel could achieve integration of over 560 Princely States in a matter of 18 months. He outdid Bismarck. In the final hour of Britain's receding glory, this was Patel's most shining victory. It was an incomparable event in world history. Not only for its speed, but for its being totally non-violent: a peaceful Gandhian revolution. He befriended the Princes, not turned them into potential enemies.

However, complexities of the implications of the "Imperial strategy" were to be resolved by stages. Each was designed, without allowing it to be publicly known, to strengthen Jinnah's position as its sole implementer. In 1945, he had no hold over the Muslim majority provinces of Punjab, Sind and the NWFP, without whose willingness the creation of Pakistan was next to possible. Nor did Jinnah have full backing in the Muslim minority provinces. He was yet to be invested with the status of a sole spokesman. He was to be helped to achieve this through three stages:

a) the Simla Conference of May-June 1945
b) the General Elections of end-1945
c) the Cabinet Mission Plan of May-June 1946

Since 1937 Britain had started strengthening Jinnah's position. This was to be after Congress had captured power, post-1937 elections, in eight out of eleven provinces. Viceroy Lord Linlithgow considered it necessary to make a counter move. He wrote to the Secretary of State: "Jinnah is our man, and we accept him as a representative of all Muslims." He took steps to remove the most stumbling hurdle from Jinnah's path—the Punjab Premier Sikander Hayat. His Unionist Party—a coalition of Muslims, Hindus and Sikhs—had been ruling since 1926. And Sikander Hayat believed: "If Pakistan meant Muslim raj in Punjab, he would have nothing to do with it. He wanted a free Punjab in which all communities would share self-government."[6]

In 1937 itself, Linlithgow had forced Sikander to reach an agreement with Jinnah, under which the Muslim members of his party were to be allowed to become members of the League simultaneously. But Sikander had got a clause included in the agreement, stating: "That will not affect the continuance of the present coalition of the Unionist Party."[7] In 1938, with "eyes blazing with indignation", Sikander had told Penderel Moon: "Pakistan would be an invitation to them (the Muslims) to cut the throat of every Hindu bania… Pakistan would mean a massacre."[8]

Sikander's successor, Khizr Hayat Khan Tiwana, was an equally committed secularist. But the Simla Conference (as discussed later) had weakened his position. He looked to Patel for what the latter had nearly achieved in Sind but had failed in the final hour of his victory. Because of Azad's "despotism" in Sind, Patel had refused to visit Punjab for party alignments. Consequently, the weak coalition Azad had worked out could not last long. On gaining power, the League had started victimisation of Muslim officers who had supported Khizr.

Nevertheless, Patel continued to enjoy Khizr's confidence. On the League's large-scale victimisation of Muslim officers who had supported Khizr, he sought Patel's help especially in the case of one ICS officer, Nasir Ahmed. Patel's reply was most accommodating: "I fully sympathise with him in his difficulties, and am prepared to do my best to accommodate him."[9]

Patel's large-heartedness lay in his generosity. Had Azad not come in his way in Sind and thereby marred his proposed visit to Punjab post-1945 general elections, the League would have lost Punjab, but also the NWFP, besides Sind—indeed the whole of what constituted later West Pakistan.

a) The Simla Conference

The Simla Conference, called by Viceroy Lord Wavell in June-July 1945, was the first stage of implementation of Churchill's "Imperial strategy". Ostensibly, it looked as if Britain was liberalising her rule by offering membership to political parties on the Viceroy's Executive Council. Nobody, including the Congress, could suspect its hidden motives: to boost Jinnah's position as implementer of the "strategy". Immediately after granting Jinnah two major gains, Wavell called off the conference, and thus saved Jinnah from facing opposition from leading liberal Muslim leaders at the conference. Jinnah's gain lay in two major respects.

The first in itself was the most important, as it was to clear the path to the creation of Pakistan. West Pakistan was to comprise Punjab, the NWFP and Sind. In the NWFP, Congress position was impregnable. In Sind, it was for Jinnah far from stable. Punjab was the stronghold of the Unionist Party—a Hindu-Muslim-Sikh coalition since 1926. The later had to be dislodged. Jinnah's victory there would automatically make the NWFP and Sind fall into his lap.

Wavell did that most despotically by refusing to accommodate a Unionist Muslim on his proposed Executive Council. A former Governor of Punjab, Bertrand Glancy, correctly forecast that: "the Unionist Ministry will not last unless a Unionist Muslim gets a seat on the Executive Council."[1] Wavell's refusal sounded the death-knell of the Unionist Party in due course, but it had cleared the way for Jinnah to capture Punjab in the end. Still, for the time being, suspense hung over fear of Patel upsetting his applecart, as he had almost done in Karachi in January 1946—post-general elections.

Wavell's second favour to Jinnah was on all-India basis, but especially so in the Muslim minority provinces. It was the granting of "parity" to the Muslims with the caste Hindus. Purposefully Wavell left the scheduled castes out, so as to enable Jinnah to buy them out, and thus increase his numbers.

Gandhi had first "threatened to ban the conference unless the stipulation of parity between Hindus and Muslims was removed."[2] At the conference when Wavell proposed, Gandhi compromised with Azad's stand that "while the Congress did not object to the parity proposal, it had strong views about the door through which the members would enter."[3]

Having given Jinnah two solid gains, Wavell suddenly called off the conference, thereby saving Jinnah from embarrassment he would to face from, apart from the Congress, liberal Muslim loaders attending the conference. He helped Jinnah emerge unscathed as a wrecker. Congress President Maulana Azad had legitimate reasons to deny Wavell the initiative by himself staging a walkout. Rather than that he quietly swallowed the insult heaped on his person by Jinnah when the latter refused him a handshake.

Wavell began his meetings with twenty-one political leaders of all shades of opinion, individually and in groups, including the provincial Chief Ministers, on June 25th. His initial moves generating hope soon turned into disappointment and invited doom when he attempted to mollify Jinnah and win his support by equating him with Gandhi as the two recognised leaders of the Congress and the League; as also by suggesting that his proposed Executive Council would include an "equal proportion of caste Hindus and Muslims".

This was a give-in which Gandhi opposed by telling the Viceroy: "You will unconsciously but equally surely defeat the purpose of the conference if the parity between Hindus and Muslims is unalterable. Parity between the Congress and the League is understandable. I am eager to help you and the British people, but not at the cost of fundamental and universal principles."[4] In spite of his foretelling Wavell of the doom of his plan, Gandhi and the Congress did not show any averseness to their helping the Viceroy in the success of his efforts.

In contrast, Jinnah was enigmatic: "studiously non-committal". He wanted to play for time. He proposed the postponing of the conference by a fortnight. Wavell refused to oblige him, and Jinnah and other Leaguers attended it "without more demur". He had, however, already scored his first victory in the parity between caste Hindus and Muslims. This emboldened Jinnah to put forward another unreasonable demand: his right to nominate all the Muslim members of the proposed Council, including representatives of the Punjab Unionist Party and Congress Muslims. Only on such a basis would Wavell's plan be acceptable to Jinnah.

Since no guarantee was being given by the Viceroy that the Muslim members would be selected only from the League's list,

Jinnah refused to submit his list. After this, the League should have forfeited its right to participate in the conference. But in Wavell's ignoring such a vital point lay the beginnings of the failure of the conference.

Wavell had the opportunity of breaking down Jinnah on July 9th. But he didn't. At their meeting, Wavell records, Jinnah "finally refused to give me his list of names, though he left himself a loophole at the end by asking me to write to him, which I have done this morning. He was obviously in a high state of nervous tension, and said to me more than once, 'I am at the end of my tether... I ask you not to wreck the League.' He is obviously in great difficulties; but they are largely of his own making by his arrogance and intransigence. He fears now to be made the scapegoat for the failure of the conference; and yet will not give up anything of his claim to represent all Muslims."[5]

Yet Wavell ignored all that, as also the opposition Jinnah faced from a number of prominent Muslim leaders, including Dr. Khan Sahib, Chief Minister, NWFP; Khizr Hyat Khan Tiwana, Chief Minister, Punjab, and Sultan Ahmed, a former Executive Councillor. In his talks with Wavell, Sultan Ahmed had "not much to say, except to inveigh against Jinnah's bad manners and the absurdity of his claim to represent all Muslims."[6]

July 11th proved a fateful day. Wavell offered Jinnah four seats for the League Muslims and reserved one for a Unionist Party Muslim nominee. Jinnah's outright rejection—this time in a clash not with the Congress but with Muslim interests in Punjab—led Wavell to, rather enigmatically, call off the conference virtually *sine die* merely on the ground that his list was "not acceptable to the Muslim League". Wavell's action shocked Patel, and invited his sharp, cynical comment, "We were called all the way to Simla. What for? Just to be told that nothing could be achieved without Jinnah's cooperation! They knew perfectly well that would not be forthcoming."

In H.V. Hodson's critical analysis: "Wavell had in effect capitulated to Jinnah. His proposal for a representative of the Punjab Unionist Party—which had held office since 1926 under

Fazl-i-Husain, Sikander Hyat Khan and Khizr Hyat Khan Tiwana and represented all three communities—in the Government was entirely reasonable, and might well have been accepted by the Congress in lieu of their own nomination of a Mussalman, for the evidence is that they came to Simla in a mood to conform. Jinnah's control of the Muslim League was at that time far from complete. The Unionist Party was still strong, and Liaquat Ali Khan favoured a settlement. There were still many uncommitted Muslims in the country... if the Viceroy had been as adamant as Jinnah, the latter would have been obliged himself to give in... the destruction of the Unionist Party, which paved the way for Partition of Punjab, would have been averted, and... an effective all-community political Government of India would have operated... Right or wrong, the moment was a critical one in the whole story?"[7]

Much to Patel's regret, Azad failed to capture that moment as Congress President. Azad could have boycotted the conference before Wavell capitulated to Jinnah. The boycott would have robbed Jinnah of the honour of a wrecker in the eyes of Muslims, as also the recognition he got as the sole spokesman of the entire community. Jinnah was allowed to play the role of big brother in dictating his terms—refusal even to accept Khizr's right to nominate a Unionist Muslim on Wavell's proposed Executive Council. Patel would have acted more positively—rather somewhat aggressively—in two ways. The first was to be seen later in Sind when he nearly succeeded in throwing Jinnah into isolation, and, second, when he threatened Wavell of the Congress' resignation from the Interim Government, thereby creating a crisis for the British Government, which it could ill-afford as it wanted to hand over power and quit. If Jinnah could play the politics of a recalcitrant, why couldn't Patel? He would have preferred, unlike Gandhi and Azad, to be as uncompromising as Jinnah ever was.

Wavell ignored his assurance to Azad that "no party to the conference would be allowed to obstruct settlement out of willfulness",[8] whereas he allowed his plan to be wrecked by

Jinnah's "intransigence and obstinacy". Wavell's capitulation resulted in India's moving from then onwards towards Jinnah's demand: "divide and quit". The failure of the conference boosted his personal prestige and political stature. The impression created was: who could defy Jinnah when Wavell couldn't? Not only did it ruin the prospects of a settlement of India's political future, it damaged beyond repair the strength of the Unionist Party in Punjab and caused its ultimate demise. It was this critical moment that paved the way for Jinnah's Pakistan, Punjab being its cornerstone. And it was this critical moment that, if handled with firmness and fairness, could have saved India's unity and averted Partition.

Minus the League, all other parties would have accepted Wavell's plan. Gandhi was in a conciliatory mood. So was Patel, who had stated on the third day of the conference, "We have no enmity with the British. If there is a change of heart in our British rulers, we shall not pursue our quarrel"; whereas at the time of the Cripps Mission in 1942 he had said, "We would rather be ruled by dacoits than by the British." Wavell, thus, failed to grasp the hand of friendship Gandhi and Patel had extended. "Many people, including some of his official advisers, thought he was wrong to accept Mr. Jinnah's veto without even a struggle, and that a great chance of setting India on the road to united self-government had been needlessly abandoned... Some observers thought that Lord Wavell's sudden abandonment of his plan was the decisive move that made the Partition of India inevitable."[9]

A shrewd Jinnah fully exploited the situation. Asked "why he had spurned the Wavell plan when he had won his point of parity for the League with the Congress", his reply "stunned" Durga Das, an Indian journalist, "Am I a fool to accept this when I am offered Pakistan on a platter?" Durga Das's "painstaking inquiries" revealed that "a member of the Viceroy's Executive Council had sent a secret message to Jinnah" on behalf of the diehards in London that "if Jinnah stepped out of the talks, he would be rewarded with Pakistan."[10]

The Conservatives were out of power in Britain, but they could play their game through the diehard Civil Servants in India—men like Francis Mudie, Olaf Caro and others. At such a time when Jinnah's image and stature had been artificially inflated and communal passions were getting hold of the people's minds, the Labour Government, which had just succeeded the Conservatives, prematurely announced its intention "to convene as soon as possible a constitution-making body "by first holding elections" so that the will of the Indian electorates may be known.

b) General Elections

The general elections, held end-1945, was a deliberate attempt to help Jinnah emerge as the chief spokesman of the Indian Muslims. This was Wavell's second gift to Jinnah post-Simla conference as implementer of Churchill's "Imperial strategy". The election results proved that. He won every Muslim seat in the newly elected Central Legislative Assembly, and 442 out of 509 Muslim seats in the eleven provinces combined. Reginald Maxwell, a former Home Member, had earlier correctly stated that "a general election will only produce a new version of the old body without any new ideas."[1] Patel too thought that nothing would be settled by the elections. He had several reasons: thousands of Congressmen would be still in prison; the Congress, having been out of politics, hadn't had the time to prepare itself for the polls; and the elections would be held without new electorates who had become eligible during the past five years. And yet, ironically, the Congress under Azad agreed to take part in the elections.

The results further inflated Jinnah's ego, hardened his attitude and turned him more aggressive, uncompromising and intractable. Yet, the Muslim majority provinces were not completely under his control. Punjab, Sind and even Bengal were opposed to his type of virulent communalism. The Congress could have benefited from this, if Patel was allowed to handle the situation. But Azad's direct interference did not permit Patel to form anti-Jinnah fronts either in Sind or in Punjab.

In Punjab, Jinnah still faced a very difficult task. The Punjabis were, by and large, not unhappy with the Hindu-Muslim-Sikh coalition in power, the Unionist Party, whose founder, Fazl-i-Husain, and his successor as Premier on his death, Sikander Hyat Khan, had warned Jinnah "to keep his finger out of the Punjab pie... We cannot possibly allow 'provincial autonomy' to be tampered (with) in any sphere and by anybody, be he a nominee of the powers who have given us this autonomy, or a president of the Muslim League."[2] According to the ex-Governor, Henry Craik, "moderate Muslims in Punjab do not really like... Pakistan."[3] Even Sikander admitted that once the Punjabi Muslims realised that Pakistan would mean partition of their province, "they would think twice before blindly following Jinnah."[4] Nevertheless, largely on account of Linlithgow's tacit support, Jinnah claimed to have secured from Sikander a pact under which a Muslim League party was to be established in the Punjab Assembly, and that the party was to be subjected to the control and supervision of the All-India Muslim League and the Provincial League.

Sikander's death in 1941 created a vacuum very much in Jinnah's favour, and to the great disadvantage of Sikander's successor, Khizr Hyat Khan Tiwana. Because of Sikander's "constant submission to Jinnah and unwillingness to stand up to him", he left the party with a split image. In comparison, Khizr was "a man of the highest courage—far more resolute than Sikander... Jinnah soon realised that in Khizr he had a tougher man to deal with than Sikander. He, therefore, set himself to undermine his position."[5] At Sialkot, Jinnah "roaring like a lion", called for the dismissal of the Punjab Governor and asked for "the head of the Premier on the charger."[6] Khizr found himself in a most difficult situation—between the devil and the deep sea. On the one hand, he faced Jinnah; on the other, the powerful, landowning, now pro-Jinnah, Muslim families of the Daultanas, the Noons and the Hyats, led by no less a person than Sikander's son, Shaukat Hyat Khan. The third group he faced comprised, though individually, the Hindu jats led by Chottu Ram and the Sikhs. They were his major partners in the coalition. Khizr's ill-luck was also due to the repercussions in his province of the formation of the League Ministry in the neighbouring NWFP, unfortunately for him in a coalition with the Akalis, and in the formation of which the British had a direct hand—being nominated by the Government rather than elected by the Provincial Legislature.

The Congress, on the other hand, suffered from a lack of unity. Patel, because of his organizing ability and party control, had enjoyed full powers as Chairman of the Parliamentary Board during the 1937 elections. Not so this time. Azad had curbed Patel's powers as Chairman of the Parliamentary Sub-Committee by retaining to himself overriding powers as Chairman of the Board. Of this Patel wrote to Nehru as early as November 15, 1945: "Maulana is unwilling to give authority, nor is he prepared to deal with the proposals himself."[7] Patel and Azad differed and clashed—first over Congress support to non-party organisations. With an eye on the desertions he feared, Patel wrote to Rajendra Prasad on November 10th: "We shall be liquidating the Congress altogether if we allow independent organisations of the Muslims, Sikhs and the Depressed Classes... to have their own Provincial Election Boards from which alone candidates are to be set up and Congressmen are expected to come under that banner."[8] When Patel was approached by Master Tara Singh on the growing Akali discontent, Azad advised him by telegram on November 14, 1945: "If Akalis approach you, please refer them to me."[9] Later, on February 14th, he told Patel, "the Board may dispose (of) nominations (from) remaining provinces after which I shall dispose (of) appeals if any." The irrepressible Patel countered by saying, "There can be no appeal against Central Board's decision. Besides, such a course would encourage indiscipline and endless disputes."[10]

Azad, however, stuck to his position, "If any appeal would be filed... you would send it to me, and I shall decide it in consultation with you." Patel told him bluntly, "... if such authority were vested in you, there should have been a specific provision in the Working Committee's resolution. Besides, if you were the appellate authority, you cannot at the same time be the Chairman of the Board, whose decisions are appealable to you alone. This is a strange procedure." He confronted Azad with what the latter did not expect, "in view of your attitude, I propose to immediately tender my resignation from the Central Board as well as the Working Committee... I regret very much to say that I have to take this action at a very critical juncture, but I feel that the treatment that has been given to me is, to say the least, unexpected and underserved and, hence, no alternative is left to me."[11] The following day Patel informed Gandhi, "I am finding it hard to carry on with Maulana. He is behaving as a despot... I have asked him to relieve me."[12]

Azad felt rattled. Anxious to avert a major crisis within the party, he offered his apologies to Patel by writing on February 28th: "I assure you that I had not viewed this matter in the light you have taken it, nor was I under the slightest impression that I am taking a decision against the decision of the Board." Seeking "a generous attitude" from Patel, Azad pleaded, "We have been working together for the last twenty-six years in perfect unison. Every morning and evening of our public life has passed in amity and concord."[13] Because of such despotism and his uncompromising behaviour at Karachi earlier in the month, Azad had not only forfeited Patel's confidence, but a breach had been caused in their relationship at a time when the Congress could ill-afford such disunity at the top. It impaired the party's strength in putting up a strong, united front against the Muslim League, which enjoyed a greater cohesiveness under the single command of Jinnah. Patel would have been more than a match for the latter, had he been allowed, in his words, "to cripple the League's strength" by attacking Jinnah at his weakest—in the Muslim majority provinces of Sind and Punjab where he faced opposition from provincial leaders.

In early 1946, Sind politics took a dramatic turn which, Patel thought, could help him defeat Jinnah for all times to come. The occasion was the formation of a Ministry in Sind following the Assembly elections. Patel and Azad were to reach Karachi on January 31st. Patel arrived there on that day, but Azad could make it only on February 3rd. Patel had no patience to wait for Azad. Prior to his departure from Bombay when he was told of Azad's late arrival, he had sarcastically remarked, "Whether he goes there or not, I am leaving."[14] He would have preferred if Azad didn't go to Karachi, as he thought his way of handling the issue could prove disastrous. Patel had expressed his fears to Pant in a letter of January 29th prior to his leaving for Karachi: "The Sind elections have turned out to be very encouraging, and if the situation is handled properly, we may be able to bury Pakistan once for all in that province. But Maulana Saheb insists on going there personally. So, the local people are full of apprehensions. You know how things are handled by him."[15]

Patel and Azad went to Karachi on different missions. Patel's was to defeat Jinnah by preventing him from forming a League Ministry as that would pave the way for Jinnah to gain Pakistan. Azad's mission was to seek the formation of a Congress-League coalition. He seemed unconcerned with Jinnah's strategy of turning down such moves in the end. He had done the same earlier in the Bhulabhai Desai-Liaquat Ali Khan talks on a Congress-League coalition at the Centre, whereby he had humiliated the Congress in the eyes of Muslims.

Patel's hopes rested on his winning over Ghulam Hussain Hidayatullah to his side, in the same way he had won over Allah Bux and had defeated Jinnah in 1938. Hidayatullah had been "an outspoken enemy of the Lahore Resolution" and his "success in the assembly owed nothing to Jinnah".[16] His great confidant, B.R. Patel, confirms that he was "not for Pakistan; nor did he have, like Abdullah Haroon, committed love of Jinnah. If Pakistan were to come, he would jump at it, as his main aim was to be in power as the Premier of Sind. But in the prevailing situation, he was anxious to maintain neutrality, as he had as many good friends among the Hindus as among his own community."[17] In 1936 Hidayatullah had formed a Hindu-Muslim coalition against Jinnah's wishes. In February 1945, again, Hidayatullah as Chief Minister had defied Jinnah by taking into his Ministry Maula Bux, a brother of Allah Bux, without his signing the League pledge; and he had even accepted Maula Bux's suggestion to release Congress MLAs. Patel's shrewd eye did not miss that, but more particularly what had happened on October 20th on Jinnah's arrival in Karachi on his fateful mission—formation of a League Ministry. Jinnah was putting up with Hidayatullah, but the host "entrained for Hyderabad within three hours of Jinnah's arrival."[18] Hidayatullah did so purposely for two reasons. First, to avoid an entanglement in the dispute between the rival factions in the Sind Muslim League which "continued unabated". Secondly, he wanted "to avoid antagonising his Hindu supporters, which he would have done if he had openly identified himself with Jinnah and his policies."[19]

Patel had good reasons to consider the election results "very encouraging". The Congress had won 22 seats against the League's 27, but formed a solid block of 30 out of a House of 60 with the support of Nationalist Muslims and the Syed group, each with four seats. In spite of this support, the fate of the Congress in Sind hung by a thread. Patel was, therefore, anxious to strengthen that by hooking Hidayatullah, who was more practical and politically experienced than Syed whom Azad favoured; also, that way alone he could upset Jinnah's applecart. With Congress support and his own, Hidayatullah could have mustered a strength of 35 or more, whereby he would have had a stable Ministry, free from dependence from Jinnah and the European group. It was Patel's strategic move, well-planned and purposefully directed towards Jinnah's defeat in Sind. Patel considered a defeat in Sind to prove contagious—to be followed by a similar one in Punjab, where conditions seemed, perhaps, more favourable. The loss of Sind and Punjab would have sounded the death-knell of Jinnah's politics in the sub-continent. In Patel's view, Hidayatullah was, like Khizr Hayat Khan in Punjab, non-communal and uncommitted; and compared to others in Sind, he was far more adept in State politics. He could have been less reliable than Syed, but Patel needed his "reliability" for the time being—just to break Jinnah's back and no more perhaps. Syed, on the other hand, had been a staunch Muslim Leaguer. His nationalism was recent and skin-deep. According to the *Sind Observer*, Syed wanted "self-determination to establish a Sindhi Pakistan without interference from the League High Command."[20]

Patel's talks with Hidayatullah, prior to Azad's arrival in Karachi, were most encouraging, and seemed to be bearing the fruit Patel desired. Hidayatullah, reportedly, held out the promise that, if made the Premier, he would not only accept Congress nomination, but also help Patel bury Pakistan in Karachi, where Jinnah had been born. Patel even succeeded in getting round the local Hindu Congress leaders, whose main opposition to Hidayatullah's leadership was that he was "very corrupt"; but Patel knew that so were some of the Hindu leaders. Sarcastically, but approvingly, Patel had therefore asked them, "How much does he want? A crore!" No price seemed enough for Patel to pay if he could defeat Jinnah and kill the prospects for Pakistan. Patel was optimistic of a victory, the like of which he had achieved single-handed in the same city in 1938, when Jinnah had gone there to form a League Ministry following the 1937 provincial elections. With a view to showing off his status and power, Jinnah had on that occasion taken to Karachi with him Sikander Hyat Khan and Fazlul Huq, both of whom were to become later the Premiers of Punjab and Bengal respectively, but as non-Leaguers. The galaxy of League leaders assembled hailed Jinnah as "the Great Guide and Commander of the Muslim community."

Jinnah succeeded in winning over to his side not only most of the highly splintered Muslim members of the Sind assembly but also the keyman among them, Allah Bux. Patel was alerted. From Bombay he pulled wires; and when the League meeting took place for Jinnah to clinch the deal, "much to the astonishment of every one, Allah Bux backed out of the agreement". Jinnah was "shocked" by such "gross breach of faith in resiling". His pride was hurt; but, according to Stanley Wolpert, he "still felt it worth fighting", and sent his closest Sind deputy, Abdullah Haroon, "to appeal that night to Allah Bux at home, but concluded next morning that the latter "was in the hands of the Congress party". It was "a most bitter pill for Jinnah to swallow. He had laboured long and hard for an independent province of Sind... Now the Sardar, Congress's strong man, the shrewd organisational hand beneath Nehru's idealistic velvet glove, had snatched this plum from Jinnah's lips just as he was about to savour its sweetness." Wolpert adds, "He would never forget, or forgive, Sardar Patel for having "cheated" him of Sind, "robbing" his home province out from under him at the very meeting of the League."[21]

In 1946 Patel could not repeat a 1938. His moves were not free from Azad's interference. Patel's optimism began to fade with the arrival of Azad in Karachi on February 3rd. Azad, unlike Patel, favoured a Congress-League coalition. Syed offered him his group's "welcome". But a major support reportedly came, though without Jinnah's prior approval, from M.H. Gazdar, President of the Sind Provincial Muslim League. Gazdar had "a chat with Maulana Azad in the plane while *en route* to Karachi from Delhi" and he made it known that "the Congress President favours an all-party Government in Sind, including the League."[22] Patel was totally opposed to such moves. He had made his views known in his statement earlier, "The Congress is no longer going to knock at the door of the League. The Congress has tried to settle with the League many times. But it has been kicked out every time... If Pakistan is to be achieved, Hindus and Muslims will have to fight it out. There will be a civil war. We are determined to take power into our hands."[23] This was a public confirmation of what Patel had written to Gandhi still earlier on December 28th: "... yesterday the Aga Khan invited me to his place... He spoke to me that better would it be if we have a settlement with Jinnah. I said, 'We, i.e. the Congress, would not like to initiate talks with him; for, he abuses us in season and out of season, and, in fact, he does not genuinely wish for a settlement.' To this he said, 'Jinnah is now in a better mood.' I rejoined: 'I utterly disbelieve it.' As we have decided not to have any truck with him, he might be making such a show in order to tempt us to his snare. But, on our part, we have decided not to make any suggestion for a talk with him."[24]

In total disregard of Patel's views and his strategy. Azad

went ahead with his Congress-League coalition plans without approval of the Congress Working Committee. At Karachi, he invited the League to join the proposed coalition by nominating two Ministers. He did not succeed, because of Jinnah's malicious disinterestedness; whereas he had himself stood in Patel's way in his nearly successful talks with Hidayatullah. In the new situation, Patel was forced to accept a compromise and lend support to Azad's alternative proposal—to bring together Syed, Maula Bux and others to form a coalition Ministry without the League—without Hidayatullah—in the fond hope, Patel wrote to Lalji Mehrotra, that "with the combined efforts of Syed and Maula Bux, it will be possible to make a breach in the League ranks which are none too solid."[25] That was poor consolation. Patel was full of apprehensions. The patchwork nature of the arrangement reached was quite brittle to break any time. Hidayatullah succeeded soon with his threat to "break the present coalition".[26] The League Government too could not achieve stability. As late as September 1946, Wavell reported to Pethick-Lawrence of the continuing deadlock in the Sind legislature, with neither party willing to spare a member for the Speaker's seat. Pro-League Governor Mudie recommended to Wavell "dissolution" of the Assembly in the hope that a fresh election would help the Muslim League capture all the Muslims seats in "the present state of communal feeling."[27]

Defeated and frustrated, Patel returned to Bombay on February 5th, before the coalition was born and the Ministry formed. Since the coalition was resting precariously on a slender majority, the very first blow proved fatal with the defection of a Nationalist Muslim to the League. This gave the Governor his opportunity to install the League Ministry under Hidayatullah with the support of the Europeans. In a letter to Lalji Mehrotra, Patel wrote: "... the League Ministry is, in fact, not a League Ministry but a Mudie Ministry supported now openly by the European block."[28] Mudie went further in his effort to purchase Hidayatullah, about which the Chief Justice of Sind, Godfrey Davis, wrote to Patel: "He is anxious that I should resign from my office of Chief Justice... So,

I believe, that Sir Ghulam's nephew could be made a permanent judge of our Chief Court at once."[29]

The situation in Punjab for the Congress was more favourable than in Sind, though, as Patel said, it required tactful handling. The Congress enjoyed two advantages. First, there was no Mudie to support Jinnah out and out, and Governor Evan Jenkins was a pro-Unionist and not a pro-Pakistani. Secondly, Khizr, the Premier, who had won a majority in the elections, was a staunch anti-Leaguer. Patel was to visit the province along with Azad to give direction to the Congress in provincial politics. Embittered by his experience in Sind, he was reluctant to go there; and then something happened between him and Azad that brought the matter to a dead-end. Patel wrote to Azad on February 23rd: "From your conversation on the phone, I understood that my going to Lahore is likely to embarrass you and that I should rather not go there."[30] As Congress President, Azad had reserved to himself the task of conducting electoral matters in the Muslim majority provinces whose importance lay in holding the key to Pakistan, but Patel's services had been required in these provinces merely to provide funds amounting to a few lakhs of rupees for fighting the elections. With that job now over, Azad could afford to give less importance to Patel's services. And that is what Azad did in Sind, Punjab and elsewhere, arrogating to himself the powers Patel had enjoyed as Chairman of the Parliamentary Board during and after the 1937 elections. Patel realised his overall responsibility to the party and the country, and was, therefore, unsparing in his criticism of the electoral arrangements Azad had reached, as also the selection of candidates. He had written to Azad earlier on December 21st: "I have already sent a cheque for Rs.50,000, but I am afraid we are wasting good money for nothing, and Congress reputation will in the end suffer badly... I am afraid we have mishandled the whole Punjab situation." He considered it to be "very unwise" that the Congress "should be mixed up with such a shady transaction" with the Ahrars.[31] Patel referred to an Ahrar candidate who joined the League even after his nomination had been declared valid. The 1931 agitation in Kashmir, according to

Prem Nath Bazaz, was "aggressively communal". To this agitation, the Ahrars had sent as many as 4,500 volunteers.

More serious were the Azad-Patel differences over the reorganization of the Congress parliamentary party in Punjab. Azad was opposed to Gopichand Bhargava's election as the legislative party leader, no matter if Bhargava enjoyed, more than anyone else, Khizr's confidence. Azad's election of Bhim Sen Sachar, who had hardly anyone's backing, at such a critical time was the weakest point in the Congress strategy. About this vital matter Patel had warned Azad earlier on January 10th: "The most important question, so far as Punjab is concerned, is the determination of our attitude towards the Unionist Party, because soon after the elections are over there will not be time left to settle this matter."[32] Still earlier on December 25th, Patel had impressed on Sachar, "I am distressed to find that even good Congressmen are not united in Punjab... Instead of this muddle at this critical juncture, if we could secure a big group in the new Assembly, which cannot be ignored, it would be something; otherwise all the sacrifices of the past three years, the enthusiasm of the people and the awakening of the masses will result in nothing, and the energy and the expense of all of you will, in the end, be wasted. Punjab is a key province. Can nothing be done to make Congress workers realise their sense of responsibility at this critical period?[33]

Patel's assessment found confirmation in Asaf Ali's letter to Patel that Khizr was "anxious to come to some sort of a compromise with us." Maulana Daud Ghaznavi also wrote to Patel on January 4th. "Both the Unionists and the Akalis are struggling to make use of the Congress in order to achieve power for themselves."[34] In a situation where both the Unionists and the Akalis were wooing the Congress, no matter if with the intention of downing the Muslim League so as "to achieve power" for themselves, the Congress held the trump card which Patel wanted to play adroitly and turn the tide of provincial politics in his party's favour. But the Congress failed to rise to the occasion. Sachar's leadership proved weak, vacillating, ineffective and, indeed, leaderless. He did not enjoy the confidence of Khizr;

he was also impolitic in estranging the already not-too-happy Congress-Akali relations by making a suggestion that on Khizr's proceeding to the UK a Muslim should officiate as acting Premier. This killed Baldev Singh's claim which he had hopefully nursed. He apprised Patel of the situation in general in his letter of January 5th: "growing complications within the local Congress ranks... have prevented any possibility of mutual confidence between Malik Sahib (Khizr) and local Congress leaders", with the result that "it has not been possible to arrive at any arrangement for post-election cooperation as between the Congress and Malik Sahib's party." He further stated: "If some collaboration with Malik Sahib is still contemplated, if only to keep the Muslim League out, it is most essential now not to encourage anti-Gopichand partymen... Malik Sahib has made it plain that, if the Congress do want his collaboration, he should not be made to accept men on whom he cannot rely. He is quite prepared to have the collaboration of Dr. Gopichand and of such Congressmen on whom Malik Sahib and Gopichand can agree."[35]

A settlement with the Unionists and the Akalis was most essential for the Congress on two grounds: One, to defeat Jinnah in Punjab, which Patel considered as the "key province of Pakistan." Two, for the party's future well-being after its debacle in Sind. In November the Congress had received a big jolt in "the *volte-face* of Abdul Qayum and the somersault of Mian Iftikhar-ud-Din" in the NWFP and Punjab respectively, following which, according to Prof. Abdul Majid Khan, "the sincerity of almost every Nationalist Muslim in this part of the country is being questioned and his *bona fides* being impugned."[36] And when Maulana Daud Ghaznavi, President of the Provincial Congress for several years, resigned, Patel wrote to Nehru on July 19th: "Maulana Daud has played false to us in a crisis. It seems he was waiting for an opportunity for an excuse to go over to the other side. He was made Congress President in Punjab by Maulana (Azad). We had to spend a lakh of rupees for his election alone, and he was given a safe joint constituency, from where he got in by a majority of Hindu votes... it is difficult for us to trust the best of them."

With these somersaults had begun Patel's disenchantment with the Nationalist Congress Muslims. He further wrote to Nehru: "The Punjab situation is in a hopeless muddle... Sachar wants to resign his leadership. Maulana placed him there, and I have asked him to obtain his permission. It seems the coalition is scrapping."[37]

In Bengal too Azad's election strategy failed. The political arrangements he arrived at were imperfect, politically unwise and lacking in down-to-earth forthrightness. He behaved, as Patel complained to Gandhi, like an autocrat, even when his indifferent health deprived him of speed and personal direction. At a time of deepening crisis, while the Congress suffered from disunity and dispiritedness, Jinnah gained in strength by leaps and bounds. A three-member Bengal Election Board was formed on October 19th during Azad's absence at Kurseong near Darjeeling. He was the Board Chairman. Other members were Ashrafuddin, who was in jail, and P.C. Ghosh, who, having got fed up with frustrating party affairs mainly on account of Sarat Bose's activities, wanted to resign. Patel stopped him with the advice in his letter of November 16th: "Your attitude... is unfortunate. Any resignation at this stage is likely to injure our cause. Why can't you make your own position felt and fight from within to carry your point?"[38] Patel himself was leading such a fight from within. Earlier, on October 26th, he had told Ghosh that the composition of the Board was "not a very satisfactory arrangement. Independently you will be able to do nothing without obtaining the consent of the Chairman who is not there." He had asked Ghosh, "Will the responsibility of selections and running the elections devolve on the small committee of these three persons? Or, will you form another board? I hope that all efforts will be made to present a united front in these elections against all opposition to the Congress, either from the Hindu Mahasabha or the Muslim League, or any other anti-Congress group." Laying emphasis on the need of the hour, Patel wrote: "This is a question of now or never. Bengal has suffered tremendously in the past five years, and it is for us to make or mar the future of Bengal. The Congress must present a united front and sink all its personal differences".[39] Patel also expressed his apprehensions to Sarat Bose in a letter he wrote on January 9th: "If you will not be careful, the experience of the Central Assembly elections will be repeated, and if Shamsuddins and Ashrafuddins are the type of people with whom we have to deal, then God help us!"[40] Gandhi's appeal to the Bengal Congress could be effective only if he had first settled the differences between Azad and Patel. His failure was in allowing the party to drift and suffer in the end.

Azad had kept the selection of candidates in Bengal in his hands. Patel admitted to having "no knowledge about these", as he had been kept out of this business. He wrote to Rajendra Prasad on November 10th: "My own advice would be to contest every one of the seats in the province (Bengal); and, as far as possible, on the Congress tickets."[41] His views were the same as those expressed by Syed Naushar Ali, Speaker of the Bengal Legislative Assembly, in a letter of December 23, 1945 to Azad and a copy to Patel. He wrote: "I should like to tell you frankly that the more I think about the matter the more I feel convinced that the Muslim seats in the Bengal Legislative Assembly should be contested directly on the Congress ticket." Naushar Ali felt that "non-League Muslim candidates run on a ticket other than that of the Congress will have to face all the difficulties and disadvantages of Muslim Congress candidates without any of the advantages." He, therefore, considered this as "nothing short of a blunder", to "encourage or induce them to keep away from the Congress." Naushar Ali thought that "a clear decision to contest the Muslim seats on the Congress ticket, coupled with an assurance of adequate financial assistance and vigorous propaganda, would inspire confidence in non-League Muslims and make them bold to openly join the Congress and contest the election on a Congress ticket." He felt that "a Congress army thus formed of Hindus and Muslims will present a front too strong for the Muslim League to fight with"; and he saw in the Bengal famine, for which the League Ministry "is mainly responsible", "a golden opportunity" worth exploiting under a programme that would appeal to the masses, namely a suitable economic programme added to the main issue, "Quit India", or "immediate transfer of power". Naushar Ali felt convinced that "the Congress, with adequate funds and backed by the Jamiat-ul-Ulema and the Nationalist Muslim students, will carry the day."

Azad, however, pursued a self-chosen path. He did not care for Naushar Ali's advice. Nor did he listen to Patel's complaint in his letter of January 2nd: "A Muslim board was formed after I left, of which I was not informed. Shamsuddin, the Secretary of this board, joined the League immediately after that... the proper course all over India would have been to contest the elections on Congress ticket. The independent machinery will give us no more seats in Bengal, but I have subordinated my opinion in these matters both in Punjab and in Bengal and elsewhere to yours without question."[42] Shamsuddin's defection hit the Congress in Bengal below the belt—in an identical manner as of Qayum's in the NWFP and Iftikhar-ud-Din's and Daud Ghaznavi's in Punjab. Such somersaults had a cumulative effect all over India.

The political situation in the NWFP was totally different from the prevailing in Bengal, Punjab and Sind. As a Muslim majority province, it had been for the past many years an impregnable stronghold of the Congress, primarily because of the prestige and status enjoyed by Dr. Khan Sahib and Khan Abdul Ghaffar Khan. The two brothers were rock-like firm as nationalists and were Congressmen to the core, bearing no traces of communalism. They were the product of the secular Pathan mind, unsullied by the machinations of the British in the rest of India. Khan Sahib had headed the province as Premier since 1937. Ghaffar Khan was the leader of the Khudai Khidmatgars (God's servants) or Redshirts, who were truly non-violent, and who had spread among the virile Pathans a love for the Congress, especially for Gandhi—after whom Ghaffar Khan was reverentially known as the "Frontier Gandhi". Such a stronghold developed cracks—and with that a loosening of the Congress hold—following the Khan Sahib Ministry's' resignation in 1939; but more particularly soon after the imprisonment of the Khan brothers during the "Quit India" movement in 1942. The Muslim League got its opportunity to form a government with official support and thereby secure a foothold in the NWFP. By October 1945, such a hold, especially in the urban areas, in Asaf Ali's assessment, had grown "pretty strong"; and in the following year League propagandists had begun infiltrating into the countryside. Ghaffar Khan seemed somewhat dispirited; and Asaf Ali reported to Patel that his "attitude and speeches, far from proving helpful, have caused considerable weakness. Whatever happens, he must be persuaded—and only the Mahatma can influence him—to take up election work in right earnest." Herein lay neglect of the NWFP. And yet the Congress won a decisive victory, winning 21 out of 38 Muslims seats and 11 out of 22 non-Muslim seats, thus securing 32 out of a total 50 seats in the Legislative Assembly.

Patel emerged as the saddest man in view of the Congress failure in Bengal, Punjab and Sind, as also the waning of Congress influence in the NWFP. His faith in Azad had been shaken. He had denied Patel the opportunity to play a decisive role in the 1945 elections; though after 1946, Patel played a far more decisive role in shaping the future of the country. But in 1945, of all Congress leaders, Patel alone had to bear the burden of collecting lakhs of rupees to finance the election machinery of even non Congress candidates whom Azad had put up; and who, on Azad's authority, had promised to romp home and upset Jinnah's applecart. His disappointment over the failure of Azad's strategy, in spite of his warnings, was deep; and his frustration was to last thereafter. Added to this was Gandhi's failure to mend the fences when time was still on the side of the Congress—in Sind, Punjab and even Bengal. Had Gandhi asked Azad to step down from the presidential chair prior to the provincial elections instead of mid-1946 for his secretive role during the Cabinet Mission talks, history might have taken a different course.

Azad had written two letters—one to Wavell and the other to the Cabinet Mission, without consulting Gandhi and without the knowledge of his colleagues on the Congress Working Committee. For presentation of the Congress case to the Mission, Azad was given a brief embodied in the notes prepared by Nehru, to which Patel had given his concurrence. Azad, however, took the liberty of making two "private and unauthorised interventions" in his negotiations: "venturing the view that he might be able to get the Congress to agree to some form of grouping of provinces for optional subjects", but "the Mahatma was unwilling to go as far as Azad in meeting the Muslim fears and Muslim League demands. Gandhi was shocked at Azad's informal initiatives vis-à-vis the Mission." To the Congress, the grouping of the provinces was "on a communal basis". Gandhi and Patel seemed to have felt dismayed, because Azad believed that in a federation "especially so in the grouping" "all Muslims can pull their weight together"; and the Partition "would be injurious to Muslim interests." Further, "many Muslims would, inevitably, be left in India and would be treated as aliens." Patel feared something still graver from India's point of view. Under the grouping India would have been sandwiched between two hostile, anti-Indian Muslim blocs of Pakistan.

Gandhi was "deeply hurt" when Sudhir Ghosh conveyed to him what Cripps had told him, "Well, Sudhir, there is a letter that the Maulana wrote to the Viceroy. He did say in this letter that he would see to it that no Muslim name was included in the Congress list, and if his own name was proposed he would not agree to the inclusion of his name."

Ghosh adds, "I then understood why the Maulana had refused to be a Congress nominee in the Government (Interim) in spite of all Gandhi's pleading."[43] Gandhi was so upset as to have asked Azad to step down from the Congress presidentship. Azad's reluctance was understandable. Whoever be the Congress President that year would be invited to head the Interim Government. But "it was at the insistence of Gandhi that he (Azad) consented to resign."[44]

Who should be the next Congress President? For the first time since the party's formation in 1885, the issue assumed a real meaning. It virtually meant choosing the Prime Minister of independent India. Patel was the overwhelming choice of twelve out of fifteen Pradesh Congress committees. Nehru's name had not been even proposed. Brushing aside a democratic procedure, Gandhi made Patel withdraw his name in favour of Nehru—for the third time since 1929! What influenced Gandhi not to back the man who had contributed most to his satyagrahas, built a formidable party machine for him, and had been ever by his side rocklike to fortify his strength to face political storms over the past three decades, is not known. One can only speculate on an event which could have changed the destiny of India. Jayaprakash Narayan and the Socialists were anti-Patel. And so were Azad and the Nationalist Muslims.

Kripalani, who was the General Secretary, says, "It is on record that the Maulana did not want to resign to give place even to Jawaharlal... And it is also on record that Gandhi, in his letter to the Maulana, had suggested Jawaharlal's name."[45] Kripalani admits that in accordance with the expressed wish of Gandhi, "I sent a paper round proposing the name of Jawaharlal... It was certain that if Jawaharlal's name had not been proposed, the Sardar would have been elected as the President. The Sardar did not like my intervention. I have since wondered if, as the General Secretary, I should have been instrumental in proposing Jawaharlal's name in deference to Gandhi's wishes in the matter... But who can forecast the future? On such seemingly trivial accidents depends the fate of men and even of nations."[46]

Azad's private secretary, Humayun Kabir, however, gives a somewhat different version. According to Kabir, "Gandhi had thought of Sardar Patel as the next President of the Congress. This was virtually choosing Patel to be the first Prime Minister of India. Maulana Azad intervened by proposing Nehru's name before Gandhi could put forward Patel's name. I think this was the last, and perhaps the most powerful, cause of antipathy between Patel and Azad." Azad had "at the time thought that Patel's views were somewhat narrow, but, I think, towards the end of his life, he had changed his views."[47] A week before his death, Kabir told *The Statesman* that Azad "in his last days had come to believe that Patel would have made a better Prime Minister than

Nehru."[48] Rajagopalachari too expressed his regret for having not supported Patel in becoming the Prime Minister. A similar regret was expressed by Jayaprakash Narayan in 1972, when he stated, "Rajaji once unburdened his heart by publicly confessing to a wrong he had done to Sardar Patel. I find myself in a similar situation: the dominant feeling within me today is one of self-reproach, because during his lifetime I was not merely a critic but an opponent of the Great Sardar."[49] This and other events since 1945 resulted in Patel's remaining no longer Gandhi's "yes man" or a "blind follower", as he had been since 1917.

Patel had a similar disappointment with Nehru as the new Congress President. He wrote to D.P. Mishra on July 29th: "Though the President has been elected for the fourth time, he often acts with childlike innocence, which puts us all in great difficulties quite unexpectedly… He has done many things recently which have caused us great embarrassment. His action in Kashmir, his interference in the Sikh election to the Constituent Assembly, his press conference immediately after the AICC are all acts of emotional insanity, and it puts tremendous strain on us to set matters right." Yet he told Mishra in a spirit of generosity becoming of an elder, "In spite of all his innocent indiscretions, he has unparalleled enthusiasm and a burning passion for freedom, which make him restless and drives him to a pitch of impatience when he forgets himself. All his actions are governed by a supreme consideration of reaching the cherished goal with electric speed. His mind has been exhausted by overwork and strain. He feels lonely and he acts emotionally and we have to bear with him in the circumstances." Of such circumstances he wrote: "We are passing through a critical period, and our life's work may either yield successful results, or our hopes may all be dashed to pieces by sheer foolishness on our part; and the cup which is full of nectar and which is very near our lips may drop down from our hands before we can taste even a drop of it. The situation is full of perplexities and difficulties, but on such occasions seasoned soldiers have to hold their feet firmly and tightly on the ground and brave the tumult and storm through which the country is passing."[50]

The Congress, nevertheless, suffered from lack of unity. There were, unlike Jinnah's League, too many leaders. Such disunity had surfaced during the war years and continued thereafter. At the Simla conference in 1945, the shrewd British had correctly diagnosed the state of the Congress party affairs. Sitaramayya too arrived at such a diagnosis when he wrote: "While the Muslim League spokesman was one single, individual leader... the Congress had more than one leader: a non-official leader in Gandhi, an official leader in Maulana, a *de facto* leader in Jawaharlal and a dynamic leader in the Sardar. This four-pronged leadership and diplomacy not only stood in glaring contrast with the unity of command in the League, but also served to widen the range of possibilities for the Viceroy to exercise his appeals and exhortations on different temperaments, in different ways and to different purpose."[51]

Azad repeated the role he had earlier played at the Simla Conference. He seemed to have not cared to know the role the League was going to play, about which former Punjab Governor Bertrand Glancy had correctly forewarned: "a very serious danger of the elections being fought, so far as the Muslims are concerned, on an entirely false issue... The uninformed Muslim will be told that the question he is called on to answer at the polls is: are you a true believer or an infidel and a traitor."[52] This is what seemed to have happened. Azad had every valid reason to have boycotted the elections, and not let Jinnah come out stunningly victorious.

The Congress was, thus, a divided house. In the circumstances, it became inevitable that the elections should have proved disastrous for the Congress, and, as a consequence, a drift towards India's Partition set in.

c) The Cabinet Mission Plan

Lord Wavell's speech in the Central Legislature on 28th January 1946 raised new hopes. Patel was led to say: "The ship has reached the shore... the freedom of India is at hand."[1] Yet, nobody could judge what sort of freedom it would be. Would it fulfil Jinnah's dream, or the aspirations of the Congress? Nevertheless, as a follow-up to Wavell's speech, the Labour Government announced on February 19, 1946 its decision to send out to India a high-powered Cabinet Mission comprising Lord Pethick-Lawrence (Secretary of State), Stafford Cripps (President of the Board of Trade) and A.V. Alexander (First Lord of the Admiralty) to negotiate a settlement with Indian political leaders.

The day after their arrival in India on March 24th, Pethick-Lawrence testified to their sincerity by stating: "... in our negotiations, we shall not seek to provide for anything that is incompatible with the freedom of India... The precise road towards the final structure of India's independence is not yet clear, but let the vision of it inspire us all in our renewed efforts to find the path of cooperation."[2] And yet he added by way of allaying the misgivings of the Muslims, "While the Congress are representative of large numbers, it would not be right to regard the Muslim League as merely a minority political party—they are, in fact, majority representatives of the great Muslim community."[3] This was what Wavell had done at Simla by equating the Congress and the League as representatives of caste Hindus and the Muslims. Cripps categorically stated that they had not come to adjudicate between rival claims in India, but to find out the means for the transfer of power to Indian hands. Even Attlee had stated in the House of Commons, "We are mindful of the rights of minorities, and the minorities should be able to live free from fear. On the other hand, we cannot allow a minority to place its veto on the advance of the majority."[4] Such double-talk was an attempt to placate Jinnah more than the Congress.

In such a climate of politically whetted appetite, the Cabinet Mission could not have had smooth sailing, especially because of Jinnah's unbending attitude. He adopted the usual sphinx-like enigmatical attitude by not giving out at any time the slightest inkling of his mind, but demanding to know of the other's first and then summarily dismissing the proposition as if with the authority of an oracle. Cripps found it "impossible to pin him down to anything beyond vague phrases."[5] So did it prove at the end of the Mission's labours, in spite of the fact that the three-tier grouping of India was intended, apart from preserving the territorial integrity of the country, to pacify and bring round an uncompromising Jinnah at the cost of sacrificing the interests of other communities. While in Group A (Madras, Bombay, United Provinces, Bihar, Central Provinces and Orissa) the Congress was given a majority, in Group B (Punjab, the NWFP and Sind) and Group C (Bengal and Assam) the League was given a dominating position. The allocation of seats in Group B was 22 to the Muslims against 13 to the rest, whereas the ratio of Muslims to non-Muslims in Group C was 36 against 34. This amounted to virtually conceding Pakistan in Group B and C. Even with this, Jinnah was reluctant to accept the plan. The main hitch was on the right of a province to opt out of a Group if it so desired.

Assam's merger with Bengal in Group C proved the main bone of contention and sounded the death-knell of the plan. Grave fears, aroused by the League's communal politics, were entertained by the Assamese. After the merger, they felt, manoeuvring would be entirely in the League's hands. Such apprehensions found an echo in the Great Calcutta Killing of August 16, 1946; and later in March 1947 when the Muslim League set up an "Eastern Pakistan Fort" in Rangpur district of the League-dominated Bengal, which bordered Assam's Goalpara district. On March 10th, an "invasion" of Assam was staged in the town of Mankachar by 25,000 League volunteers by holding parades. Similar activities were indulged in some places in Assam too. The Provincial League President, Maulvi Abdul Hamid, had come out with the declaration: "Pakistan would be established in Goalpara in a day and in Assam in a week", while the Governor of Assam reported to the Viceroy: "The Muslim Leaguers of Bengal seem to be in a militant mood and have resolved to send large batches to Assam."[6] To allay the Assamese fears, Nehru, in his first statement as the new Congress President, stated on July 10th that Assam would enjoy the right to opt out of the Group. Jinnah lost no time in not only condemning the Congress stand, but also in rejecting the Mission's proposals. Nehru was blamed for a tactical error, even when he did not hide the naked truth and even when that would have been the final attitude of the Congress because of Jinnah's dubious mind.

With Assam as part of undivided Bengal in Group C in the north-east and undivided Punjab as part of Group B in the north-west, there would have been two solid, hostile blocks of Jinnah's Pakistan. Sandwiched between the two would have been an India with a weak Centre and splintered with the Princely States grouped into confederations, as planned by the Political Department. How could this have been acceptable to the Congress, least of all to Patel? His strategy would have been one of discreetness in not poking the smoldering embers, as Nehru had unwittingly done, by being openly critical of the plan's "option" clause at such a delicate stage of the Mission's negotiations. He would have waited for Jinnah to have opened his mouth, which he never did first, whereby he reserved his right to veto what the other said. In the end Patel's attitude would have been even harsher than Nehru's. One judges this from Wavell's impression of his reaction during the early discussion stage, "Patel's face of cold angry disapproval was a study... in *khadi*, but wearing it more like a Roman toga and with rather a Roman face, powerful, clever, uncompromising, very seldom speaking, but listening with obvious disapproval"; and when Jinnah claimed the right of a Group to secede after five years, "Patel", according to Wavell, "exclaimed triumphantly, there we have it now, what he has been after all the time... the damage had been done in Patel's mind, and he had been given a handle for his contention that the League are not really in earnest about entering a Union and mean to get out as soon as possible."[7]

That was on May 6th. Patel expressed his candid views privately in a letter of June 15th: "We do not accept the groupings as proposed in the Scheme, nor do we accept the interpretation of the Cabinet Mission in this respect."[8] Later he openly stated that he was "not at all sorry that the State Paper had gone... had we accepted the plan, the whole of India would have gone the Partition way." Patel's regret was, "In our anxiety to placate the Muslim League, we have diluted nationalism to such an extent that it has almost lost its original genuine appearance."[9] However, at that delicate moment, he preferred to watch, tight-lipped, developments in the Muslim majority provinces of Bengal, Sind, Punjab and the NWEP after the formation of groups, as he expected, "cracks and quarrels in the Muslim League everywhere"; for, he argued, "Nobody wants to sacrifice one's own provincial patriotism, and I have little doubt that this formation of groups will create dissensions in the Muslim League itself."[10] Hodson quotes Patel having expressed the view that "as soon as the Viceroy announced the prospective partition of Bengal, the Bengali Muslims would break from the League in order to preserve the province as a whole, and the same might possibly follow in Punjab."[11]

Jinnah rejected the plan in a mood of deep frustration. He felt he had been thrown off the high horse he had been riding so far. He felt defeated. Not only did his hope of gaining Pakistan seem to have receded from the horizon, but he also suffered loss of face with his partymen and the Muslims at large. He came to the conclusion that it was "hopeless to solve the Indian problem by peaceful and amicable means." This gave inspiration and direct encouragement to his lieutenants to talk openly and loudly of "blood and iron". The Nawab of Mamdot (Punjab) was the first to rattle the sabre when he declared on July 13, 1946 in Lahore: "I ask the Mussalmans to be prepared... if there were to be a war, we shall accept the challenge." And on July 29th the Bengal League Premier, H.S. Suhrawardy, came forward with the threat, "Let the Congress beware that it is not going to fight just a handful of people fighting for power, but a nation which is struggling for its life, and will ensure that life. We await the clarion call of the Quaid-i-Azam."[12] Such a call for "Direct Action" came on July 30th when Jinnah declared in Bombay, "This day we bid goodbye to constitutional methods... Today, we have also forged a pistol and are in a position to use it."[13]

Jinnah's threat was real and serious, though, in a letter to

Rajagopalachari, Cripps tried to defuse it with the hope that his "bark will prove worse than his bite."[14] Rajagopalachari wrote to Patel, "Jinnah's declaration of civil war has come! I fear this would throw the British (Government) into confusion, and a moral breakdown might result... Now that Jinnah and the League are certain to create trouble, it has become our unavoidable and bounden duty to accept that challenge. We cannot refuse any offer about the Interim Government now..."[15] The "breakdown" was to be seen in Wavell's Breakdown Plan, which proposed "a partial withdrawal to northern India... a partial withdrawal to the Muslim majority provinces of North-West and North-East India is the only practicable course we can see." Wavell's *Journal* discloses that, in a telegram to the Cabinet in London on June 3rd, the Viceroy proposed "in the event of a break with the Congress, to give, in effect, independence to Southern and Central India and to maintain the existing position in North-West and North-East India."[16] Rajagopalachari had earlier favoured conceding Pakistan to Jinnah and was the brain behind the Gandhi-Jinnah talks in 1944. Now he veered round to Patel's outlook and policy, though belatedly. It was a vindication of what Patel had stood for and strongly advocated. Rajagopalachari told him, "The violence of Jinnah's chagrin is the measure of wisdom of our decision at a critical moment. It is all due to your firm and thoughtful stand."[17]

Patel was all for that. No other Congress leaders had the courage to say what he had said at the Meerut session of the Congress in November 1946 that "the sword will be met with the sword." Earlier on May 8th, during his interview with Patel, Wavell had got an insight into his tough mind, and of this he has recorded, "He was, to begin with, uncompromisingly hostile to any settlement, except on the basis of complete Hindu supremacy; and said that they were bound to have it out with the Muslims sooner or later, and that it was better to have a conflict now and get it over... he is always likely to be on the side of direct action and, if necessary, violence."[18] Patel's failure to defeat Jinnah at his game was primarily due to the hostility he encountered within the Congress. Gandhi, being totally committed to non-violence, abhorred bloodshed, even if the other side adopted it as a weapon; while Nehru's emotional attachment and obsessive concern for the Muslim community had rendered him incapable of retaliation, even as a necessity. Jinnah benefited both from the Congress schizophrenia and the British moral breakdown; and the two combined to result in a political stampede on the part of the British, which ended in Britain's surrender of power to India and Pakistan.

Jinnah's rejection of the plan put the Mission in a quandary. It caused serious disappointment to the members, who had stretched themselves to the maximum in their attempt to accommodate Jinnah. According to Wavell, "Jinnah over-called his hand in the end, and was too uncompromising on the non-League issue."[19] Jinnah seemed to have lost favour with Pethick-Lawrence and Cripps, though not with Wavell. Cripps expressed the hope to Rajagopalachari, "I trust his withdrawal... will not lead to any stopping of the work by others."[20] Such work lay in Britain's orderly withdrawal from India through early transference of power, and that could be effected only through, as a first step, the formation of an Interim Government. Jinnah feared joining the Interim Government for two reasons: first, his chances of getting Pakistan might recede for ever; and, second, his League would lose its minority importance on the British withdrawal from India. Hodson learnt that Jinnah "evinced a deep sense of relief upon his return to his old tactical position, and upon his no longer bearing responsibility for a strategic compromise—the Cabinet Mission plan—which he had accepted only because he feared that if he rejected it, the Congress would be left not only in British favour as the time for independence approached, but also in actual power as the Interim Government of India."[21] Patel, who was jockeying for such a position, realised the danger inherent in a drifting situation, and was only too keen to gain power. Wavell held a somewhat similar view. According to H.V.R. Iengar (ICS), he reportedly told the Secretary of State that "administration in India had reached the point of collapse...

the only solution of the Indian problem was to hand over the Government of the country to whichever party was prepared to accept the responsibility."[22]

The talks having failed, Patel returned to Bombay. Every evening he paced up and down the terrace of his Marine Drive flat, having with him always appreciative listeners, like K.M. Munshi and others, to be the recipients of his "spicy and vigorous comments on men and things." But Munshi found him passing his days "like a caged lion… crouching watchfully and patiently, waiting for some bar of the cage to break so that he could pounce upon the prey."[23] Patel's restlessness had a streak of expectancy: formation of the Interim Government by the Congress, to the exclusion of the League, following his successful negotiations with Pethick-Lawrence and Cripps in the Congress acceptance of the Mission's long-term plan, even at the risk of a break with Gandhi. He told his Private Secretary, V. Shankar, that "he felt convinced that, if the Congress had not accepted the plan with its own interpretation, a League Ministry would have been installed with Jinnah gathering together the flotsam and jetsam… (which) would have done incalculable harm to Indian's future. The country would have rapidly slid into civil war."[24] Iengar flew to Bombay to see Patel, to acquaint him with Government thinking and to plead with him "to accept the offer from the Viceroy which would be forthcoming in a day or two." V.P. Menon too sent an ICS officer to see Patel with a message from Wavell, "Would he agree to help? If the Congress was offered office, would it accept on an assurance that, for all practical purposes, the Viceroy's Executive Council would be treated as a Dominion Government? Or, would it insist upon a formal declaration of Dominion Status, which, for practical and legalistic reasons, appeared to be out of the question?"[25] Patel conveyed his "pledged word" that he would exercise all his influence to see that the offer was accepted. Wavell felt as much concerned about Jinnah's "Direct Action" as was Patel; and Wavell was "convinced that the Congress must enter the Government to prevent chaos spreading in the country."[26] He was also convinced that "Patel is more like a leader than any of them (Congressmen), and might become the easiest to do business with."[27]

Wavell got the Secretary of State's approval by conveying to him on August 5th, what an "unimpeachable source" had told him about Patel's attitude, "He told the informant that if the Congress were asked to form an Interim Government, he would insist on their agreeing. He thought Nehru had temperamental objection to taking on responsibility and was frightened of the Muslim League on the one side and the Congress Socialists on the other. Patel was, however, convinced that the Congress must enter the Government to prevent chaos from spreading in the country... He would be prepared to resign from the Working Committee if his view was not accepted."[28] Patel expressed his satisfaction, rather prematurely, in a letter dated August 16th to a friend: "The Congress President has been invited to form the Interim Government, and for the first time the British Government have shown the Muslim League its proper place. They have thus given proof of their *bona fides*... If the British Government and the Congress play the game well, I have no doubt that we shall see India free sooner than many people imagine, and neither the League nor any other group of people or interests, however strong or powerful, will be able to stop it."[29] A day earlier he had written to another friend: "There is hardly any conflict now left with the British Government, and it is for us now to frame a Constitution of free India."[30] Patel erred in being so optimistic too soon, and ignored to see what could be lurking beneath the green grass. He had placed too deep a faith in Cripps, if not in Wavell. But Wavell was an incalculable factor. He could not be trusted at all, he was to prove so soon.

Jinnah reacted like a wounded lion. "Direct Action" in Calcutta was his weapon to achieve three objectives: to confuse the British and force them to concede Pakistan; to browbeat the Hindus in Calcutta, and secure transference of the Muslims of Bihar to Calcutta by forcing a Hindu exodus, thereby altering the population pattern of Calcutta; and to prepare ground for a Muslim League "invasion" of Assam, securing thereby incorporation in a future Pakistan the whole of Bengal and Assam. "Direct Action" was also to ensure that Calcutta would remain with East Pakistan. Under "Direct Action", Calcutta witnessed an "orgy of killing, loot and arson, incredible in its manifestation of communal savagery and hatred: corpses piled one on top of the other like corn sacks in a railway yard, headless bodies sprawled on the streets, walls bespattered with blood everywhere, shops broken open and rifled, cars burnt without intervention by the police". The streets of Calcutta "flowed with blood". About 6,000 people were killed, of whom 4,500 happened to be Muslims. As a face-saving device, not only did Suhrawardy carry his war on the Hindus to Noakhali and other places in East Bengal, but he also cast his evil eye on non-League Muslims. He had stated, "The League should see that no Nationalist Muslims existed within eight days."[31] Fazlul Huq, a former League Chief Minister, was physically coerced into signing the pledge of the Muslim League, while Naushar Ali, ex-Speaker of the Bengal Legislative Assembly, was humiliated and ultimately driven out from his own house.

With the League excluded from the Interim Government, Patel's manoeuvring threw Jinnah into isolation where he would have stewed in his own juice. The consequences could have been serious: a possible exodus from his party, like the one earlier if the Congress Ministries had not resigned in 1939. However, Jinnah's "Direct Action" forced Wavell to change his mind in his favour. According to Hodson, "after Wavell had seen the horrors of Calcutta, his determination to secure a coalition Government hardened."[32]

Patel saw a great danger lurking in Wavell's move. By pulling Jinnah out of his isolation, Wavell seemed to be rehabilitating him, as he had done at the Simla conference; but this time Jinnah was to gain a much stronger position. As Jinnah's aide, Ghazanfar Ali, gave out, "We are going into the Interim Government to get a foothold to fight for our cherished goal of Pakistan... The Interim Government is one of the fronts of Direct Action campaign."[33] After the first Council meeting held on September 4th, Wavell recorded of the Congress Ministers, "I do not trust them by a yard." Yet he spoke of Patel the next day, "he was very reasonable and sensible in his arguments (unlike Jinnah) and is certainly the most impressive of the Congress leaders and has the best balance."[34] Earlier, on August 19th, Patel had told Gandhi that Wavell had asked Nehru, "Would you mind if I invite Jinnah once more and persuade him?" Patel's firm attitude was, "... we are unable to accept his suggestion as it was fraught with the difficulties ahead. Not only that, it would change the entire context of things and that the Viceroy had better keep himself out of it as it was a matter for us to invite him or otherwise."[35] Wavell had ignored Jinnah's press statement of the 18th, "The Muslim League was not prepared to surrender..."[36]

What was in Jinnah's mind? A surrender not by the League but by the British and the Congress—the former by responding to his call (Divide and Quit) and the latter accepting the *fait accompli*, submitting to his demand of Pakistan. For his success, he had only to rely upon his "Direct Action", which Suhrawardy launched in Noakhali and Tippera on October 14th. Of this Patel wrote to Cripps: "What is happening in East Bengal is much worse, and the Calcutta incident pales into insignificance before Noakhali."[37] In a letter to Wavell, Nehru described the happenings in East Bengal as "mass slaughter... far worse than the Calcutta killings." In Calcutta and Noakhali the Hindus and the Muslims played Jinnah's game of "civil" war. Noakhali was followed by trouble in Bihar towards the end of October, and from there it spread to Western U.P., Punjab and the NWFP. This suited Jinnah much more than the Congress, with the British playing the role of non-interfering, inwardly bemused spectators.

Wavell displayed total indifference to the worsening law and order situation in the country. Patel considered his attitude somewhat partial insofar as he was blind to the happenings in Calcutta and East Bengal, but not so in Bihar where he sent his Deputy Private Secretary Ian Scott ostensibly on a mission. Patel lodged his protest and a warning, "We are somewhat mystified at this sudden activity, and should like to be enlightened as to the purpose and scope of his (Scott) mission... I would like to make it clear that any interference with, or bypassing of, the Ministry, particularly now that peace has been restored and the Ministry from all accounts has been doing all that is possible under most difficult circumstances, would create a major crisis." Patel emphatically stated, "Whilst I have all my sympathy for the victims and sufferers of Bihar, I wish to bring to your notice that there is a strong feeling that the unfortunate sufferers from East Bengal have not been able to enlist adequate sympathy and attention from official quarters."[38] In a letter to the Chief Minister of Bihar, Patel stated, "You must have seen Jinnah's statement in the Press today (November 26th). He talks of transfer of population... Scott also proposes the transfer of some of these people (evacuees in camps) to Bengal. My impression, reading the report of Scott, has been that even a confirmed League member would not have made such a report. It is an effort to put the League into power in these areas at the expense of the Government and (through) the use of Government machinery."[39]

Patel did not slacken his pressure on Wavell by way of reminding him of his duty to act. The power to act lay with Wavell, not with Patel as Home Member of the Interim Government because of provincial autonomy under the 1935 Act. In a letter of October 20th, he reminded Wavell of Ghazanfar Ali's outburst and asked him, "Is the Interim Government to be the arena of party politics and intrigues and for driving in the very partition wedge which the long-term arrangement (under the Cabinet Mission plan) had withdrawn once for all and replace it by grouping, which in itself seems to be voluntary?"

He reminded Wavell, "If wrangles over Partition and fomenting of trouble are to take the place of the immediate work of the administration, it would be a question for the Congress to revise its attitude about shouldering the burden it has taken over in response to your invitation."[40] Again in a note to Wavell of October 25th, Patel stated, "It would, indeed, be a tragic paradox if we who have undertaken the responsibility of the Government of India should be powerless to do anything to terminate the reign of terror..."

Patel referred to the powers Wavell possessed under the Government of India Act and stated, "I and my colleagues, whom I have consulted before writing this, are emphatically of (the) opinion… that we should recommend to Your Excellency that you should immediately exercise the powers attaching to you special responsibility as Governor-General and take all steps necessary to take over the duties of law and order in the affected areas, if not in the whole of Bengal, from the hands of the present Government of Bengal who have totally failed in their duties in that respect."[41]

In this game of cornering, Patel was outmanoeuvred by Wavell. On the day Patel had suggested a Cabinet meeting, Wavell gave a broadcast speech inviting the League to join the Interim Government. Although many, including Patel, were aware of the working of Wavell's mind in this regard, the timing and the manner of invitation was to them like a bolt from the blue. A senior Cabinet member N.V. Gadgil records, "I was stunned and immediately phoned Vallabhbhai. He said he was equally shocked. There was a fatal contradiction between the firm policy which we had decided upon in dealing with the League and the advice given to the Viceroy by Nehru. This became evident within a week or so. The leaders of the League had realised that without power, they would lose their hold on the Muslims. On the other hand, if they entered the Government, they would achieve Pakistan by sabotage inside and disorder outside."[42]

As early as June 12th, Patel had forewarned Wavell that "Jinnah would only use his position in the Interim Government for purely communal and disruptive purposes and to break up India." Wavell had, however, assured Patel that he was quite certain that would not be Jinnah's attitude, and that he could trust him "to see that any attempt by Jinnah or either party to make the Interim Government a battleground of communal politics, instead of an instrument of administering India, would be prevented". Wavell further records that "Patel was not all convinced."[43]

The League's entry into the Interim Government was the beginning of the end of India's unity. Earlier the threat was from outside, which could be warded off if the British so desired; now it was from within, and the rulers found themselves caught in the crossfire. The Leaguers created a deadlock in the working of the Government machinery, and were insulting to Nehru in not giving him the recognition he deserved as Vice-President. Worst still, as Patel experienced, with the League's entry, "every, Muslim officer was an advance guard of the League... India's administration began to be openly balanced in favour of the Muslims."[44] Patel was also to face a situation of near confrontation within the party, as "Rajaji tried to conciliate the League members, and the combination of Rajaji and Nehru in this respect was insurmountable even for the mighty Sardar... Often he would let himself go in sheer exasperation."

Gadgil has further recorded, "The Congress members of the Executive Council were subject to open criticism by the League in the Assembly, and it was obvious that Jinnah encouraged them. The Congress party was overwhelmed by the thought that it was responsible for the administration and handicapped by feeble leadership."[45]

A defeat stared Patel in the face. Instead of the League, it was now the Congress that had begun losing all along the line. Things had gone out of control, and the new dangers demanded a drastic move. At the Meerut session of the Congress, not only did Patel warn the League that "the sword will be met with the sword", but the session decided that the party should quit the Interim Government if the League boycotted the Constituent Assembly. The British could not afford to let the Congress create a crisis which would have been far more serious than the one created by the League, insofar as it would have made it difficult for them to transfer power and quit. Attlee lost no time in countering such a step by calling to London the Indian leaders with the declared purpose of reconciling the Congress-League differences. It was found to be an impossible task, as the League was well entrenched to fight on two specific fronts: to demolish the edifice of the Interim Government by stalling its working, and thereby letting the administration at the Centre and in the provinces break down completely. Secondly, to prevent the Constituent Assembly from being called. A complete deadlock in the Government was more to Jinnah's advantage than to the advantage of the British or the Congress. Hodson says, "The British could not stay indefinitely in India until the parties were agreed." Taking advantage of this, Jinnah demanded, "If the British were going, they had better to at once, or else draw up a constitution and make an award. They should give the Muslims their own bit of country, however small, where they could live, if necessary, on one meal a day."[46]

Patel was opposed to the Congress going to London. He feared it to be a snare for the Congress. Jinnah's position, because of the League's membership of the Interim Government, was now much stronger than before. Patel had announced the Congress decision on November 29th, "The League and the Viceroy will go to England day after tomorrow. The Congress and the Sikh representatives will not go."[47] His reasoning was, "The invitation, in spite of all denials to the contrary, means either the reopening of the question or putting pressure on the Congress to make some more concessions to the League." And that is what took place in London. Patel, however, accused the League and the Viceroy of an "open alliance", and stated, "The Viceroy gave us an assurance, and so did Jinnah to the Viceroy at the time of the League's entry into the Interim Government. He has repudiated his assurance publicly and now they want to placate him. Every time the League takes a recalcitrant attitude, they try to placate it. The result is that the League gets stronger and stronger, and its attitude of violence gets encouragement. It is a misfortune that the British Government is unable to take a firm stand and call off the bluff."[48] Nehru was not scheduled to go to London. Yet, moved by Attlee's personal appeal, he decided to go, believing that "refusal to accept the invitation may be regarded as an act of discourtesy."

"Nehru", Patel told Cripps, "left India full of hopes for a message of goodwill and sympathy, but he returned sadly disappointed. He now realises his mistake and the amount of harm that has been done to India by his having accepted the invitation." Complaining that "there is very little understanding over there of our difficulties here", Patel bluntly told Cripps, "You called the League delegation there at a time when there was some realisation that violence is a game at which both parties can play and the mild Hindu also, when driven to desperation, can retaliate as brutally as a fanatic Muslim. Just when the time for settlement was reached, Jinnah got the invitation, and he was able to convince the Muslims once again that he has been able to get more concessions by creating trouble and violence." Every action of Wavell since the Great Calcutta Killing, he told Cripps, "has been in the direction of encouraging the Muslim League and putting pressure on us towards appeasement."

Patel assertively stated, "If you think that Assam can be coerced into accepting the domination of Bengal, the sooner you rid yourself of that illusion the better." He had no hesitation to tell Cripps, "With great difficulty, we were able to build a bridge between England and India by our joint efforts—and you know my own contribution. I regret to say that the sense of faith and confidence about the sincerity of Britain that was created by our settlement is fast being dissipated, and the bridge is about to crack or collapse." Stating that "the solution has now been made more difficult, nay, almost impossible", Patel sadly pointed out, "You know when Gandhi was strongly against our settlement, I threw my weight in favour of it... All of us here feel that there has been a betrayal."[49]

For the Congress, the battle was lost. The ground Patel had gained, after so skilful a manoeuvring, slipped from under his feet. Now he had no chance of having the upper hand. Hereafter the upper hand was Jinnah's, to whom Attlee capitulated in London in the same manner, though for different reasons, as Wavell had at Simla in 1945. But the Congress lost ground primarily because of Nehru's capitulation twice—first to Wavell on the issue of the League's entry into the Interim Government without repudiation of its 'Direct Action' resolution; and, second, to Attlee by agreeing to attend the London talks, which turned out to be like summons from a court to hear the judgment. Without giving anyone a chance to speak, Attlee only announced the British plan for the future of India, "His plan clearly indicated that the country was going to be partitioned."[50] The deciding factor was Attlee's judgment, "the Bengal Muslims can draft the constitution of Assam."[51] To Patel, Nehru or the Congress, this was unacceptable.

Britain was not, in reality, concerned as to who won or lost. Her main anxiety was how to get out of India, and how to preserve her own position in India, whether united or partitioned. The London conference was her last resort to bypass the situation. Otherwise, Patel wouldn't have let them go so easily. Like Jinnah, he too would have exploited Britain's weakness: her helplessness to act without the Congress acceptance of Partition. Here the trump card was with the Congress, not with Jinnah; nor with the British. He seemed to be wanting to play it to his advantage. Even if this involved anarchy and civil war, Patel was ready for it. This could have been like the American war of independence—more to unite the country than to bifurcate it. In the end, perhaps, Jinnah might not have got his Pakistan, and Britain would have lost India for good. However, as matters stood then, the once great Empire builders and rulers, the British, had shown up unmistakable signs of weakness, vacillation and defeatism, which indicated the path leading to the end of the Empire. Theirs was a surrender to Jinnah by consensus. And at such a critical stage when India had been placed on a razor's edge, Britain, overlooking Jinnah's role as a wrecker, served as a prelude to India's Partition.

19

Verdict on Assam, Blow to Unity

Attlee's verdict on Assam favouring Jinnah on 6th December 1946 left the Congress with no option but to agree to India's Partition. The Congress could not go against the wishes of the overwhelming Hindu population of Assam. Jinnah returned from London with a glimmer of hope, though not yet certain as to when he would achieve his Pakistan. Earlier he had lost all along the line, and had even been thrown into isolation. Now, he seemed to be advancing hopefully towards his long cherished goal. The new interpretation given to the provinces joining the Groups in the British Government's statement of December 6th and Lord Pethick-Lawrence's clarification of it in the House of Lords on December 17th totally changed the situation. The December 6th statement said, "The decisions of the Sections should, in the absence of agreement to the contrary, be taken by a simple majority vote of the representatives in the Sections' and that "the provinces have a right to decide both as to grouping and as to their own constitutions." The statement "threw a veritable apple of discord into Indian politics." It was contrary to the earlier understanding given to the Congress. In a letter of June 15th, Wavell had told Azad, "The Delegation and I are aware of your objections to the principle of Grouping. I would, however, point out that the statement of May 16th does not make Grouping compulsory. It leaves the decision to the elected representatives of the provinces concerned sitting together in Sections. The only provision which is made is that the representatives of certain provinces should meet in Sections so that they can decide whether or not they wish to form Groups."[1]

The Congress Working Committee described the new situation emerging from the December 6th statement as "full of peril for the future". In a statement on December 22nd, it recalled that the statement of May 16th had laid down that "there should be a Union of India embracing both British India and the States"; that "all subjects other than Union subjects and all residuary powers should vest in the provinces", and that "provinces should be free to form Groups". It, therefore, pointed out: "The provinces were intended to be autonomous, subject to the Union controlling certain specified subjects. Paragraph 19 laid down, *inter alia*, the procedure for Sections to meet for decisions to be taken as to whether Groups should be formed or not, and for any province to elect to come out of the Group in which it might have been placed." The Congress' "objection was not to provinces entering Sections, but to compulsory Grouping, and the possibility of a dominating province framing a constitution for another province entirely against the wishes of the latter. This might result in the framing of rules, and the regulation of franchise, electorates, constituencies for elections and the composition of the legislature which might seriously prejudice, or even nullify, the provision for a province subsequently to opt out of a Group."[2] It was feared that since sections B and C would meet on their own accord, the new statement "would authorise the formation of a second Constituent Assembly for sections B and C, and that would be Pakistan against the protest of the Congress." The Congress suggestion that the disputed interpretation be referred to the Federal Court was rejected. Pethick-Lawrence stated in the House of Lords of December 17th, "The British Government do not consider that this issue is one which it is desirable to refer to the Federal Court."[3]

The Congress was thrown into a dilemma. An agitated AICC met on January 5th, 1947, to consider the implications of the new development. Some members felt that "Jinnah's, or the League's or the Muslim's triumphs were fast mounting up, not as a result of any active movement they had ever initiated in life, but of the attitude of negation, and, at the outside, of passive resistance on all occasions."[4] Assam members dominated the AICC session, as they were primarily concerned with the outcome of the December 6th statement. They were "anxious to see that the pledges made solemnly by the Congress High Command that Assam would not be forced into the C Section are honoured in the spirit in which they were made." They were critical of Nehru's role in two respects: First, he had "straightaway agreed to the provinces going into Sections" in a broadcast on September 2nd on becoming Vice-President in the Interim Government, which was contrary to the official Congress statement on May 25th. They looked upon this as a "breach of understanding". Secondly, because Nehru, "may be much against his own wishes but wholly against the wishes of his wiser colleagues, went to England and entangled himself and the country in a development from which it was not easy for him or the country to escape."[5]

With the Congress well cornered, Jinnah's civil war entered the final phase for the capture of the Muslim majority provinces *as a whole*. To achieve this, he intensified an on-surface non-violent civil agitation against the non-League Ministries of Punjab and the NWFP. Punjab was his main target, as it held the key to his Pakistan; while the NWFP, by staying out, would have created problems of homogeneity of Pakistan, and even caused loss of international importance. In January itself the League started civil agitation in both the provinces. In Punjab, its claim was that since the Premier represented a minority of the Muslim legislators, Khizr Hayat Khan Tiwana had no right to rule. In the NWFP, its fight was for civil liberties on behalf of the small urban Muslim population it represented. In both, under the garb of a peaceful agitation, the League attempted to poison the minds of the Muslim masses with the communal virus and prepare them for a grim fight against the Punjab Hindus and Sikhs, and thereby coerce the Congress into accepting the League's demand for Pakistan.

The Punjab Government arrested all the top Leaguers. But Khizr could not afford to deal with the agitators sternly on his own, even when his Governor, Evan Jenkins, was a pro-Unionist and anti-Leaguer, unlike Mudie in Sind or Olaf Caroe in the NWFP. There was a lack of support from the Congress. Khizr and his British Home Secretary suggested to Bhim Sen Sachar, the Congress Legislative party leader and Finance Minister in Khizr's coalition Government, that "if the Hindus were to start a counter-agitation resulting in a clash with the Muslim Leaguers, the Government would get an opportunity to come down with a heavy hand on the League."[6] Sachar lacked courage to do so, as this would have been against the official Congress policy, but more particularly, contrary to the policy of Azad whose nominee he was. Failure of the Unionist Government to take strong action against the League agitators strengthened Jinnah's position even among non-League Punjab Muslims, who now looked upon him as the new Messiah and started jumping onto his bandwagon.

In the NWFP elections, the Congress victory had been decisive. But the League's advantage lay in a pro-League Governor, Olaf Caroe, as also the backing it enjoyed of the local British Civil Servants. Encouraged by their attitude, the League launched a Punjab-style agitation against Dr. Khan Sahib's Congress Ministry in the urban areas only where it enjoyed some influence. Dr. Khan Sahib could have handled the situation had it not been made worse by Nehru's Frontier visit in September after joining the Interim Government as Vice-President. The visit was taken as a challenge by the Muslim League and it increased the tempo of its agitation. Sardar Abdur Rab Nishtar described it as "a deliberate encroachment on the League preserve." True or untrue, it mattered little in the climate of 1946, surcharged with communal hatred. It placed in the hands of the League a highly sensitive issue which it could easily communalise and exploit to its advantage. Jinnah looked upon the visit as a godsend to show how unpopular Nehru and the Congress were among the Muslims of the NWFP, especially of the tribal areas. The League inflamed communal passions in two ways: by publicising the Pathans wounded in the communal rioting at Garmukhteshwar in Uttar Pradesh; and by publicly displaying a few reportedly burnt pages of the holy *Koran* by the Hindus.

Nehru's decision to visit the NWFP was his own. He was in charge of Foreign Affairs in the Interim Government. He was overconfident of his personal hold on the people, no matter if they were Muslims. Blinded by his overconfidence and his status consciousness, Nehru brushed aside not only Patel's advice *not to go*, but also Dr. Khan Sahib's *not to visit*. According to Mehr Chand Khanna, the Finance Minister, Caroe "did not favour the idea of Nehru's projected visit to the Agencies. A plot was hatched to create trouble. The Congress Ministry got an inkling of this, and Dr. Khan Sahib and his colleagues advised Nehru to cancel his programme of visiting the Agencies, but Nehru thought that any change in his programme would be attributed to a weakness on his part."[7] Nehru failed to realise the danger lurking in his visit: it could prove a fatal mistake that would cost the Congress the NWFP. Caroe admitted later that "this visit of Nehru's to the Frontier, more than anything else, made Partition inevitable."[8] The British utilised the agitation as the basis for the holding of the referendum later. Nehru did not appreciate that Dr. Khan Sahib enjoyed no authority in the tribal area he was visiting. The five Tribal Agencies were directly under the charge of Caroe as the Crown Representative.

A hot reception awaited Nehru. He travelled in Khanna's car flanked by the Khan brothers. In the violent attacks the Pathans indulged in, not only was the car heavily damaged, but even Nehru was hurt. An explosive situation, with the backing of officials, was whipped up in some of the NWFP towns. Peshawar suffered its worst fate by remaining completely closed and cut off for over a week, following a total breakdown of law and order. This, according to Khanna, was pre-planned: "to create trouble and to demonstrate that the Congress Ministry was ineffective, the police were withdrawn to the barracks and the city was left to its fate." When the Provincial Congress and the Khudai Khidmatgars decided to risk entry into the city with a view to restoring normalcy, the Chief Secretary, de la Fargue, advised Dr. Khan Sahib "to avoid a clash at any cost, as the Governor has orders ready to dismiss the Ministry in that event."[9]

Following this good trip, in Shahi Bagh all the Khudai Khidmatgars surrendered their arms and about 10,000 of them, led by Dr. Khan Sahib, Khan Abdul Ghaffar Khan and Mehr Chand Khanna, entered the city in columns of fours in military formation. The city gates were opened without any clash and the Khudai Khidmatgars were posted at different points in the city to maintain law and order. This helped the Congress Government in regaining control of the city and enhancing its prestige. Caroe was uninfluenced by this show of non-violent power, which the Leaguers and officials witnessed as silent spectators. A committed Caroe suggested to Dr. Khan Sahib that he would help him and his Cabinet colleagues "continue as Ministers in Pakistan if they dissociated themselves from the Hindu Congress."[10]

The stage-managed violent reception to Nehru and the communal violence in parts of the NWFP gave Wavell his opportunity to conclude that the Pathans had "no intention of being ruled by Hindus and resented Nehru's visit."[11] Chief Secretary de la Fargue, on the other hand, told Mountbatten that "a free and clean election in the province was more likely to return the Congress to power than the League, even if Section 93 Government had been interposed; that the Governor... was biased against his Congress Government; and that his continuance in office was a menace to British prestige."[12] The communally surcharged atmosphere and the approaching transference of power did cause some dents in the Congress position in the NWFP. Such dents, however, could not throw Dr. Khan Sahib out of power. He remained entrenched as the NWFP Chief Minister till Jinnah took over as Governor-General of Pakistan and dismissed him. In the prevailing vitiated climate in the NWFP and the Congress acceptance of Partition, under which there was hardly any possibility of the NWFP remaining within India, the Congress influence declined, though not necessarily of the Khan brothers.

Azad said later, "The Khan brothers were certainly right

in claiming that a large section of the people in the Frontier supported them. They had, however, exaggerated the extent of their influence."[13] There was some erosion of authority, though not to the extent it was blown up by the Leaguers and the British Civil Servants. By the time the referendum was to be held, Abdul Ghaffar Khan and his followers had started "thinking of having a separate homeland for the Pathans." A feeling of helplessness seemed to have overtaken the minds of the Congress leaders both at the Centre and in the province: "to placate the Muslim League, it was given out that the newly-formed Pakhtoonistan would be within Pakistan, but the demand was rejected outright."[14] Such was the new shape of politics in the NWFP in the wake of the June 3 Plan.

By mid-June Ghaffar Khan had an infructuous meeting with Jinnah, while earlier in May, Dr. Khan Sahib is reported to have told Mountbatten that "no referendum was necessary; for, we were all for Pakistan and considered our province an integral part of it."[15] Patel was of the view that the Khan brothers' "influence is on the wane."[16] Patel believed that to fight a lost battle in the NWFP would not be an act of wisdom as it would come in the way of the Congress taking over power in India. He was guided by the pragmatic policy of strengthening the foundations of the new State, rather than dream of something that was distant and impossible. Another contributory factor to the lessening of Patel's interest in the NWFP was the Frontier Congress's decision, under Gandhi's advice, to boycott the referendum so as to avoid bloodshed. Patel concurred with Nehru that, apart from being unsure of the results, boycott would mean "accepting the Muslim League's dominance in the NWFP—in effect a surrender to the Muslim League agitation."[17]

As Home Member in the Interim Government, Patel's major task was to ensure safe sailing for the ship of State, which he could do only by underscoring the grave mischief the Leaguers, especially those in the Government, were deliberately indulging in with a view to stoking the communal fires they had themselves lit in Punjab and the NWFP. He drew Wavell's attention to many such occasions of serious indiscretions on the part of his Muslim League colleagues. In his letter of February 14, 1947, he quoted Ghazanfar Ali having stated: "Mohammed Bin Kassim and Mahmud of Ghazni invaded India with armies composed of only a few thousands, and yet were able to overpower lakhs of Hindus. God willing, a few lakhs of Muslims will yet overwhelm crores of Hindus." Patel laid emphasis again on what he had written earlier: "the impropriety of the Muslim League members of the Central Government issuing public statements criticising the conduct of the Punjab Government in grossly disparaging terms." He also stated: "The parallel drawn is significant, particularly in regard to Ghazni's invasion, which consisted of repeated raids on India in which Hindus were killed in thousands and temples were destroyed… A more flagrant breach of the rules of responsibility incumbent on members of the Central Government would be difficult to find. Instances like this only serve to strengthen our conviction that a corporate body like the Central Government has ceased to exist and that the sooner the present state of affairs is put an end to the better."[18]

The Congress troubles were more due to Wavell's tolerance of Jinnah's and his colleagues" explosive outbursts. Nehru wrote to Patel of his meeting with Wavell on January 2nd: "…our talk was very revealing about his persistent attitude to push the Muslim League on. We are going to have all manner of additional difficulties."[19] In the circumstances, the only thing Patel could do was not to relent his pressure on Wavell, lest the Congress point of view should go by default. He did so also from a noble motive. He told Wavell of January 26th: "I feel that there is still time to prevent this dangerous tendency from becoming further accentuated, and stop matters from passing from unfair criticism to open encouragement to defiance." Patel went on to suggest that "if they wish to continue in their course, the only honourable course for them is to resign."[20] Wavell refused to budge. He merely spoke to Liaquat Ali—and that too in a casual manner. In the second week of February, Nehru wrote to Gandhi: "We are drifting everywhere and sometimes I doubt if we are drifting in the right direction. We live in a state of perpetual crises, and have no real grip of the situation."[21] Communal disturbances were spreading unabated. Patel, therefore, wrote to Wavell: "I would impress upon you, with all the earnestness at my command, the desirability—in fact the necessity—of enforcing martial law in the worst affected areas." Wavell merely replied: "I do not think that martial law, which has many grave disadvantages, is at present necessary."[22]

The Congress-League conflict assumed another dangerous proportion when the League refused to join the Constituent Assembly. Upon this the Congress and minority members of the Interim Government demanded the resignation of the League representatives. This was not for non-participation in the Constituent Assembly only, but also for a total rejection of the Cabinet Mission scheme and for a programme of Direct Action, which the League had not withdrawn. Liaquat Ali countered it with the contention that it was the Congress which had not in fact accepted the Mission Plan and demanded of the British Government to see that the Congress "did keep on the rails laid down by the Mission for the Constituent Assembly." Liaquat Ali even challenged the Congress right to be in the Interim Government. Wavell was "in sympathy with the Muslim League's contention and was himself of the view that the Congress had not in fact accepted the Cabinet Mission Plan."[23] He asked the British Government to call upon the Congress to confirm that the relevant passages of its resolution dealing with Sections and Groupings, which had given rise to Muslim League doubts, were not intended to limit or qualify the Congress acceptance of the Cabinet Mission Plan. The Secretary of State was doubtful if such a step would improve the situation. About this time (February 13th), Nehru, in a letter to Wavell, reiterated his demand for the resignation of the League members from the Interim Government. Patel sounded more forthright and firm when he made it clear that the Congress would withdraw from the Interim Government if the League members were allowed to remain in it. He insisted, "The League must either get out of the Interim Government, or change its Karachi decision."

The British Government found itself in an inextricable situation—badly entangled in a web of its own making. It realised that to ask for the resignation of the League representatives from the Interim Government would have "serious repercussions in India and in the Muslim countries of the world", to allow the Congress to resign would lead to "even more disastrous consequences."[24] It also realised, in V.P. Menon's view, that "the Central Government was a house divided against itself. In further communal disorders, it was doubtful if the loyalty of the Army and the Services could be relied upon." Menon also records that the British Government seemed to have "now exhausted all its resources to bring about an agreement"[25] between the Congress and the League. Apparently forced by such circumstances, Attlee announced on February 20th HMG's definite intention to take the necessary steps to effect the transference of power to responsible Indian hands by a date not later than June 1948. Attlee further announced: "HMG will have to consider to whom the powers of the Central Government in British India should be handed over on the due date, whether as a whole to some form of Central Government for British India, or in some areas to the existing provincial Governments, or in such other way as may seem most reasonable and in the best interests of the Indian people."

The February 20th statement, according to Hodson, meant "an open licence for Pakistan in some form or other."[26] Penderel Moon too thought likewise: "This announcement meant Partition, and Partition within the next seventeen months."[27] Viscount Templewood, who, as Secretary of State for India, had piloted the Government of India Bill of 1935 through the House of Commons, considered Attlee's announcement as "unconditional surrender, at the expense of many to whom we have given specific pledges for generations past, which would lead to a division of India under the worst possible circumstances." To him the decision seemed "to imperil the peace and prosperity of India." Lord Simon too lent his support to such a view. But it was Halifax who "turned the scales" by supporting the Labour with the significant observation: "... the truth is that for India today there is no solution that is not fraught with the gravest objection, with the gravest danger. And the conclusion that I reach—with all that can be said against it—is that I am not prepared to condemn what HMG are doing, unless I can honestly and confidently recommend a better solution."[28] The London *Times* wrote: "Muslim separatism is deriving encouragement from the language of the White Paper." All said and done, the British decision was an act of betrayal, even a surrender—not "a mission of fulfillment", as Attlee claimed it to be.

Nehru welcomed Attlee's statement as "wise and courageous." Patel maintained his discreet silence. But the statement was a masterpiece of jugglery, conveying no definite meaning except that the British had decided to quit India in their helplessness. They were not in a position to maintain any longer the autocratic Empire, whose close-knit fabric they had built over the past century and a half. Nor could they any more give protection to the minorities whom they had pampered and built up as a counterpoise to the Hindus under their divide-and-rule policy. The announcement automatically derecognised the Interim Government. It seemed clear that the British would not hand over power to any Central Government singly controlled either by the Congress or the League. Absence of a clear-cut solution made confusion worse. Equally disturbing was Attlee's reference to the Indian States that "HMG do not intend to hand over their powers and obligations under Paramountcy to any Government of British India. It is not intended to bring Paramountcy, as a system, to a conclusion either than the date of the final transfer of power..." In British India, power may be handed over "in some areas to the existing provincial governments."

Attlee's announcement was an invitation to anarchy and chaos. Its repercussions were to be seen at their worst in Punjab, where some of the staunchest Muslim Unionists, hitherto strong supporters of Khizr, began wavering in their loyalty to their Premier. To Khizr, the hardest blow came from his main prop, Muzzafar Ali Quizalbash, "most of whose family members had by then fallen prey to the Muslim League propaganda" and who accused Quizalbash of "betraying the interests of his own community." One day Khizr told Quizalbash, "Muzz. This is the time to fight these communal forces. Let us go all out to fight the Muslim League."[29] Quizalbash kept mum. He wasn't the same—a strong Unionist and an anti-Leaguer. Mentally he had crossed over to the other side of the fence. The blow to Khizr was shattering. He began losing heart. Fed up with a hopeless situation he announced at midnight of March 2nd-3rd, "The basic fact of the situation is that the province has been suddenly confronted with the main constitutional problem, and, in conformity with the policy to which I have throughout adhered, the responsibility for dealing with this problem on behalf of the Muslims must continue to vest in the Muslim majority party. Needless to say, my Muslim colleagues and I will continue to support the Muslim demand for self-determination."[30] That was a surrender to Jinnah.

On coming to know of his decision to resign, Sachar told Khizr, "Is it for this that we had joined you?" With eyes filled with "tears of remorse and helplessness, and a heart overwhelmed with anguish", Khizr replied, "You also say so, Sachar! Don't you feel my position?"[31]

Such a surrender to Jinnah, according to some, might have been stalled or reversed, had Azad allowed Patel a free hand in reaching such party alignments in Punjab as would have given the Coalition Government the much-needed cohesion—and power to fight Jinnah.

Punjab Congress and Akali leaders thought that Khizr's decision was calculated to facilitate the installation of the Muslim League in power in Punjab prior to the transference of power. This would have had disastrous results. Out of fear and anxiety, the Hindus and Sikhs took out in Lahore, capital of the province, processions on March 4th and held protest meetings--just in the manner the League had done a few days earlier. But unlike earlier occasions, the police showed partiality and vindictiveness by firing on Hindu Sikh mobs, killing a few and wounding many. Nothing like that had happened during the League's 34-day agitation. The Muslim mobs had been tolerated; even treated with indulgence.

Sachar met the Governor to know why "this discrimination was made today, while the police did not think it worthwhile to take any action against the League demonstrators a few days ago", even when they had been unruly on many occasions and injured a few senior police officials, some of whom were Englishmen. In a League demonstration in Amritsar on February 24th, described by a Government communiqué as "exceedingly serious", a Sikh constable was beaten to death, the Additional District Magistrate brutally assaulted, a murderous assault made on a Sub-Inspector of Police, besides injuries to 29 constables.[32] And yet no action was taken.

The communal clash in Lahore on March 4th was a signal, and a good excuse, for the League to launch its Calcutta-type Direct Action in the cities of Amritsar, Rawalpindi, Multan, including the rural areas of the last two, and Jhelum, besides Abbottabad district of the NWFP. In no time, all West Punjab was aflame. Large, well-organised mobs, sometimes 3,000 to 4,000 strong, armed with sten-guns and Bren-guns and led by demobbed military jawans, attacked defenceless Hindus and Sikhs in villages and towns, perpetrating abominable crimes, especially on women and children. Gandhi's Secretary Pyarelal states: "The similarity of the pattern followed by the rioters in all these places pointed to a deliberate and well-conceived plan. By mid-day of March 19th 1947, according to a statement by A.A. MacDonald, Chief Secretary to the Punjab Government, the campaign launched by the Muslim League had cost in casualties 2,049 Hindus and Sikhs and 1,103 seriously wounded."[33] Nehru, who visited some of the riot-affected areas, saw "ghastly sights" and "heard of behaviour by human beings which would degrade brutes." Moved by such sights, the British Deputy Inspector-General of Police, Rawalpindi, J.A. Scott, observed on March 21st, "I could never believe that such barbarous acts as were committed on innocent people in the rural areas of Rawalpindi district could be possible in Punjab."[34]

Patel suffered deep frustration due to Wavell's refusal to act; and such a feeling was heightened by his inability to act on his own as India's Home Minister, the provinces being outside his jurisdiction under the Act of 1935. He urged Wavell to act before it was too late. But he had to suffer Wavell's refusal. Yet, he wrote to him in a prophetic vein: "I still feel more severe action is required. From the latest telegram (from the Governor of Punjab) you will notice that the situation in Eastern Punjab is full of explosive possibilities, and any prolongation of the disturbed conditions in the North and Western Punjab might bring about a flare-up at any time."[35] Wavell even ignored Patel's friendly advice that "firm and determined action of the kind I have suggested within the next few days will enable you to hand over to your successor a better legacy than you received from your predecessor."[36]

Patel was the first among Congress leaders who realised the implications of Attlee's statement of February 20th; even much earlier than foreign commentators. He acted quickly, not allowing events and individuals to overtake him. In 1946, Azad had come in his way during the Ministry formation at Karachi. Now, he feared, Gandhi might play the same role. His advantage this time, however, lay in Nehru being no longer a neutral as in 1945-46. He was with Patel, not with Gandhi. Of their relationship, Pyarelal records: "Sardar Patel... thought in terms of reciprocity—uniform action in Bihar and Bengal and elsewhere. The League would come to its senses only when it realised that violence was a game 'at which both parties can play' ...Pandit Nehru's was an idealistic approach... Sardar Patel, the matter-of-fact realist, was at times very critical of what appeared to him as the disjointed idealism of his colleague (Nehru). But, however much they disagreed with each other, neither of them could agree with Gandhi... A widening gulf separated them from their erstwhile oracle. Sardar Patel was the first to recognise it. The recognition came late to Pundit Nehru, and he continued to struggle against it almost to the last."[37]

It was at Patel's initiative that the Congress Working Committee passed a resolution on March 8th favouring a division of Punjab. The resolution stated, "The tragic events have demonstrated that there can be no settlement of the problem in Punjab by violence and coercion, and that no arrangement based on coercion can last.

Therefore, it is necessary to find a way out which involves the least amount of compulsion. This would necessitate a division of Punjab into two provinces, so that the predominantly Muslim part may be separated from the predominantly non-Muslim part."[38] For Gandhi, the resolution was like a bolt from the blue, "it was as if the abyss had suddenly opened under his feet. He had not been consulted or even forewarned."[39] He wrote to Patel: "Try to explain to me your Punjab resolution if you can. I cannot understand it." Unlike on earlier occasions, this time Patel's reply was terse, matter-of-fact, "It is difficult to explain to you the resolution about Punjab. It was adopted after the deepest deliberation. Nothing has been done in a hurry, or without full thought. That you had expressed your views against it, we learnt only from the papers. But you are, of course, entitled to say what you feel right."

He further told Gandhi, "The situation in Punjab is far worse than in Bihar... The military has taken over control. As a result, on the surface the things seem to have quietened down somewhat. But no one can say when there may be a burst-up again. If that happens, I am afraid, even Delhi will not remain unaffected." Lending his support to Patel, Nehru wrote to Gandhi that the resolution was "the only answer to Partition as demanded by Jinnah."[40]

Partition was a dilemma the Congress faced the post-Attlee policy statement of 20th February 1947. Gandhi's solution lay in his surrender to Jinnah (see next chapter). Patel's was a bold approach: practical, pragmatic, earliest to achieve so as to recreate an integrated, homogeneous India. Reginald Coupland had written about this in 1945 in *India: A Re-Statement* (Oxford): "An India deprived of the States would have lost all coherence. They stand between all four quarters of the country... India could live if its Muslim limbs in the north-west and north-east were amputated, but could it live without its midriff?" Prevailing conditions left no other choice for Patel, and was decidedly the best for India in 1947.

Through his Punjab resolution, Patel wanted to end the vicious stalemate the Congress had tolerated for so long; and thereby: first, to grasp the power that was coming; secondly, to gain as much territory for India as possible, and, thereby, save non-Muslim minorities from the fate they had already suffered in Calcutta, Noakhali, Punjab and the NWFP. Patel was out to frustrate Jinnah's ambition to secure the whole of Bengal and Assam, and, on gaining power, to frustrate British efforts to create in the Princes a third force—a third Dominion. Through the resolution, Patel was forestalling, as well as checkmating, any move on Gandhi's part. Gandhi, indeed, made such a move with Mountbatten in the suggestion to hand over India as a whole to Jinnah for the sake of preserving the country's unity and integrity. Possibly, the resolution was also a step to prevent Gandhi from running to Jinnah's court, as he had done in 1944 when Patel was in jail. However, Patel gave Munshi two reasons. First, "the Congress being pledged to non-violence, it was not possible for it to resist Partition." With the Muslim League having already unleashed violence and the British Government "sitting tight over the country with its police and army", resistance would "mean the end of the Congress". Secondly, "if Partition were not accepted there was bound to be a long drawn-out communal strife in cities, in some rural areas, and even regiments and police forces would be torn by communal dissensions."[41] Prospects for immediate independence would have, thus, been lost—and never to return for many years. Prudence lay with Patel in grasping the opportunity.

Since India faced Balkanisation, Patel's Punjab resolution was like catching the bull by the horns—a masterly strategy in many ways. Pyarelal considers it as "an eleventh hour attempt on the part of the Congress to wean the Muslim League from the principle of Partition by confronting it with the logical consequences of its doctrine, if it persisted in its demand for the division of India. It was partly also an effort, in the event of India's Partition, to salvage the non-Muslim majority area of that province from the Muslim League rule... The assumption was that, confronted with the prospect of being left with a 'truncated, moth-eaten' Pakistan... the League would not press for its demand for Partition."[42] Patel disclosed his mind to Kanji Dwarkadas on March 12th, four days prior to the passing of the Punjab resolution, "If the League insists on Pakiştan, the only alternative is the division of Punjab and Bengal. They cannot have Punjab as a whole or Bengal without civil war... a strong Centre with the whole of India, except Eastern Bengal and a part of Punjab, Sind and Baluchistan, enjoying full autonomy under that Centre, will be so powerful that the remaining portions will eventually come in."[43] That sounded like loud thinking, though it could not be termed wishful. If his reference to civil war gives a clue to the working of his mind, it could have been an American-type war of independence. But the Punjab resolution was, essentially, to set the divided Congress house in order, so that it could present a united front at a time when transference of power was on the anvil.

20

Transfer of Power

Attlee's statement of February 20th was a clear indication of Britain's decision to surrender to Jinnah's demand: "divide and quit". The statement's implementation, however, required a surgical operation which was not an easy task, and for which Attlee needed someone possessing a personality far different from Wavell's: more dynamic, not merely charming but charismatic too, and decisively domineering. His choice fell on the Admiral of the Fleet, Lord Mountbatten. He was all that, and much more—dashing, debonair and handsome. On top of it, he was connected with the royal family. Mountbatten's appointment as the new Viceroy of India was made simultaneously with the February 20th statement.

Mountbatten arrived in New Delhi on March 22nd, and was sworn in Viceroy and Governor-General of India the next day. He made three significant departures from the past in order to win over the Indian leaders and people. First, he broke tradition by announcing, through his speech at the swearing-in ceremony, that his was not a normal Viceroyalty that had in the past sought perpetuation of the British rule. Secondly, prior to his being sworn in, he invited Gandhi and Jinnah for an informal introduction. Mountbatten knew that Jinnah's position was irrevocable; but not so of Gandhi's, particularly after the Punjab resolution of the Congress. His purpose was to derive gains from Gandhi's position of isolation. Thirdly, besides drawing Nehru under the spell of his magnetic charm, Mountbatten saw to it that he won over a stern realist in Patel by proving that, unlike Wavell, he meant business. Mountbatten won Patel's confidence by making a matter-of-fact admission of the Indian situation, "India in March 1947 was like a ship on fire in mid-ocean with ammunition in the hold." That was the conclusion Patel had arrived at earlier, and he had, time and again, urged Wavell to extinguish the fire through the imposition of martial law.

That Mountbatten had no plan of his own was his advantage. Unlike Wavell, he could stand squarely with all the political leaders. It was a completely uninhibited Mountbatten who moved on the Indian political scene free from the hard prejudices of Wavell, but with the informality of an adventurist determined to do business with one and all. Wisely, his plan of action was none other than befriending Nehru and Patel, particularly the latter who was the heavyweight of the party. But he won them over in different ways: Nehru with the friendliness of a family member; Patel with his earnestness to deliver the goods at last: freedom for India at the earliest. If Mountbatten could do that on behalf of the British Government, Patel, Mountbatten had come to realise, could do so on behalf of the Congress. "It was not long before he recognised the near-equal importance of Sardar Vallabhbhai Patel"[1] in any negotiations. Mountbatten also recognised that "Nehru had always seemed to need a stronger figure to give him confidence, a wiser or more self-assured man whose judgment would guide or confirm his own. In the early days it was his father, Motilal Nehru; for most of his life it was Mahatma Gandhi; in Cabinet and in Congress politics in these crucial days it was Sardar Patel."[2] He hoped to tackle Jinnah though pressure and threat, which Wavell had refused to do even when he could.

Hardly a month had passed for Mountbatten in his new post when he had a taste of Patel's bluntness. Patel told him, "You won't govern yourself and you won't let us govern."[3] That's what Wavell had done, and thus allowed Indian affairs go from bad to worse. Patel had also demanded of the Viceroy, "If you will not act yourself, then turn over full authority to the Central Government and let us stop the Muslim League war in Punjab and the NWFP; let us stop the Muslim League army being mobilised in Bengal to attack Assam; let us govern."[4]

With Patel, Mountbatten's approach was "somewhat apprehensive at his first meeting... who has the reputation of being the strong man in the Congress High Command, but he very quickly detected a twinkle in the Sardar's eye. His approach to the whole problem was clear and decisive. India must get rid of the Muslim League."[5] Mountbatten alone could help Patel achieve that through Partition. In comparison, Nehru's was a near surrender to Mountbatten on the latter's emotional appeal, "Mr. Nehru, I want you to regard me not as the last Viceroy winding up the British Raj, but as the first to lead the way to the new India." The trick worked. An "intensely moved" and smiling Nehru confessed, "Now I know what they mean when they speak of your charm being so dangerous."[6]

Opposition to his plan, Mountbatten knew, could come from Gandhi. He must clear him out of his way by handling him in a masterly manner. He saw to it that his first interview with Gandhi on March 31st was "deliberately taken up with reminiscence, the first hour and a quarter with Lady Mountbatten present to help produce the air of friendliness". Thereafter, when Mountbatten was alone with Gandhi, he "deliberately avoided all reference to the immediate political situation, to allow time for them to progress along the path of understanding and friendship."[7] At his second meeting with Gandhi on April 1st lasting two hours only a quarter of an hour was "taken up with solid business", with "a further long excursion into the Mahatma's life-story."[8] Growing impatient with such deliberate rigmarole, Gandhi came out with the "astonishing proposal": to dismiss the present Cabinet and call upon Jinnah to form a new one of his choice, no matter if it were an all-Muslim Government at the Centre.

Gandhi's "master-plan" was discussed at Mountbatten's staff meeting on April 5th. It was described as "an old kite flown without disguise". It was also thought that "Mountbatten should not allow himself to be drawn into negotiation with the Mahatma, but should only listen to advice."[9] Mountbatten did exactly that, to avoid incurring Gandhi's displeasure or hostility. However, sensing opposition from Patel and Nehru, Gandhi himself relieved Mountbatten of the anxiety by withdrawing his proposal. Gandhi accepted his defeat by telling Mountbatten that "he is personally handing over all future negotiations to the Working Committee."[10] Gandhi had been influenced in his proposal by Azad in an effort to resurrect the Cabinet Mission Plan, with a view to preserving India's unity no matter at what cost. Such efforts in April 1947 were like flogging a dead horse. They ran counter to the rapid tide of events. At a time when India was going to be given her freedom, and was going to be partitioned, Patel was not prepared to leave the Central Government in the hands of Jinnah. This would have amounted to political suicide. Like Patel, Auchinleck, the Commander-in-Chief, too had come to the conclusion that there was no alternative to Partition and by mid-April even Mountbatten was "beginning to think that Pakistan was inevitable". In such a situation, Patel would rather accept immediate transference of power, and thereby not only save India from a permanent domination of the Muslim minority, but also achieve a much bigger objective in the integration of Indian States.

Mountbatten's tackling of Jinnah was as masterly as was of Gandhi, though not as easy. Their first meeting turned out to be "a vital encounter". Jinnah was "reserved, haughty and aloof; and as Mountbatten admitted, "My God, he was cold. It took most of the interview to unfreeze him." True to his ways, Jinnah "started off the conversation quite blankly"—rather demanding, "I will enter into discussion on one condition only."

Not letting him go further, Mountbatten interrupted, "Mr. Jinnah, I am not prepared to discuss conditions or, indeed, the present situation until I have had the chance of making your acquaintance and knowing more about you yourself." According to Campbell-Johnson, "Jinnah was completely taken aback by Mountbatten's attitude, and for some while did not respond...

But in the end his mood softened and he duly succumbed to Mountbatten's desire to hear him recount the story of the Muslim League's rise to power in terms of his own career." Jinnah's talk helped Mountbatten tell him his instant decision: "... a surgical operation. An anaesthetic is required before the operation."[11] That role Mountbatten was to perform himself.

Jinnah was visibly shaken by Mountbatten's mention of a surgical operation. He had all along thought that he would get away without it—getting what he considered to be his Pakistan, a decision regarding which should be his and none else's. When applied to Punjab and Bengal, as demanded by Patel, the operation would strike at the heart of his dream of having in his Pakistan the whole of Punjab, the whole of Bengal and even the Hindu majority province of Assam as envisaged in the Grouping plan of the Cabinet Mission. For the first time, Jinnah was challenged over the inherent contradiction of his Pakistan demand. Or else, Suhrawardy wouldn't have made frantic efforts to keep Bengal united under fictitious autonomy. A helpless Jinnah allowed himself to be exposed to his contradictions when he begged of Mountbatten, as he had done earlier with Wavell, "not to destroy the unity of Bengal and Punjab, which had national characteristics in common: common history, common ways of life, and where the Hindus have stronger feelings as Bengalis or Punjabis than they have as members of the Congress."[12] Having brought Jinnah down from the high horse he had so far proudly ridden, Mountbatten could triumphantly proclaim, "Jinnah can negotiate with me, but my decision goes."[13] And the decision in the end lay in the division of Punjab and Bengal, which Jinnah had to accept ruefully, regretfully terming his Pakistan "truncated and moth-eaten".

The situation was both dangerous and baffling. The two-day Governors' conference on April 15th-16th proved revealing, with each Governor reporting on the state of affairs in his province. Caroe wanted an election to be held in the NWFP which his Premier, Dr. Khan Sahib, opposed as he had won it only in 1945. Mountbatten considered the NWFP a liability without which

Pakistan could not have been created. J.D. Tyson, Secretary to the Governor of Bengal, Frederick Burrows, thought that, on Partition, East Bengal would become a "rural slum". For this reason, Suhrawardy was "frightened of Partition" and was "ready to play with the Hindus". The industrial development of Chota Nagpur was, hence, "part of Suhrawardy's concept for the building up of an independent Bengal". He enjoyed the support of the Governor and the European group, and was confident of winning over some of the provincial Congress leaders. Mountbatten, however, feared that "east Bengal might contract out". Evan Jenkins, who gave "a lucid analysis of the implications of Punjab partition", spoke of "the possible growth of anti-Pakistan opinion in Punjab and Bengal". Jenkins had, therefore, suggested an "Operation Solomon" for Punjab and "put forward the possibility of a statistical boundary commission."[14]

Suhrawardy's move for "a sovereign, independent and undivided Bengal in a divided India", which would have in all probability included Assam because of geographical contiguity and support from the European planters, was a shrewd development from Pakistan's point of view, but an ominous one from India's. Suhrawardy had not only secured the backing of the Governor, but had also gained the support of Sarat Chandra Bose and Kiran Shankar Ray, leader of the Congress party in the Bengal Legislative Assembly who belonged to East Bengal. Suhrawardy proceeded further to achieve his ends by employing muscle-power to cow the rest of the leaders, as well as the Hindu public, both through the clandestine "Azad Pakistan S.S. Headquarters, Calcutta", and his public speeches. The HQ issued leaflets in Bengali warning supporters of Bengal partition, which was described by a senior Bengal Congress leader, N. Dutt Mazumdar, in a letter to Patel as a "loaded pistol... ready to correct us (Hindus) from the path of partition of Bengal and resistance against the creation of Pakistan." One such leaflet stated: "Bengal must be an independent, sovereign and united State... must be called "Azad Pakistan" and the Muslims, by virtue of their numerical strength, will be the dominant power... Youths of Muslim Bengal are now prepared to sacrifice their last drop of blood to attain, and afterwards defend, what they love to call Pakistan". Suhrawardy even threatened that "Calcutta will be sacked and burnt in case the Partition idea is favoured."

K.C. Neogy, Syama Prasad Mookerjee and other Bengal leaders thought Patel alone could resolve the situation. Neogy, therefore, wrote to him: "... all our eyes are turned towards you in the hope that you will not fail to take whatever action is possible to save Bengal and Calcutta from utter ruin and bloodshed." Patel replied, "This cry of a sovereign, independent Bengal is a trap in which even Kiran Shankar may fall with Sarat Babu. The only way to save the Hindus of Bengal is to insist on partition of Bengal." To Mookerjee, Patel gave the assurance, "You can depend on us to deal with the situation effectively and befittingly. The future of the Hindus of Bengal is quite safe, so long as they stand firm and continue to give us such support as only they can."

On Patel fell the great task of weaning Sarat Bose and Kiran Shankar Ray from Suhrawardy's machinations. Boldly did he tell the Bengal leaders: "Bengal cannot be isolated from the Indian Union. Talk of the idea of a sovereign republic of independent Bengal is a trap to induce the unwary and unwise to enter into the parlour of the Muslim League. The Congress Working Committee is fully aware of the situation in Bengal... Bengal has got to be partitioned if the non-Muslim population is to survive." No other Congress leader did talk with such clarity and assertiveness. Patel wrote to Sarat Bose diplomatically: "I am sorry to find that you have isolated yourself so completely from all-India politics, and even in provincial politics you have not kept in touch with us. In these critical times, we cannot afford to be stand-offish and must pool our resources and take a united stand. Vital matters, which will leave their mark on generations to come, have to be settled; and in such a settlement, it behoves all of us to contribute our best to the combined strength of the Congress." Patel also wrote to Kiran Shankar Ray: "Both Sarat Babu's and your names are implicated in these allegations, and I feel that it is in your interest to see that such rumours do not gain further currency.

These are undoubtedly critical times, and the issue of Partition is of paramount importance. It is incumbent on all Congressmen to set aside personal predilections and to stand united on the official policy of the Congress. Individual expression of views must fit into that policy, and there should not be any discordant note. As a disciplined Congressman, I am sure you will appreciate this advice."[15] That had its desired effect. Bengal was saved. Jinnah described the new Congress demand for partition of Bengal and Punjab as "a sinister move actuated by spite and bitterness."[16]

Not long after his arrival in India and following his interviews with Indian leaders, Mountbatten had conveyed to Attlee the definite conclusion he had reached—that "India cannot be ruled any more from England, but India can be ruled from India". He also impressed upon London that, if the transfer of power was not effected quickly, there was the grim possibility of no authority being left in some parts of the country to whom power could be handed over. This would have made difficult early withdrawal of the British from India. To achieve that, Mountbatten acted without losing time. He sent his plan to London with Ismay and Abell on May 2nd—just 41 days after he had set foot on Indian soil; and he seemed to be in such a desperate hurry that he wanted to make a formal announcement about it on May 17th. Meanwhile, he moved to Simla for a cool recess. Nehru had gone there by special invitation as his guest. On May 10th the plan came back "revised and approved by London". Mountbatten showed it to Nehru whose reaction was violent. The plan, Nehru felt, would cause a further breakdown of the Central authority and would provoke civil conflict and chaos; and encourage the Balkanisation of India by making the provinces initially independent successor States. Nehru saw in the proposal concerning the States "a direct invitation, at least to the major States, to remain independent kingdoms, presumably as allies or feudatories of Britain."[17] This would have created many "Ulsters" in India.

For the first time an overconfident, domineering Mountbatten found himself thrown overboard into a deep crisis. He least expected from a friend like Nehru "a bombshell of the first order".

His mission in India faced a disastrous end—bigger than that of Wavell's because he had come to India in a conquering mood. His buoyancy had been built on the wide authority entrusted to him by Attlee. Nehru's reaction violently shook Mountbatten. Campbell-Johnson narrates its shattering effect on Mountbatten: "His hair was somewhat dishevelled, but he was still marvellously resilient. He told us that only a hunch on his part had saved him from disaster. Without that hunch, 'Dickie Mountbatten', he said, 'would have been finished and could have packed his bag'. We would have looked complete fools with the Government at home having led them up the garden path to believe that Nehru would accept the plan".[18] But "the fateful hour found a man and an idea to match it."[19]

It was V.P. Menon who came to Mountbatten's rescue, and it was on May 11th. Urgently summoned to see him, Menon found Mountbatten in "a very ruffled state", nervously walking up and down in his room". At his request, Menon pulled out from his dusted records a scheme for transfer of power he had prepared during Wavell's time, which, for lack of interest shown by those in power then, had remained a personal document. It envisaged, way back in 1946, early transfer of power on the basis of Dominion Status to two Central Governments, and separation of the Muslim majority areas from India. After securing approval of Mountbatten and Nehru, Menon sat down to prepare an alternative draft plan. In the two or three hours at his disposal, he started dictating to one stenographer after another. He had barely got the draft into shape when Eric Mieville came and took it away to the Viceroy merely to allay his anxiety, as also to secure Nehru's approval. By dinner time Mountbatten had "completely regained his buoyant spirits and good cheer", primarily because Nehru had considered the approach contained in Menon's plan to be "on proper lines and that it would not be unacceptable to the Congress."[20]

In regard to Congress acceptance, Patel mattered more than the rest. The position he commanded was summed up by G.S. Bozman, his British Secretary of the Information Department: "From his day-to-day experience of his chief, Vallabhbhai Patel, he was convinced that he was the strong man among the Indian leaders. Any discussions which failed to recognise this fact were likely to be unfruitful. He was essentially a practical man with whom business could be done, but if he was left out, he was in a position to invoke a veto just as crippling as anything known at UNO."[21] In order to safeguard the position of his new draft plan and to keep him informed of the latest development at Simla, Menon sent Patel a copy of the plan by a special messenger, so as to reach him before dawn. Patel was "delighted by the turn of events". He assured Menon that "there would be no difficulty in the Congress accepting Dominion Status."[22] Nehru was, however, worried about the Congress acceptance of India's membership of the Commonwealth, which was a condition for the transference of power. He had been since his return from the Soviet Union in 1927 an anti-imperialist. At such a critical moment, Patel came to his rescue when he told a worried Nehru on the telephone, "Leave that to me. That's my business."[23] Patel's hold over the Congress was absolute.

Following Menon's June 3rd Plan draft, Patel and Mountbatten veered to almost identical attitudes. Their roles became complementary, both in regard to the transfer of power and the integration of the Indian States. Mountbatten reported to have stipulated two things: creation of Pakistan not merely to satisfy Jinnah, but also to meet the desires and designs of the British imperialists; and, second, India's membership of the Commonwealth. The latter was essential to secure Churchill's support to the passage of the Indian Independence Bill in the House of Lords where the Conservatives enjoyed a majority. According to Mountbatten, Churchill saw in such membership "the chance of holding on to some vestige of the Empire in the form of the Commonwealth... And he went out and gave full support. That's how we got the legislation through." That made easy what Mountbatten wanted: the earlier withdrawal from India. So did Patel desire—the earliest assumption of power. Pyarelal quotes Patel having made a condition in this respect: that "in two months time, power should be transferred and an

Act should be passed by Parliament in that time, and if it was guaranteed that the British Government would not interfere with the question of the Indian States. We said: 'We will deal with that question. Leave it to us. You take no sides. Let Paramountcy be dead'."[24]

Another major hurdle to overcome was approval by Attlee and others in London, as also its acceptance by Jinnah. London, however, appreciated that the plan offered Britain the best possible way to hand over power to India with dignity and honour, no matter if that would be by casting aside the pledges given to the minorities and the Princes. A disturbing development, however, took place during Mountbatten's absence in London. Jinnah dropped "a carefully timed and placed bombshell" with his demand for a 800-mile "corridor" to link West and East Pakistan. By releasing the news exclusively through Reuters, Jinnah was "ensuring for himself the greatest possible coverage in the British Press", and thereby, according to Campbell-Johnson, "to exert the maximum pressure on London at this critical stage in the Viceroy's deliberations with the Government ... the technique of releasing it seems to have been copied from Stalin."[25] Patel dismissed Jinnah's demand as "fantastic and absurd". Nehru was critical of the British for their surrender to Jinnah since Linlithgow, but more specifically since Wavell's Simla conference by bluntly stating that Jinnah "accepts what he gets and goes on asking for more. There could be no one-sided commitments."

Mountbatten was not going to let that happen this time. He was determined not to lose the initiative he had gained with HMG's approval of the plan and the Congress acceptance of it. On these two gains alone depended the success of his mission in India—to stage a British withdrawal from the sub-continent. He outmanoeuvred Jinnah. He strengthened his hands by managing to secure a trump card, which he was to play at the appropriate moment. From London he brought with him a message from Churchill to Jinnah, which stated that "it was nothing less than a matter of life and death for Jinnah to accept the Plan."[26] Mountbatten had his "dramatic midnight encounter" with Jinnah on June 2nd-3rd. Jinnah proved as intractable as ever. He categorically refused to give in writing his acceptance of the Plan, which Mountbatten was to announce the following day. Mountbatten again outmanoeuvred Jinnah by having as "a second witness" in Ismay who was pro-Jinnah. No amount of pressure could make Jinnah "agree to a firm acceptance from the Muslim League". His only assurance was that he would make his best endeavours. According to Campbell-Johnson, "Mountbatten then reminded Jinnah that the Congress party was terribly suspicious of this particular tactic, which he always used, whereby he waited until the Congress party had made a firm decision about some plan, and then left himself the right to make whatever decision suited the Muslim League several days later". Mountbatten warned him that "Nehru, Kripalani and Patel had made an absolute point that they would reject the Plan unless the Muslim League accepted it simultaneously with themselves; and, furthermore, accepted it as a final settlement."

"Nothing Mountbatten could say would move him; he once more took refuge behind the excuse that he was not constitutionally authorised to make a decision without the concurrence of the full Muslim League Council, and pointed out that he could not in any case call this Council meeting for several days". An exasperated Mountbatten had to tell Jinnah, "If that is your attitude, then the leaders of the Congress party and Sikhs will refuse final acceptance at the meeting in the morning; chaos will follow, and you will lose your Pakistan, probably for good."

Jinnah shrugged his shoulders and said, "What must be, must be."

Mountbatten then sternly spoke, "Mr. Jinnah! I do not intend to let you wreck all the work that has gone into this settlement. Since you will not accept for the Muslim League, I will speak for them myself. I will take the risk of saying that I am satisfied with the assurances you have given me, and if your Council fails to ratify the agreement, you can place the blame on me. I have only one condition, and that is that when I say at the meeting in the morning, 'Mr. Jinnah has given me assurances which I have accepted and which satisfy me', you will in no circumstances contradict that, and that, when I look towards you, you will nod your head in acquiescence." Jinnah's reply to the proposition itself was "to nod his head without any verbal undertaking." Mountbatten's final question was: Did Jinnah consider that he (Mountbatten) would be justified in advising Attlee to go ahead and make his announcement tomorrow (June 3rd)? To this Jinnah replied: "Yes"; and it was "on this last assurance Mountbatten and Ismay both felt that the maximum possible measure of acceptance had been wrung out of him."[27]

Having cleared the decks, Mountbatten was now poised for his final act: the announcement of the June 3 Plan to hand over power to the two new Dominions of India and Pakistan on August 15, 1947, the date having been advanced from June 30, 1948. He was yet apprehensive of the unpredictability of Gandhi. At his Press conference on June 4th, he got wind from Devdas's question that Gandhi (his father) might be highly critical of the Plan at his prayer meeting. Mountbatten met Gandhi prior to that, and invited him to the Viceroy's House. "Gandhi", according to Campbell-Johnson, "was clearly in a state of some distress, feeling under the first impact of the Plan that his lifelong efforts for the unity of Hindus and Muslims had fallen about him. But Mountbatten, summoning all his power of persuasion, urged him to consider the Announcement not as a Mountbatten but as a Gandhi Plan; in all sincerity he had tried to incorporate Gandhi's major concepts of non-coercion, self-determination, the earliest possible date of British departure, and even his sympathetic views about Dominion Status." Once again, Mountbatten "carried the day". Gandhi told his prayer meeting: "The British Government is not responsible for Partition. The Viceroy has no hand in it. In fact, he is as opposed to division as Congress itself, but if both of us—Hindus and Muslims—cannot agree on anything else, then the Viceroy is left with no choice." According to Campbell-Johnson, "never surely had a Viceroy achieved such swift and decisive conquest over Gandhi's heart and mind."[28]

Patel and Nehru had a big hand in Mountbatten's success.

Without such support to his Plan, he could not have won over Gandhi, nor overcome the obduracy of Jinnah. Their central approach was identical: to get rid of Jinnah, "to hear no more of him and eliminate his nuisance value." Their approach, however, originated from different premises. Nehru's was largely emotional. Patel's was that of a hard, matter-of-fact realist. Nehru thought that by "cutting off the head, we will get rid of the headache"; and thereby he would be free from the insults he had to bear, as India's *de facto* Prime Minister, at the hands of the League members of the Interim Government. Patel's main consideration was that they had got, to his satisfaction, seventy-five to eighty per cent of India which they could "develop and make strong according to their genius". Mountbatten wrote to his mother on June 14th: "I must stress the importance of Patel in the agreements so far reached. He has a rough exterior and uncompromising manner. His achievements tend to remain below the surface, but he was probably the first of the Congress High Command to realise that the 20th February statement implied Partition if a political settlement by June 1948, or before, was to be achieved. Having absorbed that vital implication, he has never wavered and has stood firm against inner voices and neutral indecisions that have sometimes afflicted his colleagues. Patel's realism has also been a big factor in the acceptance of the Dominion Status formula."[29]

Implementation of the Plan imposed on Patel another onerous task—the division of assets and liabilities between the two new Dominions. In the Partition Council, his was the decisive voice on behalf of India. Since his frustrating experience as Vice-President of the Interim Government, Nehru leaned over Patel completely. Chandulal Trivedi, the Governor of Orissa, whom Mountbatten called to New Delhi about mid-June for preparation of a plan for the division of the Armed Forces, was told by Nehru, "The Sardar will tell you what he wants."

With no pretensions of his status, Patel told Trivedi, "I am no expert. I am rather a layman. Only I wish you to see that India is not let down."[30] Patel undertook Partition Council work in a business-like manner—brief, quick, firm, yet flexible. Like a sentinel, he guarded the country's interests, and expected the same from others, especially the ICS officers who were working with him on the task. The Council set up a Steering Committee of two senior officials. H.M. Patel represented India; Mohammed Ali, Pakistan. They were assisted by ten expert committees to decide on such multifarious, wide-ranging matters as total assets and liabilities, records and personnel, central revenues, currency and exchange, economic controls, trade, foreign relations and domicile and nationality of the inhabitants of British India and the position of Indian nationals abroad.

Patel gave full freedom to the Civil Servants and Armed Forces officers serving on various expert committees. Their negotiations with their counterparts, therefore, produced quick, satisfying results, with practically no hurdles to stall their progress. Prior to the start of their work, Patel invited them to his residence for an introductory talk. His speech was brief, but very appealing. He gave them confidence and infused into them a new spirit by telling them, "We are entrusting you with work of great national importance. It has to be done in a very short time. You will have to work very hard, as you have never done before. All I would like to tell you is that all my life I have enjoyed working for the country, and I have been working very hard. I invite you to share in the same pleasure."[31] That galvanised them into ceaseless activity.

Patel's success in the stupendous task of Partition was due to many factors. He had "an eye for the essential, and yet no detail escaped his attention. He defended with determination every Indian interest", and had "no difficulty in reconciling it with generosity and goodwill for Pakistan". And his attitude of give-and-take contributed to the working out Partition smoothly, expeditiously, without much wrangling. The Pakistanis were considerably impressed by his approach and outlook. Their sentiments were voiced by Abdur Rab Nishtar at the concluding session of the Partition Council. While taking leave of Patel, Nishtar "admired his statesmanship, applauded his constructive approach, and affirmed that the Pak Ministers would continue to look upon him as their elder brother."[32]

The surgical operation to "divide and quit" by August 15, 1947 marked the culmination of the British policy of "divide and rule". It meant the end of Mountbatten's mission in India: to extricate his country from the deepening Indian crisis that had already begun exploding here and there, though it had not yet wholly engulfed India. Mountbatten averted that most cleverly, efficiently and expeditiously with the British withdrawal in mid-1947, rather than waiting for a withdrawal by mid-1948 as Attlee had announced earlier. For Patel, the withdrawal was the starting point of another great mission: to consolidate the two vastly different Indias—British and Princely India—into a strong, united, homogeneous Union.

21

Integration of States

Patel's decision on unification of India went back to December 1939 when he had declared with a seeming premonition: "The red and yellow colours on India's map have to be merged into one. Unless that is done, we cannot have swaraj."[1] Patel undertook that task on the transference of power. Mountbatten had confidence in his wisdom and ability to do that most amicably and successfully.

Patel had, as Home Member in the Interim Government, come to know of the Political Department's designs to Balkanise the Indian States. He was then a helpless witness. The Princes were under the exclusive charge of the Viceroy as Crown Representative, but were directly responsible to the Secretary of the Political Department, who, in turn, could directly report to the Secretary of State in London. The British were to terminate Paramountcy simultaneously with the transference of power to India, so that they could make the Princes independent, and thus enable them to negotiate, individually or jointly, with the new Government in British India on equal terms. This was an attempt to implement Churchill's "Imperial strategy", of which Wavell records in his *Journal* on March 29, 1945: "He seems to favour partition into Pakistan, Hindustan, Princestan, etc."[2] This was the tip of the iceberg. What was being manoeuvred underneath hardly anyone could see or know. Patel was no exception.

Such manoeuvring followed the two pronouncements of the Cabinet Mission: the Memorandum of May 12th, and the Plan of May 16th. The former stated: "When a new fully self-governing or independent Government or Governments come into being in British India... HMG will cease to exercise the powers of Paramountcy... the rights of the States which flow from their relationship to the Crown will no longer exist and that all the rights surrendered by the States to the Paramount Power will return to the States. Political arrangements between the States, on the one side, and the British Crown and British India, on the other, will thus be brought to an end. The void will have to be filled either by the States entering into a federal relationship with the successor Government or Governments in British India, or, failing this, entering into particular political arrangements with it or them."[3] As Patel commented later, "Nobody could have been so innocent or ignorant as to presume that overnight small rulers could be converted into 'Their Majesties!' That position would have been full of dangerous possibilities and potentialities."[4] In its statement of May 16th, the Mission virtually put a seal on the States' sovereign status by declaring, "Paramountcy can neither be retained by the British Crown nor transferred to the new Government."[5]

The Cabinet Mission made another dangerous move in the suggestion that for the seats allotted to the Princes in the Constituent Assembly, the Chamber of Princes should nominate a Negotiating Committee for parleys with its counterpart from British India. Two dangers lurked in that. Since "practically every matter which concerns the States has been committed to the care of the States Negotiating Committee", Patel wondered "whether their Negotiating Committee has to settle the question of determining the method of election of States' representatives to the Constituent Assembly, or whether the Negotiating Committee has even a wider field of discussing other subjects concerning the States." Further he wrote to Munshi: "Another important question for us to decide is whether the Constituent Assembly will have any say in the matter of grouping of States, which the Chamber of Princes might decide on, or which any group of States independently might agree upon." He also told Munshi in his letter of December 7, 1946: "You know efforts are being made to form groups of States, either independently or under the inspiration of the Chamber of Princes."[6] Not much later, such fears came out in the open when Bhopal and Conrad Corfield, Secretary of the Political Department, began organising the Princes into blocs.

An accident of history changed the course of events and determined the fate of the country. An official file, casually falling into his hands after taking charge of Home in the Interim Government in September 1946, opened Patel's eyes to the dangers India faced. Bastar, whose "Raja was a minor and a weakling and the Prime Minister a foreigner" and which had rich mineral and other resources, was being "mortgaged to Hyderabad State by means of a long lease." and was to be "exploited to the prejudice of India." The Political Department evaded Patel's inquiries. He was told that those in-charge of the department were "the guardians of the minor and that they could enter into the contract in the interests of the minor." Patel told them that "they were now going away and they should not bother about their wards. Their guardianship would now devolve on us, and they should do nothing without our agreement, or which was contrary to the interests of the people." Not satisfied with the Political Department's response, Patel sent for the Ruler. "When I saw the ruler," he records, "how young and inexperienced he was! I felt that it was a sin to make him sign such an agreement. It was then that I was made fully conscious of the extent to which our interests were being prejudiced in every way by the machinations of the Political Department, and came to the conclusion that the sooner we were rid of these people, the better. Their main aim was to further their own interests and to cause as much damage to India as possible. I came to the conclusion that the best course was to drive out the foreigners even at the cost of partition of the country. It was also then that I felt that there was only one way to make the country safe and strong—and that was the unification of the rest of India".[7]

In a letter of February 2, 1947, Patel explained himself further: "Sovereignty in England vests in the people of England and not in His Majesty the King... No man in his senses in the modern world believes that sovereignty vests in any single individual, whether he be a prince or a monarch, a Czar or a Hitler."[8] On February 26th, after Attlee's policy statement of February 20th, Patel wrote to a friend: "From June 1948, there will be no Sovereign in India, and Paramountcy will evaporate in the air."[9] By such utterances, he was forewarning the British and checkmating their designs in India. No other Indian leader had Patel's boldness and courage. Later, after the transference of power, he grew still bolder to state: "Paramountcy can never be annihilated. It must ever reside in the Central authority; for, it belongs to the people. Whoever will challenge it will perish."[10] That was a warning to the Princes playing into the hands of Bhopal and Corfield.

Nevertheless, from January onwards till he had power in his hands, Churchill's Princestan worried Patel. His fears were later confirmed by some of the Indian Diwans of the States. No less a person than Corfield himself admitted at Mountbatten's Staff meeting on March 26th that he was supporting Bhopal's conspiracy with some Princes against their joining the Indian Union, and that he was making efforts to set up the "Princes as a potential Third Force"[11]—which was another name for Churchill's Princestan. At a conference of Residents and Political Officers, held in the second week of April, Corfield asked them "to enable the States to stand on their feet, to encourage them to hold together and, at the same time, to cooperate fully with British India."[12] There was also a sinister motive in the Political Department's proposal to hand over to the States the Crown Representative's police force. Ingeniously, Patel killed the proposal by immediately changing the name to the Central Reserve Police. In the hands of the States, the force could have been a source of potential mischief.

Patel maintained his characteristic coolness: an attitude of conciliation and compromise rather than confrontation, and yet he was firm in his resolve, and, when an occasion demanded, he was blunt in expressing his views. In an effort to woo the Princes, he told them, "There are many in the country who believe in the total elimination of the Indian States. Gandhi and I dream of the old world in the fond hope that the Princes will once again create *Ram Rajya*. That is the policy of the Congress, which desires to befriend the Princes on such a basis." In contrast, Nehru's occasional outbursts scared the Princes. V.P. Menon characterised as "a rather inauspicious start" Nehru's speech in the Constituent Assembly on December 21st (1946) on the crucial resolution on the appointment of a Negotiating Committee for talks with a similar body of the Chamber of Princes. Nehru said, "I regret, I say frankly, that we have to meet the rulers' Negotiating Committee. I think that, on the part of the States, there should have been on the Negotiating Committee representatives of the people of the States. I think even now the Negotiating Committee, if it wants to do the right thing, should include some such representatives; but I feel that we cannot insist upon this at this stage."[13] Even much later, Nehru's attitude had remained unchanged. Speaking at Gwalior on April 19th, he gave the Princes "a virtual ultimatum either to join the Constituent Assembly or to be treated as hostile." According to Hodson, Mountbatten "privately rebuked him," for two reasons: first, it would scare the Princes from joining the Indian Union; and, second, "for his demagogy, especially as a Member of the Interim Government who ought not to speak in such terms without Cabinet approval. Pandit Nehru took this castigation meekly, explaining that he was speaking in a personal capacity as President of the States People's Conference."[14]

Nehru's speech in the Constituent Assembly (December 21, 1946) helped Bhopal and Corfield in the hardening of the Princes' attitude. The Standing Committee of the Chamber of Princes held many meetings and even sought the Political Departments' advice on several issues. At their Bombay conference on January 29th, the Princes resolved that the constitution of each State, its territorial integrity and the succession of its reigning dynasty shall not be interfered with by the Union, nor should the existing boundaries of a State be altered except by its free consent. Far more alarming was their decision that the Constituent Assembly was not to deal with questions affecting the internal administration or constitutions of the States. The resolution "provoked a good deal of controversy"; in particular, "public opinion was considerably agitated over the statement made by some rulers that, if the fundamental propositions were not accepted by the Congress, they would boycott the Constituent Assembly."[15]

That amounted to playing the Bhopal game, and thereby play into the hands of Jinnah. Cochin and Baroda were the only States who were not party to the Bombay resolution. The Maharaja of Cochin had announced earlier on July 30th his decision to participate in the proceedings of the proposed Constituent Assembly through popular representatives elected by the State's Legislative Assembly. Now, Baroda, guided by its Diwan, B.L. Mitter, announced its decision to join the Constituent Assembly on February 8th when the two Negotiating Committees met. The majority of the Princes were still with the Chamber of Princes under Bhopal's influence. Bhopal seemed to have received a shot in the arm with Travancore and Hyderabad joining his battle. C.P. Ramaswami Aiyar, the Diwan of Travancore, said on March 17th that his State "will be an independent State and will revert to the 1750 status."[16] On behalf of the Nizam, Dr. Syed Abdul Latif had earlier declared on February 27th that Hyderabad would "automatically become a kingdom" on the transfer of power and that the Nizam would proclaim himself "His Majesty the King of Hyderabad."[17] This was just after Attlee's statement of February 20th.

Addressing the joint meeting of the two negotiating Committees on February 8th, Patel and Nehru suggested that, even when it did not form part of the agenda, the two committees should decide, in the larger interest of the country, on the manner in which the States representatives could enter and participate in the work of the Constituent Assembly. The proposal did not find favour with the rulers, Bhopal as the Chancellor pointing out that the Chamber of Princes "by its resolution of January 29th had laid down certain fundamental propositions on which they wanted satisfactory assurances before they could enter the Constituent Assembly." Bhopal's was a deep game. On the second day of the meeting he deliberately attempted to keep the Princes' attitude irreconcilable by, once again, laying emphasis on the imperative need for adhering to the Bombay resolution. He stated that he was prepared to discuss how "a satisfactory settlement of the fundamental's could be secured" either formally or informally with somebody competent to do so, and in the meanwhile proposed a postponement of the discussions. Patiala checkmated Bhopal's move for a deadlock through postponement by seeking a clarification of the position as it had emerged from the previous days' meeting. Because of Nehru's "persuasive approach" and "conciliatory statement, the atmosphere became more friendly."[18]

The meeting was adjourned till March 1st. The two committees asked the Secretaries of the Constituent Assembly and the Chamber of Princes to jointly work out a scheme for distribution of the seats allotted to the States. At such a time when the two committees could have, if left to themselves, worked out a mutually acceptable solution, Attlee's statement of February 20th threw overboard whatever limited progress the talks seemed to have made. The statement served as an encouragement to Bhopal and his group of Princes to sit on the fence by declaring Britain's intentions "not to hand over their powers and obligations under Paramountcy to any government of British India", as also "not to bring Paramountcy, as a system, to a conclusion earlier than the date of the final transfer of power."

At the scheduled meeting of March 1st, Patel, sensing trouble ahead, assumed a stern attitude and spoke to the Princes in a mixed tone of frankness and deliberate pessimism. He is reported to have said, "Freedom is coming. But I am afraid it may not last long. Before that happens, nothing may be left of the Princes as well."[19] It was a stern warning, which turned the tide in his favour. Such pessimism on the part of India's "iron man" surprised many Princes, especially Bikaner and Patiala, on whom, because of the closeness of their States to Pakistan and because of the happenings in Punjab, a new realisation had dawned: how vulnerable their

States could be to new dangers. They, therefore, refused to follow Bhopal's policy in their negotiations with the Congress. Impressed by the realism of Patel, the Bikaner-Patiala group assured him of its cooperation in achieving a united, strong India. Prime Minister K.M. Panikkar informed Patel, on March 10th, of Bikaner's decision to participate in the Constituent Assembly. Patel replied, "I am glad that so many Princes are getting out of the cordon (of Bhopal). Let us hope that they will come in now... You have seen what is happening in Punjab. I hope there will be no sympathy from any quarters for the Muslim League any more, not even amongst any of the Princes."[20]

The Bikaner-Bhopal differences were in the limelight with the absence of the two rulers at Mountbatten's swearing-in ceremony on March 24th. Since both were Mountbatten's "two oldest personal friends in India", and in view of "the importance attached by the Princes to ceremonial etiquette", their absence could not be explained except as "a good indication of disunity and crisis in their ranks". Both of them saw Mountbatten later to give their explanation. Their interviews "revealed the full scale of the split among the Princes." According to Campbell-Johnson, "This is a great grief to Bhopal, who feels that Bikaner and the other 'dissidents', by allowing themselves to take part in the Constituent Assembly, are becoming the tools of the Congress and undermining the whole bargaining position of the States... Bhopal thought the time-limit was quite impossible, and, if enforced, must involve bloodshed and chaos." That sounded Jinnah-like to some of the Princes. Bikaner, on the other hand, held Bhopal responsible for the split, "who, by his attitude to the Interim Government, had caused the communal issue to be raised among them (Princes)".

The real danger, however, lurked in the support Bhopal had of Corfield, who, at his meeting with Mountbatten on March 26th, "argued with some bitterness that Bikaner, by taking his place in the Constituent Assembly, had seriously weakened the bargaining power of the Princes."[21] With his backing, Bhopal continued with his efforts to influence the Princes. As Chancellor, he got his Secretariat to circulate a memorandum for the meetings of the Standing Committee, which recommended a policy of "wait-and-see". Bikaner now openly questioned "the advisability and wisdom" of such a policy. He countered Bhopal's move by circulating among the Princes a statement, which argued: "Even if the Muslim League ultimately decided not to participate in constitution-making, it is beyond question in the interests of the States as a whole, interspersed as they are with territories in British India, that, by June 1948, a strong Central Government should be created which can take over power. The only safe policy for the States, therefore, is to work fully with the stabilising elements in British India to create a Centre… which would safeguard both the States and British India in the vacuum that would be created by the withdrawal of the British Government… The interests of the people of the States obviously lie in joining hands with British India in establishing a strong Centre. And they are keenly alive to that necessity. If the Princes were to help in attaining that object, then the interests of the people and the Princes would continue to remain identical." Bikaner was followed by Patiala, who, in a public statement, deprecated the policy of "sitting on the fence."

The Maharajas of Bikaner and Patiala together forged a new group among the Princes, which, though still in a minority, was openly anti-Bhopal and pro-India. Their point of view had its salutary influence on the Princes' meeting on April 2nd. As a result, the original draft was "watered down", and another one was adopted instead, which reiterated the "willingness of the States to render the fullest possible cooperation in framing an agreed constitution and towards facilitating the transfer of power on an agreed basis." Seeing the situation going out of hand, Bhopal played a trump card by suggesting to Patiala, who was Pro-Chancellor, that the rulers who held offices in the Chamber should adhere to its recommendations, "not withstanding any personal differences of opinion." Patiala retorted by saying that his holding the office imposed no obligations on his Government, nor on his pursuing a policy "he considered necessary in the interests of his State." He told Bhopal that he was sending his representatives to the Constituent Assembly because he felt that "the stage for the States" participation in the constitution-making process had definitely come, and that any delay in doing so would be prejudicial not only to his own interests, but also to the wider interests of the country." Menon characterised the wind of change as "the beginning of the end of the united front put up by the Chamber of Princes".[22]

Patel saw in the opening of a big chink in the Chamber of Princes Bhopal had built as a bastion to give the Congress a strong fight. His statesmanship lay in turning the disunity among the Princes to his advantage. Now he rode among them like a rancher, gently shepherding his scattered flock back home. The operations had to be completed before the "return'" of Paramountcy to the Princes on August 15th. Patel told the Princes on April 15th, "In a short time India will be free... I congratulate those Princes who have wisely sided with the Congress. Only those Princes will be able to rule who carry their people with them; those who fail to do so will find their thrones disappear... Many of the Princes are yet sitting on the fence, waiting to see what shape coming events will take... I appeal to such Princes to join us now. It would not behove them to do so in the hour of their defeat."

Patel further told them, "Many Princes seem to believe that they should collect arms to establish their authority. But India is not the same today as she was when the British came here... In the end, every State will have to come in. But those who come in last will deny themselves the honour they will enjoy now. It will be said of those who come in now that they helped bring about unity and establish peace in India. The rest will be classed as mere spectators." He, however, assured the Princes, "We want to uphold the Princes' prestige, their honour... Those amongst them who have ability, intelligence and bravery can take up leadership of the Army. They can also enjoy the glory of serving India abroad as our Ambassadors. What for are you rotting in your small pits? Come out into the open ocean of national life."[23]

Patel's speech had its salutary effect. He won over many important Princes to his side. Baroda, Bikaner, Cochin, Jaipur,

Patiala and Rewa took their seats in the Constituent Assembly on April 28th. This set the ball rolling; and, as a result, other States began coming in one after another. Yet some kept aloof. An official document says: "Bhopal... was acting as an agent of Pakistan,... he was circulating to other rulers false statements to the effect that, as a result of the efforts of his group of rulers, the Instrument of Accession was being revised, and that, if all of them stood firm, they would be able to obtain or extract more favourable terms."[24] He attempted to establish his sincerity with the Princes by telling them that the lapse of Paramountcy would take place prior to the actual transfer of power, so that they could be in a better position to bargain with the successor Government. Yet, Bhopal succeeded in misleading many States, especially those strategically placed. Jodhpur, Jamnagar and even Travancore were among them.

The concept of lapse of Paramountcy was, according to Menon, "the greatest disservice the British had done us as well as the rulers."[25] Patel held the same opinion. The disservice lay in the June 3 Plan which was to sow the seeds of disruption by making Paramountcy lapse simultaneously with the transfer of power on August 15th; whereas under the Cabinet Mission Plan, Paramountcy would have lapsed "only after the constitution had been set up and power transferred to the successor Governments". Even as late as June 3rd, when the Pakistan demand had been conceded, Corfield and Jinnah endeavoured to aggravate the situation for India by trying to establish the States' sovereign status under the Plan. Jinnah stated on June 18th that every Indian State was a sovereign State and that the States were "fully entitled to say they would join neither Constituent Assembly." Liaquat Ali was more explicit in stating, "The Indian States will be free to negotiate agreements with Pakistan or Hindustan as considerations of contiguity or their own self-interest may dictate..."[26] This was fishing in Indian waters not without purpose. If he could force acceptance of his interpretation, Jinnah expected accession to Pakistan not only of Kashmir, Hyderabad and Bhopal, but also Indore, Jodhpur, Junagadh, Jamnagar and even Baroda.

Corfield's stress on the Government of India being not a successor to the functions and powers of the Crown Representative and the Political Departments was a deliberate and mischievous twisting of the facts in contradiction of what Viceroy Reading had told the Nizam in March 1926: "...the sovereignty to the British Crown is supreme in India, and, therefore, no ruler of an Indian State can justifiably claim to negotiate with the British Government on equal footing." In the transference of power, the Government of India was assuming such supremacy as a successor to the British Government. Corfield's views also had ominous overtones in respect of the British Government's instructions to Mountbatten that the Government of India could take over the residencies only if the Princes agreed. Mountbatten also admitted that he was not entitled to force a State to continue to accept an Agent of the Central Government in its territory. He was convinced that it was for the States to decide whether to send representatives to either Delhi or Karachi or receive representatives from the successor Governments. This amounted to declaring each State independent.

The situation as it prevailed on June 3rd had dangerous potentialities. Patel told Menon that "if we did not handle it promptly and effectively, our hard-earned freedom might disappear through the States' door."[27] Events rushed past like a hurricane, leaving many baffled by its speed and befogged by the resultant uncertainties which hung over the horizon. Many Princes lost their moorings. But Patel held fast to his anchorage. Panikkar echoed Patel's thoughts when he told him in March 1947: "Paramountcy is like a string that holds together all the 500 odd precious stones and pearls: remove the string, all of them will fall apart. And then it will be our job to collect them again and find out a formula that binds them to us." Such a string had broken with the Bikaner-Patiala group joining the Constituent Assembly. Bhopal and Corfield had attempted to mend the string not only through the formation of autocratic federations of groups of States, but also through various provisions of the June 3 Plan which favoured the Princes' position. They were outmanoeuvred by Patel. Bhopal faced the futility of his efforts in Patel's success in Jodhpur, Kathiawar and even Travancore. He realised the wisdom of what C.S. Venkatachar had told Corfield as early as February when the latter believed that he and his clan could "prop them up… The Princes will have no bargaining power the moment two independent Dominions are created and power transferred to the two Central Governments, which will be so strong as to shift the balance of power in their favour and against the Princes."[28]

Patel's assumption of charge of the newly-created States Department (not a Ministry yet) on July 5th was significant in the prevailing confused, complex and dangerous situation. The new department was to replace the Political Department without the latter's functions, powers and even records. With Patel these things mattered little. He was capable of creating his own functions and powers that suited the nation's interests. And he did create them. Princes were drawn towards him because of his powerful personality, which gave them firm assurance of a new, hopeful future in an atmosphere of unsuspecting, benign friendship of one who exuded humanity, humility and broad-mindedness. Ample evidence of this was seen in Patel's policy statement on taking charge as Minister of States. The statement was acclaimed as a masterpiece of diplomatic finesse, reflecting Patel's transparent sincerity. He stirred up the nobler sentiments of the Princes by recalling the Princes' proud, glorious past, when ancestors of some had played highly patriotic roles in the defence of their family honour and the freedom of their land.

Patel proudly told the Princes that among them "I am happy to count many as my personal friends." He reminded them, "It is the lesson of history that it was owing to her politically fragmented condition and our inability to make a united stand that India succumbed to successive waves of invaders. Our mutual conflicts and internecine quarrels and jealousies have, in the past, been the cause of our downfall and our falling victims to foreign domination a number of times. We cannot afford to fall into those errors or traps again." He told them, "We are on the threshold of independence… The safety and preservation of the States, as well as of India, demand unity and mutual cooperation between its different parts." Patel urged the Princes to consider that in the exercise of Paramountcy, "there has undoubtedly been more of subordination than cooperation", and that "now that British rule is ending, the demand has been made that the States should regain their independence. Insofar as Paramountcy embodied the submission of States to foreign will, I have every sympathy with this demand, but I do not think it can be their desire to utilise this freedom from domination in a manner which is injurious to the common interests of India, or which militates against the ultimate Paramountcy of popular interests and welfare, or which might result in the abandonment of that mutually useful relationship that has developed between British India and Indian States during the last century."

Patel grew somewhat sentimental when he told them, "We are all knit together by bonds of blood and feeling, no less than of self-interest. None can segregate us into segments; no impassable barriers can be set up between us… I invite my friends, the Rulers of States, and their people, to the councils of the Constituent Assembly in this spirit of friendliness and cooperation in a joint endeavour, inspired by common allegiance to our motherland, for the common good of us all." In the same breath Patel gave them the assurance that "it is not the desire of the Congress to interfere in any manner whatsoever with the domestic affairs of the States." He further assured them: "They (the Congress) are no enemies of the Princely Order, but, on the other hand, they wish them and the people under their aegis all prosperity, contentment and happiness. Nor would it be my policy to conduct the relations of the new department with the States in any manner which savours of the domination of one over the other; if there would be any domination, it would be that of our mutual interests and welfare."

In a masterly peroration, Patel declared, "We are at a momentous stage in the history of India. By common endeavour, we can raise the country to a new greatness, while lack of unity will expose us to fresh calamities. I hope the Indian States will bear in mind that the alternative to cooperation in the general interest is anarchy and chaos, which will overwhelm great and small in a common ruin if we are unable to act together in the minimum of common tasks. Let not the future generations curse us for having had the opportunity but failed to turn it to our mutual advantage. Instead, let it be our proud privilege to leave a legacy of a mutually beneficial relationship which would raise this sacred land to its proper place amongst the nations of the world and turn it into an abode of peace and prosperity."[29]

Patel received profuse felicitations from many a Prince, big and small. Bikaner's rich compliment was: "May I take this opportunity of sending you my very best wishes in the onerous duties which have fallen upon you... The fact that one of the most respected and mature statesmen and leaders of your experience and judgment has been chosen is, I feel, a happy augury. It is most gratifying to recall that you have always shown a realistic and cordial attitude towards the States. The friendly hand that you have so spontaneously extended to the Princes and States, as evidenced by your statement, is, I need hardly assure you, greatly appreciated by us. We are confident that we may look forward to an association of full cooperation with you and a sympathetic understanding at your hands of the very important problems vitally affecting the States at the present transitional stage, thus enabling the States at take their due and honoured place in the future Union of India, in the making of which we are all proud to give our wholehearted support. I know that the interests of the Princes and States are safe in your hands."[30]

Mountbatten's preference for Patel to Nehru was for good reasons. "I am glad to say", he wrote, "that Nehru has not been put in charge of the new States Department, which would have wrecked everything. Patel, who is essentially a realist and very sensible, is going to take it over."[31] He told the Princes at his last conference with them on July 25th, "In India the States Department is under the admirable guidance of Sardar Vallabhbhai Patel... You can imagine how relieved I was, and I am sure you will yourselves have been equally relieved, when Sardar Vallabhbhai

Patel, on taking over the States department, made, if I may say so, a most statesmanlike statement of what he considered were the essentials towards agreement between the States and the Dominion of India."[32] Mountbatten thought that Patel, being the "strongest pillar of the Cabinet", alone could help him fulfil his assurance to the King on two matters: India's membership of the Commonwealth, and fair treatment for the Princes.

In dealing with the Princes, the roles of Patel and Mountbatten were complementary. Mountbatten got Patel's strong support for the Commonwealth membership, and his pursuit of the middle path in the integration of the States. Patel, on his part, felt satisfied with Britain's decision that the Indian States could not enter the Commonwealth as a Dominion. Patel secured another point. While giving his consent to India's memberships of the Commonwealth, he made it a condition... "Let Paramountcy be dead. You do not directly or indirectly try to revive it in any manner... The Princes are ours, and we shall deal with them."[33] Hodson records a meaningful dialogue between Patel and Mountbatten prior to the former's acceptance of the charge of the States Ministry. Patel said, "I am prepared to accept your offer provided that you give me a full basket of apples."

"What do you mean?" asked Mountbatten.

"I'll buy a basket with 565 apples, but if there are even two or three missing, the deal is off."

"This," said the Viceroy, "I cannot completely accept, but I will do my best. If I give you a basket with, say, 560 apples, will you buy it?"

"Well, I might." replied Patel.[34] That nearly settled the Princes problem so far as Patel was concerned.

C.P. Ramaswami Aiyar, who, as the Diwan of Travancore, was the first to declare a revolt against his State joining the Indian Union, accused the British of duplicity: their "inconsistent and dissimilar approaches" to the Princes and the Congress. "The British Rulers and Lord Mountbatten," he writes, "could be justly charged with trying to please both the parties, and finally giving way with an ill-grace to the inevitable force of Indian political pressure. If it had been made clear from the first that the Indian States could not expect to maintain themselves as self-governing entities, the history of the negotiations might have taken a different course. A great deal of avoidable confusion and misunderstanding was created by ambiguous utterances by various authorities." C.P. quotes Mountbatten having told the Princes, "My scheme leaves you with all practical independence that you can possible use."[35]

Patel on his part showed tact and diplomacy in his handling of the Princes. They feared his firmness, even his wrath; but they could enjoy his genuine friendship if they did not override the country's interests. Presiding over a press conference addressed by Menon on July 5th, Patel gave a blunt warning, "Whoever denounces such agreements takes the responsibility for the consequences."[36] And yet, no one could match his humility. He showed profuse consideration in giving Their Highnesses what they passionately loved: their regal status, their royal splendour, their scintillating titles, and, above all, the Princely Order. Patel had come to a decision, about which Reginald Coupland had speculated in 1945, "An India deprived of the States would have lost all coherence. They stand between all four quarters of the country... India could live if its Muslim limbs in the north-west and north-east were amputated, but could it live without its midriff?"[37] And that is what Patel instinctively meant when he stated, "Hyderabad is, as it were, situated in India's belly. How can the belly breathe, if it is cut off from the main body?"[38] The States formed India's heart and Patel's genius lay in preserving, integrating and strengthening that heart at all costs, and thereby saving India from the frightening prospects of Balkanisation. Patel prevented a situation which was "fraught with the gravest danger to the integrity of the country"; and falsified what prophets of gloom had predicted that "the ship of Indian freedom would founder on the rock of the States."

Jinnah could not forgive India, in particular, Patel, for forcing him to accept in the end, when the British were to leave India, a Pakistan that was "truncated and moth-eaten". It was the end of his dream, which the British from Churchill to Attlee had, purposefully, built to serve Britain's own interests. They had nearly succeeded but for the "man of iron" in Patel, who blocked their way like a massive rock. The failure of British diplomacy was to be seen in Attlee's policy statement of 20th February 1947. Jinnah could not forgive Patel and made all efforts to secure accession or association of Jodhpur, Junagadh, Kathiawar, and even the far-off Hyderabad, not forgetting the "invasion" of Kashmir through Frontier tribesmen.

a) JODHPUR

Jinnah's fishing in the distant waters of Travancore and Hyderabad was to achieve his objective of weakening the Government in New Delhi. Kathiawar, including Junagadh, was on Jinnah's priority list, but that did not provide so favourable a situation to Pakistan as Jodhpur. The State lay across Pakistan's border; and was most strategic from the point of view of making inroads into the heart of India. "The case of Jodhpur," admits H.V. Hodson, "illustrates the lengths to which Jinnah was prepared to go in order to wean States from India."[1] Events in Jodhpur took a dramatic turn with the sudden demise of Maharaja Umed Singh in June 1947 and the succession to the throne by his son, Hanwant Singh, who was young, rash, headstrong and given to irresponsible, emotional outbursts. Hanwant Singh's father had cast his lot with India, and was among the first few Princes whose representatives took their seats in the Constituent Assembly on April 28, 1947.

On the occasion of the Rajtilak (crowning) ceremony on June 21, the new Maharaja announced that Jodhpur would continue to be associated with the Constituent Assembly of India. He even expressed the desire that Jodhpur, in close association with participating States in the Assembly, would work wholeheartedly for the formation of a Union of India. But the presence of Bhopal in Jodhpur was a most disturbing factor in an otherwise quiet situation. He had flown in, ostensibly, to offer his felicitations to the young Maharaja; but he had a secret mission—that of an emissary of Jinnah. On the latter's behalf, he was to arrange a few meetings in New Delhi at Jinnah's residence, at which Bhopal, along with his Legal Adviser, Mohammad Zafrullah, was to be present to assist Jinnah in winning over Jodhpur, and thus weaning the Maharaja away from India. Jinnah harboured a grand plan—a Karachi-Jodhpur-Bhopal axis, which was looked upon by Patel as "a dagger into the very heart of India." This way Jinnah wanted to avenge Patel's forcing on him a truncated Pakistan. Jodhpur's defection would have given a fatal blow to Patel's dream of unification of the Rajput States, which stretched along Pakistan's eastern border and Rajput's disunity, distrust and friction in the past had helped the Mughals to build their Empire in India. Jinnah seemed to be angling for a similar role for Pakistan, with Jodhpur repeating history by playing a quisling.

C.S. Venkatachar, the Prime Minister of Jodhpur, came to know about Bhopal's secret mission from whispers floating around the palace. Deeply concerned over what was ominously taking shape, he sent H.V.R. Iengar, Home Secretary to the Government of India, a handwritten note through a special messenger, so as "to avoid being spied upon", giving news of the "utmost gravity for the very stability of India." The note also stated that "the ruler had been approached by Jinnah and had been persuaded to stay out of the Indian Dominion."[2] Iengar took the note to Patel and apprised him of the "gravity of the situation." A great danger lurked in Bhopal, Indore and a few other Central India States forming an independent federation under Bhopal's leadership with ultimate accession to Pakistan. Bhopal expected Baroda to join his group on Jinnah's promise that he would be allowed to exercise control over his port of Bedi Bandar on the Saurashtra coast. Jinnah was hopeful of roping in the Jamsaheb of Nawanagar as well in his grand plan.

Jodhpur was hesitant to see Jinnah alone. He took with him the Maharajkumar of Jaisalmer. Jinnah's argument with Jodhpur was, "As long as the Central Government in India is weak, we are both strong... Your Highness, I sign on the dotted line, and you fill in the conditions."[3] The ambitious Maharaja was tempted by four offers: a sea-outlet through the use of Karachi as a free port, free import of arms and continuance of manufacture of firearms in his State, jurisdiction over the Jodhpur-Hyderabad (Sind) railway, and a large supply of grain for famine relief. This was Jinnah's "basket of apples", which Bhopal had already successfully sold to Jodhpur. The Maharaja seemed to be so happy with the offer that he invited the Maharana of Udaipur to join the Bhopal plan. The reply was to shock Jodhpur: "My choice was made by my ancestors. If they had faltered, they would have left us a kingdom as large as Hyderabad. They did not. Neither shall I. I am with India."[4] Bikaner also refused Jodhpur to accompany him to Jinnah.

Anxious not to let the fish escape from his net, Jinnah at his meeting with Jodhpur, signed a blank sheet of paper and gave it to Maharaja Hanwant Singh along with his own fountain pen, saying: "You can fill in all your conditions". The Maharaja was prepared to line up with Pakistan. He then turned to the Maharajkumar of Jaisalmer and asked him whether he would follow suit. Jaisalmer's one condition was, "If there was any trouble between the Hindus and the Muslims, he would not side with the Muslims against the Hindus." This was "a bombshell that took Maharaja Hanwant Singh completely by surprise."[5] Zafrullah tried to make light of the whole affair and pressed Jodhpur to sign the instrument. The Maharaja could not immediately make up his mind. Taking advantage of his vacillation, the Maharaja's A.D.C. Col. Thakur Kesari Singh, whispered into his ear, "Your Highness, before you sign, you must ask your mother." The Maharaja greatly respected her. Known as Rajdidi, she was "a woman of great character, power and influence."[6] The Maharaja suggested to Jinnah that he would go back to Jodhpur and return the next day.

Since power had not yet been transferred, Patel could only exercise patience. He had no authority to deal with the Princes officially and his approach to Bhopal could only be through Mountbatten as the Crown Representative. Mountbatten took up the matter with Bhopal, telling him that Patel had received information that "His Highness had made contact with the young Maharaja of Jodhpur and induced him to come with him to Jinnah. That at this meeting Jinnah had offered extremely favourable terms on condition that he did not sign the Instrument of Accession, and that he had even gone as far as to turn round and say to the Maharaja of Jodhpur, "Here's my fountain pen! Write your terms and I will sign it." Bhopal gave an evasive version of the story. But Mountbatten took the opportunity to warn Bhopal: "I pointed out to His Highness that no amount of friendship would enable me to protect either himself or his State or the new ruler of the State, if the future Government of India thought that he was acting in a manner hostile to that Government by trying to induce an all-Hindu State to join Pakistan."[7]

Patel, thus, faced three extremely intrepid, intractable and unpredictable men in Jinnah, Bhopal and Jodhpur. The first was astute and clever, proudly basking in the glory of his victory in getting away with Pakistan, and now hunting for opportunities to stir up trouble for India by other ways. The second was a peerless Machiavellian who carried influence with some of the Princes as Chancellor of the Chamber of Princes. And the third, the Maharaja of Jodhpur, was headstrong, emotional and impulsive, capable of committing any rash act irrespective of the consequences.

The Maharaja returned to New Delhi after a three-day stay at Jodhpur for a final round of talks with Jinnah and Bhopal. He didn't seem to be the same as earlier—apparently subdued by his mother's talk, as also by what his guru, a swami, reportedly told him, "How could a Hindu State like Jodhpur agree to accede to Pakistan which will be a Muslim State?" Yet, Venkatachar did not leave matters to chance. He followed him to New Delhi to keep a watch on his moves. V.P. Menon too moved into the arena of manoeuvring. He was informed that unless he handled the Maharaja "quickly, the chances were that he might accede to Pakistan."[8] It was decided, as part of strategy, that before Patel stepped into the scene, Mountbatten might handle the Maharaja first. The latter agreed to do so, rather hopefully. Before Bhopal could get in touch with the Maharaja on Jinnah's behalf, Menon contacted the young Prince and told him that Mountbatten, who was still the Crown Representative, would like to see him.

Without losing time, Menon drove the Maharaja to the Viceroy's House. Mountbatten explained to the Maharaja that from a purely legal standpoint, there could be no objection to Jodhpur's acceding to Pakistan, but he should not overlook the fact that his was a predominantly Hindu State: if acceded to Pakistan, "his action would surely be in conflict with the principle underlying the Partition of India on the basis of Muslim and non-Muslim majority areas; and serious communal trouble inside the State would be the inevitable consequence of such affiliation."[9] The Maharaja remained non-committal. He tried to put Mountbatten off by asking for "impossible concessions". An exasperated Mountbatten used all his persuasive powers—first as a well-wisher, and then as his "uncle" by telling him in plain language that "his father had been a great personal friend of mine, having been on the Prince of Wales' staff with me in 1921-22 ... he had been supporting my scheme for the accession of the States to the Dominion of India, and that Jodhpur would have acceded if he had not died. To me it was tragic that his successor should not follow the wisdom of his father, and should have been misled by Jinnah...." Mountbatten admits: "I could not get the Maharaja to agree then and there, although I had obviously shaken him, and I then conceived the idea of getting V.P. Menon to take him to see Sardar Patel before returning to Jodhpur..."[10]

The Maharaja saw Patel at the latter's residence. Patel was "extremely polite, exceedingly courteous, but firm in tone". The conversation between the two was very brief. The awe-inspiring looks of Patel made the Maharaja somewhat shaky. He faltered in tone. Patel purposely put up a show that was an anti-climax to what had happened at the Maharaja's meeting with Mountbatten. He treated him with overflowing kindness and disarming smiles. The conversation between the two briefly was:

Patel: I hear Your Highness has met Lord Mountbatten.

Maharaja: Yes, Sardar.

Patel: So, what talk did you have with him?

Maharaja: No... thing.... Sardar.

Patel: I also hear Your Highness has met Jinnah and have decided to remain independent.

Maharaja: Yes, Sardar.

Patel: Well, I have no comments to make. Your Highness is free to stay out, if you like. But if there is trouble in your State as a result of your decision, you will not get the slightest support from the Government of India.[11]

According to Iengar, "there was a clear warning that there *would* be trouble in the State", and Patel "left the ruler in no doubt that the move initiated by Jinnah was dangerous not only to India, but to the ruler himself."[12] Patel closed the conversation with a mild admonition by saying that the Maharaja's father, who was his friend, had left him to his care as a ward; and if he did not behave as he should, Patel would have to act the role of a guardian to discipline him! The Maharaja felt unnerved. He broke out in a cold sweat. Sobered, subdued, he quietly got up from his seat and told Patel in a mollified voice, "Well Sir, I have decided to go back to Lord Mountbatten and sign the Instrument of Accession right now."

One drama was over. Another one began soon after at the Viceroy's House. Even when the Maharaja had committed himself to Patel, he could still give Menon a slip and motor down to Bhopal's residence. Menon could not allow that. He himself drove the Maharaja straight to Mountbatten. Immediately after the Instrument of Accession had been signed, Mountbatten went out of the room. During his short absence, in a fit of emotional outburst, narrates Menon, the Maharaja "whipped out a revolver, leveled it at me and said, 'I refuse to accept your dictation.' I told him that he was making a very serious mistake if he thought that by killing me, or threatening to kill me, he could get the accession abrogated. "Don't indulge in juvenile theatricals."[13] Just when the incident was over, Mountbatten returned to the room. Menon told him what had happened. He wisely made "light of the episode and turned it to a jest" by patting the Maharaja on his back and telling him, "Don't show such bravado! Let us now finish the business first."

In the settlement of the Jodhpur affairs, a great calamity was averted. Both Patel and Mountbatten played their respective but complementary roles. The ultimate success was, nevertheless, due to Patel. He made Jinnah suffer a humiliating defeat. It was for Bhopal too. Patel's greatest gain, however, was winning the abiding loyalty of the Maharaja. While the Maharaja struck a deep, warm, lifelong friendship with Menon, his relations with Patel grew deeper and warmer from then onwards. He gave Patel the reverence he would have offered to his late father. His devotion to Patel led the Maharaja to serve him as an "errand boy", who happily flew in his aircraft from Prince to Prince and from State to State carrying Patel's messages. He always felt proud to accompany Patel to various places, wearing "a spotless white, jewel-buttoned coat and Jodhpuris, with a coloured turban and a leather belt across his left shoulder replete with a revolver and cartridges."

An interesting incident of such devotion took place on March 29, 1949 when the Maharaja accompanied Patel in an Indian Air Force aircraft to Jaipur to attend the inauguration of the Union of Greater Rajasthan the following day. Beyond Alwar, the aircraft forcelanded owing to engine trouble. Passing through valleys and hills, the pilot Bhim Rao, showed great skill in manoeuvring the aircraft to avoid dashing against one of the hills. There was also the danger of the aircraft bumping on stony ground, and of the fuel tank catching fire. In such tense moments, the Maharaja's corpulent body provided a diversionary amusement to all, including Patel, with Shankar suggesting that the Maharaja would have to be the last to go, if his figure got stuck in the exit, there would be no chance for the others to get out! The Maharaja took all this in good humour, and even participated in such light conversation. But the danger of a tragedy was real. Patel, however, looked unruffled. The aircraft landed on a soft, sandy, dry river-bed near the village of Shahpur. All got out—the Maharaja, of course, the last! They rested for a while under a tree. Hearing the noise of the landing, the villagefolk came running to witness the accident. Coming to know who was involved, they fetched a few cots. Patel was "calm and composed", and enjoyed folk music and folk dance offered by a group of village boys and girls.

The nearest town, Sikar, was several miles away. The Maharaja thought of indulging in some purposeful adventure—walking some distance in search of the main road and finding some transport which could carry Patel and his party to Jaipur. He stood near the centre of the road, trying to stop the passing cars and trucks. But the drivers, on seeing a bulky man with two revolvers hanging on either side of him, would press the accelerator and speed away. His appearance frightened many a car-owner too. Meanwhile, K.B. Lall, Administrator of the United States of Matsya, on securing information from a bystander, reached the place where Patel was resting. He happened to be travelling by car from Alwar to Jaipur to attend the same function. Seeing him, Patel gave a broad smile and enquired how he managed to reach there. Lall gave a light-hearted reply, "A note from his Private Secretary called him to his duty!"

Humorously, Patel quipped, "Somehow you manage to turn up from somewhere in critical situations."[14] Lall found Patel settled comfortably in a chair which had been detached from the aircraft. He appeared composed, with no trace of worry or annoyance or agitation. He was content with the situation he was in. But his mind was set on Jaipur. He asked how long it would take him to reach those who would be anxiously waiting to receive him. On being requested by Lall to get into his car, he insisted on waiting for the Maharaja's return. But time was running out, and he could not delay his departure if he were to reach Jaipur on time. He wanted Lall and others to satisfy him that they would take care of the Maharaja, and that adequate arrangements would be made for every one.

The sun had set. Dusk was settling down. The journey to Jaipur was long. Reluctantly Patel agreed to Lall's suggestion, but on the assurance that the Maharaja would be looked after. He thought that he would meet him on the main road. Not seeing him there, he organised a search. It was unsuccessful. Lall followed Patel in another car, keeping a watch-out along the road. At some distance, he recognised the Maharaja standing on the roadside, still in search of a vehicle! Maharaja Hanwant Singh was head-strong but he was essentially a simple-minded and sincere human being. He proved to be the most lovable of the Princes, whose courage and patriotism flowered under the paternal affection of Patel. The Prince died in a plane crash in 1952.

At the other end, in the Jaipur palace, the scene was equally dramatic--the uncertainty getting on everybody's nerves. A whisper by someone into the ear of the Maharaja of Jaipur broke the gloom. M.K. Vellodi records that "the effect was electric. The Maharaja jumped out of his chair and yelled with joy and hugged the Jamsaheb... all of us on the terrace hugged each other... In a matter of minutes we saw a small group of people approaching the palace on foot with a petromax light leading the way. It was the Sardar and his retinue. We were transported with joy, and when he came on to the terrace we nearly wept (*in sheer joy*!). The Sardar put his arms round the Jamsaheb and broke into a broad grin. He was as cool as a cucumber..."[15] That was characteristic of him: calm, unperturbed, unruffled even amidst grave crises.

b) JUNAGADH

In Junagadh's accession to Pakistan on August 15th, Patel saw "the first danger sign for splitting India again." He admitted, "After Partition, we had a huge problem. Those who partitioned the country had mental reservations. They thought that this Partition was not the last word, and they started the game immediately thereafter. Among the Kathiawar States, they went to Junagadh and got its accession to Pakistan.... We woke up in time and those who tried to play the game saw that we were not sleeping."[1] The situation in Junagadh was in marked contrast with that of Jodhpur; and one which was much to Patel's disadvantage. In the case of Jodhpur, he had foiled Jinnah's efforts to entice the

Maharaja; in Junagadh, he was presented with a *fait accompli* by a Muslim ruler.

The gravity of the situation further increased by Mountbatten's recognising Junagadh as "Pakistan territory" in his report to the King, in which he stated: "My chief concern as Governor-General was to prevent the Government of India from committing itself on the Junagadh issue to an act of war against what was now Pakistan territory." Further in the report, Mountbatten gave out what seemed to be his major role in India as her Governor-General: "But at the same time I was aware that, in the wider aspect, my own physical presence as Governor-General of India was the best insurance against an actual outbreak of war with Pakistan."[2] That he wanted to safeguard Pakistan's position, Mountbatten confessed to Nehru much later, "Pakistan is in no position even to declare war, since I happen to know that their military commanders have put it to them in writing that a declaration of war with India can only end in the inevitable and ultimate defeat of Pakistan."[3] However, Mountbatten's views expressed to the King seemed contrary to the advice he gave the Princes on July 25th: to recognise "geographical compulsions which cannot be evaded", as also "the communal majorities of the ruler's subjects."[4] Mountbatten had also told the Princes, "You cannot run away from the Dominion Government which is your neighbour any more than you can run away from the subjects for whose welfare you are responsible."[5]

In spite of such professions, Mountbatten made a serious attempt to play a role in Junagadh which was not in India's interest. He had no control over Jinnah's actions, but he thought he could use his position as Governor-General in averting a war with Pakistan by binding India to three conditions: first, reference of Junagadh to the UNO; second, Indian troops should not enter Junagadh territory; and, third, offer of holding a plebiscite in Junagadh. Patel was far too clever and strong-willed to fall into a trap laid by Mountbatten; whereas Nehru failed in that respect in Kashmir. In Hyderabad too Mountbatten played a similar role: to secure for the Nizam association, not accession, to India.

As Monckton has opined: association could be terminated, not accession, with the latter being a permanent commitment.

Reluctantly, Patel agreed to a plebiscite, even when Jinnah had not asked for it. But he rejected outright the first two. The first would have, by giving Pakistan *locus standi* in Junagadh, internationalised the issue, as it happened later in the case of Kashmir. Patel's terse comment was, "There was a grave disadvantage in being the plaintiff in such cases."[6] Mountbatten overlooked the fact that in Junagadh's accession to Pakistan would lie "Jinnah's tactical shrewdness. He must have seen—or, if he did not see, it certainly turned out—that the accession of Junagadh to Pakistan placed India in an acute dilemma from which any escape could be turned to the advantage of Pakistan."[7] There was also the danger of Pakistan securing a foothold in Junagadh by landing troops through its port of Veraval, a course she secretly adopted later in Kashmir by sending tribal invaders there. Once Pakistani troops were on Junagadh soil, it would have been difficult for India to dislodge them from there. A graver danger would be Jinnah's claim to Hyderabad on the Nizam's accession to Pakistan and to Kashmir for reasons of the State's contiguity to Pakistan and its people being predominantly Muslims. Patel refused to oblige Mountbatten on two grounds. The first, according to him, was the "forcible dragging of our eighty per cent of Hindu population of Junagadh into Pakistan by accession in defiance of all democratic principles."[8] The second was that accession would have set up a dangerous precedent. On Campbell-Johnson's admission, it "would automatically be a direct challenge to the essential validity of the whole accession policy, with disastrous effects both upon the Kathiawar States and upon the Hyderabad negotiations."[9] Junagadh brought home to Patel's critics "the possibilities of disintegration if the policy of accession had not been implemented."[10]

The situation in Junagadh presented certain complications. The ruler, Nawab Mahabatkhan Rasulkhanji, was an eccentric, who "loved dogs to excess" and he was said to have owned 800 of them, "each with its human attendant, and to have spent

20 lakhs of rupees (£150,000) on a wedding for two of them, for which he proclaimed a State holiday." His Diwan, Shah Nawaz Bhutto, was a Muslim League politician from Karachi and father of Zulfikhar Ali Bhutto, who later became the Prime Minister of Pakistan. But what supported India's claim was that, unlike Jodhpur, Junagadh had no contiguity with Pakistan by land, though it could establish a direct link with Karachi through its port of Veraval—just 300 miles away. Landlocked Junagadh was separated from Pakistan by the territories of Kutch, Baroda, Nawanagar, Porbandar and Gondal. Junagadh's map, according to H.V. Hodson, had "absurd complexity": "fragments of other States were embedded in Junagadh, and fragments of Junagadh were embedded in other States, while an arm of Junagadh separated one substantial outlying portion of the Maratha State of Baroda from another and from the sea."[11] Whatever geographical impediments, Jinnah expected Junagadh's accession to give Karachi mastery over the Arabian Sea. Equally important was the fact that Jinnah wanted Junagadh to serve as a test case on the basis of which he could claim Kashmir. He built his hopes on another calculation, about which Pyarelal writes: "Right till the end of the British rule in India, Jinnah and the Muslim League had ridden in triumph on the 'heads I win, tails you lose' principle... Junagadh marked the turning-point."[12] This was entirely due to Patel's toughness, whereas Mountbatten's suggestions would have given Jinnah the veto the British had purposely placed in Jinnah's hands to wreck political talks since the Simla Conference in 1945.

Patel called Junagadh's accession to Pakistan an act of perfidy. As early as April 11, 1947, the Muslim ruler had camouflaged his real intentions by stating that "what Junagadh pre-eminently stands for is the solidarity of Kathiawar, and would welcome the formation of a self-contained group of Kathiawar States."[13] Accession to Pakistan was purposely not mentioned. Junagadh seemed to be adhering to the policy advocated by Corfield, though the Diwan of the State, Abdul Kadir Mohammed Hussain, categorically repudiated, on April 22nd, allegations that Junagadh was thinking of joining Pakistan. In May, Kadir left for Europe for medical treatment, handing over charge to Bhutto. In spite of this change of Diwanship, Junagadh's representative at the rulers' conference on July 25th, Nabi Baksh, told Mountbatten that his intention was to advise the Nawab to accede to India. He had also given a similar impression to Patel when he called upon him, as also to the Jamsaheb of Nawanagar, his neighbour. This was despite the fact that Junagadh had already secretly recruited to the State forces Baluchis and Hurs from Pakistan, and a decision had been taken that the local Bahauddin College was to be affiliated to the Sind University in Karachi.

Hodson thinks that handling of Junagadh "would be full of traps, and there was good reason to suspect that some of those traps had been deliberately laid by Pakistan." Hodson justifies his suspicion from the fact that Bhutto obeyed Jinnah's advice, given on July 16th, "to keep out under all circumstances until August 15th."[14] With the termination of Paramountcy, Bhutto could take an independent decision. Meanwhile, Jinnah assured Bhutto that he would not allow Junagadh to starve as "Veraval is not far from Karachi." Jinnah's assurance was to allay Bhutto's fears which he had expressed in his communication: "Junagadh stands all alone surrounded by Hindu rulers' territories and British Indian Congress provinces. We are, of course, connected by sea with Pakistan. If geographical position by land was fairly considered, Kutch, Jamnagar and other territories adjoining Junagadh geographically should be considered connected with Pakistan, as they once in the past actually formed part of Sind. Though the Muslim population of Junagadh is nearly 20 percent and non-Muslims form 80 per cent, seven lakh Muslims of Kathiawar survived because of Junagadh. I consider that no sacrifice is too great to preserve the prestige, honour and rule of His Highness and to protect Islam and the Muslims of Kathiawar."[15]

Patel saw dangerous implications of the Jinnah-Bhutto conspiracy. If Junagadh were allowed to accede to Pakistan, Menon thought, "its detachment would turn it into a hothouse plant with no powers of survival." What worried him most was "the immediate potentialities for turmoil when stability was the crying need of the hour. The Nawab's action would have undesirable effects on law and order in Kathiawar as a whole. It would extend the communal trouble to areas where at present there was peace. There was also the fear that it would encourage the intractable elements in Hyderabad." In one of his bellicose utterances, Hyderabad's Razakar leader, Kasim Razvi, confirmed this when he said, "Why is the Sardar thundering about Hyderabad when he cannot control even little Junagadh?"[16]

Junagadh's accession to Pakistan on August 15th was kept a closely guarded secret. Mountbatten, the Crown Representative, was kept in the dark by the Political Department, the Residents and Agents keeping mum. And so was the British Government—the Paramount Power. The Government of India too had no inkling. It came to know about it on the 17th from newspaper reports. On an enquiry being made, Junagadh simply confirmed the news. Pakistan having not yet formally accepted the accession, India moved into the matter constitutionally by inviting the attention of the Pakistan High Commissioner to India to the invalidity of accession on grounds of Junagadh's geographical contingity to India, the composition of its population and the need for consulting the views of the people. Pakistan was discreetly silent. Even a reminder sent on September 6th evoked no response. Jinnah expected that nothing serious would take place. Mountbatten would not let India take precipitate action; Britain would hesitate to take sides; and Nehru would show his usual hesitancy in taking a firm decision. Through this haze of inaction he would carry the day—surreptitiously achieving Junagadh's accession. He had made one serious miscalculation—Patel's capacity to act strongly and quickly, bypassing all the rest—even Mountbatten.

As Jinnah expected, Nehru showed constitutional inhibitions and wanted to pursue a policy of soft-pedalling. On Nehru's suggestion, a telegram addressed to Liaquat Ali was sent on September 12th. It indicated India's willingness to abide by the verdict of the people of Junagadh. This was playing into Jinnah's hands, as he could expect the same in Kashmir later—people's right for self-determination. Lest India's message was ignored like the earlier ones, the telegram was personally carried by Ismay to Karachi. He also carried Mountbatten's message to Jinnah that, if Pakistan accepted Junagadh's accession, it would lead to a dispute between the two Dominions, and that if Jinnah wanted any State to accede to Pakistan, he could not have chosen a worse State. Pakistan merely telegraphed on September 13th confirming acceptance of Junagadh's accession.

The Junagadh crisis, according to Campbell-Johnson, erupted as if from "a wholly unexpected quarter", and "in the welter of great events immediately before and after the transfer of power, Junagadh was simply overlooked."[17] Not only did Pakistan take advantage of this, but also seemed to have bracketed Junagadh with Hyderabad and Kashmir. Repudiating such a situation, Patel was ready to go on the warpath. He rejected Nehru's soft-pedalling in the suggestion that "it would be desirable for us to send a message to the British Government about the Junagadh affair" with the polite comment: "I am not quite sure whether we need say anything to the British Government at this stage."[18] Patel was not willing to let India revert to the pre-Independence years and allow the British to play their earlier partisan role which was pro-Muslim and pro-Jinnah. He proved vindicated by such partisan role of Britain later in Kashmir and Hyderabad. Patel was confident of acting on his own, untroubled by what worried Nehru and Mountbatten: the former with an exaggerated notion of international opinion; the latter by an anxiety which reflected the mood of a Briton, fearing that a war might knock Pakistan out of existence.

Junagadh's decision sent a wave of indignation and protest among the people and Rulers of Kathiawar—Nawanagar, Bhavnagar, Morvi, Gondal, Porbandar and Wankaner. All condemned it as strongly as they could. The Junagadh affair turned the rulers to Patel for handling the situation in the same manner as he had in Jodhpur. Junagadh's accession made the Kathiawar rulers anti-Jinnah. The Maharaja of Dhrangadhra asked the Nawab of Junagadh in a personal letter to reconsider the decision as it was opposed to geographical compulsions, and, no less, the wishes of the people; and that failure to reverse it would cause disruption of Kathiawar. The Nawab's reply was: "The Indian Independence Act did not, and does not, require a ruler to consult his people before deciding on accession. I think we are making an unnecessary fetish of the argument of geographical contiguity. Even then, this is sufficiently provided by Junagadh's sea coast with several ports which can keep connection with Pakistan."[19]

The Jamsaheb rushed to New Delhi personally to tell Patel that the rulers and people of Kathiawar were greatly agitated over Pakistan's attempt to encroach on Indian territory, and how difficult it would be to restrain the people of Kathiawar from retaliation, and that, if the Government of India did not take "immediate and effective steps', the Kathiawar States would "lose faith in the will and ability of the Indian Dominion to carry out all the obligations arising from their accession to India".[20] Mountbatten and Ismay were concerned not so much with this as with deterring India from any physical action. Mountbatten had long talks with Nehru and Patel. He did not have much difficulty in carrying conviction with Nehru; with Patel it was a difficult task. According to Campbell-Johnson, Mountbatten "reiterated Ismay's thesis that the whole manoeuvre was almost certainly a trap and part of a wider campaign which Jinnah might be expected to launch for the express purpose of presenting Pakistan to the world as the innocent weak State threatened by the ruthless aggressor."[21] Patel remained unconvinced. World opinion did not weigh so much with him. He was primarily concerned with saving Junagadh from falling into the hands of Jinnah. If he agreed to withhold action, it was in deference to the wishes of Mountbatten and Nehru.

Two developments pushed the crisis to a boiling point. One was Liaquat Ali's reassertion on September 25th that the Nawab had every right to accede to Pakistan regardless of the State's territorial location. The other related to the Nawab's declaration of accession of Babariawad and Mangrol to India as invalid, claiming both as integral parts of Junagadh territory. Junagadh refused to withdraw its troop sent to Babariawad. For Patel, it was "an act of aggression, which must be met by a show of strength, with readiness in the last resort to use it."[22] To avert war, Mountbatten sought a solution in a reference to the UNO. Patel rejected the suggestion on the ground that Junagadh was not a disputed matter, but was a case of blatant interference on the part of Pakistan. Had the issue been referred to the UNO, Junagadh would have gone the way of Kashmir. Mountbatten expected that Nehru and Gopalaswami Ayyangar would lend him their support. Since they did not, his proposal was dropped. Patel also rejected Mountbatten's other suggestion that the Central Reserve Police, and not the Indian Army, should be entrusted with the task of occupation of Babariawad and Mangrol. To Patel, the suggestion meant "taking unnecessary risks; he was firm that the operation should be handled by the Indian Army."[23]

Avoiding direct violation of Junagadh territory, Indian troops, under a newly created command, the Kathiawar Defence Force, were deployed in the adjoining States with a view to "creating steadying effect all over Kathiawar"; and carry out occupation of Babariawad and Mangrol on November 1st. Simultaneously, the people of Kathiawar, under the leadership of Samaldas Gandhi, formed a provisional Government with headquarters at Rajkot and recruited volunteers. This was, obviously, with Patel's blessings. Meanwhile, over two and a half months' political stalemate and economic stagnation had reduced Junagadh to near bankruptcy, resulting in a steep fall in the State's revenues and leading to a fast deteriorating food situation. Since no help reached from Pakistan, the Nawab saw "the writing on the wall and fled to Karachi, together with his family, many of his dogs, and all the cash and negotiable assets of the State Treasury."[24]

From Karachi, the Nawab authorised Bhutto to use his "judicious discrimination as the situation demanded" and "to negotiate with the proper authorities".[25] Bhutto wrote to Jinnah on October 27th, telling him of "the fading of Muslim ardour for accession", as also: "Today our brethren are indifferent and cold. Muslims of Kathiawar seem to have lost all enthusiasm for Pakistan."[26] A completely dispirited Bhutto called a meeting of the Junagadh State Council on November 5th, which decided: "The position arising out of the economic blockade, interstatal complications, external agitation and internal administrative difficulties make it necessary to have a complete reorientation of the State policy and a readjustment of the relations with the two Dominions, even if it involves a reversal of the earlier decision to accede to Pakistan."

In pursuance of the State Council's resolution, Bhutto opened negotiations with Samaldas Gandhi on November 7th through Capt. Harvey Jones, a senior member of the Council for handing over power. The Muslim Jamiat of Junagadh desired that the administration be handed over to the Government of India. Bhutto, therefore, told the Indian Regional Commissioner in Kathiawar, N.M. Buch, that the Government of India could take over the administration. When Buch rang up Menon at New Delhi, he was at Nehru's residence. It was past midnight. On Nehru's advice, Menon drafted two telegrams: one to Buch; the other to the Prime Minister of Pakistan. The latter was to convey India's decision to concede to the request of Bhutto, and to assure Pakistan that "the Government of India has no desire to continue this arrangement and wished to find a speedy solution in accordance with the wishes of the people of Junagadh." Pakistan was also assured of India's desire "to discuss this question and other allied matters affecting Junagadh with representatives of Pakistan at the earliest possible moment." From Nehru's residence, Menon motored to Patel's and woke him up at that past midnight hour to seek his approval to the drafts. Nehru was obviously toeing the Mountbatten line, whereas Patel was "strongly of the opinion that an offer of a plebiscite should not be made", since the Nawab had fled and Bhutto had "voluntarily offered to hand the State over to the Government of India." Patel's view was that "in these circumstances, to commit ourselves to a plebiscite in regard to accession was unnecessary and uncalled for."[27] Ultimately, under pressure, Patel agreed to Nehru's sending a telegram to Pakistan, but rejected the offer of a plebiscite.

Patel, however, took the earliest opportunity the following

day (November 10th) to clarify his views. He had no difficulty in carrying the Cabinet with him in the decision that India could not agree to a joint India-Pakistan plebiscite in Junagadh. He yielded only to the other part—a plebiscite under the UNO auspices, though subsequent developments ruled that out. However, Liaquat Ali stated that since Junagadh had acceded to Pakistan, neither the Diwan nor the ruler could negotiate a temporary or permanent settlement with India, and that it was a violation of Pakistan territory and a breach of international law. Since Junagadh was the States Ministry's responsibility, Patel had the upper hand in playing a master tactician's game. Underestimating Patel, Mountbatten and his advisers had hoped that "Patel would be satisfied for a decision on the occupation of Junagadh itself to lie in the pending tray until greater problems were safely resolved." Mountbatten was "tactfully left in the dark." By the time he discovered what was afoot, troops were already on the move. According to Campbell Johnson: "All these developments were only brought to Mountbatten's notice late in the evening (of November 8th). It is the first time since the transfer of power that the Government have carried out a major act of policy without fully consulting or notifying him in advance of the event. He feels this may be due to Patel's and V.P.'s (Menon) desire to spare him embarrassment."[28]

It was due to Patel's firm handling of the Junagadh crisis that the storm blew over in no time. The Government of India took over the Junagadh administration on November 9th. On the 13th, Patel visited Junagadh. He was given a rousing reception. Addressing a mammoth public meeting on the grounds of the Bahauddin College, he assured the people that India would abide by their wishes. And then, dramatically, "by way of oratorical flourish, asked the audience to indicate whether they wished the State to accede to India or Pakistan. Over ten thousand hands were immediately raised in favour of accession to India."[29] Patel also did some plain speaking, "The action of the Nawab of Junagadh would be a lesson to those who are persisting in their chimera of attachment to an authority with which they have no natural ties...

The State is no property of a single individual. Paramountcy has lapsed—certainly not by the efforts of the Princes, but by those of the people."[30]

A plebiscite, as Patel had promised, was held on February 20, 1948, which went overwhelmingly in favour of India. Out of a total of 201,457 registered voters, 190,870 exercised their franchise. Only 91 cast their vote in favour of accession to Pakistan. A referendum was held at the same time in Mangrol, Manavadar, Babariawad, Bantwa and Sardargarh, which showed that out of 31,434 votes cast in these areas, only 39 went in favour of Pakistan. Jossleyn Hennessy, of *The Sunday Times*, and Douglas Brown, of *The Daily Telegraph*, who were in Junagadh at that time, confirmed that "they could find little fault with the manner in which the referendum was conducted."[31] Patel was the recipient of congratulations from many quarters for his "crowning success", especially the Princes who eulogised his "noble efforts" in achieving "a unique victory over Junagadh without causing loss of life and property." All Kathiawar Princes and people felt grateful to Patel for "preserving the integrity and unity of Kathiawar by (his) timely action."[32]

c) KATHIAWAR

The Jamsaheb of Nawanagar's position in Kathiawar was strategically no less important than that of the Maharaja of Jodhpur in Rajasthan. If the unification of the Rajasthan States largely depended on Jodhpur, equally so was that of Kathiawar on the attitude of the Jamsaheb, who, unlike the Maharaja of Jodhpur, commanded a position of respect and influence among the Princes of Kathiawar. A sinister situation, similar to that in Jodhpur, was developing in Jamnagar around May-June 1947. On July 1st, B.L. Mitter, Diwan of Baroda, wrote to Nehru: "The Jamsaheb is reported to be negotiating with Jinnah regarding his port of Bedi Bander. If this port and Veraval, the Junagadh port, come into the orbit of Karachi, Bombay will be seriously affected."[1] And with the accession of Veraval and Junagadh to Pakistan, the whole of Kathiawar would have come under Jinnah's domination.

Much earlier, on November 22, 1946, Mitter had informed Patel: "The Princes Chamber is playing Jinnah's game… The Jamsaheb has bought his immunity by selling his soul to the Political Department. His confederation plan is sponsored by the department."[2] Mitter wrote to Patel on March 26, 1947 that the Chief of Wadia (in Kathiawar) had told him, "The Jamsaheb was strengthening his armed forces… was aspiring to be the overlord of Kathiawar."[3] About mid-June, a gathering of Kathiawar Rulers, with the Jamsaheb as the leader, met in a secret conference at Mount Abu under the presidentship of the Resident. The view propagated was that "if Travancore can declare its independence, the Kathiawar States, being maritime States, can do likewise… they can rule without any interference from Delhi and develop their ports and they need not depend upon India for anything." The conference decided to form a "Union of Kathiawar", comprising as many as seven States, which were Jamnagar, Bhavnagar, Gondal, Porbandar, Morvi, Dhrangadhra and Junagadh. In the event of its accession to Pakistan, Junagadh "would enter into an offensive and defensive treaty" with the Union. Mitter also told Patel, "The Resident is helping and the Jamsaheb has promised to put up a crore of rupees in furtherance of the scheme… The Resident and the Political Agent are out to Balkanise India." There was something sinister in granting Junagadh the right to either "declare separate independence or to join Pakistan."[4] The move unmistakably implied severance of links with India. Jinnah expected Junagadh to play a role in Kathiawar similar to Bhopal's in Central India after its accession to Pakistan.

The situation in Kathiawar was more complex and difficult than the one in Jodhpur. In the latter, Patel had to face the challenge of a single ruler; in Kathiawar, seven rulers were uniting to declare their independence. And while Maharaja Hanwant Singh was young and immature and Patel could treat him as a boy, the Jamsaheb was "a tower of strength". Patel watched the developments with deep concern but with equanimity, waiting for an opportunity when he could act. Such an opportunity arrived on May 11th. The Jamsaheb and some other rulers were halting for a short while at the New Delhi airport, on their way to some Rajput States to sell the confederation idea. The Jamsaheb's brother, Himatsinhji, informed Patel of this. Patel sent him in his car to bring the Jamsaheb to his residence for lunch. Accompanied by Her Highness and Himatsinhji, the Jamsaheb lunched with Patel. The meeting proved momentous. It changed the course of events. Patel's influence on the Jamsaheb was irresistible. The Nawanagar ruler seemed to have been won over by Patel at his very first meeting. Happy over the outcome, Mitter wrote to Patel on the 14th: "You have converted the Jamsaheb. Now you will have to fashion the Kathiawar and Gujarat units for the Union."[5]

Patel was cautious in expressing his opinion: "The Jamsaheb had come here yesterday (May 11th)... He is still hopeful of his confederation scheme succeeding, and he has gone to Kotah for that purpose. Udaipur has already joined the Constituent Assembly and I do not know whether it will join the confederation now. From his talk I understood that all the Kathiawar States, except for Junagadh and Bhavnagar, have joined the (proposed) confederation. I have, of course, expressed no opinion about the merits of this scheme."[6] Patel, however, made the Jamsaheb appreciate the dangers India faced from Pakistan all along the border from Rajasthan to Kathiawar. Events in Jodhpur and Junagadh more than convinced the Jamsaheb of Patel's logic in checkmating Jinnah's designs to destroy India's unity. A hopeful indicator of Jamsaheb's mind, as also of the Maharaja of Dhrangadhra, was what they told Menon by way of a warning that "with Shah Nawaz (Bhutto) in the saddle, there was a possibility of Junagadh going over to Pakistan."[7]

The decks having been cleared, Patel got into action to face Jinnah's challenge through the unification of the Kathiawar States. Since he came from Porbander, Gandhi was "intensely interested" in it; and in its achievement was the fulfillment of Gandhi's dream. For Patel it meant political consolidation of the country in a big way. The unification was highly necessary like the unification of the Rajput States. It was complex, as it involved 222 States of great diversity and covering an area of over 22,000 square miles. As many as 46 States had an area of two or less than two square miles; the smallest one had an area of 0.29 square miles, a population of 206 souls and an income of Rs.500 a year! Many of the States had scattered pockets of territory outside their own boundaries. Such a chaotic state of affairs rendered law and order poor and even unmanageable, hampered trade and encouraged extensive smuggling. "In fact, all the worst effects of political fragmentation were to be seen in Kathiawar." Patel inaugurated the United State of Kathiawar on February 15, 1948. Speaking on the occasion, he paid handsome tributes to the Jamsaheb and other rulers who had joined the Union. He said, "But for their vision, wisdom and patriotism, the happy result you are seeing today would not have fructified. It was Mahatma Gandhi's dream that Kathiawar should be united, and it gladdens my heart that the dream of such unification has come true."[8]

The Jamsaheb significantly replied, "It is not as if we were tired monarchs who were fanned to rest. It is not as if we have been bullied into submission. We have by our own free volition pooled our sovereignties and covenanted to create this new State, so that the United State of Kathiawar and the unity of India may be more fully achieved." It was a tribute as much to Patel as to the rulers of Kathiawar when Nehru described the events as "a great step forward... one of the most notable in contemporary Indian history", and called it "a far-sighted act of statesmanship."[9] Nehru was more specific when he wrote to the provincial Chief Ministers on February 20th: "Six months ago, it would have been considered an idle dream to think of an administrative merger of the hundreds of Kathiawar States, let alone such a merger accompanied by full responsible government. The peninsula was ridden by factions and jealousies; and it was a crazy patchwork of States of varying degrees of sovereignty with only one thing common, namely, autocratic rule. On the February 15th, the whole of the peninsula became one unit under one responsible Government. This is an achievement for which Sardar Patel has deservedly won high tribute."[10] Mountbatten wrote to Patel: "...

it appears that you have again scored a brilliant success in your handling of the Kathiawar States' problem."[11]

d) HYDERABAD

Hyderabad, to Patel, seemed to have mattered much more than Kashmir. Situated as it was in India's belly, he naturally asked: "How can the belly breathe if it is cut off from the main body?"[1] That would have sounded the death-knell of Patel's dream of One India; and the cancer of disunity and divisiveness would have spread to totally Balkanise the country. Alan Campbell-Johnson too saw a frightening situation developing in an independent, Pakistan-dominated Hyderabad. During his interview, the Nizam gave him "a lecture in forcible terms on the Muslim philosophy of life"[2]; and his bigotry naturally gave direct encouragement to the State's most fanatic Muslim zealots, the Razakars. The second danger Campbell-Johnson saw was in Hyderabad's various "sponsored" acts as "acts to display its status as an independent nation." Such acts related to "moral and physical violations of the Standstill Agreement": a loan of Rs.20 crores to Pakistan, the State Congress leaders' imprisonment without trial, and the "most provocative was the activity of Kasim Razvi."[3] Patel felt an irresistible itch for action for early settlement with the Nizam on the same basis as with other Princes. But he withheld action in deference to Mountbatten's policy of restraint, often irritating and frustrating to him. Patel thoroughly distrusted Hyderabad's Prime Minister, Mir Laik Ali, who was till September 1947 Pakistan's representative in the United Nations. But far more disquieting was Jinnah's statement, "I require Hyderabad as an active ally, not as a neutral in such a war."[4] It was perhaps an oblique reference to Kashmir.

In settling with Hyderabad, Patel's most formidable obstacle lay in Mountbatten's outlook and his convincing of Nehru to his point of view: to prevent the Indian Army from moving into Hyderabad—in the same way as he had unsuccessfully tried to prevent movement of Indian troops into Junagadh. Walter

Monckton, the Nizam's Constitutional Adviser, was a friend of Mountbatten, whose services Mountbatten had secured for the Nizam for conducting negotiations with India. Monckton had stated that "he felt there was no fundamental difference of approach between Mountbatten and himself. He would continue to look for the formula which would allow statutory independence for Hyderabad, and which, while containing no direct reference to the word "accession", would incorporate it on a *de facto* basis."[5] Both Mountbatten and Monckton thus wanted the Nizam to have "association" with India, not accession, which was not acceptable to Patel. Patel also failed to understand Mountbatten's asking India alone "to adopt ethical and correct behavior towards Hyderabad and to act in such a way as could be defended before the bar of world opinion."[6] Such moralisation had little value for Patel as the Nizam showed no qualms in trampling on all codes of moral conduct; and the UNO too was devoid of such a lofty outlook. Campbell-Johnson admitted that "both the Nizam and his Government are very volatile statesmen, pursuing a very inconsistent and wavering line of policy."[7] In such a situation, it was but natural that Mountbatten should have found in Patel "a much sterner and less conciliatory leader than Pandit Nehru."[8]

Patel had turned sterner and less conciliatory by the anti-Indian activities of the British Secretary of the Political Department, Conrad Corfield, and his British diehard Residents and Agents in the States. Added to this was Monckton's highly intriguing role: "Even before Attlee's February statement, Monckton (who was in touch with Jinnah through Bhopal) was testing the possibility of Conservative party support for appeals by Jinnah and the Muslim Princes for separate membership of the Commonwealth. In mid-January he was in touch with the chief creator of the 1935 Act, Samuel Hoare (now Lord Templewood), and was "much encouraged" by their measure of agreement. In April 1947 Monckton was "in touch with Templewood about the acquisition of port facilities at Marmagoa, in Portuguese Goa, with a rail linkage to be built from the State to the sea." One Alexander Roger, a businessman who had "important contacts among the Portuguese authorities, was employed as an intermediary." Monckton himself is reported to have visited Portugal in April before reaching India. He is quoted to have stated that "for the Nizam to join India would be political suicide"; and "if we go warily, we shall very likely outlast them" (the Indian Government). Monckton was "sanguine of Hyderabad's survival", and believed that "if HMG would maintain relations with Hyderabad, then Pakistan would recognise it, as would Egypt and Saudi Arabia."[9]

Monckton's presence in Hyderabad from April onwards was sufficient encouragement to the Nizam to step up his activities aimed at achieving independence. In fact, even before Britain's transference of power, plans were afoot for the transfer of Bastar to Hyderabad. Panikkar wrote to Patel on May 19th; "A very serious and extremely dangerous intrigue is taking place" in Bastar, where the Nizam's Government has been given a mining lease, the right to extend the Nizam's railway to Bastar and to acquire 15,000 square miles of rich mineral deposits. He stated: "It is a part of the dangerous intrigue to strengthen the Nizam in every possible way, e.g. by the sale of the Bren gun factory... This intrigue with the Nizam has to be scotched, otherwise the whole of Hindustan will be undermined." An alarmed Nehru wrote to Patel: "... the Hyderabad Government has come to an arrangement with the Birmingham Small Arms Company for supply of arms." He also informed Patel that Hyderabad had placed "an order for four crores of rupees worth ammunition with Mr. Kral, calling himself representative of the Czechoslovakian Government."[10] On June 12th, after the announcement of the June 3 plan, the Nizam issued a *firman*, which declared that "the departure of the Paramount power... will mean that I shall become entitled to resume the status of an independent sovereign." The Nizam had "set his heart on becoming a 'Third Dominion' of the British Commonwealth."[11] The Nizam had been advised, early in June, not only to declare his "independence", but also to recruit Britishers to the State forces, to ask for Goa as part of his State, to demand a corridor between Hyderabad and Goa and apply for membership of the United Nations.[12]

The Nizam, on whom the King had conferred the title of "Faithfull Ally to the British Government" was shocked and disappointed to find that the Indian Independence Bill before the British Parliament did not provide for Dominion Status to Indian States. He protested against "the way in which my State is being abandoned by its old ally, the British Government, and the ties which have bound me in loyal devotion to the King Emperor are being severed."[13] Mountbatten dispelled all doubts when he told the Nizam's delegation on July 11th that HMG would not agree to Hyderabad becoming a member of the British Commonwealth except through either of the two Dominions of India or Pakistan. This humbled the Nizam's pride, but did not dishearten him as he had other plans up his sleeve: to gain time by engaging India in prolonged constitutional negotiations through Monckton, to make preparations for a military confrontation with India by purchase of arms through foreign sources, and to build up the Ittehad-ul-Mussalmeen so as "to arm himself with a view to crushing the Hindu subjects"[14], and to encourage at the same time migration of Muslims from some of the Indian provinces and States to his State.

It was on Monckton's advice that the Nizam wrote to Mountbatten on August 8th that "he could not contemplate bringing Hyderabad into organic union with either Pakistan or India", but was prepared to enter into a treaty which guaranteed the integrity and independent identity of his State under three conditions: in the event of a war between India and Pakistan, Hyderabad would remain neutral; Hyderabad should have the right to appoint Agents-General wherever it thought fit; and if India seceded from the British Commonwealth, Hyderabad would be free to review the situation *de novo*. Seeing such dangerous trends, Patel could not restrain himself from telling Mountbatten sternly on August 24th: "... I wish to let Your Excellency know my mind before you meet the (Nizam's) delegation. I see no alternative but to insist on the Nizam's accession to the Dominion of India. The least variations in the Instrument of Accession, or arrangement regarding the State's association with the Dominion in regard to the three subjects, would not only expose me to the charge of breach of faith with the States that have already joined the Dominion, but would create the impression that advantage lay in holding out rather than coming in, and that, while no special merit attached to accession, a beneficial position could be secured by keeping out. This is bound to have most unfortunate consequences in our future negotiations for accession to the Union." Patel also informed Mountbatten: "I have authentic information that the recent activities of the Ittehad-ul-Mussalmeen are designed almost to create a feeling of terror amongst the non-Muslim population, so that its agitation in favour of the independence of Hyderabad, with possible alliance with Pakistan, should flourish."[15]

It was distressing, even humiliating, to Patel's sense of national pride to let Mountbatten, a foreigner and a Britisher responsible for the partitioning of the country, handle negotiations which primarily concerned him and his Ministry of States. But he had to swallow his pride by agreeing to this arrangement, which helped Nehru and Patel to set aside their different approaches and overcome, though temporarily, the frequent quarrelling between them. The administrator in Patel saw the problem "in somewhat simplistic strategic terms", and "instinctively felt that India could not survive with a hostile force in its belly, as it were". The politician in Nehru, on the other hand, was "preoccupied with the emotional problems of the huge Muslim minority in India. He was anxious that nothing should be done to hurt their feelings, and he thought that any rough treatment of the Nizam, the premier Muslim Ruler, would seriously hurt their feelings." In order to resolve their differences, "Pandit Nehru suggested that the matter may be left for negotiations by Lord Mountbatten. Although Sardar Patel felt most strongly on the subject, he agreed to this proposal..."[16] To Patel, this was sheer appeasement, very much in contrast with Nehru's treatment of the Maharaja of Jammu and Kashmir. Nevertheless, for the sake of harmony and ultimate achievement of what he desired, Patel agreed to Nehru's suggestion but kept the reins in his hands, as Hyderabad, unlike Kashmir, was under the State Ministry's charge. His firm grip neither allowed Hyderabad to be internationalised, as it happened with Kashmir, nor permitted the slightest shift in his irrevocable attitude. He knew his mind better than anyone else. And he also knew the action he was to take in the end. If such action was delayed, it was due to the combined opposition Patel faced first from Nehru and Mountbatten and later from Nehru and Rajagopalachari; and also to the massive heart-attack he suffered early in March 1948. In order to ensure a close watch on Mountbatten's negotiations, as also to apply a brake on him whenever it became necessary, Patel made his most trusted lieutenant, V.P. Menon, a co-negotiator.

What role was Monckton playing? He himself disclosed this in his note of September 15th to the Nizam's Executive Council: "My object has been to advise a course calculated to obtain for Hyderabad the maximum degree of real, practical independence, compatible with its prosperity and security… that Hyderabad is landlocked in the belly of Hindustan; that Pakistan is not yet in a sufficiently established state to be able to give effective help; that, if Hyderabad is to remain independent, she must stand on her own feet… The guiding principle has been to avoid executing an Instrument of Accession." Monckton then explained what an agreement of "association", as opposed to "accession", means: that "a treaty or agreement, short of accession, preserves independence in law, whereas accession destroys it and involves merger or organic union; that, when circumstances change, e.g. if Pakistan and Hyderabad grew strong enough to warrant it, the treaty can be denounced… once a State has acceded to the Dominion, it will find it hard to extricate itself." Monckton revealed his mind when he said, "I wanted the negotiations to continue for Hyderabad as long as possible after 15th August… the longer they continue the better for us… we have a breathing space to get ready for the economic and political conflict if it comes… I know that Patel was and is against any extension of time to Hyderabad and that the Governor-General prevailed over the Cabinet of the Dominion to allow him personally two months' time to see whether he and I, who had known each other intimately for many years publicly and privately, could find a compromise satisfactory to both sides."[17]

Encouraged by Monckton's note, the Nizam wrote to Mountbatten on September 18th that, short of accession, Hyderabad was "ready and willing" to make a treaty of association with India. "Simultaneously with this approach to us," writes Menon, "the Nizam got into contact with Jinnah with a view to securing the services of Zafrullah Khan as the President of his Executive Council," Zafrullah could not be spared as he was to lead the Pakistan delegation to the UNO. After this an uncertainty hung over Hyderabad. Delegation after delegation, with leaders and members changing now and again, began visiting New Delhi for negotiations with Mountbatten. Yet, no agreement was in sight. About mid-October Patel got completely fed up and wanted to break off the negotiations. This upset Mountbatten. He pleaded, "It would be a great pity if the negotiations were to break down." Towards the end of October, the Nizam wrote to say that "if the negotiations with the Government of India were to break down, he would immediately negotiate and conclude an agreement with Pakistan." Patel felt so annoyed at the Nizam's impertinence that he told Menon that "the only decent course for us was to send back the new delegation by the very same plane by which it has arrived."[18]

If Patel held back, it was because of Mountbatten's persuasion and Nehru's submission to Mountbatten. This was despite what a member of the Nizam's Executive Council Aravamudh Aiyangar, had written, to Gopalaswami Ayyangar on September 25th, with the request that it be passed on to Patel" "The Berar legislation was the joint handy work of Monckton and Ali Yavar Jung... Ali Yavar Jung, though he is considered to be not so very extreme in his views, is sufficiently mischievous and unreliable." He also wrote; "There is absolutely no doubt that every Englishman is pro-Pakistan or pro-Muslim. Griggson, who was till recently Revenue Member, and Major Maunsell, who was Secretary to the Resident, have got employed in Pakistan. Savidge, who is the Director General of Revenue, is going to Pakistan. Anderson, who was the Director General of Police, is in quest of employment in Pakistan."[19]

The situation within Hyderabad had worsened with the outbreak of serious communal riots in Secunderabad on August 25th. The police were entirely manned by Muslims. They were "unwilling to protect the life or property of a Hindu", and "armed Pathans, Rohillas and Arabs are allowed to roam about without let or hindrance, terrorising the people." This caused an exodus of the Hindus. Aiyangar wrote on August 29th: "... the local Muslim League, which has been well organised and supplied with arms, is only waiting for an opportunity to attack the Hindus *en masse*... if Hyderabad joins the Union, there will be mass slaughter on an large scale." Again he reported on October 23rd "... one Lancaster landed at Begumpet aerodrome direct from Pakistan. It is suspected that it contained arms and ammunition."[20]

Earlier on September 19th, Patel had told Mountbatten: "The Nizam has mortgaged his future to his own Frankenstein, Ittehad-ul-Mussalmeen."[21] True to this description, the Razakar leader, Kasim Razvi, mounted a tirade against Patel. He said on October 14th, "Patel belongs to the class of Hitler... Our Government is temperamentally like Chamberlain, which has no courage to face the opponent. It is afraid merely by the name of accession. Mountbatten, like a Daniel, has come in to remove both of these from this intricate position."

Razvi then said, "Why not somebody asks this so-called Government (of the Nizam), what is there to prevent carrying on negotiations with Pakistan and other Muslim and non-Muslim countries after the Hyderabad Independence Act and His Majesty the Nizam's *firman*?" And he went on to answer, "There is nothing to prevent. It is merely the threat of Patel."[22]

Amidst such bewildering confusion and deepening dangers, Mountbatten saved the situation for Hyderabad by playing a magician's role in pulling out of his hat a Standstill Agreement with Hyderabad on November 25th. His co-negotiator, V.P. Menon, believed that Mountbatten was "sanguine and it would allow heads to cool and hearts to soften, and that before the expiry of the Agreement the Nizam, like all other rulers, would accede to India."[23] Such hopes even Nehru did not entertain. He wrote to Patel on November 25th: "I have just heard on the radio that the Hyderabad agreement has been signed. Congratulations. Whether this puts an end to the trouble there or not is a matter of doubt." Patel's reply was pragmatic: "The Nizam has yet to sign the agreement. I only hope there will be no last-minute hitch... Nevertheless, it gives us breathing time and gives the Nizam plenty of scope to think over and to deal with the Frankenstein which he has created in his Ittehad-ul-Mussalmeen."[24] A year later India had to resort to "Police Action" in Hyderabad. Patel had seen its inevitability from the beginning. He could not carry it out because of Mountbatten's opposition. By the time the "Police Action" was taken, Mountbatten had left India. It was now Nehru whose vehement opposition Patel had to encounter.

The proposed Standstill Agreement bestirred the Nizam to conspire for his independence. He demanded that the newly appointed Agent-General, K.M. Munshi, should be only a Trade Agent, and that the ceremonials on his assuming charge should be the same as those for the Hyderabad Agent-General to India. On this basis the Nizam seemed to be planning to have ambassadors between two independent countries. His second demand was speedy withdrawal of Indian troops and supply of arms and ammunition for the Hyderabad army and police. And thirdly, Hyderabad's declared intention to appoint agents in several foreign countries. Hyderabad had already appointed a Public Relations Officer to Pakistan without reference to India. On January 30, 1948, the leader of the Hyderabad delegation visiting New Delhi, Moin Nawaz Jung, openly stated that the demand for independence in Hyderabad was the reaction to the demand for accession on the part of India. It had taken hardly two months for Mountbatten to be proved wrong. Instead of the heads cooling and hearts softening, Hyderabad was moving towards confrontation.

Purposefully, the Nizam pursued a policy of drift, of buying time, which he explained in a cable of January 6, 1948 to Monckton who was in London: "I agree with your opinion that no good of our hurrying up making long term agreement with the Indian Union at the beginning of the year, but to wait and see what further developments arise before we do it, namely, towards the end of the year. Besides, we must see how Kashmir and Junagadh's case is going to be settled by UNO. After that we can think about our own affair. Is Lord Mountbatten going to get an extension after April next, as was rumoured before? In any case, since he has got no power, what help he can give to us is obvious. In that case, his being in office or not does not affect us materially. So, we must manage our affairs in the best way we can, after taking everything into consideration."[25] The Nizam's objectives in gaining time were: to further build his armed strength through acquisition of more arms, and completion of new airfields; to initiate "a large-scale programme of converting Harijans to Islam"[26], and to encourage the Ittehad-ul-Mussalmeen's efforts "to get Muslims to migrate to Hyderabad" and even "induce ex-army Muslims or those in active service to join the Hyderabad army."[27] Patel had to tell Mountbatten that "the period of two months, which we have agreed to give the State to make up its mind, is being utilised for preparations rather than for negotiations... I am convinced that it would neither be proper nor politic for us to agree to any arrangement other than the Instrument of Accession already settled between us and other States."[28] The Nizam, realising that Patel "will not be bamboozled into a surrender even to the slightest extent", changed his strategy: to bank on Nehru who was "more accommodating than Sardar Patel", and pin "faith to the chance of having a better reception when C.R. (Rajagopalachari) becomes Governor-General."

From his sick-bed at Dehra Dun where he had retired for convalescence after the heart-attack in March 1948, Patel watched with exasperating helplessness the growing instransigence of the Nizam, failure of Mountbatten's efforts, and a growing feeling in Hyderabad that India was "not in dead earnest to take action". When Laik Ali called on him on April 16th at Dehra Dun, Patel told him with stunning bluntness: "You know as well as I do where power resides and with whom the fate of the negotiations must finally lie in Hyderabad. The gentleman (Kasim Razvi), who seems to dominate Hyderabad, has given his answer. He has categorically stated that, if the Indian Dominion comes to Hyderabad, it will find nothing but the bones and ashes of one and a half crores of Hindus. If that is the position, then it seriously undermines the whole future of Nizam and his dynasty." Patel made it clear: "The Hyderabad problem will have to be settled as has been done in the case of other States. No other way is possible. We cannot agree to the continuance of an isolated spot which would destroy the very Union which we have built up with our blood and toil. At the same time, we do wish to maintain friendly relations and to seek a friendly solution. This does not mean that we shall ever agree to Hyderabad's independence. If its demand to maintain an independent status is persisted in, it is bound to fail."

Many reasons hardened Patel's attitude. On March 26th, Laik Ali himself had told Munshi that the "Nizam was willing to die a martyr and that he and lakhs of Muslims were willing to be killed." Immediately thereafter, Razvi, in a speech on March 31st, "indulged in a good deal of sabre-rattling and urged the Muslims of Hyderabad not to sheathe their swords until their objective of Islamic supremacy had been achieved." He exhorted the Muslims "to march forward with the Koran in one hand and the sword in the other to hound out the enemy." But the most sinister part of the speech was his declaration that "the forty-five million Muslims in the Indian Union would be our fifth columinists in any showdown." Razvi "perpetrated an even more grotesque verbal aggression" when he asserted on April 12th, "The day is not far off when the waves of the Bay of Bengal will be washing the feet of our Sovereign", and that he would "hoist the Asaf Jahi flag on the Red Fort in Delhi."

It was mid-May. In a month's time Mountbatten was to say good-bye to India. He had achieved a lot from the viewpoint of Britain. But Hyderabad lay heavy on his heart. He had failed to do anything for Britain's "Faithful Ally", and was worried if, after he had gone, Patel could be restrained from sending troops into Hyderabad. He was, therefore, anxious "to make one final effort to bring about agreement between Hyderabad and India"—motivated as he was by the desire "to end his fateful career in India in a blaze of glory by presenting an association with Hyderabad, whatever form it took." Mountbatten's success depended on Patel's acceptance of his "plan". So, he flew to Dehra Dun early in June in his personal aircraft, taking with him Nehru, Rajendra Prasad, Gopalaswami Ayyangar and Baldev Singh—all of whom were "confident he (Patel) would not agree" to his "plan", as Monckton, who had drafted it, admitted to Mountbatten that "the terms were now so heavily weighed in Hyderabad's favour that it would be a miracle if India accepted."

Mountbatten's meeting with Patel was momentous. On it hinged the fate of India and of Hyderabad. "Soon after arrival", records Mountbatten, "I gave the paper to Patel to read. He grunted, 'Imperitenence—I will never initial it.' I then dropped the subject... After lunch Sardarji became quite emotional, and spoke of the debt India owed me. 'How can we prove to you our love and gratitude? Whatever you ask for, if your wish is in my power, it will be granted.' I hardened my heart, for I too was affected, and replied: 'If you are sincere, sign this document.'

"Sardarji was visibly taken aback. 'Does agreement with Hyderabad mean so much to you', he asked in a low voice. 'Yes...'. Patel initialed the draft... The others, although astonished, accepted this, and I flew to Delhi very elated at my success... Monckton could hardly believe his luck and flew back at once to Hyderabad with it." Mountbatten's elation was, however, short-lived. "Then," he admits, "an astonishing thing happened. The Nizam and his advisers now rejected their own draft." Monckton was told by Laik Ali, "We shall fight to the last man."

"To this," Monckton replied, "You will be in the first aeroplane to Karachi" (if India sent her troops). And unhappy Mountbatten records: "The situation was indeed 'lost' by Hyderabad through the intervention of Kasim Razvi... But for India, it spelt 'victory'. Now their conscience would be clear if they had to intervene in Hyderabad."[31]

With Mountbatten's departure, a major roadblock seemed to have been removed. Patel did gain a free hand, but not full freedom. Nehru and he differed, not so much on what India was to do—"Police Action"—but when to do it. With Patel it was *now*; with Nehru, *later*. Nehru told the Chief Ministers on July 1st, "We are ready at short notice to invade Hyderabad. But we propose to wait for developments and to avoid such invasion if we can help it, because of the other consequences that it is bound to bring in its train."[32] In contrast, Patel was categorical—unwavering and assertive. In his speech at the inauguration of Patiala and East Punjab Union on July 15th, he restated his earlier declaration, "If Hyderabad did not behave properly, it would have to go the way that Junagadh did. The former Governor-General, Lord Mountbatten, thought that he would be able to secure a peaceful settlement... Although I was doubtful whether the efforts would succeed, I let him try."[33]

Patel was now in a new mood, as if he had been unfettered. This was reflected by what he told Munshi over the telephone. Munshi records; "Next day (next to Mountbatten's departure) I heard Sardar's voice over the phone, vibrating with good cheer: 'Well Munshi! How are you? Is everything all right? What about your Nizam?' 'Oh, he is all right,' I said. Then I told him about Zaheer's suggestion—'Settlement!'. As if he had never heard of any such thing. 'What settlement?' His jocose queries were a sure sign of his mood. He now felt himself to be the master of the game. 'The Mountbatten settlement,' I said. 'Tell him that the Settlement has gone to England,' he replied caustically and laughed."[34]

Patel also publicly stated, "The terms and the talks which Lord Mountbatten had have gone with him. Now the settlement with the Nizam will have to be on the lines of other settlements with the States. No help from outside, on which he seems to rest his pathetic hopes, would avail him."[35] In the twenties, the British Resident, William Barton, had "twisted the Nizam's tail and asserted the Paramountcy of the Crown."[36] Now it was Patel's turn to make the Nizam accept Free India's suzerainty over Hyderabad.

Patel's path was not yet all that clear. Mountbatten's policy still dominated Nehru's mind. Four days prior to Mountbatten's departure, Nehru had stated, "We will pursue an open—door policy so far as these proposals (offered by Mountbatten) are concerned, and the Nizam is welcome to accept them any time he chooses."[37] This was not acceptable to Patel, as Nehru's outlook indicated three things: first, his unwillingness to act now after all that had happened or was happening in Hyderabad; second, his unwillingness to shed Mountbatten's influence; and, third, his favouring a policy of drift, which the Nizam had successfully managed with the support of Mountbatten, whose latest proposals had failed, "because Jinnah did not want Laik Ali to settle with India".

Patel was critical of Nehru's outlook in a letter of June 21st to Gadgil: "I am rather worried about Hyderabad. This is the time when we should take firm and definite action. There should be no vacillation; and the more public the action is the greater effect it will have on the morale of our people, both here and in Hyderabad, and will convince our opponents that we mean business... There should be no lack of definiteness or strength about our actions. If, even now, we relax, we shall not only be doing a disservice to the country, but would be digging our own grave."[38]

The Hyderabad situation was climaxing towards confrontation. On August 2nd, Laik Ali told the State Legislature, "Hyderabad has decided to refer its case to the United Nations." Bitterly speaking of the Indians, he said, "They may coerce us. They may subject us to any ordeals. They may overrun us by their military strength. We cannot give up our stand. We shall not give up our freedom." Earlier he had told a Muslim deputation that "if the Union Government takes any action against Hyderabad, a hundred thousand men are ready to join our army. We also have a hundred bombers in Saudi Arabia ready to bomb Bombay."[39] Reporting this to Patel on August 3rd, Munshi called this a "bluff" and added, "But the rumours are so persistent that there are some bombers in Pakistan, Saudi Arabia or Makalla, a small State in Arabia..."

Munshi further said, "During the last fortnight, the atrocities of the Razakars have become utterly irresponsible, and loot, murder and rape are going on in more than one district."[40]

By early July, Hyderabad "bore the appearance of a camp". Gun-running from Goa by land and from Karachi by air had been accelerated. On July 6th, India's Secretary-General, Girija Shankar Bajpai, informed India's High Commissioner in London, Krishna Menon, "of gun-running by air into Hyderabad from airfields near Karachi." Engaged in these operations was an Australian, Sidney Cotton, who smuggled arms and ammunition into Hyderabad by night, landing his aircraft either at Bidar or Warangal. Simultaneous with this, India's Air Commander-in-Chief, Thomas Elmhirst, reportedly warned the Defence Minister, Baldev Singh, that "if these gun-running aircraft (six Lancasters) were loaded up with bombs, he could be powerless to intercept them with the aircraft at his disposal."[41] Pakistan's complicity was clear from what Pakistan's General Gracey told India's General Bucher on August 30th "any coercion of Hyderabad would put Pakistan in an impossible position should civil disorder break out in India."[42] To Patel, this was Pakistan's veiled attempt to checkmate India's action in Hyderabad. Pakistan's hostility was also seen in her cashing a portion of the Rs.20 crore Government of India securities which the Nizam offered to Pakistan as a loan. Further, the Nizam's UN delegation had first visited Karachi prior to proceeding to the USA. Reference to the UNO had been made on Monckton's advice in the expectation that it would delay "Police Action"; and that even "the UNO might get India to accept the modifications to the rejected Mountbatten drafts."[43]

Patel had written to a friend from Dehradun on July 1st: "Hyderabad remained unsolved because of my prolonged illness. Nearly four months I have remained out of action."[44] He was now ready to act—and act quickly and positively. He told Munshi, "The bullock-cart must, some time or the other, come out of the rut."[45] He called to Dehradun General J.N. Chaudhuri, who was to lead the operations, and subjected him to a cross-examination for his personal assurance before he gave the army the word

"Go". Chaudhuri records what Patel told him, "If I did well, I would take the credit; but if things went wrong, I would be blamed, but whatever I did, I would be supported. This was the wonderful thing about working with Sardar Patel. He gave a feeling of intimacy."[46] His wholehearted backing and unflinching faith in men under him not only spurred them into action but helped them to final victory.

However, in a democratic set-up, Cabinet sanction was essential for the "Police Action". Patel faced a formidable task in overcoming Nehru's reluctance to go that far. At one of the meetings of the Defence Committee, of which Nehru was the Chairman, "there was so much bitterness that Sardar Patel walked out." Seeing his seat vacant, Menon told a Rotary meeting in Bombay, "I too walked out five minutes later." This seemed to have shaken Nehru out of his complacent mood; it mellowed his opposition, though not completely. Later, at a meeting attended by the Governor-General (Rajagopalachari), the Prime Minister and the Home Minister (Patel) and Secretary of the States Ministry (Menon), "it was decided to order troops into Hyderabad."[47] Despite such a decision, Patel had yet to face the Hamlet in Nehru.

That's what happened the night preceding the "Police Action". The British Commander-in-Chief of the Indian Army, General Bucher, persuaded Nehru that "even at that late stage the campaign should be called off as militarily risky and hazardous on grounds of internal security in the whole country."[48] About midnight on September 12th, after he has spoken to Nehru, Bucher attempted "a rare feat" in pulling Patel "out of bed at that hour" and advised him to at least postpone the action for fear of air attacks on Bombay and Ahmedabad. Patel reminded Bucher, "how London had suffered during the Great War, and coolly assured him that Ahmedabad and Bombay both could stand up to an attack if it came." Bucher, writes Munshi, "was hesitant throughout. He overestimated the capability of the Hyderabad army, underestimated that of his own troops, and knew not the ability of Sardar... to deal with the problems of internal law and order. Like most Englishmen, he was unable to realise that no price was too high to be paid for eliminating the Razakar menace which threatened the very existence of India."[49] Patel had reportedly told Nehru, when contacted on telephone, "to forget about it and go to sleep as he himself was doing." In Iengar's view, "the verdict of history will be that the Sardar was right"[50]—a verdict with which Nehru wholeheartedly agreed later.

Indian troops marched into Hyderabad in the early hours of September 13th. The campaign was named "Operation Polo", and lasted barely 108 hours. A jubilant Patel, responding to the Jamsaheb's congratulations, wrote to him: "The whole operation went through like a machine."[51] The Nizam was reduced to a bundle of nerves; Razvi, the fire-spitting and sabre-rattling hero, looked woebegone in a military barrack. For its remarkable speed and astonishing success, the army earned a handsome tribute from Patel, who wrote to Bucher: "I should like to send you and officers and men under your command my sincerest felicitations on the successful conclusion of the Hyderabad operations. The speed and the skill of these operations cannot fail to extort admiration even from our severest critics, and I have no doubt that history will record these operations as a masterpiece of efficiency, organisation and all-round cooperation. The Indian Army has added one more chapter to its glorious record of achievements, and I should like to convey to you and through you to all those who have had a hand in these operations my personal thanks for the part which each one has played in it. We are really proud of them all."[52] Bucher had, nevertheless, admitted to his sister in a letter of April 4th: "The real trouble there (Hyderabad) seems to be that the Nizam has become bound hand and foot to the Ittehad-ul-Mussalmeen... The Indian policy is one of reasonableness insofar as this is practicable."[53]

On September 23rd the Nizam withdrew the Hyderabad case from the UNO, where Patel had sent as leader of the Indian delegation, Ramaswami Mudaliar, whom he had selected on merit, brushing aside party considerations, uninfluenced by the fact that throughout his political life he had been an opponent, and "whose very religion was enmity to the Congress."[54] Patel complimented

Mudaliar, "I should like to say how much I appreciated the skill and ability with which you represented India's stand on Hyderabad before the Security Council."[55] India's success was a personal triumph for Patel. Not only did "Operation Polo" remove the "cancer" from the belly of India, but it also belied the hopes of the prophets of doom. Nehru was most happy with the outcome. His fears and doubts had been belied. He wrote to the Chief Ministers on September 21st: "What has happened in Hyderabad has created a situation which should lead to a stabilisation of the communal situation in India, or rather to a progressive elimination of the communal sentiment..." He wrote again on October 4th: "I have a feeling that India has turned the corner more specially since these Hyderabad operations. We are on the upgrade now. The atmosphere is different and better..."[56]

Congratulatory messages poured in from the Hindus, the Muslims and even foreigners. Akbar Hydari, Governor of Assam, whose father was the Nizam's long-time Prime Minister, wrote to Governor-General Rajagopalachari: "... the Hyderabad crisis has passed away like a bad dream. It is a miracle that the whole affair passed off so smoothly, leaving, as far as one can judge, no bitterness behind in the minds of the people of either community." From Switzerland, the Jamsaheb wrote to Patel: "Here I am just rejoicing on your splendid success over Hyderabad, and in fact over the Security Council." Ali Zaheer, India's Ambassador to Iran, wired from Teheran: "Heartiest congratulations on the success of your plan in Hyderabad. Obviously the time for operations was well chosen." The firebrand Muslim Leaguer, H.S. Suhrawardy, who was responsible for the "Great Calcutta Killing", congratulated Patel on his "policy regarding Hyderabad, the operations and their successful outcome." He observed, "I also take the liberty of offering you most sincerely my very best thanks and congratulations on the speech that you made just before the Hyderabad surrender. It has been widely appreciated by the Muslims in India." And even Monckton could not help writing to Nehru: "I want to tell you how relieved I am that the action which you were eventually driven to take did not result in large-scale communal troubles. I know how anxious you were not to take action at all, and how hard you struggled to avoid it... everyone who wants to see a peaceful and prosperous India will rejoice, as I do, that the episode is quietly finished."[57]

Patel visited Hyderabad in the last week of February 1949. Nehru had preceded him. But Patel was the first Indian to have been received personally by the Nizam at the aerodrome. His courteous treatment of the defeated Nizam not only dispelled the latter's fears, but cemented a friendship between the two. To the people of Hyderabad, Patel spoke in sincere, plain, straightforward language. He told the Osmania University students, "Now we must draw a curtain on the past. Everyone in the country should join together in making India a great country. People must maintain complete communal amity; for, we have all been born and brought up on the Indian soil, and we have to live and die together on the same soil."

Speaking in the Fateh Maidan, Patel told the people of Hyderabad that they were "now a part of India—in fact, the heart of India." He asked them to appreciate the realities of the post-Partition situation: "India has become two. Those who were responsible for starting the agitation for the two-nation theory have got what they wanted. But there are still some in the country who cherish the same ideas. To them I will say that their rightful place is in the other country. It is better for such people to go to Pakistan, for their God is there... I warn such people that if they ever dreamed that they can get any assistance from outside, or that others outside can interfere in the affairs of Hyderabad, they are insane. The affairs of Hyderabad are an internal problem for the people themselves to decide." Patel was, however, generous in his advice to the Muslims of Hyderabad: "In the poisoned atmosphere of the past, many people did things that they should not have done... The dust of the turmoil is now settling down. The turbid waters are now getting clearer. These people should refrain from raising the dust again, and making the water muddy again. They should forget the past. They should purify the atmosphere by going along the right path."[58]

On Patel's return to New Delhi, the Nizam wrote him an amiable letter: "I was glad to get an opportunity of making my acquaintance with you… and hope that this will prove to be a happy augury for the future of the premier State of Hyderabad…" Patel's large-hearted reply was: "I was happy to learn that Your Exalted Highness had adapted yourself so readily to changed conditions. As I told Your Exalted Highness, while error is a human failing and divine injunctions all point to forgetting and forgiving, it is the duty of human beings to contribute their share to this process by sincere repentance and by employing the period that is left in discharging their duties to their people and to their God." A grateful and an extremely happy Nizam again wrote to Patel on May 12th: "… Your great personality is a valuable asset for India at this crucial period when the whole world is in turmoil."[59]

During his second visit to Hyderabad in the first week of October 1950, Patel told a mammoth public meeting in Fateh Maidan, "We are prepared to forget and forgive, but if anyone wishes to be a martyr and gets his name registered in God's book as such, how can we help it?" He was more categorical in telling them, "I do wish to say to the Muslims that they are equals, that they have equal rights as Indian citizens, and that they are entitled to live in peace and in complete protection of the law and Government. At the same time, every Indian citizen, whether he is a Hindu or a Muslim, will have to behave as an Indian, feel as an Indian and act as an Indian, and the sooner he realises this the better. Some might think that Pakistan is a place of pilgrimage for them. If they really believe that this is so, it is their duty to leave without any delay. We shall place no difficulty in their path. We are really committed to give such facilities, and we wish to do so. Such a departure would be in the interests not only of the man who feels this way, but also in the interests of the Muslims of India."[60]

The Nizam felt concerned with the deteriorating health of Patel. He wrote on November 25th: "During your second visit to Hyderabad, I noticed that due to indifferent health and advancing age, you found some difficulty in walking, even a short distance, without the help of a stick. I, therefore, venture to send a trifling present to you in the shape of a walking-stick. The ivory handle of this stick, which came in my possession along with other old articles of my family, dates back to nearly half a century, and I am taking the liberty of sending the same to you as a token of my goodwill and appreciation of what you have done for Hyderabad State and also for my dynasty. It is my honest conviction that all those who, like myself, have received due consideration and sympathy at your hands must be grateful to you, since they have fully realised that, even under the changed conditions of the world, whatever they enjoy is due to your staunch support and guidance. I am writing this not merely to please or flatter you, but, believe me, this is my genuine feeling which compels me to express my personal sentiments in these few lines." The Nizam again wrote on the 30th: "I trust that you will soon be restored to your normal health, as, in my opinion, India is in need of your valuable services and guidance, specially at a time when the whole world is passing through a crisis... so, let us hope that nothing serious will happen that may mar the peaceful condition of India."

Owing to bad health, Patel could not reply to the Nizam's letter of November 30th. But his reply of December 1st to the Nizam's letter of November 25th—barely fifteen days before his death—summed up the philosophy that governed his States policy: "In dealing with the States, my aim has been to secure the interests of India with the maximum amount of goodwill and in a spirit of full accord and understanding. I am very glad to find that this has been fully reciprocated by the Rulers of Indian States, and it has given me real pleasure to know that Your Exalted Highness shares that response... These are difficult times, and one must subordinate one's own interests to the larger interests of the country."[61]

Patel's Hyderabad success had double significance. On the personal level, it was his crowning glory: vindication of what he had stood for and unwaveringly advocated, despite the opposition he had from Mountbatten and Nehru. On the national level, it was a historic achievement: the integration of 564 Princely States. Writing in *The Christian Science Monitor*, W. Gordon Graham called Patel the man "who by his decisiveness resolved the great Hyderabad crisis", and significantly observed: "Hyderabad, a State covering 80,000 square miles in the heart of peninsular India, was at that time in the grip of an unscrupulous minority which aimed at secession from India. Had the bid succeeded, India might not have survived as a political unit. This situation needed a man of iron who would not balk at coercive action, and in the Sardar, India had, at that vital moment, just the man."[62] An equally glowing tribute came from General Bucher who was gracious in his ungrudging admission, "I take no credit to myself for the success of the Hyderabad operation. In all the circumstances from beginning to end, I was not prepared to say, 'Go', until every possible development had been thought out and guarded against. The Sardar was, in my opinion, a very great man indeed... Undoubtedly, he was right when he decided that either the Government of Hyderabad must accept the Indian Government's conditions, or else the State would have to be entered in order to eliminate the Razakars."[63]

Patel's quick, bold step and instant success had two implications. First, it killed for good the British policy of creating Hyderabad as the "Third Dominion", of which, according to Munshi, "Arthur Lothain was a great protagonist... it is even possible that he himself had presented the idea to the Nizam in the first place; at any rate, Conrad Corfield, the Adviser to the Crown Representative, was its active sponsor", while Monckton was "the most formidable instrument of the Nizam's policy."[64] Secondly, as Patel put it, "Hyderabad was like an ulcer which had been operated upon."[65] The "Police Action" not only performed such operation, but also saved India from Balkanisation and thereby ensured unification of India into a single, homogeneous country. Hyderabad's integration prevented, as Munshi has put it, the creation of "a second Pakistan in the 'belly' of India, an intensely hostile State separating the North from the South."[66]

e) TRAVANCORE

The redoubtable C.P. Ramaswami Aiyar, a super-egoist like Jinnah, dreamt of a status completely independent of a Union Government headed by Nehru and Patel. His was the first State to have raised the banner of revolt, even when he was its non-Travancorean Diwan. C.P. declared on May 9, 1947, in an interview with *The Hindu* that if it was not possible to frame a constitution for the country as a whole without dividing it, Travancore would have "no alternative but to declare herself a free and independent State, and to take all necessary steps for it."[1] C.P. was an acknowledged intellectual, the Diwan of a premier State, and a stalwart who had occupied the centre of the political stage during the Home Rule movement. He was Secretary to its founder, Annie Besant. This was in 1916-17, prior to Gandhi's emergence on the political horizon. The seriousness of his revolt lay in Travancore's strategic position: a premier Hindu State at the southernmost tip of India, with a sizeable seaboard, and ancient maritime tradition. And it was trotted out that, with the discovery of uranium deposits, for Travancore "the lapse of Paramountcy now assumes new strategic significance."[2]

Patel was among the first to have sensed that C.P. was spearheading a dangerous move among the Indian States. According to K.M. Munshi, his "intransigence gave a new ray of hope to those Princes who had been dreaming of evolving a 'Third Force' out of the States."[3] They were, indeed, "dreaming of a State League and looking to the wizard of Travancore, who at least has a seaboard for the export of his coconuts and uranium."[4] C.P. had, however, isolated himself from the major Hindu States, including his neighbour, Cochin, whom Patel had won over earlier. The Maharaja of Cochin had said on April 27th: "The States are subservient autocracies and helpless under the subjugation of a Superior Power." He had, therefore, advised his brother Princes "to play a useful part in the country's future by willingly assuming the role of constitutional rulers."[5] But C.P. derived his inspiration and arrogance from the support he enjoyed of Bhopal and Corfield. In spite of such a discouraging situation, it was diplomatic of Patel to have written to C.P. a short but sweet letter, breathing friendliness, on May 31st, and timed it with C.P.'s visit to New Delhi to see Mountbatten prior to the announcement of the June 3rd Plan. Patel's intention was to soothe C.P.'s pride and to wean him away from the dangerous path he was pursuing.

Patel's letter to C.P. read: "It is in my nature to be a friend of the friendless. You have become one by choice, and I shall be glad if you will come and have lunch with me tomorrow at 1 p.m." Patel was rather impish in the use of the words "friendless" and "you have become one by choice", as these few words conveyed what C.P. had, unfortunately, reduced himself to—an isolated man. C.P., nevertheless, remained intractable, infatuated as he was with overpowering pride—a pride born out of his mistaken, though deep-rooted belief in his personal friendship with the British. The young Maharaja of Travancore had allowed himself to be led by the nose, especially in C.P's hoodwinking Patel with the fallacious argument that no one could negotiate as the State was ruled "in the name and on behalf of the tutelary deity, Sri Padamanabha." Mischievously did Patel retort: how could Travancore rulers allow the Lord to become subservient to the British Crown?

C.P. rode the high horse from which, he was sure, nobody could dismount him. His reply to Patel's invitation mirrored his character and reflected his mood: "I appreciate your letter, and the kind thought underlying it. It, however, so happens that the 'friendless' person referred to has an engagement with a person for lunch today, and he cannot therefore, avail himself of your generous invitation. Hoping for better luck later on, and renewing my thanks for the friendliness displayed by you."[6] The person C.P. was lunching with was Mountbatten; and "later on" C.P., instead of finding "better luck", had to eat humble pie.

At the States Negotiating Committee's meeting with Mountbatten on June 3rd, C.P. "pleaded for a loosening or lapse of Paramountcy before the transfer of power, in order to strengthen the bargaining power of the States and enable them to negotiate on equal terms with the prospective Dominion Governments." Obviously, C.P. felt encouraged by Mountbatten's reply that he would consider "the premature lapse of Paramountcy in special cases if it could be proved that its continuance was a handicap to negotiation."[7] Brimming with hope and confidence, C.P. was bold to announce on June 10th, Travancore's decision to declare itself independent on August 15th. He asked the people of the State to stand "solidly by His Highness" on "a matter of life and death", made "a fervent appeal to the great traditions and glorious heritage, unique history and unquestioned patriotism of Travancoreans", urging them "to cogitate and decide whether they wished to cherish their freedom and independence, or preferred to be submerged and absorbed as an adjunct to a dominion in a divided India, or be a colony or dependency." He held out the alluring prospect of Travancore being "destined to be the saviour of South India."[8]

C.P. roused people's emotions by raising the slogan: "Travancore for the Travancoreans"; and he went on to say, "The future for the next hundred years at least of Travancore is in the making... The Maharaja does not act, has not acted, will not act as an autocrat. He conceives himself as the trustee and the spearpoint of Travancore's activities and of Travancore's will, and I am making this appeal on behalf of the Maharaja and with his special permission, and on behalf of the dynasty he represents." He asserted, "There is no question that Travancore is ever going to enter the Constituent Assembly. There is no question that Travancore is now going to join the Indian Union. Travancore will be an independent State, and will function as an independent State from August 15th. I have told the Viceroy—and this is no secret—that from the next day, next to the 2nd of this month on which I met him, namely the 3rd instant, I propose to prepare Travancore to fulfil its role and play its part as an independent State."

The demagogue in C.P. raised the emotional appeal to a still higher pitch, "I may tell you that the Maharaja is prepared for the worst that may happen. This is clear. Either this State fulfils its destiny—as by its resources, by the intelligence of its people, by the equipment of its people, by the education of its people, by the history of its people, it is fit to do; or, on the other hand, if this State prefers inglorious existence, prefers to be submerged and suffocated, then His Highness is prepared for every step that may have to be taken, for every risk that may have to be faced." And with a dramatic touch, he added, "...from the 15th of August no power on earth, short of an open war for which we are prepared, can prevent Travancore from declaring its independence ... from the 15th of August Travancore will be an international entity ... people may laugh at us, people may deride us for the time being, but we shall be in exactly the same position as any State in the world. If Switzerland, if Norway, if Sweden, if Denmark can be independent, notwithstanding their small area, notwithstanding their small population, notwithstanding their small revenue, I do not see why Travancore should not be. Travancore wants to live its own life. Travancore wants to pursue its own ideals. It is distinct and separate from the rest of India by its culture."[9] C.P.'s rhetoric was an empty burst of eloquence, hidden under which was his anti-India, pro-Jinnah game. This became unmistakably clear when C.P. announced his intention to appoint a Trade Agent in Pakistan.

On the heels of C.P.'s declaration had come that of the Nizam of Hyderabad on June 12th. Such developments had grave portents. V.P. Menon thought that "these events gave rise to apprehensions lest other States should adopt a similar attitude and India be split into fragments."[10] Jinnah was quick to add fuel to the fire by stating on June 17th that "constitutionally and legally, the Indian States will be independent sovereign States on the termination of Paramountcy and they will be free to decide for themselves to adopt any course they like; it is open to them to join the Hindustan Constituent Assembly or the Pakistan Constituent Assembly, or decide to remain independent... Neither the British Government, nor the British Parliament, nor any other power or body can compel them to do anything contrary to their free will and accord."[11] And since the major States had during the Second World War strengthened their armed forces and the Indian States comprised two-fifths of India, their "return to a state of complete political isolation", in Menon's opinion, was "fraught with the gravest danger to the integrity of the country."[12]

R.K. Shanmukham Chetty, a former Diwan of Cochin, voiced his grave concern over C.P.'s stand on June 22nd, stating, "The most disquieting feature of the Indian political situation is not so much the fact of division or the potentialities of communal troubles, but the declaration of some of the Indian States that they intend to remain as independent sovereign States on the termination of British Paramountcy... the creation of the separate State of Pakistan may not be a damaging blow to India's prestige or influence .... The real danger to the unity and prestige of India is the attitude of certain Indian States. If a considerable number of Indian States chooses to follow the example of Travancore and Hyderabad, it would mean the Balkanisation of India." Shanmukham Chetty, therefore, regretted, "It is one of the ironies of fate that the Diwan of Travancore, who has been the champion of pure Indian nationalism and a strong Central Government, should now make an alliance with Jinnah."[13]

Gandhi could not withhold his voice of deep concern. He stated on June 25th: "If the Travancore Diwan were allowed to have his way and his example were followed by others, India would be split up into several States—a disaster too dreadful to contemplate. Those many States would need an Emperor, and the Emperor who was leaving might even return with redoubled force."[14] Patel had earlier unequivocally stated at the AICC meeting on June 16th, "Probably the statesman who made declaration of independence and sovereignty did not understand the implications of those terms. So long as the Congress continued to have a foothold in Travancore, there is no question of independence and sovereignty."[15]

C.P. indulged in sabre-rattling again on June 23rd and continued doing so almost throughout July. K.P.S. Menon, who later became India's Foreign Secretary, thought that C.P. had declared Travancore independent "in a moment of megalomania", which had led him to the next step when "he expressed his intention to establish diplomatic relations between Travancore and Pakistan, and even selected a retired police officer for the post of Ambassador of Travancore in Karachi."[16] Travancore sat on a powder-keg. Afraid of an explosion, C.P. resorted to repression, which was a reminder of 1938 when he had faced a somewhat similar situation and to check which "he and his Gestapos searched through every nook and corner and preyed upon unarmed victims, who had asked for freedom to live and work, talk and write, associate and organise, (and) subjected them to oppression."[17]

On July 10th, Pattom A. Thanu Pillai, President of the Travancore State Congress, informed Patel by telegram that C.P. "attempts suppression of public opinion… terrorist organisations composed of *goondas* are formed throughout country under control of police and other Government agencies to wreck public meetings and assault public men… Life of public men is in danger. Members of (these) organisations parade public streets armed with *lathis*, knives and other weapons… Life and property insecure… Conditions rapidly degenerating into widespread violence… Travancore is subjected to unbridled dictatorship by an irresponsible non-Travancorean Diwan."[18] When C.P.'s "rogue elephant politics got worse" with the indiscriminate loosening of its fiery temper, the Keralite in K.M. Panikkar felt so emotionally stirred as to decide to jump into the fray and fight C.P. face to face. He gave up his decision on Patel's advice that "there was no need for me to do any such thing and he would solve the Travancore problem himself."[19] Patel was "furious and determined, if necessary, to deal severely with Travancore."[20]

Two events, almost simultaneously happening, took the situation to its climax, then to its ludicrous descent, and, finally, to its quiet passing away and getting lost in the pages of history. One was, according to insiders, Patel's direct handling of the Maharaja, who, being in his early thirties, had proved incapable of standing up to C.P. Patel telephoned the Maharaja and asked him in a voice that was soft, firm but blunt, "Who is standing in your way?" The second was an attempt on C.P.'s life on July 25th by the State Communists when he was attending a cultural function at Trivandrum. The first unnerved the Maharaja; the second, C.P. Both felt rattled. Immediately after the incident, the Maharaja communicated to Mountbatten his decision to accede to India; while a humiliated, defeated, mollified C.P. wrote to Patel from his retirement at Ootacamund on November 11th: "May I take this opportunity to convey to you my sincere felicitations over the forthright and unequivocal policy adopted and maintained by you during the present time of crises and momentous decisions. I have differed from you on several occasions, but cannot refrain from paying my tribute to the consummate talents of leadership manifested by you and Pandit Jawaharlal Nehru at this juncture." In his characteristic magnanimity, Patel replied: "We both know how much we have differed in the past. But, in spite of those differences, I have always regretted that we could not make use of your undoubted talents in a wider sphere of activities." C.P.'s praise for Patel increased as time passed. He wrote to Purushottam Tricumdas on March 27, 1948: "...generally speaking, all the great Kshatriya rulers—descendants of the Sun and Moon—behave like mendicants and sycophants, and have no more spirit than a parcel of frightened rabbits or sheep. They deserve (their) fate, and I congratulate Patel on the brilliant results of his downright policy."[21]

Forgetting the past, Patel was anxious to harness C.P.'s services in the Government. He was motivated to do so not so much by the request he had received from Mountbatten to rehabilitate C.P., as by his own conviction. Patel, therefore, suggested to Nehru, in a letter of May 6, 1948, C.P.'s appointment as India's Ambassador to the USA, in the belief that "his abilities and talents should be utilised by us in the service of the country." He impressed on Nehru, "Men like Sir C.P. Ramaswami Aiyar start with a great advantage in external fields, as they carry a prestige and a position which comparatively unknown personalities have to build up, and their already established contacts provide a useful stepping-stone for further efforts in that direction." Patel tried to mollify Nehru's deep-rooted prejudice with the plea, "I know how bitterly he has been opposed to us, but I do feel that we should be generous and forgiving in our adversary's defeat, and that we should not let go waste his undoubted talents and capacity." Patel suggested, "Irrespective of party or personal considerations, therefore, we should have in Washington a very able and competent man. I feel that we have such a man in Sir C.P. Ramaswami Aiyar, and that if only we could rise above the past, we could utilise him."

Nehru could not forget C.P.'s past and he could not rise above it. He rejected Patel's suggestion with the comment, "I feel quite clearly that C.P. would not be the right man for Washington, or any of the important ambassadorial posts. This has nothing to do with his past, except that the past has created a prejudice against him among large numbers of people in India and his appointment would be very unpopular." Nehru also stated, "I have received advice from the US that while his capability and intellect were greatly admired, he is looked upon as a man out of touch with developments and rather lopsided in his approach. If that was the reaction in America itself, you can well imagine reactions elsewhere... C.P. talks unrestrainably about world politics and this is likely to create difficulties."[22] With that, the matter ended, and C.P. continued to hibernate in political wilderness. Patel could not oblige Mountbatten. More importantly, his failure was the country's loss. C.P.'s presence in the U.S., as Mountbatten must have thought, could have contributed to securing stable, happy Indo-American relations. Since the matter related to foreign affairs, the decision rested with Nehru.

The inauguration of the United State of Travancore and Cochin on July 1st, 1949 was one of the happiest and momentous events for Patel. He could not attend the inaugural function in Trivandrum owing to ill-health. But his message described the union as "the culminating point of the policy of consolidation of States which was inaugurated not more than eighteen months ago; and which, with the cooperation and assistance of the rulers and the support and consent of the people of the States, has been my proud privilege to implement." Not taking all the credit for himself, Patel paid handsome tributes to all those concerned with its success: "It has also been my unique pleasure to find among the Princes and the people, a willingness to make sacrifices in the cause of the country—that sense of public duty which only true patriots can exhibit, and that realisation of the urgency and pre-eminence of the country's interests which calls forth the best and the truest in human beings. The Rulers of Travancore and Cochin, the two Premiers and their colleagues and the local Congress organisations have given by this act of union an unmistakable proof of these virtues, and the complete unity of purpose and devotion to duty thus symbolised by them are a happy augury for the success of this unique enterprise."[23] The historic significance of Patel's success was underlined by Mountbatten: "The adherence of Travancore, after all C.P.'s declaration of independence, has had a profound effect on all the other States and is sure to shake the Nizam."[24] Patel's was a major victory.

f) BHOPAL

Bhopal's challenge to India's unity was far more pernicious than that posed by Ramaswami Aiyar on behalf of Travancore, or even by the Nizam of Hyderabad; whereas his surrender had a great drama. Apprising Gandhi of the dangers inherent in the situation, Patel wrote to him on August 11th: "For the last fifteen days I have been occupied with the Princes. It is so taxing. There seems to be no end to the Nawab of Bhopal's intrigues. He is working day and night to cause a split among the Princes and to keep them out of the Indian Union. The Princes are weak beyond measure. They are full of selfishness, falsehood and hypocrisy." Gandhi's reply showed the great confidence he had in Patel, "We are faced with difficulty, and difficulties seem to be increasing.... The problem of the States is difficult. But I know you will successfully tackle it."[1]

Bhopal was sly and aggressive, who surreptitiously but swiftly moved from one Prince to another, tempting one and all to join hands with him in torpedoing Patel's dream on One India.

He played his game from a position of advantage. He enjoyed encouragement and active support of the Political Department and its powerful Secretary, Conrad Corfield. He was also manoeuvring at the behest of Jinnah. The British had amputated India only in the west and in the east. Bhopal's machinations aimed at dismembering India criss-cross in a multiple fracture. From Kashmir to Kanyakumari and from Kathiawar to Eastern India, the country would have been fragmented into many independent States. Such Balkanisation would have been the worst in Indian history. Only Patel seemed to possess the strength of a Hercules and the political acumen of a Chanakya to meet the formidable challenge and avert the catastrophe. He did that with rare boldness and wisdom, and succeeded in making Bhopal lick the dust.

Bhopal had two objectives: to establish the Princes as a potential "Third Force" on behalf of Corfield; and, on behalf of Jinnah, to secure their accession to Pakistan, if not immediately but ultimately. Along with the Residents and Agents, he endeavoured to persuade the Hamlets among the Princes to form independent confederations outside the Indian Union. As Jinnah's emissary and one of his "closest advisers", Bhopal was "not averse to playing an important role in the higher politics of Pakistan"[2] later by migrating to that country. Before that he was to secure either accession of Hindu States to Pakistan, or their staying out of the Indian Union as independent entities with diplomatic ties with Pakistan. The crafty shepherd was confident of satisfying both Corfield and Jinnah by driving the fear-stricken, bewildered lambs among the Princes into the pens each was building to rope them in.

All this bravado was by a Muslim ruler of a small, predominantly Hindu State. The ruler, Nawab Hamidullah Khan, enjoyed a status and influence with the British and the Princes out of proportion to the State's population, area and revenue. It stood no comparison with the larger and richer States like Kashmir, Hyderabad and Travancore, or the Rajasthan States which glowed with the pride of a glorious heritage, or the

Kathiawar States whose maritime traditions descended from the misty dawn of the Indus Valley civilisation. Bhopal's importance was all due to its dynamic, articulate and crafty ruler, who was in the forefront of the Princely Order by virtue of his personality as a Muslim ruler who could be a most trusted ally of the British. He ascended the throne in May 1926 and came into prominence at the time of the Round Table Conference in 1931. With the British support, he became Chancellor of the Chamber of Princes first from 1931 to 1932, and again from 1943 till his resignation under force of circumstances in 1947. His second term coincided with the most crucial period of Indian history when the future of a united India was on the anvil. K.M. Panikkar, who was Secretary to the Chamber during 1931-32, writes: "One year's stay in Bhopal had taught me that Hamidullah was a Muslim partisan and an enemy of the Hindus. I was certain that he manoeuvred to gain the Chancellorship at this time (1943) to strengthen the voice of the Muslims and to weaken the Hindu claims with the instrumentality of the Hindu Princes"[3], who, looking upon the Political Department as "their patron saint, became tools of Bhopal."[4]

Bhopal packed the Chamber Secretariat with pro-Pakistani Muslims. Assured that the Secretariat would play his game and hopeful of many Hindu Princes' support, Bhopal played an anti-Indian role in the proceedings of the States Negotiating Committee on the issue of the Princes joining the Constituent Assembly. He attempted to browbeat weak, vacillating Princes by prophesying "bloodshed and chaos" in the States if a time-limit on their joining the Constituent Assembly was imposed. He tried to influence them by word of mouth, besides pressing into service his Pakistani dominated Secretariat, to make them adopt a policy of "wait and see." In spite of the shrewdness Bhopal possessed and the patronage he enjoyed of the Political Department, Patel outmanoeuvred him, and made him suffer a humiliating defeat at the hands of the Maharajas of Bikaner and Patiala. And also through a vocal opposition built up within and outside the Chamber by the States Prime Ministers—Diwans Mirza Ismail of

Mysore, V.T. Krishnamachari of Udaipur, Panikkar of Bikaner and B.L. Mitter of Baroda. This resulted in the weakening of Bhopal's position, and was naturally a matter of "great grief to Bhopal". Yet, because of Corfield's support and inspiration from Jinnah, Bhopal continued, undeterred, to persuade the Princes sitting on the fence to keep off the Bikaner-Patiala group.

Panikkar and some other Diwans believed that Bhopal was "acting as an agent of Pakistan", and that "Bhopal came forward as the standard-bearer for Hyderabad", having entered into "a compact with the Nizam whereby the former (Bhopal) agreed to use the Chamber to rally Hindu Princes to undermine Hindu power in India and the Government of Hyderabad was to finance this devious scheme."[5] Bhopal had every hope of success. Like Jinnah, he believed that "a government in India, weakened by the hostility of the Hindu Princes to the Congress, would not dare to offend Muslim public opinion and impose its will on the Nizam." He was of the firm opinion that Hyderabad, as large as England and having a population of 17 million and a revenue of Rs. 20 crores, would survive; and that his "tiny island in a Hindu ocean" could do so "in association with Hyderabad."[6] Such a dream turned sour with Britain's change of mind to transfer power on August 15, 1947, and not by June 1948 as decided earlier; and in this regard Patel had played a decisive role. The speed at which events moved left the Princes bewildered. Bhopal suffered, as his isolation increased thereafter. Yet, his "evil genius was not quite played out"—right till he acceded to the Indian Union.

Simultaneously with the announcement of the June 3rd Plan, Bhopal resigned from the Chancellorship of the Chamber of Princes on the ground that "Bhopal State would, as soon as Paramountcy is withdrawn, be assuming an independent status."[7] He went so far as to say that Bhopal would negotiate directly with the successor Governments of British India, which meant either Pakistan or Hindustan. Bhopal felt so embittered, and even frustrated, that he refused to attend the meeting of the Rulers and States representatives called by Mountbatten on July 25th in his capacity as the Crown Representative. He dismissed it with the contemptuous remark that the rulers had been "invited like the Oysters to attend the tea-party with the Walrus and the Carpenter." Mountbatten regretted to say, "I have spent more time on Bhopal's case than on all the other States put together... it would be a tragedy if he were to wreck the State by failing to come in now."[8]

As August 15th drew nearer, Bhopal realised that his game was up. He also realised that in losing the battle to Patel, and not to Mountbatten, he might lose all in the end. He found himself "in an anomalous and difficult position". So, he approached Mountbatten to find out whether he could sign a Standstill Agreement without acceding to India. What lay behind this move, can only be conjectured upon. He perhaps wanted to see how strong Patel would be after the transfer of power. Would he be exercising full control or partial or none at all? On that basis he wanted to formulate his strategy. He was, however, told that this was not possible. Thereupon, he sent his Constitutional Adviser, Zafrullah, to seek clarification of the terms of accession from V.P. Menon. This could not inspire confidence in Bhopal's intentions, especially so because of Zafrullah's credentials. Zafrullah was an ardent Pakistani, who was soon to represent the Muslims on the Radcliffe Boundary Commission and later as Pakistan's nominee in the UNO to argue Pakistan's case on Kashmir and Hyderabad. Menon told Bhopal that there could be no exception, and he would have to join on the same terms as any other ruler. At his meeting with Mountbatten on August 11th, Bhopal sought his help to save face. He wanted his accession to be announced ten days after the creation of the Dominion of India—i.e. by August 25th. Mountbatten expressed his helplessness unless Patel agreed. Patel was generous to grant Bhopal's request, even when Bhopal had something up his sleeve.

After the announcement of his accession on August 25th, Bhopal wrote to Patel on the 26th. The letter was in the nature of his gratitude for the spirit of accommodation Patel had shown, and an open confession of his guilt. He wrote: "By the time you receive this letter, you will have heard the news that I have decided to join the Union of India... I do not disguise the fact that while the struggle was on, I used every means in my power to preserve the independence and neutrality of my State. Now that I have conceded defeat, I hope that you will find that I can be as staunch a friend as I have been an inveterate opponent. I harbour no ill feelings towards any one; for, throughout I have been treated with consideration and have received understanding and courtesy from your side. I now wish to tell you that so long as you maintain your present firm stand against the disruptive forces in the country and continue to be a friend of the States, as you have shown you are, you will find in me a loyal and faithfully ally."

He further told Patel, "I shall stand by you and if ever you need my assistance in maintaining communal harmony, you have only to say the word and I will do everything in my power to help."

Patel's reply reflected a generous, forgiving heart. He wrote: "Quite candidly, I do not look upon the accession of your State to the Indian Dominion as either a victory for us or a defeat for you. It is only right and propriety which have triumphed in the end, and in that triumph, you and I have played our respective roles. You deserve full credit for having recognised the soundness of the position and for the courage, the honesty and the boldness of having given up your earlier stand, which, according to us, was entirely antagonistic to the interests as much of India as of your own State. I have noted with particular pleasure your assurance of support to the Dominion Government in combating disloyal elements, irrespective of caste, creed or religion, and your offer of loyal and faithful friendship."[9]

With this, the anti-Indian front of the Princes Bhopal had built, collapsed. There followed total confusion among the rulers of his group. They were completely "routed"; and were so crestfallen that they sought interviews with Patel, looking for some saving grace in his forgiveness. One such ruler was the Maharaja of Indore, Bhopal's closest ally. "Erratic and bad-mannered", he did not, like Bhopal, attend the Rulers' meeting Mountbatten had called on July 25th. On July 30th, Mountbatten sent six of his fellow Maratha Princes, headed by Baroda, to Indore with "a personal letter from the Viceroy urging the Ruler of Indore to come to Delhi."[10] The Maharaja insulted his brother Princes by declining to see them. Baroda told Menon that "all of them were waiting in the Maharaja's drawing-room when he came in and went past them on his way upstairs as though they did not exist."[11] With Bhopal's having fallen from his earlier "high" position, Indore realised his position was no longer safe. Along with Bhopal, he saw Mountbatten on August 4th, and was given "a dressing-down of painful severity."[12]

For what was Bhopal playing Jinnah's game? Obviously for a price. In return for the services rendered, Bhopal hoped to succeed Jinnah as Governor-General of Pakistan. The succession story saw the light of day immediately on Jinnah's death on September 11, 1948, when the *Civil and Military Gazette* of Lahore published a news-despatch from its New Delhi correspondent, apparently inspired by the Nawab himself, which purported to say that Bhopal would succeed Jinnah as Governor-General of Pakistan. The ruling clique looked upon the news with disfavour, characterising it as sinister. A usurper appeared to be coming to Pakistan to become the head of the State. An agitation was whipped up. A procession went through some of the main streets of Lahore staging a protest. A worked-up crowd gathered outside the newspaper office on the Mall, and made a bonfire of copies which carried the news. The Christian News Editor got so many threatening telephone calls that he had to seek police protection.

The story finds confirmation in Bhopal's admitting to Nehru of the possibility of his being "called upon to serve" Pakistan as Governor-General after Jinnah, though he qualified this by stating: "There can be no question of it as long as Mr. Jinnah is alive." ("Selected Works of Jawaharlal Nehru: Quest for Communal Peace", Second Series, Vol. VII, p.8, footnote 9). Bhopal had lodged with Mountbatten his Instrument of Accession in a sealed envelope for handing it over to the Ministry of States on August 25th, "unless the Nawab instructed otherwise".

According to H.V. Hodson, "three days before this period of grace expired", Bhopal had a long talk with Patel and then saw Mountbatten, when he explained the reasons for his hesitation: "he had ambitions to play a big role in the Muslim world in the future, and he feared that if he acceded, Jinnah would denounce him as a traitor to the Muslim cause." Bhopal had flown to Karachi to meet Jinnah, who, though "sufficiently magnanimous" towards the Nawab, must have by then seen opposition from Liaquat Ali and other Muslim leaders. It was thereafter, on his return from Pakistan, that the State of Bhopal acceded to India and "its ruler decided not to resign his *gadi* to his daughter, as he had intended to do in order to take office in Pakistan."[13]

g) KASHMIR

Patel can appropriately be called the Saviour of Kashmir. But for his timely action, Srinagar would have fallen into the hands of marauding Pakistani raiders. By his timely visit to Srinagar in most inhospitable climate, he averted the tragedy. Had Srinagar fallen, India would have lost the Valley for good. Being in charge of Kashmir, he rose to the occasion and risked his life at the call of duty.

November 4, 1947, was a fateful day for Srinagar. The people shivered with the fear of what had happened earlier at Baramulla: looting and burning of shops and houses, brutal killing of men and raping of women. Religion mattered little to such brutes. Srinagar's fate hung by a thread. The Pakistani raiders, fully armed and outnumbering Indian troops, were just four miles outside the city limits in the village of Shalateng for their final assault. In anticipation of the expected victory, Jinnah was reported to be at Abbottabad "expecting to ride in triumph into Kashmir."[1] Srinagar and its leaders were undergoing a traumatic experience. General L.P. Sen, then a Brigadier in command of 161 Brigade, found a paralysis creeping over the city in fear of the approaching doom that had already befallen Baramulla and some other Valley towns. The fear struck Sheikh Abdullah no less. Ian Stephens, Editor of *The Statesman* records his interview with him on the lawns of the Nedou's Hotel in Srinagar: "As a Kashmiri with ancestral recollections of previous incursions up the same route, he had felt personally outraged." Abdullah spoke to Stephens bitterly, "If they had to attack, Mr. Stephens, why in Heaven's name couldn't they go to Poonch to help the people there against that autocrat? Why must they rush towards Srinagar, looting and burning?"[2] The autocrat was the Maharaja, whose Muslim troops in Pooch had revolted against him and killed some of their Hindu fellow soldiers.

Abdullah seemed worried about his future. Would Jinnah spare him for his defiance in not letting him have his prize—the beautiful Valley of Kashmir? Jinnah was bad-tempered, uncompromising, dictatorial and ruthless. He caused the eclipse of the most powerful Congress leaders of the NWFP—Dr. Khan Sahib, the Premier, and his brother Khan Abdul Ghaffar Khan, known as the Frontier Gandhi. Abdullah also could not overlook the fate of the Punjab Premier, Khizr Hayat Khan Tiwana, who had to run away from Jinnah's reach by asking Patel to arrange his passage by sea from Bombay to London. Unlike them, whom India could render no help, Abdullah could secure such help, and save his position only if the State acceded to India and he influenced the future course of events through his friendship with Nehru. From Nehru he later secured, first, the exile of the Maharaja from the State so as to have unbridled power in his hands; and thereafter he got his "independence" through Article 370 of the Indian Constitution.

On that fateful morning of November 4th, when Srinagar faced the grim prospect of falling into the hands of marauding tribesmen and the people shivered both in fear of the impending calamity and the biting cold weather, Patel, accompanied by his daughter, Maniben, and Sardar Baldev Singh, the Defence Minister, flew into Srinagar. He went straight to the Brigade Headquarters to know of the situation from Brigadier Sen. Interestingly, Sen records, "Sardar Patel had closed his eyes soon after I had begun the briefing, and I assumed that he was feeling the effects of the air journey and had fallen asleep. The briefing completed. I looked at Sardar Baldev Singh and asked him a direct question, 'Am I expected to eject the tribesmen from the Valley regardless of the fate that may befall Srinagar, or is the town to be saved?' Sardar Patel stirred. The Tiger had not been asleep, and had heard every word of the briefing. A strong and determined man, and one of few words. 'Of course, Srinagar must be saved', he snapped. 'Then I must have more troops, and very quickly,' I answered, adding, 'and if it is possible, I would like to have some artillery'."

"Sardar Patel rose. 'I'm returning to Delhi immediately,' he said, 'and you will get what you want as quickly as I can get them to you.' On reaching the vehicle park, I called forward my jeep and asked him whether I could drive him to the airfield. 'No, Brigadier', he replied, 'don't bother to come to the airport to see me off. You have got more important things to do than wasting your time doing that.' He then climbed into his own vehicle and, with a wave of his hand, was off. That evening I got a message that two battalions of infantry, one squadron of armoured cars and a battery of field artillery were being dispatched to the Valley by road. The engineers had bridged the numerous culverts on the road from Pathankot to Jammu, and the Valley could now receive large bodies of troops by surface transport. This was heartening news, as the airstrip was beginning to look like a ploughed field. Sardar Patel had lived up to his reputation as a man of action."[3]

Patel's visit saved the situation in two ways: first, prompt military support to Indian units insufficiently equipped both in men and materials, which alone could prevent Srinagar from falling into the hands of tribesmen. Capture of Srinagar would have given Pakistan a permanent foothold in the Valley, and Pakistan would have easily secured the Maharaja's accession. India would have thus lost Kashmir for good. Secondly, Patel could apprise Nehru and the Government of the real situation in the Valley. This saved Sen from the embarrassment he was facing on account of a contradictory report sent by an Army officer of his rank, General (then Brigadier) B.M. Kaul, whom Nehru had deputed to report. "He had", according to Sen, "painted a picture of complete calm, and of the situation being more than well in hand, and had suggested that the number of troops in the Valley was adequate and could easily cope with what was no more than a band of ill-trained hooligans".[4] Kaul's report and the one sent by the local Army commanders angered Nehru: "to receive two diverse reports on the situation in the Kashmir Valley over a matter of hours was more than he could tolerate."[5] Patel's visit was, however, timely. It clarified the confusion, boosted the morale of the local Army commanders with his firm assurance, and even ended any hesitancy the Government had in its help to the Army.

Patel's visit was no doubt hazardous. He was 72. It was November, and there could have been early snowfall. The real hazard lay in the narrow air passage between Jammu and Srinagar. Under cover of a thick fog, a slight error of judgment in poor visibility could have landed his plane in Pakistan territory. Calling him "rock-like in his appearance and demeanour, which bred confidence in him to an extraordinary degree", General Roy Bucher, Commander-in-Chief of the Indian Army, narrates, "... the Sardar ordered an aircraft of the Indian Air Force to be put at his disposal to take him, his daughter and some members of his staff to Kashmir, so that the Deputy Prime Minister could see for himself what was happening there. When he was told the journey would be extremely hazardous, and that the Commander-in-Chief might not approve of it, the Sardar said, "Not to worry about the Commander-in-Chief's opinion, but get me an aircraft".

"This flight", concedes Bucher, "did result in reinforcements being sent to Kashmir."[6] Clearance of the tribesmen from the Valley was thus achieved, and with that ended Pakistan's adventure in Kashmir.

Patel's second strategic step to save Kashmir was to send V.P. Menon to Srinagar, soon after the raiders were on the move from Baramulla, with instructions that the Maharaja should at once move to Jammu and be out of Pakistan's reach. Abdullah and Bakshi Ghulam Mohammad made capital out of this by alleging that the Maharaja "collected all his valuables, loaded them into all the trucks he could lay hands on, and bolted with his family to Jammu." Sen lost no time to scotch this canard, whose ill-conceived intent poisoned the minds of the Kashmiri Muslims against the Dogra Hindus of Jammu, and even against India in course of time. Sen bluntly stated that the "statement was not wholly accurate... Nor had the Maharaja 'bolted' ... He had been persuaded for political reasons to leave Srinagar and take up residence in another part of his State. Had he remained in Srinagar and fallen into tribal hands, his functions as Maharaja would have been dictated to him."[7] Abdullah had himself shifted his family to a safer place in India.

"It was, perhaps, unfortunate," writes Sen, "that Sheikh Abdullah and Bakshi Ghulam Mohammad were both away from the Valley during the winter of 1947-48. This was a crucial period... Sheikh Abdullah gave me the impression that he was not going to be boxed up in the Valley... Kashmir had suffered a severe blow from the raiders, and Sheikh Abdullah would have been wiser not to leave the Valley and its people at a time when they required all help, guidance and alleviation."[8] Sen refers to another alarming motive of Abdullah: "...as the military situation improved, he had become obsessed with his own importance. His interest had veered from the tackling of the many pressing problems which demanded his undivided attention and time, to the building up of his popularity with the masses."[9] Further, both the Sheikh and the Bakshi stubbornly refused to accept the logic of the Maharaja's action; and they used it as a convenient stick to stoke the fire they had lit of anti-Dogra feelings among the Kashmiris.

Patel's third strategic step was to establish and strengthen expeditiously, defying climate and terrain, the State's territorial integration with India through a communications system: telegraph, telephones, wireless, but, the most important, an all-weather road for transport of men and materials to Srinagar. Till Partition, Kashmir had two motorable road-links with India: one from Abbottabad to Srinagar; the other via Sialkot to Jammu and

Srinagar. India's only link had been snapped with Sialkot having gone to Pakistan, though it did not alter the State's contiguity with India. Patel took upon himself the task of building the road-link. He had an assurance from the Minister of Communications, Rafi Ahmed Kidwai, that "although the normal time for the completion of such construction is two months, it may be possible to complete it much earlier."[10] As a vital link, a road was hurriedly constructed from Pathankot to Jammu, which ran almost parallel to the Pakistan border. Not only was this road to be made good for heavy vehicular traffic, but the portion between Jammu and Srinagar had to be widened and improved. The real difficulty lay in the construction of a bridge over the Ravi at Madhopur. It had to be completed in just eight months before the onset of a heavy monsoon.

Patel's anxiety and his efforts are evident from an account of the Minister for Works, N.V. Gadgil. Towards October-end, one day after the Cabinet meeting, he writes, "Vallabhbhai took out a map, and, pointing to the Jammu—Pathankot area, said that the sixty-five mile road between the two towns had to be made capable of carrying the heavy army traffic before July 1948, i.e. within eight months. 'You must see to it,' he said. I said: 'You do not feel the rivers and rivulets, hills and mountains on the map. This is one of the mountainous parts of India, and besides, a number of rivers flow through it. This is the Defence Ministry's work. They should undertake it.' The Sardar said, 'We are not giving it to the Army. You have to do it.' I said, 'All right, if you say so, it is done'."[11]

And it was done. Within a fortnight, the necessary steel parts of three long bridges and numerous culverts had been assembled at the worksites. Seventy special trains brought to Pathankot materials and men. Ten thousand workers came from long distances, and the entire workforce numbered over 40,000. It was a round-the-clock job. The 54-mile road and 11 miles of bridges and culverts were completed within Patel's stipulated period.

Nehru declared the bridge open on July 7th,1948. Major-General Williams, a Britisher in charge of the M.E.S., addressing

Gadgil at the inaugural function, said, "Your boys have done it. They have done the impossible. I had said earlier that the work cannot be completed within the stipulated time. I take back my words."[12] Not only did the bridge establish a road link between India and Kashmir, but it was an engineering feat. Some American newspapers published illustrated articles under the heading, "*India can do it.*" Patel was generous in complimenting Gadgil, both verbally and in writing. Behind the success of the project lay Patel's resolute mind. It had to be executed at all cost—with certain ruthlessness. Andrew Mellor, the London *Daily Herald* correspondent, sensed such ruthlessness when he interviewed Patel after his visit to Kashmir: "I saw him one evening, and was describing the difficulties of the terrain for Indian troops moving through the passes from Jammu… I had seen several guns which had rolled over at road curves and fallen hundreds of feet. It seemed to me that these difficulties were appalling, if not insurmountable. 'The roads are so bad that a lot of vehicles cannot, in my opinion, be got up,' I said. 'They must be got up,' he replied, 'and they will be.' They were."[13]

Patel's three strategic steps—his visit to Srinagar on November 4th, his asking the Maharaja to shift from Srinagar to Jammu, and the building of a permanent all-weather road-link between India and the State—saved Kashmir from falling into the hands of Pakistan. And all this was done just in the nick of time. It was a touch and go affair. Patel admitted to V.T. Krishnamachari, "The Maharaja came to us very late. Had he delayed by a day, things would have been beyond redemption altogether." In reply, Krishnamachari confirmed what most people thought, "It is a blessing that, in spite of initial handicaps, the situation in Kashmir has now much improved. Kashmir and all Indian States generally owe a deep gratitude to you and the Government of India for the timely assistance which has preserved the integrity of Kashmir."[14]

Abdullah had agreed to Kashmir's accession apparently not so much on secular considerations as to ensure, first and foremost, his freedom from Jinnah, whose hatred for him is evident from

Jinnah's cynical remark, "Oh, that tall man who sings the Koran and exploits the people."[15] Liaquat Ali had contemptuously called him: "This Quisling—an agent of the Congress for many years, who struts about the stage bartering the life, honour and freedom of the people for the sake of personal profit and power."[16] The Maharaja's attitude too had a background. He drew inspiration, like the Nizam and Bhopal, from the British politicians' pronouncements on the Princes' right to exercise independence on the termination of Paramountcy, as also his fear of what Abdullah might do to him on gaining power, with Nehru's backing. If the Maharaja wobbled, it was primarily due to his being placed between the devil and the deep sea—Jinnah on one hand; Abdullah on the other. Since Jinnah's accessibility to Srinagar and Jammu was easier than India's at the time when the road-link between Pathankot and Jammu had not yet been built, the Maharaja's vacillation seemed natural.

V.P. Menon gives the Maharaja the benefit of the doubt: "In fairness to Maharaja Hari Singh, it must be said that, situated as he was, it was not easy for him to come to a decision. If he acceded to Pakistan, the non-Muslims of Jammu and Ladakh, as well as considerable sections of Muslims led by the National Conference, would definitely have resented such action. On the other hand, accession to India would have provoked adverse reactions in Gilgit and certain areas contiguous to Pakistan."[17] But the man who put him at the end of his rope was Nehru for his emotional attachment for Kashmir, the land of his ancestors; equally so far his attachment to Abdullah, for whom he had a blind eve and refused to read what was at the back of Abdullah's mind. According to Nehru's biographer, Sarvepalli Gopal, Nehru looked upon Abdullah as "an old friend and colleague and blood-brother."[18] To Nehru, Abdullah was above suspicion. He could do no wrong. Nor could he think of evil. For Nehru, Abdullah was Kashmir and Kashmir was Abdullah.

The Maharaja's vacillation and Nehru's deep-rooted hatred of the Maharaja had their origin in the happenings in Kashmir in May 1946. That was the time when in New Delhi the Cabinet

Mission was busy trying to find out a solution whereby power could be transferred to India. Ignoring that, Abdullah launched his "Quit Kashmir" agitation against the Maharaja in imitation of Gandhi's "Quit India" movement of 1942. He was sure of Nehru's backing, though the agitation, many Congress leaders conceded, was inopportune, thoughtless and malevolent, directed towards an Indian ruler, not a foreigner, and motivated by purely personal considerations. The agitation could have proved contagious, affecting other States in India, which would have come in the way of Congress efforts to gain freedom for the country. To ward off any such developments, Patel had to define the official Congress policy on June 8th, 1946 while addressing the General Council of the All-India States People's Conference: "The time has arrived when it is necessary for the Indian people to deal with the States problem on the basis of a collective approach to the Princes as a whole, and not to fritter away their energies in isolated battles... We do not want to start any movement in the States. We are not to make settlement with individual States, but with the entire Princely Order at one time. There are so many of them, and they cannot be tackled individually."[19] A year later, Mountbatten followed Patel's principle of "collective approach" in settling with the Princes by adopting the "common form accession." Mountbatten, like Patel earlier, had come to the conclusion that "separate negotiation with each state is out of the question."[20] The two pursued the same path, but their ends were different. Mountbatten's was to settle with the Princes, hand them over to either India or Pakistan and quit; Patel's was to integrate the States into an all-India pattern and build on their foundations a new, strong, homogeneous country. But Nehru's deviation from that path created the Kashmir problem.

Contradictory to the Congress States' policy, Abdullah had demanded that "Maharaja Hari Singh should quit the Valley bag and baggage and leave the Kashmiris alone to decide their future by themselves." Such a "fraudulent" slogan being anti-Dogra, Prem Nath Bazaz, a leading Kashmir Pandit leader and once a close associate of Abdullah in the National Conference, points out, "would be very welcome to the Muslims of the Valley, among whom the Nationalists (of the National Conference) had lost enormously." The slogan meant two things: one, the National Conference was "out to end the Hindu rule", and, second, "the Conference has finally determined to exterminate despotism and autocracy, root and branch." This, again, was contrary to the Congress policy towards the Princes in the rest of India—Hindus and Muslims alike. Abdullah also dreamed of a "New Kashmir". The dream was spelt out in a manifesto, which according to Bazaz, "envisaged a communist form of government." Abdullah's demand for the deposition of the Maharaja not only antagonised the Dogra Hindus of Jammu, but even stirred up apprehensions in the minds of the Valley Pandits. This led to communal riots in Srinagar. Fearing his arrest by the Maharaja, Abdullah left for Delhi by car to seek Nehru's help. But before he could cross the state border, he was taken into custody.

Nehru rushed to Srinagar to protest from within the State. He ignored the advice of his senior colleagues; also Bakshi Ghulam Mohammad's statement, in contradiction to Abdullah's stand, from Delhi where he had reached by evading arrest: "The National Conference demanded the establishment of responsible government in the State" and "did not desire to harm the Royal family in any way."[21] Nevertheless, Nehru's hasty step caused deep apprehensions in the mind of the Maharaja. Even the Kashmiri Pandits, in a telegram of June 4th, stated, "The statements of Pundit Jawaharlal Nehru... are universally condemned and resented by the Hindus of Kashmir. By encouraging Sheikh Abdullah's fascist and communal programme, he is doing the greatest disservice to the people of Kashmir. His unwarranted and wrong statements... inflame Muslims against Hindus."[22] Nehru's bias in favour of Abdullah was evident from what he had said in August 1945 at the annual session of the National Conference at Sopore in the Valley, "If non-Muslims want to live in Kashmir, they should join the National Conference or bid goodbye to the country... If Pandits do not join it, no safeguards and weightages will protect them.[23]

Nehru left Delhi on June 18th for Srinagar. At Lahore on the 19th, he warned the Maharaja that "there can be no peace unless Abdullah was released."[24] For defying the ban on his entry into the State, he was detained at Uri. Nehru's action did not carry support of the Congress High Command. Azad, the President, summoned him back over the telephone. Patel voiced his disapproval by saying that Nehru had "taken action individually as President of the All-India States Peoples' Conference on his own responsibility."[25] Privately, he characterised it as an act of "emotional insanity".[26] He further clarified the position, "The Congress, as an organisation, has kept out of this movement in Kashmir. We have managed to ease the situation by calling him (Nehru) back from Kashmir, and arranging to send him there again to fulfil his mission with the permission of the State." Prior to his second visit on July 24th, Nehru assured Patel, "It is not my intention to raise any major issues in Kashmir at this stage… I do not propose to hold public meetings and the like…"[27]

This time there was a marked change in Nehru's attitude and pronouncements. After interviewing Abdullah in jail, he admitted that "the leaders of the National Conference had committed a mistake by starting the Quit Kashmir movement, but it was not fair to leave them to their fate."[28] None of the senior Congress leaders appeared to have shared Nehru's views. Kripalani, who visited Srinagar in May, had stated that he was convinced that the "Quit Kashmir movement was abusive and mischievous… the Maharaja was a son of the State", and it was, therefore, "absurd to ask him to quit"; and that "there could be no comparison between the Quit Kashmir agitation and the Quit India movement."[29] He also disapproved of the slogan denouncing the Treaty of Amritsar.

Nehru's unsuccessful visit created more problems than it solved. Nehru took Abdullah's continuance in jail as an affront to his person. His defeat and frustration drove his hatred towards the Maharaja deeper. This created bitter apprehensions and hatred in the mind of the Maharaja towards India's future Prime Minister. That was during mid-1946. A different anxiety, however, overtook the Maharaja when the British decided to transfer power and quit India. Like other Indian Princes, he began to wobble: whether to remain independent, or to accede to Pakistan under pressure; for, India had no direct road-link with the State at that time, though the State had contiguity with India. Abdullah's growing anxiety was mainly on personal account. It posed a threat to his future. Casting aside his pride, he climbed down from his earlier stand and sent the Maharaja a message from his prison cell, advising him "to at once accede to the Indian Union and not to remain independent as the leaders of the Muslim Conference wanted him to do."[30]

A new wind of change blew in September with the appointment of a new Prime Minister, Mehr Chand Mahajan. Nehru's first act was to ask him "to see that Sheikh Abdullah was set free."[31] Nehru pursued the matter by writing to Patel on September 27th: "Your advice will naturally go a long way either to the Maharaja or to Mahajan... We have definitely a great asset in the National Conference, provided it is properly handled. It would be a pity to lose this. Sheikh Abdullah has repeatedly given assurances of wishing to cooperate and of being opposed to Pakistan; also to abide by my advice."[32] On Patel's advice Abdullah was released. On coming out of prison, he called upon the Maharaja and offered him a *nazarana* as a token of his loyalty. The letter he had sent earlier from the prison read: "In spite of what has happened in the past, I assure Your Highness that myself and my party have never harboured any sentiment of disloyalty towards Your Highness's person, throne or dynasty... I assure Your Highness the fullest and loyal support of myself and my organisation... Before I close this letter, I beg to assure Your Highness once again of my steadfast loyalty and pray that God may grant me opportunity enough to let this country attain under Your Highness's aegis such an era of peace, prosperity and good government that it may be second to none and be an ideal for others to follow."[33] The Maharaja understood that Abdullah's profession of loyalty was a mere pretence. He told Mahajan that Nehru had "a soft corner for the Sheikh and was very friendly with him, and as the

Sheikh's ambition is to become the Prime Minister of Kashmir, he would take the earliest opportunity to prevail upon Pandit Nehru to put him in power. Once in power, he would revive his 'Quit Kashmir' move and become all powerful himself."[34]

Kashmir acceded to India on October 26th. The handing over of the Instrument of Accession was preceded by high drama at Nehru's residence in New Delhi. Present there were Nehru, Patel, Menon and Mahajan. When Mahajan suggested that "Srinagar must be saved at any cost from loot and destruction" by immediate military aid, Nehru made light of a serious issue, which meant life or death for the Valley, by making a romantically hopeful observation that "even if the town was taken by the tribesmen, India was strong enough to retake it." Mahajan repeated his insistence on immediate military aid, to which Nehru bluntly replied that "it was not easy on the spur of the moment to send troops, as such an operation required considerable preparation and arrangement, and troops could not be moved without due deliberation merely on demand." Perhaps, he wished to consult Mountbatten. But such dilly-dallying made Mahajan retort, "Give us the military force we need. Take the accession and give whatever power you desire to the popular party (Abdullah's). The Army must fly to save Srinagar this evening, or else I will go to Lahore and negotiate terms with Jinnah." Nehru flared up, "Mahajan, go away." Mahajan was getting up from his seat to leave the room when Patel detained him by saying, "Of course, Mahajan you are not going to Pakistan." At this tense moment, a piece of paper was handed over to Nehru which changed his mood and altered the course of events. He loudly proclaimed, "Sheikh Sahib also says the same thing." Abdullah was sitting in the adjoining room listening to the conversation. According to Mahajan, Abdullah "strengthened my hands by telling the Prime Minister that military help must be sent immediately. This came as a timely help for the success of my mission to New Delhi."[35]

Immediately thereafter, Patel, through a broadcast over All-India Radio, commandeered all the aircraft available in India with the private airlines. This made it possible to start the aerial operations the very next morning. And on October 27th, with relief and satisfaction, people saw aircrafts taking off one after another from the small, civil airfield of Safdarjung. A relieved Gandhi told Patel, "...At one time I was feeling very miserable and oppressed when I heard this. But when the Kashmir operation began, I began to feel proud of them, and every aeroplane that goes with materials and arms and ammunition and requirements of the Army, I feel proud." Gandhi justified his view, "Any injustice on our land, any encroachment on our land should... be defended by violence, if not by non-violence... If you can defend by non-violence, by all means do it; that is the first thing I should like. If it is for me to do, I would not touch anything, either a pistol or revolver or anything. But I would not see India degrading itself to be feeling helpless." Patel congratulated the Indian Air Force personnel, "When Srinagar was touch and go, when we wanted to put our Army in Srinagar, and when the Air Force was asked to carry the Army and all its requirements quickly, it did it with wonderful speed; and if we had been late by twenty-four hours, the whole game would have been lost. That is the work which you have done, and which will be written in letters of gold in the history of Freedom. We are proud of you."[36]

The Maharaja's accession to India brought to an end a most costly indecision on his part, which was due to, besides his distrust of Abdullah and Nehru, Mountbatten's advice through Ismay that he should "hold a referendum at once on the question of whether his people wished to accede to India or Pakistan."[37] The Maharaja felt that the suggestion smelled foul. He also saw certain contradictions in Mountbatten's stand. First, his suggestion did not emerge from the Indian Independence Act. Secondly, the proposal of a referendum appeared to him very much similar to the one Mountbatten had imposed on the NWFP—to satisfy the wishes of Jinnah more than of the inhabitants—the Pathans. In the case of Kashmir, the suggestion would have given Pakistan an edge over India: ultimately giving Pakistan a much larger territorial base and thus making it more stable.

Patel's role in clearing the climate of distrust and indecision and bringing the Maharaja closer to India was of great importance. He had advised the Maharaja on July 3rd with such disarming frankness, "I am sorry to find that there is considerable misapprehension in your mind about the Congress. Allow me to assure Your Highness that the Congress is not only not your enemy, as you happen to believe, but there are in the Congress many strong supporters of your State. As an organisation, the Congress is not opposed to any Prince in India. It has no quarrel with the States." Patel assured the Maharaja that there would be no interference in "your domestic affairs", and showed a sympathetic mind by emphasising, "I fully appreciate the difficult and delicate situation in which your State has been placed, but as a sincere friend and well-wisher of the State, I wish to assure you that the interest of Kashmir lies in joining the Indian Union and its Constituent Assembly without any delay... all India looks up to you and expects you to take that decision. Eighty per cent of India is on this side. The States that have cast their lot with the Constituent Assembly have been convinced that their safety lies in standing together with India."[38]

Two steps taken by Patel showed the measure of his success. The first was the Maharaja's terminating Kak's services, and appointing in his place a new Prime Minister—Mehr Chand Mahajan, a former judge of the Punjab High Court, who was a Dogra from the adjoining Kangra Valley. The second was Patel's letting Kashmir have the services of Col. Kashmir Singh Katoch, about which he wrote to the Defence Minister, Baldev Singh, on September 13th. "You know the difficulties of the State, and I feel that at this juncture it would be most useful to have an officer of our own Army as Commander-in-Chief of the Kashmir forces."[39] Katoch happened to be the son of General Janak Singh, a former Prime Minister of Kashmir. Such strategic moves on Patel's part placed India in a more advantageous position than Pakistan. But these earned Jinnah's wrath, as he saw in them the prospect of Kashmir slipping out of his hands. His frustration led to the tribal invasion. Indication of Pakistan's designs was available to General Thimayya. As India's nominee on the Boundary Force under General Rees with his HQ at Amritsar, he had gone to Lahore some time in August and was putting up with General Mohammed Iftikhar. According to his biographer, Humphrey Evans: "While Thimayya was changing for dinner, his host's other guests arrived. Most of them were Pakistani officers. When Thimayya returned to the drawing-room, he caught part of their conversation. He overheard that Probyns Horse would be located at Gulmarg and the 13th lancers at Pahalgam. The Pakistani officers were dividing the Kashmir territory between their regiments and were talking about how pleasant these posts would be. This was the first time Thimayya heard of the Indo-Pakistani conflict over Jammu and Kashmir State."[40]

Besides the capture of the Kashmir Valley, the tribal invasion had other compelling considerations: to avert the serious trouble Pakistan was expecting in the NWFP with the withdrawal of the Army from the Frontier and the menacing presence of the Pathans in Punjab, especially in Lahore. They posed a serious challenge to law and order, and to the stability of Pakistan. The situation in the NWFP arose following Britain's decision to abandon her "Frontier commitments", "if a Pakistan Army was to be created." Withdrawal from the Frontier military posts was carried out in great fear under "Operations Curzon". Of such fears Birdwood records: "When Major-General R.E. le Fleming and Brigadier R.S. Steed were leading their men away and closing a stage of history with all the care and precaution ... a few miles away the Political Agent for South Waziristan, Påtrick Duncan, was busy trying to restrain the Mahsuds from their advance onto their prize around which for years they had played their own particular form of hide and seek." Birdwood confirms, "The troops had fully expected the tribesmen in their exuberance to harass the final retreat. But whether through tribal preoccupations farther afield in Kashmir, or whether in recognition of a new era of comparative freedom, the Razmak garrison escaped unscathed."[41]

Trouble was brewing in Lahore as well. It was sensed by G.M. Sadiq, later to become Chief Minister of Jammu and Kashmir. He visited Lahore first on October 6th and later on October

18th for talks with Liaquat Ali on the future status of Kashmir. Liaquat Ali questioned as to why Abdullah hadn't himself come to Lahore, but had instead gone to New Delhi. When Sadiq suggested that he could arrange Abdullah's visit on October 25th, Liaquat Ali said, "It would be too late." By the 18th itself, Sadiq realised that "Pakistan had already finalised her plans of a tribal invasion of the Valley." And it was on the 20th that the tribesmen captured Muzaffarabad. Lahore, as Sadiq saw, was "full of Pathan tribesmen", who moved about in groups under leaders. Sadiq "sensed a danger and thought that Pakistan was up to some mischief." When he complained to his host, Daultana, a leading Muslim League leader, of attempts on his life in the mistaken belief that he was an Indian agent, Daultana admitted that "the Government itself was facing the danger they (Pathans) were posing to the law and order situation in the city."[42]

In the tribal invasion of Kashmir, Pakistan was thus attempting to save her own skin by diverting tribesmen to Kashmir. Her complicity in this also finds support from what General Sen learnt from General Messervey, Commander-in-Chief of the Pakistan Army at the time of the invasion, during the latter's visit to the Jat Regiment, of which he was Colonel, in Ambala in 1955. Sen writes: "One evening I asked him a straight question as to whether he was aware of the preparations being made to invade Kashmir. His answer to me was: 'Yes'. Akbar Khan's office was very close to his and he had been told to give Akbar Khan all the help he required."[43]

The unexpected and prompt airlifting of Indian troops to Srinagar made Jinnah fly into a rage. Not prepared to lose the Valley at any cost, he ordered General Gracey, who was officiating for Messervey, "to send troops into Kashmir to seize Baramula and Srinagar, also the Banihal Pass and to send troops into Mirpur district of Jammu."[44] That seemed a well thought-out plan to seal the fate of the small Indian force in the Valley from all strategic directions, and present India with a *fait accompli*. Gracey did not carry out the orders. Instead, he invoked the help of Auchinleck. The latter reached Lahore and forced Jinnah to cancel his order.

"I simply told him", he writes, "that if he persisted in his plan to send the Pakistan Army against India, all British officers (and there were many, including General Gracey, the C-in-C., in important posts) would be withdrawn at once as it was inconceivable that British officers, commissioned by the British Sovereign, should lead Pakistani troops against Indian troops similarly commanded."[45] Auchinleck reported to the Chiefs of Staff, London, on his meeting with Jinnah on October 28th, "General Gracey emphasised the military weakness of Pakistan, while I pointed out the incalculable consequences of military violation of what now is territory of the Indian Union in consequence of Kashmir's sudden accession."[46] Jinnah cancelled his order to Gracey, but, instead, he lent open support to the invasion of Kashmir by the Frontier tribesmen. And the man who was entrusted with the task of mobilising tribesmen was Sheikh Mahboob Ali, the Political Agent in the Malakand Agency, who had engineered the violent attack on Nehru during his visit to the Frontier in September 1946. He was "behind the invasion of Kashmir by tribesman". The Chief Minister of the NWFP, Abdul Qaiyum Khan, was "encouraging the tribesmen to go into Kashmir and even collecting Frontier Scouts and militia transport for a tribal invasion."[47]

In India, Patel was moving fast to give Kashmir greater political stability. The first step in that direction was the proclamation of general amnesty by the Maharaja, who had the assurance of Patel in a letter of October 2nd: "I have no doubt that this would rally round you the men who might otherwise have been a thorn in your side. I can assure Your Highness of my abiding sympathy with you in your difficulties; nor need I disguise the instinctive responsibility I feel for ensuring the safety and integrity of your State."[48] The tribal invasion on October 20th gave Abdullah his opportunity to seek a foothold in the State Administration. It was Patel who made that possible. He alone could influence the Maharaja and his Prime Minister, not Nehru. He had long discussions with Abdullah in New Delhi, following which Patel pleaded with Mahajan in his letter of October 21st: "He seems to me genuinely anxious to cooperate and sincerely desirous of assisting the State... at the same time, as is natural, he feels that unless something is done and is done immediately to strengthen his hands... it would be impossible for him to do anything substantial. I myself feel that the position which Sheikh Abdullah takes up is understandable and reasonable... it is my sincere and earnest advice to you to make a substantial gesture to win Sheikh Abdullah's support."[49] As a result, it was decided to install an interim, popular government on the Mysore model. While Abdullah was to be the Prime Minister, Mahajan as one of the Ministers was to formally preside over the Cabinet meetings. Such an arrangement was to act as a brake on Abdullah's anti-Maharaja politics, as also to give the Dogras of Jammu a feeling of confidence and hope about their status in the future set-up.

It didn't work out as planned or hoped for. As soon as Abdullah assumed powers as Head of the Administration, he changed to his original colours and threw to the winds the understanding he had given both to the Maharaja and Patel. An anxious Mahajan wrote to Patel on November 22nd: "Sheikh Sahib, I suppose, is in no hurry about it (formation of interim Government), having got dictatorial powers, which are being exercised in a dictatorial manner, regardless of all rules and forms of law."[50] Abdullah's unexpected somersault turned Kashmir into a complicated affair, both internally and internationally. Responsibility for the former was Abdullah's; for the latter, Mountbatten's. It was Mountbatten's in two respects: first, committing India to a plebiscite in the State; and, secondly, making Nehru refer Kashmir to the UN Security Council. Mountbatten was giving effect to his offer of a plebiscite to Jinnah at his meeting with him in Lahore on November 1st, even when Jinnah told him that it was "redundant and undesirable... objected so strongly to a plebiscite". Mountbatten had gone to Lahore to discuss with Jinnah Kashmir, as also Junagadh and Hyderabad. He was, as he has admitted, "unbriefed and unauthorised" by the Government of India. The plebiscite proposal, he also admits in the note he wrote to Nehru on his return from Lahore, he had "drafted out in the aeroplane" while flying from New Delhi to Lahore, which "I had not yet shown to my Government but to which I thought they might agree."[51] This was no ordinary presumption, and of which Nehru's Cabinet colleague Ajit Prasad Jain complains, "Mountbatten did not have plenipotentiary powers on behalf of India, and he talked as an ex-Viceroy who had a major hand in partitioning the country." Besides, should Mountbatten have committed India on plebiscite when Jinnah had not welcomed the proposal?

Mountbatten had a purpose in going to Lahore, even without Nehru and Patel, but with Ismay who was known to have pro-Pakistani proclivities. Both were Britishers whose first duty was to serve the interests of their country—to see the continuance of Pakistan as a separate entity. The offer of a plebiscite was to appease Jinnah and mollify his pride, which had been hurt on the cancellation of his orders to Gracey to march troops into the Valley. Mountbatten sought to overcome Jinnah's deep-seated hatred of India by speaking to him "not as Governor-General of India but as the ex-Viceroy who had been responsible for Partition." Mountbatten asked Jinnah to appreciate that "Pakistan was in a much weaker position than India, not only from the obvious military point of view, but, I was sure, the world would think they were in the wrong"; and "war, whilst admittedly very harmful for India, would be completely disastrous for Pakistan and himself."[52]

Mountbatten's visit was the outcome of a British commitment: to save Pakistan from direct military confrontation with India. But actually it was a follow-up of Auchinleck's visit, when, in return for his cancellation of his orders to Gracey, Jinnah had agreed to Auchinleck's suggestion that "he (Jinnah) and his Prime Minister should meet Mountbatten, Nehru, the Maharaja of Kashmir and his Prime Minister at a round-table conference to try to find a way out of the present dangerous situation." Auchinleck had, thus, "prevented the outbreak of a war between India and Pakistan. Mountbatten was eager to act upon the initiative put into his hand by Auchinleck."[53]

Even though Auchinleck had sidelined Patel, Mountbatten realised his indispensability. He was only too keen to take him to Lahore along with Nehru, so as to ensure acceptability of his proposals. Nehru could not accompany him because of his sudden illness. Patel refused point-blank. According to Hodson, Patel thought that "Pakistan being the aggressor, such a visitation would smack of Munich and imply an admission of guilt." Cynically did he remark: "For the Prime Minister to go crawling to Jinnah, when we were the stronger side and in the right, would never be forgiven by the people of India."[54] According to Auchinleck's biographer, John Connell, prior to Mountbatten's departure for Lahore, there was "strong resistance to the whole idea" (of his visit) at the Cabinet meeting held on the afternoon of October 28th, when "comparisons were made with Neville Chamberlain's visit to Hitler at Godesberg in 1938. Vallabhbhai Patel, in particular, made this opposition clear to the Governor-General."[55] If Mountbatten still preferred to go to Lahore on November 1st, it was on the strength of Nehru's support.

Patel was opposed to any more appeasement of Jinnah, as it would further boost his ego and make him grow still haughtier and overbearing. And at Lahore, Mountbatten had found Jinnah just that: "unstatemanlike, inept and bad mannered." Mountbatten was bombarded with invectives against India, and he had to be on the defensive throughout. Patel wouldn't have stood such insolence, and there would have been a clash of two strong-willed personalities, aggravating thereby the already deteriorating relations between the two countries. But, Patel, as he had realised, would have had the disadvantage of being in Jinnah's "court" as a plaintiff. Many, therefore, have wondered why Mountbatten should have gone to Lahore alone? Couldn't he have postponed the visit till Nehru recovered? But from the British point of view, Mountbatten's visit had to be on the heels of Auchinleck's efforts to placate Jinnah; and Ismay's attempt on November 1st "to cheer him up out of his depression."[56] However, Nehru stood by Mountbatten by making "a big broadcast" offering a UN-controlled plebiscite in Kashmir.

Reference to the UNO sucked India into the vortex of international politics. It turned Kashmir into an intractable problem and a pawn in the hands of world powers. Mountbatten's haste avoided prior consultation with Patel, who happened to be on a short tour of Assam and returned to New Delhi two days after the reference had been made. Had Mountbatten and Nehru waited, Patel, they feared, would have come in Mountbatten's way, as he had earlier in the case of Junagadh when Patel did not allow a reference to be made to the UNO. As if to fulfil a formality, Nehru wrote to Patel on January 7th, 1948: "During your absence, the Kashmir situation, more specially in regard to the reference to the UNO, had developed, and we have had to take a number of decisions. We have missed you here because your advice would have been valuable, but we could not afford to postpone our decisions owing to the urgency of the matter." Patel was outspoken in his reply: "Perhaps any comment from me at this stage, when part of the delegation has already left and arrangements for others have already been made, is unnecessary... but the delegation has grown unwieldy and I feel that the inclusion of Sheikh Abdullah in the delegation might lead to some complication."[57]

Campbell-Johnson thought that "Sheikh Abdullah's flamboyant personality might easily 'swamp the boat'."[58] Patel's unofficial comment on India's going to the UN, however, was, "Even a District Court pleader will not go as a complainant."[59] India was rushing to the "court", not the aggressor; and she was to regret her well-intentioned action later when the UNO treated the plaintiff and the aggressor alike. With an oblique reference to the role of Mountbatten, Ismay and some others, Patel expressed his views to Arthur Henderson, British Under Secretary of States, though much later: "Unfortunately, it is my experience that the attitude of an average Englishman in India is instinctively against us... we should never have gone to the UNO... at the UNO, not only has the dispute been prolonged but the merits of our case have been completely lost in the interaction of power politics... we were so terribly disappointed at the attitude of your delegation... it was, we maintain, the attitude of Noel Baker that tilted the balance against us. But for his lead, I doubt if the USA and some other powers would have gone against us."[60]

It did not take long for Nehru to come round to Patel's view, and to realise that India had committed a great mistake by taking an irreversible step. The situation could have been avoided, had Nehru adhered to Patel's Junagadh policy. He confessed in the first week of January 1948 that the Kashmir issue "has been raised to an international level by our reference to the Security Council of the UN and most of the great powers are intensely interested in what happens in Kashmir."[61] A month later Nehru admitted that the Kashmir issue "has given us a great deal of trouble... the attitude of the great powers has been astonishing. Some of them have shown active partisanship for Pakistan."[62] In May he again said, "We feel that we have not been given a square deal."[63] *The Times*, London, quoted Patel's long-held contemptuous view of the Security Council, "an insecurity Council and a disturber of the peace."[64]

Apart from Abdullah, Patel did not consider a wise choice the appointment of Gopalaswami Ayyangar as leader of the Indian delegation. At best a good bureaucrat, he and the demagogue in Abdullah put up a petitioner's poor show: they did not make a forceful presentation, but simply moaned. Patel had suggested C.P. Ramaswami Iyer's name, because he was an intellectual, a statesman and a diplomat with many foreign contacts, especially in the USA and the UK. He would have been more than a match for Zafrullah, Pakistan's representative, who, on hearing Ayyangar's appointment, cynically remarked, "You are offering me Kashmir on a platter!"

That was a mere dig at India. But real trouble began at home with Abdullah's success in making Nehru take away Kashmir from Patel's charge. He achieved this by driving a wedge between Nehru and Patel. The incident that sparked a bitter controversy between the two related to a transaction of Rs.20 lakhs, which Patel complained to Ayyangar, was "put through by the Prime Minister's Secretariat with Sheikh Abdullah, without the Ministry concerned coming to know of it until at a late stage." Patel pointed out that "the Ministry of States has its own Financial Adviser, and, therefore, it makes it all the more incumbent that a transaction involving any financial commitment, either on the part of a State or of ourselves, should be centered in the Ministry of States." Ayyangar had already admitted to Patel that "strict official correctness would require the course suggested by you" and that he was acting "merely as a post office". Nehru lost his patience and temper, and he wrote to Patel: "The present issue relates to Kashmir. This raises all manner of connected issues—international, military and others—which are beyond the competence of the States Ministry as such... All this was done at my instance, and I do not propose to abdicate my functions in regard to matters for which I consider myself responsible."

In taking away Kashmir from the States Ministry and placing it under the charge of Ayyangar who was Minister without Portfolio, Nehru was acting under Abdullah's influence. To all intents and purposes, he was discarding Patel for Abdullah, ignoring how Patel had stood by his side both as a loyal friend and as a pillar of strength through the tempestuous, nerve-wracking, fateful months preceding and following the transfer of power. This was especially so in two respects: Nehru's returning from the London conference with Attlee in December 1946 as "a broken reed", completely dispirited; and Patel's significant role in securing Kashmir's accession to India. Nehru's action was an affront to Patel. He wrote back: "Your letter of today (December 23, 1947) has been received just now at 7 p.m. and I am writing immediately to tell you that it has caused me considerable pain... your letter makes it clear to me that I must not, or at least cannot, continue as a member of Government, and, hence, I am hereby tendering my resignation."[65] The letter does not seem to have been delivered, presumably at Gandhi's intervention. But Mountbatten himself would not have allowed Patel to leave the Government, as he had acted in a similar situation later in January 1948.

Having cleared the decks, Abdullah was now poised for his next assault: to send the Maharaja into exile, which he achieved with remarkable ease and speed with Nehru's help. The new arrangement placed Abdullah beyond Patel's reach. And Patel thus became a helpless spectator of the morbid drama in Kashmir, of which Nehru himself became a victim in 1953 when Abdullah challenged Nehru's authority and conspired to become Sultan-e-Kashmir. Ironically, for Abdullah's sake, Nehru had denied the Maharaja just treatment, which he deserved especially in view of fair treatment being meted out to the Muslim rulers of Bhopal and Hyderabad, who had played an anti-Indian role. However, before the Maharaja's abdication, Abdullah secured the exit of Mahajan from Diwanship, so as to weaken the position of the Maharaja by denying him the support of a trusted legal adviser.

Nehru lent support to Abdullah by inveighing against the Maharaja in his letter of December 30th to Patel: "The Maharaja, unfortunately, is terribly shortsighted and has a way of doing the wrong thing... I fear he will get into great trouble if he does not appreciate the present situation and act accordingly."[66] Pained by Nehru's attitude, the Maharaja wrote to Patel on January 25th: "I have been perusing with some interest the proceedings that are taking place before the Security Council... Unfortunately, I have been more or less ignored in this matter. It should not be forgotten that the matter of accession is either for me, or, according to the view of the Government of India, for me and my people. It is not a matter either for the Government of India's or for the Pakistan Government's decision. To which Dominion the State should accede... I alone am the authority to decide."[67] Nehru mistakenly inferred from it the Maharaja's intention to cancel the accession, failing to appreciate that the Maharaja had abdicated his right to do so, having signed the Instrument of Accession.

Developments in Kashmir were alarming, Rising above personal discouragements, and even affronts, Patel served the interest of the country by playing the role of an honest broker: to bring about stability and harmony in the State through reconciliation between Abdullah and the Maharaja. It was easier for him to handle the Maharaja, but not so Abdullah. His fears proved true when Abdullah was explosive at a press conference on September 29th, of which Patel complained to Nehru, "We, the Maharaja and Sheikh Abdullah himself came to a settlement last March (1948). That settlement has not only been faithfully adhered to by the Maharaja, but in certain respects he has acquiesced in departures from the settlement to the advantage of Sheikh Abdullah." Patel further pointed out, "I am not aware of any single instance... in which the Maharaja has obstructed or resisted any of the popular reforms. As a constitutional head, he may have asked for reconsideration in one or two matters, but this could hardly be treated as the subject of a grievance. It is undignified and constitutionally improper for a Prime Minister (Abdullah) to attack the constitutional head of his administration, knowing full well that the latter is not in a position to defend himself or to retaliate. On top of it, to insinuate that he is trying to retain power, or that he has strong friends in India, or that he could buy friends, is, in my opinion, to say the least, most unfortunate."[68]

Patel also wrote to Abdullah the same day in an effort to bring him to the path of reasonableness: "I had hoped... with practically no resistance or obstruction from the Maharaja in regard to the many schemes of reforms which you have introduced and are introducing, you would now accommodate yourself to your new constitutional relationship with him. I had never imagined that you would ventilate your grievance in public, and I had thought that at least in fairness to ourselves and, having regard to the agreed arrangements between ourselves, if you had any grievance, you would first come to the States Ministry and seek a satisfactory solution through our medium." Patel argued with Abdullah, "No one knows better than you that today the Maharaja is powerless to resist your wishes. Even if he feels inclined differently, on merits he has to endorse your wishes if you pressed them. It is within my knowledge that he has deferred to your wishes in matters which concerned him intimately... I am, therefore, unable to comprehend your reference to his trying to retain power."

Patel even wrote to Ayyangar: "I myself feel bitterly that, after all that we have done for him (Abdullah) and the sympathy and understanding which we have extended to him, he should have indulged in such direct and unbecoming attacks on the Maharaja, who, he knew, would be unable to hit back..." Ayyangar admitted to Patel, "...I had been told orally by persons who had been present there (at Abdullah's press conference) of a good deal that he had said but had not appeared in the newspapers. What was not reported in the papers, I gathered, was even more unjustifiable than what did appear." In his letter to Patel, Nehru admitted: "I entirely agree with you that some of the statements that Sheikh Abdullah made in regard to the Maharaja were very indiscreet and should not have been made." Yet, he held a brief on his behalf: "Sheikh Abdullah is, I am convinced, a very straight and frank man. He is not a very clear thinker and he goes astray in his speech as many of our politicians do. He is, of course, obsessed with the idea of meeting the challenge of Pakistan and keeping his own people from being influenced by Pakistan's propaganda."[69]

By the first week of October 1948, Abdullah had grown so bold as to become "a law unto himself"; and he demanded, "... the choice is finally between the Maharaja and the people, and if the choice is not soon made, it might lead us into very serious trouble, both militarily and politically. The only alternative is that His Highness should abdicate in favour of his son."[70] Patel minced no words in reminding Abdullah. "You seem to be in the peculiar position of having been misunderstood, apart from many others, by all the three of us—Jawaharlal, Gopalaswami and myself. Jawaharlal has written to me and, I believe, spoken to you also, taking exception to your attitude at the press conference. Similarly, Gopalaswami has done the same and spoke to you the very next day... There is no disposition on your part either to understand our point of view or to strike a new line as demanded by the changed situation. I am quite convinced that the grossly prejudiced view which you have taken of the matters referred to is not likely to mend matters; instead, it is likely to make them worse and more complicated." Patel further told Abdullah, "You do not seem to realise that both you and we ourselves owe the technical correctness of our position in regard to Kashmir to the Maharaja's signing the Accession and his calling upon you to form the Ministry. Without that, neither we nor you would have been where we are... I am also surprised that you, who had a different attitude towards His Highness when you were in jail, as is typified in your letter to him, a copy of which is with me, should now speak in such terms of him."[71]

Such advice cut no ice with Abdullah. He continued to be high-handed: uncompromising, overbearing, dictatorial. He could do so, as he knew Nehru would not let him down because of his hatred for the Maharaja. Patel failed to save the Maharaja, as Nehru ultimately came round to Abdullah's view which he expressed in his letter of April 17, 1949 to Patel: "… it was highly desirable that the Maharaja should take some kind of leave and not remain in Kashmir."[72] In glaring contrast, Abdullah was growing bolder with his despotic utterances. In an interview with Michael Davidson, of *The Scotsman,* he said, "Accession to either side cannot bring peace. We want to live in friendship with both Dominions. Perhaps a middle path between them… an independent Kashmir must be guaranteed not only by India and Pakistan, but also by Britain, the United States and other members of the United Nations." Ayyangar complained to Patel, "…reading between the lines, I suspect a plan, the first step of which is this blessing by the Premier of Kashmir of the idea of an independent Kashmir, and this public expression of his conviction that accession to India will not bring peace, and the final step of which may well be perhaps one of the greatest betrayals of history."

Patel was simply complying with Nehru's wishes when he undertook the painful task of the Maharaja leaving the State on April 29th, about which he wrote to Nehru on May 11th: "… I explained to him the whole position and commended to him my view that, in the circumstances of his relations with the Ministry and the situation created by the reference to the UNO and the plebiscite issue, it should be best for him to absent himself from the State for some time and to make the Yuvraj Regent." Nehru added further poignancy to the Maharaja's "sense of shock and bewilderment" by suggesting to Patel, "I do not think any period should be fixed for the Maharaja's absence from Kashmir. The matter had better be left vague." The Maharaja could not help telling Patel, "I would not be human if I did not express my sense of keen disappointment and bewilderment at having been called upon to make such a sacrifice of personal prestige, honour and position... while Sheikh Abdullah has been allowed to depart, from time to time as suited his inclinations, from the pledged and written word, to act consistently in breach of the loyalty which he professed to me prior to his release from jail and the oath of allegiance which he took when he assumed office, and to indulge openly along with his colleagues in a campaign of vilification and foul calumny against me, both inside the State and outside, I should have had to be driven from position to position—each of which I thought I held on the advice of the States Ministry."[73]

Thus was paved the way for the Maharaja's exile from the State. He left in May, never to return. Around August, B.N. Mullik, Director, Central Bureau of Intelligence, spent ten days in the Valley and wrote his assessment of the situation. Patel totally disagreed with him. According to Mullik, "He suspected that the Sheikh was not genuine and was misleading Pandit Nehru... He apprehended that Sheikh Abdullah would ultimately let down India and Jawaharlal Nehru, and would come out in his real colours... Events, as they turned out subsequently, proved that the Sardar was right and I was not. Within three years, we found ourselves fighting against Sheikh Abdullah. Sardar Patel was dead by then... Probably, things would not have come to this pass at all if the Sardar was still alive, because Sheikh Abdullah had a very wholesome respect and fear of him."[74]

Patel was officiating for Nehru during the latter's absence in Europe in October-November 1948, when the Constituent Assembly debated some amendments to Article 370. Abdullah could not contain his anger over the Assembly's right to do so. To him, Article 370 was to be "an executive act of the Government of India as distinguished from Parliament", to "exclude altogether the Parliament of India from having any say regarding the Constitution of Jammu and Kashmir"; and that only the State Assembly could "revise or annul any action taken by the Government of India".[75] In that burning anger, Abdullah cast aside the respect the House commanded of each member and

Sardar Patel

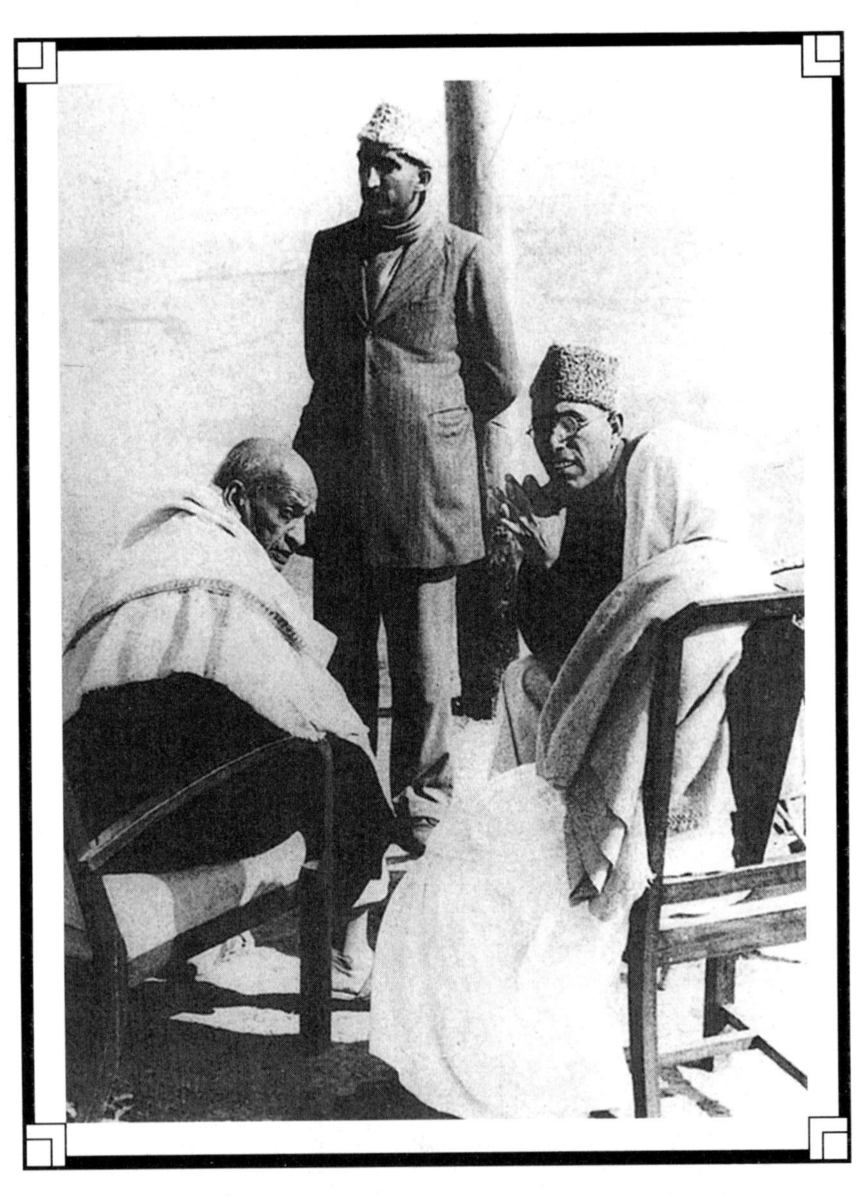

The saviour of Kashmir with Sheikh Abdullah, Bakshi Ghulam Mohammad and Manibehn Patel at Srinagar airport on November 4, 1947. This visit turned the tide in India's favour

(top) President Rajendra Prasad flanked by Prime Minister Nehru on his left and Deputy Minister Patel on his right
(below) Sardar with General Cariappa, the first Indian C-in-C

First Cabinet with Lord Mountbatten.
L to R: Dr. John Mathai, Rafi Ahmed Kidwai, Sardar Baldev Singh, Jawaharlal Nehru, Lord Mountbatten, Sardar Patel, Maulana Abul Kalam Azad, Jagjivan Ram, Rajkumari Amrit Kaur
Standing L to R: R.K. Shanmukham Chetty, Jairamdas Doulatram, K.C. Neogy, Syama Prasad Mookerjee, B.R. Ambedkar, N.V. Gadgil, Gopalaswami Ayyanagar, Mohanlal Saxena

Partition Council Meeting:
L to R: (clockwise) Sardar Baldev Singh (Akali); Kripalani, Sardar and Nehru (Congress); Mountbatten; Jinnah and Nishtar (Muslim League)

At Birla House, New Delhi, Sardar with
(L to R) Dr Rajendra Prasad Abdul Ghaffar Khan, Sarojini Naidu,
Kripalani and Manibehn

IAS Probationers
(1948 batch) with
Sardar Patel

With Rajaji and Manibehn Patel

AIR

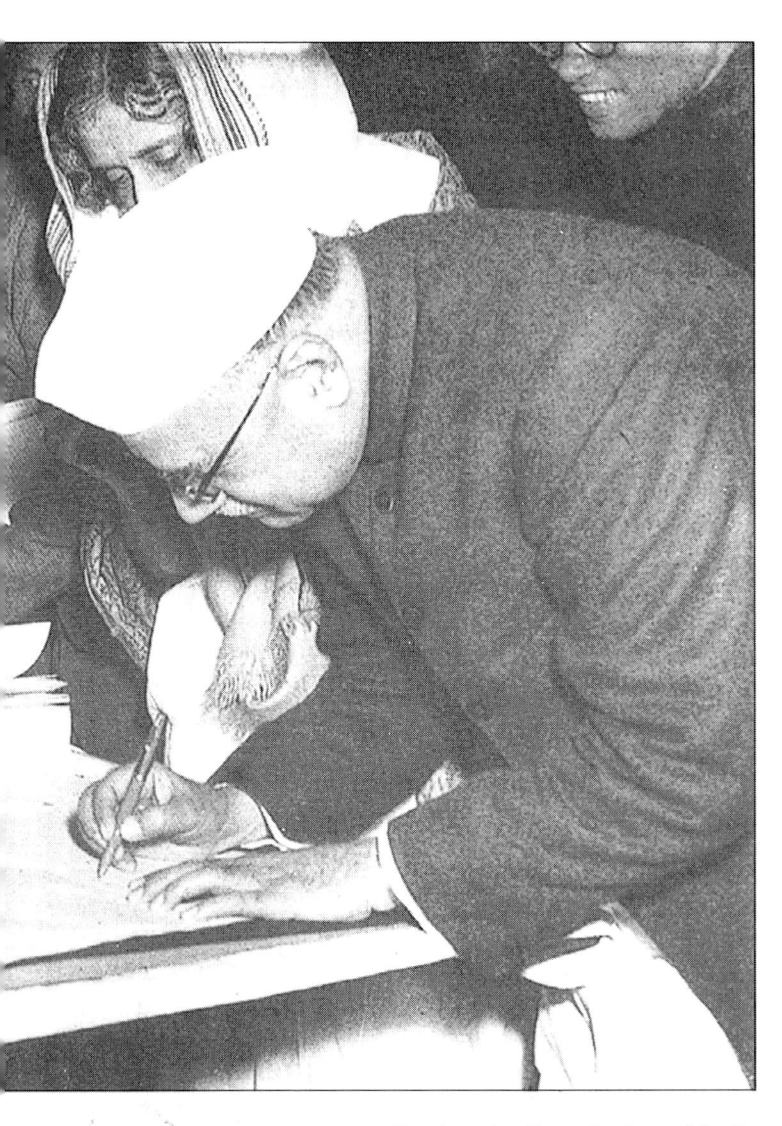

Signing the Constitution of India
on January 24, 1950

(opposite page) Sardar's broadcast to the nation
on March 14, 1949

(top) A proud mother with her five sons:
(L to R) Vithalbhai, Somabhai, Narsibhai, Vallabhbhai. *(standing)* Kashibhai
(below) Addressing the final session of the Constituent Assembly
on January 24, 1950

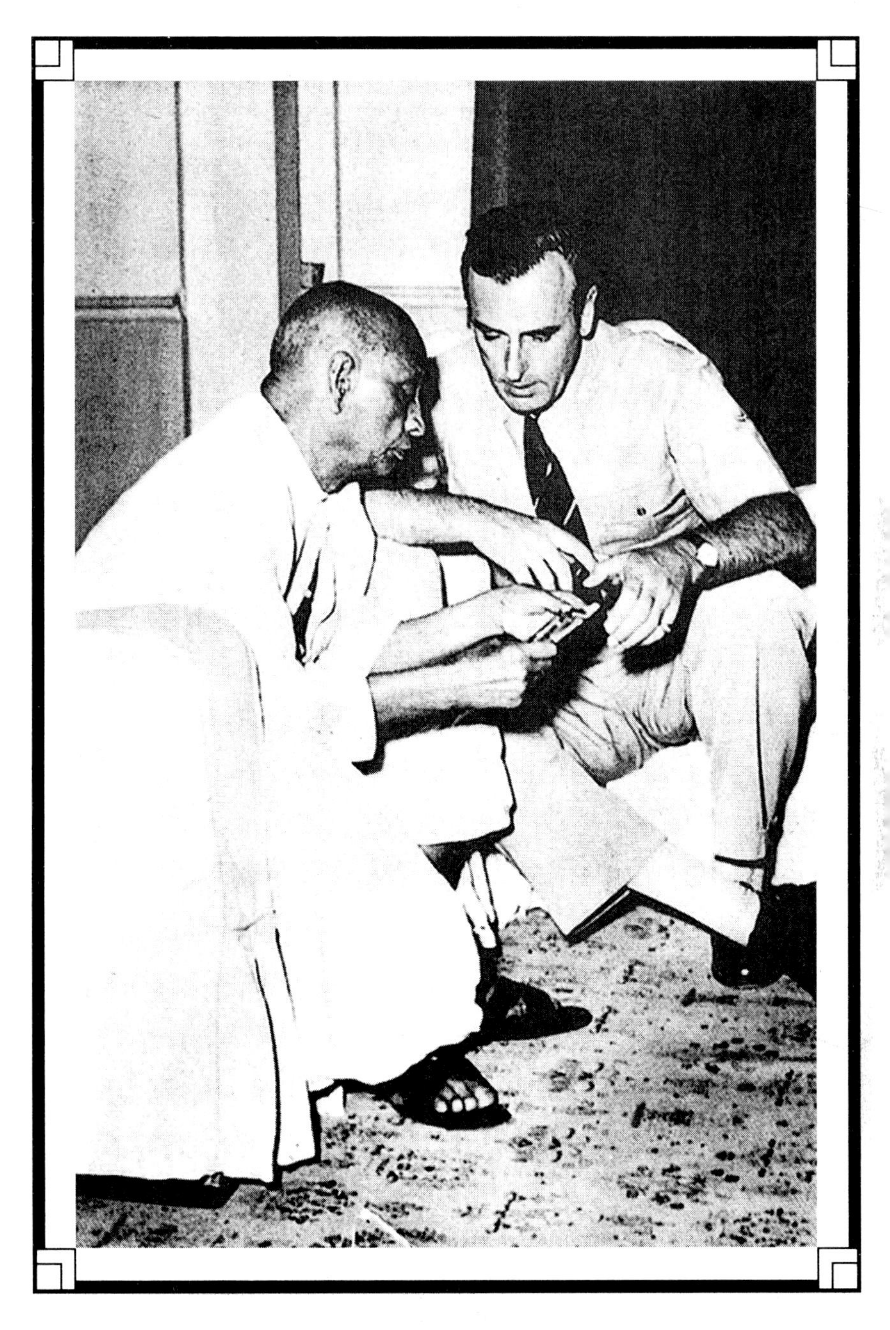

Mountbatten's parting visit to Sardar at Dehra Dun, June 1948

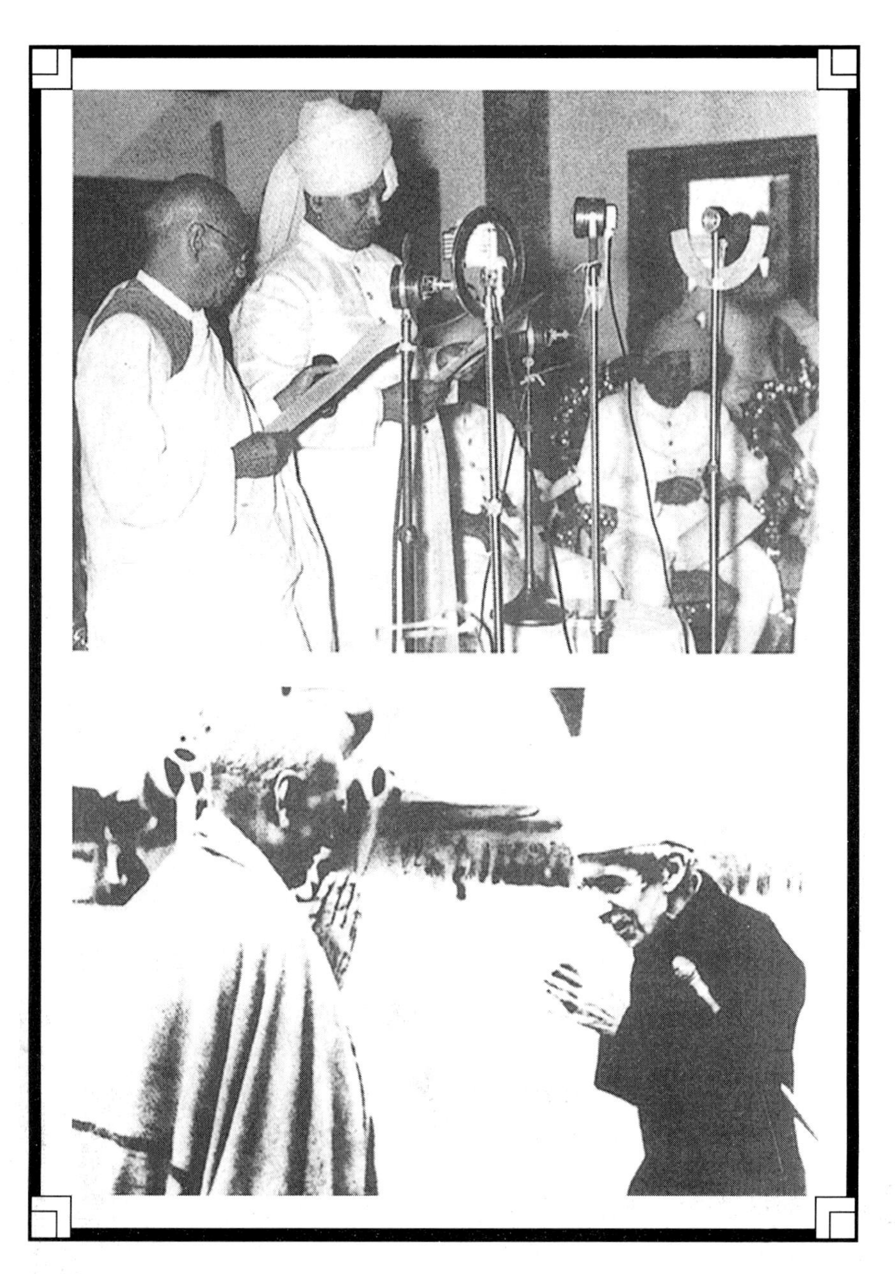

(top) Sardar administering oath of office to the Jamsaheb of Nawanagar as Rajpramukh of the United State of Kathiawar
(below) The Nizam of Hyderabad welcoming the Sardar at the Begumpet airport, an honour which he seldom extended to others

Patel administering the oath to the Maharaja of Jaipur on his being sworn in as the Rajpramukh of Greater Rajasthan

With members of his family on his 74th birthday

(top) President Rajendra Prasad carrying the urn containing Sardar's ashes for immersion in the Ganga at Allahabad. Also seen is U.P. Chief Minister, Govind Ballabh Pant

(below) The final journey, 1950

walked out in protest with the threat that he was going back to Kashmir. It was a virtual boycott. Patel could not take up cudgels with Abdullah, as the debate was on. Later he sent Mahavir Tyagi to the railway station to deliver a stern message. Abdullah had settled down in his compartment when Tyagi stepped in to tell him, "Sheikh Sahib, the Sardar says you could leave the House, but you cannot leave Delhi."[76] A speechless Abdullah got down from the train, cancelling his departure.

Evidently, Patel alone, not Nehru, could strike such fear in Abdullah; and he alone could have tamed the "Lion of Kashmir", if he so desired. But he did not. He preferred to ignore, with apparent unconcern, Abdullah's arrogance, high-handedness and self-righteousness; he even reluctantly accepted Abdullah's anti-Indian outbursts—only registered his protests with Ayyangar so as to quieten his troubled conscience. All this was not without reason. The unceremonious manner in which Kashmir had been taken away from his charge had caused him considerable sorrow and pain. As a result, he had adopted a bystander's attitude, though offering help whenever called upon and he rendered such help as a matter of duty to the country. He avoided a direct clash with Nehru for two reasons: Nehru's sentimental love for Kashmir; to ensure his own freedom in handling Hyderabad. He, therefore, witnessed with acute sorrow Abdullah's high-handedness in getting rid of the Maharaja's Prime Minister and Constitutional Adviser, Mehr Chand Mahajan; and; thereafter, sending the Maharaja himself into an indefinite exile. Both were with Nehru's support, no matter if they lacked constitutional validity.

What mattered most to India was Article 370. Its genesis lay in Nehru's agreeing to Abdullah's having a separate Constitution for the State. Even President Rajendra Prasad was "taken back"[77] when Abdullah conveyed to him Nehru's acceptance of such a proposal. A day or two prior to Nehru's departure for Europe, Abdullah arrived in New Delhi for its implementation. Nehru entrusted the drafting of the Article to Munshi, Ayyangar and Abdullah. According to Munshi, "Abdullah was unhappy with the Article we drafted, and though he was scheduled to support the Article before the Constituent Assembly", Munshi feared he might absent himself from the proceedings.[78] Instead, Abdullah chose to lodge his protest in person with a walkout.

On his part, Nehru left India at a very crucial moment without settling the confusion and bitterness the Article caused then, and without foreseeing that soon it would turn into a festering sore. However, Nehru left a most difficult task in the hands of Ayyangar: to get it adopted by the Constituent Assembly. Prior to that, the Article had to have the approval of the Congress parliamentary party. At the party meeting, the issue raised "a storm of angry protests from all sides and Gopalaswami found himself a lone defender, with Maulana Azad an ineffective supporter."[79] Ayyangar got so unnerved that he appealed to Patel "to come to his rescue." Patel's magnanimity prevailed upon him to save an ugly situation from getting out of hand. With least difficulty he got the party's approval the very next day, and thus paved the way for its presentation to the Constituent Assembly. He, however, told Ayyangar the bitter truth which others feared to utter in public: "Whenever Sheikh Sahib wishes to back out, he always confronts us with his duty to people. Of course, he owes no duty to India or to the Indian Government, or even on a personal basis to you and the Prime Minister who had gone all out to accommodate him." After Nehru's death, Abdullah had no qualms even to state: "We shall not hesitate to secede from India if we are not assured a place of honour and dignity in terms of the safeguards provided for the people of the State under Article 370 of the Constitution."[80]

Nehru had himself come round to Patel's view later in 1962, when he told Mullik of Abdullah's "communal activities throughout the period he had acted as the National Conference leader. It was the Pakistani aggression which had mellowed him a little for a short time, because the tribals had committed gruesome atrocities on the Muslim population in the Valley. But, as soon as he became Prime Minister, he came out in his true colours once again and started his anti-Hindu activities... his entire outlook and behaviour was based on the fact that the Kashmir Valley had a Muslim majority."[81]

Patel also proved vindicated both in regard to the reference to the UNO and the plebiscite issue. Ayyangar admitted to Patel in his letter of June 5, 1948: "The ways of the Security Council have been extraordinary, and in dealing with the Kashmir question, it has behaved in a manner which has surprised even a person like me... As you say, we have entangled ourselves with a set of persons who will not see things straight..."[82] Even Nehru, in a letter of October 27th to Patel from Paris, lamented over foreigners' attitude towards Kashmir: "...this business of a plebiscite and the conditions governing it, fills people's minds. Of course people cannot get rid of the idea that Kashmir is predominantly Muslim and, therefore, likely to side with Muslim Pakistan."[83] In August 1949, when the American Ambassador and the British High Commissioner wanted to see Nehru with a view to persuading him to accept arbitration by Admiral Nimitz of the UN Kashmir Commission, Nehru confessed to Patel: "All this barrage is, I suppose, meant to sweep us away."[84] Nehru further veered round to Patel's original view when in July 1950, five months before Patel's death, he admitted to him that in the circumstances prevailing in Kashmir and "in the world situation today... a plebiscite is unreal."

What would have been the fate of Kashmir under Patel? This has been speculated by, among others, Jayaprakash Narayan and M.N. Roy—one a Socialist, the other a Communist; but both pro-Nehru and inveterate opponents of Patel. Narayan thought that the Kashmir issue, being left to Nehru, "proved to be unfortunate for the nation. Because of Panditji's mishandling, the issue did no longer remain an internal affair, as it should be, but is smouldering as an international issue in the United Nations and its Security Council, making it possible for Pakistan to rake it up every now and then. Many a veteran leader in the country maintains that had the matter been handled by the Sardar (and it fell within his domain), he would have found a satisfactory solution, and thus prevented its becoming a perennial headache for us and a cause of bitterness and animosity between India and Pakistan."[85] H.V. Kamath, MP, says that Patel once told him that "if Jawaharlal and Gopalaswami (Ayyangar) had not made Kashmir their close preserve, separating it from my portfolio of Home and States, he would have tackled the problem as purposefully as he had already done in Hyderabad."[86]

Patel did not believe in carrying the Kashmir operations half way through. He would have preferred the Indian Army not to halt at Uri, but to advance beyond—possibly up to Muzaffarabad. General S.P.P. Thorat confirms that "our forces might have succeeded in evicting the invaders, if the Prime Minister (Nehru) had not held them in check and later ordered the cease-fire... obviously, great pressures must have been brought to bear on him by the Governor-General... Panditji was a great personal and family friend of Lord Mountbatten."[87] Capture of Domel and Muzaffarabad, which Nehru later considered of "primary importance", could have been possible only if the Indian Air Force had carried the war further afield and bombarded the bases from which the reinforcements came. Mountbatten wouldn't let that happen, while Patel couldn't force his way as he could in Junagadh earlier and in Hyderabad later.

One, however, gets an indication of Patel's mind while he was acting as Prime Minister. He sent for Air Marshal Thomas Elmhirst, Chairman of the Chiefs of Staff Committee, with whom he wanted "to discuss a point relating to the Kashmir war". Elmhirst writes: "He was not well, and the meeting was in the sitting-room of his home, and we were alone. He said something to this effect, 'If all the decisions rested on me, I think that I would be in favour of extending this little affair in Kashmir to a full-scale war with Pakistan... let us get it over once and for all, and settle down as a united continent'." According to Elmhirst, Patel was "obviously a man of action, of few words, frank, straightforward and unequivocal... whose intelligence, firmness and strength of character I much admired."[88]

M.N. Roy's speculation over Patel's attitude towards Kashmir was: "...I am inclined to believe that it was as realistic as his attitude towards Partition. Nevertheless, once the die was cast by the gambler's megalomania, the Sardar had no choice but to play the game. But one could be sure that he loathes the stupidity clothed in the glamour of popular heroes."[89] What would have been Patel's attitude? An attempt has been made to find out an answer in the Postscript.

h) GREATER RAJASTHAN

The whole of Rajasthan brimmed over with centuries-old ancestral pride on March 30, 1949 when Patel inaugurated at Jaipur the Union of Greater Rajasthan—almost as large as Italy, comprising 14 States with a combined population of over 15 million and an area of more than 128,000 square miles. Patel evoked such pride, in particular among the Rajput Princes and nobles—resplendent in their rich brocades, conspicuous in their manly beards and multi-coloured turbans and Jodhpuris—assembled to hear him state, "What we have achieved today is merely the fulfillment of the desires and aspirations of Maharana Pratap."[1] Patel's tribute to Pratap took in one sweep the proud Rajputs back three and a half centuries and reminded them not only of the nationalist fervor that coursed through the veins of Pratap, who fought the Mughals till death for the freedom of his motherland, but also of the circumstances under which some quislings from among the brave Rajputs had surrendered to Akbar, body and soul.

It was a reminder of how Akbar's Empire was "the outcome of the coordination of Mughal prowess and diplomacy and Rajput valour and service."[2] Prior to fighting Pratap, Akbar had secured the submission of Jaipur, Bikaner and Jaisalmer and the services of able Rajput generals like Man Singh. And it was diplomatic of him to have cemented his relationship with the Rajputs through marriage alliances. History seemed to be repeating itself, though somewhat differently, in 1947. Akbar's realism that his Empire could not be built without the subjugation of the Rajputs appeared to have been the motive for Jinnah's designs on Rajasthan and Kathiawar through his manoeuvres to secure the accession of

Jodhpur and Jaisalmer in Rajasthan and Junagadh in Kathiawar. Patel defeated all such moves, and even put to an end to fissiparous tendencies and internal feuding among the Rajput Princes and Kathiawar Rulers. In Greater Rajasthan he was proud to have "achieved a unity most unknown in the past recorded history."[3] Patel was equally proud to say in his speech at Jaipur that with the union of Rajput States, Indian unity "can now be said to be complete."

The forces arrayed against Patel were formidable. Rajasthan was not merely a jigsaw puzzle of many Rajput States which could discourage anyone, but it was also like steel armour, not so easily penetrable. Glorifying in their ivory-tower aloofness, the highly sensitive Princes were too proud of their status, privileges, ancestry, territories and, no less, the number of guns the British had conferred upon them to be fired in their honour on ceremonial occasions. They did not concern themselves with the reality that all that they enjoyed was in name only—under the watchful eye of the Resident and at his pleasure; and the regal splendour was permitted by the British to feed their ego. Rajasthan, therefore, required careful handling; and Patel believed that "any word or action there affected the entire region." The ruling class, the Rajputs and the Muslims were "considerably agitated." A procession in Jaipur "openly indulged in anti-Congress and anti-Indian slogans." Jodhpur "was no better". Patel, therefore, proceeded slowly, playing cool and showing imperturbable and almost inexhaustible patience in his handling of the Rajasthan Princes. Wisely he aimed at promoting friendliness rather then arousing opposition and enmity with them, or amongst them. Patel's policy in this "strategically important region" lay in his belief: "It would be best to avoid upsetting the feudatory element. That element can be tackled by us as soon as possible when the proper time comes and things are ripe."[4]

Between the States' accession by August 15th, 1947 and the formation of the Union of Greater Rajasthan in March 1949, Patel waited for more than nineteen months for implementing Pratap's dream. It was a patient wait. The task was complex, delicate, difficult and could prove explosive. The highly sensitive pride of the Rajput rulers was their steel armour. Patel could penetrate it only through political manoeuvring, which required two prerequisites: first, integration of the neighbouring small Rajput States so as to break the back of the bigger ones; and, second, since the Rajput States were like a hornet's nest, Patel wanted to put his finger into it only when the wasps had lost their sting, and their aggressiveness was diluted. He expected opposition mostly from Bikaner, Jaipur and Jodhpur, and not from Udaipur whose ancestor was Maharana Pratap. Patel, therefore, according to Thakur Jaswant Singh, once Prime Minister of Bikaner and a close relation of the Maharaja, proceeded diplomatically to "cut through the complex but delicate tangle without a violent shake-up which would have harmed India as much as the Princes."[5]

Jaswant Singh, who had closely watched the emergence of the new politico-geographical pattern of States in Rajasthan from Bikaner, his home State, further explains Patel's strategy: "The mastermind that he was, Sardar Patel looked for the earliest opportunity to achieve his objective." Such an opportunity came to him on its own with Gandhi's assassination, "when rumours of Alwar's and Scindia's complicity in the crime were in the air." Patel did not hesitate to strike; if he succeeded, it was because of not only his boldness but also because time seemed to be on his side. Both the rulers had been badly shaken by the prevailing hostile opinion among their subjects, even when they had no direct involvement. Both rushed to Delhi to clear their position with Patel. While Scindia "complied with whatever the Sardar wanted", Alwar was ordered to stay on in the capital till the inquiry was completed. It was this surrender that made Patel's task easier—the formation of the United States of Matsya on March 17, 1948 comprising Alwar, Bharatpur, Dholpur and Karuali. By this Patel "killed the nefarious designs the jats and Rajputs from these States, particularly Alwar and Bharatpur, seemed to be hatching." Thereafter, Patel proceeded with the integration of the Maratha States of Gwalior, Indore and Malwa in Madhya Bharat, to be followed by the Rajasthan Union comprising smaller States of Kotah, Banswara, Bundi, Dungarpur, Jhalawar, Pratapgarh, Shahpura, Tonk and Kishengarh.

The importance and prestige of the Rajasthan Union considerably increased with the Maharana of Udaipur joining it and being appointed its Rajpramukh. In February 1948, the United State of Kathiawar had been inaugurated, and in July was formed the predominantly Sikh Patiala and East Punjab States Union. With the formation of these new unions, Patel "achieved a sort of encirclement of the States of Bikaner, Jaipur and Jodhpur, which were holding out from any union."[6]

Such "encirclement" was the outcome of the onrush of events let loose in the wake of Britain's early withdrawal from India. Patel rose to the occasion and proved himself a skilful navigator who steered the Indian ship through a raging storm to safe anchorage. The storm did not settle down with Independence on August 15th but continued thereafter. Many States looked for opportunity to take advantage of situations favourable to them. Alwar in particular was bellicose till Gandhi's assassination. Mountbatten sought a way out. "With the willing concurrence of Patel," he addressed a group of Princes in the first week of January 1948, at which "Alwar alone saw fit to remonstrate" According to Campbell-Johnson: "In a high-pitched and querulous voice, he observed: 'If the people wish to live in hell, one should not compel them to live in paradise.' When Mountbatten was trying patiently to explain the advantages to the Princes and their families entering the Indian Union Diplomatic Service, Alwar interrupted him to say: "This should not be a favour. If Menon can be States Secretary, why not Bikaner?" Mountbatten replied sharply, "I am not here dispensing favours, I am just trying to make common sense of the situation".[7] Even thereafter Alwar continued with his tantrums. On one occasion he likened his position as ruler to that of "an ant stuck up in a lump of jaggery, prepared to lose its legs and arms, even its life, in the effort to resist attempts to dislodge it from the source of sweetness and sustenance."[8] Bertland Glancy, the head of the Political Department, once, observed: "...Harvey (the Chief Minister) was to the Maharaja of Alwar like a red bag to the bull..."[9] The Chanakya in Patel understood well the Princes' mentality and bent them to his will, but his paternalism was far gentle and humane.

Patel felt much distressed over the news that Gandhi's assassination had been celebrated in Alwar with the distribution of sweets. He wanted "to proceed against both the Maharaja and Dr. Khare". Alwar being "the hotbed of dissident elements, a threat to the central Government so close to Alwar could not be tolerated." Patel decided to act against the advice of Mountbatten and others. He placed Alwar under house arrest in Delhi, along with his Prime Minister, N.B. Khare. Patel's anger was, perhaps, fuelled by Mountbatten's advice that, "in terms of the Indian Independence Act transferring power to the Princes, the States, even though they had signed the Standstill Agreement, were foreign territories where the Indian Government did not exercise any extradition rights."[10] Patel could not accept this. To him in a free India, it sounded illogical. The British had themselves never accepted such a position; for them Paramountcy of the Crown was always supreme. Patel was, therefore, determined to prove that on behalf of Independent India, he alone exercised such rights. Before the house arrest of Alwar, Patel had seen to it that he segregated Bharatpur from him; and thereby killed any designs Alwar and Bharatpur were reportedly hatching among the Jat Rulers of the region. Patel's second bold step was to send Indian troops to Alwar to take control of the State.

Having thus created the right climate, Patel visited Alwar to talk to the people face to face, and thereby disprove Alwar's claim to speak on their behalf. At a public meeting on February 25th, he bluntly said, "Small States cannot subsist as independent entities any longer without endangering Indian unity... Many rulers have realised their duty by merging themselves in bigger entities. Rajasthan has to march with the times." In the same breath he tickled their Rajput pride and roused their dormant nationalist patriotism with the observation, "It is your privilege and duty to bear the sword. It is equally your responsibility to ensure that the sword is not used to harass the weak, but to protect them. You should use it in a manner that the world will say, you are the inheritors of an ancient civilisation and are true to the real traditions of the chivalry of Rajasthan."[11]

Patel had thus prepared the ground for his next step—the formation of the Matsya Union on March 17th. From his sick-bed at Dehra Dun, where he had retired for convalescence following a massive heart-attack in Delhi, Patel sent an inspiring message on the occasion: "The future of our Motherland lies in unity and strength. The need is for different units to draw together and not to drift apart."[12] The formation of the Union was a victory for Patel. His "firmness, combined with gentleness, paid dividends"; and the happy ending lay in the Maharaja's agreeing to "an honourable compromise in the formation of the Matsya Union."[13] Patel rewarded the Maharaja by making him Up-Rajpramukh.

The formation of the Matsya Union opened the way to the formation of similar other Unions in quick succession in the neighbouring States: on March 25, 1948, the Union of Rajasthan, comprising new States and Principalities, with headquarters at Kotah; in early April, the Union of Vindhya Pradesh (Rewa and the States of Bundelkhand); on July 15th the PEPSU (Patiala, Kapurthala, Nabha, Jind, Faridkot, Malerkotla, Nalagarh and Khalsia); and on May 29th, the Union of Malwa comprising 25 big and small States. Patel's message on each occasion had a historic significance—meant as a lesson for the Princes to take seriously. He told the Rajputs of the smaller Union of Rajasthan, "Placed as they are today, small units, unable to support themselves according to modern requirements, cannot afford to remain in precarious isolation. The history of the world in the last two centuries amply demonstrates that it is only by coming together that smaller States can retain their distinctive culture, safeguard their economic interests and take their due share in the political life of the country."[14] He reminded the Rulers of Vindhya Pradesh: "For several centuries in the past, Central India had been the cockpit of this great subcontinent. Under a strong imperial regime, it was generally either a transit route for armies on the march or a stepping-stone for expeditions to the South. Under a weak

Central Kingdom, it was divided up into small principalities under a feudal rule, which made any progress or prosperity impossible." Patel told them, "The consequence has been that this tract of land, intended by a bounteous nature to flourish in wealth and plenty, has been one of the most backward tracts of India." He was, therefore, happy "to find that both the rulers and the people of Rewa and Bundelkhand States have decided to pool their resources in order to bring out to the full the glory of this ancient territory..."[15]

Patel was particularly appreciative of the Maharaja of Patiala for showing "commendable public spirit" in the formation of the PEPSU. Patel stated that even when Patiala "could stand on its legs" and enjoyed separate representation in the Constituent Assembly, the Maharaja, who, along with Bikaner, had broken up Bhopal's anti-Indian designs, had "willingly agreed to pool the resources of his State with those of the other States in Punjab, and by so doing he has enabled us to build up a unit comparable in size and population to some of the largest units which we have hitherto formed."[16]

Besides the Jat, Rajput and Sikh Princes, Patel also roped in the equally proud Maratha Princes, whose domain since the days of the Maratha Empire had extended right up to Central India and who had matched their strength with the powerful Mughal and Sikh rulers. The bigger ones amongst them were Gwalior (Scindia) and Indore (Holkar). In his message on the inauguration of the Union of Malwa, Patel stated, "The inauguration of the Malwa Union brings into reality a dream which many a patriotic Indian has cherished for long. Malwa has been a historical, geographical, economic and territorial entity since ancient times. It has witnessed many a scene of splendour, glory and greatness. It has been the seat of Hindu empires, the exploits of which have adorned the pages of Indian history. Nature has been bountiful to Malwa and its people, but history and fate have often been unkind. After hundreds of years, Malwa is now on the threshold of what I hope and pray shall be a period of uninterrupted peace and prosperity."[17]

As for the surrender of the Maratha Princes, Scindia was

completely swept off his feet and became one of Patel's most ardent admirers. His devotion to India's master-builder did not die with Patel's death in 1950. There was no portrait of Patel in the Central Hall of Parliament till 1954, while that year, on Azad's death, Nehru lost no time in asking his Parliamentary Affairs Minister to write to Members of Parliament for subscriptions for a portrait of Azad. Scindia felt much irked by such an unceremonious omission of Patel. He got a portrait made and presented it to Parliament for installation. The unveiling ceremony was performed by the President of India, Dr. Rajendra Prasad. Speaking on the occasion, the Maharaja of Gwalior (Scindia) said with a sense of pride and gratitude, "Here is the man whom I once hated. Here is the man of whom I was afraid. Here is the man whom I admire and love."[18] Maharaja told General Thorat, "If we Princes have to have our throats cut again, we will undoubtedly choose the Sardar and V.P. (Menon) to do it."[19]

Around June 1948, Patel discerned certain "dangerous trends" in Bikaner and Jaipur, which, according to Jaswant Singh, "if acquiesced in, could have been taken as acceptance of the States' independence in their relations with each other." The Nawab of Loharu had acceded to Bikaner, and the Chieftain of Lawa to Jaipur. Patel saw dangers lurking in the intriguing advice Mountbatten had given him in the case of Alwar, and felt concerned over the new developments. He wondered if Paramountcy was still alive after it had been laid to rest on India's becoming independent. Patel's instant decision was that he must bury the ghost if it were still alive and hovering around. The solution, as he viewed, lay in the formation of Greater Rajasthan, whereby he could clip the wings of Bikaner, Jaipur or Jodhpur. Patel's earlier United States of Rajasthan was a move in that direction.

What contributed to Patel's efforts was the announcement by the Maharana of Udaipur of his decision to join the Union of Greater Rajasthan. The break away of Udaipur upset the Maharajas of Bikaner and Jaipur. The former sent Jaswant Singh to Udaipur to dissuade the Maharana from taking this step. Bikaner considered it "a major landslide in the Rajasthan Princely Order".

Apart from appreciating the winds of change, the Maharana of Udaipur was ever distrustful of the Houses of Bikaner, Jaipur and Jodhpur, as his ancestors were since their sell-out to Akbar and his descendants. And a similar drama Jodhpur had re-enacted with Jinnah only the previous year. Udaipur was thus Patel's "biggest prize", and through the formation of the Union of Rajasthan earlier he had killed for good any possibility of the Rajput rulers joining hands and forming themselves into a more or less independent confederation. Patel could now make further moves and "look forward confidently to tackle Bikaner, Jaipur and Jodhpur" in the hope of fulfilling his dream of Greater Rajasthan.

Prior to his proceeding to Udaipur for the installation of the Maharana as the Rajpramukh of the United States of Rajasthan, Patel cleverly mollified the pride of the Maharajas of Bikaner and Jaipur by writing to them personal letters in a tone which "left them with no heart to send him a reply in the negative. He (Patel) was merely seeking their consent, not imposing his will on them. Bikaner, Jaipur and Jodhpur seemed to have considered the changing scene in the neighbouring Rajput States. And the Maharana of Udaipur had let them down by not standing with them in their fight for a viable status for each one of them individually. With these developments, Bikaner, Jaipur and Jodhpur saw that one by one all the States to the north, east and south of their territories had given in to Sardar Patel."[20] With sweet reasonableness, Patel sought—and indeed secured without difficulty—their permission to his announcement at Udaipur of their consent to the formation of the Union of Greater Rajasthan.

Patel's historic speech at Udaipur on January 4, 1949 was "a precursor to the revolution that gripped Rajasthan in the next two months." He said on the occasion, "... my main purpose in coming here is to announce a big decision that we have taken after conferring with the rulers of the four big States of Rajasthan (i.e. Jaipur, Jodhpur, Bikaner and Udaipur). For a long time we and these rulers were considering the question of forming a 'Greater Rajasthan'. There was general realisation that in the conditions of India today, there was no gain but distinct harm in isolated existence; and, for the welfare of Rajasthan and India as well, United Rajasthan was indeed essential." Then, announcing the decision, Patel said, "The rulers whom I have referred to have authorised me to make the announcement. The Maharana of Udaipur and the Maharajas of Jaipur, Jodhpur and Bikaner have all accepted the formation of Greater Rajasthan." Underlining its significance, Patel stated, "The greatness of the hour requires us to realise the value of this step... You have to think of the gain that would accrue to Rajputana when all these big States will be together in a common administrative structure. No longer would it become you to act like a frog in a well... Every stone in Rajasthan speaks of a thrilling story of the valour of a Rajput; his devotion to duty and his spirit of self-sacrifice... in spite of these prodigies of valour, we became slaves... The safety of India and Rajputana lies in the formation of Greater Rajasthan."[21]

Thus came, what Patel called, "a momentous and historic occasion"—the fulfillment of Maharana Pratap's dream; equally so of Patel's. March 30, 1949 was a day of Rajasthan's glory and pride. Patel specially flew from Delhi to Jaipur to inaugurate the Union of Greater Rajasthan. At the inaugural ceremony, while the Maharaja of Jaipur was installed as Rajpramukh, the Maharana of Udaipur, in keeping with his dynasty's tradition, was made Maha-Rajpramukh. Jaipur being senior, Bikaner could not be accommodated. Bikaner felt very sore about it. Patel felt equally bad. Bikaner's role had been historic, indeed patriotic. Along with Patiala, he had smashed the opposition Bhopal had built, as Chancellor of the Chamber of Princes, against the rulers' joining the Indian Union. It was Bikaner, not Jaipur, who had frustrated the designs of the Political Department, and this alone had enabled Patel to handle the Princes individually. Realising the extreme sensitiveness of the proud, high-strung Rajput Princes, Patel wisely decided not to stir up the hornet's nest—the Princely hierarchy in Rajasthan. It could also have been beyond constitutional propriety. Bikaner's pride was deeply hurt. In a huff, he handed over his State to the new Union of Greater Rajasthan by wire from Bombay on April 7th prior to his sailing for Britain, where he later died.

The inaugural ceremony was held in the Durbar Hall of the Rambagh Palace. In keeping with Gandhian ideals, it was bereft of the usual princely pomp and show. But the occasion was most momentous—it opened up a new chapter in the history of Rajasthan. The Durbar Hall presented many pleasing, noteworthy contrasts. Congressmen in their Gandhi caps, *khadi kurtas* and *dhotis* rubbed shoulders with the hitherto aloof and proud Rajput Princes and nobles. While administering the oath of office to the Maharaja of Jaipur, Patel himself, in his homespun, plain, white *khadi* dress and *chappals* looked utterly dissimilar to the Maharaja's full-dress military uniform together with a "golden" turban. The Maharaja was a young man of 38; Patel was past 72. They also contrasted in their build—one nearly towering over the other. Yet, Patel was a figure of serene dignity and robust confidence born of the status and power he enjoyed as the maker of the Princes' destiny.

Pride, however, did not mar his humility. This was fully reflected in his speech, in which he said, "... I am being praised and congratulated for what I have been able to do in the sphere of the States. But if those who deserve these congratulations and all that praise, it is the rulers, who have sacrificed so much for the cause of their country. If they had not wholeheartedly supported us, we could never have changed the history of this country as we are doing today."[22]

22

Outdoing Bismarck

Stafford Cripps thought that it would take at least ten to fifteen years to liquidate the Indian States and to merge them with the rest of India. It was "a welcome surprise to him—and a great tribute to the ability of Sardar Patel—that the integration of the States with the rest of India has not taken even ten to fifteen months."[1] K.M. Panikkar praised it in glowing words, "How all these grand and grandiose title-holders were swept under the carpet of history in the twinkling of an eye! Many are amazed that Vallabhbhai Patel was able to sweep them away in so short a time. The *Puranas* say that Parasurama fought twenty-one battles before he could exterminate the Kshatriya princes, but the new Parasurama needed no battle to make a clean sweep of kingship in India. One by one they queued up to sign their Instrument of Accession, collected their pensions and left with good grace."[2] Patel was gentle to them, persuasive, but firm—under no circumstances willing to barter away India's interests. His feat was revolutionary—perhaps unique in world history for its speed and bloodlessness. He was himself the executioner of the revolution he had dreamed of in 1938 when he had publicly stated, "The Princes should be made to dissociate themselves from their reign. They should be given annual pension, and we should ourselves rule."[3]

For such a historic achievement, Patel has been compared with

Bismarck who had, likewise, consolidated Germany by integrating a handful of Princely States, and who was considered "the greatest master of diplomacy" in Europe. President Zakir Hussain considered Patel "even greater than Bismarck, because he has unified the country within a short time and without much noise and trumpeting."[4] President V.V. Giri stated that Patel possessed "the organising ability of Bismarck, the astute statesmanship of Chanakya and the single-minded devotion to the cause of national unity of Abraham Lincoln."[5] Patel's task was stupendous; even more complex than Bismarck's: 562 States were reduced to 26 administrative units of the Indian Union, and democracy was extended to 80 million people comprising 27 per cent of India's population in a matter of months, not years. "When the British left India," writes Foreign Secretary K.P.S. Menon, "the unity even of divided India was in danger. Some 560 Princely States had been left in the air. It was open to them to adhere to India, to accede to Pakistan, or to remain independent... It almost looked as if India was going to be Balkanised. But this danger was averted by the firm handling of the Princes by a man of iron, Sardar Vallabhbhai Patel."[6]

Patel and Bismarck possessed totally dissimilar personalities: differing from each other in physical appearance, mental make-up and the means each employed in achieving the ends. Bismarck struck awe through his "fierce moustache, huge jackboots, a spiked helmet and a sword"; he was "a civilian despite his military tunic." Patel had, in contrast, the looks of a simple, unsophisticated peasant, with whom he had completely identified in his traditional dress of *dhoti, jubba,* waistcoat and a pair of countrymade *chappals*. Patel's round clean-shaven head made him look like a venerable Buddhist monk, while in his toga-style dress, he reflected the dignity and grandeur of a Roman consul. Patel's Gandhian humility was fully mirrored in his statement after his victory in the "Police Action" in Hyderabad, "On the chessboard of this world, we are like small or trivial pawns, and are instrumental, at times for small or bigger events... Let us express our gratitude to God."[7]

Bismarck was a thoroughbred aristocrat and a crafty dictator, "always impulsive and always exaggeratedly nervous of the aggressive designs of others";[8] whereas Patel was ever cool and unruffled, possessing the serenity of "a volcano covered with snow", and devoid of malice and unscrupulousness. If he did not like someone, he did so openly. Bismarck had "no friends, only sycophants".[9] Patel's friendships were deep and lasting, but he suffered neither fools nor flatterers. Unlike Bismarck, Patel was a born democrat but a party disciplinarian who remained content throughout his political life with a number two role—first under Gandhi and later under Nehru. Yet, he played a role independent of either. Because of his forceful personality and his hold over the party machine, Patel wielded the weapon of people's support, and ruled through the Princes" willing surrender; whereas Bismarck ruled through a policy of "blood and iron", court intrigue and ruthlessness. Bismarck "did not value the princes nor respect them," as Patel did. Bismarck also "trusted no one else. Suspicion grew with power."[10] Patel, in comparison, secured the lasting trust and friendship of the Princes.

Patel's approach was Gandhian—non-violent, high-minded, principled statesmanship, which believed in befriending, rather than in eliminating the Princes. Khrushchev perhaps appreciated its significance much more than others when, during his visit to India in 1956, he observed, "You Indians are an amazing people! How on earth did you manage to liquidate the Princely rule without liquidating the Princes."[11] On occasions, however, Patel did not hesitate to speak to them harsh truths to make them realise the consequences of their own actions. He, indeed, spoke to them homely truths in a homely manner, in a paternal tone which was invariably kind, but sometimes admonishing, so as to make them understand the great lesson of Indian history: one of fragmentation through disunity, succumbing to successive waves of invaders. According to Panikkar, it was Patel's "understanding and vision that killed the suspicions of most Princes."[12]

Patel achieved all this through sympathy, conciliation, accommodation. He was free from rancour and revenge. He did not believe in any kind of harassment. At the very start he convinced them that he meant business by such plain-talking, "My humble advice to the Princes is: they cannot remain isolated. They cannot remain outside the Constituent Assembly. It would be suicidal on their part to exploit the Hindu-Muslim differences in British India. If any member of the Princely Order desires to establish Paramountcy, he is mistaken. They cannot establish that Paramountcy which the British are relinquishing. Paramountcy vests in the people." He also told them, "If they are anxious to maintain peace and order in the country and cherish the ideal of a united and prosperous India, they should cooperate with, and take part in the efforts now being made of building the future of India on sound and firm foundations."[13] He warned them, "With the exit of the foreign power, the Princes will have to adjust themselves to the democratic order. The days of those rulers who do not command the confidence of their subjects are numbered... These days, no state can afford to live in isolation." At the same time he used soothing words, "Many of them are the descendants of great and benevolent rulers of the past ages."[14] The Princes can survive only as "trustees of the people."[15]

Simultaneously, Patel advised the people to change their outlook towards the rulers, "They are ours, and we can make them understand and appreciate our point of view... the days of vilifying the Princes, calling them names and maligning them are gone."[16] He set an example by being gentle and forgiving, generous and gracious, considerate and loyal to those who put their trust in him. He openly acknowledged, "None is more conscious than myself that all this could not have been achieved but for their willing cooperation and their intense patriotism, which was latent but which has just blossomed forth in all its fullness with the acquisition of independence of the country."[17]

Unlike Patel, Bismarck was "a political conspirator, not a fighting man, by nature and by experience."[18] Patel too was a fighting man, but as a Gandhian. He could not dream of conspiracy as a means to achieve the ends, whereas Bismarck's "greatest gift was in packing the cards, not in playing the hand...

he had gained power by court-intrigue and never learnt a better trick." To Bismarck , "his family was always more important than any political affairs";[19] Patel had completely detached himself from his family: he had kept his son at bay; and he did not leave behind any property for his unmarried daughter.

In dealing with the Princes, Patel was neither disdainful nor proud, neither intolerant nor dictatorial, but certainly firm—unbudging from his resolve. His diplomacy varied to suit an individual Prince, or a situation. Where coaxing and cajoling failed, he would thunder to bring them round. He followed Chanakya's four-fold policy of persuasion (*sama*), money (*daam*), punishment (*dand*) and division (*bhed*). His policy of integration began with *sama* in Junagadh and ended with *dand* in Hyderabad. Not given to vacillation, he was sterner and firmer than other Congress leaders. The Princes knew that he could be the best of friends and the worst of foes when the country's interests were at stake. He understood the weaknesses of the Princes, and therefore consciously upheld the pride of their status by strictly adhering to protocol while writing to them. Yet, in such correspondence, he could be courteous or reprimanding, the reprimand varying from soft to harsh.

Patel subdued the Maharaja of Jaipur by bluntly telling him, "Maharajdhiraj, your guns have got rusted." Thereby he indirectly asked for his surrender. In a sterner manner he dealt with the Maharaja of Indore, a close ally of Bhopal, when he came to see Patel on August 19, 1947 in his Rolls Royce with two uniformed ADCs, one of them an Englishman. At Patel's austere Aurangzeb Road residence, the Maharaja talked "very excitedly with lots of gestures... in his haw-haw accent... he went on for almost ten minutes at a breathless pace." Patel, who wore "the usual scowl on his face", sat through the meeting "with his head down staring at his feet, and then suddenly he stood up and said very loudly, "You are a liar,"[20] and walked away. The Maharaja was completely dumbfounded. Indore's activities since the transfer of power had not been "particularly glorious." He had been "acting as a stooge of Bhopal" and he had tried "desperately hard to sabotage the whole accession scheme." He had "at one time very nearly succeeded in weaning away some of the leading rulers who had already agreed to sign the Instrument of Accession. Even after signing the accession, he did not permit the State officials to celebrate Independence Day on August 15th and obstructed the celebration of the day by his people. His accession was thus "half-hearted and insincere" and "not inspired by patriotic motives, but as an act of surrender after he had lost the battle." Patel, therefore, gave the Maharaja a taste of his annoyance, which resulted in his surrender through a letter of November 17th: "Since I met you in Delhi, I have been doing all I can to follow the very sound and affectionate advice you gave me as a friend."[21]

Patel was no less blunt with the Maharaja of Baroda. Baroda was the first to have sent his representatives to the Constituent Assembly, besides giving a lead to other Princes in signing the Instrument of Accession. Yet, suddenly, he staged a somersault. Jinnah's influence seemed to have worked on him, and so did Junagadh's accession to Pakistan. He had also come under the umbrella of Indore. What was more, Baroda wanted "to emulate the Nizam". At the time when the Junagadh trouble broke out and the whole of Kathiawar and Gujarat were in turmoil, Baroda tried to be cheeky with Patel by offering conditional help: in return, he should be "declared the King of Gujarat and Kathiawar, so as to have sovereign powers"; and that he should be given "jurisdiction of all the six agencies, viz. Mahikanta, Rewakanta, Sabarkanta, Palanpur, Western India States and the Gujarat States along with whatever power the Dominion Government enjoys today over them." Patel was not the man to stomach such insolence. He told Baroda bluntly that "the Government of India did not need his help", and warned him that "his territorial ambitions would spell nothing but disaster." Patel wrote to him in April 1948: "You have referred to the part which you played in the solution of the problems of constitutional relationship of Indian States with the Indian Union. It was, perhaps, fortunate that at that time you happened to be outside India and the prevailing local intrigues did not affect you. But I should like to remind you that when we were in difficulties about Junagadh, our approach to you met with a reply which shocked me beyond words. You bargained about your own position at a time when India was in difficulties."[22]

Patel's handling of a communally-motivated Akali agitation in Patiala after the formation of PEPSU in July 1948 gave proof of his skill and tact, but for which the situation could have turned dangerous, as it had gathered momentum among the Sikh masses. It had shades of the Muslim League mentality, which had been inspired by Master Tara Singh, who had shifted his headquarters from Amritsar to Patiala. The objective of the agitation seemed to be to gain an independent Sikh State. This would have further split north-west India, already cut into two halves on the creation of Pakistan. The Akalis had hoisted the State flag over the fort, instead of the national flag, and inside they had started a round-the-clock recitation from the *Guru Granth Sahib*, which was equally holy to the Hindus. Reportedly, the agitation had the Maharaja's covert and Prime Minister Gian Singh Rarewala's overt support. Sikh *jathas* roamed about in the city, causing great panic and even an exodus of the Hindus. Even when the agitation was not directed towards them, they could have been an easy target in order to force the Government to yield to their demand.

Patel moved step by step as on a chessboard from his residence in New Delhi. First, he called the Maharaja of Patiala to New Delhi. What transpired between the two, no one knows. But the Maharaja returned looking "woebegone and agitated." Apparently, he had been given a dressing down, and had been virtually put under "house arrest" when told to stay on in New Delhi for the next few days. Thereafter Patel sent for Rarewala, who was also the Maharaja's maternal uncle. Reportedly, he was taken to task for his failure to curb the agitation. Sarcastically, Patel asked him, "How far is Patiala from Ambala? How long would it take to reach there?"

Not catching the hint, Rarewala replied, "Thirty-four miles, Sir. It will take an hour to reach by road."

"No, no", thundered Patel, "I did not mean the distance by road, but as the crow flies, so that minimum time is lost in moving the Army from Ambala by air to encircle Patiala and raze it to the ground... a dirty city with narrow lanes, so that a new city could come up from its ruins." A badly shaken Rarewala now understood the hint. He requested Patel to allow him to go back to Patiala and handle the situation. Rarewala got the flag replaced, and the *Guru Granth Sahib* removed from the fort.

That was not the end of the Akali agitation. It erupted in 1950 when the Sikhs seemed to have taken to the "war path". Nehru was heckled while addressing a public meeting at Fatehgarh Sahib. The Sikhs were attending the *Jor Mela* there in thousands. The Akalis found the occasion suitable for demanding a Punjabi *suba*. Patel flew into Patiala. He addressed a mammoth gathering on the stadium grounds. The Sikhs came in large numbers. They were mostly volatile refugees from West Pakistan. A great majority of them were followers of Master Tara Singh, and were intent upon creating disorder. During the course of Patel's speech, some from amidst the crowd shouted pro-Akali, pro-Punjabi slogans. Patel silenced them by a warning clothed in satirically descriptive language, "The doctor operates only when the boil is fully ripe, so that the bleeding is the minimum and the patient suffers from as less pain as possible. We had adopted such a course in Hyderabad. We had been urged to operate there earlier. But we did not till the time was ripe, and everything turned out to be so well. It has come to my hearing that our Sikh brethren wish to set up a Khalistan. If it is so, let them dare have a go at it! But I want to tell them that Hyderabad showed its teeth, and we had to pull them out. If our Sikh brethren wish to do the same, they would meet with the same fate. The Government of India has enough strength to face the situation. We turned the British out of India, (they) being foreigners. But the Rajas and Maharajas are like our children or brothers. They are, therefore, ours. We can make them understand. If, however, children refuse to understand, they have to be made to do so, even, if necessary, by slapping."[23] The reprimand had a salutary effect. The audience retreated into a pin drop silence.

Having secured the Princes' accession by August 15th, Patel's next task was merger—the first essential step towards integration and consolidation of the varying patterns of the states and the provinces into a single territorial mould. The Princes' opposition was not unexpected, as it meant a surrender of their territories to neighbouring provinces or their unionisation with larger States. At Cuttack, Patel had his first brush with the Princes of Orissa and Chhattisgarh States in December 1947. Their merger—the first ever—with the neighbouring provinces of Orissa and the Central Provinces was desirable because of the stubborn attitude of the Princes numbering 41. The biggest one amongst them had an area of 4,000 square miles and a population of 10 lakhs; and the smallest, 46 square miles and a population 20,000. According to V.P. Menon, "our success or failure at Cuttack was bound to have a great psychological effect on rulers all over India; and we could not, therefore, risk a failure". Patel was determined to have his way. The rulers were, Menon had been warned by a former official of the Political Department, "supposed to be intractable", though "the situation in Orissa was clamouring for immediate attention, and we had no alternative but to tackle it."

Patel, accompanied by Menon, reached Cuttack on December 13th for a face-to-face meeting with the Princes. Patel's inaugural address to the Ruling Chiefs' conference he had convened was "a most persuasive speech". He told the rulers, "I have come to Cuttack to tender friendly advice to the rulers, not as a representative of the old Paramountcy or of any foreign power, but as a member of a family trying to solve a family problem." He also told them that "the safety of the rulers, as well as of their people, was in danger" and that "the situation demanded immediate solution." Orissa as "a federal unit could only thrive and progress if it was a compact whole and was not torn as under by multifarious jurisdictions and authorities which ruined its compactness."[24]

In spite of such reasonableness, Patel encountered rough weather. He was quick to nip evil in the bud. When a 21 year-old Prince started his speech with the words, "My people want...", Patel snubbed him with the remark: "They are not your people, Your Highness. They are my people. Leave them to me." Patel delivered a similar snub to a saffron-robed Prince, who started talking about Princely duty, with the remark: "Your Holiness(!) is not fit for Princely duties." To the Maharaja of Mayurbhanja who said he had transferred power to his Ministers, Patel administered a snub by leaving him "out of the discussion" with the remark: "I will deal with Your Highness later."[25]

Patel addressed a mammoth public meeting in Cuttack on December 14th, during which he warned the Princes, "I have met some rulers today, and I have told them that they cannot carry on in the manner they did in the past. They must transfer their power to the people... Today the people of Orissa are agitated over the rulers. There would be no rulers if the people as such did not recognise them. They must move with the times. Let them cease to be like frogs in the well. These are the days of democracy, and the rulers too must put their trust in the people."[26]

The same evening Patel boarded the train for New Delhi. He was unhappy, as his success was not complete. The rulers were much more unhappy over possible repercussions. They sent him a message that he should delay his departure. Patel agreed to stay on for an hour. At the end of the hour, they signed the agreement. Two days later, when the Princes met Patel in New Delhi, they against adopted dilatory tactics, despite the agreement. They put forward legal arguments to justify their demand to be left as separate entities and not to be merged with Orissa. When they hinted at taking legal opinion, Patel said in anger, "Your Highnesses may consult lawyers, but I make the law." Undeterred, the rulers then shifted their ground with the suggestion that they be allowed to form a Union of their own. Patel firmly put this down with the remark, "I am prepared to leave each of Your Highnesses as a separate unit, but will not allow Your Highnesses to form a Union. Remember, if any of Your Highnesses wants my help to deal with your people, I will not come to your help."[27] That was enough to dampen their spirits, and to reduce them into submission.

The Orissa "battle" with the Prices thus ended in Patel's victory. It was to prove a precursor of many such victories for Patel in other states. The Governor of Orissa, Dr. K.N. Katju, called the merger of the Eastern States "a great epoch-making change ushered in in the Indian States by the vision and statesmanship of Sardar Patel. On December 14, 1947, in the Government House at Cuttack, he first set his hand to the wheel of this great revolution."[28] Patel himself looked upon this as "a dramatic beginning", however small, in distant Orissa, which "gradually swept over the whole of the sub-continent." Mountbatten compared Patel's fine achievement with that of Napoleon in his letter of December 23, 1947, "I personally have for long thought that the principle of mediatisation of States, which was adopted by Napoleon in the Central European principalities in the beginning of the last century, is the right answer for the small and uneconomic States."[29]

The merger of the Eastern States, as Patel had correctly forecast, "electrified the whole atmosphere." With it began his ingenious merger plan, under the impact of which the "Indian States could not long remain the citadels of autocracy. The bastions gradually began to give way."[30] The bloodless revolution he ushered in, integrated within two years the vast sub-continent, interspersed as it was with Princely States and British India provinces, into a single mould. To pave the way for such integration, Patel first consolidated the States into viable Unions, replacing the earlier Instrument of Accession signed by individual Princes with fresh agreements with the new Unions. He did this fully realising that "integration without consolidation would represent a collection of bones without flesh and blood. It will lack that vitality and spark which alone make life possible."[31]

In the conduct of his bloodless revolution, Patel moved step by step as a great strategist. The first was the accession, made easier by the dissolution of the Chamber of Princes, which gave Patel his opportunity to deal with them individually. Like a wise, kindly, but resolute shepherd, he roped in nearly all the "sheep" into his pen by August 15th, when Paramountcy was to lapse. The second was the merger: merger of 219 States, involving a total of 84,774 square miles and a population of 120.18 lakhs, with adjacent provinces such as Orissa, the Central Provinces,

Bihar, Madras, East Punjab and Bombay. This was followed by consolidation of 22 States into units like Himachal Pradesh and Kutch, covering a total area of 19,061 square miles with a population of 14.37 lakhs. Then came territorial integration of 294 States to create new viable Unions of Saurashtra, Matsya, Vindhya Pradesh, Rajasthan, Madhya Bharat, and Patiala and the East Punjab States, involving a total area of 150,000 square miles and a population of 237.64 lakhs. Finally, the creation of larger Unions of States like Kathiawar, Cochin-Travancore and Greater Rajasthan. By the time India became a Republic on January 26, 1950, a new order had emerged with identical units constituting the Union of India.

Patel took legitimate pride in his achievement. "Had anyone," he asked, "dreamt a year or two ago that a third of India would be integrated in this fashion? This is the first time in history after centuries that India can call itself an integrated whole in the real sense of the term."[32] He drew a pertinent historical comparison: "Centuries ago, it was the proud privilege of Kalinga to arouse awakening in a great monarch… Few had dreamt, and none had imagined, that it would be the same land that will usher in a revolutionary change which would achieve for India the same measure of unity, strength and security which India had once attained under that distinguished ruler, Asoka."[33]

Prior to his departure from India on completion of his tenure of office, Mountbatten wrote to Patel on June 19th: "There is no doubt that by far the most important achievement of the present Government is the unification of the States into the Dominion of India. Had you failed in this, the results would have been disastrous. But since you succeeded, no one can see the disastrous results that have been avoided. I feel no one has given you adequate recognition of the miracle which you and your faithful V.P. (V.P. Menon) have produced. Nothing has so added to the prestige of the present Government than the brilliant policy you have followed with the States."[34] Patel had achieved what Sayajirao, the Maharaja of Baroda, had told the Aga Khan in 1908: "The first thing you will have to do when the English are gone is to get rid of all these rubbishy States. I tell you, there'll never be an Indian nation until this so-called Princely Order disappears."[35]

An eloquent tribute to his genius, though not directly paid to him, is to be found from what Lord Curzon wrote about the Princes to Lord Hamilton in August 1900: "For what are they for the most part, but a set of unruly and ignorant and rather undisciplined schoolboys? What they want more than anything else is to be schooled by a firm, but not unkindly, hand; to be passed through just the sort of discipline that a boy goes through at a public school..."[36] Patel proved the ideal schoolmaster. None could have been more kind and firm than he. Patel's paternalism was unlike the autocracy of the British, or the iron hand of Bismarck. It was humane, benevolent, essentially Gandhian.

In that lay Patel's genius and his crowning glory. Of all the Congress leaders, according to Archibald Nye, Patel was a real leader in the military sense. To John Gunther he looked "rather like a Roman emperor in the heroic tradition."

23

A Secularist with a Difference

Patel was a secularist. No less than Gandhi and Nehru. His secularism, like Gandhi's, was traditional in its acceptance of religion as a humanising force for promotion of non-violence, tolerance, compassion and love; it stemmed from the secular Hindu culture and outlook. Unlike Gandhi and Patel, Nehru was "a secular phenomenon without formal religious foundations". Being of the Western concept, Nehru's secularism had "no vestige of religiosity in it". It was non-religious to the extent of bordering on atheism. Patel differed from both Gandhi and Nehru insofar as their secularism permitted unqualified compromise and appeasement—a give-in-to-win policy which set no limits to win over the Muslims. The ends of all the three were the same; only the approach differed. The difference lay in Patel's opposition to dilution of nationalism by surrendering to the Muslim minority the right to be on par with the majority in the Interim Government, and giving it a prominence and status in political affairs inconsistent with that accorded to other minorities. It amounted to, as events proved, placing a veto in their hands. His was the approach of a pragmatist; essentially of an administrator who believed that a satisfactory solution could be reached only through striking the right balance between conflicting interests. And that it could not be a one-sided game, as it turned out to be with Gandhi and Nehru who felt that in the end the Muslim minority would see reason and the country would remain undivided.

Such a balance Patel attempted to achieve through plain-speaking to both the Hindus and the Muslims. He asked the former, on India's gaining Independence, "to forget the past, because it is a manly virtue to do so... in India every Muslim should feel that he is an Indian citizen and has equal rights as an Indian citizen."[1] At the same time he told the Muslims that "there is no place here for those who claim separate representation... For a community to think that its interests are different from that of the country in which it lives is a great mistake." He, therefore, advised them to realise that "the future of a minority—any minority—is to trust the majority"; that they should "make friends with others and create a change in the atmosphere. You will then have more than your quota, if you really feel for the country in the same manner as the other people."[2]

Patel's advice was in no way different from the one tendered by Dr. M.A. Ansari in the early twenties; and by Mrs. Indira Gandhi over half a century later in 1983. Ansari had told the Muslims, "The true safeguard of a minority is the goodwill of the majority." And Mrs. Gandhi's advice to the Muslims was that "no minority can survive if the majority were irritated."[3] Over a decade later, in 1995, Rafiq Zakaria repeated Patel's advice to the Muslims: "The Indian Muslims must cultivate the Hindus... remove the cobwebs of religious prejudices and historical distortions which have bedeviled their relations with the Hindus."[4] Patel's thinking was the same as theirs. He desired harmony on a reciprocal basis—not give-in-to-win; and his abolition of separate representation was a progressive step in that direction—integration of the communities, rather than keep them in watertight compartments as the British had done.

Patel was secular both in speech and action, though he never hesitated in telling, or pursuing the truth, no matter how unpalatable. His historic speech at Lucknow on January 6th, 1948 was of the same genre. His tone and approach were, however, aggressive. The provocation came from the deliberations at the

Lucknow Conference Mussalman-e-Hind towards the end of December 1947, which was attended by Azad and about 70,000 Muslims. *The Statesman* columnist, "Observer", reported: "As I sat listening to most of the speeches, I could not help feeling that the conference had succeeded in taking over where the Muslim League had left off (inside India) after August 15th. Some of the speeches were of the mischievous and rabble-rousing type and in this, surprisingly enough, the ball was set rolling by Dr. Syed Mahmud of Bihar, a Nationalist Congress Muslim, who said: 'I can tell Hindus and Sikhs that Muslims may be finished in India, but they should know that they also in that case would not survive.' Maulana Hafiz-ul-Rahman, Vice President of the Jamiat-ul-Ulema-e-Hind, made one of the most provocative speeches… From behind a cleverly laid-out smokescreen of praise for Mahatma Gandhi and Pandit Jawaharlal Nehru, the Maulana was firing mischievous insinuations against certain other leaders" (obviously, Sardar Patel). In the columnist's "considered opinion", "the conference has been a new edition of the League at its fretting and fuming worst. The speeches delivered had the familiar ring about them of the malicious Pirpur Report, which proved once one of the most effective weapons in the League propaganda armoury in inflaming Muslim masses."[5]

Immediately following on its heels was Patel's Lucknow speech. It was an answer to "rabble-rousing" by the Muslim conference. He told the Muslims, "I am a true friend of the Muslims, although I have been described as their greatest enemy. I believe in plain-speaking. I do not know how to mince matters. I want to tell you frankly that mere declarations of loyalty to the Indian Union will not help you at this critical juncture. You must give practical proof of your declarations. I ask you why you do not unequivocally denounce Pakistan for attacking Indian territory with the connivance of Frontier tribesmen. Is it not your duty to condemn all acts of aggression against India?... In the recent All-India Muslim Conference, why did you not open your mouth on Kashmir.? …in the Constituent Assembly, one of the Lucknow Muslim Leaguers pleaded for separate electorates and reservation of seats. I had to open my mouth and say that he could not have it both ways. Now he is in Pakistan."

Patel, therefore, advised the Muslims, "Those who want to go to Pakistan can go there and live in peace. Let us live here in peace to work for ourselves." Earlier in the same speech, Patel had significantly observed, "Today, I think of those days when in this city of Lucknow, the foundation of the two-nation theory was laid. It was said Muslim culture and tradition were not akin to those of the Hindus. The Muslims were a separate nation." Patel pointed out: "Muslim Leaguers call me their greatest enemy. Formerly they used to call Mahatma Gandhi Enemy Number One. Now they think Gandhi is their friend, and have substituted me in his place. But I too speak the truth... I want to say a word as a friend of the Muslims and it is the duty of a good friend to speak frankly: It is your duty now to sail in the same boat (with the Hindus and others) and sink or swim together. I want to tell you very clearly that you cannot ride on two horses. You select one horse, whichever you like best."[6] Many considered the speech historic. It was full of meaningful words compulsively uttered by one whom Mountbatten described as "a very stern realist"; and who, he thought, had "the courage to rise above popular sentiment ... (when) the interests of the country demanded a different line."[7]

Patel's Lucknow speech contained the basic truth of the situation prevailing in India after the creation of Pakistan. He was greatly irked by the communal stance of the Nationalist Muslims at the Lucknow conference. His speech was not, as he himself claimed, anti-Muslim. To him it was the only way to solve the Hindu-Muslim problem: by inducing the Muslims to think rightly, and by cleansing the Indian waters of the bad fish. But his Lucknow speech created a storm. Khaliq-uz-Zaman and other Leaguers, staying behind in India, openly dubbed Patel the "strong man of Hindudom in the Congress." The Nationalist Muslims, who dared not do so out of fear of him, mounted an attack on him secretly.

Azad, Hafiz-ul-Rahman and others stormed Gandhi with

complaints. Nehru preferred to remain neutral. But they secured the support of the Socialists led by Jayaprakash Narayan and Achyut Patwardhan. Gandhi publicly stated, "I know the Sardar... His method and manner of approach to the Hindu-Muslim question, as also to several other questions, is different from mine and Pandit Nehru's. But it is a travesty of truth to describe it as anti-Muslim. The Sardar's heart is expansive enough to accommodate all." Gandhi, nevertheless, admitted that Patel was no longer his "yes-man"; he was "too masterful" to be anybody's "yes-man". His revilers were "isolating the Sardar and making a scapegoat of him ...showering gratuitous praise on Nehru and him."[8]

Added to the above was the bad name given to Patel on two issues concerning Pakistan, but of no direct concern to the Indian Muslims. The first was the dispatch of Pakistan's share of arms and ammunition remaining in India, and of India's left in Pakistan. Pakistan had slowed down movement of India's share, and diverted to Kashmir whatever she received from India. General Thorat felt much concerned about the situation. Especially so because of the attitude of the British Commander-in-Chief of the Indian Army, General Roy Bucher, who "insisted that we continue sending Pakistan's share to her." Of this Thorat records: "I implored him to stop, or at least slow down this movement as Pakistan had done, but all I received in return was a stern warning that not withstanding what Pakistan did, we were to fulfil our obligations faithfully. In sheer disgust I sought an appointment with Sardar Patel, and explained my dilemma to him. He looked at me with the shade of an amused smile and said:

'Why have you come to me? You should have gone to the Prime Minister.' Then without waiting for my reply he went on: 'All right don't be too prompt in doing your duty.' I said: 'Sir, but these are the orders of the C-in-C. What will I tell him when he discovers it?' This time he smiled openly. 'Surely you can tell a plausible lie for the delay. I am with you'."

"From then onwards there was a sharp decline in the quantities of arms and ammunition sent to Pakistan... I do not know if the C-in-C discovered the ruse; if he did, he said nothing to me."[9]

The second issue was the Cabinet decision to withhold payment of Rs.55 crores to Pakistan, due to her as part of her share of assets on Partition. Patel was adamant in supporting the decision. But Gandhi was equally adamant to have his way. His main consideration was to create a feeling of confidence and friendliness with the Muslims of India and Pakistan. To force a decision in his favour, Gandhi resorted to his most potent weapon—the fast with which he had pricked the Hindu conscience in the past. This time his fast was aimed at pricking Patel's conscience. The issue drove a wedge between Gandhi and Patel on the one hand, and between Nehru and Patel on the other. Under such heavy pressure, Patel had to yield. But the surrender was accompanied by his resignation from the Government. Patel handed over his letter of resignation to Gandhi, who decided to have him released from the Ministry. V.P. Menon, who came to know of it, rushed to Mountbatten, who thought that Patel's exit would spell disaster, and a possible split in the Congress party which may lead to civil strife. Mountbatten saw Gandhi, and told him that without Patel the Government would not run, arguing: "Patel has his feet on the ground, while Nehru has his in the clouds."[10] Patel's resignation thus remained with Gandhi. On Mountbatten's persuasion, Gandhi called Patel for a meeting with him, which took place just before his assassination on January 30th. It was at this meeting that Gandhi got a promise from Patel that he would look upon Nehru as his leader. Such a promise Patel kept till the end, no matter under what pressures and circumstances.

Patel's disillusionment with the Congress policies and attitudes towards Muslim politics had begun in 1945 with the Simla Conference, at which his party had surrendered to Wavell, and yielded to the dictates of Jinnah in two fundamental respects: in agreeing to parity between the caste Hindu and the Muslims; and, second, only the League were to represent the Indian Muslims. An equally contributory factor was the ineffectual role of the Nationalist Muslims in the provincial elections of 1945-1946. Patel had felt their failure more than Gandhi and Nehru, because of its serious repercussions, and also because of his single-handedly pouring into the election campaigns huge sums of money. He had written to Azad on November 18th, 1945: "It must be understood between us that no seats should be lost for want of money."[11] Patel felt further disillusioned by the defections, as mentioned earlier, to the Muslim League of prominent Nationalist Muslims like Abdul Qayyum Khan in the NWFP and Mian Iftikhar-ud-Din in Punjab.

Much worse was the anti-party role of Azad as the Congress President in his commitment to the Cabinet Mission and Wavell without consultation with Gandhi and the Congress Working Committee. To the former he had reportedly supported the idea of the three-tier Grouping of India under a loose Centre; to the latter, a commitment that the Congress would nominate no Nationalist Muslim on the Interim Government. In the Grouping, Jinnah would have got away with Bengal, Assam and Punjab as they existed; and in regard to the Interim Government, the Congress was surrendering its representation of the Muslims. The breaking-point for Patel reached on two issues: first, when Azad insisted that the Congress should surrender one Hindu seat in the Interim Government in favour of a Nationalist Muslim, which would have changed the ratio from parity to six against four; and, second, when the Nationalist Muslims desired reservation, if not separate representation.

Patel was dead set on killing the ghost of separatism for good, come what may—opposition, unpopularity and what not. There was no question of yielding under any circumstance or pressure. Patel undertook such a task as Chairman of the Advisory Committee on Minorities set up by the Constituent Assembly. His first step was to neutralise Jinnah's agents provocateurs left behind in India, people like Khaliq-uz-Zaman. Patel had referred to him in his Lucknow speech for having pleaded for separate electorates and reservation of seats in the Constituent Assembly. This was after the creation of Pakistan for which he had fought tooth and nail—much more than the Muslims in Punjab and Sind. And it was he who had gone away to Pakistan after he had pledged loyalty to the Indian Flag on August 14-15th.

Patel's thoughts were reflected by Pant in a speech in the Advisory Committee, "Let not the lesson of history be lost. It is a lesson which should burn deep in the hearts and minds of all minorities that they can find their protection only from the people in whose midst they live; and it is on the establishment of mutual goodwill, mutual trust, cordiality and amity that the rights and interests not only of the majority but also of the minorities depend. This lesson of history, I hope, will not be forgotten... There is the unwholesome and, to some extent, degrading habit of thinking always in terms of communities and never in terms of citizens." Khaliq-uz-Zaman's attitude was "cautiously obstructive"; while "the Nationalist Muslims, who acted under the guidance of Maulana Azad, urged reservation with weightage". Two leading Nationalist Muslims, Abdul Qaiyum Ansari and Maulana Hafiz-ul-Rahman, demanded insertion of a provision in the Constitution "to the effect that Muslim Qazis should be appointed to administer *Shariat* laws and a Muslim Minister placed in charge of waqfs", which Munshi had described as "going back on the equality before law established in the country for over a century and a half."

Patel conduced the deliberations in a masterly manner. He acted like a silent giant, quietly setting into motion manoeuvres through his confidants like Pant and Munshi, and yet discreetly avoiding to impose his will. He chose to be diplomatic, not autocratic. Since no decision could be reached on the issue of reservation of seats and weightage in the sub-committee, he had the matter referred to the Advisory Committee. There too he allowed the discussion to be free and frank. "All the time", according to Munshi, "the Sardar, as Chairman, sat in stolid silence, interrupting the discussions only by some humorous remarks." At the same time he looked for the right man for the right job. He found in Tajamul Husain an energetic spokesman for the Muslims. Husain's forthright criticism of the Nationalist Muslims emboldened Begum Aizaz Rasul to put forward her point of view: namely, now that Pakistan has been formed, in the interests of the Muslims who are left in the country, it would be better not to isolate themselves from the general community by asking for reservations." At the Shia Political Conference, Ali Zaheer from Uttar Pradesh and Tajamul Husain from Bihar had supported joint electorates without reservation and weightage. But the Muslim representatives on the Advisory Committee were still divided in their attitude to reservation of seats. Patel could have forced his decision, but, in fairness to them he did not and preferred to postpone the decision.

The Advisory Committee took up the matter on May 11th. The atmosphere was tense. Jinnah had died eight months ago; and seventeen months had passed since the British had left India. But the ghost of separateness they left behind was still haunting the minds of some of the Muslim representatives. Growing wiser by the decisions of the Shia Conference, the Nationalist Muslims decided not to press for reservation, leaving it for the Muslim Leaguers to give the crucial verdict and face the consequences. Having been in the forefront of Jinnah's struggle for Pakistan, they were placed on the horns of a dilemma. "Afraid of being severely attacked by the Nationalist Muslims", Begum Aizaz Rasul "could not summon up courage to speak". This was despite the fact that at the earlier meeting, Tajamul Husain had, "in a vehement speech, criticised the Nationalist Muslims for seeking reservation, indirectly attacking Maulana Azad", and had "urged upon the Muslim representatives to forget the past and help in creating a secular State". In the absence of Tajamul Husain, according to Munshi, "there was no one to propose that the Muslims did not want reservation, and the fate of the most important issue—joint electorates without reservations—hung in the balance. When the item was called out, there were a few anxious moments of silence. The Sardar looked at me significantly. I, in my turn, whispered to Begum Rasul, who was sitting next to me, that the Sardar expected her to speak. Ultimately, somehow, she summoned up courage and walked up to the lectern. She pleaded in a very hesitant manner for abolition of reservations for Muslims left in India; they were an integral part of the nation, she said, and should play their part in the general electorate."

Hardly had she resumed her seat when Patel, anxious to outmanoeuvre Azad, closed the issue with the statement, "I am very glad that the Muslims are unanimously in favour of joint electorates without reservations. We will now adjourn." His two-hour-long tactful patience won him a victory. It was his great triumph, when H.C. Mookerjee's motion was carried in the Advisory Committee by a majority of 58 to 3. Following this Patel made a most generous statement in the Constituent Assembly, "It is up to the majority community, by its generosity, to create a sense of confidence in the minorities, and so also it will be the duty of the minority communities to forget the past and to reflect on what the country has suffered owing to lack of the 'sense of fairness', which the foreign rulers thought was necessary to keep the balance between community and community." He further observed, "If the minorities have honestly come to the conclusion that, in the changed conditions of this country, it is in the interest of all to lay down real and genuine foundations of a secular State, then nothing is better for the minorities than to trust the good sense and sense of fairness of the majority and to place confidence in them... In the long run it would be in the interest of all to forget that there is anything like majority or minority in this country, and that in India there is only one community." He had the boldness to utter the harsh truth later in May: "A minority that could force the Partition of the country is not a minority at all."

At the Advisory Committee meeting, Nehru described Patel's triumph as a "historic turn in our destiny", and said, "It means not only discarding something that was evil, but turning back upon it and determining with all our strength that we shall pursue a path which we consider fundamentally good for every part of the nation." Frank Anthony, the Anglo-Indian leader who had played an active role in the deliberations of the Advisory Committee, expressed appreciation of Patel's readiness "to understand the real feelings and psychology of the minority mind." He also confirmed that the decisions reached were the result of unanimous agreement; and that "they represent no imposed decisions; they represent decisions which have been arrived at as a result of friendly understanding and compromise... We have set our sails in the right direction... In our march towards the goal, the minorities must be in the vanguard. Any minority which thinks it can flourish on sectarianism is asking for ruin and death."[12]

Frank Anthony has given a convincing picture of Patel as a secularist in his "thumb-nail sketch" of his first meeting with him which was primarily to secure safeguards for his community, the Anglo-Indians. "In the popular mind", he writes, "he had been invested with an awesome aura, as the "Iron Man" of India. That *nom de guerre* suggested not only a hard but even ruthless approach to administrative and political problems... As I sat down, I scrutinised the Sardar. His heavy-lidded, half-closed eyes and sphinx-like manner did not help in my assessment. I stated the case of the community before him rather fully, setting out the historical and political position, and also the special economic needs of the community. Beyond a few non-committal, monosyllabic grunts, he did not interrupt me. I wondered how much he had taken in. To my surprise, he then put me a series of *staccato* questions which no other leader had asked. I realised then, what further contacts and subsequently increasing close association only helped to confirm, here was a man with a crystal-clear mind, who could see to the core of a problem within the shortest possible time."[13] After he was fully satisfied, Patel graciously gave Anthony what he had come to ask for—the Anglo-Indian representation in the Constituent Assembly.

Among the Muslims, Jinnah's hitherto Leaguers seemed most satisfied with Patel's policies and actions. They could appreciate the realities much more than the Nationalist Muslims. According to Begum Aizaz Rasul, Jinnah had "permitted the Leaguers to go into the Constituent Assembly probably with the same intention which had persuaded him to let the Muslim League enter the Interim Government earlier"—to wreck it from within. Begum Aizaz Rasul appreciated Patel's patience and spirit of accommodation. Some time in September 1947 she told Patel of Jinnah's promise to her to create a Minorities Board in Pakistan.

Patel's spirited reaction was, "I am very glad you have spoken to Jinnah. I will wait for his decision, as it will make our position easier and help us in our deliberations." Begum Aizaz Rasul laments: "Three months passed in waiting. The Sardar kept his patience, holding in abeyance the discussion in the Minorities Commission. But the patience of the Muslim Leaguers left behind in India was exhausted, and it became apparent that we must take our fate in our own hands."[14]

No matter how much Patel differed with Gandhi and Nehru, and even with Azad and the Nationalist Muslims, he was totally non-communal. His secular outlook was born of an administrator—discreet, judicious and unbiased. And he had quite a few admirers from among rational Muslims. They included politicians like Asaf Ali and Ali Zaheer, and civil servants like Akbar Hydari. Pyarelal confirms, "He was looked upon by some as an enemy of the Muslims and Pakistan. Nothing could be more erroneous... One had only to see him in the company of his Imambhai—the late Imam Saheb Bavazir, Gandhi's South African comrade, and the late Abbas Tyabji to realise that in him there was no tinge of antipathy towards the Muslims as such... After the establishment of the Interim Government, one of his most favourite officers was the Inspector-General of Special Police—a Muslim."[15] Patel's treatment of the Nizam and of the Nawab of Bhopal also gave proof of his secularism.

Patel's was, indeed, a large, secular heart, which prevented serious rioting or an exodus of Muslims from those areas where he was more than a "king"—Borsad, Broach or Surat with large Muslim populations. Genuinely and effectively he imposed law and order to afford protection to the minority community.

K.B. Lall gives an account of Patel's deep concern. Around August 20, 1947, Patel was having a meeting with V.P. Menon, H.M. Patel and Lall at his residence, when a man rushed into the room, bitterly complaining about the murders being committed and asking him to do something to stop them. According to Lall: "The Sardar's face suddenly darkened with pain. In a voice filled with agony, he asked Lall (since he was a resident of Delhi) to do something effective about the matter." Because of lack of time, nothing could be immediately done. Meanwhile, Patel had his second shock, when a man ran into him room, shouting that some Muslims had been stabbed to death near his residence. "His face," says Lall, "showed tremendous grief. The agony of helplessness was writ large on it." With some annoyance, he asked Lall what had been done. Time had not permitted to put any plan into action. An "impatient and angry" Patel "muttered in great anguish" to Lall: "Why can't you get on with the job?" The Delhi Emergency Committee was the outcome, and within a couple of days the situation was brought under control.[16]

Patel's Lucknow speech, however, revealed two things: first, how much he had moved away from Gandhi—not in regard to secularism, but in the manner it should be achieved and sustained. Secondly, how much he was worried about the past continuing to poison Hindu-Muslim relations in Independent India. As a pragmatic, far-seeing politician, he was anxious that people's minds should be rid of such poison, and that the generations to come should be different from the generations the British had nurtured as separate nations living together in the same land. Ignoring his nature of a hard leader, Patel had lent his support to Gandhi on the Khilafat issue, unmindful of the strong, convincing criticism with which others had assailed Gandhi. Among the latter were C.F. Andrews, Jinnah and even Nehru. On the issue of Khilafat, Andrews had written to Gandhi: "... the Khilafat demand (for an Ottoman Empire) would surely cut the ground under the Indian demand for independence... will you or will you not accept Arab and Armenian and Syrian independence in lands which are obviously theirs, and not of the Turks?"[17] Talking to Durga Das, "Jinnah deplored the Khilafat agitation, which had brought the reactionary *mullah* element to the surface... The Hindu leaders had not realised that this movement would encourage the Pan-Islamic sentiment that the Sultan of Turkey was encouraging to buttress his tottering empire and dilute the nationalism of the Indian Muslim."[18]

As a "blind follower" of Gandhi, Patel had ignored all such

criticism. He had declared at the Fourth Gujarat Political Conference held at Ahmedabad in August 1920, "What is the plight of our Muslim brethren? The Turkish empire has been broken up into pieces. The Sultan is held as a prisoner in Constantinople. Syria has been swallowed up by France... while our Government (the British) has laid its hands on Mesopotamia and Palestine." Patel called this "a flagrant breach" of the sacred word given to the Indian Muslims by the Prime Minister during the time of the war. "Such an injustice, on which there can be no two opinions in India." Patel said, "has rent the heart of the entire Muslim community with pain." He, therefore, emphatically stated, "The Hindus cannot remain unmoved when the Muslims are in such an agony. If the Hindus desire the Muslims' friendship, they must share their sorrow."

A year later, in 1921, at Broach, Patel again spoke for his master, "Hindu-Muslim unity is yet like a tender plant. We have to nurture it extremely carefully over a long period; for our hearts are not yet as clean as they should be. We have got into the habit of suspecting each other, and efforts will be made to break this unity. But a golden opportunity lies in cementing such unity forever through the Khilafat. It is the Hindus' duty to help protect Islam by rendering every possible assistance to the Muslims and expressing full faith in the goodness of that community." Later in September, Patel was bitterly critical of the Government over the arrest of the Ali Brothers, "When the Government saw that the Non-Cooperation Movement had shaken the British throne, it arrested the Ali Brothers... The people have seen through the Government's game. Their faith in the Ali Brothers remains unshakable."[19]

Such faith could not be sustained because of the rise of Pan-Islamism in the early 1920s in the wake of the failure of Non-Cooperation. There was the Moplah massacre of the Hindus, and a most serious riot in Kohat. Both happenings sent a shiver down many spines. The atrocities committed by the Moplahs were so "blood-curdling" as to make B.R. Ambedkar regret that "certain Khilafat leaders were so misguided as to pass resolutions of congratulations to the Moplahs on the brave fight they were conducting for the sake of religion." Even two Britishers, Theodore Morrison and J. Campbell Ker, considered "the Moplah atrocities as the direct sequel to the appeals of racial hatred generated during the Khilafat agitation." An appalled Annie Besant wrote: "... we do not want to see another specimen of the Khilafat raj in India."

The concept of Hindus and Muslims as two nations was born not with Jinnah, the creator of Pakistan, but with the Aga Khan and poet Mohammad Iqbal. The Aga Khan stated in 1929, "The Muslims of India are not a community, but a nation... and (have) a population outnumbering in the aggregate the total even of the pre-war German Europe."[20] The following year, Iqbal supported the creation of a Muslim India by observing, "I would like to see Punjab, the NWFP, Sind and Baluchistan amalgamated into a single state. Self-government within the British Empire, or without the British Empire, the formation of a consolidated North-West Indian Muslim State appears to me to be the final destiny of the Muslims, at least of North-West India..." Iqbal surpassed the limits of bigotry in his Presidential address at the Allahabad session of the Muslim League the same year, "I confess to be a Pan-Islamist... The mission for which Islam came into this world will ultimately be fulfilled: the world will be purged of infidelity and the worship of false gods; and the true soul of Islam will be triumphant."[21] The Congress refused to see the end towards which India was moving—Partition. At the time of the Kohat rioting, an extremely sad Gandhi merely complained that there was "a snake under his quilt". The apostle of non-violence couldn't have killed it; had he been a hard realist, he would have at least taken the fangs out. The snake was allowed to grow, and force Partition of India. Would that have happened if Patel had a free hand, at least since 1945-46?

Jinnah said good-bye to New Delhi on August 7, 1947. Prior to his departure for Karachi, Begum Aizaz Rasul and some other League leaders "discussed with Jinnah about the fate of the Muslims who were staying back in India"—especially the U.P. Muslims who had "formed both the brain and the physical strength of the Muslim League."[22] But for a vague promise to create a Minorities Board in Pakistan, Jinnah had nothing to offer. He was silent; even coolly indifferent. His mind was preoccupied with the new role he was to play as head of the Dominion of Pakistan. The fulfillment of his dream seemed to have eclipsed the issue of the Indian Muslims. They were now the responsibility of India. Patel saw in the Indian Muslims a forlorn community let down by Jinnah, and split into three broad groups: the first, led by Khaliq-uz-Zaman, were ready to play Jinnah's game of weakening India; the second were the Nationalist Muslims under Azad, who now desired to play the League's game by demanding continuation of reservations, if not separate electorates; and the third were the bewildered Muslim Leaguers.

Patel's solution sought the Muslims as a community to dissociate themselves from the past, and merge into the mainstream of India's socio-economic-political life as equal and responsible citizens of the State. He firmly held the view, "The idea that I am anti-Muslim is an invention made to discredit me. Of course, I hate the Muslim League. They have, particularly Jinnah, spread the poison that... has led to this tragedy of Partition. But there are 70 million Muslims in India. It is our business to see that they are safe and free... I have known nothing so poisonous as the teaching of Jinnah and the Muslim League that it is impossible for the Hindus and the Muslims to live together. It is a horrible thing to preach. It is also false, but could be so easily true if persisted in day after day. Our problem number one is to disprove Jinnah and his evil teaching." Patel's Lucknow speech was a move in that direction: to decontaminate the climate polluted by Jinnah and the British. But he was checkmated by Gandhi and Nehru, so as not to annoy Azad and his group of Nationalist Muslims.

Subsequent years proved the truth and soundness of what Patel had told the Muslims in January 1948 at Lucknow. Jayaprakash Narayan repeated that advice nineteen years later, in 1967, when he asked the Indian Muslims not to forget that "Partition has left a deep wound" in the hearts of the Hindus; and reminded them that "many of the Muslims and Muslim leaders who made

India their home, particularly in Bihar and Uttar Pradesh, were passionate advocates of Pakistan", on account of which there was still "so much mistrust in their heart". Narayan emphasised that "the healing of the hearts and minds will not depend only upon the behaviour of the majority community." Narayan's warning was, "We do not realise on what a veritable volcano of disruption we are sitting. We also tend to forget the history of our country from ancient times down to the British conquest." And Narayan repeated what Patel had said in 1948, "I fear that what I am saying may arouse bitter anger... I am speaking as a friend, as one who is deeply concerned about the future of Indian Muslims, and of the future of our country as a nation."[23]

Patel's advice was as "a friend of the Muslims". Patel had attempted to reach the core of the problem, and find a solution as a rational secularist: a solution based on his fundamental belief in what he had once said, "A nation forgets the lessons of history only at its peril... It will be a folly to ignore realities. Facts take their revenge if they are not faced squarely and well."[24]

24

A Friend of Labour and Capitalists

Patel claimed to be "a friend of labour and the poor as well", and of the capitalists too. That was in true Gandhian spirit. The Socialists, his bitter critics, however, branded him as a friend only of the Rajas and the capitalists. But Patel's friendship, whether with labour and the poor, or with the Rajas and the capitalists, had only one criterion—it must serve the larger interests of India: the unity of the land and the economic well-being of her people. Being the son of a peasant, a leader of many a peasant satyagraha and labour movement, Patel's love for labour was longer and deeper. He stated with a sense of pride, "I can claim longer association with organised labour than probably many labour leaders of today. I served my apprenticeship under that great leader of men and that great friend of labour, Mahatma Gandhi."[1]

Patel's association with Ahmedabad's Textile Labour Association was from its inception in 1917. President Rajendra Prasad considered him to be "one of the earliest among the Congress leaders to interest himself in organising labour. His interest in it began even before the Non-Cooperation movement and he had always been one of the pillars of strength of the Ahmedabad Labour Union..."[2] In 1920 he served as Chairman of the BB & CI Railway Workers' Union. "I wonder," said Rajendra Prasad, "if anyone can claim as much constructive work as he accomplished." Patel could thus legitimately claim, "I am also a friend of the Socialists. Unlike many who indulge in the parrot cry of Socialism, I have no property of my own. Before you talk of Socialism, you must ask yourself how much wealth you have created by your own labour... By experience, I am convinced that what is necessary is for us to learn how to produce wealth, and then to produce (it) and thereafter to think what to do with it."[3] His great fear was that the territorial and administrative unity he had achieved for India might "flounder on the economic rock." He, therefore, thought that the key to the improvement of India's economic situation lay in increased production; also that "the foundations of prosperity are often laid on self-denial."[4] For achieving success, he set the maxim: "Produce and then distribute equitably", together with the warning: either produce or perish.

Patel's thinking was pragmatic and crystal-clear. It suffered from no inhibitions of ideology or sentimentalism. As a "stern realist", he called a spade a spade. "My convictions", he once explained, "are firm and not based on any theories, but on experience and a practical approach to the many problems."[5] He spoke out of conviction when he stated, "In the task ahead, we have to take labour and capital with us. If we fail to do so, we are doomed to disappointment. I have no doubt whatsoever that conflict between labour and capital—and, may I say, also the Government—at this stage would be nothing but ruinous to the country."[6] And he gave a warning, "No country can prosper without industry; nor can labour, in the modern sense, survive without industry."[7] He gave labour a homely example, "If there is no water in the well, none can draw any to drink."[8] He asked the industrialists to understand that: "labour is a driving force for the stabilization of our freedom and no Government can afford to ignore what should be due to them." His advice to labour was that: "strikes are a strategy of the Communists to catch votes in their favour to ascend to power."[9] He also said: "Nationalisation is worthwhile only if we can manage to run the industries. We have neither men nor the resources even to run our administration"; and that "industry has to be established before it can be nationalised. India, industrially, is yet in an infant stage." He told labour, "Like Gandhi, I want to make the capitalists understand where their true duty lies. I cannot succumb to the prevalent fashion to pose as a leader, or to attempt to gain leadership by abusing Princes and capitalists without rhyme or reason."[10]

Patel felt that labour had "fallen into evil ways", and its organisers knew "only one thing and believe only in one method—that is to prop up their leadership by strikes."[11] He regretted that "labour is out to have its demands fulfilled at the point of a bayonet"[12], and had developed the psychology that "labour should produce less and get more money." Labour, Patel thought, "is not being properly led, and must be rescued... Firmness in dealing with labour agitators and in restoring discipline among labour ranks is indisputably necessary. If we cannot be firm, we might cease to govern. The Government cannot allow intimidators to function with immunity."[13]

Keeping the country's interests in view, Patel introduced a Bill in the Constituent Assembly, which provided for "the prevention of strikes in certain essential services." Strong opposition came from pro-Left Congress quarters, especially the Socialists. Yielding under pressure, Nehru withdrew the Bill in Patel's absence from the House on the plea that "he had to go out of Delhi on an important engagement."[14] The withdrawal was, obviously, against Patel's wishes, particularly when he had assured labour, "I myself am all for your getting the legitimate fruits of your labour. The Congress stands by you. Where then is the need for strikes, go-slow tactics or stoppage of work?" He, in fact, held the view, "what labour is entitled to must be settled, and settled satisfactorily and peacefully. But for that the correct method is not stoppage of work, nor sabotage, but arbitration."[15] Patel's simple argument was, "Arbitration had shown the way in Ahmedabad. There is no reason why it should not be successful elsewhere."[16]

Ahmedabad's was a shining example of a most successful labour-capital relationship, in the development of which, Patel played a crucial role under Gandhi's leadership. The textile workers, led by Anasuyaben Sarabhai and Shankerlal Banker, resorted to a strike in 1918, which Gandhi's Secretary, Mahadev Desai, called a "righteous struggle". The millowners were led by Anasuyaben's brother, Seth Ambalal Sarabhai. The strike and the subsequent organization of labour in 1920 under *Majoor Mahajan* was Gandhian insofar as it preferred negotiations and arbitration to strike as a means of settling disputes. An Arbitration Board was set up under the chairmanship of the British Collector of Ahmedabad, G.E. Chatfield. It had three representatives from either side. Gandhi, Patel and Shankerlal Banker represented the workers. Chatfield admired the Gandhian approach to settle peacefully, on the basis of truth and non-violence, labour-capital disputes. Even the Commissioner of the Northern Division, F.G. Pratt, told both the millowners and the workers, "It pleases me very much that there is a settlement between you. I am thoroughly convinced that so long as you follow Gandhi Saheb's advice and do what he tells you, you will fare well and secure justice. You have to remember that Gandhi Saheb and his associates, both men and women, have suffered much, taken a great deal of trouble and shown love and compassion for you. You should remember that always." The millowners Representative, Ambalal, expressed equally noble sentiments: "... if the workers revere Gandhi Saheb, the millowners do no less. On the contrary, they revere him even more. I hope that mutual goodwill among us will remain for all time."[17]

Such hopes were given concrete shape during the strike of 1923, when Gandhi and Patel helped in the framing of an agreement between the two sides. It was Patel's positive role that averted the ruin of the industry. Credit went to both the parties for adopting a Gandhian outlook and approach. Labour circles of Ahmedabad admitted that "the mentality and attitude of the employers have also been of considerable help ...they do not entertain pride or arrogance where business interests are concerned; they are willing and ready to talk and negotiate not only with union officers but even with workmen directly." Labour leaders even helped the Textile Labour Association develop into a truly non-political organisation of massive size and power, with a membership of over 70 per cent of the total work force in Ahmedabad.

The Association has engaged itself for over three quarters of a century now in labour welfare activities; and such activities have contributed towards an integrated development of the workers' socio-economic life. Education has been given the pride of place: schools for children, reading-rooms and libraries for adults, and hostels and homes for workers' girls where they are taught professions like embroidery, tailoring, cooking and even music. Scholarships are given to the deserving. The Association has also been looking after the health and hygiene of its members. Gymnasiums help the workers and their children build their health. Apart from credit and consumer stores societies, cooperative banking offers financial help to the needy. And above all, the Association helps its members to own houses through cooperative housing societies. Ahmedabad has thus proved to be Gandhi's "laboratory for making experiments in truth and non-violence in the field of labour." Such a development, along with the satyagrahas in Champaran and Kheda, taking place almost simultaneously, marked the resurgence of India's national life on Gandhian principles. It was a potent alternative to the Communists' class struggle.

Patel's real worry was not the Socialists but the Communists. He looked upon the former as inexperienced and misguided young friends, but not foes. His regret was that they had thrown reason to the winds in their romantic adventurism with the Communists, and exposed themselves to the contradiction of standing divided between Marx and Gandhi. Patel had a deep hatred for the Communists; for, they, not believing in Gandhi's concept of non-violence, fomented discontent and unrest through strikes and sabotage, and struck terror through violence. Even when Nehru was conciliatory towards the Communists, Patel had vowed: "Assault, murder and pillage among poor villagers is hardly the way to bring about Communism. It is a blot on Communism itself. I have said before, and let me warn again, that

I will root out such people".[18] He accused them of extraterritorial loyalty, and also of betraying India. Such a role the Communists had been playing surreptitiously since 1919. The First World Congress of the Communist International, held in Moscow in April 1919, had declared; "Gandhism is more and more becoming an ideology directed against mass revolution. It must be strongly combated by Communism." The Fifth Congress, held in 1924, called upon the Indian Communists to "bring the trade union movement under their influence. They must reorganise it on a class basis and purge it of all alien elements," and this was to be achieved by infiltrating into the Congress though a Trojan Horse, which they found in the Socialists.

The All-India Trade Union Congress was founded in 1920 with Gandhi's blessings. Its inaugural session was presided over by Lala Lajpat Rai, and attended by a galaxy of Congressmen including Motilal Nehru, Jinnah and Mrs. Annie Besant. As directed by the Fifth Congress, the Communists got into action and created disorderly scenes at the AITUC session held at Calcutta in 1924, with the delegates raising Communist slogans. Greatly alarmed, the President of the session, C.R. Das, warned the organisers of labour in India "not to be misled by European ideals and catchwords", as "their problem was different from that of the West, and that the same solution did not apply to the conditions of both." The year 1924 witnessed a number of strikes taking place in India and 1925 saw the birth of the Communist Party of India.

By 1927 the Communists had gained control of the Kanpur session of the AITUC by securing help of the radical elements in the Congress. They got a party member elected as one of the Secretaries. They celebrated their success by observing in Bombay May 1 as Labour Day. It caught Nehru's imagination. He had just returned from a visit to Russia, fired with radical thinking. He lent support to May Day by suggesting to Anasuyaben to change celebration of Labour Day in Gujarat from December 4th to May 1st. The suggestion was turned down, being alien in spirit; but its impact was to be seen in later years when May Day began to be celebrated throughout India. Nehru also lent support to the Communists by acting as their defence counsel in some of the court proceedings against them.

Up to now the Communists had functioned from outside the Congress. In 1935 they received instructions "to infiltrate into the Congress, gain confidence of the Congress leaders and, if possible, capture the Congress party's leadership". This they were supposed to achieve by disrupting the Congress "by misguiding and setting one Congressman against another by means of subtle propaganda ... while, on the one hand, even important individual leaders like Sardar Vallabhbhai Patel were subtly attacked as being the leaders of the reactionary right wing; on the other, they praised Jawaharlal Nehru and tried to keep Gandhi out of controversy." They were successful in drawing within their orbit Jayaprakash Narayan. He was the General Secretary of the Socialist Party and the Communists used him in arriving at "a united front agreement with the Socialists in 1936." Much to Patel's chagrin, this served the Communists as "a door thrown open to them to get into the Congress." This also proved one of the causes that led to an open clash in 1937 between Nehru, the Congress President-elect, and the Gandhian Old Guard, of which Patel was a leading member. Patel's annoyance with the Socialists led him to dub them "sappers and miners" of the Communist party.

M.R. Masani, a leading socialist, realised the potential dangers of Communist infiltration and he resigned from the Congress Socialist Party in 1939. He resigned because the party lacked courage to take action. The Communists fully exploited their position by breaking up the All India Student's Federation and the All-India Kisan Sabha, and took away with them big chunks of these two organisations. It was in 1940 that Jayaprakash Narayan woke up to the new danger. He has made "a generous admission of his error" in his booklet, *Socialist Unity and the Congress Socialist Party*. The Socialists expelled the Communists from the party. "Obviously late by several years... already sufficient damage had been done, and the Socialist party lay crippled and weak."[19]

Patel could not sit helpless like the Socialists, nor adopt

Nehru's lukewarm, almost neutral, attitude. He was not willing to allow the Communists dominate the labour force. In 1938 he got the Hindustan Mazdoor Sevak Sangh organised under his chairmanship. It was to be a specialised agency to train workers on Gandhian principles. He acted so, as he could not get the Communists expelled from the party for lack of support from Gandhi and Nehru: the former because of the principle of coexistence he believed in; the latter because of his Leftist leanings. Patel's argument was: "The preoccupation of the Congress with the political struggle gave an opportunity to certain sections of the people to exploit the situation to their advantage... placing before labour visions of unrealisable Utopia."[20]

The Communists continued to be members of the Congress. The going was good for them so long as Russia and Britain opposed each other in the Second World War; and the Communists were with the Congress in its opposition to India being made belligerent without her people's consent. With Russia and Britain becoming allies against Germany, the Communists staged a somersault by openly proclaiming the Soviet Union as "the Fatherland of Indian peasants and workers"; and, in consequence, lending a full hand to the Government's war effort. The launching of "Quit India" in 1942 prevented Patel from taking early action against the Communists; and during the next three years when the Congress leaders were in jail, the Communists got their best opportunity to exploit the situation and consolidate their hold over labour.

On his release from prison in 1945, Patel expressed his unhappiness over two things: the Communists' betrayal of India; and labour had been injected with "the strike fever." Since freedom appeared to be round the corner, he felt worried over labour being "at the crossroads"; and stated that if the Congress took "the right road and contribute all their energies to the task of strengthening the country, India will have a glorious future. But if they are misled and take the wrong path, they will go down into the ditch; and it will lead everyone—labour as well as all others—to destruction and ruin."[21] Patel took two steps to resolve the situation. The first was the Communists' expulsion from the

Congress in 1945; the other was the setting up, in May 1947, of a Congress-guided and controlled trade union organisation—the Indian National Trade Union Congress (INTUC).

Acting democratically, Patel had the Communists investigated by a sub-committee comprising Nehru, G.B. Pant and himself. The committee's judgment, which followed an opportunity given to eight Communist members of the AICC to explain their conduct, was: "It leaves no doubt whatsoever about the validity of the charges framed against them. It is clear from their reply that they have been actively opposing and obstructing the policy and the programme of the Congress for a considerable time. They are still acting in a hostile manner so as to undermine and injure the prestige and position of the Congress organisation. They have altogether forfeited the confidence of the Congress and are unworthy to occupy any responsible or elective place in the Congress. Conscious of their guilt, the Communists resigned from all subordinate Congress committees and also from the primary membership of the Congress."

Patel did not stop with that. He took a historic step in the establishment of the INTUC as a counterpoise to the AITUC. Almost entirely at his initiative, the INTUC was born in May 3rd, 1947, primarily to combat, according to its Secretary, Gulzarilal Nanda, "the anti-labour and anti-national role the AITUC had been playing", as also to "voice the genuine demands for realizing the aspirations of the working class", and taking "the necessary steps to protect and promote the interests of both the workers and the country." The INTUC had a two-day session, held in New Delhi on May 3rd and 4th, presided over by Patel. It was inaugurated by the Congress President, J.B. Kripalani. The number of unions represented at the inaugural session was around 200 with a total membership of 575,000, which seemed to be a heartening beginning for the Congress after it had lost touch with labour.

In his presidential address, Patel made a forthright speech, in which he stated, "The debt that the AITUC owes to the Congress is immense. Many eminent Congress leaders were associated with the AITUC for several years from the beginning. Much of the prestige that it now enjoys arose from its association with such Congress leaders as Lala Lajpat Rai, C.R. Das, Pundit Jawaharlal Nehru, Netaji Subhas Chandra Bose and others, who have been its Presidents on various occasions... The Communists, who are in the dominant position in the AITUC, have little scruples as regards the means to be adopted so long as they are helpful to them in discrediting the Congress and defeating its programmes. In their blind opposition to the Government, the Communist labour leaders have thrown all regard for national welfare to the winds. We are passing through one of the worst crises that faces a nation at any time..."

Patel explained "... Strikes are launched on all conceivable pretexts and in utter disregard of the workmen's own interest and well-being. Nothing is achieved through these strikes, except chaos and misery all round. No progress is possible unless there is the requisite atmosphere of peace and security. The strike-mongers... are now turning their attention to the railways and coalmines... their success in these new fields would be nothing less than a calamity for the whole nation." Patel made an impassioned appeal to labour: "The workers of India are only a section of the people and not a class apart. Their culture and their tradition form part of the common heritage of the people of India. In organizing them and seeking the redressal of their grievances, ways and means have to be evolved in consonance with our own conditions. No mere grafting or transplantation of a foreign ideology and method, howsoever suited to the conditions elsewhere, is likely to yield healthy results here. What is required is an indigenous movement having its roots in the Indian soil. Such a movement has for long been in existence and has attained a remarkable degree of success through a number of unions in several centres. But, generally speaking, these unions have held themselves aloof from the AITUC. Today, they are coming together to form a new national organisation. It is to be hoped that the new organisation would give the correct lead to the working class and strive to establish social justice, peace and security, and that its constitution and working would be essentially democratic, giving every one of its constituent units ample scope for free expression of views and action."[23]

In a broadcast over All-India Radio in November 1949, Patel said the "the Government, industry and labour must all play the game in a spirit of national service", and asked the vital question: "Who flourishes if the country sinks into economic slavery? Who sinks if the country prospers? Let that be our ruling sentiment; let that be our ruling thought. Let the industrialists concentrate on getting the maximum out of their plants and machinery. Let labour lend its helping hand to the industrialists to exploit their resources to the maximum national advantage. It will be Government's duty which it must discharge to ensure that the decks are cleared for action and there are no impediments, no bottlenecks and no red-tape. The wheels must move with clock-like precision and perfect smoothness, and there must be no mutual fault-finding."[24] In this tripartite partnership, Patel assured the working class on another occasion, the Government would not "submit to the exploitation of labour". He also stated: "The cry of nationalisation is being raised merely to cause panic. If you get panicky, you fall into the trap. You should yourself realise that industry is to be established before it can be nationalised." His advice to both labour and industry was that the "profit motive is a great stimulant to exertion and rules human conduct in whatever walk of life it may be, whether it is the capitalist, the middle classes, the labour or the agriculturists... transcending everything must be a high sense of civic consciousness and national duty."[25] He was also bold enough to say: "All talk of giving no compensation to the zamindars is dangerous, and, if translated into practice, it would amount to worse than robbery."[26]

In an interview with Dorothy Norman, an American journalist, Patel told her: "Theoretical Socialism, industrial Socialism, are not suited to India. Gandhian Socialism is... Socialism of a country such as Britain must necessarily be different from that of India. Our country is vastly populated... here in India, Socialism should develop on a co-operative basis, rather than as a result of State ownership". He clarified: "After the monsoon is over, what are the people to do? You cannot simply displace them by developing large-scale machinery overnight and a highly industrialised economy. We must develop a co-operative system in India whereby all can be used gradually, but soundly. We must develop the use of small-scale machinery and cottage industries on a controllable basis."[27] Patel's views were the same which he had expressed in January 1935 after the formation of the Socialist Party of India the previous year: "True Socialism lies in the development of village industries. We do not want to reproduce in our country the chaotic conditions prevalent in the Western countries consequent on mass production." The pragmatist in him stated in November 1949: "The time for preparing paper schemes has gone. We cannot indulge any longer in the pastime of conjuring before our vision idealistic utopias... It is no use our offering to a hungry man a rich fare some time hence. Similarly, it is no use overloading an already bewildered mind with confusing ideas... The time has come, if it was not there already, for clear-cut policies and for strong and determined action."[28]

Patel's economic thinking was thus simple, coordinated, unideological, down-to-earth—applicable in equitable measure as much to labour and the poor as to the Rajas and capitalists. He was neither an ideologue, nor a slave to the capitalists, who were ever at his beck and call. *The Times*, London, wrote in its editorial on his demise: "In all his dealings with big business, his personal integrity was not questioned: he was the master, not the servant, of those who provided the Congress with its funds. Because he knew their strength and their weakness, he could shape men to his purpose. That purpose was Indian freedom."[29] Essentially, Patel was a Gandhian—a friend and well-wisher of all—of labour and the poor, and not the least of the Rajas and the capitalists. Dorothy Norman discovered in him "a gentle person, for all the strength; a man of great simplicity with but one thought—the well-being of the future India."[30]

25

The Great Administrator

Amidst deepening crisis in the Interim Government, the Secretary of State decided in October 1946 to stop further recruitment to the Indian Civil Service, with indication of the possibility of termination of his connection with the Services earlier than the date of the constitutional changes. Such a step had dangerous implications. A breakdown prior to the transfer of power in the already depleted Services, with some members showing anti-India bias and some others pro-League, endangered the country's administrative unity. The British had built their Empire on the foundations of such unity through the "Steel Frame." Such a "Frame" was all the more needed in a newly-born democratic India, yet riddled with fissiparous tendencies. Patel felt more than any other leader that only a single, all-India Administrative Service could help him preserve what the British had built and through which they had ruled over India.

Patel was quick to act. He called a conference of the provincial Chief Ministers (then called Prime Ministers) in New Delhi and spoke to them with such stern confidence: "The sooner the Secretary of State's control is ended and the present structure wound up, the better."[1] After a tour of India, Leonard Mosley had confirmed, what Patel was already aware of, that "emotionally, the majority of British Civil Servants in India were pro-Muslim."[2] To meet boldly the new challenge, Patel ordered the immediate replacement of the ICS with a new Indian Administrative Service.

Patel's decision was not to the liking of the Chief Ministers. They favoured provincial (State) civil servants who could be under their complete control "in order to ensure their pliability." According to B.K. Nehru, a senior member of the ICS, "it was only he (Patel) who could force down the throats of unwilling and very powerful heads of provincial Governments the concept of the all-India service." Nehru admits that Patel, "with his much longer vision and his greater grasp of the essential requisites for the Rule of Law", successfully convinced the Constituent Assembly on October 10, 1949 by saying: "The Union (of India) will go, you will not have united India, if you do not have a good all-India Service which has independence to speak out its mind." Patel considered "an efficient, disciplined, contented Service... a *sine qua non* of sound administration under a democratic regime."[3]

Time being short, no competitive examination for recruitment could have been held earlier than July 1947. Patel could not wait that long. A beginning had to be made by recruiting the first batch from amongst demobilised Armed Force personnel, who joined the newly-started IAS training school in Metcalfe House in Delhi in April 1947. That was a bold step. Britain hadn't yet decided whether and when to abdicate power, least of all announcing a date of transfer of power. Patel's move was to prevent any possible breakdown in the administration. The Service's continuity was to ensure not only that, but equally so to maintain law and order, already strained to a break-point.

Patel told the probationers of the first batch on April 21st that "the days of the ICS of the old style are going to be over", and that the formation of the IAS in its place was "both significant and epoch-making—an unmistakable symptom of the transfer of power" from foreign to Indian hands. The IAS, he said, "marks the inauguration of an all India Service officered entirely by Indians and subject completely to Indian control", and, "the Service will now be free to, or will have to, adopt its true role of national service without being trammelled by traditions and habits of the past." Patel offered the probationers a few words of paternal advice: "The days when the Service could be masters are over... Perhaps, you are aware of a saying regarding the Indian Civil Service—that, it is neither Indian nor civil, nor imbued with any spirit of service... Your predecessors had to serve as agents of an alien rule; and, even, against their better judgment, had sometimes to execute the biddings of their foreign employers... A Civil Servant cannot afford to, and must not, take part in politics. Nor must he involve himself in communal wrangles. To depart from the path of rectitude in either of these respects is to debase public service and to lower its dignity."[4]

As an administrator in charge of Home, Patel's immediate task was to grapple with the problems the country was facing, political as well as administrative. Patel had, as Girija Shankar Bajpai, Secretary General to the Government of India and the seniormost ICS, assessed it, "a double task: conservative, in the good sense of the word, in what had been provinces in the old India; creative in the Indian States. Neither was easy. To the ordinary stresses of a transition caused by the withdrawal of trained personnel, which had wielded all power for a hundred years, was added the strain of Partition and the immense human upheavals and suffering that followed it." Bajpai thought: "The fate of our new State hung in the balance during those perilous months... That, despite some oscillation, the scales stayed steady was due not only to the faith of the people in its leaders, but to the firm will and strong hand of the new Home Minister—Sardar Patel."[5]

Patel's unique success as the Great Administrator was due to his qualities of head and heart: the former gave him the strength of mind—an iron-will; the latter, a considerate, accommodating spirit. He was neither a hidebound person, nor an ideologue. He was a stern realist. His flexibility helped him adopt a strategy that suited a particular situation, without changing his basic concepts. He realised, more than his colleagues, that in the solution of administrative problems, only the Civil Servants could act as his faithful agents—not the politicians. Patel's realism was admitted by British historian Judith Brown: "Patel, as Home Minister in the Interim Government, was well aware that in the turbulent days of 1946-47, the ICS, whatever its previous image in the eyes of Congressmen, was a bastion against chaos and the disintegration of Government." Patel was "partly instrumental in persuading other Congressmen that continuity in administration must be maintained. Clearly the Service was a source of stability."[6] He, therefore, turned to those members of the ICS who had opted to serve Free India. He needed them as much as they needed him. The British had left them orphaned; while Prime Minister Nehru and pro-Left Congressmen openly aired their hostility towards them as a class.

With shrewdness, tact and generosity, Patel helped them overcome their predicament by extending his hand of friendship. Early in 1947, he invited about thirty to forty senior Civil Servants to his residence and talked to them, much to their surprise, in a manner none had done before—utterly informal, free from the rigid mannerism of their former bosses. His talk was brief, realistic, transparently sincere and patriotic. Prefacing it with a narration of how he and his colleagues had for years worked with "only one burning desire—to serve the country", Patel invited them "to dedicate themselves equally to the service of the country." He did not promise them "in return anything more than the joy which he himself and his colleagues had experienced through such single-minded devotion to what they regarded as the supreme duty, and which he was certain they too would experience." Patel offered the Civil Servants "equality" of consideration, if only they too would respond and work as untiringly and unceasingly as he and his colleagues, whether in or out of Government, had been doing for the people of the country."[7]

Patel's concept of the Civil Service emerged from the belief he held and which he once expressed to his Home Secretary H.V.R. Iengar: "It would be a bad day if people did not look up to officials holding high positions. Ministers come and Ministers go, but the permanent machinery (the Civil Service) must be good and firm, and have the respect of the people."[8] Coincidentally, nearly a hundred years before, Lord Macaulay had expressed identical views in the British Parliament: "The character of the

Governor-General is less important than the character of the Administrator by whom the administration was carried on."[9] The British Civil Servants were, thus, the real founders of the Empire. In a Free India, Patel looked upon the ICS and their successors in the new Service (the Indian Administrative Service) as "partners with him in the task of administration". He "selected people, trusted them, and gave them their head, subject to overriding policy being settled by him." Bajpai once ruefully told Iengar that "he was just a scribe waiting for the oracle to speak." Nehru, according to Iengar, "did not think of us, as a class, as being particularly distinguished." To the ICS officers individually, he was "most kindly and considerate", but he often maintained an ivory tower aloofness; and in discussions he "started off with certain fixed convictions which he would not allow anyone to discuss with him." Further, unlike Patel, "Nehru, with all his great qualities, did not have any particular feeling for administration, or the genius required for getting the maximum work out of the large heterogeneous mass of Government servants all over the country."[10] Patel was a patient listener, who possessed an open mind and a willingness to benefit from others' experience. He had the administrator's tact and ability to carry others along with him, even when the final judgment remained his. He imposed his decisions democratically—not through blatant imposition, but through willing acceptance.

As an administrator, Patel was a class by himself. He conducted his work mostly from his residence—not by reading files till midnight, but by giving decisions on briefings by his Secretaries. His method of settling official matters was short and swift, involving the minimum of time and achieving the maximum of results. His Secretaries visited him with their briefs to obtain orders. Though verbal, he always stood by them. He had a photographic memory.

Earlier in his working with Patel, Iengar had an intriguing experience. One day he had discussed with him an important issue concerning a political leader who had threatened a fast unto death and with dire consequences if his conditions were not accepted immediately. Iengar carried in his pocket the letter he had received from the leader concerned in the expectation that Patel would surely like to see it before giving his decision. The issue was discussed on the basis of verbal briefing. Patel gave his decision, showing no interest in seeing the letter. For Iengar this was something unusual. Out of sheer curiosity, he asked Patel "whether he did not want to read it himself", and interestingly records: "He turned to me and asked whether I had not told him all that it contained, and whether there was any point which I had forgotten to mention. I said, 'No'. I had given him a gist of all the important points in it. He then refused to look at the letter."[11]

On another occasion, Patel asked Iengar what he thought of a political leader who happened to be a senior Congressman. Iengar felt uncomfortable. He politely told him that "it sounded a little comic to me that he should consult me about that particular gentleman", as Patel "knew a great deal more about him than the official machinery." Iengar adds: "He turned to me and gravely said that I was making a mistake. 'I may have moved about with him a great deal,' he told me, 'but how do I know that my impression of the man is not a prejudiced one? It is of the greatest use to me to know what you or the official machinery think. Your appreciation of the person may be based on facts, of which I have no knowledge. Between my own knowledge and what you are able to tell me, I may be able to get a balanced picture'." According to Iengar, "he wanted to make the fullest use of the knowledge and experience which the Civil Service had acquired. To him they were the people with whom it was worthwhile discussing a problem before he took a decision."[12]

Patel's democratic spirit gave his officers full freedom to express their views without fear or restraint. He expected of them to think and act independently to the best of their knowledge and ability, without shirking their responsibility. He once stated: "My Secretary can write a note opposed to my views. I have given that freedom to all my Secretaries. I have told them, 'If you do not give your honest opinion for the fear that it will displease your Minister, then, please, you had better go. I will bring another Secretary.' I will never be displeased over a frank expression of opinion." For, he said, "these people are the instruments. Remove them, and I see nothing but a picture of chaos all over the country."[13] One day he asked Law Secretary Shavax A. Lal to give him his opinion on an issue raised by Mountbatten when he was still the Viceroy and Governor-General. Lal "just had a somewhat unpleasant experience of a straightforward but rather unpalatable opinion" given by him to one of Patel's Cabinet colleagues. He, therefore, asked him if he wanted his honest opinion. Patel, according to Lal, "flared up and said tartly: 'Does Government pay you Rs.4,000 a month for your dishonest opinions? It is your duty to give an honest opinion, and it is for me to accept it or not.' Lal was very much impressed. "After this introduction, "he records," I knew where I stood and never hesitated to speak my mind whenever the Sardar consulted me."[14]

The Government faced an extremely difficult administrative problem over the implementation of the Congress Working Committee resolution directing it to take immediate steps towards the formation of a linguistic Andhra State. Iengar, as Home Secretary, was, however, opposed to making a move in the matter. Being in a quandary, he asked Patel: "Sir, the gentlemen who have passed this resolution include Shri Jawaharlal Nehru, Maulana Azad, Dr. Rajendra Prasad and you yourself. All of you are Cabinet Ministers and you have taken this decision. What do you expect of me to do about it?" Without a moment's hesitation, Patel asked me: "Are you, or are you not, the Home Secretary?" Iengar was a little taken aback. "Of course, I am", he replied. "Then," Patel said, "do your duty as Home Secretary. Prepare a note to the Cabinet stating what exactly in your judgment are the implications of the proposal and how they should be further examined. It must make no difference to you who are the parties to the Working Committee resolution. You must clearly and frankly analyse the whole problem." Iengar did exactly that, "subjecting to a cold analysis" the decision which Patel and others had taken. As a result, the proposal to create the State of Andhra before the Constitution came into force was postponed. In fact, such a linguistic State could never materialise so long as Patel was alive. After the Cabinet meeting, Iengar called on Patel and told him rather in a lighter vein: "I have succeeded in getting you as Home Minister to overrule yourself as Sardar Patel of the Congress Working Committee!"[15] Patel openly stated that the formation of linguistic provinces would "unmistakably retard the process of consolidation of our gains, dislocate our administrative, economic and financial structure, let loose... forces of disruption and disintegration." He did not allow that to take place so long as he was alive. Nehru could not resist pressures, and yielded to the creation of the first linguistic State of Andhra in December 1952. That was two years after Patel had passed away.

Iengar gives a classic example of Patel standing by his Home Secretary. He had to take a most crucial decision in the absence of Patel and other senior Ministers from New Delhi, including the Prime Minister. The decision brooked no delay. Iengar acted on his own to the best of his knowledge and ability. Later when Iengar reported to him the action he had taken, Patel "shook his head with evident disapproval and said that, if I had consulted him beforehand, he would have taken a different decision. I pressed my arguments. He then patiently explained to me the reasons."[16] Iengar further states: "I was very unhappy about this, but he asked me not to worry and said that every human being makes mistakes. When the matter subsequently came up before the Cabinet, he told them that the decision was his, and there the matter ended. The incident made a striking impression on me."[17]

An equally striking example of Patel's trust in the Civil Servants is typified by the confidence he reposed in his redoubtable States Secretary, V.P. Menon, which he enjoyed to a degree as no other Civil Servant perhaps did, even when he was a non-ICS. Such confidence Patel had expressed as early as July 1946 when he told him: "Menon, you and I are working for a common purpose. Let there be no mistake about our determination to achieve Independence. If the British are under the impression that they can hang on because of the difference of opinion between the

Congress and the League, they are mistaken. We will not consider any sacrifice too great to achieve our objective."[18] A year later, in July 1947, after Menon had secured Patel's approval to the basic contents of the draft Instrument of Accession, he "did not trouble him with the changes which the draft underwent from time to time without affecting its main features". The *Hindustan Times* managed to get hold of a copy of the draft and published it. That very morning when Menon was with Patel, the latter mischievously put on an innocent and serious face, and pretending as if he had been ignored, told his States Secretary: "Menon, now that The *Hindustan Times* has published the Instrument of Accession, can I see a copy of it?" Menon felt puzzled. Even fear gripped his mind. Was the old man really annoyed? Within seconds a faint smile lit up Patel's somber face, and he said "he was only joking." And Menon happily records: "The Sardar had that saving sense of humour which is so great an attribute, especially in a man of his position and responsibility."[19]

Patel gave his Secretaries a status which commanded respect. As Secretary, Menon enjoyed a status far more powerful than he had enjoyed as Reforms Commissioner under Wavell and Mountbatten, even when he had played a crucial role in the preparation of the June 3 Plan. Under Patel, Menon could rub shoulders with the tallest among the Princes and get the integration plans executed expeditiously. He used "the device of countering resistance or recalcitrance with the threat of taking them to the Sardar."[20] As Home Secretary, Iengar also enjoyed a similar status. He was with Patel one day when the Maharaja of Patiala arrived. Since he was the Rajapramukh of PEPSU, Iengar volunteered to wait in the drawing-room outside till he finished with the Rajapramukh. Patel disagreed, but invited the Maharaja to his bedroom and offered him "to take another chair till my work was finished." Next morning lengar asked Patel why he had shown "such exceptional courtesy" to him. The reply was typical of an administrator: "It was nothing personal, but he felt that the position of a Secretary to the Government of India was a very high one and should be maintained at a high level in public estimation."[21]

Patel's greatness as an administrator was born of his personal qualities: he was ever cool, even tempered, alert, never losing the reins of command—no matter how grave the occasion. His light-heartedness and humour would help others reach decisions with composure. Thomas Elmhirst, the Air Chief, recalls a meeting of the Emergency Committee in New Delhi in August 1947 when "Delhi appeared to be in the hands of armed Sikhs. The city was certainly not under the control of the police or Armed Forces. "Mountbatten was asked to take the chair. On either side of him sat Nehru and Patel, and those present included some of the Cabinet Ministers, as also General Rob Lockhart, the Army C-in-C, and Elmhirst by special invitation. According to Elmhirst: "There was fear in the highly charged atmosphere as views were expressed as to how the Government could regain control. Someone expressed a view that was absurd. Sardar Patel laughed heartily, and made a remark that caused most of us to laugh. The tension was broken, and he followed up with a wise suggestion that brought general agreement."[22]

In handling public matters, Patel was free from bureaucratic pride or outlook. He was practical, just and fair. Once he understood a complaint, none could be more accommodating and generous. After the formation of the Congress Ministry in Rajasthan, the jagirdars of Bikaner were "faced with many problems of vital importance". A deputation of them, led by Thakur Jaswant Singh, waited upon Patel, but failed to meet him, as "the Rajasthan Ministry had prevailed upon Shankar and Maniben to see that we did not get the interview." According to Jaswant Singh, "for weeks we had to cool our heels in Delhi without the interview." Every time Patel was approached, Shankar would say: "Sardar Sahib has no time." Jaswant Singh was a member of the Constituent Assembly. Yet, he admits: "I was afraid of approaching the Sardar directly. At last, one day I took courage and met him in the lobby. Seeing me approach the Sardar, Shankar hurriedly joined us and bluntly told me: 'For some days Sardar Sahib will have no time.' I stared at the Sardar, who sympathetically told me that he would see the deputation the following day. Shankar again intervened by saying that the Sardar's whole day was already booked. I was assured by the Sardar not to worry. Jaswant Singh narrates further: "Next day I received a phone call that the Sardar would see the deputation at 3 pm. On arrival, we were told by Shankar that only 15 minutes had been allotted to us, and in view of the Sardar's bad health and other engagements, we should not take longer time. As we were ushered in, we found Maniben and Shankar sitting with the Sardar. We had hardly opened our lips when Maniben began talking of the atrocities committed by the jagirdars and the Princes. Fifteen minutes thus passed away, and Shankar told us that the time was up and that the doctor and others were waiting. We were dumb-founded. The Sardar looked at us with sympathy and affectionately told us: 'Never mind the doctor and others. They can wait. You have not told me what you want. Take your own time.' Encouraged by these words, we poured out our heart, taking more than one hour. The Sardar patiently heard us, much to the embarrassment of Maniben and Shankar. And in a few days time, we got our redress."[23]

Though accommodating and generous, Patel could be unsparing in upbraiding erring colleagues and irresponsible politicians. He treated them all with the same yardstick, though his style of reproach or expression of dissent would vary in degree from individual to individual. The administrator in him was conscious of the other's status. Patel's genius lay in changing his mood and style, which was in direct proportion to the individual concerned. His correspondence reflects matter-of-fact directness of the head rather than the impulsiveness of the heart. He strictly adhered to administrative discipline, being governed by the spirit of law. As Home Minister, he considered it his duty to preserve and promote administrative etiquette. He pulled up Dr. B.C. Roy, Chief Minister of West Bengal, for showing discourtesy to the Prime Minister: "I was distressed to find you writing to the Prime Minister like this. Had it been a personal letter, or had you been talking to him, perhaps as an elder, you could afford all this liberty. But in an official communication to him as Prime Minister, I had expected that you would be deferential as is appropriate to the dignity of the high office that he holds, as well as the office which you yourself occupy as serving your own interest."[24]

Patel was no less critical of Govind Ballabh Pant, Chief Minister of Uttar Pradesh, for declaring open a Congress exhibition at Varanasi showing pictures of atrocities committed by the police during the "Quit India" movement in 1942. It amounted to undermining the administration. He wrote to Pant: "... The punishment of persons who were concerned with the 1942 atrocities is quite a different matter... But the caricaturing of official activities in the manner reported in the Press at a time when we are in office is open to serious objection. This is likely to affect the morale of the police force which, in the present emergency, can hardly be considered proper. It is also likely to agitate the public mind against the Services. For obvious reasons, this must be avoided if administrative efficiency is to be maintained in these difficult times."[25]

Patel's wrath could be seen when he handled trouble-shooters. Jainarain Vyas, President of the Rajasthan Provincial Congress Committee, incurred it for getting a resolution passed by his Provincial Congress Committee calling upon Hiralal Shastri and his ministers to resign. Patel was furious and unsparing in his admonition: "You should understand that Hiralal Shastri as Premier is not responsible to the PCC, which cannot appropriate to itself functions of the legislature. He owes his Premiership not to election as leader, or to the mandate of PCC, but to my choice of leadership at the unanimous request of all of you..." Patel went further to warn him: "... your persistence in the undesirable and harmful course which you have adopted will merely recoil on you. I am quite sure the tactics you have adopted are a disservice to the organization we all belong to, and are injurious too, though your narrow outlook may make it appear as serving your own interest."[26]

Patel did not spare even his non-Congress Cabinet colleagues. John Mathai was one such person, who was the Railway Minister, whose services Patel had specially secured from J.R.D. Tata. He could not tolerate Mathai's acting bureaucratically in the matter of quick transport by rail of the refugees from West Punjab and the NWFP, who were awaiting "timely assistance to escape from (their) sad and almost desperate plight." He wrote to him: "... I find that the progress made in securing reasonable rail communication is slow and entirely out of keeping with the requirements... It must be borne in mind that evacuation must claim prior and almost sole attention during the present emergency..."[27] Unwilling to accept Mathai's explanation, Patel wrote back: "I am surprised and distressed at the tone and content of your letter... You were obviously in a temper, but I am not going to emulate it... You have apparently assumed that I wrote my letter to you as Home Minister. I have sufficient sense of responsibility to realise that as such I have no business, save in my capacity as a Minister of the Cabinet with joint responsibility, to express myself in relation to the duties and functions of another Ministry. But as Deputy Prime Minister, it has fallen upon me, in the absence of the Prime Minister, to coordinate in Delhi the various measures being taken for the evacuation and relief of refugees."[28]

Non-adherence to administrative discipline and correct official procedure caused an open clash between Patel and Nehru in December 1947 on two major issues. The first, as already referred to in the chapter on Kashmir, related to Gopalaswami Ayyanger's bypassing the States Ministry in authorizing the East Punjab Government to loan motor vehicles to the tune of Rs.20 lakhs to Kashmir under Abdullah's pressure. The second issue related to Nehru's sending Iengar, then his Principal Private Secretary, to Ajmer, instead of going there himself as he had informed Patel, to inquire into the communal disturbances over the head of the Chief Commissioner, who was Iengar's senior. Patel immediately wrote to Nehru: "I am surprised—perhaps 'shocked' would be a more appropriate description—to hear that you sent Iengar to Ajmer-Merwara..." When Nehru contended that "if I am to continue as Prime Minister, I cannot have my freedom restricted and I must have a certain liberty of direction", Patel sent a sharp reply: "I have no desire to restrain your liberty of direction in any manner, nor have I ever done so in the past. It is also not my desire to hustle you, or to embarrass you, in any manner, but when it is clear to us that on the fundamental question of our respective spheres of responsibility, authority and action there is such vital difference of opinion between us, it would not be in the interest of the cause which we both wish to serve to continue to pull on longer... The question of your resignation or your abdicating your functions does not arise at all. I am at one with you in that the decision may be taken with dignity and goodwill, and I will strain every nerve to help you doing so, but you will not, I am sure, want me to continue long as an ineffective colleague."

Nehru sought Gandhi's arbitration on his differences with Patel in a long note he submitted to him on January 6, 1948, to which Patel answered the Mahatma: "I have tried my best to appreciate what he (Nehru) says on that subject (Hindu-Muslim relations), but howsoever much I have tried to understand it on the twin basis of democracy and Cabinet responsibility, I have found myself unable to agree with his conception of the Prime Minister's duties and functions. That conception, if accepted, would raise the Prime Minister to the position of a virtual dictator, for he claims 'full freedom to act when and how he chooses.' This, in my opinion, is wholly opposed to democratic and Cabinet system of government. The Prime Minister's position, according to my conception, is certainly pre-eminent; he is first among equals. But he has no overriding powers over his colleagues; if he had any, a Cabinet and Cabinet responsibility would be superfluous. In my view, the Prime Minister, as the leader of the party and the head of the whole administration, is inevitably concerned that Cabinet decisions are effective and that there is no conflict between one Ministry and another. But the entire responsibility for implementing the policy of Government rests upon the Ministers and ministries under them which are concerned with the subject matter of the Cabinet decisions. The Prime Minister has, accordingly, the right to ask for information from the Minister concerned, as well as the right to consult and advise on the lines of policy to be adopted and even the manner in which the policy is to be implemented. But the responsibility for the implementation of the policy must be that of the ministry concerned and of the Minister-in-charge, and the Prime Minister should influence action by way of consultation with and advice to the Minister. I feel sure that this position of the Prime Minister not only fully safeguards his preeminence and makes him an effective head of the administration, but is also fully in accord with democratic principles and rules of ministerial and Cabinet responsibility."[29]

Gandhi did not have the time to resolve the differences between Nehru and Patel. His assassination, however, did that job. A surge of sentimentalism in the wake of his martyrdom drifted away the dark clouds which had hung over Nehru and Patel, and united the two to jointly shoulder the burdens of an infant State which had gained her freedom less than six months earlier. Gandhi's last visitor, before his assassination, was Patel, from whom he extracted a promise that he would look upon Nehru as his leader. Patel's surrender was a sacrifice, perhaps unparalleled in history, on two counts. He enjoyed majority support in the party; and Nehru's leadership was not through the democratic process of election, but through nomination by Gandhi.

Patel hadn't spared Wavell or Mountbatten or Churchill either. He had told Wavell on February 14, 1947 that "a corporate body like the Central Government has ceased to exist, and that the sooner the present state of affairs is put an end to, the better."[30] And in view of the deteriorating law and order situation, Patel did not hesitate to tell Mountbatten: "Since you have come out here things have got much worse. There is a civil war on and you are doing nothing to stop it. You won't govern yourself and you won't let the Central Government govern. You cannot escape responsibility for this bloodshed."[31] His firmness was on occasions tinged with "a delightful sense of humour". At their first meeting on March 25, 1947, when Mountbatten expressed pleasure that his first Cabinet meeting went off "so smoothly", Patel told him "with a twinkle in his eye, that this was only because all the members had previously decided not to give me a stormy passage the first time."[32]

Perhaps, the most telling illustration of the punch and power of Patel's pen may be cited from the manner he silenced Winston Churchill, who, as late as June 1948, while "bemoaning the disappearance of the title of Emperor of India from the Royal titles", had the audacity to make the derogatory remark that the Government of India had been handed over to "men of straw". In reply, Patel called Churchill "an unashamed imperialist at a time when imperialism is on its last legs", and "the proverbial last ditcher for whom obstinacy and stupid consistency count more than reason, imagination or wisdom." Patel gave a grim warning from his sick-bed in Dehra Dun: "I should like to tell His Majesty's Government that if they wish India to maintain friendly relations with Great Britain, they must see that India is in no way subjected to malicious and venomous attacks of this kind and that British statesmen and others learn to speak of this country in terms of friendship and goodwill."[33] Churchill, great as he was, despite his being a blue-blooded, diehard Conservative and unabashed anti-Indian, however, took Patel's attack in good spirit. He conveyed to Patel through Anthony Eden, during the latter's visit to India, that he had "thoroughly enjoyed the retort... he had nothing but admiration for the way the new Dominion had settled down to its tasks and responsibilities, particularly those involving relations with the Indian States. Churchill had specially said that the Sardar should not confine himself within the limits of India, but that the world was entitled to see and hear more of him."[34]

Patel's was an administrator's pen: precise, direct, sometimes biting but always strong. It could be soft and soothing, or cut through like a razor. But he was ever discreet in the use of words. His effectiveness lay in his restraint, in his unerring judgment, fair-mindedness and inflexible determination. Iengar calls him a "genius in the art of administration" who had "a tremendous capacity for listening—and listening patiently and carefully—before he made up his mind. And, thereafter, he was a rock."[35] And "after listening and reflection", when he had made up his mind, then "you knew that a giant had got up and moved inflexibly into action."[36] Rising above his person, Patel took "a broad and generous view of things", and was "generous and forgiving in his adversary's defeat."

Patel did not forget those who executed his plans—the ICS. He never doubted their loyalty, appreciated their work and offered them full protection by acting as their Godfather. He told the Constituent Assembly: "I need hardly dilate at length on the necessity of maintaining their discipline and morale, and keeping them contented. In no other circumstances can we get out of the Services loyal and efficient service except by trying to appreciate their difficulties and their work... it is our duty to see that the machine with which we have to work is kept in good humour and good temper."[37] Later on October 10, 1949, Patel again told the House: "I must confess that in point of patriotism, in point of loyalty, in point of sincerity and in point of ability, you cannot have a substitute. They are as good as ourselves."[38]

Philip Mason, himself a distinguished British member of the Indian Civil Service, has called Patel "a natural administrator who did not seem to need experience." Everything came to him instinctively, instantly and intuitively. His watchword was speed. His decisions never brooked delay or interference. They were decisive. H.V.R. Iengar once said: "I often used to wonder where exactly lay the strength of the Sardar. There he was, mostly conducting his business from his sick-bed or lying reclined on a chair in his drawing-room, always exquisitely polite and never once raising his voice. His politeness was really impeccable. I believe the truth of the matter was twofold. The first is that he listened, patiently to all sides of a case before making up his mind, but once he made up his mind nothing would shake him from his decision. The other is that he had the capacity to say 'No' to requests which he felt should not be accepted... the Sardar was absolutely firm..."[39]

An emotional bond united the Civil Servants to Patel—so much so that when he died, the ICS Association met on December 16, 1950 to condole his loss. Bajpai, who presided, being the most senior, rose to say: "We meet today to mourn the loss and to pay tribute to the memory of a great patriot, a great administrator and a great man. Sardar Vallabhbhai Patel was all three—a rare combination in any historic epoch and in any country... History holds many examples of the fruits of freedom squandered by lack of attention to stability and order, the twin foundations of society..." which Patel provided. Bajpai referred to the "ties of trust between the Sardar and the Services" and to the "keenness and warmth of his personal interest in their welfare. A smaller man might have allowed old-time prejudices to raise a curtain of suspicion between him and those who had served an alien regime." Bajpai concluded: "That we should deeply mourn the loss of one who gained freedom for us in our time, and sought successfully to impact to it the durability that comes from stable conditions and administrative strength is but natural."[40]

Patel belonged to that class of administrators who are born, not made; who lead, but are not led. Foreign correspondent O.M. Green wrote on his demise: "There is no obvious successor to Vallabhbhai Patel. Men of his stamp are not born every day."

26

Gandhi, Nehru, Patel

Patel, according to Gandhi's close associate Kaka Kalelkar, belonged, by tradition, to the illustrious class of Shivaji and Tilak, though his reverence for Gandhi was of a blind devotee.[1] With Bal Gangadhar Tilak, he had many similarities—physical as well as temperamental; with Shivaji he shared the genius of a General who had commanded some of Gandhi's most successful satyagraha—Kheda and the Dandi March or the Salt Satyagraha. Patel played the role of Deputy Commander in the first; in the latter, that of John the Baptist. Vinoba Bhave held the view that Patel was "the accurate bowman of Gandhi's struggle, his disciple and his GOC. He knew no retreat... It was due to his presence in the Government that the people of India could keep courage and feel secure, just as in the time of Shivaji the people remained brave and unbroken due only to his personality."[2]

Patel and Tilak carried with dignity a heavy, impressive, domineering face resting on a well thick-set bodyframe. Both were of a stern character: iron-will, indomitable courage, incorruptible integrity, austere living and a life full of suffering and sacrifice. Mahavir Tyagi gives a moving account of Patel's simplicity and sacrifice. One evening he was with Patel in the Circuit House, Dehra Dun, where he was convalescing after his massive heart-attack. Tyagi happened to be in a jocular mood. Seeing Maniben, Patel's devoted daughter, wearing a *khadi* sari with a big patch covering a torn portion, he made fun of her: "Maniben, you think yourself to be 'great', being the daughter of a man who has, within a year, established a far-flung 'empire'. Not so was of Rama's or Krishna's, nor Asoka's, Akbar's, or of the British! As the daughter of one who is the 'Sardar' of big Rajas and Maharajas, don't you feel ashamed of wearing such a sari?" Teasing her further, Tyagi said: "If you happen to go round my town, people will take you for a beggar and offer you some money."

Patel burst into laughter, deriving full pleasure out of the banter and jocularly observed: "The bazaar is full of people. By evening she will be able to collect a good amount!" Dr. Sushila Nayyar interjected to reveal the truth behind the patched sari: "Tyagi, Maniben spends the whole day in looking after Sardar Saheb. Then she has to find the time to write her diary and spin yarn on the *charkha*. Of the yarn thus spun, clothes are stitched for Sardar Saheb, as he doesn't purchase cloth from the *khadi bhandar*. When his *dhotis* and *kurtas* are torn, Maniben makes her clothes out of them." To this Patel again added a touch of humour by observing: "She is a poor man's daughter. How can she afford to have good clothes? Her father doesn't earn at all?"[3]

Devotion to duty was the hallmark of the character of both Tilak and Patel. Tilak was writing his editorial for the *Kesari* when a telegram announced the death of his young son. He put the telegram aside, finished the editorial, and then went home grief-stricken. Patel acted likewise. He was arguing a criminal case at Borsad when a telegram was delivered to him in the court-room. He read it, quietly put it in his pocket, continued with his arguments without betraying emotions. He had told himself: "One life has gone. Let me save another."[4] When he had finished his arguments, the judge asked him out of curiosity: "Mr. Patel, may I take the liberty of enquiring as to what the telegram was about." In a depressed mood, Patel said: "My Lord, my wife is dead." Patel's devotion to duty saved a life.

Like Tilak, Patel placed duty above his person. And like Tilak, Patel carried inside him the fire of revolt. Yet, he preferred Gandhi to Tilak as his guru. For, Gandhi, unlike Tilak, was not an individual crusader, but a man of mass action who converted Tilak's revolutionary *mantra*—"Swaraj is my birthright, and I will have it"—into a clarion call for the nation; and Tilak's mass contact into mass struggle for national regeneration, again through Tilak's four-fold programme: *swadeshi*, boycott, prohibition and national education. It was Gandhi, not Tilak, who aroused Patel's dormant national spirit.

To Patel, Gandhi was a rebel-god, who seemed to have descended upon India to free his people from the bondage of the British. Patel's view of Gandhi was none other than Annie Besant's who had once exclaimed: "Why! His eyes are like the eyes of Christ". And soon, like Christ, Gandhi began "drawing people to himself like a magnet." Patel was one of them, but the most precious from Gandhi's point of view. Unlike Nehru, Patel's was a total surrender: one of "not to reason why" but "to do or die"; and he prided himself on being called Gandhi's blind follower. Their companionship was highly complementary. In Yusuf Meherally's view: "Vallabhbhai at long last found a leader the like of whom the country had not seen for centuries—not since the days of Asoka and Akbar. The Mahatma had found a lieutenant that those Emperors would have given a kingdom to get."[5] Patel saw in Gandhi "a tremendous revolutionary force in action", as also "the idealised personification of vast millions". And of Patel, Nehru has testified: "Perhaps, in the whole of India Gandhi has had no more loyal colleague than Vallabhbhai—a man strong and unbending in his work, and yet devoted to him personally and to his ideals and policy. I could not claim to have accepted these ideals in the same ways."[6]

Being an idealist, a sentimentalist and a visionary, Nehru's attachment to Gandhi was emotional, not spiritual. He was more of a Marxian Socialist than a Gandhian Socialist, whereas Patel was a Gandhian without being a Socialist. Nehru, in his own words, "always felt attracted towards big machinery" as the key to economic prosperity; whereas Patel, like Gandhi, believed that "our salvation can come only through the farmer". Nehru was, as Gandhi described him, "more English than Indian in his thoughts and make-up." Patel was "a born kisan", the son of the soil; also a soldier who kept "his feet firmly on the soil." The difference between Gandhi and Nehru, unlike Gandhi and Patel, was essentially one of age. They belonged to two different generations, two different classes, two different upbringings. Theirs was a clash between India's ancient past and the modern West; between youth and age. Patel was in this respect much nearer to Gandhi than was Nehru. And it was Patel, rather than Nehru, who provided the much-needed muscle power to Gandhi's soul force.

Gandhi and Patel were like Marx and Lenin. In the Bardoli satyagraha, the British had linked his name to the Soviet revolutionary. Like Marx, Gandhi was a political thinker and inspirer; while Patel, like Lenin, was a master of practical politics. It was a combination of their political philosophy and organisational skill which "transformed the Congress into a mass party geared for militant action." Yet, Gandhi's weakness for Nehru was that of a father. Ironically, while Gandhi and Patel drifted apart, Nehru and Patel drew closer to each other in the Interim Government and, thereafter, for a year or so. Theirs was not an ideological camaraderie, but an outcome of the new humiliating situation Nehru found himself in *vis-a-vis* the Muslim League members, who did not give him the respect he deserved as Vice-President of the Interim Government. This made Nehru feel the necessity of having a strong man by his side. The two worked together in harmony and helped India pull through the turbulent and dangerous months preceding and following the transference of power. Patel enjoyed Nehru's tremendous confidence, which is evident from his letter to him at the time of the formation of India's first Government: "As formalities have to be observed to some extent, I am writing to invite you to join the new Cabinet. This writing is somewhat superfluous because you are the strongest pillar of the Cabinet." Patel's reply was equally warm and sincere: "Our attachment and affection for each other and our comradeship for an unbroken period of nearly 30 years admit of no formalities. My services will be at your disposal, I hope, for the rest of my life and you will have unquestioned loyalty and devotion from me in the cause for which no man in India has sacrificed as much as you have done. Our combination is unbreakable and, therein, lies our strength."[7]

Such sentimental effusions could not cement relations between Nehru and Patel. They began drifting apart from December 1947 onwards—first on the issue of Nehru's bypassing the States Ministry under Patel by giving direct to Sheikh Abdullah a loan of Rs.20 lakhs followed by his taking away Kashmir from his charge, and soon afterwards following Patel's January 6th Lucknow speech in which he was critical of the Indian Muslims' attitude towards the Indian Union. However, when the patch-up came on Gandhi's assassination, Patel replied to a highly sentimental letter from Nehru: "I am deeply touched—indeed overwhelmed—by the affection and warmth of your letter of February 3rd. I fully and heartily reciprocate the sentiments you have so feelingly expressed. We both have been lifelong comrades in a common cause. The paramount interests of our country and our mutual love and regard, transcending such differences of outlook and temperament as existed, have held us together... Recent events had made me very unhappy, and I had written to Bapu (Gandhi) when I was going to Bombay, appealing to him to relieve me, but his death changes everything, and the crisis that has overtaken us must awaken in us a fresh realization of how much we have achieved together and the need for further joint efforts in our grief-stricken country's interests."[8]

They agreed to resolve their differences. But theirs could not be the unity of hearts. Their strong individualistic temperament, outlook and ways of functioning asserted now and again to end up in a clash. As a matter of principle, and being a strict disciplinarian, Patel avoided interference with Nehru's specific responsibilities, no matter if these concerned Tibet, Goa or even Kashmir. Yet, he did not withhold, in the interest of the country, his sound, mature advice and cooperation. In Kashmir, his wholehearted support was merely to help Nehru extricate himself out of a web of difficulties he had himself created. So far as the ministries under his charges were concerned, he did tolerate

Nehru's interference as Prime Minister up to a point. He showed sufficient patience in the Hyderabad "Police Action", which was the direct responsibility of the States Ministry under him. Yet, he secured first Nehru's consent in the Cabinet decision, though the "Police Action" was launched under his orders. Nevertheless, whenever party or Government affairs troubled Nehru, Patel rushed to his side, and acted as his best counsellor. He tried to help Nehru overcome frustration, which he expressed to Patel in his letter of March 29, 1950: "I see every ideal that I have held fading away and conditions emerging in India which not only distress me, but indicate to me that my life's work has been a failure."[9]

Nehru's mind had been "greatly troubled", and he had been "exploring various avenues of thought and action."[10] Nehru uncovered his disturbed state of mind to Patel in his letter of February 20, 1950. Patel promptly replied soothingly: "I am very distressed to feel that you have been so much agitated and troubled. If I had any hint from you, I would certainly have rushed to (have) a discussion with you in an attempt to relieve your mind. I quite appreciate the sense of oppression which weighs over your mind, but we should do nothing which should make confusion worse confounded." In reply, Nehru assured Patel: "I shall, of course, take no step without full discussion with you." He confessed that he had been agonised over "the difference in outlook between Parliament as a whole and me", and admitted: "They put up with me because of their friendliness towards me and their affection and a certain past record and habit of doing so. But they go farther and farther away from me in mind and heart. This produces unhappiness all round and frustration."[11]

Within five days of such camaraderie, Patel was much pained to receive a letter from Nehru which cast doubts on the usefulness of their association. Nehru wrote on March 26, 1950: "Lately, however, new developments have taken place which have made me doubt seriously whether this attempt at joint working serves a useful purpose, or whether it merely hinders the proper functioning of Government". Patel felt "personally pained and hurt". For, in the same letter Nehru had written: "We have been close friends and colleagues, in spite of differences of opinion, for thirty years or so, and we have passed through numerous crises together... We have a good deal of affection and respect for each other, and this has helped us a great deal in the past to face problems together."[12]

Patel wrote back that Gandhi had "expressed his considered opinion that both you and I should continue to collaborate in the service of the country since the consequences of any separation would be disastrous to its interests. I have striven to my utmost to execute these last words of Bapu. I have, according to my lights, striven to strengthen your hands as much as I could, while giving expression to my views frankly and sincerely. I have given you my loyal support, often at times subjecting myself to considerable self-restraint... We have differed on some matters, but have recognised that such differences were natural, and have adjusted ourselves in order to evolve an agreed policy." Patel bluntly told Nehru: "Hitherto I have been sustained in my heavy burden by the thought that I had your trust and confidence. But I am shaken in the belief by the manner in which you accepted statements made by those interested persons without even verifying from me as to what I had stated and in what context and manner. I have no desire to continue if I cannot fulfil the mission entrusted to me by Bapu in his last moments and strengthen your hands, or if you entertain any suspicion about my loyalty to you; or if you think I am an obstacle in the implementation of your policies."[13]

Nehru's attitude compelled Patel to decide on quitting the Government. Before he could put in his resignation, Nehru found his boat rocked by the storm that swept across East Pakistan; he needed now the strong man in Patel to be by his side. The storm had darkened Indo-Pakistan relations; but no less Nehru's own future with West Bengal rising in revolt. The crisis had been developing since January 1950 when, in a fresh outbreak of communal violence, the police themselves had assaulted the Hindus, thereby giving encouragement to the local rowdies to raid the houses of the Hindus in Dacca. Of such happenings, India's Foreign Secretary S. Dutt records:

"They plundered and burnt houses and attacked men, women and children. These brutalities were accompanied by the abduction and forcible conversion of Hindu women to Islam and desecration of Hindu places of worship." In Calcutta, the Hindus retaliated. But it was not mass action, but only "stray assaults", which the Government put down with a heavy hand, whereas "swift retaliation on the Hindus followed in East Bengal. In Dacca, a huge Muslim crowd went on the rampage on February 10, 1950... in less than twenty-four hours, many thousands of Hindus, who had been living for generations in the city, had to leave their homes and seek shelter in refugee camps. Two thousand people lost their lives, and many more were injured. What happened in Decca was repeated in many districts of East Bengal. Hundreds of thousands of Hindus now left their homes in panic and crossed over the far-flung borders of West Bengal utterly destitute".[14]

Pakistan seemed to be re-enacting in 1950 in her eastern wing what she had done in the western in 1947—with the similar objective of converting East Pakistan into a totally Muslim populated region, like the West, by driving the Hindus out of the State. A "greatly alarmed" Nehru telegraphed Liaquat Ali on February 24th, offering suggestions for restoration of "confidence and security in the minds of the minorities". But Pakistan appeared unconcerned. She was apparently happy in pursuing a two-pronged policy. Within East Pakistan, she permitted brutalities to be committed behind an iron curtain, whereas through Radio Dacca she conducted a campaign of vilification. A glaring example of this was its announcement that 10,000 Muslims had been killed in Calcutta. Nehru called this "amazing falsehood". But he needed a strong hand to deal with Pakistan. He left it to Patel to give a warning to Pakistan: either surrender territory for the rehabilitation of the refugees, or he would order "the military to mount action". U.N. Dhebar records: "This went home, and Liaquat Ali Khan came to Delhi to negotiate a pact"[15]—the Nehru-Liaquat Pack.

Patel was shrewd enough to have seen through Pakistan's game. He wrote to Nehru on February 25th: "I have carefully read the draft letter which you propose to send to Liaquat Ali Khan in reply to his regarding the 'No War' declaration. My own reading of Liaquat's letter is that he is cleverly trying to commit us to a line of procedure, both in regard to outstanding and future disputes, which would give Pakistan, in view of its complete disregard of scruples, principles or moral behaviour, a perpetual advantage over us. While everything binds us, nothing seems to bind them." Patel saw "a perpetual war of nerves, a series of accomplished facts, continuous pressure backed by persistent vilifying campaign and absolute denial of even the most glaring facts which take place in its territory are all quite familiar to us. We have had sufficient experience of the implementation of agreements with Pakistan. We have also had a bitter taste of the protection which it affords to minorities. If anybody had any little faith in the good intentions of Pakistan, East Bengal should shatter it completely." Patel's conclusion was: "We seem to be offering a counsel of peace where the spirit and mentality of war exist, and where, to the best of our information, all preparations for war are being made... I sometimes wonder whether we could really talk of peace with Pakistan..."[16] He was against submission to Pakistan, or do anything that would encourage regional fanaticism. He, therefore, asserted: "We have conceded one Pakistan: that is more than enough."[17]

The pact threw West Bengal into a raging storm of protest. Its tremors were felt in New Delhi as well. Nehru's two senior Cabinet colleagues, Syama Prasad Mookerjee and K.C. Neogy, resigned in protest, while N.V. Gadgil and John Mathai expressed their opposition in "emphatic language", though the latter's resignation was on grounds of differences with Nehru over his autocratic functioning. Finding himself in the midst of a deepening crisis and realising that the party was at Patel's beck and call, Nehru preferred to resign. At such a crucial moment, Mountbatten sought Patel's help by writing to him on 16th April: "You have for years been the 'strong man' of India. With your support, Jawaharlal cannot fail. I do not believe there is one man in the country who would stand up to you when you make up your mind, so that the support which you are in a position to give him is a matter of the highest international importance."[18] Patel had already made up his mind to help Nehru on two considerations: first, the disciplinarian in him had no option but to carry out the Government's decision; the second, his commitment to Gandhi. To Nehru's great relief, he offered to go to Calcutta, the storm centre of the "revolt", even at the risk to his health.

At a Press conference in Calcutta on the 16th itself, Patel went all out to defend the pact, which he described as "a solemn word pledged on behalf of the people of India and of Bengal", and impressed upon his audience that it was "our bounden duty to fulfil our obligation and make every honest effort to implement it. We have to do it in a manner which would enable us to say before God and man that we have done our duty." He pleaded that Nehru and he had spent "many anxious days and nights... over the ills of Bengal", and clinched the issue with an emotional declaration: "We realise that if Bengal dies, India dies; and that India cannot live without Bengal. It was with this consciousness and fully realising our duty to Bengal that we entered into this agreement, and I would like you to understand its implications in that spirit." Frankly admitting that "it was not easy for me to reconcile myself to a faith in the pledged word of Pakistan", Patel said that he had come to the conclusion, after his meeting with the Prime Minister of Pakistan, that "there was a different spirit behind the words of the Pakistan Prime Minister, and that, if we had to avert a major calamity which could completely upset the two countries, we must explore this possibility of averting a great disaster. We thought: 'Let us take this last chance'."[19]

Fifty editors attended the Press conference. "The atmosphere", Patel wrote to Nehru on 18th April, "was hostile to start with. They were all bitter and expressed complete absence of faith in the pledged word of Pakistan." Patel earnestly requested them "to view the agreement dispassionately, not on the basis of their past experience, but with a new and friendly approach to the whole scheme. I appealed for a fair trial to the agreement." Towards the end of the conference, Patel's magic worked: not only was the atmosphere "much improved", but except for one or two, "the rest were helpful and co-operative".[20] Resignations of Syama Prasad Mookerjee and Neogy had made matters difficult for Patel. Nevertheless, he succeeded in spreading "goodwill and understanding".

Over the Calcutta station of All India Radio on 21st April, Patel made a most reasoned appeal to the people to cooperate in this "big-hearted attempt to heal the wounds and to reverse the process of misunderstanding and bitterness which have unfortunately marred our relations with Pakistan." He asked them to consider in all fairness: "The question before West Bengal is not so much whether the agreement is good or bad, beneficial or harmful, but whether, in the face of the stark reality of a partitioned Bengal under two independent Governments and placed in the present set of circumstances, any other peaceful means are open to it to bring hope and faith and succour and relief to the unfortunate victims of the recent disturbances on both sides of the border." Patel said: "Let us not indulge in impotent rage or mere supercharged emotional outbursts. Instead, let us make a constructive, helpful and wholehearted contribution to the relief of suffering humanity on both sides of the border and help make their lot a more tolerable one. The lot of mortal existence is already a hard one; let us not make it harder… If we succeed, we might, in a humble way, have started an era of peace, understanding and good neighbourliness. If, God forbid, we fail, we shall have had the satisfaction of having explored the last possibility of a peaceful solution of a potentially dangerous problem."[21] Nehru appreciated Patel's role by publicly acknowledging: "I am deeply grateful to him for all he has done at a moment of crisis and difficulty. No person has worked harder for the full implementation of the agreement than Sardar Patel."[22]

Nehru and Patel differed from each other fundamentally in their outlook, attitudes and policies. Nehru was a Socialist by conviction, not by practice. Patel was a pragmatist. His only belief was in Gandhism, which he followed within the frontiers of practicability. But above all, he was a true democrat. John Mathai, who was earlier "a great admirer of Nehru and was somewhat prejudiced against Sardar Patel", doubted Nehru's credentials as a supporter of parliamentary democracy. He told M.R. Masani of his "disappointment with Nehru whose 'feet of clay' he had discovered", and that "under Nehru the Cabinet had never functioned, and all decisions were taken privately by the Prime Minister and the individual Minister concerned. Even when a decision was endorsed in the Cabinet, the Prime Minister went back on it and reversed the decision... The only time when the Indian Cabinet really functioned was when Nehru was away in Washington for a few weeks towards the end of October 1948 and when Sardar Patel was acting as Prime Minister. For the first time the Cabinet functioned with joint responsibility; and the acting Prime Minister conducted meetings as the British Prime Minister would have."[23]

Because of their towering personalities, both Nehru and Patel were paternalistic: Nehru's paternalism was autocratic; that of Patel was democratic. However, according to C.D. Deshmukh, there existed between Patel and Nehru "an unstable equilibrium, each making allowances for the other for the sake of peace. But it was uneasy partnership... Between them, harmony meant compromise for safeguarding the interests of the country—the essence of all Governments."[24] In the preservation of such harmony, Patel's contribution was more than Nehru's for two reasons: first, as he admitted, "our work is over, but, unfortunately, the second line is not ready"; secondly, after his massive heart attack, Patel was a man in a hurry, racing against time to accomplish "the mission" entrusted to him by Gandhi, which could be ensured only by the partnership. A few months before his death, Masani asked Patel why he did not take over as Prime Minister and let Nehru function as Leader of the Opposition party and build up a two-party democratic system which the country badly needed. Patel's reply was: "... there is no certainty that he would be alive for even a few months more. If he were to take this step and then pass away, the consequences for the country could be disastrous. Nehru would be back again. It was better to continue with this uneasy combination."[25]

The pragmatist in Patel had other reasons as well for his partnership with Nehru. Nehru was a valued colleague in whose company he had fought shoulder to shoulder in the freedom struggle for thirty long years under the same guru. Patel did not like to break with him at the fag end of his political career. It was his guru who had nominated Nehru for that position, and he had, without hesitation, endorsed that decision. Nehru was like a younger 'brother' whom he loved from the depths of his heart, despite political differences. He confessed this in a letter to a friend on September 25th 1948: "I am taking this opportunity to clear your mind of the misimpression you have got about myself and Jawaharlal going to part. There is absolutely no truth in the matter. We cannot think of doing so at this juncture… Of course, there are differences of opinion between us, as all honest people have. But that does not mean that there would be any difference between our mutual regard, respect, admiration and confidence."[26] On Nehru's birthday on November 14th, 1949 Patel spoke with such warm feelings: "I am very glad to be broadcasting today, the birthday of my dear brother Jawaharlal. The day is twice blessed: not only are we celebrating a great national event, but we are also welcoming him back with all our heart after an eventful tour abroad. Our birthday gift to him is loyalty and devotion."[27] And his last birthday greetings to Nehru, a month before Patel's death, had the same ring of sincerity and friendliness: "My affectionate greetings on your birthday. Relations between us transcend formalities, and I need hardly say anything more than this: it is my fervent and heartfelt prayer that you may live long and well to lead the country through all difficulties and establish in it an era of peace, happiness and prosperity."[28]

Yet, Patel was a man of unbending mind and strong convictions. Let alone Nehru, he did not hesitate to differ from his guru when the interests of the country demanded it. On his own admission: "For several years, Gandhi and I were in perfect agreement. Mostly we agreed instinctively; but when the time for a big decision on the question of India's independence came, we differed. I felt that we had to take independence there and then. We had, therefore, to agree to Partition. I came to this conclusion after a great deal of heart-searching and with a great deal of sorrow. But I felt that if we did not accept Partition, India would be split into many bits and completely ruined."[29]

In spite of their dissimilar origins, upbringing, temperaments and even beliefs, Gandhi, Nehru and Patel formed a perfect troika, highly complementary to one another. Gandhi belonged to the *bania* class with a genius for negotiation and compromise, possessing a personality so magnetic as to attract, inspire and lead millions. Nehru was a thoroughbred aristocrat, a weak, vacillating politician, a Western-type intellectual wedded to woolly Socialism, a visionary and a theoretical revolutionary. His was a split personality. Adoring millions fell under the spell of his irresistible charisma; and yet he could not identify himself with the masses and adopt their lifestyle, as Gandhi and Patel did. He remained distant and aloof even in their midst.

Unlike Gandhi and Nehru, Patel was a born *kisan*. He possessed a peasant's stern character and sturdy common sense; and he was a down-to-earth realist. Such realism was seen not only in his successful handling of complex State affairs, but also in his simple-hearted humour reflecting subtle meaning. Post-Dandi March, Patel and Madan Mohan Malaviya were undergoing their second trial in Bombay. As a Gandhian, Patel refused to make a statement. But the learned Malaviya delivered a long one. Tired of listening, Patel told him: "Panditji, why teach *Bhagvad* to buffalo!"—the magistrate. Post-Independence, Ramakrishna Dalmia obliged Jinnah by buying his New Delhi bungalow, for which he paid a good price. It was immediately requisitioned for the Netherlands Ambassador. Dalmia sought its release under the pretext of opening there a cow protection committee. He called upon Patel, who, being unconvinced, told him" "Sethji, how can you protect the sacred cow from a house where beef has been cooked and eaten?" Later in 1950, when Nehru was to send a Red

Cross team to Korea as part of the Peace Mission, Patel jocularly advised him: "Mere bandaging will not help. Send a brigade!" The suggestion had a deep meaning.

If Gandhi inspired the masses as an oracle, it was Patel who organised them into a fighting force. Gandhi admitted that Patel felt the pulse of the peasants better than he did. Later, when India was undergoing birth-pangs of independence, it was again Patel who confronted boldly and effectively the problems and anxieties of the new developments. He put back on its feet a completely broken down law-and-order machinery; he arranged for expeditious evacuation of millions of Hindus and Sikhs caught in the communal holocaust in Wet Pakistan, he got settled with speed and harmony the vexatious issue of the division of assets and liabilities between India and Pakistan on Partition; and achieved a smooth, satisfactory integration of the Indian States. He dissolved the Princely Order, but spared the Princes.

A comparison has been drawn between Patel and Nehru by two eminent journalists—Ian Stephens, Editor of *The Statesman*, and Andrew Mellor, *The Daily Herald* Representative in New Delhi between 1947 and 1949. Stephens writes: "I much liked the tough old Sardar, even when in disagreement with his views; he had always been very cordial and frank. Five minutes with him were in my experience worth fifteen with Pandit Nehru".[30] According to Mellor: "The broad and heavy features, the great head and generally unmoving, almost unblinking gaze from eyes which were extremely penetrating could not fail to have a considerable effect. With Nehru, the charm immediately reached out and one felt his humanity and friendliness. Patel was altogether different. He gave a feeling of aloofness, almost grimness, and certainly inspired awe. Nevertheless, I know that he was personally kind and patient... Patel may have been a politician at the beginning, but certainly at the end he was a statesman of unrivalled skill, acumen and wisdom... his actions showed a pattern of unshakeable determination. He was very different indeed from Gandhi and Nehru—the one a Mahatma with all the strange atmosphere surrounding him, the other an intellectual often prone to deep human doubts and fears about his course of action."[31] To Pattabhi Sitaramayya, the Congress historian, Patel's was "a composite make-up: sharp in intellect, quick in understanding, firm in decision, unrelenting in action and indefatigable in energy... He does not suffer fools, much less rogues."

All three—Gandhi, Nehru, Patel—were great leaders, fired with limitless zeal, possessed of unquestionable sincerity to the cause of the country's freedom, for which they sacrificed a lot. Gandhi's genius welded the troika into a potent force that jointly waged a non-violent struggle against the British for well over three decades. Their roles can be compared to the great Hindu Trinity: Brahma, Vishnu and Siva. Gandhi represented Brahma—the creator and the inspirer. Nehru reflected Vishnu's soft, gentle looks, a nobility of character and humanism that transcended barriers of caste and creed. And Patel proved, like Siva, the destroyer and unifier—the builder and consolidator of Modern India.

27

The Last Journey

Patel wrote to an old co-worker after Gandhi's death: "Bapu has left us. His life's mission was over."[1] That was literally true. Partition had turned Gandhi into a living corpse. He had himself remarked: "My life's work seems to be over. I hope God will spare me further humiliation." About himself Patel had once stated: "In the past, attempts have been made by fanatic Muslims and other interested persons on my life. But I have escaped by the grace of Providence... To take the life of any person is not in the hands of an individual or group of persons. It rests with God only. If my work is finished in this world and I am wanted elsewhere, my life will end. But it will be only in the manner in which it is destined to end and in no other way."[2] Gandhi's mission ended on India's gaining freedom. Patel's was over with the integration of the States and with the inauguration on January 26, 1950 of a Republican Constitution for India. He had by then completed his great task of repainting India in "one colour", about which he stated with a sense of pride on May 14, 1950: "There are no differences now between the States and provinces. All units will practically be governed by a uniform set of laws. In the history of India, there never was such consolidation of the land as it is today."[3] No longer were there red and yellow patches criss-crossing a vast, diverse land, which the British had strategically built and diplomatically maintained as two watertight units to perpetuate their rule in India. The British achieved this thought two Indias—British India and Princely India. Patel's last major historic act was his support to Nehru on the Nehru-Liaquat Pact in mid-April 1950.

Patel's week-long stay in Calcutta proved strenuous for his ailing body. The visit caused a serious setback to his health. Doctors advised a sea voyage, which he undertook in early May from Bombay to Cochin by the *INS Delhi*. This did not do him much good. His health continued to decline. Despite this, he led a fully preoccupied life, which caused further strain. October came with two new worries: one concerned developments in Nepal and Tibet; the other, a further deterioration in his health. He felt greatly perturbed over the internal happenings in Nepal and the Chinese incursion into Tibet. India's internal security was seriously threatened. Over the impregnable Himalayas loomed a new danger for the first time in history. The architect of India's unity could not remain unconcerned. In a public address on 9th November 1950, Patel said: "... a peaceful country like Tibet has been invaded. It may not survive, but we did not think that it would so happen. We were maintaining friendly relations with China. But China did not accept our advice. We did not know what will be its outcome.... But when one is affected by the vanity of one's power, one does not realise what one is doing.... In Nepal, the people are quarrelling amongst themselves. The ruler himself went to take shelter in the Indian Embassy... The borders of Assam, Pakistan, Kashmir and Burma are just adjacent to Nepal. That makes our whole border exposed to danger." He further observed: "Fire is raging on all sides... we should protect our country, if possible by non-violence, but, if necessary, by violence."[4]

In the second week of November, Patel had his old intestinal trouble. He wrote to Rajagopalachari on the 16th: "My intestine trouble still persists and there is some pain which is occasionally quite severe."[5] On December 7th there was recurrence of his heart trouble. By the 10th he had abdominal trouble again. With some improvement in his condition the following day, doctors decided to shift him from the cold of New Delhi to the mild climate of

Bombay. His flight on the 12th was in a way a sentimental journey about which he seemed to have had some premonition. It was reflected in his Independence Day message on 15th August: "In my life, I have now reached a stage when time is of the essence. Age has not diminished the passion which I bear to see my country great and to ensure that the foundations of our freedom are well and securely laid. Bodily infirmity has not dimmed my ardour to exert my utmost for the peace, prosperity and advancement of the Motherland. But 'the bird of time has a little way to fly, and lo! It is on the wing'."[6]

For his forty-five-year-old daughter, Maniben, the last three days of Patel's struggle with life were most excruciating—oscillating between hope and despair. She had looked after him for decades most devotedly, remaining a spinster to serve her father as a house-keeper and as a political helper, ever keeping a vigil on him by day or by night—always by his side whether in the scorching heat of Delhi or in the freezing cold of Kashmir which they specially visited in November 1947. Her heart was torn apart to see the life of her father slowly ebbing away. Hers was a great personal loss: parting company with a life-long companion, they being the only two souls in the house. When narcotics failed to have any effect, records Maniben, "half awake, half in stupor, his mind was full of thoughts, and words would come out of his mouth—words referring to some work or other. To the last he was thinking of the nation."

Patel's condition worsened on the night of December 14th. He expired on the 15th at 9:37 in the morning. The whole country plunged into deep mourning. At Bombay, a sea of people surged towards Birla House. President Rajendra Prasad, Prime Minister Nehru and other leaders, including Central Ministers and Chief Ministers, flew in to pay their last homage to their departed colleague. His body lay dressed in his familiar *dhoti, jubba* and waistcoat, as millions of his countrymen had seen him during the past half a century of his political career. Paying her last homage, Maniben put a saffron mark on his forehead and "garlanded him with a hank of yarn" spun by her. His face presented a picture of sublime serenity. A green *tulsi* leaf between his lips was the only indication of death. Besides a mass of fresh flowers, a copy of the *Bhagvad Gita* lay open on his body.

At the cremation, Nehru having broken down under emotional strain, Rajagopalachari delivered the funeral oration, in which he nostalgically recalled: "Thirty-two years ago, when Gandhiji was with me at Madras, one morning he asked me, 'Have you met Vallabhbhai Patel? Do you know that I have found in him a most trustworthy man, staunch and brave? You should meet him'. I did meet him some time later... What was Vallabhbhai who departed from us early this morning? ... What inspiration, courage, confidence and force incarnate Vallabhbhai was... We will not see the like of him again."[7] Nehru paid a most touching tribute in the Indian Parliament when he said: "early this morning, he had a relapse, and the story of his great life ended. It is a great story, as all of us know, as the whole country knows, and history will record it in many pages and call him the builder and consolidator of the New India and will say many things about him. But, perhaps, to many of us here, he will be remembered as a Great Captain of our forces in the struggle for freedom and as one who gave us sound advice in times of troubles as well as in moments of victory, as a friend and colleague on whom one could invariably rely, as a tower of strength which revived wavering hearts when we were in trouble. We shall remember him as a friend and a colleague and a comrade above all; and I, who have sat here on this bench side by side with him for these several years, will feel rather forlorn, and a certain emptiness will steal upon me when I look at this empty bench."

Nehru further said: "... Many calamities have fallen on us, bringing distress to our people. But the greatest of these calamities and sorrows has been the passing away from amongst us of a giant among men. Sardar Vallabhbhai Patel was a dear and valued comrade in the brave days of our struggle for freedom, a rock full of wisdom and determination, a rock of patient strength to whom instinctively all of us went for guidance. Later, when we occupied the seats of Government, inevitably some of the heaviest burdens fell on him, and history will record how he discharged that duty."

Nehru concluded: "His name will always be remembered not only as that of a great leader in the fight for freedom, but as a great builder, unifier and consolidator of New India. That is a proud title to fame which he well deserved."[8]

Patel was, indeed, a Great Captain, whose role, in spite of his voluntary acceptance of number two position first under Gandhi and later under Nehru, was in reality second to none. He played a most significant and triumphant role and could say with a sense of fulfillment in his last Independence Day message: "Looking back at the broad sweep of events since we became free, my predominant feeling is one of thankfulness and relief. We are grateful to Providence for having seen the country safely out of many a critical period."[9] Patel was, indeed, the maker of history, who has left behind a history which will, apart from being ever remembered, rank with that of Asoka and Akbar. Yet, he once observed in all humility speaking introspectively at Hyderabad, "Capitals have come and gone, but India goes on as it is. Similar ideas struck me when I saw Ajanta and Ellora, their glory and their beauty and the masterly way in which art was executed. Then I felt that our existence was merely of an insect, irrespective of whether we are big or small. Those who built these caves enshrining ancient history hardly ever realised that for centuries nobody would know about them."[10]

Patel's contribution was, indeed, no less than that of Gandhi's and Nehru's. Appreciating this, *The Times*, London, editorially commented: "Little known outside his own country, 'Sardarji' neither sought nor won the international reputation achieved by Mr. Gandhi and Mr. Nehru. Yet he made up with them the triumvirate that gave shape to the India of today. His work was no less essential than theirs to the success of the national struggle for independence. It lay for the most part behind the scenes, in the committee room rather than on the platform. He first shaped the Congress Party into a disciplined engine of political power and then directed it, ruthlessly and with a single-minded determination, towards the end which his colleagues had taught the people of India to desire." He possessed "great organising ability, cold courage and inflexibility of purpose."[11]

28

Postscript

Two days before Patel's death, M.N. Roy wrote in the Radical Humanist: "On his 74th birthday (October 31st, 1949), Nationalist India has done homage to the man who has been correctly described as the master—builder of her destiny." Considering what Patel had done for the nation, Roy shared Nationalist India's reluctance "to face the problem of doing without him", but he thought that it was "idle to play the ostrich game", as Patel was "74 years old and not in the best of health." Himself a committed agnostic, Roy, nevertheless, wrote: "I sincerely join in the prayers that he may live for many years more"; but he could not silence the question: "What will happen to India when the master-builder will go, sooner or later, the way of all mortals?" Roy said: "It is easy enough to pay tribute to a successful man. But it is much more difficult to carry on the work he will leave unfinished... Nationalist India was fortunate to have Sardar Patel to guide her destiny for a generation. But her misfortune is that there will be none to take his place when he is no more..." Roy made the significant observation: "When the future is bleak, one naturally turns to the past, and Sardar Patel can be proud of his past."[1]

Patel's past was glorious. He formed the third side of the Gandhi-Nehru-Patel triangle or *Trimurti* which dominated India's political struggle for freedom for nearly three decades till Independence in 1947—and even afterwards. His post-independence years were crowned with towering achievements. These were monumental in dimensions and depth, and outstripped Nehru's.

Even as Deputy Prime Minister, Patel wielded considerable authority and influence, both in the party and the Government, though as a strict disciplinarian he gave Nehru the respect he should command as Prime Minister. However, because of his equally towering position within the party and in the country, Patel and Nehru had agreed to their respective "independence" in matters pertaining to Home and Foreign Affairs. Patel did not allow Mountbatten's or Nehru's interference in the case of Junagadh, nor in the case of Hyderabad. He was himself scrupulous in not meddling in affairs under Nehru, including Kashmir which had been taken away from his charge. But he did not hesitate to express his views, however unpalatable, whenever his help was sought or the occasion demanded.

What was Patel's attitude towards Kashmir? Hardly anyone knows or knew. He seldom opened his mind even to his intimate colleagues. While traveling with him in his car once, Vishnu Sahay, his States Ministry Secretary, heard him muttering to himself: "I will not take what's not mine; but I will not part with what's mine."[2] Dr. Rajendra Prasad told Jayaprakash Narayan: "The Sardar used to evade an answer with the remark that he had left the problem for Jawaharlal to tackle. But once he did say that when we had given away Punjab, Sind and the NWFP, of what value could the small valley of Kashmir have for us? Will the people there ever agree to live happily with us?" Rajendra Prasad said that "it was an unexpressed thought with Patel that the Valley could be separated from the State and given to Pakistan, while Ladakh and Jammu would remain with India."[3] When a peaceful solution could have possibly been thus reached, India was, as Alan Campbell-Johnson confirms, "amply provoked" by the tribesmen's invasion of the Valley. Hence, in Mountbatten's view, "the accession had indeed been brought about by violence, but the violence came from the tribes, for whom Pakistan, and not India, was responsible." As opposed to Jinnah's petulance and impetuousness, Patel was calm, cool and tremendously patient. According to Campbell-Johnson, "Mountbatten was empowered to advise him (the Maharaja) on the authority of Patel that if his decision was to throw in his lot with Pakistan and join their Constituent Assembly in advance of the transfer of power, it would not be regarded as an unfriendly act by India."[4]

Patel told M.R. Masani that, "but for Nehru, he could settle the Kashmir issue in no time by arranging that the Kashmir Valley go to Pakistan and East Pakistan to India. Both countries would benefit from such an arrangement."[5] V.P. Menon held the same view. Patel knew that Jinnah would succumb to the idea both on emotional and strategic grounds. Kashmir was nearer to his heart than East Pakistan. He could sojourn there during Pakistan's hot summer in the regal style of the Mughals. He considered that the Kashmiri Muslims were nearer to the West Pakistan Muslims culturally and ethnically than the Muslims from East Pakistan, who were closer to the Bengali Hindus in language and culture. Field-Marshal Auchinleck wrote to a friend: "Pakistan should let East Pakistan go. They will always be a millstone about their necks and a great danger, or more. Jinnah made a big mistake when he fought for their inclusion... Punjabis and Pathans will never mix with Bengalis; they are like oil and water. They differ so in every way except religion, and I always think a Bengali is a Bengali first and a Muslim second! I think myself that they should agree to separate." He wrote to another friend in December 1970: "Jinnah should not have insisted on East Pakistan. It is alien to West Pakistan in every conceivable way except religion. Much more akin to Hindu Bengal. Why cannot they do a deal over Kashmir?"[6] That appeared to be Patel's thinking too.

There was more of logic and less of emotion in Patel's thinking in the exchange of the two regions. His logic was that of an administrator who sought a quick settlement of the Kashmir issue without letting outsiders poison Indo-Pakistani relations, and without allowing time to make it more and more complicated as years pass. An exchange would have drained out the poison on which successive rulers in Pakistan whipped up anti-India hysteria. Nor would it have given foreign powers an opportunity to play power politics between India and Pakistan; and even plot with Abdullah to turn Kashmir into a sovereign "Switzerland". If Kashmir had spared the Defence Budgets of India and Pakistan from running a mad race for arms, the two underdeveloped countries would have had enough money for developmental activities aimed at the economic well-being of the poor.

Patel appeared to have had other reasons as well: the highly complementary economies of the two Bengals in agricultural produce especially jute, the harnessing of waterways, harmony through the composite culture of the two, which would have promoted and sustained India's secularism, protection to nearly 10 million non-Muslim Chittagong hill tribes, and proper control of India's eastern land borders and eastern waters through the port of Chittagong. Above all, Patel would have thereby eliminated East Bengal becoming West Pakistan's second front on India's back. In 1960 when the Naga trouble erupted, the rebels were found receiving assistance "in various ways by the authorities in what was then East Pakistan."

A similar situation had arisen in 1956 in Nepal when the King attempted to loosen Nepal's traditional ties with India by negotiating a treaty of peace and friendship with China; also inviting the Russians and the Americans to Kathmandu, and thereby turning his capital into a hotbed of international intrigue. Nehru was so much irked over the Nepal-China affair that he informed the Chinese Government that "a treaty of friendship with Nepal would, from India's viewpoint, be inopportune." His unhappiness with Nepal was expressed in his despairing statement: "They are perfectly free to go their own way, and we shall go our own."[7] Such developments were contrary to what had happened in 1950. Patel's proposal, made at the time of the King's seeking asylum in the Indian Embassy at Kathmandu and shifting him to New Delhi, would not have perhaps allowed later day developments to take place.

The Foreign Affairs Committee of the Indian Cabinet discussed whether India should give recognition to the infant Ruler. Nehru took an unusual line. He felt, according to Foreign Secretary K.P.S. Menon, that "the King's espousal of the popular cause should be taken at its face value and that he should be enabled to go back to Nepal as King." Patel differed. His eyes were focussed on the future, not on the present. He observed that "Nepal is a frontier State, that stability is the paramount consideration there and that the Ranas are in a better position to ensure stability than anyone else." Menon writes further: "Nehru's view prevails... Patel stood primarily for stability and Nehru for freedom."[8] From Patel's viewpoint, such freedom under a hereditary and autocratic rule was an anachronism, and such a rule was contradictory to socialist thinking. Patel could have hoped to establish people's supremacy in Nepal through the Ranas, but not through the King. If once achieved, a direct rapport between the two people—of Nepal and India—would have been the next step. For the two have had the same heritage: language, culture and religion.

Similar was the story of Goa, which, Nehru admitted, had been "for years an irritant and a humiliation." It was so because of Nehru's policy of procrastination, resulting in its ineffectiveness. His vacillation forced him to "cling to inaction as a means of attaining his objective." That too Nehru found it "difficult to define." As a result, he went on "postponing a decision", which allowed international pressures to grow on him, and his yielding to Goa's "close association with India, with possibly internal autonomy." Nehru was repeating Hyderabad in Goa. As he allowed time to pass, Portugal dug her feet deeper in Goa with her nearly successful efforts to internationalise the issue. The American Ambassador to India, Ellsworth Bunker, could not have otherwise suggested that "Goa might be purchased from Portugal in the manner in which the United States had bought Louisiana from France." His successor, John Galbraith, suggested that India should request the Security Council to dispatch a UN force to evict the Portuguese. Nehru was "driven gradually and reluctantly to the conclusion that his approach had failed."[9] His inaction was brought to an abrupt end by Krishna Menon who pushed an unsuspecting Nehru into the Goa fray in December 1961.

What would have been Patel's policy? K.P.S. Menon records his role in the discussion on Goa by the Foreign Affairs Committee in 1950. Different people made different proposals. Rajagopalachari was opposed to economic pressure, and suggested: "We should conquer Goa by love." He forgot that "love" could not prevent the creation of Pakistan, even when the Muslims asking for it were of Indian origin. In Goa, India faced a foreign power. "The discussion", says Menon, "went on for two hours. Sardar Patel seemed to take no interest. He kept his eyes closed for most of the time and seemed half asleep. Suddenly, he woke up and said: 'Shall we go in? It is two hour's work!' Nehru resisted the suggestion vehemently, saying that "if we, who professed to believe in non-violence, were to use violence to absorb Goa, we would be setting a bad example. Moreover, there would be international complications". Patel did not press his point, but "retired sphinx-like into silence. He is said to have remarked to a friend that Jawaharlal Nehru was proving himself to be not merely the political heir of Mahatma Gandhi but a lineal descendant of Gautama Buddha."[10]

Patel's concern was for two reasons: first, he considered Goa an inalienable part of India. Secondly, Patel was keen to redeem the assurance he had given to the President of the Goa Congress in a letter of May 14, 1946: "Your desire for reunion with Mother country is understandable, as it is natural. The Congress will not forget you when proper time for action comes. Indian independence means independence of the whole of India, in which there can be no spot or place for foreign domination however small it may be."[11] Patel could not force his way, as he did in Hyderabad, when time for such action came, as Goa, being foreign territory, was the concern of Nehru. Yet, he impressed upon the Portuguese Minister Plenipotentiary, Vasco Garin, when he called on him in New Delhi on January 25th 1949, the "great strategic importance" of Goa which India could not overlook. Referring to Junagadh, Patel told Garin "... if Pakistan had occupied Diu (a Portuguese enclave on the Gujarat coast), it would have created a highly critical situation. Nothing tells us that it will not happen in the near future. The Nizam of Hyderabad had also thought of occupying Goa with the help of British agents."[12]

Patel gave vent to his inner feelings in May 1950 when on medical advice he undertook a sea cruise by the *INS Delhi* from Bombay to Cochin. While cruising along the Goa coast, Patel asked the Captain of the ship how many miles they were from Goa. On being told the distance, he asked the Captain to take the ship nearer to Goa to let him have a look at it. When reminded of the rule governing territorial waters. Patel smiled his "turtle-like smile" and said, "It does not matter. Let's go and have a look". According to Taya Zinkin, when the ship was nearer Goa, Patel asked the Captain, "How many men have you got on board?" "800", answered the Captain. "Enough to take Goa?" Patel enquired. "I think so," replied the Captain. "Well, let us go and take it while we are here", said Patel. A puzzled Captain could not believe what he had heard, and asked Patel to repeat what he had said. Patel repeated it. This confused the Captain further. In a hesitant tone and with some trepidation, he said, "You will have to give me a written order, sir—just for the record." Patel grinned, and said, "Perhaps on second thoughts we better go back. You know that fellow Jawaharlal. He will object."[13]

The threat from China loomed larger and far more ominous than from Goa or Nepal. It threatened India's territorial integrity. In the thousands of copies of a map distributed in Sikkim and other Himalayan regions, Tibet and China had been shown as "the palm of a human hand, and Ladakh, Nepal, Sikkim, Bhutan and NEFA as its five fingers".[14] Till events hadn't disturbed his dream, Nehru had stuck to the belief that China would not launch an aggression against India. The border war, therefore, gave Nehru a rude shock, shattering his ever-green youthful health and exuberance, but, more importantly, his faith in the goodness of man and belief in the goodwill of nations. In despair he stated, "We were getting out of touch with reality in the modern world, and we were living in an artificial atmosphere of our own creation. We have been shocked out of it, all of us, whether it is the Government or the people; some might have felt it less and some more." Personal betrayal led Nehru to feel intensely, "How I worked for friendship between India and China, fought for China's legitimate interests in the world—and aggression was my reward!"[15]

Patel's vision seemed to reach far beyond Nehru's. He had foreseen China's designs as far back as June 1949 when on the 4th of the month, he had written to Nehru: "We have to strengthen our position in Sikkim as well as in Tibet. The farther we keep away the Communist forces, the better. Tibet has long been detached from China. I anticipate that, as soon as the Communists have established themselves in the rest of China, they will try to destroy its (Tibet's) autonomous existence." His advice to Nehru was: "You have to consider carefully your policy towards Tibet in such circumstances and prepare from now for that eventuality".[16] Nehru's faith in China did not permit him to listen to such advice.

About a month and a half before his death. Patel attended a Cabinet meeting called at fifteen minutes notice to discuss Tibet. This didn't give Patel time to study the relevant papers, while Nehru's mood was petulant. He snubbed N.V. Gadgil with the remark, "Don't you realise that the Himalayas are there?" Whereupon K.M. Munshi timidly ventured to say that "in the seventh century, Tibetans had crossed the Himalayas and invaded Kanauj." Nehru dismissed this as nonsense. Immediately after the meeting, Patel left for Ahmedabad, but he continued "anxiously thinking" over the problem. On his return to New Delhi, he wrote Nehru a long letter on November 7th, which showed his "uncanny vision" in discerning "as far back as 1950 the portents across our north-eastern border and the dangerous implications of our foreign policy in that direction… Every word of what he wrote has been proved true by the developments of the past seventeen years."[17]

Patel wrote to Nehru: "The Chinese Government has tried to delude us by professions of peaceful intentions. My own feeling is that at a crucial period they managed to instill into our Ambassador a false sense of confidence in their so-called desire to settle the Tibetan problem by peaceful means... The final action of the Chinese, in my judgment, is little short of perfidy. The tragedy of it is that the Tibetans put faith in us... we have been unable to get them out of the meshes of Chinese diplomacy or Chinese malevolence... it appears that we shall not be able to rescue the Dalai Lama." Patel tried to convince Nehru that "the Chinese do not regard us as their friends", and "their last telegram to us is an act of gross discourtesy not only in the summary way it disposes of our protest against the entry of Chinese forces into Tibet, but also in the wild insinuation that our attitude is determined by foreign influences. It looks as though it is not a friend speaking in that language but a potential enemy."

Patel warned Nehru: "...very soon they (Chinese) will disown all the stipulations which Tibet has entered into with us in the past. That throws into the melting pot all frontier and commercial settlements with Tibet on which we have been functioning and acting during the last half a century. China is no longer divided. It is united and strong. All along the Himalayas in the north and north-east, we have on our side of the frontier, a population ethnologically and culturally not different from Tibetans or Mongoloids. The undefined state of the frontier and the existence on our side of a population with its affinities to Tibetans or Chinese have all the elements of potential trouble between China and ourselves... Chinese ambitions in this respect not only cover the Himalayan slopes on our side, but also include important parts of Assam.... The danger from the north and north-east, therefore, becomes both communist and imperialist."

Patel suggested a number of positive steps to counter the Chinese threat. These included improvement of road, rail, air and wireless communications with Nepal, Bhutan, Sikkim, Darjeeling and the tribal areas in Assam; building of defensive lines; policing and intelligence of frontier posts to stop infiltration of spies, fifth columnists and Communists; fully manning the outposts, and ensuring loyalty of people inhabiting the regions concerned. Patel further suggested such redisposition of our forces as might be necessary, particularly with the idea of guarding important routes or areas which are likely to be the subject of dispute; an appraisal of the strength of our forces, and, in regard to Chinese entry into the UNO, "in view of the rebuff which China has given us and the method which she has followed in dealing with Tibet, I am doubtful whether we can advocate her claims any longer." Patel's was a prophetic warning, which Nehru ignored, and suffered the consequences of the war in 1962. His warning was: "Any faltering or lack of decisiveness in formulating our objectives, or in pursuing our policy to attain those objectives, is bound to weaken us and increase the threats which are so evident."[18]

In summing up, one may quote two diverse personalities expressing two diverse views: Mountbatten and J.R.D. Tata. Mountbatten wrote of him in 1966: "He will always remain in my memory as that paradox, a man of iron will, clear vision and ruthless determination, who was at heart kind, gentle and sentimental. It is given to few men to serve their country so faithfully and so well as did Sardar Vallabhbhai Patel without ever sacrificing his loyalty to those whom he called friend."[19] Tata, whose evaluation was from the viewpoint of India's economy, wrote in 1986: "I have often thought that if fate had decreed that he (Patel), instead of Jawaharlal, would be the younger of the two, India would have followed a very different path and would be in better economic shape than it is today."[20] Above all, Patel embodied Abraham Lincoln's famous lines: "With malice toward none, with charity for all, with firmness in the right as God gives us to see the right, let us strive on to finish the work we are in..." In that spirit, Patel devoted himself to his various tasks right till the end of his life, and his achievements have been so great as to have left indelible footprints on the sands of India's history.

Appendices

Appendix–I

The Bombay Chronicle, 31st October 1945

Patel at 70: Tributes

With an uncanny flair for quick decision, dramatic and unerring, the Sardar is essentially a man of action... As a man of steel and iron discipline, he is feared, but as a leader of his men, he is loved and respected. Battle-scarred and physically wrecked, he still remains undaunted and unbeaten.

Rajagopalachari: "It was on a day of unforgettable importance in my life 26 years ago, Gandhiji, while chatting with me in Madras, mentioned Vallabhbhai's name to me as one of the men I should meet and know... Those who think Sardar Vallabhbhai Patel is a hard man are thoroughly mistaken. On the contrary, it would be not far from the truth if one were to say that his is the nature of a loving and jealous woman. His affection is exacting and behind a cold and cynical exterior, he holds a highly emotional and responsive soul and untiring spirit for work. Masterful he is, but as a mother and not as a tyrant..."

Maulana Azad: "He is a bold and untiring general of India's struggle for Independence... at the age of 70, with a young man's zeal and a soldier's altertness."

Jawaharlal Nehru: "... strong of will and purpose, a great organiser, wholly devoted to the cause of India's freedom, he has inevitably roused powerful reactions. Some have disliked him because they could not fall in line with him. But the greater number of people have found in him the leader of their choice, and, working with him and under him, have laid the stable foundations of Indian freedom…"

Sarojini Naidu: "To my great comrade Sardar Vallabhbhai Patel I send my tribute of deep affection. His intrepid patriotism and implacable passion for India's freedom, his proud and stubborn power of resistance and sacrifice, his complete and unquestioning loyalty to Gandhiji have made him the central strength of our national movement. With his stern, rugged and grave exterior, he is like an iron casket that holds rare and hidden gems of devotion, sweetness and charm."

Appendix–II

New Delhi, 27th August 1947

Abolition of Separate Electorates

Sardar Patel, Chairman of the Advisory Committee on Minorities, Fundamental Rights etc., today in the Constituent Assembly (while submitting the reports of the committees) congratulated the various minorities who had taken a correct perspective of the problems and helped in arriving at unanimous conclusions on many items.

In considering his report, Sardar Patel appealed to the House to eschew heat and bitterness, to recognise the present state of affairs in the neighbouring areas and avoid the raising of controversies which would have unfortunate reactions elsewhere.

Despite bitter controversy on occasions, the Sardar said he was happy to note that the reports he was presenting were the result of a general consensus of opinion among the minorities and the majority. It was not possible to satisfy all, but the House would see that the recommendations were practically agreed ones. The Committee had taken into consideration the points of view, sentiments and feelings of the minorities big and small, and as far as possible tried to meet their wishes.

There was a complication and there were conflicting interests among the minorities themselves. There was a minority within the minority. The Committee did not take advantage of such differences, and instead of dividing themselves, presented a united front. Such difficulties which arose were sought to be solved without bitterness and controversy. He hoped the House would deal with the reports in a friendly atmosphere and with goodwill.

Referring to joint versus separate electorates and representation in legislatures, the Sardar said those issues had been discussed for over a decade, produced so much of controversy and they had suffered and paid heavily for it. But today, fortunately, they had been able to deal with them in an amicable manner and there was unanimity on the point that there should be no more separate electorates and they should have joint electorates.

On the question of weightage, they had agreed that there should be no weightage and the various communities should be represented according to the proportion of the population. He had thought it fit to agree to reservation of seats in proportion to the population of minorities. Some of the minorities had gladly surrendered their rights. They desired neither separate electorates, nor reservation, and wanted to merge into the Nation and stand on their own legs. He congratulated those who had taken that stand…

Referring to the position of the Anglo-Indians, Sardar Patel said that the community at present enjoyed certain privileges and concessions in certain services as the Railways, Posts and Telegraph, etc. To ask them to surrender these concessions at present would put them in a difficult position. They might not be prepared for it now and sufficient time should be given to them to adjust themselves.

Congratulating the Parsis for the stand they had taken, Sardar Patel said that the Parsis had voluntarily abandoned any claims for concessions. Though small, the Parsis were a very powerful community, and perhaps most wise. They knew that concessions would do more harm than any benefit, because they could make their way anywhere and in such a way that they would get more than they would secure by reservations and other methods.

Dealing with the question of representation in Services, the Sardar said that the main consideration should be that posts must go by merit. If they were to dilute the principle, the general administration would suffer.

There remained, however, the Sardar said, one matter of controversy and that was on behalf of the Muslim League and the Scheduled Castes. A point was raised that members of those communities should poll certain percentage of votes of their community to be declared successful in the elections. The matter was discussed and the Advisory Committee rejected the suggestion by a large majority.

Frank Anthony paid a tribute to the far-sighted statesmanship of Sardar Patel whose realistic approach to the question had made agreement possible in the Committee... The findings of the report were a happy augury for the future. By being generous, the majority community had assuredly harnessed the loyalty of the minorities to the tasks of nation-building facing the country. Every minority should look forward to the time, sooner or later, when it would take its place not under communal or racial label, but as part and parcel of the whole Indian community.

Like B. Pocker Sahib Bahadur, Chaudhury Khaliquzzaman pleaded for granting of separate electorates to the Muslims. Addressing Sardar Patel, he said: "You have become the final arbiters of the fates of the minorities. If you grant us separate electorates, what is the harm if the Muslim community feels it will help in determining their true representative character? After all they will appeal to you and not to any Third Power—not even to Pakistan—for redress of their grievances. I beg of you to consider the new situation in which this question is now being discussed." Earlier referring to the new factor that had emerged, namely, the disappearance of the Third Party, he said that in the light of that, if the country really visualised the situation existing today in its true perspective, much of the suspicion that hung round separate electorates would disappear. There was no longer any Third Party to whom the Muslims could go and appeal. There was no doubt that if things untoward happened anywhere, they must now go to Sardar Patel.

Replying to the debate, Sardar Patel said he was surprised that there should have been such a debate on the motion... His mind (the Sardar said) went back to the day when the question of separate electorates was first discussed. Many eminent Muslims had recorded their view that communal electorates were a serious flaw in the body politics. Many Englishmen had also admitted that the country had to be partitioned today because of separate electorates.

The Sardar said: "When Pakistan was conceded, at least it was assumed there will be One Nation in the rest of India and that there will be no attempt to thrust the two-nation theory here. It is no use saying, we shall ask for separate electorates but will abide by your decision. We have heard this for many years... Do you still want there should be two nations? Will you show one free nation which has a religious basis? If this unfortunate country is to be again oppressed by this, even after its division, then woe befall it. It is not worth living for."

Chaudhury Khaliquzzaman had said that "the British have gone and, therefore, we must forget past suspicions. The British had not intended to go so soon. They had left enough mischief behind: we did not want to perpetuate that mischief. The British had introduced communal electorates for easy administration, but the legacy left behind must be liquidated. You say you want to be loyal to the nation. May I ask you, is this loyalty?"

Sardar Patel said he had not intended to speak, but apparently there was something still wrong in the land. "If you want peace in this land—and you can do nothing either here or in Pakistan without peace—I appeal to you at least at this stage to show that everything is forgotten. I appeal to you to withdraw your amendment and pass this clause unanimously so that the world outside may understand that we have forgotten."

Pocker Sahib's amendment seeking to have separate electorates for Muslims was negatived by the House.

New Delhi, August 28, 1947

Speaking in the Constituent Assembly, Sardar Patel said: "So far as the amendment moved by the representatives of the Muslim League was concerned, he found he was under a mistaken impression. Otherwise he would have agreed to no reservation at all.

"When I agreed to reservation on population basis, I thought that our friends in the Muslim League will see the reasonableness of our attitude and accommodate themselves in the changed circumstances after the separation of the country. But I now find repetition of the same methods which had been adopted when separate electorates were introduced in the country. In spite of ample sweetness in the language used by the speakers, there is a full dose of poison in the methods adopted."

Quoting the analogy of the younger brother making suggestions to an elder brother used by a speaker, the Sardar said: "The last speaker (Nazirudin Ahmed) has said we will lose the affection of the younger brother if we do not accept the amendment. I am prepared to lose it because otherwise it would prove the death of the elder brother."

The formula suggested by the amendment had a history behind it, the Sardar said. It was known as the Mohammad Ali formula. The formula had been evolved by Nationalist Muslims to prevent separation of the communities from each other. But now separation was complete and the country was divided. He did not understand the demand for its introduction now.

Sardar Patel said: "If the process that was adopted in the past, which resulted in the separation of the country, is to be repeated, then those who want that kind of thing can have a place in Pakistan, not here. We are laying the foundations of One Nation. And those who think of dividing again and sow the seeds of disruption will have no place and no quarter here.

"You must change your attitude and adapt yourself to changed conditions, and do not pretend to say our affection is very great for you. We have seen the affection. Let there be no talk about it. Let us face realities. The point is whether you really want to cooperate with us, or want to adopt disruptive tactics. I appeal to you to have changed hearts, and not merely change your tongues, because it would not pay.

"If you think this is going to pay, you are mistaken. I know how much it costs me to protect Muslim minorities here in the present conditions and in the present atmosphere. I appeal to you to forget the past. You have got what you wanted. And remember, you are the people who are responsible for Pakistan, and not those who live in Pakistan. You led the agitation. What is it you want now? We do not want the country to be divided again.

"I sincerely tell you there will be no injustice done to you. There will be generosity towards you, but there must be reciprocity. If it is absent, then you take it from me that no soft words can conceal what is behind the words. Let us forget the past and let us be One Nation."

Appendix–III

The Times of India, 28th June 1948

Churchill's Anti-India Outburst

Addressing a rally of Conservatives yesterday, Winston Churchill accused the Socialists who, "on gaining power, threw themselves into the task of demolishing our long built up and splendid structure in the East with zeal and gusto, and they certainly have brought widespread ruin, misery and bloodshed upon the Indian masses to an extent no one can measure.

"Power has been recklessly confided to Indian political parties which in no way represent the needs or feelings of the 400 million people who had dwelt so long under the protection of the British Crown. Already there has been something like a collapse in the process of internal administration and we must expect an indefinite epoch of internecine and religious strife.

"We have witnessed the violent action of Mr. Nehru's Hindu Government against Kashmir, four-fifths of whose people are Muslims. It may be that soon this same Government, using the modern weapons we left behind, will attack the ancient State of Hyderabad with its 17 millions of people and overthrow the Government of the Nizam."

Further to the above, Churchill was reported to have arrogantly forecast: "Power will go into the hands of rascals, rogues and free-booters... These are men of straw of whom no trace will be found after a few years."

Patel's smashing reply silenced the British "bulldog". But he took it in good spirit and told Patel in a message through Anthony Eden, on a visit to India on 22nd March 1949, that he had "thoroughly enjoyed the retort", and that he had "nothing but admiration for the way the new Dominion had settled down to its tasks and responsibilities, particularly those involving relations with the Indian States." Churchill even suggested that the Sardar should "not confine himself within the limits of India, but the world was entitled to see and hear more of him."

The Times of India, 30th June 1948

Sardar Patel's Stunning Retort

In a rare moment of rage, Sardar Patel gave him a most stunning reply:

"I should like to tell His Majesty's Government that if they wish India to maintain friendly relations with Great Britain, they must see that India is in no way subjected to malicious and venomous attacks of this kind and that British statesmen and others learn to speak of this country in terms of friendship and goodwill.

"Mr. Winston Churchill, His Majesty's Leader of the Opposition and Britain's war-time Premier, while bemoaning the disappearance of the title of 'Emperor of India' from the Royal titles, has indulged in a characteristically ignorant but extremely prejudiced outburst against India and its Government... Mr. Churchill is an unashamed imperialist and at a time when imperialism is on its last legs, he is the proverbial last-ditcher to whom obstinacy and dogged consistency mean more than reason, imagination and wisdom...

"That Mr. Churchill's attack on India and its Government is both mischievous and venomous... we were fully aware of the machinations of the vested interests both in India and the

UK to hand over as difficult a legacy to India as possible. The balkanization of India was being actively promoted. Large scale disturbances were being manufactured. Vandalism at the peak of the impending departure from the scene of personal rule was actuating many of the Churchillian agents in power here.

"We, therefore, decided to drink the bitter cup and accept the lesser evil of partition, only on the condition that it commanded the support of all parties... We thought Mr. Churchill was an honourable man and would abide by the obligations inherent in the agreement... If a proof of his deep-seated prejudice and his medieval mind were needed, it would be enough to show that whilst he refers to Kashmir as being four-fifths Muslim, he has omitted to mention that Hyderabad is four-fifths Hindu, and that a creation of the 18th century, as the Nizam's State is, is suddenly, by the magic of Mr. Churchill's words, transformed into an 'ancient State'. The fact of the matter is that, to vary the words of a British statesman, whether Mr. Churchill roars like a lion or coos like a dove, it is his ignorance and blind prejudice that must come out prominently..."

Appendix—IV

Tibet: Patel's Letter to Nehru

New Delhi
7 November 1950

My dear Jawaharlal,

Ever since my return from Ahmedabad and after the Cabinet meeting the same day which I had to attend at practically 15 minutes' notice and for which I regret I was not able to read all the papers, I have been anxiously thinking over the problem of Tibet and I thought I should share with you what is passing through my mind.

I have carefully gone through the correspondence between the External Affairs Ministry and our Ambassador in Peking and through him the Chinese Government. I have tried to peruse this correspondence as favourably to our Ambassador and the Chinese Government as possible, but I regret to say that neither of them comes out well as a result of this study. The Chinese Government have tried to delude us by professions of peaceful intentions. My own feeling is that at a crucial period they managed to instil into our Ambassador a false sense of confidence in their so-called desire to settle the Tibetan problem by peaceful means. There can be no doubt that during the period covered by this correspondence the Chinese must have been concentrating for an onslaught on

Tibet. The final action of the Chinese, in my judgment, is little short of perfidy. The tragedy of it is that the Tibetans put faith in us; they chose to be guided by us; and we have been unable to get them out of the meshes of Chinese diplomacy or Chinese malevolence. From the latest position, it appears that we shall not be able to rescue the Dalai Lama. Our Ambassador has been at great pains to find an explanation or justification for Chinese policy and actions. As the External Affairs Ministry remarked in one of their telegrams, there was a lack of firmness and unnecessary apology in one or two representations that he made to the Chinese Government on our behalf. It is impossible to imagine any sensible person believing in the so-called threat to China from Anglo-American machinations in Tibet. Therefore, if the Chinese put faith in this, they must have distrusted us so completely as to have taken us as fools or stooges of Anglo-American diplomacy or strategy. This feeling, if genuinely entertained by the Chinese in spite of your direct approaches to them, indicates that even though we regard ourselves as friends of China, the Chinese do not regard us as their friends. With the Communist mentality of "whoever is not with them being against them," this is a significant pointer of which we have to take due note. During the last several months, outside the Russian camp, we have practically been alone in championing the cause of Chinese entry into the UNO and in securing from the Americans assurances on the questions of Formosa. We have done everything we could to assuage Chinese feelings, to allay its apprehensions and to defend its legitimate claims in our discussions and correspondence with America and Britain and in the UNO. In spite of this, China is not convinced about our disinterestedness; it continues to regard us with suspicion and the whole psychology is one, at least outwardly, of skepticism, perhaps mixed with a little hostility. I doubt if we can go any further than we have done already to convince China of our good intentions, friendliness and goodwill. In Peking, we have an Ambassador who is eminently suitable for putting across the friendly point of view. Even he seems to have failed to convert the Chinese. Their last telegram to us is an act of gross discourtesy not only in the summary way it disposes of our protest against the entry of Chinese forces into Tibet but also in the wild insinuation that our attitude is determined by foreign influences. It looks as though it is not a friend speaking in that language but a potential enemy.

In the background of this, we have to consider what new situation now faces us as a result of the disappearance of Tibet, as we knew it, and the expansion of China almost up to our gates. Throughout history we have seldom been worried about our north-east frontier. The Himalayas have been regarded as an impenetrable barrier against any threat from the north. We had a friendly Tibet which gave us no trouble. The Chinese were divided. They had their own domestic problems and never bothered us about our frontiers. In 1914, we entered into a convention with Tibet which was not endorsed by the Chinese. We seem to have regarded Tibetan autonomy as extending to independent treaty relationship. Presumably, all that we required was Chinese counter-signature. The Chinese interpretation of suzerainty seems to be different. We can, therefore, safely assume that very soon they will disown all the stipulations which Tibet has entered into with us in the past. That throws into the melting pot all frontier and commercial settlements with Tibet on which we have been functioning and acting during the last half a century. China is no longer divided. It is united and strong. All along the Himalayas in the north and north-east, we have on our side of the frontier a population ethnologically and culturally not different from Tibetans or Mongoloids. The undefined state of the frontier and the existence on our side of a population with its affinities to Tibetans or Chinese have all the elements of potential trouble between China and ourselves. Recent and bitter history also tells us that communism is no shield against imperialism and that the Communists are as good or as bad imperialists as any other. Chinese ambitions in this respect not only cover the Himalayan slopes on our side but also include important parts of Assam. They have their ambitions in Burma also. Burma has the added difficulty that it has no McMahon Line round which to build up even the semblance of an agreement. Chinese irredentism and Communist imperialism are different from the expansionism or imperialism of the Western Powers. The former has a cloak of ideology which makes it ten times more dangerous. In the guise of ideological expansion lie concealed racial, national or historical claims. The danger from the north and north-east, therefore, becomes both communist and imperialist. While our western and north-western threat to security is still as prominent as before, a new threat has developed from the north and north-east. Thus, for the first time, after centuries, India's defence has to concentrate itself on two fronts simultaneously. Our defence measures have so far been based on the calculations of a superiority over Pakistan. In our calculations we shall now have to reckon with Communist China in the north and in the north-east, a Communist China which has definite ambitions and aims and which does not, in any way, seem friendly disposed towards us.

Let us also consider the political conditions on this potentially troublesome frontier. Our northern or north-eastern approaches consist of Nepal, Bhutan, Sikkim, the Darjeeling [area] and tribal areas in Assam. From the point of view of communications, they are weak spots. Continuous defensive lines do not exist. There is almost an unlimited scope for infiltration. Police protection is limited to a very small number of passes. There, too, our outposts do not seem to be fully manned. The contact of these areas with us is by no means close and intimate. The people inhabiting these portions have no established loyalty or devotion to India. Even the Darjeeling and Kalimpong areas are not free from pro-Mongoloid prejudices. During the last three years we have not been able to make any appreciable approaches to the Nagas and other hill tribes in Assam. European missionaries and other visitors had been in touch with them, but their influence was in no way friendly to India or Indians. In Sikkim, there was political ferment some time ago. It is quite possible that discontent is smouldering there. Bhutan is comparatively quiet, but its affinity with Tibetans would be a handicap. Nepal has a weak oligarchic regime based almost entirely on force; it is in conflict with a turbulent element of the population as well as with enlightened ideas of the modern age. In these circumstances, to make people alive to the new danger or to make them defensively strong is a very difficult task indeed and that difficulty can be got over only by enlightened firmness, strength and a clear line of policy. I am sure the Chinese and their source of inspiration, Soviet Russia, would not miss any opportunity of exploiting these weak spots, partly in support of their ideology and partly in support of their ambitions. In my judgment, therefore, the situation is one in which we cannot afford either to be complacent or to be vacillating. We must have a clear idea of what we wish to achieve and also of the methods by which we should achieve it. Any faltering or lack of decisiveness in formulating our objectives or in pursuing our policy to attain those objectives is bound to weaken us and increase the threats which are so evident.

Side by side with these external dangers, we shall now have to face serious internal problems as well. I have already asked [H.V.R.] Iengar to send to the E.A. Ministry a copy of the Intelligence Bureau's appreciation of these matters. Hitherto, the Communist Party of India has found some difficulty in contacting Communists abroad, or in getting supplies of arms, literature, etc. from them. They had to contend with the difficult Burmese and Pakistan frontiers on the east or with the long seaboard. They shall now have a comparatively easy means of access to Chinese Communists and through them to other foreign Communists. Infiltration of spies, fifth columnists and Communists would now be easier. Instead of having to deal with isolated Communist pockets in Telengana and Warangal we may have to deal with Communist threats to our security along our northern and north-eastern frontiers where, for supplies of arms and ammunitions, they can safely depend on Communist arsenals in China. The whole situation thus raised a number of problems on which we must come to an early decision so that we can, as I said earlier, formulate the objectives of our policy and decide the methods by which those objectives are to be attained. It is also clear that the action will have to be fairly comprehensive, involving not only our defence strategy and state of preparations but also problems of internal security to deal with which we have not a moment to lose. We shall also have to deal with administrative and political problems in the weak spots along the frontier to which I have already referred.

It is, of course, impossible for me to be exhaustive in setting out all these problems. I am, however, giving below some of the problems which, in my opinion, require early solution and round which we have to build our administrative or military policies and measures to implement them.

a. A military and intelligence appreciation of the Chinese threat to India both on the frontier and to internal security.
b. An examination of our military position and such redisposition of our forces as might be necessary, particularly with the idea of guarding important routes or areas which are likely to be the subject of dispute.
c. An appraisement of the strength of our forces and, if necessary, reconsideration of our retrenchment plans for the Army in the light of these new threats.
d. A long-term consideration of our defence needs. My own feeling is that, unless we assure our supplies of arms, ammunition and armour, we should be making our defence position perpetually weak and we would not be able to stand up to the double threat of difficulties both from the west and north-west and north and north-east.
e. The question of Chinese entry into UNO. In view of the rebuff which China has given us and the method which it has followed in dealing with Tibet, I am doubtful whether we can advocate its claims any longer. There would probably be a threat in the UNO virtually to outlaw China in view of its active participation in the Korean war. We must determine our attitude on this question also.
f. The political and administrative steps which we should take to strengthen our northern and north-eastern frontiers. This would include the whole of the border, i.e.

Nepal, Bhutan, Sikkim, Darjeeling and the tribal territory in Assam.

g. Measures of internal security in the border areas as well as the States flanking those areas, such as UP, Bihar, Bengal and Assam.
h. Improvement of our communications, road, rail, air and wireless, in these areas and with the frontier outposts.
i. Policing and intelligence of frontier posts.
j. The future of our mission at Lhasa and the trade posts at Gyangtse and Yatung and the forces which we have in operation in Tibet to guard the trade routes.
k. The policy in regard to the McMahon Line.

These are some of the questions which occur to my mind. It is possible that a consideration of these matters may lead us into wider questions of our relationship with China, Russia, America, Britain and Burma. This, however, would be of a general nature, though some might be basically very important, e.g. we might have to consider whether we should not enter into closer association with Burma in order to strengthen the latter in its dealings with China. I do not rule out the possibility that, before applying pressure on us, China might apply pressure on Burma. With Burma, the frontier is entirely undefined and the Chinese territorial claims are more substantial. In its present position, Burma might offer an easier problem for China and, therefore, might claim its first attention.

I suggest that we meet early to have a general discussion on these problems and decide on such steps as we might think to be immediately necessary and direct quick examination of other problems with a view to taking early measures to deal with them.

Yours,
Vallabhbhai Patel

Post-Script

As recorded earlier, Nehru always needed a strong man by his side. Earlier in life it was Motilal Nehru, his father; thereafter it was Gandhi, and finally, since Independence, it was Sardar Patel. In April 1950, there was a near revolt by the Bengalis in Kolkata over the Nehru-Liaquat Pact in the wake of communal rioting in East Pakistan, Mountbatten wrote to Patel: "You have for years been the 'strong man' of India. With your support, Jawaharlal cannot fail. I do not believe there is one man in the country who would stand up to you when you make up your mind..."

Patel was not by Nehru's side when China annexed Tibet. The US showed its desire to help Tibet by whatever means possible. A weak-hearted, vacillating Nehru "requested that Washington refrain from publicly condemning China." Nehru accepted the new development quietly.

Nehru woke up to the realities of the grim reality in 1962 in China's undeclared war on India. Nehru's pride of a non-aligned leader hadn't permitted him to see what was happening. He was shaken from his long slumber, and in his humiliation he made an abject surrender to US President, J.F. Kennedy, of the grave fear that troubled his mind:

"... the situation in the NEFA Command has deteriorated still further. Bomdila has fallen and the retreating forces from Sela have been trapped between the Sela Bridge and Bomdila. A serious threat has developed to our Digboi oil fields in Assam. With the advance of the Chinese massive strength, the entire Brahmaputra Valley is seriously threatened, and unless something is done immediately to stem the tide, the whole of Assam, Tripura, Manipur and Nagaland would also pass into Chinese hands."

Nation suffered great humiliation. But Nehru much more. For him this was visible worldwide. Dr. Radhakrishnan echoed the nation's sentiments most correctly when he stated: "The people listened to Nehru, while Nehru believed the Chinese." His was a lost mind, and he suffered physically too. He was not the same: ever youthful and sprightly. But he didn't want to leave his seat of Prime Ministership. He preferred to continue in that pathetic state of mind and body till his death at the end of May 1964. Had Nehru listened to Patel post-1950, India's power and prestige would have been far different. Nevertheless, some may console themselves with the though: Destiny governs the lives of individuals and nations.

Appendix—V

Kashmir: Mountbatten Offers Jinnah Plebiscite

Note of a Discussion with Mr. Jinnah in the presence of Lord Ismay at Government House, Lahore, on 1st November 1947

In the course of 3½ hours of the most arduous and concentrated conversation, Kashmir took up most of the time; Junagadh took next place and Hyderabad the least. We darted about between these three subjects as well as talking about the overall policy affecting States. I have divided this note into four parts, although this was not necessarily the order in which the subjects were discussed, nor, of course, were all the remarks made consecutively.

Part I: India's Policy towards States Whose Accession Was in Dispute

I pointed out the similarity between the cases of Junagadh and Kashmir and suggested that plebiscites should be held under UNO as soon as conditions permitted. I told Mr. Jinnah that I had drafted out in the aeroplane a formula which I had not yet shown to my Government but to which I thought they might agree. This was the formula:

> The Governments of India and Pakistan agree that, where the ruler of a State does not belong to the community to which the majority of his subjects belong, and where the State has not acceded to that Dominion whose majority community is the same as the State's, the question of whether the State should finally accede to one or the other of the Dominions should in all cases be decided by an impartial reference to the will of the people.

Mr. Jinnah's first observation was that it was redundant and undesirable to have a plebiscite when it was quite clear that States should go according to their majority population, and if we would give him the accession of Kashmir he would offer to urge the accession of Junagadh direct to India.

I told him that my Government would never agree to changing the accession of a State against the wishes of the ruler or the Government that made the accession unless a plebiscite showed that the particular accession was not favoured by the people.

Mr. Jinnah then went on to say that he could not accept a formula if it was so drafted as to include Hyderabad, since he pointed out that Hyderabad did not wish to accede to either Dominion and he could not be a party to coercing them to accession.

I offered to put in some reference to States whose accession was in dispute "to try and get round the Hyderabad difficulty" and he said that he would give that his careful consideration if it was put to him.

I then pointed out that he really could not expect a principle to be applied in the case of Kashmir if it was not applied in the case of Junagadh and Hyderabad, but that we naturally would not expect him to be a party to compulsory accession against the wishes of the Nizam.

Part II: Hyderabad

I told Mr. Jinnah how much I regretted that at this serious

moment he should have been compromised by the behaviour of the Itttehad-ul-Mussalmin's delegation to Karachi.

He asked me what I meant. I told him that the two delegates, Yamin Zuberi and his companion, who had been reported by the Press as having seen him in Karachi, had returned to Hyderabad and were alleged to have influenced the Nizam into going back on his word to accept the standstill agreement which his Executive Council had passed by six votes to three. The inference had been drawn that they had carried a message to HEH from Mr. Jinnah, and that this was the cause of the latter's reversal of his decision.

Mr. Jinnah assured me categorically that he had merely seen these two men out of courtesy, for a matter of five or perhaps seven minutes. They had told him that HEH was about to sign an instrument of accession to India, and they begged Mr. Jinnah to intervene. Mr. Jinnah had replied that it was outside his power to intervene and that it was only a question for the Nizam and his own Government to decide.

I then recounted to Mr. Jinnah briefly the events which Sir Sultan Ahmed had related to me on 31 October, and Lord Ismay substantiated this account from a letter he had received from Sir Walter Monckton.

Mr. Jinnah once more affirmed most solemnly that he had nothing whatever to do with the recent reversal of the Nizam's decision. He had sent no verbal message whatsoever to Hyderabad. The advice he had tendered to HEH in writing some time ago was that he was between the devil and the deep blue sea. If he acceded to India, there would be bloodshed in Hyderabad; and if he did not accede, there would equally be bloodshed. Thus an agreement, but not accession, seemed to be the only hope.

I told him that the Nizam had sent me a letter through Sir Sultan Ahmed, dated 30 October, in which he implied that if negotiations now broke down with a new negotiating committee he might have to consider entering into an agreement with Pakistan.

Mr. Jinnah laughed and said, "That looks to me as though he

is threatening you. It has nothing to do with me. I have never discussed any form of agreement with the Nizam."

I asked him straight out whether he would be prepared to sign a standstill agreement with Hyderabad if he were asked to by the Nizam. He replied that a standstill agreement implied that there were relations or intervening factors which formed the basis for a standstill [agreement]. He could not think of any such factors between Pakistan and Hyderabad, and whereas he did not envisage wishing to sign such an agreement, he would have to examine the matter carefully, if it were put to him, before refusing.

I drew his attention to the unfortunate effect it would have if in fact he were to start negotiations with the Nizam after they had been broken off with the Dominion to which he was irretrievably linked geographically and by majority of population.

Mr. Jinnah said he would bear this in mind.

Part III: Junagadh

I read out to Mr. Jinnah the following extract from a statement made by Mr. Liaquat Ali Khan, which had been published in the *Statesman* of Friday, 21 September:

> The correct position is that the Indian Independence Act of 1947 has left all Indian States completely free to join either one Dominion or the other or to enter into treaty relations with either. Legally and constitutionally there can be no question of putting limitations on this right of the States. Muslim League leaders before 15 August and the official spokesmen of the Pakistan Government thereafter have publicly declared their agreement with this view; and have since rigorously stood by it. No objection has been raised by Pakistan to any State acceding to the Dominion of India.

I asked Mr. Jinnah if he still stood rigorously by his Prime Minister's statement. He looked somewhat uneasy but admitted that it represented the legal position. I told him I would revert to this when talking about Kashmir, but in the meanwhile wanted to know what he proposed to do about Junagadh.

He admitted that there was no sense in having Junagadh in the Dominion of Pakistan, and said that he had been most averse from accepting this accession. He had in fact demurred for a long time, but had finally given way to the insistent appeals of the Nawab and his Dewan.

I told him that in the case of Babariawad and Mangrol, it was clearly the wish of the people that they had in fact signed instruments of accession to that effect. How then could he refuse them the right of accession? He said that Mangrol's accession had been forced on him, and withdrawn almost before the ink was dry. In any event, he had persuaded the Nawab of Junagadh to accept legal arbitration.

I told him that the Government of India would not have minded the position so much if Junagadh had played the game and not interfered internally in these small States; but that they were oppressing the people, imposing fines and removing their grain. I pointed out that repeated telegrams had been sent protesting at this. Mr. Jinnah denied this, and stated categorically that neither Pakistan nor Junagadh had sent any soldiers or armed police into these States.

I told him that we had definite information that Junagadh had sent armed police into both of them, and that they were oppressing the people. Pandit Nehru had telegraphed to Mr. Liaquat Ali Khan about this, and the latter had undertaken to ask Junagadh to withdraw their forces.

When they had failed to do so, the Government of India had telegraphed, a few days back, saying that we would have to protect the interests of these States if the Junagadh forces were not withdrawn. Since they had not been withdrawn, India were going to put in forces to protect their interests, subject to a plebiscite being subsequently held in these States about final accession. They would go in under a flag of truce, with loud-hailers and inviting the cooperation of Junagadh authorities.

Mr. Jinnah lamented that the Government of India had not invited the co-operation of Pakistan before hand. I pointed out that they had in fact been unable to enforce their own orders and that so far as I was aware, Indian forces had been sent into these two States that very day.

Part IV: Kashmir

I handed Mr. Jinnah a copy of the statement of events signed by the Indian Chiefs of Staff, which I had shown to Mr. Liaquat Ali Khan. He asked if he could keep it, but I made him return the original and gave him an unsigned copy. Although he expressed surprise at the remarkable speed at which we had been able to organise sending troops into Srinagar plain, he did not question the document or my statement.

Mr. Jinnah's principal complaint was that the Government of India had failed to give timely information to the Government of Pakistan about the action that they proposed to take in Kashmir.

I pointed out the speed at which events had moved. It was not until the evening of the 24th that reliable reports had been received of the tribal incursion, and it was not until the 25th that observers had been sent up to confirm these reports. Thus the decision to send in troops had not been taken until the 26th, by which date the Maharaja had announced his intention of acceding to India. There had not been a moment to lose. I added that I could not recall the exact time, but that it was my impression that Pandit Nehru had telegraphed to Mr. Liaquat Ali Khan on the 26th, immediately the decision to send in troops had been taken.

Mr. Jinnah complained that this information should have been sent much earlier—in fact on 24 October. "If," he said, "they had on that date telegraphed saying that a critical situation was reported to be developing in Kashmir and they had sent in observers to confirm these reports and suggested that Pakistan should co-operate in dealing with the situation, all the trouble would have been ended by now."

Lord Ismay agreed that the Government of Pakistan should have had the earliest possible notification. This was the first thing that had occurred to him on his return to Delhi from the United Kingdom, and, indeed, he was under the impression that it had been done. To the best of his recollection, Pandit Nehru had told him on the 28th that he had kept Mr. Liaquat Ali Khan in touch with what was happening all the time. If this had not been done, the oversight must have been due to the pressure of events, and not because the Government of India had anything to hide.

Mr. Jinnah looked up his files and said that the telegram had arrived after the troops had landed, and that it did not contain any form of an appeal for co-operation between the two Dominions in this matter; it merely informed him of the accession and the landing of troops. Continuing he said that the accession was not a bonafide one since it rested on "fraud and violence" and would never be accepted by Pakistan. I asked him to explain why he used the term "fraud," since the Maharaja was fully entitled, in accordance with Pakistan's own official statement, which I had just read over to him, to make such accession. It was therefore perfectly legal and valid.

Mr. Jinnah said that this accession was the end of a long intrigue and that it had been brought about by violence. I countered this by saying that I entirely agreed that the accession had been brought about by violence; I knew the Maharaja was most anxious to remain independent, and nothing but the terror of violence could have made him accede to either Dominion; since the violence had come from tribes for whom Pakistan was responsible, it was clear that he would have acceded to India to obtain help against the invader. Mr. Jinnah repeatedly made it clear that in his opinion it was India who had committed this violence by sending her troops into Srinagar; I countered as often with the above argument, thereby greatly enraging Mr. Jinnah at my apparent denseness.

From this point, he went on to say that the Government of India authorities had encouraged the Kashmir Government to massacre Muslims in the Poonch and Mirpur areas. I repudiated this as obvious nonsense. He then said, "Very well, it was the Congress party that did it." I pointed out that if there had been any such massacre by Hindus in the Poonch area (which I did not deny) this had been done entirely by Kashmir Hindus and could hardly have been done with the object of inciting the tribes to invade Kashmir and come so close to capturing Srinagar, merely to afford the Maharaja an excuse for acceding to India for the purpose of obtaining help.

I then explained to Mr. Jinnah, at some length, the policy which I had consistently pursued in regard to Kashmir, namely—trying to persuade the Maharaja to institute progressive government, ascertain the will of the people and then accede to the Dominion of the people's choice before 15 August. I recounted how I had tried to persuade H.H. to do this during my visit to Kashmir in July, and how I had told him my views privately whilst driving in the car with him; but that when I had wished to have a formal meeting with him in the presence of his Prime Minister and my Private Secretary (Sir George Abell) on the last day of my visit, he had pleaded illness and gone to bed to avoid the meeting. On leaving Srinagar, I had instructed the Resident (Colonel Webb) to continue to give the Maharaja this advice officially; and finally Lord Ismay had gone up at the end of August with instructions to advise the Maharaja to hurry up and ascertain the will of the people. But the Maharaja had invariably avoided the issue, and had always turned the conversation to lighter topics.

Mr. Jinnah paid a handsome tribute to the correctness of my policy and admitted that it was I who had put the ex-Premier of Kashmir (Pandit Kak) in touch with him when he came to Delhi.

Mr. Jinnah next referred to the statement which he had issued to the Press that day and enlarged on his difficulties in not being able to have any reasonable conversation, either personally or through representatives, with the Maharaja or even with his Prime Minister; and that, not only had the Maharaja brought his troubles upon himself by this attitude, but had greatly aggravated them by the massacres to which he had incited his Dogras against innocent

Muslims. He said that even today at Jammu 90,000 Muslims were in danger of being massacred.

I told Mr. Jinnah that Pandit Nehru had expressed horror at the massacres that had taken place and had issued stringent orders that everything possible was to be done to stop them. Only the night before I had supplemented those instructions myself through an Indian Brigadier who had just returned from Kashmir and who fully agreed with the necessity for stopping any further killing of Muslims.

I informed Mr. Jinnah that we already had a Brigade Group of 2,000 men in Srinagar; that a 4th Battalion would be flown in that day, and a 5th Battalion within the next two days. I said that we should have no difficulty in holding Srinagar and that the prospect of the tribes entering the city in any force was now considered remote.

Lord Ismay suggested that the main thing was to stop the fighting; and he asked Mr. Jinnah how he proposed that this should be done. Mr. Jinnah said that both sides should withdraw at once. He emphasised that the withdrawal must be simultaneous. When I asked him how the tribesmen were to be called off, he said that all he had to do was to give them an order to come out and to warn them that if they did not comply, he would send large forces along their lines of communication. In fact, if I was prepared to fly to Srinagar with him, he would guarantee that the business would be settled within 24 hours.

I expressed mild astonishment at the degree of control that he appeared to exercise over the raiders.

I asked him how he proposed that we should withdraw our forces, observing that India's forces were on the outskirts of Srinagar in a defensive role; all the tribes had to do was to stop attacking. I also pointed out that we could not possibly afford aeroplanes to fly the Indian troops back. Lord Ismay suggested that they should march back via Banihal Pass.

I asked Mr. Jinnah why he objected so strongly to a plebiscite, and he said he did so because with the troops of the Indian Dominion in military occupation of Kashmir and with the National

Conference under Sheikh Abdullah in power, such propaganda and pressure could be brought to bear that the average Muslim would never have the courage to vote for Pakistan.

I suggested that we might invite UNO to undertake the plebiscite and send observers and organisers in advance to ensure that the necessary atmosphere was created for a free and impartial plebiscite. I reiterated that the last thing my Government wished was to obtain a false result by a fraudulent plebiscite.

Mr. Jinnah repeated that he and I were the only two who could organise a plebiscite and said that we should do it together. Lord Ismay and I went to great trouble to explain that I was a constitutional Governor-General and a Britisher, and that even if my Government would trust me sufficiently to see this through, I was sure that Mr. Attlee would not give his consent.

Mr. Jinnah complained bitterly that after the extremely generous gesture on the part of the Government of India in accepting his invitation to come to discussions at Lahore, the illness of one man should have prevented some other Minister from coming to conduct the negotiations; why, for example, could Sardar Patel not have come? It was a matter of the greatest urgency to get together on this problem, and he asked me how soon Pandit Nehru could come to Lahore.

I countered by saying that it was now his turn to come to Delhi since I had come to Lahore, and I invited him cordially to stay as my guest, when I would take him to see Pandit Nehru in his bedroom. He said that this was impossible. I pointed out that I had been to see Pandit Nehru personally in his bedroom and that I had now been to see his Prime Minister (of Pakistan) in his bedroom, and that I failed to see what was improper in this suggestion. He assured me that it was not a question of going to anybody's bedroom, but that he was so busy he simply had no time to leave Lahore while his Prime Minister was on the sick list.

I asked him afterwards if there was any single problem more serious or urgent than Kashmir. I pointed out that when one was so busy one had to arrange work in order of priority. If he admitted that Kashmir was top priority, then all other work should stand aside for it and he should come to Delhi at once. He said he regretted that this was impossible, for the whole burden of events was on his shoulders at Lahore. I explained that he need only be gone for the inside of a day and that I was anxious to return his hospitality. He said, "I would gladly come a hundred times to visit you; I just cannot manage it while my Prime Minister is ill." I asked him to come as soon as his Prime Minister was well enough to travel, and he said, "We shall have to see."

Lord Ismay pointed out that the best way to stand well in world opinion was for him now to come and return my visit and discuss Kashmir with Pandit Nehru. Mr. Jinnah said that he had lost interest in what the world thought of him since the British Commonwealth had let him down when he had asked him to come to the rescue of Pakistan.

I ended the meeting, as I had started it, by making it quite clear that I had come unbriefed and unauthorised to discuss Kashmir, since I had not had a chance of seeing Pandit Nehru after he had informed me he would be unable to accompany me. I told him I was speaking not as Governor-General of India but as the ex-Viceroy who had been responsible for partition and was anxious to see that it did not result in any harm coming to the two Dominions. He said he quite saw this but hoped that I would be able to discuss the various proposals which we had been talking about with Pandit Nehru and send him a firm telegram. I undertook to convey this message to Pandit Nehru.

Round about 5.00 p.m. it was obvious that we were going to be too late to go and see Mr. Liaquat Ali Khan again, so Lord Ismay left the room to telephone our apologies to him. I took the opportunity of Lord Ismay's absence to 'tell off' Mr. Jinnah. I told him that I considered it was unstatesmanlike, inept and bad mannered for him to issue a statement which directly accused the Government of India of "fraud and violence" in Kashmir a few hours before he expected the Prime Minister of India to come and discuss this very question in a friendly manner; and that had he been feeling well enough to come, such a studied and ill-timed insult would have been enough to send his temperature up again. I finally pointed out that Pakistan was in my opinion in much weaker position than India, not only from the obvious military point of view, but I was sure, the world would think they were in the wrong; and that this form of abuse before a discussion commenced could only put Pakistan even deeper in the wrong.

At the end, Mr. Jinnah became extremely pessimistic and said it was quite clear that the Dominion of India was out to throttle and choke the Dominion of Pakistan at birth, and that if they continued with their oppression, there would be nothing for it but to face the consequences. However depressing the prospect might be, he was not afraid; for the situation was already so bad that there was little that could happen to make it worse.

I pointed out that war, whilst admittedly very harmful for India, would be completely disastrous for Pakistan and himself.

Lord Ismay tried to cheer him up out of his depression but I fear was not very successful. However, we parted on good terms.

References

Preface

1. Sahay, Vishnu (ICS), Secretary, Kashmir Affairs: Recorded interview with author, dated 2nd April 1969.
2. Elmhirst, Air Marshal Sir Thomas, C.-in-C., Indian Air Force: letter to author, dated 8th January 1969.
3. Bucher, General Sir Roy, C.-in-C., Indian Army: letter to author, dated 6th March 1969.
4. Parikh, Narhari D.: "Sardar Vallabhbhai Patel", Vol. 1, p. vii.
5. Menon, K.P.S. (ICI), Foreign Secretary: letter to author, dated 22nd October 1968.
6. Garrett, Sir Hugh (ICS): letter to author, dated 16th August 1968.
7. The *Manchester Guardian* (now the *Guardian*), dated 16th December 1950.
8. Roy, M.N. Roy: "Men I Met", p. 15.

1. The Child, the Land, the People

1. Karandikar, M.A.: "Islam in India's Transition to Modernity", p. 152.
2. Hume, Allan Octavian, quoted by Karandikar, ibid, p. 153.
3. Bombay Gazetteer, Vol. III, Kheda and Panch Mahals (1879), p. 77.
4. ibid, p. 78.
5. ibid, p. 95.

6. ibid, p. 98.
7. ibid, p. 95.
8. ibid, p. 120.
9. ibid, (vide Bombay Government Litho Papers, 148, 1 p. 103.
10. ibid, (vide Bishop Herber's Note), p. 109.
11. ibid, p. 2.
12. ibid, p. 97.
13. ibid, p. 31.
14. Parikh, Narhari D.: "Sardar Vallabhbhai Patel", Vol. I, pp. 5-6.
15. ibid, pp. 3-4.

2. Genius of a Schoolboy

1. "This was Sardar—the Commemorative Volume", Vol. I (originally dictated by Patel in 1949 for Children's Special Number of *Shankar's Weekly*), pp. 167-68.
2. ibid, p. 168.
3. ibid, p. 168.
4. ibid, p. 206.
5. ibid, p. 207.
6. "Mahadev Desai's Diary" (Yeravada Jail), Part I, (1932-33), p. 88.

3. Pleader Whom the Police Feared

1. Parikh, Narhari D.: "Sardar Vallabhbhai Patel", Vol. I, (vide Patel's speech in 1921), p. 11.
2. ibid, p. 11.
3. ibid, p. 17.

4. A Great Ambition Fulfilled

1. Parikh, Narhari D.: "Sardar Vallabhbhai Patel", Vol. I, p. 11.
2. ibid, p. 11.
3. Mavalankar, G.V.: "Sardar Patel" an article on Patel's 70th birthday in *The Tribune*, Lahore, November 3, 1945.
4. ibid.
5. ibid.

5. A Rebel Enters Municipal Politics

1. Parikh, Narhari D.: "Sardar Vallabhbhai Patel", Vol. I (vide Patel's speech in 1921), p. 22.
2. Tiwari, A.R.: "Making of the Leader—Sardar Vallabhbhai Patel", (vide Administration Report of Ahmedabad Municipal Corporation, 1916-17), p. 6.
3. Parikh, p. 27.
4. Tiwari, pp. 13-14.
5. ibid (vide Gujarati newspaper *Prajabandhu*, June 4, 1916), p. 7.
6. ibid, p. 8.
7. Parikh, p. 31.
8. ibid, pp. 32-33.
9. Tiwari, p. 284.
10. Parikh, p. 145.
11. ibid, p. 33.
12. Tiwari, p. 235.
13. "Sardar Patel's Speeches" (in Hindu)—1918-48, p. 467. (1918-1947).
14. Tiwari, p. 33.
15. Tahmankar, D.V.: "Sardar Patel", p. 63.
16. Parikh, p. 36.

6. Gandhi's Disciple

1. The *Bombay Chronicle*, January 13, 1915.
2. ibid, January 15, 1915.
3. Mavalankar, G.V.: "Sardar Patel"—an article on Patel's 70th birthday in The *Tribune*, Lahore, November 3, 1945.
4. ibid.
5. Yagnik Indulal: manuscript article written in late twenties.
6. Ravishankar Maharaj: interview with author.

7. Gandhi's Deputy Commander in Kheda Satyagrah

1. Parikh, Narhari D.: "Sardar Vallabhbhai Patel", Vol. I, p. 89.
2. ibid.
3. ibid, p. 67.

4. ibid, p. 78.
5. ibid, pp. 49-50.
6. ibid, p. 57.
7. ibid, p. 58.
8. ibid.
9. ibid, Amritlal V. Thankkar (vide letter to the Editor, *The Times of India*), p. 53.
10. ibid, p. 58.
11. ibid, p. 59.
12. ibid, p. 60.
13. ibid, p. 61.
14. ibid, p. 62.
15. ibid, p. 63.
16. ibid, pp. 64-65.
17. ibid, p. 55.
18. ibid, p. 69.
19. ibid, p. 72.
20. ibid.
21. "Sardar Patel's Speeches" (in Hindi), pp. 3-4.
22. Parikh, p. 74.
23. The *Bombay Chronicle*, April 13, 1918.
24. ibid.
25. ibid.
26. ibid, May 28, 1918.
27. Parikh, p. 80.
28. ibid, p. 82.
29. ibid, p. 83.
30. The *Bombay Chronicle*, April 24, 1918.
31. "Sardar Patel's Speeches" (in Hindi), pp. 4-5.
32. Parikh, p. 85.
33. ibid, pp. 88-89.
34. The *Bombay Chronicle*, April 23, 1918.
35. ibid, April 20, 1918.
36. ibid, June 5, 1918.
37. Parikh, p. 88.
38. The *Bombay Chronicle*, July 3, 1918.
39. ibid.
40. "Sardar Patel's Speeches" (in Hindi), pp. 7-8.

41. The *Bombay Chronicle*, July 3, 1918.
42. Sitaramayya, Dr. B. Pattabhi: "The History of the Indian National Congress", Part I, p. 239.

8. Birth of a New Congress

1. Bose, Subhas Chandra: "The Indian Struggle: 1920-1942", p. 68.
2. ibid, p. 70.
3. Parikh, Narhari D.: "Sardar Vallabhbhai Patel", Vol. I, p. 145.
4. The Bombay Chronicle, December 28, 1921.
5. ibid.
6. "Sardar Patel's Speeches" (in Hindi), p. 44.
7. The Bombay Chronicle, ibid.
8. Parikh, p. 147.
9. ibid.
10. Jayakar, M.R.: "The Story of My Life", Vol. I (views of a chronicler quoted), pp. 501-02.
11. ibid, p. 503.

9. Nagpur Satyagraha

1. Parikh, Narhari D.: "Sardar Vallabhbhai Patel", Vol. I, p. 190.
2. ibid, p. 200.
3. ibid, p. 201.
4. ibid, p. 204.
5. ibid, p. 206.
6. ibid, p. 208-09.
7. ibid, p. 211-12.
8. ibid, p. 212.
9. ibid, p. 212-13.

10. A Satyagraha to Fight Dacoits

1. Parikh, Narhari D.: "Sardar Vallabhbhai Patel", Vol. I, p. 219.
2. ibid, pp. 220-22.
3. ibid, p. 233.

4. ibid, p. 228.
5. ibid.
6. ibid, pp. 237-238
7. ibid, pp. 239-41.
8. ibid, p. 242
9. ibid, pp. 242-43.
10. ibid, pp. 244-46.
11. *Young India*, April 6, 1924

11. Fighting Gujarat Floods

1. Parikh, Narhari D.: "Sardar Vallabhbhai Patel", Vol. I, p. 284.
2. Asher, Lakshmidas Purushottam: interview with author.
3. "Sardar Patel's Speeches" (in Hindi), p. 132.
4. Parikh, p. 288.
5. "Sardar Patel's Speeches" (in Hindi), p. 132.
6. ibid, p. 123.
7. Parikh, p. 288.
8. Parikh, p. 296.
9. ibid, p. 292.
10. ibid, pp. 295-96.
11. ibid, p. 294

12. The Lenin of Bardoli

1. Desai, Mahadev: "The Story of Bardoli", p. 107.
2. Taleyarkhan, Homi J.H.: The *Bharat*, September 10, 1950.
3. Nehru, Jawaharlal: "A Bunch of Old Letter", p. 58.
4. The *Times of India*, July 4, 1928.
5. Taleyarkhan, ibid.
6. Parikh, Narhari D.: "Sardar Vallabhbhai Patel", Vol. I, p. 379.
7. Desai, ibid, p. 5.
8. ibid, pp. 7-8.
9. Parikh, ibid, p. 153.
10. Desai, ibid, p. 7.
11. ibid, p. 20.
12. ibid, p. 12.
13. ibid, pp. 12-13.

14. ibid, p. 14.
15. ibid, pp. 14-15.
16. ibid, p. 15.
17. ibid, p. 16.
18. ibid, p. 18.
19. Parikh, ibid, p. 301.
20. Desai, ibid, p. 22.
21. ibid, p. 32.
22. ibid, p. 41.
23. ibid, p. 43.
24. Parikh, ibid, p. 304.
25. Desai, ibid, p. 46.
26. ibid, pp. 46-47.
27. ibid, p. 48.
28. ibid, p. 49.
29. Parikh, ibid, pp. 305-06.
30. ibid, p. 306.
31. Desai, ibid, pp. 54-55.
32. ibid, p. 55.
33. ibid, p. 56.
34. Parikh, ibid, p. 321.
35. ibid, p. 322.
36. Desai, ibid, p. 58.
37. Parikh, ibid, pp. 343-44.
38. Desai, ibid, p. 167.
39. ibid, p. 233.
40. ibid, p. 97.
41. ibid, p. 73.
42. Parikh, ibid, p. 318.
43. Desai, ibid, p. 97.
44. Parikh, ibid, p. 319.
45. ibid, p. 320.
46. The *Times of India*, July 4, 1928.
47. Desai, ibid, p. 235
48. ibid, pp. 108-09.
49. ibid, pp. 146-47.
50. ibid, p. 158.
51. ibid, p. 143.

52. ibid, p. 110.
53. ibid, p. 324.
54. ibid, pp. 325-26.
55. Desai, p. 126.
56. ibid, p. 108.
57. ibid, pp. 140-41.
58. ibid, p. 154.
59. ibid, pp. 155-56.
60. ibid, p. 160.
61. Parikh, p. 334.
62. Desai, p. 159.
63. Parikh, pp. 336-37.
64. ibid, p. 338.
65. ibid, p. 337.
66. ibid, p. 338.
67. ibid, p. 340.
68. Desai, p. 197.
69. Parikh, p. 346.
70. ibid, p. 347.
71. Desai, p. 232.
72. ibid, p. 222.
73. Parikh, p. 349.
74. Desai, p. 228.
75. Parikh, p. 351.
76. ibid, pp. 352-53.
77. Desai, p. 257.
78. ibid, p. 260.
79. ibid, p. 262.
80. ibid, pp. 262-63.
81. ibid, pp. 265-68.
82. Parikh, p. 374.
83. "Sardar Patel's Speeches" (in Hindi), pp. 189-90.
84. Bose, Subhas Chandra: "The Indian Struggle", p. 152.
85. Brown, Judith M.: "Modern India", p. 259.
86. ibid, p. 266.
87. Mehta, Kalyanji: Recorded interview with author.

13. "John the Baptist" in Dandi March

1. Phatak, Prof. N.R.: "Government of Maharashtra Source Material for a History of the Freedom Movement in India", Vol. III, Part III: 1929-31, p. 19.
2. Sitaramayya, Dr. Pattabhi: "The History of the Indian National Congress", Vol. I (1885-1935), p. 638.
3. Phatak, ibid, p. 14.
4. Sitaramayya, ibid, p. 639.
5. Parikh, Narhari D.: "Sardar Vallabhbhai Patel", Vol. II, p. 13.
6. Phatak, ibid, p. 12.
7. ibid, p. 16.
8. ibid, p. 17.
9. Shirer, William L.: "Gandhi: a Memoir", p. 95.
10. Parikh, ibid, pp. 6-7.
11. "Sardar Patel's Speeches" (in Hindi), edited by Narhari D. Parikh, p. 221.
12. ibid, pp. 222-23.
13. Parikh, ibid, p. 9.
14. ibid, p. 12.
15. ibid, p. 9.
16. ibid, pp. 10-12.
17. Patel, Ashabhai: Recorded interview, March 16th, 1969.
18. Brailsford, H.N.: "Subject India", pp. 232-34.
19. Patel, Ashabhai, ibid.
20. Shirer, ibid, p. 98.
21. Nanda, B.R.: "Mahatma Gandhi", p. 298.
22. Shirer, ibid, p. 71.
23. ibid, p. 96.

14. President of Karachi Congress

1. Majumdar, R.C.: "Struggle for Freedom", Vol. XI, p. 464.
2. Nehru, Jawaharlal: "Jawaharlal Nehru: An Autobiography", p. 265.
3. Nehru, Jawaharlal: "A Bunch of Old Letters", p. 61.
4. Sitaramayya, B. Pattabhi: "The History of the Indian National Congress" (1885-1935), p. 767.

5. Parikh, Narhari D.: "Sardar Vallabhbhai Patel", Vol. II, p. 50.
6. "Sardar Patel's Speeches" (in Hindi), pp. 245-51.
7. Parikh, ibid, p. 55.
8. ibid, p. 56.
9. Shirer, William: "Gandhi a Memoir", p. 126.

15. A "Mother to Gandhi"

1. Desai, Mahadev: "Yeravada Jail Diary" (in Hindi from Gujarati), Vol. II, p. 18.
2. ibid, Vol. I, p. 7.
3. Parikh, Narhari D.: "Sardar Vallabhbhai Patel", Vol. II, p. 136.
4. ibid, pp. 91-92.
5. Desai, Vol. I, p. 8.
6. Parikh, p. 112.
7. ibid, p. 108.
8. ibid, p. 112.
9. ibid, p. 96.
10. ibid, p. 93.
11. ibid, p. 94.
12. ibid, p. 95.
13. Desai, ibid, p. 274.
14. ibid, p. 68.
15. ibid, Vol. III, p. 56.
16. ibid, Vol. I, p. 199.
17. ibid, p. 32.
18. ibid, p. 28.
19. Parikh, Vol. II, p. 95.
20. Desai, Mahadev, Vol. I, p. 143.
21. ibid, Vol. II, pp. 162-63.
22. ibid, pp. 170-71.
23. ibid, Vol. III, p. 134.
24. ibid, p. 44.
25. ibid, Vol. I, p. 375.
26. ibid, Vol. III, p. 138.
27. ibid, Vol. II, p. 8.
28. ibid, Vol. III, p. 221.
29. ibid, Vol. I, p. 177,

30. ibid, p. 164.
31. ibid, p. 174.
32. ibid, p. 206.
33. ibid, p. 45.
34. ibid, p. 156.
35. Shirer, William L.: "Gandhi: A Memoir", pp. 155-56.
36. ibid, p. 105.
37. Desai, Vol. II, p. 87.
38. ibid, Vol. I, p. 175.
39. ibid, Vol. III, p. 277.
40. Parikh, Vol. II, p. 136.

16. The Party Boss

1. Desai, Mahadev: "Mahadevbhai's Diary" (Yeravda Jail), Vol. II, p. 10.
2. Nehru, Jawaharlal: "A Bunch of Old Letters", p. 120.
3. ibid, p. 118.
4. ibid, pp. 156-157.
5. Brecher, Michael: "Nehru—A Political Biography", p. 221.
6. Sitaramayya, B. Pattabhi: "The History of the Indian National Congress", Vol. II, p. 8.
7. ibid, p. 13.
8. Nehru, ibid, p. 175.
9. ibid, p. 178.
10. ibid, pp. 197-98.
11. ibid, pp. 182 and 185.
12. Sitaramayya, ibid, p. 7.
13. Masani, M.R.: Recorded interview with author, July 25, 1969.
14. Meherally, Yusuf: "Leaders of India", Vol. I, p. 61.
15. Nehru, ibid, pp. 174-75.
16. Nehru, Jawaharlal: "Autobiography", p. 602.
17. Brecher, ibid, p. 223.
18. Sitaramayya, ibid, p. 31.
19. Parikh, ibid, pp. 218-19.
20. Nehru, Motilal: "Selected Works of Motilal Nehru", Vol. II, p. 356.
21. Parikh, ibid, p. 220.

22. ibid, p. 221.
23. ibid, p. 222.
24. Sitaramayya, ibid, p. 43.
25. Parikh, ibid, pp. 230-31.
26. ibid, p. 233.
27. ibid, p. 234.
28. ibid, pp. 234-35.
29. ibid, p. 235.
30. ibid, pp. 237-38.
31. ibid, p. 248.
32. ibid, p. 249.
33. ibid, p. 251.
34. ibid, p. 252.
35. ibid, p. 253.
36. ibid, pp. 254-55.
37. ibid, p. 283.
38. ibid, pp. 284-85.
39. ibid, p. 288.
40. ibid, p. 289.
41. ibid, p. 287.
42. Mishra, D.P. (then one of three Mahakoshal Ministers): interview with author, January 3, 1970.
43. Nehru, Jawaharlal: "Autobiography", pp. 338-39.
44. Parikh, ibid, p. 270.
45. ibid, p. 389.
46. ibid, p. 390.
47. ibid, p. 391.
48. ibid, pp. 393-94.
49. ibid, p. 396.
50. Sitaramayya, ibid, p. 113.
51. ibid, p. 115.
52. Roy, M.N.: "Men I Met", p. 16.
53. ibid.
54. Bose, Sarat Chandra: Letter to Gandhi, March 21, 1938, published in "Dr. Rajendra Prasad: Correspondence and Select Documents", Vol. 3, p. 214.
55. Bose, Subhas Chandra: "Indian Struggle", p. 333

17. The God that Failed

1. "Sardar Patel's Speeches" (in Hindi), edited by Narhari Parikh, pp. 431-32.
2. ibid, pp. 433-34.
3. ibid, pp. 435-36.
4. ibid, p. 437.
5. ibid, p. 375.
6. Linlithgow: quoted by John Glendevon in "The Viceroy at Bay: Lord Linlithgow in India 1936-1943", p. 87.
7. ibid, p. 196.
8. ibid, p. 49.
9. ibid, p. 148.
10. Mazumdar, R.C.: "Struggle for Freedom", p. 577.
11. Moon, Penderal: "Divide and Quit", p. 20.
12. "Sardar Patel's Speeches" (in Hindi), pp. 459-60.
13. ibid, pp. 460-61.
14. ibid, p. 462.
15. Sitaramayya, ibid, p. 145.
16. ibid, p. 133.
17. ibid, p. 197.
18. ibid, p. 201.
19. Kanungo, Nityanand (former Governor of Bihar): Letter to author dated February 8, 1969.
20. Sitaramayya, ibid, p. 133.
21. ibid, p. 206.
22. Dwarkadas, Kanji: "Ten Years to Freedom", p. 55.
23. Sitaramayya, ibid, p. 212.
24. "Sardar Patel's Speeches" (in Hindi), p. 477.
25. Parikh, Narhari D.: "Sardar Vallabhbhai Patel", Vol. II, pp. 434-35.
26. Sitaramayya, ibid, p. 292.
27. ibid, p. 294.
28. Parikh, ibid, p. 464.
29. Congress Working Committee War Resolution at Allahabad, published in "Dr. Rajendra Prasad: Correspondence and Select Documents", Vol. 5, p. 221.
30. Sitaramayya, ibid, p. 341.

31. "Sardar Patel's Speeches" (in Hindi), p. 526.
32. ibid, p. 513.
33. ibid, pp. 516-18.
34. ibid, p. 520.
35. ibid, p. 541.
36. ibid, pp. 544-50.
37. U'ren, C.W.E.: Letter to author dated March 18, 1969.
38. Sitaramayya: "Feathers & Stones: My Study Windows", pp. 391-95.
39. ibid, p. 46.
40. ibid, p. 24.
41. ibid, p. 15.
42. Venkataramani, M.S. and Srivastava, B.K.: "Quit India", p. 238.
43. "Sardar Patel's Speeches" (in Hindi), p. 551.
44. Ramakrishnan, S.: recorded interview with author, dated July 26, 1980.

18. Churchill's "Imperial Strategy"

1. Lord Wavell: "The Viceroy's Journal", p. 120.
2. "The Untold Story of India's Partition" by Narendra Singh Sarila, Oriental & Indian Collection, British Library, p. 25.
3. The "Transfer of Power" 1942-4, Vol. I: the Cripps Mission, January-August 1942, Document 208, pp. 282-84.
4. ibid, Document 375, p. 468.
5. Wavell to Henderson, 21st May 1946, quoted in Ayesha Jalal's "The Sole Spokesman", p. 200.
6. John Glendevon: "The Viceroy at Bay", p. 198.
7. G.D. Khosla: "Stern Reckoning: A Survey of the Events leading upto and following the Partition of India", p. 312.
8. Penderel Moon: "Divide and Quit", p. 20.
9. Patel's letter of 27th July 1947 in reply to Khizr Hayat Khan's of the 26th instant.

18 (a). The Simla Conference

1. Wavell: "The Viceroy's Journal", p. 144.
2. ibid, p. 143.

3. Hodson, H.V.: "The Great Divide: Britain, India, Pakistan", p. 123.
4. ibid, p. 121.
5. Wavell, ibid, p. 153.
6. ibid, p. 151.
7. Hodson, ibid, pp. 124-25.
8. Sitaramayya, Dr. Pattabhi: "The History of the Freedom Movement in India", p. 666.
9. Hodson, ibid, pp. 126-127.
10. Durga Das: "India from Curzon to Nehru & After", p. 216.

18 (b). General Elections

1. Sitaramayya, B. Pattabhi: "The History of the Indian National Congress", Vol. II, p. 656.
2. Jalal, Ayesha: "The Sole Spokesman: Jinnah, the Muslim League and the Demand for Pakistan", p. 21
3. ibid, p. 77.
4. ibid, p. 83.
5. Moon, Penderel: "Divide and Quit", pp. 38-39.
6. Sitaramayya, ibid, p. 538.
7. "Sardar Patel's Correspondence", Vol. II, p. 74.
8. "Sardar's Letters—Mostly Unknown"—I (Birth Centenary, Vol. IV, Years 1945-46), p. 11.
9. "Sardar Patel's Correspondence", Vol. II, p. 146.
10. ibid, p. 57.
11. ibid, pp. 59-61.
12. "Sardar's Letters—Mostly Unknown"—I (Birth Centenary, Vol. IV, Years 1945-46), p. 161.
13. "Sardar Patel's Correspondence", Vol. II, p. 62.
14. Mehrotra, Lalji: recorded interview with author, dated January 21, 1985.
15. "Sardar's Letters—Mostly Unknown"—I, Vol. IV, p. 46.
16. Jalal, Ayesha, ibid, p. 109.
17. Patel, B.R. (ICS): recorded interview, February 13, 1985.
18. The *Times of India*, October 23, 1945.
19. Mehrotra, Lalji, ibid.
20. Jalal, Ayesha, ibid, p. 165.

21. Wolpert, Stanley: "Jinnah of Pakistan", p. 164.
22. The *Bombay Chronicle*, February 4, 1946.
23. ibid, January 15, 1946.
24. "Sardar's Letters—Mostly Unknown"—I, Vol. IV, p. 177.
25. "Sardar Patel's Correspondence", Vol. III, p. 94.
26. ibid, M.S.M. Sarma's letter to Patel, p. 100.
27. The "Transfer of Power 1942-47", Vol. VIII, p. 429.
28. "Sardar Patel's Correspondence", Vol. III, p. 98.
29. ibid, p. 96.
30. ibid, Vol. II, p. 60.
31. ibid, p. 47.
32. ibid, p. 297.
33. ibid, pp. 280-81.
34. ibid, p. 290.
35. ibid, pp. 299-300.
36. ibid, p. 277.
37. ibid, Vol. III, pp. 75-76.
38. "Sardar's Letters—Mostly Unknown"—I, Vol. IV, p. 12.
39. "Sardar Patel's Correspondence", Vol. II, pp. 121-22.
40. "Sardar's Letters—Mostly Unknown"—I, Vol. IV, p. 45.
41. ibid, p. 11.
42. "Sardar Patel's Correspondence", Vol. II, p. 52.
43. Ghosh, Sudhir: "Gandhi's Emissary", p. 167.
44. Kripalani, J.B.: "Gandhi: His Life and Thought", p. 250.
45. ibid.
46. ibid, pp. 248-49.
47. Kabir, Humayun: Letter to author, July 22, 1969.
48. The *Statesman*, July 25, 1969.
49. *Bhavan's Journal*, December 22, 1974, p. 35.
50. "Sardar Patel's Correspondence", Vol. III, pp. 153-54.
51. Sitaramayya: "The History of the Indian National Congress", Vol. II, p. 798.
52. The "Transfer of Power", Vol. VI, pp. 71-72.

18 (c). The Cabinet Mission Plan

1. Mazumdar, A.K.: "Advent of Indian Independence", p. 213.
2. Sitaramayya, ibid, p. 791.

3. Hodson, ibid, p. 134.
4. ibid, pp. 133-34.
5. ibid, p. 135.
6. Das, Manmath Nath: "Partition and Independence of India", pp. 120-22.
7. Wavell, ibid, pp. 258-259.
8. "Sardar's Letters—Mostly Unknown"—I (Vol. IV), p. 206.
9. "Sardar Patel's Correspondence", (1945-50), Vol. III, p. 105.
10. ibid, pp. 108-09.
11. Hodson, ibid, p. 235.
12. The *Calcutta Review*, December 1949: "Mass Migration from West Punjab", p. 183.
13. Hodson, ibid, p. 166.
14. "Sardar Patel's Correspondence", Vol. III, (Rajagopalachari quotes Cripps in his letter to Patel) p. 38.
15. ibid, pp. 248-49.
16. Wavell: "The Viceroy's Journal", p. 285.
17. "Sardar Patel's Correspondence", Vol. III, p. 249.
18. Wavell, ibid, p. 261.
19. ibid, p. 315.
20. "Sardar Patel's Correspondence", Vol. III, p. 38.
21. Hodson, ibid, p. 164.
22. Iengar, H.V.R.: "Vallabhbhai Patel: a birthday memorial lecture at Surat Municipal Corporation", October 31, 1973, p. 6.
23. Munshi, K.M.: "Pilgrimage to Freedom", Vol. I, p. 108.
24. Shankar, V.: "My Reminiscences of Sardar Patel", Vol. II, p. 146.
25. Munshi, pp. 108-09.
26. Wavell, ibid, p. 329.
27. ibid, p. 315.
28. The "Transfer of Power 1942-47", Vol. VIII, p. 190.
29. "Sardar Patel's Correspondence", Vol. III, pp. 40-41.
30. ibid, p. 72.
31. ibid, (G.L. Mehta's letter to Patel), p. 179.
32. Hodson, ibid, p. 168.
33. "Sardar Patel's Correspondence", Vol. III, p. 303.
34. Wavell, ibid, pp. 346-47.
35. "Sardar's Letters—Mostly Unknown"—I, Vol. IV, p. 238.

36. ibid, p. 239.
37. "Sardar Patel's Correspondence", Vol. III, p. 182.
38. ibid, pp. 175-76.
39. ibid, p. 174.
40. ibid, p. 302.
41. ibid, pp. 303-04.
42. Gadgil, N.V.: "Government from Inside", p. 17.
43. Wavell, ibid, p. 291.
44. Gadgil, ibid, p. 17.
45. ibid, p. 18.
46. Hodson, ibid, p. 175.
47. "Sardar Patel's Correspondence", Vol. III, p. 190.
48. ibid, p. 290.
49. ibid, pp. 314-15.
50. Gadgil, ibid, p. 19.
51. "Sardar Patel's Correspondence", Vol. III, p. 314.

19. Verdict on Assam Blow to Unity

1. Sitaramayya, Pattabhi: "The History of the Indian National Congress", Vol. II, p. 817.
2. ibid, p. 816.
3. ibid, p. 815.
4. ibid, p. 819.
5. ibid, p. 820.
6. Sachar, Bhim Sen: recorded interview, April 4, 1969.
7. Khanna, Mehr Chand: recorded interview, March 31, 1969.
8. Hodson, H.V.: "The Great Divide: Britain—India—Pakistan", p. 282.
9. Khanna, ibid.
10. ibid.
11. Wavell: "Viceroy's Journal", p. 377.
12. Hodson, ibid, p. 283.
13. ibid, pp. 278-79.
14. Khanna, ibid.
15. The *Statesman*, May 20, 1955.
16. Pyarelal: "Mahatma Gandhi—the Last Phase", Vol. II, Gandhi's letter of June 6 to Nehru, p. 268.

17. ibid, p. 270.
18. "Sardar Patel's Correspondence", Vol. IV, p. 6.
19. ibid, p. 1.
20. ibid, p. 5.
21. Pyarelal, ibid, p. 3.
22. "Sardar Patel's Correspondence", Vol. IV, p. 12.
23. Menon, V.P.: "The Transfer of Power in India", p. 336.
24. ibid, p. 337.
25. ibid, p. 338.
26. Hodson, ibid, p. 200.
27. Moon, Penderel: "Divide and Quit", pp. 62-63.
28. Menon, ibid, pp. 340-41.
29. Sachar, Bhim Sen: Recorded interview, April 4, 1969.
30. The *Calcutta Review*, December 1949, "Mass Migration from West Punjab", p. 185.
31. Sachar, ibid.
32. The *Calcutta Review*, ibid, pp. 186-87.
33. Pyarelal, ibid, pp. 10-11.
34. The *Calcutta Review*, ibid.
35. "Sardar Patel's Correspondence", Vol. IV, p. 13.
36. ibid, p. 12.
37. Pyarelal, ibid, p. 16.
38. ibid, p. 11.
39. ibid, p. 3.
40. ibid, p. 35.
41. Mazumdar, A.K.: "Advent of Indian Independence", (K.M. Munshi's letter dated December 4, 1962, quoted), p. 410.
42. Pyarelal, ibid, pp. 11-12.
43. "Sardar's Letters—Mostly Unknown"—II (Vol. V), p. 209.

20. Transfer of Power

1. Hodson, H.V.: "The Great Divide: Britain—India—Pakistan", p. 220.
2. ibid, p. 215.
3. Campbell-Johnson, Alan: "Mission with Mountbatten", p. 72.
4. Das, Manmath Nath: "Partition and Independence of India",

quotes "Record of Viceroy's Interview No. 90 with Patel, April 24, 1947", p. 52.
5. Campbell-Johnson, ibid, p. 46.
6. ibid, p. 45.
7. ibid, p. 51.
8. ibid, p. 52.
9. ibid, p. 55.
10. ibid, p. 61.
11. ibid, pp. 56-57.
12. Jalal, Ayesha: "The Sole Spokesman: Jinnah, the Muslim League and the Demand for Pakistan", quotes "Record of Mountbatten's interview with Jinnah, April 8, 1947", p. 252.
13. Campbell-Johnson, ibid, p. 57.
14. ibid, p. 65.
15. "Sardar Patel's Correspondence", Vol. IV, pp. 36-47.
16. Menon, V.P.: "The Transfer of Power in India", p. 355.
17. ibid, p. 363.
18. Campbell-Johnson, ibid, p. 89.
19. Hodson, ibid, p. 299.
20. Menon, ibid, p. 365.
21. Campbell-Johnson, ibid, p. 68.
22. Menon, ibid, p. 365.
23. Hodson, ibid, p. 309.
24. Pyarelal: "Mahatma Gandhi—the Last Phase", Vol. II, quotes Patel's speech in the Constituent Assembly in November 1949, p. 154.
25. Campbell-Johnson, ibid, p. 94.
26. ibid, p. 97.
27. ibid, pp. 102-103.
28. ibid, p. 110.
29. ibid, pp. 117-18.
30. Trivedi, Chandulal M. (ICS): Recorded interview, July 26, 1970.
31. Patel, H.M. (ICS): Recorded interview, July 25, 1970.
32. Lall, K.B. (ICS): Letter to author, May 17, 1974.

21. Integration of States

1. "Sardar Patel's Speeches" (Hindi translation from Gujarati by Narhari D. Parekh), p. 445.

2. Wavell: "Viceroy's Journal", p. 120.
3. "Sardar Patel—In Tune with the Millions"—I (Vol. II), Appendix I, p. 330.
4. ibid, p. 37.
5. Munshi, K.M.: "Pilgrimage to Freedom", quotes p. 150.
6. ibid, pp. 151-52.
7. Mehtab, Harekrushna: "Beginning of the End", Patel's Preface, pp. 8-9.
8. "Sardar Patel's Correspondence", Vol. V, p. 401.
9. ibid, p. 407.
10. "Sardar Patel—In Tune with the Millions"—I (Vol. III), p. 57.
11. Campbell-Johnson, Alan: "Mission with Mountbatten", p. 46.
12. Menon, V.P.: "The Story of the Integration of the Indian States", p. 79.
13. ibid, pp. 70-71.
14. Hodson, H.V.: "The Great Divide: Britain—India—Pakistan", pp. 358-59.
15. Menon, ibid, p. 71.
16. The *Indian Express*, March 18, 1947.
17. ibid, February 28, 1947.
18. Menon, ibid, pp. 72-73.
19. Himatsinhji, Maharaj, Major-General: Recorded interview, September 6, 1970.
20. "Sardar Patel's Correspondence", Vol. V, p. 384.
21. Campbell-Johnson, ibid, pp. 43-46.
22. Menon, ibid, pp. 75-78.
23. "Sardar Patel's Speeches" (in Hindi), pp. 592-95.
24. "Sardar Patel's Correspondence", Vol. V (Note by A.S. Pai of the States Department), pp. 342-43.
25. Menon, ibid, p. 94.
26. Hodson, ibid, p. 361.
27. Menon, ibid, p. 94.
28. Venkatachar C.S. (ICS): Recorded interview, May 17, 1969.
29. "For a United India" (Speeches by Sardar Patel), pp. 3-5.
30. "Sardar Patel's Correspondence", Vol. V, p. 392.
31. Hodson, ibid, p. 364.
32. Munshi (K.M.) Papers: "Indian Constitutional Documents", Vol. II, pp. 415-16.

33. "Sardar Patel—In Tune with the Millions"—II (Vol. III), p. 125.
34. Hodson, ibid, pp. 367-68.
35. The *Hindu*: C.P. Ramaswami Aiyar's review of E.W.R. Lamby's book, "The Transfer of Power in India", March 21, 1958.
36. Menon, ibid, p. 100.
37. Coupland, Sir Reginald: "India—A Re-Statement", p. 278.
38. "For a United India" (Sardar Patel's Speeches), p. 11.

21 (a). Jodhpur

1. Hodson, H.V.: "The Great Divide—Britain, India, Pakistan", p. 379.
2. Iengar, H.V.R. (ICS): "Sardar's Ways: Focus on Main Tasks", The *Indian Express*, May 31, 1965.
3. Venkatachar, C.S. (ICS): recorded interview, May 17, 1969.
4. Munshi, K.M.: "Pilgrimage to Freedom", p. 163.
5. Menon, V.P.: "The Story of the Integration of the Indian States", p. 116.
6. Venkatachar, ibid.
7. "Sardar Patel's Correspondence", Vol. V, Appendices, pp. 515-16.
8. Menon, ibid, p. 117.
9. ibid.
10. Mountbatten of Burma, Earl: Memorandum of March 17, 1976.
11. Iengar, H.V.R.: recorded interview, April 25, 1975.
12. Iengar, "Sardar's ways...", The *Indian Express*, May 31, 1965.
13. Menon, ibid, p. 117.
14. Lall, K.B. (ICS): letter to author, June 24, 1970.
15. Vellodi, M.K. (ICS): "Air Accidents to Remember", The *Indian Express*, June 9, 1972

21 (b). Junagadh

1. "Sardar Patel—In Tune with the Millions"—II (Vol. III), pp. 4-5.
2. Hodson, H.V.: "The Great Divide—Britain, India, Pakistan", p. 430.

3. "Sardar Patel's Correspondence", Vol. I, p. 220.
4. Campbell-Johnson, Alan: "Mission with Mountbatten", p. 192.
5. ibid, p. 141.
6. Menon, V.P.: "The Story of the Integration of the Indian States", p. 138.
7. Hodson, ibid, p. 430.
8. "Sardar's Letters—Mostly Unknown", II (Vol. V), p. 74.
9. Campbell-Johnson, ibid, p. 192.
10. Menon, ibid, p. 112.
11. Hodson, ibid, p. 428.
12. Pyarelal: "Mahatma Gandhi—the Last Phase", Vol. II, p. 490.
13. Menon, ibid, p. 125.
14. Hodson, ibid, p. 429.
15. Menon, ibid, pp. 128-29.
16. ibid, p. 127.
17. Campbell-Johnson, ibid, p. 191.
18. "Sardar Patel's Correspondence", Vol. VII, p. 335.
19. Menon, ibid, p. 129.
20. ibid, p. 130.
21. Campbell-Johnson, ibid, p. 194.
22. Menon, ibid, p. 138.
23. ibid, p. 141.
24. Hodson, ibid, p. 438.
25. Menon, ibid, p. 143.
26. Hodson, ibid, p. 438.
27. Menon, ibid, pp. 143-44.
28. Campbell-Johnson, ibid, p. 237.
29. Menon, ibid, p. 147.
30. "Sardar Patel—In Tune with the Millions"—I (Vol. II), p. 62.
31. Menon, ibid (quoted), p. 149.
32. "Sardar Patel's Correspondence", Vol. VII, pp. 392-93.

21 (c). Kathiawar

1. "Sardar Patel's Correspondence", Vol. V, p. 475.
2. "Sardar's Letters—Mostly Unknown"—I (Vol. IV), p. 256.
3. ibid, II, Vol. V, p. 17.
4. ibid, p. 20.

5. ibid, p. 19.
6. ibid, p. 18.
7. Menon, V.P.: "The Story of the Integration of the Indian States", p. 126.
8. "For a United India: Speeches of Sardar Patel" (1947-50), p. 31.
9. Menon, ibid, p. 197.
10. Nehru, Jawaharlal: "Letters to Chief Ministers", Vol. I, p. 67.
11. "Sardar's Letters—Mostly Unknown"—II (Vol. V), p. 22.

21 (d). Hyderabad

1. "For a United India: Speeches of Sardar Patel" (1947-50), p. 11.
2. Campbell-Johnson, Alan: "Mission with Mountbatten", p. 329.
3. ibid, p. 360.
4. Hodson, H.V.: "The Great Divide—Britain, India, Pakistan", p. 382.
5. Campbell-Johnson, ibid, p. 198.
6. ibid, p. 295.
7. ibid, p. 199.
8. Hodson, ibid, p. 478.
9. More, R.J.: "Escape from Empire: The Attlee Government and the Indian Problem", pp. 305-08.
10. "Sardar Patel's Correspondence", Vol. VII, pp. 29-30, 38.
11. Munshi, K.M.: "Pilgrimage to Freedom", Vol. I, p. 166.
12. The *Indian Express*, June 7, 1947.
13. Menon, V.P.: "The Story of the Integration of the Indian States", p. 317.
14. "Sardar Patel's Correspondence", Vol. VII, letter dated August 31, 1947 from Aravamudh Aiyangar, member, Nizam's Executive Council, to Gopalaswami Ayyangar, p. 56.
15. ibid, p. 109.
16. Iengar, H.V.R. (ICS): The *Indian Express*, "On Working Together", September 18, 1969.
17. "Sardar Patel's Correspondence", Vol. VII, pp. 59-60.
18. Menon, ibid, pp. 323, 327, 329, 330.
19. "Sardar Patel's Correspondence", Vol. VII, p. 67.
20. ibid, pp. 46, 53-54, 87.

21. ibid, p. 111.
22. ibid, pp. 80-81.
23. Menon, ibid, p. 337.
24. "Sardar Patel's Correspondence", Vol. VII, pp. 125-26.
25. "Sardar Patel's Correspondence", Vol. VII, p. 134.
26. ibid, p. 118.
27. ibid, K.M. Munshi's letter of May 17, 1948 to the Nizam, p. 158.
28. ibid, p. 110.
29. ibid, pp. 105, 95.
30. Menon, ibid, pp. 354-55, 348, 350-52.
31. "This was Sardar—Commemorative Volume", Vol. I, pp. 244-45.
32. Nehru, Jawaharlal: "Letters to Chief Ministers" (1947-64), Vol. I, p. 147.
33. "For a United India", ibid, p. 40.
34. Munshi, K.M.: "The End of an Era: Hyderabad Memories", p. 177.
35. "For a United India", ibid, p. 41.
36. Menon, K.P.S. (ICS): "Many Worlds Revisited: An Autobiography", p. 314.
37. Menon, V.P., ibid, p. 368.
38. "Sardar Patel's Correspondence", Vol. VII, p. 217.
39. Munshi, ibid, pp. 190, 180.
40. "Sardar Patel's Correspondence", Vol. VII, p. 194.
41. Bucher, General Sir Roy: Letter to author, December 19, 1968.
42. ibid.
43. Munshi, ibid, p. 202.
44. "Sardar's Letters—Mostly Unknown—II (Vol. V), p. 307.
45. Munshi, ibid, p. 217.
46. Chaudhuri, General J.N.: An Autobiography, p. 146.
47. The *Times of India*, August 6th, 1958.
48. Iengar, H.V.R.: The *Indian Express*, "On Working Together", September 18, 1969.
49. Munshi, ibid, pp. 239, 237.
50. Iengar, ibid.
51. "Sardar Patel's Correspondence", Vol. VII, p. 242.
52. Bucher, General Sir Roy: Letter to author, December 19, 1968.
53. ibid, April 4, 1948.

54. Panikkar, K.M.: "An Autobiography", p. 154.
55. "Sardar Patel's Correspondence", Vol. VII, p. 647.
56. Nehru, Jawaharlal: "Letters to Chief Ministers", Vol. I, pp. 206-7.
57. "Sardar Patel's Correspondence", Vol. VII, pp. 266, 241, 246, 250, 255.
58. "Said the Sardar"—speeches published by Hyderabad State Congress, pp. 1, 5.
59. "Sardar Patel's Correspondence", Vol. VII, pp. 309-10, 315.
60. "Said the Sardar", ibid, pp. 47-49.
61. "Sardar Patel's Correspondence", Vol. VII, pp. 375-77.
62. Graham, W. Gordon: *The Christian Science Monitor*, February 1, 1951.
63. Bucher, General Sir Roy: Letter to author, December 19, 1968.
64. Munshi, ibid, p. 34.
65. "Sardar Patel—In Tune with the Millions"—I (Vol. II), p. 276.
66. Munshi, K.M.: "Pilgrimage to Freedom", Vol. I, p. 175.

21 (e). Travancore

1. The *Bombay Chronicle*, May 10, 1947.
2. Campbell-Johnson, Alan: "Mission with Mountbatten", p. 54.
3. Munshi, K.M.: "Pilgrimage to Freedom", Vol. I, p. 165.
4. "Hyderabad in Retrospect", a The *Times of India* publication (February 1949), comprising articles by an ex-official of Hyderabad, p. 18; K.M. Munshi, in his "Pilgrimage to Freedom", credits these to Ali Yavar Jung, p. 165.
5. The *Indian Express*, April 27, 1947.
6. Patel Papers (unpublished letter).
7. Hodson, H.V.: "The Great Divide—Britain, India, Pakistan", p. 362.
8. The *Bombay Chronicle*, June 11, 1947.
9. Koshy, M.J.: "Last Days of Monarchy in Kerala", pp. 271-72.
10. Menon, V.P.: "The Story of the Integration of the Indian States", p. 90.
11. The *Bombay Chronicle*, June 18, 1947.
12. Menon, ibid, p. 91.
13. The *Bombay Chronicle*, June 23, 1947.

14. ibid, June 25, 1947.
15. ibid, June 16, 1947.
16. Menon, K.P.S. (ICS): Letter to author, February 24, 1970.
17. Koshy, ibid, p. ii.
18. "Sardar Patel's Correspondence", Vol. V. pp. 446-47.
19. Panikkar, K.M.: "An Autobiography", p. 162.
20. Munshi, ibid, p. 165.
21. "Sardar Patel's Correspondence", Vol. VI, p. 375.
22. ibid, pp. 370-72.
23. "Sardar Patel—In Tune with the Millions"—II (Vol. III), pp. 74-75.
24. Hodson, ibid, vide *Viceroy's Personal Report* No. 15, August 1, 1947, p. 378.

21 (f). Bhopal

1. Pyarelal: "Mahatma Gandhi: the Last Phase", Vol. II, p. 332.
2. Campbell-Johnson, Alan: "Mission with Mountbatten", p. 147.
3. Panikkar, K.M.: "An Autobiography", p. 138.
4. ibid, p. 148.
5. ibid.
6. ibid, p. 151.
7. Hodson, H.V.: "The Great Divide—Britain, India, Pakistan", p. 365.
8. ibid, p. 375.
9. "Sardar Patel's Correspondence", Vol. V, pp. 361-63.
10. Hodson, ibid, p. 376.
11. Menon, V.P.: "The Story of the Integration of the Indian States", p. 119.
12. Hodson, ibid, p. 376.
13. Hodson, ibid, p. 427.

21 (g). Kashmir

1. Campbell-Johnson, Alan: "Mission with Mountbatten", p. 225.
2. Stepens, Ian: "Horned Moon", p. 211.
3. Sen, Lieut-Gen. L.P.: "Slender was the Thread", pp. 76-77.
4. ibid, p. 53.

5. ibid, p. 54.
6. "This was Sardar—Commemorative Volume", Vol. I, pp. 252, 53, 55.
7. Sen, ibid, p. 81.
8. ibid, p. 160.
9. ibid, p. 139.
10. "Sardar Patel's Correspondence", Vol. I, p. 49.
11. Gadgil, N.V.: "Government from Inside", p. 63.
12. ibid, p. 65.
13. Mellor, Andrew, London *Daily Herald* correspondent in New Delhi: letter to author, November 18, 1968.
14. "Sardar's Letters—Mostly Unknown"—II (Vol. V), pp. 90-91.
15. Durgadas: "India: From Curzon to Nehru", p. 270.
16. Campbell-Johnson, ibid, p. 244.
17. Menon, V.P.: "The Story of the Integration of the Indian States", pp. 394-95.
18. Gopal, Sarvepalli: "Jawaharlal Nehru", Vol. III, p. 263.
19. "Sardar Patel's Correspondence", Vol. I, pp. lxxxviii-ix.
20. Hodson, H.V.: "The Great Divide", pp. 371 and 373.
21. Bazaz, Prem Nath: "The History of Struggle for Freedom in Kashmir", pp. 256-58.
22. "Sardar Patel's Correspondence", Vol. I, All-State Kashmiri Pandit Conference's telegram, June 4, 1946, p. 1.
23. Bazaz, ibid, p. 248.
24. "Sardar Patel's Correspondence", Vol. I, The *Hindu* quoted, p. xcii.
25. ibid, p. 6.
26. ibid, Vol. III, p. 154.
27. ibid, Vol. I, p. 10.
28. Bazaz, ibid, p. 262.
29. ibid, p. 272.
30. Bazaz, ibid, quoting The *Hindustan Times* of June 7, 1947, p. 318.
31. Mahajan, Mehr Chand: "Looking Back" (autobiography), p. 126.
32. "Sardar Patel's Correspondence", Vol. I, pp. 46-47.
33. ibid, p. 130.

34. Mahajan, ibid, p. 129.
35. ibid, pp. 151-52.
36. "Sardar Patel—In Tune with the Millions"—I (Vol. II), p. 318.
37. Ismay: "The Memoirs of Lord Ismay", p. 433.
38. "Sardar Patel's Correspondence", Vol. I, pp. 32-33.
39. ibid, p. 37.
40. Evans, Humphrey: "Thimayya of India: A Soldier's Life", p. 264.
41. Birdwood, Lord: "A Continent Decides", pp. 89-90.
42. Sadiq, G.M.: Letter to author, June 26, 1969.
43. Sen, Lieut-Gen. L.P.: Letter to author, June 26, 1969.
44. Connell, John: "Auchinleck: a Biography of Field-Marshal Sir Claude Auchinleck", p. 930.
45. Auchinleck, Field Marshal: Letter to author, January 7, 1969.
46. Connell, ibid, p. 930.
47. Hodson, H.V.: "The Great Divide—Britain, India, Pakistan", p. 447.
48. "Sardar Patel's Correspondence", Vol. I, p. 42.
49. ibid, pp. 61-62.
50. ibid, p. 96.
51. ibid, p. 73: Mountbatten's note of a Discussion with Jinnah in Lahore on November 1, 1947.
52. ibid, pp. 80-81.
53. Connell, ibid, p. 932.
54. Hodson, ibid, p. 458.
55. Connell, ibid, p. 932.
56. "Sardar Patel's Correspondence", Vol. I, Mountbatten's Note on his visit to Lahore, pp. 80-81.
57. ibid, pp. 148, 151.
58. Campbell-Johnson, ibid, pp. 262-63.
59. Sahay, Vishnu (ICS), recorded interview with author, April 2, 1969.
60. "Sardar Patel's Correspondence", Vol. VI, p. 387.
61. Nehru, Jawaharlal: "Letters to Chief Ministers", Vol. 1, p. 43.
62. ibid, p. 61.
63. ibid, p. 119.
64. The *Times* of London, October 2, 1948.
65. "Sardar Patel's Correspondence", Vol. I, pp. 119-22.

66. ibid, p. 135.
67. ibid, p. 157.
68. ibid, p. 227.
69. ibid, pp. 229-33.
70. ibid, p. 238.
71. ibid, pp. 241-45.
72. ibid, p. 263.
73. ibid, pp. 266-69.
74. Mullik, B.N.: "Kashmir", pp. 14-17.
75. Chaudhary, Valmiki: "President & Indian Constitution", pp. 257-58.
76. Tyagi, Mahavir: Interview with author, also narrated by Prakash Vir Shastri (MP) in *Swatantra Jyoti*, Sardar Patel Number, 1973, p. 27.
77. Valmiki, ibid, p. 298.
78. Munshi, K.M.: Letter to author dated December 17, 1968.
79. Shankar, V.: "My Reminiscences of Sardar Patel", Vol. II, p. 61.
80. Jagmohan: "My Frozen Turbulence in Kashmir", p. 107.
81. Mullik, ibid, p. 102.
82. "Sardar Patel's Correspondence", Vol. I, pp. 201-02.
83. ibid, p. 249.
84. ibid, p. 294.
85. Narayan, Jayaprakash: *Bhavan's Journal*, "Sardar Patel: A Reappraisal", December 22, 1974, p. 37.
86. Kamath, H.V.: *Bhavan's Journal*, "Sardar Vallabhbhai Patel: Some Memories", January 16, 1982, p. 63.
87. Thorat, Lieut-Gen. S.P.P.: "From Reveille to Retreat", p. 101.
88. Elmhirst, Air Marshal Thomas: Letter to author, January 18, 1969.
89. Roy, M.N.: "Men I Met", p. 17.

21(h). Greater Rajasthan

1. "Sardar Patel—In Tune with the Millions"—II (Vol. III), p. 69.
2. Majumdar, Dr. R.C.: "An Advanced History of India", p. 449.
3. "Sardar Patel—In Tune with the Millions"—II (Vol. III). p. 70.
4. "Sardar's Letters—Mostly Unknown"—II (Vol. V), p. 61.

5. Singh, Thakur Jaswant: Recorded interview, March 5th-7th, 1970.
6. ibid.
7. Campbell-Johnson, Allan: "Mission with Mountbatten", p. 263.
8. Lall, K.B. (ICS): Letter to author, June 24th, 1970.
9. Menon, K.P.S. (ICS): "The Secret Department and I", The *Sunday Standard*, September 12, 1976.
10. Lall, K.B.: ibid.
11. "For a United India: Speeches of Sardar Patel", (1947-50), p. 34.
12. "Sardar Patel—In Tune with the Millions"—I (Vol. II), p. 90.
13. Lall, K.B., ibid.
14. "Sardar Patel—In Tune with the Millions"—I (Vol. II), p. 92.
15. ibid, pp. 94-95.
16. ibid, pp. 97-98.
17. ibid, p. 101.
18. Singh, Thakur Jaswant, ibid.
19. Thorat, Lieut-Gen. S.P.P.: "From Reveille to Retreat", p. 119.
20. Singh, Thakur Jaswant, ibid.
21. "Sardar Patel—In Tune with the Millions"—II (Vol. III), pp 35-37.
22. ibid, pp. 69-70.

22. Outdoing Bismarck

1. Ram, Jagjivan: "The Great Administrator", The *Statesman*, October 31, 1950.
2. Panikkar, K.M.: "An Autobiography", pp. 190-91.
3. "Sardar Patel's Speeches" (in Hindi), p. 363.
4. Hussain, Dr. Zakir: The *Statesman*, November 1, 1968.
5. Giri, V.V.: The *Times of India*, November 1, 1969.
6. Menon, K.P.S. (ICS): "Many Worlds Revisited: An Autobiography", p. 262.
7. "Sardar's Letters—Mostly Unknown" - II (Vol. V), p. 129.
8. Taylor, A.J.P.: "Europe: Grandeur and Decline", pp. 101-02.
9. ibid, p. 88.
10. Taylor, A.J.P.: "Bismarck: The Man and the Statesman", pp. 200, 195.

11. Menon, K.P.S.: The *Sunday Standard*, September 12, 1976.
12. "Sardar's Letters—Mostly Unknown" - II (Vol. V), p. 56.
13. "Sardar Patel's Correspondence"; Vol. V, p. 512.
14. "Sardar Patel—In Tune with the Millions"—I (Vol. II), p. 6.
15. "For a United India", p. 8
16. ibid, pp. 57-58.
17. "Sardar Patel—In Tune with the Millions"—I (Vol. II), p. 82.
18. Taylor, "Bismarck", p. 108.
19. Taylor, ibid, pp. 258-59.
20. Singh, Khushwant: (former Editor, The *Illustrated Weekly of India*): Recorded interview.
21. "Sardar Patel's Correspondence", Vol. V, pp. 342-43, 347.
22. Menon, V.P.: "The Story of the Integration of the Indian States", pp. 418-19.
23. Prasad, Pandit Badri, a member of the Maharaja's personal staff: interview.
24. Menon, ibid, p. 163.
25. Senapati, N. (ICS): Letter to author dated April 24, 1969.
26. "Sardar Patel—In Tune with the Millions"—I (Vol. II), pp. 68-69.
27. Senapati, ibid.
28. Katju, Dr. K.N.: "This was Sardar", Commemorative Vol. I, p. 22.
29. "Sardar's Letters—Mostly Unknown"—II (Vol. V), p. 39.
30. "Sardar Patel—In Tune with the Million"—II (Vol. III), p. 92.
31. ibid, p. 108.
32. "Sardar Patel—In Tune with the Million"—I (Vol. II), p. 106.
33. "Sardar Patel—In Tune with the Million"—II (Vol. III), p. 93.
34. "Sardar's Letters—Mostly Unknown"—II (Vol. V), p. 183.
35. "The Memoirs of the Aga Khan", p. 301.
36. "The Evolution of India and Pakistan (1858 to 1947): Select Documents" (HMG), p. 425.

23. A Secularist with a Difference

1. "Sardar Patel—In Tune with the Millions"—II (Vol. III), pp. 168-69.
2. ibid, pp. 155, 156, 160.

3. The *Times of India*, February 19, 1983.
4. The *Indian Express*, September 12, 1995.
5. The *Statesman*, December 28, 1947.
6. "For a United India: Speeches of Sardar Patel" (1947-50), pp. 64-67.
7. "Sardar's Letters—Mostly Unknown"—II (Vol. V), p. 182.
8. Pyarelal: "Mahatma Gandhi—the Last Phase", Vol. II, pp. 716-7.
9. Thorat, Lt.-Gen. S.P.P.: "From Reveille to Retreat", pp. 100-01.
10. "Sardar Patel's Correspondence", Vol. I, p. Liii.
11. "Sardar's Letters—Mostly Unknown"—I (Vol. IV), p. 16.
12. Munshi, K.M.: "Pilgrimage to Freedom", Vol. I, pp. 200-210.
13. Anthony, Frank (MP): Letter to author, October 31, 1968.
14. Aizaz Rasul, Begum Kudsia: Letter to author, February 10, 1970.
15. "This was Sardar"—Commemorative Volume (Vol. I), p. 149.
16. Lall, K.B.: Letter to author, June 24, 1970.
17. Andrews, C.F.: "His Life and Times" by P.C. Roy Chaudhury, p. 61.
18. Durga Das: "India—From Curzon to Nehru & After", p. 77.
19. "Sardar Patel's Speeches" (in Hindu), pp. 16, 34, 41.
20. Karandikar, M.A.: "Islam in India's Transition to Modernity", pp. 177, 191.
21. Majumdar, Dr. R.C.: "Struggle for Freedom", p. 536, 534.
22. Aizaz Rasul, ibid.
23. *Searchlight:* "The Ranchi Riots" by Jayaprakash Narayan, September 13, 1967.
24. "Sardar Patel—In Tune with the Millions"—I (Vol. II), pp. 285-87.

24. A Friend of Labour and Capitalists

1. "For a United India: Speeches of Sardar Patel" (1947-50), p. 109.
2. *Harijan*, January 26, 1951, p. 418.
3. "For a United India", p. 133.
4. ibid, p. 109.
5. "Sardar Patel—In Tune with the Millions"—I (Vol. II), p. 244.

6. "For a United India", pp. 94-95.
7. "Sardar Patel—In Tune with the Millions"—I (Vol. II), p. 244.
8. "For a United India", p.128.
9. "Sardar Patel—In Tune with the Millions"—II (Vol. III), p. 178.
10. "Sardar Patel—In Tune with the Millions"—I (Vol. II), pp. 44, 246, 18.
11. "For a United India", p. 136.
12. "Sardar Patel—In Tune with the Millions"—II (Vol. III), p. 185.
13. "Sardar Patel—In Tune with the Millions"—I (Vol. II), pp. 246-47.
14. "Constituent Assembly of India (Legislative) Debates", Vol. II, Part II, February 4-March 18, 1949, pp. 876, 1164.
15. "For a United India", pp. 100, 136.
16. "Sardar Patel—In Tune with the Millions"—I (Vol. II), p. 245.
17. Desai, Mahadev: "A Righteous Struggle", p. 35.
18. "For a United India", p. 81.
19. Ramanujam, G.: "Story of Indian Labour", pp. 15, 17, 39, 40.
20. "Sardar Patel—In Tune with the Millions"—I (Vol. II), p. 255.
21. "For a United India", p. 98.
22. Report of Congress Sub-Committee with Nehru Memorial Museum & Library, New Delhi, G-23/Part 2/1945/46—Communists.
23. Ramanujam, ibid, pp. 54-59.
24. "Sardar Patel—In Tune with the Millions"—II (Vol. III), pp. 210-11.
25. "For a United India", pp. 95, 107.
26. "Sardar Patel—In Tune with the Millions"—I (Vol. II), p. 26.
27. Norman, Dorothy, American journalist, The *Hindustan Times*, January 21, 1951.
28. The *Hindustan Times:* "Nation's unrelenting struggle for existence", November 15, 1949.
29. The *Times*, London, December 16, 1950.
30. Norman, Dorothy, ibid.

25. The Great Administrator

1. The *Times*, London, October 23, 1946.

2. Mosley, Leonard: "The Last Days of the British Raj", p. 6.
3. Nehru, B.K. (ICS): "Thoughts on Our Present Discontents", pp. 97-98.
4. The *Bombay Chronicle*, April 21, 1947.
5. The *Statesman*, December 16, 1950.
6. Brown, Judith M.: "Modern India", p. 347.
7. *Harijan*, a tribute by a Civil Servant, January 26, 1951, p. 439.
8. Iengar, H.V.R.: "The Image of the Police", The *Indian Express*, September 8, 1966.
9. Punjabi, Kewal L. (ICS): "The Civil Servant in India".
10. Iengar: "Administration in India: a Historical Review", pp. 34-40.
11. ibid.
12. ibid.
13. "Sardar Patel—In Tune with the Millions"—II (Vol. III), p. 129.
14. Lal, Shavax A. (ICS): Letter to author, January 6, 1970.
15. Iengar: "Making of Decisions by Government", The *Indian Express*, February 4, 1964.
16. Iengar: "Officials and Ministers", The *Indian Express*, July 8, 1964.
17. Iengar: "Administration in India", p. 40.
18. *Harijan*, January 26, 1951, p. 422.
19. Menon, V.P.: "The Story of the Integration of the Indian States", p. 111.
20. Shankar, V. (ICS): "My Reminiscences of Sardar Patel", Vol. I, p. 185.
21. Iengar, "The Image of the Police", The *Indian Express*, September 8, 1966.
22. Elmhirst, Air Marshal Thomas: Letter to author, January 8, 1969.
23. Singh, Thakur Jaswant: Letter to author, August 15, 1962.
24. "Sardar Patel's Correspondence", Vol. IX, p. 35: letter dated December 6th, 1949.
25. ibid, Vol. V, p. 325: Letter dated January 31, 1947.
26. ibid, Vol. VIII, p. 557: Telegram dated June 12, 1949.
27. ibid, Vol. IV, pp. 320-21: Letter dated September 1, 1947.
28. "Sardar's Letters—Mostly Unknown"—II (Vol. V), p. 248.
29. "Sardar Patel's Correspondence", Vol. VI, pp. 9-13, 22.

30. ibid, Vol. IV, p. 6.
31. Das, Manmath Nath: "Partition and Independence of India", Record of Viceroy's Interview No. 90 with Patel, April 24, 1947, p. 52.
32. Mountbatten: "His Final Act of Friendship"—"This was Sardar": Commemorative Volume (Vol. I), p. 241.
33. "Sardar Patel—In Tune with the Millions"—I (Vol. II), pp. 305, 307.
34. Shankar, V.: "My Reminiscences of Sardar Patel", Vol. I, p. 126.
35. Iengar: "Making of Decisions of Government", The *Indian Express*, February 4, 1964.
36. Iengar: "Sardar Patel—A Man of Decision", The *Indian Express*, May 7, 1964.
37. "Constituent Assembly of India (Legislative) Debates", Vol. II, Part II, February 4 to March 18, 1949, p. 1451.
38. "Sardar Patel—In Tune with the Millions"—II (Vol. III), pp. 123-24.
39. Iengar, H.V.R. (ICS): "Vallabhbhai Patel: A Birthday Memorial Lecture" at Surat Municipal Corporation, October 31, 1973 (unpublished paper with author).
40. The *Statesman*, December 16, 1950.

26. Gandhi, Nehru, Patel

1. *Mangal Prabhat* (Hindi journal): "Long Live Sardar" by Editor Kaka Kalelkar, January 1951, p. 373.
2. *Harijan*: "GOC of the Non-Violent Army" by Vinoba Bhave, January 26, 1951, p. 419.
3. *Meri Kaun Sunega* (Who shall listen to me?) by Mahavir Tyagi, pp. 58-59.
4. Films Division, Government of India: Documentary on Sardar Patel, July 21, 1970.
5. The *Bharat*: "Sardar Patel" by Junius, October 31, 1951.
6. Nehru, Jawaharlal: "Autobiography", p. 287.
7. "Sardar Patel's Correspondence", Vol. IV, p. 537.
8. ibid, Vol. VI, pp. 30-31.
9. ibid, Vol. x, p. 23.
10. ibid, p. 1.

11. ibid, pp. 6-8.
12. ibid, pp. 9-10.
13. ibid, pp. 14, 15, 21.
14. Dutt, Subimal (ICS): "With Nehru in Foreign Office", pp. 52-53.
15. "This was Sardar"—Commemorative Volume (Vol. I), pp. 262-63.
16. "Sardar Patel's Correspondence", Vol. X, pp. 104-107.
17. ibid, p. 125.
18. ibid, p. 90.
19. ibid, pp. 112-13.
20. ibid, p. 117.
21. "For a United India: Speeches of Sardar Patel", pp. 83, 84, 88, 89.
22. "Sardar Patel's Correspondence", Vol. X, p. 148.
23. Masani, M.R.: Letter to author, July 25, 1969.
24. Deshmukh, C.D. (ICS): Letter to author, June 25, 1970.
25. Masani, ibid.
26. "Sardar's Letters—Mostly Unknown"—II (Vol. V), p. 301.
27. "For a United India", pp. 110-11.
28. "Sardar Patel's Correspondence", Vol. IX, p. 290.
29. "Sardar Patel—In Tune with the Millions"—I (Vol. II), pp. 277-78.
30. Stephans, Ian: "Horned Moon", p. 111.
31. Mellor, Andrew: Letter to author, November 18, 1968.

27. The Last Journey

1. "Sardar's Letters—Mostly Unknown"—II (Vol. V), p. 284.
2. "Sardar's Letters—Mostly Unknown"—I (Vol. IV), p. 298.
3. "Sardar Patel—In Tune with the Millions"—II (Vol. III), p. 101.
4. ibid, pp. 328-29.
5. "Sardar Patel's Correspondence", Vol. X, p. 461.
6. "For a United India: Speeches of Sardar Patel" (1947-50), p. 164.
7. "This was Sardar"—Commemorative Volume (Vol. I), pp. 448-49.
8. ibid, pp. 447-48.
9. "For a United India", p. 163.
10. Shankar, V.: "My Reminiscences of Sardar Patel", Vol. II, p. 123.

11. The *Times*, London, December 6, 1950.

28. Postscript

1. Roy, M.N.: "Men I Met" (reprinted from the *Radical Humanist*, December 13, 1950), pp. 15-16.
2. Sahay, Vishnu (ICS): Recorded interview, April 2, 1969.
3. Narayan, Jayaprakash: "Sardar's Immortal Legacy" in *Swatantra Jyoti* (Hindi journal), Sardar Patel Special Number 1973, p. 13.
4. Campbell-Johnson, Alan: "Mission with Mountbatten", pp. 229, 240.
5. Masani, M.R.: Letter to author, July 25, 1969.
6. Shahid Hamid, Major-General: "Disastrous Twilight", p. 293.
7. Gopal, Sarvepalli: "Jawaharlal Nehru", Vol. III, pp. 180, 35.
8. Menon, K.P.S. (ICS): "Memories and Musings", p. 46.
9. Gopal, ibid, pp. 191-95.
10. Menon, K.P.S.: "Many Worlds Revisited: An Autobiography", pp. 273-74.
11. "Sardar's Letters—Mostly Unknown" I (Vol. IV), p. 211.
12. Gaitonde, P.D.: "The Liberation of Goa", p. 54.
13. Zinkin, Taya: "The New Cabinet", the *Bharat Jyoti* (Sunday edition of the *Free Press Journal*), April 22nd, 1962.
14. Gopal, ibid, p. 33, quoted from A. Pant's *Mandala*.
15. ibid, pp. 223, 237.
16. "Sardar Patel's Correspondence", Vol. VIII, p. 136.
17. Munshi, K.M.: "Pilgrimage to Freedom", p. 175.
18. "Sardar Patel's Correspondence", Vol. X, pp. 336-41.
19. Mountbatten, Lord: from an article written by him, of which a xerox copy given to author.
20. Tata, J.R.D.: "Keynote", p. xiii.

Bibliography

Books

1. A.K. Majumdar: Advent of Indian Independence
2. Ajit Prasad Jain: What Really Mattered
3. Alan Campbell-Johnson: Mission with Mountbatten
4. Anthony Read & David Fischer: The Proudest Day: India's Long Road to Independence
5. A.P.J. Taylor: Bismarck—The Man and the Statesman
6. A.P.J. Taylor: Europe—Greatness & Decline
7. Ayesha Jalal: The Sole Spokesman: Jinnah, the Muslim League and the Demand for Pakistan
8. Bridwood, Lord: A Continent Divides
9. B.K. Nehru (ICS): Thoughts on Present Discontent
10. Bombay Gazetteer, Vol. III
11. B.N. Mullik: Kashmir
12. B.R. Nanda: Mahatma Gandhi
13. C.D. Deshmukh: The Course of My Life
14. Charles Kincaid: Great Men of India
15. Conrad Corfield: The Princely India I Knew
16. C.F. Andrews: His Life and Times
17. Constituent Assembly of India (Legislative): Vol. II, Part II (1949)
18. Constituent Assembly of India (Legislative): Debates Vol. II, Part II, 18th March 1949
19. Dhananjay Keer: Dr. Ambedkar—Life and Mission
20. Durga Das: India from Curzon to Nehru and After
21. D.V. Thamankar: Sardar Patel

22. Encylopedia Britannica
23. Evolution of India and Pakistan: 1858 to 1947: Select Documents (H.M.G)
24. Firoz Chand: Lala Lajpat Rai
25. For a United India (speeches of Sardar Patel)
26. G. Ramanujam: Story of Indian Labour
27. H.M. Patel (ICS): Rites & Passage—a Civil Servant Remembers
28. H.N. Brailsford: Subject India
29. Harekrushna Mahtab, Chief Minister of Orissa: Beginning of an Era: Preface by Sardar Patel
30. H.V. Hodson: Great Divide: Britain-India-Pakistan
31. Humphrey Evans: Thimayya of India
32. H.V.R. Iengar (ICS): Administration in India
33. H.V.R. Iengar (ICS): Vallabhbhai Patel: Birthday Memorial Lecture (Surat)
34. Ian Stephens: Horned Moon
35. General J.N. Chaudhri: An Autobiography
36. Ismay, Lord: The Memoirs of Lord Ismay
37. K. Ishwara Dutt: Congress Cyclopedia: Indian National Congress (1885-1920)
38. Jawaharlal Nehru: A Bunch of Letters
39. Jawaharlal Nehru: Autobiography
40. Jawaharlal Nehru: Letters to Chief Ministers
41. Jamnadas Dawarkadas: Political Memoirs
42. J.B. Kripalani: Gandhi: His Time and Thoughts
43. John Connel: A Biography of Field Marshal Sir Claude Auchinleck
44. John Glendevon: The Viceroy at Bay (Lord Linlithgow)
45. Judith M. Brown: Modern India
46. Kanji Dawarkadas: India's Fight for Freedom 1913 to 1937
47. Kanji Dawarkadas: Ten years to Freedom 1938 to 1947
48. Kewal L. Punjabi (ICS): The Civil Servant in India
49. K.M. Munshi: Pilgrimage to Freedom
50. K.M. Munshi: End of an Era—Hyderabad Memories
51. K.M. Munshi: Indian Constitutional Documents
52. K.M. Panikkar: An Autobiography
53. K.P.S. Menon (ICS): Many Worlds Revisited—an Autobiography

54. K.P.S. Menon (ICS): Memories and Musings
55. Leonard Mosley: The Last Days of the British Raj
56. M.A. Karandikar: Islam in India's Transition to Modernity
57. Mahadev Desai: The Story of Bardoli
58. Mahadev Desai: The Righteous Struggle
59. Mahavir Tayagi: *Meri Kaun Sunega* (Hindi)
60. Margaret Bourke-White: Halfway to Freedom
61. Manmath Das: Partition and Independence of India
62. Maulana Azad: India Wins Freedom
63. Mehr Chand Mahajan: Looking Back (autobiography)
64. Memoirs of Aga Khan
65. Minoo Masani: Bliss Was It In That Dawn
66. Michael Brecker: Nehru—a Political Biography
67. M.J. Koshy: Last Days of Monarchy in Kerala
68. Motilal Nehru: Selected Works
69. M.N. Roy: Men I Met
70. M.R. Jayakar: The Story of My Life
71. M.S. Venkataramani & B.K. Srivastava: Quit India
72. Narhari D. Parikh: Sardar Vallabhbhai Patel Vols. I & II
73. N.R. Pathaik (Prof.): Government of Maharashtra Source Material for History of Freedom Struggle in India, Part III
74. Narendra Singh Sarila: Untold Story of India's Partition
75. N.V. Gadgil: Governant from Inside
76. Pattabhi Sitaramyya: The History of the Indian Congress Vols. I & II
77. Penderel Moon: Divide & Quit
78. Penderel Moon: Strangers in India
79. Philip Woodruff: The Men Who Ruled India—the Guardians
80. Prem Nath Bajaj: History of Struggle for Freedom in Kashmir
81. Pyarelal: Mahatma Gandhi—the Last Phase, Vols. I & II
82. P.A. Gaitonde: The Liberation of Goa
83. Rajendra Prasad: Correspondence & Select Documents
84. Rajiv A. Kapur: Sikh Separatism
85. Raj Thapar: All These Years
86. R.C. Majumdar: Struggle for Freedom
87. R.C. Majumdar: Advance History of India
88. R.J. Moore: Escape from Empire—Attlee Government and the Indian Problem

89. Report of Indian States Committee 1928-29
90. Robert Bryan: Great Men of India
91. Robert Dayne: The Life and Death of Mahatma Gandhi
92. Sardar Patel Correspondence Vols. I to X
93. Sardar Patel: In Tune with the Millions, Vols. II & III
94. Sardar Patel's Letters: Mostly Unknown, Vols. I to III
95. Sardar Patel: Speeches in Hindi (from Gujarati)
96. Said the Sardar (speeches published by Hyderabad State Congress)
97. Sarvepalli Gopal: Jawaharlal Nehru, Vols. I to III
98. Sen, Lieut.-Gen. L.P.: Slender was the Thread
99. Shahid Hamid (Major General from Pakistan): Dangerous Twilight
100. Shiva Rao, B: Indian Freedom Movement: Some Notable Figures
101. Stanley Wolpert: Nehru: A Tryst with Destiny
102. Stanley Wolpert: A New History of India
103. Stanley Wolpert: Tilak & Gokhale
104. Stanley Wolpert: Jinnah of Pakistan
105. Sri Prakasa: Pakistan—Birth & Early Years
106. Subhas Chandra Bose: The Indian Struggle
107. Subimal Dutt (ICS): With Nehru in Foreign Office
108. Sudhir Ghosh: Gandhi's Emissary
109. This was Sardar: Commemorative Volume I
110. Tata, J.R.D.: Keynote
111. Thorat, Lieut.-Gen. S.P.P.: From Reville to Retreat
112. Tiwari, A.R.: Making of a Leader: Sardar Vallabhbhai Patel
113. Transfer of Power: 1942-1947 (H.H.G.), Vol. XII
114. V. Rangaswami: The Story of Integration: a New Interpretation
115. Vincent Smith: Oxford History of India
116. V.P. Menon: Transfer of Power in India
117. V.P. Menon: Integration of Indian States
118. Wavell, Lord: the Viceroy's Journal
119. Wikipedia (Syed Ahmed)
120. William Shirer: Gandhi: a Memoir
121. Yusuf Meharally: Leaders of India

Newspapers

Bharat:
1950: September 10
1951: October 31
Bhavan's Journal:
1974: December 22 (Jayaprakash Narayan's reappraisal of Patel)
1952: January 16

Bombay Chronicle:
1915: January 13/15
April 2
1918: April 13 / 17 / 20 / 23 / 24 / 28 / 30
June 3 / 5 / 8
July 3
1920: August 31
September 9 / 10 / 11 / 16
1921: December 28
1934: October 26
1945: October 1 / 15 / 31
1946: January 9 / 15 / 17 / 26 / 29 / 30 / 31
February 1 / 2 / 5 / 7 / 9
April 1
1947: April 10 / 11 / 15 / 16 / 21
May 5 / 10 / 20 / 26
June 10 / 11 / 13 / 14 / 16 / 18 / 23 / 24 / 25
July 2 / 3 / 5 / 7 / 10 / 11 / 12 / 13 / 18 / 19 / 23 / 24 / 25 / 26 / 28 / 30
August 4 / 12 / 20 / 28 / 29
September 13 / 26

Calcutta Review (Calcutta University):
1949: December

Eastern World (London)—author's contributions
1951: February—Patel
October—Gandhi
1959: October—Gandhi
1960: August—Nehru

1961: August—Nehru
December—Patel
1962: November—Patel
1964: May—Nehru
1969: July-August—Gandhi (centenary)

Free Press Journal:
1951: December 18

Harijan:
1951: January 26

Hindu—author's contributions, which form part of my book "Great Indians"
1970: October 2—Gandhi (centenary)
1989: October 23—Nehru (centenary)
1991: June 30 – Patel
September 1—Maulana Azad
September 29—Gandhi
December 22—Jinnah
1992: January 26—Gandhi
1993: January 24—Lajpat Rai
July 18—Tilak
October 31—Patel
1994: January 30—Madan Mohan Malaviya
May 15 – Bipin Chandra Pal
October 9—Annie Besant
November 6—Surendranath Banerjea
1996: June 23 – Bankim Chandra Chatterjee
November 24—Aurobindo Ghose
1997: March 2 – Patel
August 10—C.R. Das
July 13—Patel
1998: March 8—Dadabhai Naoroji
July 26—Gandhi

Hindustan Times—author's contributions
1949: November 15
1959: November 14—Nehru (at 70)
1964: July 19

1980: October 31—Patel
1981: January 10—Gandhi

Illustrated Weekly of India—author's contributions
1950: October 29—Patel
1969: October 5—Gandhi (centenary)
1970: October 25

Indian Express:
1947: February 28
March 18
June 7
1951: December 16
1964: February 4
May 4
June 8
1965: May 31
1966: September 8
1969: September 18
1972: June 9
2006: June 25

Economic Times:
1974: October 27
1975: July 6
1978: October 31
1979: May 13

Manchester Guardian—author's contribution
1950: January 25

Mangal Prabhat:
1951: January

Modern Review:
1920: February / June
1922: February
1937: November
1949: January

Searchlight:
1967: September 13
Statesman:
1921: April 3
1950: October 31
December 16
1955: May 20
1968: November 1
1969: July 25—Gandhi (centenary)—author's contribution

Sunday Standard:
1976: September 12

Swantantra Jyoti:
1973: Sardar Patel Number

Times of India (Mumbai):
1886: May 12
1889: October 4
1928: July 4
1929: May 8
1945: October 23
1947: October 3 / 5
1948: June 30
1949: October 4
March 2 / 5
1958: August 6
1964: May 13
1968: November 1
1969: August 24—Gandhi (centenary)—author's contribution
1970: July 12—Gandhi—author's contribution
September 26—Gandhi—author's contribution
1971: April 4—Gandhi—author's contribution
1977: January 16—Gandhi—author's contribution
1981: December 4
1987: August 14
November 2

Times, London:
1946: October 23

1948: October 2
1950: December 16

Young India:
1924: April 6
1950: October 16

Index

I

J

K